My Lai

PIVOTAL MOMENTS IN AMERICAN HISTORY
Series Editors
David Hackett Fischer
James M. McPherson
David Greenberg

James T. Patterson
Brown v. Board of Education: A Civil Rights Milestone and Its Troubled Legacy

Maury Klein
Rainbow's End: The Crash of 1929

James McPherson
Crossroads of Freedom: The Battle of Antietam

Glenn C. Altschuler
All Shook Up: How Rock 'n' Roll Changed America

David Hackett Fischer
Washington's Crossing

John Ferling
Adams vs. Jefferson: The Tumultuous Election of 1800

Joel H. Silbey
Storm over Texas: The Annexation Controversy and the Road to Civil War

Raymond Arsenault
Freedom Riders: 1961 and the Struggle for Racial Justice

Colin G. Calloway
The Scratch of a Pen: 1763 and the Transformation of North America

Richard Labunski
James Madison and the Struggle for the Bill of Rights

Sally G. McMillen
Seneca Falls and the Origins of the Women's Rights Movement

Howard Jones
The Bay of Pigs

Lynn Parsons
The Birth of Modern Politics: Andrew Jackson, John Quincy Adams, and the Election of 1828

Elliott West
The Last Indian War: The Nez Perce Story

Glenn C. Altschuler & Stuart M. Blumin
The GI Bill: A New Deal for Veterans

Richard Archer
As If an Enemy's Country: The British Occupation of Boston and the Origins of Revolution

Thomas Kessner
The Flight of the Century: Charles Lindbergh and the Rise of American Aviation

Craig L. Symonds
The Battle of Midway

Richard Moe
*Roosevelt's Second Act: The Election of 1940
and the Politics of War*

Emerson W. Baker
*A Storm of Witchcraft: The Salem Trials
and the American Experience*

Louis P. Masur
*Lincoln's Last Speech: Wartime
Reconstruction and the Crisis of Reunion*

David L. Preston
*Braddock's Defeat: The Battle of the
Monongahela and the Road to Revolution*

Michael A. Cohen
*Maelstrom: The Election of 1968
and American Politics*

Also by Howard Jones

To the Webster-Ashburton Treaty
Mutiny on the Amistad
A New Kind of War
Dawning of the Cold War
Union in Peril
Prologue to Manifest Destiny
Abraham Lincoln and a New Birth of Freedom
Crucible of Power
Death of a Generation
The Bay of Pigs
Blue and Gray Diplomacy

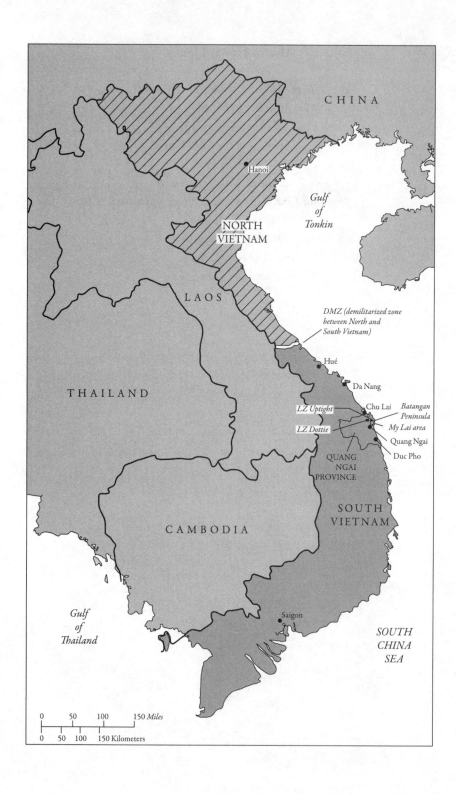

CHINA

Hanoi

NORTH
VIETNAM

Gulf
of
Tonkin

LAOS

DMZ (demilitarized zone
between North and
South Vietnam)

Hué

THAILAND

Da Nang

Chu Lai

LZ Uptight

Batangan
Peninsula

LZ Dottie

My Lai area

Quang Ngai

Duc Pho

QUANG
NGAI
PROVINCE

SOUTH
VIETNAM

CAMBODIA

Gulf
of
Thailand

Saigon

SOUTH
CHINA
SEA

0   50   100   150 Miles

0   50   100   150 Kilometers

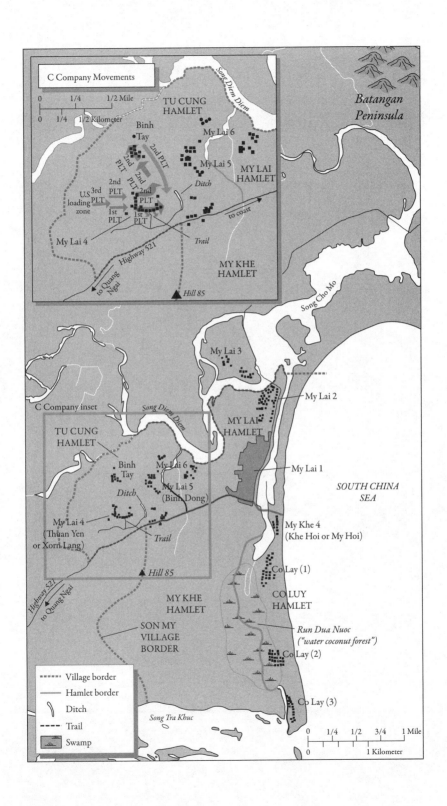

C Company Movements

0   1/4   1/2 Mile
0   1/4   1/2 Kilometer

TU CUNG HAMLET

Song Diem Diem

Binh Tay

My Lai 6

My Lai 5

MY LAI HAMLET

2nd PLT

2nd PLT

2nd PLT

2nd PLT

U.S. loading zone

3rd PLT

2nd PLT

1st PLT

1st PLT

Ditch

to coast

My Lai 4

Trail

Highway 521

MY KHE HAMLET

to Quang Ngai

▲ *Hill 85*

Batangan Peninsula

Song Cho Mo

C Company inset

Song Diem Diem

TU CUNG HAMLET

Binh Tay

My Lai 6

My Lai 5 (Binh Dong)

Ditch

My Lai 4 (Thuan Yen or Xom Lang)

Trail

▲ *Hill 85*

My Lai 3

My Lai 2

MY LAI HAMLET

My Lai 1

SOUTH CHINA SEA

My Khe 4 (Khe Hoi or My Hoi)

Co Lay (1)

CO LUY HAMLET

MY KHE HAMLET

SON MY VILLAGE BORDER

Run Dua Nuoc ("water coconut forest")

Co Lay (2)

Highway 521

to Quang Ngai

Song Tra Khuc

Co Lay (3)

- - - - - Village border
———— Hamlet border
〕 Ditch
- - - - Trail
▨ Swamp

0   1/4   1/2   3/4   1 Mile
0   1 Kilometer

MY LAI

Vietnam, 1968, and the
Descent into Darkness

HOWARD JONES

OXFORD
UNIVERSITY PRESS

OXFORD
UNIVERSITY PRESS

Oxford University Press is a department of the University of Oxford.
It furthers the University's objective of excellence in research, scholarship,
and education by publishing worldwide. Oxford is a registered trade mark of
Oxford University Press in the UK and certain other countries.

Published in the United States of America by Oxford University Press
198 Madison Avenue, New York, NY 10016, United States of America.

Library of Congress Cataloging-in-Publication Data
Names: Jones, Howard, 1940– author.
Title: My Lai : Vietnam, 1968, and the Descent into Darkness / Howard Jones.
Description: New York, NY: Oxford University Press, [2017] | Series: Pivotal moments in
American history | Includes bibliographical references and index.
Identifiers: LCCN 2016042464 | ISBN 9780195393606 (hardback : acid-free paper)
Subjects: LCSH: My Lai Massacre, Vietnam, 1968. | Vietnam War, 1961–1975—Atrocities. |
Calley, William Laws, Jr., 1943—Trials, litigation, etc. | Vietnam War, 1961–1975—United States. |
Vietnam War, 1961–1975—Moral and ethical aspects. | BISAC: HISTORY / Military /
Vietnam War. | HISTORY / United States / 20th Century.
Classification: LCC DS557.8.M9 J77 2017 | DDC 959.704/3—dc23
LC record available at https://lccn.loc.gov/2016042464

1 3 5 7 9 8 6 4 2
Printed by Edwards Brothers Malloy, United States of America

For Mary Ann and for the lost generation
...on both continents

A special tribute to Warrant Officer Hugh C. Thompson,
Specialist-4 Glenn W. Andreotta, and
Specialist-4 Lawrence M. Colburn
for personifying the essence of good character
in the midst of horrific circumstances

To the Reader

The words "My Lai" have become synonymous with the atrocities committed by U.S. soldiers in Son My Village, South Vietnam, on March 16, 1968. Indeed, the *Viet Nam News* in Hanoi in March 2008 referred to "My Lai (now Son My)" in describing the commemorative events on the fortieth anniversary of the "My Lai Massacre."[1] In truth, however, four massacres occurred on that day—in the subhamlets of My Lai 4, My Khe 4, Binh Tay, and Binh Dong. No one can know what happened in those places without *knowing* what happened in each one. To grasp the full measure of these events, the following account is graphic and detailed.

Last Train to Nuremberg

Last train to Nuremberg!
Last train to Nuremberg!
Last train to Nuremberg!
All on board!
Do I see Lieutenant Calley?
Do I see Captain Medina?
Do I see Gen'ral Koster and all his crew?
Do I see President Nixon?
Do I see both houses of Congress?
Do I see the voters, me and you?

Who held the rifle? Who gave the order?
Who planned the campaign to lay waste the land?
Who manufactured the bullets? Who paid the taxes?
Tell me, is this blood upon my hands?

If five hundred thousand mothers went to Washington
    Saying,
"Bring all our boys home without delay!"
Would the man they came to see, say he was too busy?
Would he say he had to watch a football game?

In this song, folk singer Pete Seeger expressed his feelings toward those he held responsible for the My Lai massacre. Excerpts from the lyrics appeared in a booklet available at the Son My War Remnant Site in My Lai: *A Look Back upon Son My* (Quang Ngai, Vietnam: Son My Vestige Site Management Board, 2009), 55–56.[2]

Contents

Contents

Acknowledgments

I want to extend a special thank-you to my former graduate student from Hanoi, Nhung Walsh, who is the bedrock of this book. A few years ago, Ronald Spector of George Washington University sent her my way to work on a master's degree in history. Afterward, she focused on her interest in art while helping me on this project in more ways than I ever could have imagined. A constant source of encouragement, she located materials, including (with the assistance of her husband, Joe) making digital copies of the CID documents in the Colonel Henry Tufts My Lai Collection at the University of Michigan, arranging my interviews of three survivors of the My Lai massacre, interviewing the commanding officer of the 48th Viet Cong Battalion in Pinkville, and translating and transcribing the notes on these interviews for my use. Furthermore, she put me in touch with Lawrence Colburn, the young gunner on the helicopter piloted by Chief Warrant Officer Hugh Thompson, who first reported the massacre to superiors and brought about a ceasefire. Throughout the long process, Nhung emphasized the importance of incorporating the Vietnamese side into the narrative and remaining objective in telling the story. I cannot thank her enough.

This book is the product of nearly a decade of research and writing, improved immensely by the generosity of friends and colleagues who read all or parts of the manuscript and offered many valuable suggestions. I am deeply indebted to Bill Allison, Gary Andrasko, Lawrence Colburn, William G. Eckhardt, Tony Freyer, Sharony Green, Ken Hughes, Ralph Levering, Kyle Longley, Pete Maslowski, William Hays Parks, Kevin Peraino, Don Rakestraw, Roger Spiller, Earl Tilford, and Nhung Walsh.

Sad to say, two of my favorite people passed away before the book appeared, Gary Andrasko and Larry Colburn. I am especially grateful to Gary not only for his extensive written comments on the manuscript but for the many hours we spent together, in my home, on the phone, and in email exchanges discussing every issue imaginable in the My Lai massacre and its aftermath. I am also deeply thankful to Larry for spending many hours detailing his experiences at My Lai and for exemplifying true courage and character. I can only hope they would have been pleased with the outcome.

Various institutions and archivists facilitated my research. The Earhart Foundation in Michigan once again supported my research, this time in the National Archives in College Park, Maryland, and the Nixon Library in Yorba Linda, California. For guiding me through the rich collections in the National Archives, I thank Richard Boylan, Marie Carpenti, Stanley Fanaras, and Martin Gedra. Stefan Papaioannou, a graduate student at the University of Maryland now teaching at Framingham State University, also assisted my research. For locating files at the Nixon Library, I wish to express my appreciation to Gregory Cumming, Pam Eisenberg, Meghan Lee-Parker, and Ryan Pettigrew. The Library of Congress in Washington, DC, provided online accessibility to the vast amount of materials amassed by the Peers Inquiry, the Hébert Subcommittee hearings in Congress, and many other documentary collections. The University of Michigan Library in Ann Arbor, Michigan, granted permission to digitize the CID records. For directing me to the huge collection on My Lai materials at the Vietnam Center and Archive at Texas Tech University in Lubbock, Texas, I want to thank its director, Stephen Maxner, and Vietnam veteran and historian Ron Milam, whose own work has profited from his association with the center. Mary Nelson in Special Collections at the Wichita State University library helped facilitate my use of the court-martial proceedings in the Ernest Medina case. And John Wilson, Vietnam archivist at the Lyndon B. Johnson Library, brought the William Westmoreland Papers on My Lai to my attention.

Others helped along the way and deserve thanks: Michael Bilton for graciously providing copies of the materials he and Kevin Sim used in writing *Four Hours in My Lai*; Tyra Brock and Patricia Causey at the University of Alabama Library for helping secure Interlibrary Loan materials; Lawrence Colburn for numerous phone conversations and emails that furnished eyewitness information on the events in My Lai 4 and afterward; Celina Dunlop from the *Economist* in the United Kingdom, who discovered the tapes of the Peers Inquiry and shared a documentary film she helped produce; William G. Eckhardt for providing insight into the legal issues involved in the Ernest Medina trial along with descriptions of his experience in courtroom battles with Medina's defense attorney, F. Lee Bailey; Christoph Felder, a German filmmaker who shared his first-rate documentary on My Lai; Al Fleming, long-time friend of William Calley, for trying at least two times over the course of five years to convince him to grant an interview; Tony Freyer for sharing his expertise in military and civil law; Joe Glatthaar for facilitating my contact with William G. Eckhardt; Stephen McGuigan for repeatedly making emergency house calls to resuscitate my computer either by slaying a virus or providing repairs; Colonel (Retired) Ngo Duc Tan for his personal account of commanding the 48th Viet Cong Battalion in My Lai; William Hays Parks for discussing international law and land warfare over lunch in Tuscaloosa and in numerous email exchanges; Dorothy Peacock, a nurse in a medical team sent to Quang Ngai Provincial Hospital on the eve of the Tet Offensive and My Lai massacre, who invited me to sit in on her course, This Was My Vietnam, given at the Osher Lifelong Learning Institute at the University of Alabama; Pham Thanh Cong, a survivor of the My Lai 4 massacre, for consenting to interviews and sending his notes of a meeting at My Lai in 1998 with Kenneth Schiel, the first soldier from Charlie Company to return to the scene; Tyler Pritchard, my undergraduate research assistant at the University of Alabama, who gathered many materials on My Lai and arranged my contact with Al Fleming; Earl Tilford for sharing his military expertise and facilitating my meeting with William Hays Parks to discuss *The Law of Land Warfare* and the My Lai case; Tran Van Duc for relating his experience and that of his mother at My Lai; Bruce Uhler for putting me in touch with Jim Andreotta, who provided a photograph of his cousin Glenn for this book; Vo Cao Loi and his uncle Vo Cao Tai, both survivors of the My Khe 4 massacre, who provided firsthand information on that day as well as Mr. Loi's providing a Vietnamese map of the area; the numerous other Vietnamese who described their experiences in My Lai to U.S. Army investigators; and my nephew Robert Dean Jones II, who offered to tell his Facebook friends about this book, and my own contacts on Facebook and LinkedIn who expressed encouragement and support.

I also want to express my gratitude to the great number of students I have had at the University of Alabama in courses on the Vietnam War and American foreign relations. They challenged my ideas and forced me to sharpen and substantiate them while reminding me of the importance of being objective in class and in my writings. Special thanks and admiration go to Mark Folse and Michael Stedman, both outstanding students and veterans of America's wars in Iraq and Afghanistan, Mark as a marine and Michael as an officer in the army. Both young men were in combat and tried to help me understand the fear of the unknown and the unseen that ran through their minds on the night and morning before combat. I deeply respect their honesty, dedication, and bravery.

I would be remiss if I did not thank the office staff of the Department of History at the University of Alabama for their support: Christina Kircharr, Ellen Pledger, and Morta Riggs.

There is no way to adequately express my appreciation to Oxford University Press for its accepting my proposal to contribute another book to the Pivotal Moments in American History series. Timothy Bent continues to be the kind, patient, personable, and understanding editor, who is so adept in his craft of streamlining awkward passages that I consider myself fortunate to have worked with him a second time. Alyssa O'Connell, his assistant, has been extraordinarily helpful, dependable, and friendly, particularly in finding and securing photographs for the book. She also arranged for me to work again with Alice Thiede, who did a magnificent job in drawing the maps for this volume, just as she had done for my earlier work, *The Bay of Pigs*. Joellyn Ausanka once more has demonstrated her remarkable skills in facilitating the book's passage through the production process. She made excellent decisions in choosing Ben Sadock as copy editor and Peter Brigaitis and his wife Marie Nuchols as indexers. They all are gifted in their crafts of putting finishing touches on a manuscript.

Special thanks goes to my three mentors who provided expert advice and continued encouragement throughout my professional career from graduate school at Indiana University to my many years at the University of Alabama: Professors Maurice G. Baxter and Robert H. Ferrell at Indiana University, and my longtime colleague at the University of Alabama, Professor Forrest McDonald.

Finally, I could not have completed this work without the continued support and love of my family: Mary Ann (and our late son Howie); our daughters Deborah Ann (and Jimmy) and Sharise Lynn; our grandson Timothy (and Kari); our granddaughters Ashley (and Mary Beth) and Lauren Ryan; and my brother Bob (and Ruth)—all have shown genuine interest in what happened in My Lai.

Mary Ann is my confidant and closest friend, a gentle and loving soulmate who hates violence and became emotionally shaken when hearing my stories of My Lai. She nonetheless stressed the importance of detailing the atrocities as a means of reducing the chances of their happening again. In the end, I agreed with her that to delete such descriptions would leave the mistaken impression that nothing extraordinary took place in My Lai on March 16, 1968.

Howard Jones
Northport, Alabama
Winter 2016

Editor's Note

On the morning of March 16, 1968, members of Charlie Company of the 1st Battalion, 20th Infantry Regiment, 11th Brigade of the 23rd Americal Infantry Division of the U.S. Army entered the Vietnamese village of Son My—including the hamlet called My Lai 4. Their search-and-destroy mission was intended to root out Viet Cong soldiers from what was thought to be an enemy stronghold. Finding no Viet Cong present, they nonetheless proceeded to murder some five hundred noncombatants. Over several hours, they burned huts to the ground, slaughtered livestock, gang-raped women, mowed down defenseless civilians, and even killed some fifty infants and toddlers, three years old or younger.

Army higher-ups, though informed of the war crimes, covered them up. But a few soldiers could not keep quiet. One man from another brigade who heard the horrific tales alerted politicians and Pentagon brass. Internal Army investigations in time verified many of the accounts. Journalists brought the story to the attention of the American public, who recoiled in horror.

Howard Jones's *My Lai: Vietnam, 1968, and the Descent into Darkness* recreates this infamous episode and reveals its significance in American history. Assembled with diligence from nearly five decades' worth of journalistic accounts, interviews, Army reports, trial transcripts, and government documents, Jones's gripping narrative takes the reader from the encampment where Charlie Company nervously awaited the start of its mission to the chaos of the blood-dimmed hamlet where the carnage occurred—then to the courtrooms where Lt. William Calley and others later stood trial, and ultimately to the White House, where President Richard Nixon and National Security Adviser Henry Kissinger discussed devising a "game plan" for maximum political advantage. History from below is fused to history at the top, revealing how the story of My Lai is inextricably linked to the broader story of the Vietnam War itself.

Far from a philippic, *My Lai* recovers the feelings of fear, confusion, and desire for revenge that turned the anxious young men into brutes during an increasingly chaotic war. Just after the Tet Offensive—the failed North Vietnamese military campaign that nonetheless made many Americans despair of ever conclusively winning the war—U.S. commanders moved on "Pinkville," a Viet Cong redoubt along the South China Sea that included My Lai. In the weeks between Tet and the fateful day of the massacre, the American soldiers saw comrades injured and killed by land mines, encountered children carrying out military work, and heard the nighttime shrieks of a G.I. being tortured and skinned alive.

The morning hours of March 16 are reconstructed and told in riveting—albeit excruciating—detail. The reader, facing one atrocity after another, cannot help considering the questions that the whole country would soon be debating: Did the soldiers act on orders, or were they out of control? Was Lt. Calley, the only one of the men to serve time for his crimes, a ringleader or a scapegoat or both? Was this sadistic behavior inevitable in wartime, an expression of man's inner beast, or a specific failing of specific individuals under specific circumstances—in particular amid a war that had become not only a military but also a moral quagmire?

The aimlessness and uncertain purpose of the Vietnam War may have made it easier for Charlie Company's men to sink into depravity. But not everyone did. Even in a morally disorienting situation, principled choice was possible. Hugh Thompson, a helicopter pilot who flew in support of the mission, recoiled when he came upon the mass slaughter in progress; he not only tried to save a handful of civilians but reported what he saw up the chain of command. Others, like Sergeant Jay Buchanon, resisted the urge to shoot indiscriminately and kept faith with their training not to kill the unarmed.

Beyond the exhaustive, harrowing account of the bloodbath, *My Lai* recounts the tortuous sequence of events that would inscribe it enduringly in the national consciousness and in history books. We see senior military officials choosing to ignore reports of the soldiers' savagery and authorize a whitewashed account of their mission. We see the unraveling of the cover-up, triggered by a helicopter gunner named Ronald Ridenhour, who heard about the massacre from a friend in Charlie Company, got confirmation from others in the ensuing months, and blew the whistle. We see the young investigative reporter Seymour Hersh chasing down the story, getting CBS's *60 Minutes* to air an interview with one of the perpetrators who remained tormented by his own role in the killing. We see the trials that followed, as prosecutors struggled in vain to build an ironclad case against others besides Calley—their acquittals amounting to yet more proof that nothing about the Vietnam War seemed to go right.

The My Lai massacre was a decisive event in the trajectory of the Vietnam War and what it came to symbolize. The disclosure of the atrocities not only moved public opinion further against an already unpopular war; at a time when Americans were doubting long-treasured notions of national virtue, it raised fundamental and unsettling questions about who were the good guys and bad guys in Vietnam, and why we were there at all. For the G.I.s, it deprived them of the hero's welcome that had greeted their predecessors. Lurking behind these immediate concerns were even deeper ones about America's professed role as the leader of the free world. The cover-up, too, mattered: It exacerbated a gnawing public distrust in the military and the government, feeding what would in time become a debilitating lack of faith in official institutions. Yet as dark deeds often do, the actions of Charlie Company also led eventually to stronger and clearer rules of conduct for American soldiers in wartime and a resolve within the military to resist the pressures toward cruelty that war inevitably brings.

Nearly a half century later, some wounds of the Vietnam War remain unhealed. And the capacity of men, no matter their nation of their birth or the cause for which they fought, to descend into barbarism still hasn't lost its power to shock.

David Greenberg

Abbreviations

ARVN	Army of Republic of Vietnam
CIA	Central Intelligence Agency
CID	Criminal Investigation Division
DMZ	Demilitarized Zone
GPO	Government Printing Office
IG	inspector general
JDE	John D. Ehrlichman
KCL	Kings College, London
KIA	killed in action
LBJL	Lyndon B. Johnson Library
LC	Library of Congress
LHCMA	Liddell Hart Centre for Military Archives
LZ	landing zone
MACV	Military Assistance Command, Vietnam
NA	National Archives
NARA	National Archives and Records Administration
NLF	National Liberation Front
NSA	National Security Archive
NSC	National Security Council
NSD	National Security Defense
NVA	North Vietnamese Army
PFC	private first class

POF   President's Office Files

PRC   Presidential Recordings Program

RG   Record Group

RNL   Richard Nixon Library

SP4   specialist fourth class

SP5   specialist fifth class

SVN   South Vietnam

UCMJ   Uniform Code of Military Justice

UPI   United Press International

USARV   U.S. Army, Vietnam

VATTU   Vietnam Center and Archive, Texas Tech University

VC   Viet Cong

VWCWG   Vietnam War Crimes Working Group

WSU   Wichita State University

My Lai

Prologue

I

On March 16, 1968, in Son My Village in South Vietnam, more than five hundred people—nearly half of them teenagers or younger—were slaughtered by soldiers of the United States Army. Today most people call this the My Lai Massacre, though "My Lai" actually refers to a group of villages—My Lai 4 and the neighboring subhamlets of Binh Tay and Binh Dong in Tu Cung Hamlet, and My Khe 4 in Co Luy Hamlet, all of them located in Quang Ngai province, a mainly agricultural region in what was then the northern coast of the Republic of South Vietnam and what is today the central coast of the People's Republic of Vietnam. At the time, the villages lay squarely in the region the U.S. Army called "Pinkville," designating it as under Communist control—either by the Viet Cong, the Army of the Republic of North Vietnam, or some combination of the two. The victims, all civilians, were shot, bayoneted, or killed by grenades, and left where they lay—on the trail, in a drainage ditch, in bunkers, yards, pathways, wells, and rice paddies, or in their homes.[1]

In the years that followed, despite efforts at documentation—by Americans, Vietnamese, and international observers—it has proven difficult to settle on the final death toll. In March 1970, the preliminary findings of the U.S. Army arrived at a figure of 360, including two hundred in My Lai 4 (some bodies brought to the ditch from neighboring Binh Dong); seventy in Binh Tay; and ninety in My Khe 4. But later in that same report, its writers asserted that the number might be more than four hundred, reflecting an estimate made by another ongoing investigation—both taking place nearly two years after the event. On April 11, 1968, less than a month after the killings, the village chief of Son My reported a total of 490 civilian deaths, four hundred of them in Tu Cung Hamlet (including My Lai 4 and Binh Tay) and the other ninety in Co

Luy Hamlet (including My Khe 4). That same month, the Viet Cong claimed five hundred civilians killed. Today, nearly fifty years after "My Lai," etched into the wall at the Son My War Remnant Site are the names of 504 men, women, and children.[2] Most parties now accept that number as accurate, though some still contend the actual number is smaller.

The chief perpetrator of the killings—particularly along the trail and in the ditch at My Lai 4—was William Laws Calley, Jr., a twenty-four-year-old U.S. Army second lieutenant who headed one of the three platoons in Company C ("Charlie Company") of the 1st Battalion, 20th Infantry Regiment, 11th Brigade of the 23rd (Americal) Infantry Division.

Three years later, in March 1971, a court martial in Fort Benning, Georgia, found Lieutenant Calley guilty of murdering at least twenty-two civilians and sentenced him to life in prison.

In the course of his four-month trial, Calley maintained his innocence, insisting that he had followed orders. He expressed his regret but only that the war itself had required him to do what he had been trained to do in boot camp and Officer Candidate School: to kill. War was the culprit, Calley argued. Those responsible for the fighting, not just in Pinkville but in Vietnam as a whole, bore the chief responsibility for My Lai.

Had My Lai resulted from the depraved actions of one individual— though he was far from alone, as there were more than one hundred men in Charlie Company—or had it been perpetrated by an entire command structure, even by the war with which it quickly became indelibly associated? Who bore responsibility for what everyone eventually acknowledged was a terrible tragedy?

Almost from the start, the U.S. Army realized that everything hinged on the question of orders—the chain of command. That was without question why the army kept the massacre quiet until the press and other news media made it public knowledge in November 1969, principally due to the investigative efforts of the American journalist Seymour Hersh, whose prize-winning articles on My Lai and the cover-up provided the basis for headlines around the country and around the world. He then followed these stories with two books, *My Lai 4* in 1970 (which won the Pulitzer Prize for International Reporting) and *Cover-Up* two years afterward.

The national exposure polarized Americans. On the one hand, it fed opposition to the Vietnam War (which a majority of Americans were now against). Placed within the context of other major events in this era—the Tet Offensive (which had occurred only weeks before My Lai and exerted a powerful and direct influence over it) and the invasion of Cambodia followed by the Kent State shootings—My Lai helped to unite a widely disparate number of Americans against the war, a group that included liberals and conservatives, hawks and doves from both political parties and from every level of society and section of the country. To them the My Lai massacre became both the result and the symbol of what was wrong about the Vietnam War. The army, they said, had turned the war into a contest over body counts, making a My Lai predictable if not almost inevitable. The war had transformed young American men into mass murderers, "baby killers."

To others, Calley became if not a hero, then at least a scapegoat for a flawed military policy that hampered the efforts of American forces to fight communism. Their reaction to his conviction hardened and deepened their support for the war. Calley and the other GIs in Charlie Company had done their duty in killing those villagers who aided the enemy. The soldiers had been following orders and doing the dirty work of those above them. A court-martial decision had energized a national debate by convincing Americans on both sides of the issue that a conspiracy had been at work.

During the long course of the war in Southeast Asia, other atrocities occurred, perpetrated by all sides in what was, after all, a brutal civil war, one that long preceded 1968. But none came close to My Lai in either the number of victims or the deeply personal—the murderously intimate—nature of their killing. The Vietnam War ground on until the ceasefire in January 1973, nearly five years after My Lai, followed by the withdrawal of the last U.S. troops more than two years later. But for many Americans, My Lai had laid bare the war, revealing that it was unwinnable and that, in the process of fighting for democracy and a way of life, America had lost its moral compass.

II

This book, the culmination of nearly a decade of research and writing, is an attempt to offer a balanced and accurate account of the massacre and its aftermath. One major challenge involves acknowledging that the story of My Lai is to a great degree the story of how it has been told. Who said what to whom and when? What testimony was offered to which organization or institution or journalist or jury? It goes without saying that everyone who has written or spoken about My Lai has had an agenda—whether to blame or defend American policy in Vietnam, the U.S. Army, the Viet Cong, the war itself, even the victims.

If at first My Lai was covered up, it soon exploded with details. Transcripts of interviews and testimonies abound—hundreds of thousands of pages. Some of the soldiers and officers at My Lai, along with their commanders at the base from which they organized and launched the assault on Pinkville, told their stories multiple times—to army investigators, congressional committees, radio and television news commentators, and judges and juries as witnesses in as many as three or four court appearances. Sometimes they were consistent and forthright; sometimes they were less so; many changed their accounts, subtly or dramatically, over time. Perhaps most important, we also now have the records of a number of Vietnamese who were questioned immediately after, and over the course of years, about what happened.

As anyone who works on My Lai knows, accounting for what happened in March 1968 is complicated by the major investigations that took place in the midst of the heated and divisive debate over U.S. involvement in Vietnam. Every statement or assertion became subject to rigorous examination, dissected and parsed by all parties. Those arguments and debates themselves have entered the record to become part of the "evidence."

The Pentagon became concerned about atrocity claims at My Lai and other places in Vietnam and carried out an investigation beginning in 1970, whose findings remained unavailable for nearly a quarter of a decade. When declassified in 1994, the records of the Vietnam War Crimes Working Group in the National Archives revealed more than three hundred allegations of murder and assault during the course of the war.

None came close to what happened in My Lai. The army first came under pressure to undertake an investigation in the spring of 1969, about a year after a Vietnam veteran named Ronald Ridenhour heard of the My Lai massacre from other GIs who were there. Outraged, he wrote a letter, dated March 29, 1969, to thirty military and governmental leaders (including the newly inaugurated President Richard Nixon), exposing what happened and calling for an investigation. The result was an inquiry by the inspector general's office, chaired by Colonel William Wilson. The Wilson inquiry led to a round of testimonies from soldiers, the most important of which was that given by Private Paul Meadlo of Lieutenant Calley's platoon. Meadlo's accusations convinced Wilson that American soldiers in Pinkville had engaged in something truly horrific.

Based on the inspector general's revelations, the army's Criminal Investigation Division (CID) began an inquiry in August 1969 that gathered more testimony and information supporting the atrocity claims. A key moment came when army photographer Ronald Haeberle, who had been in Pinkville, revealed that he had taken color pictures of the victims and brought them to the CID investigators. Suddenly the visual evidence was everywhere, from black-and-white photographs appearing in newspapers and on TV to color reproductions on display in *Life* magazine on December 5, 1969. These CID materials are available for perusal in the Colonel Henry Tufts Collection on My Lai at the University of Michigan in Ann Arbor (Tufts headed the inquiry). The color photographs, along with the black-and-white photographs taken by Haeberle, are on the Library of Congress website at http://www.loc .gov/rr/frd/Military_Law/Peers_inquiry.html.

To determine whether there had been a cover-up, the army established the Peers Inquiry, a panel of investigators chaired by Lieutenant General William R. Peers and comprised of both military and civilian attorneys. The Peers commission took more than four hundred testimonies from civilian and military personnel (some more than once), amassing thousands of pages of information in examining whether the earlier army investigations, which had been undertaken in Vietnam shortly after My Lai—instigated by the report of a helicopter pilot, Warrant Officer Hugh Thompson, who had hovered over the area and observed what happened—had been honest and thorough. To do this, the commission went beyond its narrowly defined mandate to look at the events occurring on March 16, 1968.

The Peers Inquiry began its work in the Pentagon on December 2, 1969, and presented its final report to the public on March 17, 1970. It accused dozens of officers, up to the division level, of suppressing evidence, and it recommended bringing charges of assault, murder, and rape against a large number of soldiers. The document containing its findings was 225 pages in length, a greatly redacted summation of twenty thousand pages of testimony set out in thirty-two books, along with six additional volumes containing five hundred documents. The entire collection became open to the public in late 1974 and is available on the Library of Congress website as well as on DVD. The "My Lai Tapes" of the testimonies are in the National Archives in College Park, Maryland, thanks to the efforts of Celina Dunlop of the *Economist*. Peers also wrote an insightful book on the subject, *The My Lai Inquiry* (1979).[3]

Virtually competing with the Peers commission was a subcommittee of the House Armed Services Committee, chaired by F. Edward Hébert of Louisiana. The Hébert Hearings resulted in a published report in 1970 that suggested a concerted effort by the subcommittee to undermine the allegations of mass killing made by Hugh Thompson. Six years later, the full records of the hearings became public and are on the Library of Congress website at http://www.loc.gov/rr/frd/Military_Law/ML_investigation.html.

There are other important sources. Calley of course testified at his court martial, but he also shared his most intimate thoughts about his role at My

Lai in extensive interviews with journalist John Sack. Much of this information Sack recorded in Calley's words in a book titled, *Lieutenant Calley: His Own Story* (1971). Sack also presented most of this material in a three-part article in *Esquire* magazine, "The Confessions of Lt. Calley" (Nov. 1970, Feb. 1971, Sept. 1971). The Richard Nixon tapes relating to My Lai are among these sources, including those in the Presidential Recording Program of the Miller Center of Public Affairs at the University of Virginia and the Richard M. Nixon Library in Yorba Linda, California. The Vietnam Center and Archive at Texas Tech University houses the My Lai Collection, a rich archive of testimonies and other documentary materials, much of it accessible over the Internet. Douglas Linder has put together a valuable website titled "Famous American Trials: The My Lai Courts-Martial."

The transcripts for both the Calley trial and the other major trial involving My Lai, that of Calley's immediate superior, Captain Ernest Medina, are available. The court-martial transcript for Calley's trial is in the National Archives in College Park, Maryland; the transcript for Medina's court martial is in the Special Collections of the University Libraries at Wichita State University in Wichita, Kansas. Also valuable for the Calley trial is the first-hand coverage provided by journalist Richard Hammer in his book, *The Court-Martial of Lt. Calley* (1971). For the Medina trial, perhaps the most useful (if self-serving) account is that written by his defense attorney, F. Lee Bailey—*For the Defense* (1975).

In the years following the trials and commissions, My Lai has come up again and again. In December 1994, for example, a major conference on My Lai took place at Tulane University in New Orleans, where Hugh Thompson, Ronald Ridenhour, Seymour Hersh, best-selling novelist and Vietnam War veteran Tim O'Brien, and others discussed My Lai in front of a large audience. Historian David Anderson edited these discussions in a book titled *Facing My Lai: Moving Beyond the Massacre* (1998). Also important to any examination of My Lai are the videos produced by PBS-TV (Barak Goodman, *American Experience*: "My Lai"; Judy Woodruff, *Frontline*: "Remember My Lai"—an award-winning film produced by Kevin Sim and Michael Bilton of Yorkshire Television in the United Kingdom and first shown on BBC-TV) and CBS-TV (Mike Wallace, *60 Minutes*). Of the numerous books on My Lai, the most complete account is that by Michael Bilton and Kevin Sim, *Four Hours in My Lai* (1992).

Despite the many testimonies, no single person could offer the full story. Both the American soldiers and the Vietnamese were scattered throughout the villages during the Pinkville campaign and actually witnessed only parts (or even none) of what happened. The My Lai story is therefore a collection, a composite, and by its very nature incomplete and partial. That is why it has also been a subject for novelists, filmmakers, and poets. What happened there has been interpreted and exploited by political leaders across the ideological spectrum; it has been fodder for lawyers, military leaders, congressmen, philosophers, and psychologists.

As I learned during the process of writing this book, among the most important sources of information, if also the most painfully and ironically overlooked, are the accounts of those Vietnamese who were actually there—the survivors of the massacre. I have included those accounts in the narrative.

Telling such a multifaceted and multilayered story has proved both captivating and challenging. For every view expressed by either a participant or a writer (then and later), there is a counter view. Fifty years later, disagreements persist over numerous aspects of the story, even the core narrative, which involved Lieutenant Calley and those under his command, as well as those under the command of Captain Medina, whose participation and responsibility still cause debate.

Many uncertainties remain. They always will. But it is clear that My Lai, once what happened there came into focus, raised a basic moral question, one that had not been posed since the post–World War II war crimes tribunals in Tokyo and Nuremberg—both of which were evoked during the Calley and Medina trials and thereafter. One figure in particular took center stage—General Tomoyuki Yamashita, commander of those Japanese forces in Manila who committed mass murder and atrocities in 1945. Yamashita was convicted of war crimes. The Supreme Court in 1946 upheld his conviction, and he was hanged. The controversy over the Yamashita conviction, and its relevance to My Lai, is clear: although the general did not personally direct or order the atrocities in the Philippines, he was guilty because he should have known they might happen and did nothing to prevent them. For a very good reason, mention of "Yamashita" struck cold fear into the hearts of everyone in positions of command in Vietnam, from General William Westmoreland on down.

The My Lai massacre became a legal and moral issue by raising the fundamental question of right and wrong, and it grew into a national policy issue by galvanizing the antiwar movement and ultimately helping to end America's involvement in Vietnam. It also brought on reforms within the Army aimed at preventing more atrocities. Only by following these events in their proper sequence can one understand how My Lai became a pivotal moment in America's history.

More important is the question I will pose at the beginning and at the end our story: Why did a massacre take place at My Lai?

I have my own reason for writing this book, but it is not, I hope, a complex one. The Vietnam War is long over, the generation that fought it heading gradually but inexorably into oblivion. What happened at My Lai needs to be recounted to and by every generation, including my own. What we make of it is for each one of us to decide.

PART I

Pinkville

One

NINETEEN SIXTY-EIGHT STARTED WITH CHAOS. On January 30–31, tracers from heavy artillery fire streaked across the dark sky and the ground shook from the blasts of shells. North Vietnamese Army (NVA) and National Liberation Front (Viet Cong) forces had launched an offensive, a full-scale assault on South Vietnam that violated the traditional truce celebrating the Lunar New Year, known as Tet. The attack raised serious questions about White House assurances that it had turned the corner in Vietnam. Opposition to the war had escalated in the United States over the previous few months, leading the Lyndon Johnson administration to pursue an aggressive public relations campaign, intended to restore faith in the war effort by forecasting imminent victory. But Communist strategists made a mockery of this optimism by engineering a massive operation that shattered White House credibility. Nineteen Viet Cong sappers armed with explosives blew a hole in the wall of the U.S. embassy in Saigon and invaded its grounds, killing and wounding several Americans, whose bloody images appeared in newsreels and photographs all over the world. The U.S. Marines only regained control of the complex the next morning after a seven-hour firefight.

The Communist offensive had spread simultaneously across South Vietnam, hitting nearly all forty-four provincial capitals—including Quang Ngai City, a small settlement in the northern sector of Quang Ngai Province that had become the gateway to Viet Cong territory. A strong counterattack by the government's ARVN (Army of the Republic of Vietnam) forces soon drove the seriously depleted Viet Cong units from the city, leaving them vulnerable to attack during their retreat, yet able to escape because the region was under ARVN jurisdiction, and it refused either to give chase or to permit Americans to enter what they called in wartime slang "Indian country."

Situated a mere six miles away, along the South China Sea and just below the Batangan Peninsula, was a Viet Cong stronghold known to Americans as "Pinkville," because of the distinctive coloring on U.S. Army maps that signified a thickly populated area. The commander of 24 Corps, Lieutenant General Melvin Zais, declared Pinkville a vital part of the three most dangerous provinces south of Da Nang—"the birthplace of the Viet Minh, and now the Viet Cong. You find mothers, fathers, sisters, brothers, grandmothers, and grandfathers a part of this insurgent movement."[1]

Located in Pinkville was the coastal fishing village of My Khe (known to Americans as My Lai 1), which allegedly housed the headquarters of the Viet Cong's fabled 48th Local Force Battalion. Farther inland were nearly four hundred Vietnamese living in the reputed Viet Cong hotspot of My Lai 4, one of several subhamlets in Son My Village that protected Pinkville's western flank. Tet made Pinkville the focal point of U.S. military action in this bitterly contested area.[2]

I

The Tet Offensive is the backdrop to the tale of two U.S. soldiers stationed in Vietnam: Captain Ernest Medina and William Calley, a young second lieutenant and platoon leader under his command. Medina was a ten-year veteran and Latino who had built a successful career in an Anglo-dominated officer corps after graduating fourth in his class of two hundred from Officer Candidate School (OCS). Following two tours in Germany and one in Fort Riley, Kansas, he trained at Schofield Barracks in Hawaii in preparation for assuming command of Charlie Company of the 1st Battalion, 20th Infantry Brigade, in late December 1966 at the age of thirty. Success at his new post virtually assured him of promotion to major and a long career in the service. Calley, for his part, had compiled a far less impressive record, joining the company in Hawaii in mid-September of 1967 after graduating from OCS at Fort Benning, Georgia, in the bottom quarter of his class and without knowing how to read a map or use a compass.[3]

Medina was a highly respected officer from New Mexico, where his father worked on a farm and his mother had died of cancer when he was less than a year old. Moving to Colorado to live with his grandparents, Medina spent his last five teenage years with the National Guard before joining the army at twenty. Stern but fair, he bore down on the raw recruits he commanded in Hawaii, molding them into the best company in the battalion. "Mad Dog," as Medina became known, drove his men so hard that they won numerous awards in camp.[4]

Calley was born in 1943 and raised in an affluent neighborhood in Miami, where he lived with his parents and three sisters in a two-story stucco house. Weighing less than 130 pounds and quite short—five foot three—he did not stand out. Yet he had a number of friends and appeared to blend in well. Nicknamed "Rusty" due to his reddish hair, Calley occasionally got into trouble but had no criminal record or history of violence and never used drugs.

Then his life took a downward turn. His father developed diabetes, and his mother was stricken with cancer. The family lost its construction business and had to give up its Miami home and move to its vacation cabin in North Carolina. The young Calley not only switched schools and lost friends, but he split his high school years between military school and public school when he ultimately returned to Miami to live and graduated in the bottom quarter of his class in 1962. Afterward, he entered nearby Palm Beach Junior College, flunking out in a single year with four Fs, one D, and two Cs. The army provided the chance for a new direction in life, but it rejected him because of hearing problems. All alone, twenty-one, he drifted from one small job to another—including bellhop, salesman, short-order cook, car washer, dishwasher, railroad conductor on a freight train, and insurance company investigator.[5]

Calley was going nowhere in the summer of 1966 when he came to the turning point in his life while job hunting in San Francisco: Two letters from his draft board caught up to him, ordering him back to Miami's Selective Service Office for a reassessment of the army's rejection of him two years earlier. Already in violation of the law for not reporting earlier, he immediately began the long drive home, but his car broke down in Albuquerque, New Mexico, and he had less than five dollars in his pocket. "What am I going to do?" Calley asked the sergeant at the army's local recruitment office in Albuquerque. "You enlist." Calley called his home induction center, which agreed not to draft him if he joined the army—which he did.[6]

Calley had never held a position of authority or shown any sign of leadership qualities, but his demeanor changed drastically in the army. After eight weeks of basic training at Fort Bliss, Texas, he attended clerical school at Fort Lewis in Washington State, where he did well, before entering OCS at Fort Benning in response to the army's urgent need for junior officers in Vietnam. The Citadel, West Point, and the Virginia Military Institute had been unable to fill the growing demand, and the Reserve Officer Training Corps (ROTC) had fallen out of favor on many college campuses. The army immediately needed more recruits from OCS—which opened the door to Calley.

At Fort Benning, in an accelerated training program at Infantry School, Calley learned how to attack while never mastering the other part of officer

training: how to convince an army of "grunts" (slang for infantrymen), aver-
aging under twenty years of age—younger than those who had fought in
either of the world wars or Korea—to follow his orders in battle. As one of his
commanding officers put it, Calley lacked both "command presence and command voice," liabilities that dogged him throughout his time in uniform.[7]

Calley became mesmerized by his teacher at OCS, a rough hulk of a
sergeant clad in gym shorts and T-shirt who demonstrated the art of killing
without a weapon. While future commanders sat in rapt attention, the sergeant selected a young soldier from the group, gruffly called him to the front,
and promptly kicked him in the kidney. As the soldier rolled on the ground in
agony, Calley apparently was appalled and transfixed.[8]

With the first man staggering back into the group and another "volunteer" warily taking his place, the sergeant stood ready with another demon-
stration. This one he "really kicked, or he flipped…with karate and *WHAM*,"
Calley related years later to journalist John Sack. The sergeant would "stomp"
on the soldier "right between the eyes: pretend to, and push his nose right
into his brain. Or stomp on his solar plexus: his ribcage, to push splinters into
his lungs. And then stomp on his heart to smash it."[9]

The sergeant then taught them how to kill silently with a garrote, readily
available in Vietnam in the form of a jungle vine to wrap around the enemy's
neck. A knife or bayonet created noise, he warned. "Don't slit a man's throat
if you don't want a sound: an *ughughugh* sucking sound, and don't stab a man
in the back anytime. A back has so many muscles," he emphasized with a
haunting sincerity, that "you'll never get a bayonet back out." The best place
to stab the enemy from behind was down through the shoulder, "the left
shoulder, preferably, where the heart is, that's how to kill someone best."[10]

This was combat Audie Murphy style, Calley thought in recalling the
most decorated combat soldier of World War II and a massive box office draw
in the Hollywood action movies of the 1950s—"*Kick in the door, run in the
hooch, give it a good burst*—kill. And get a big kill ratio in Vietnam. Get a big
kill count."[11] Murphy starred in more than forty movies, many of them
violence-ridden Westerns. His most popular movie was *To Hell and Back*, the
story of his life, which appeared in 1955 when Calley was a boy of twelve.

After graduating from OCS ranked 120 in a class of 156, Calley joined
Charlie Company, knowing that basic training had been the first stop on the
road to Vietnam. In preparation for his tour of duty, Calley took a class called
Vietnam Social Environment, which focused on the culture and history of its
people, and he attended Jungle Warfare School, where instructors taught
guerrilla tactics and the treatment of noncombatants. He and other soldiers

in Vietnam were required to carry two cards, the "Nine Rules" and "The Enemy in Your Hands," both calling for humanitarian treatment of civilians and captives. Americans were guests of the Vietnamese and were to treat everyone, including and especially women, with respect while avoiding "loud, rude, or unusual behavior."[12]

On the day before Calley left for Vietnam, the instructor selected him to deliver a three-minute orientation titled "Vietnam Our Host." "Oh god, what a farce that was," he declared years later. With the men horseshoed around him on the floor and visibly bored, he shouted, "Wake up! We're going to Vietnam! Wake up! Because it's our host—" He then read the "Do's" and "Don't's" of soldierly behavior in Vietnam to his non-listening comrades. "Do not insult the women. Do not *assault* the women." And above all, "Be polite."[13]

A vast body of international law covered guidelines—the rules of engagement—for dealing with both combatants and noncombatants in war, but few trainees or officers were familiar with or understood its intricacies. First Platoon staff sergeant and squad leader L. G. Bacon was an experienced military man who served under Calley in Vietnam and later provided an army inquiry valuable insights into what information reached the GIs and whether it had an impact on their behavior. After more than ten years in the army, he could not remember a single instance in which he and his men underwent meaningful training on the rules of land warfare. They learned about the proper handling of prisoners of war but received little guidance on the treatment of civilians and what to do if they witnessed war atrocities.[14]

The situation was no different with Medina. Though the leader of Charlie Company, he, too, had never seen a copy of the rules of engagement, nor had he read anything about the treatment of detainees, Viet Cong or otherwise. In a one-day orientation in Vietnam, he received verbal directives to evacuate civilians or move them toward friendly forces. He learned to yell *"Dung lai"* (stop) in the event that an unarmed Vietnamese tried to run away. If that did not work, he could fire a warning shot. Then he could shoot to disable. And he was under instructions not to shoot women and children.[15] Beyond these basic directives, Medina and his men would have to improvise in the heat of combat.

Even if the soldiers and commanders had received proper instruction, the directives were subject to flexible interpretation. Article 4 of the Hague Convention of 1907 on the Laws and Customs of War on Land, for example, appeared to clarify proper wartime behavior but was ambiguous. All "personal belongings, except arms, horses, and military papers," remained the property of prisoners of war. But what about rice or other items that were potentially helpful to the enemy? Article 23, furthermore, declared it illegal to confiscate or destroy enemy property but included an exception that would have enormous ramifications—unless "demanded by the necessities of war." What "necessities of war" meant, of course, was a matter of conjecture. Article 25 prohibited the "attack or bombardment" of undefended homes or buildings. Yet what constituted a *defended* bunker or place of refuge that made it open to attack? Article 28 prohibited the "pillage of a town or place," and yet, as with the property stipulations mentioned above, what if the items in question were valuable to the enemy? Where was the line between confiscation and "pillage"?[16] These exceptions made the guidelines virtually meaningless.

The rules of engagement were the U.S. military's attempt to adhere to the Nuremberg principles of 1946, set out during the German war crimes trials. Among their assertions was the stipulation that a person following an order of either his government or a superior officer was not thereby freed of his "responsibility under international law, provided a moral choice was in fact possible to him." Article 6 of the charter of the Nuremberg Tribunal contained a list of war crimes that included "murder or ill-treatment of prisoners of war" and "plunder of public or private property, wanton destruction of cities, towns, or villages, or devastation not justified by military necessity."[17]

The United States was a signatory nation to the Geneva Conventions of 1949, which upheld these same principles. Article 3 assured humane treatment to persons not participating in the hostilities, including enemy forces who had put down their weapons. At no time was it acceptable to commit murder or to torture, mutilate, humiliate, or degrade detainees. The Geneva Conventions also required providing medical assistance to the sick and injured.[18]

Aside from the rules of engagement and the Geneva Conventions, the U.S. Army Field Manual 27-10 of July 1956 followed international law in providing commanding officers with a detailed explanation of acceptable combat behavior. Titled *The Law of Land Warfare*, the manual was a revised and expanded version of the War Department's pamphlet *Rules of Land Warfare*, issued in October 1940. According to the 1956 manual, American military personnel were to protect "both combatants and noncombatants from unnecessary suffering" by safeguarding "certain fundamental human rights of persons who fall into the hands of the enemy." Military needs did not relieve the soldier of legal obligations. "Every violation of the law of war is a war crime," reads section 499.[19]

Perhaps the most far-reaching part of the Army Field Manual was section 501, which appeared to follow the so-called Yamashita Principle. In the Japanese war crimes trials following World War II, the American Military

Tribunal sentenced General Tomoyuki Yamashita to death for crimes committed by his soldiers in the Philippines. Even though the defense argued that Yamashita was not personally aware of his men's actions, the key to the decision was the prosecution's claim that he was involved in a series of similar crimes committed under the supervision of Japanese officers and NCOs under his command. His headquarters were adjacent to or within two POW camps in which a number of atrocities took place. Moreover, Yamashita personally ordered the executions of two thousand Filipinos in Manila suspected of being guerrillas and was the source of a number of orders to execute pro-American Filipinos. These violations were so widespread, the tribunal concluded, that Yamashita must have been responsible. The defense appealed his conviction, but the U.S. Supreme Court upheld the decision in 1946, and he was hanged.[20]

The Yamashita trial did not establish strict liability, as is popularly believed, but it did hold commanders responsible for controlling their soldiers. It is not clear whether the military tribunal decided there was sufficient circumstantial evidence to prove Yamashita had actual knowledge of the crimes and planned and ordered them, or that he knew about them and did nothing to stop them. It is clear, however, that the tribunal determined that a commander must make every effort to prevent war crimes even if they were not responsible for all crimes by subordinates. The issue was not what he knew but what he *should* have known concerning violations from reports, and then whether he failed to investigate or take corrective action. Were this determined, he shared the guilt of the principals who committed the crimes. Dereliction of duty was criminal negligence.[21]

According to the Army Field Manual, should troops become engaged in "massacres and atrocities" against noncombatants, the commander giving the orders "may" be as responsible as the perpetrators. He could not plead ignorance of a violation. He also was responsible if he had "actual knowledge, or should have knowledge" from reports indicating that his troops either committed or were about to commit war crimes and did nothing to stop them. Furthermore, section 507 declared that troop commanders must guarantee punishment for war crimes committed by their forces.[22]

Section 509b of *The Law of Land Warfare* seemed less clear about whether a soldier had the right to disobey what appeared to be an illegal order. The army asserted that its forces must "obey only lawful orders but opened the door to interpretation by adding three qualifications: that no one could expect soldiers in war to determine the legality of an order, that rules of war are sometimes subject to dispute, and that no one could justify a war crime committed as an act of retaliation.[23]

Lest uncertainty remain, the commanding general of the III Marine Amphibious Force of MACV (Military Assistance Command, Vietnam) included on his distribution list further directives on reporting suspected war crimes. Anyone knowing or hearing about an alleged war crime was to immediately notify his commanding officer. The commanding general would select an officer to submit a "report of investigation."[24]

II

These laws and regulations did not particularly preoccupy Calley, whose priority, as with most if not all American soldiers in Vietnam, was personal security, not protecting civilians in combat areas. What he learned at base camp did not relate to treatment of the enemy but to warnings about them, generally referred to as "gooks," "dinks," "slopes," and "slants." Treat every Vietnamese as an enemy, including the children. According to Calley, during his testimony at his court martial, the children were "even more dangerous" than adults. They warned of Americans arriving, threw hand grenades, and gathered and distributed mines and booby traps—at times planting the mines. No one at OCS spoke of "innocent civilians" in Vietnam, he explained. The Viet Cong made the decision to hide among the populace, making it nearly impossible to distinguish between civilian and combatant. Calley used the words "fear," "hatred," "hostility," and "frustration" to describe his inability to identify the enemy. He always felt uneasy about the villagers.[25]

The countryside belonged to the Viet Cong, Calley emphasized to Sack. "Be sharp! On guard! As soon as you think these people won't kill you, ZAP! In combat you haven't friends! You have enemies!" He promised himself, *"I'll act as if I'm never secure. As if everyone in Vietnam would do me in. As if everyone's bad."*[26]

He would not be alone in this belief. As Vietnam veteran and popular writer Philip Caputo put it: where trust did not exist and body counts became the only yardstick of victory, the rule in the bush was, "If it's dead and Vietnamese, it's VC."[27]

In *A Rumor of War*, the memoir of his marine experiences in Vietnam, published in 1977, Caputo confirmed Calley's observations at his trial, noting how the stress of search-and-destroy missions in the jungle led to short tempers. The truth—that all Viet Cong were Vietnamese but not all Vietnamese were Viet Cong—was not readily apparent when both sides were Vietnamese. War "can arouse a psychopathic violence in men of seemingly normal impulses," but the type of war waged in Vietnam deteriorated into an "absolute savagery" that was unlike any other conflict. American lives were at stake in an environment in which they could not be sure who or where the enemy was.[28]

It was unnerving to American soldiers to fight in Indian country with no battle lines, against a ghost-like guerrilla army without uniforms that hid among the populace and employed a labyrinth of jungle trails and tunnels. Anyone Vietnamese was responsible for their plight—or so they came to believe during endless hours in the heat, humidity, and incessant pounding rain of the monsoon season.

Dry season was no better. Long patrols trudged forward, the soldiers with heavy backpacks that tugged in the opposite direction as they worried about whether their M-16 assault rifles, which frequently malfunctioned, would work at crunch time.[29] And all this in temperatures that soared to more than a hundred degrees and humidity trailed not far behind. Sweat drenched their clothing and rolled off the sweatbands on their foreheads as they pressed forward through clouds of dust or groin-high grass or hacked through the bush with its towering bamboo and banana trees and wire-like wait-a-minute vines. Dense and razor-sharp elephant grass could rise up to fifteen feet in height, making it difficult to see more than three feet ahead.

In Vietnam, misery came in many forms for American soldiers like Calley and Medina. Whether during the advance or waiting in ambush in foxholes or brush, they fought a relentless war against flies, mosquitoes, fire ants, spiders, chiggers, centipedes, leeches, ticks, honeybees, rats, snakes, and every other pest of nature that walked, crawled, or flew. The monsoon season brought some relief from the stifling heat, but that was of little consolation to soldiers slogging through mud and muck while being hammered by the monotonous and seemingly unending rain. Massive flooding churned up scores of snakes, many of them poisonous, slithering amid a sticky, lava-like mud that bogged down everything and everyone in its path, particularly those already debilitated by trench foot, jungle rot, blackwater fever, malaria, and dysentery. Yet far worse than the pitiless environment was the stress of interminable, mind-numbing patrols, the so-called search-and-destroy operations that kept the soldiers in the bush for weeks, prey to all these afflictions, as well as mines, booby traps, and snipers.[30]

Calley and his comrades in arms hoped that basic training had prepared them for everything Vietnam could throw at them. After OCS, Calley entered six months of accelerated training at Fort Benning as a junior officer in mid-March 1967, where he felt confident he had learned the essentials of command. The gold bars on each shoulder attested to his qualifications for leading a platoon into battle.[31]

Medina for his part had hoped he had inherited a group of young men who knew how to kill with or without weapons, both in long-range and hand-to-hand fighting, and would obey orders without hesitation. Drill sergeant Kenneth Hodges helped to prepare the soldiers in Charlie Company for both types of fighting and never admitted to such a thing as an illegal order. To question a command in the heat of battle could cost the lives of fellow soldiers. Charlie Company had learned the two most fundamental rules of being a soldier: *Shoot to kill and do not question orders.* As Calley asserted to Sack, OCS and final training in Hawaii had taught him and others to kill.[32]

Charlie Company did not appear to be unique. Almost 90 percent of its non-commissioned officers (NCOs) had graduated from high school, which was slightly above the norm in the army. The soldiers' ages ranged from eighteen to twenty-two, with the median at about twenty-two, and about half of them were African Americans or Latinos. Only about a dozen came from Robert McNamara's pet program, Project 100,000, an attempt by the secretary of defense to rescue disadvantaged youths from the streets and put them in uniform. Fred Widmer, a high school graduate from Pittsburgh, proudly declared that he and his new comrades were "a cross-section of just your general, basic young people at that point in time. We were from all over the country. You know—East Coast, West Coast, blacks, whites, Mexicans—there was nothing special about us. We were just your common, ordinary teens.... Having grown up with parents that came from World War II and people that were in the Korean War and everything, being exposed to their generations, yeah, you felt it was basically your duty to go ahead and go to war." Charlie Company was typical of most units in Vietnam, in which blacks and whites stayed separate, and it was composed of the usual blend of American youths, coming from cities as far east as Richmond, Virginia, and as far west as Portland, Oregon, along with many points in between, both small towns and farm areas north and south. This cross section of America cut across racial, ethnic, and religious lines, making the infantry company appear representative of the nation as a whole.[33]

On December 1, 1967, Charlie Company rose at four in the morning to depart from Hawaii on a chartered Pan American Airways flight, covering the 6,060 miles to Da Nang Air Base in South Vietnam, in about twelve hours. Not long afterward, the men were airlifted seventy-six miles south to their new home, Quang Ngai Province, a longtime hotbed of Viet Cong activity.[34]

Almost immediately, Lieutenant Calley's relationship with Captain Medina became strained. Calley made every effort to impress him. In Hawaii he had grown to like and respect Medina: "A man would have to commission close to a half million officers before he had someone equal to Captain Medina," Calley declared to John Sack in his as-told-to book. "A real leader." That camaraderie, if it ever existed, rapidly disappeared. Within weeks of arriving in Vietnam, Medina routinely referred to him as "Lieutenant Shithead"—in front of the other soldiers.[35]

Calley had established a reputation for ineptitude early. On his first foray into the bush in mid-December 1967, he forgot to bring hand grenades and had to rush back to the ammunition center, where he had to uncrate them. Medina, as his men recollected, was livid over the delay. "Calley, I would relieve your ass in a goddamn second!" he threatened his junior lieutenant at one point, as recounted by Sack. On a nighttime ambush set up in a cornfield with no place to camouflage themselves, Calley heard rustling in the stalks sometime after midnight and suspected that the Viet Cong were sneaking up on them in the darkness. He panicked and called for a massive and continuous firing of yellow flares, which lit up the area for miles—not realizing the enemy could see them as well.

When Medina became aware of the lighted skyline, he phoned Calley: "Now what in the goddamn hell?"

"It's a dark and rainy night and—"

"You nitwit!" Medina stormed. "You're without a doubt the most stupid second lieutenant on the face of this earth!"

"Yes sir. I know sir. I'm stupid sir. What should I do?"

"Turn off them goddamn lights!"

Four hours later, dawn came with no further incident.[36]

According to most accounts, Calley seemed oblivious to the cutting remarks. Charlie Company, he boasted, again in his book with Sack, "was really made for war! We were mean! We were ugly!" With his rifle held low and his helmet pulled down, he thought, "*This is my day*! And these are my men! We're rough and we're tough, and Charlie's here: Charging Charlie! To end this damned war tomorrow!"[37]

Others besides Medina were unsure of Calley and expressed their concerns to journalist Seymour Hersh. SP4 Robert Maples of Freehold, New Jersey, declared that Calley would do anything to make himself into a "hero" and a "good boy" in front of Medina. Another member of Charlie Company, Private Roy Wood of Richmond, Virginia, marveled that Calley had even made it through OCS: "He couldn't read no darn map and a compass would confuse his ass." The Peers Inquiry confirmed these assessments, declaring that Calley appeared to have been the only one of Medina's three platoon leaders not referred to as a "nice guy" by his subordinates. "A little kid trying to play war," observed SP4 Charles Hall from Columbus, Ohio—liked by few and hated by many.[38]

Another platoon member, PFC Michael Bernhardt from New York City, remembered sharing these concerns with his group. Soon after his assignment to Charlie Company, he declared years afterward, "I knew there was something wrong. You could smell it and feel it." The men felt "no sense of community, no sense of duty or responsibility, no sense of pride." Bernhardt recalled that Medina had difficulty controlling his troops. "They were just like a bunch of street thugs doing whatever they wanted to do." Lacking discipline, they were "leaderless, directionless, armed to the teeth, and making up their own rules out there." To them, Bernhardt sarcastically added, "the epitome of courage and manhood was going out and killing a bunch of people."

Adding to this problem was what Bernhardt identified as the "three pillars" of the war effort. There was, he said, the "free-fire zone," which meant the freedom to shoot anyone who moves; the "search-and-destroy mission," which Bernhardt termed the "portable free-fire zone," one you could "tote" wherever you went—"just another way to shoot anything that moves"; and, last, there was the body count, which in a war of attrition provided the chief means for "measuring the success or failure of whatever you're doing." Given these three elements of war in Vietnam, Bernhardt concluded, "It doesn't take a genius to figure out how it's going to end up."[39]

Like Wood and others, Bernhardt detested Calley and was mystified that he had made it through OCS. Bernhardt remembered that, on one occasion in the field after Tet, he had just emerged from searching an underground bomb shelter when he saw Calley with his pants down and a woman kneeling before him while he held a .45 pistol to her head. "I really, really wanted to kill that guy but there were just too many guys around," Bernhardt recalled. "I saw him as pure evil…rotten to the core." If the men of Charlie Company "were kind of waiting for someone to tell them what the hell to do, to make some kind of moral judgment for them," that someone was not Calley.[40]

On its arrival in Vietnam, Charlie Company merged into the newly formed Americal Division, a mixed division of three infantry brigades, the 11th, 196th, and 198th. They broke down into infantry battalions comprised of three companies in each, which in turn broke down into platoons and the platoons into squads. The brigades had once been part of Task Force Oregon, formed in the spring of 1967 as the first army unit to conduct operations in Quang Ngai Province. In late September, the army re-designated the unit as the 23rd, or Americal, Division, a name derived from a division formed during World War II when the American Army defended the French colonial island of New Caledonia in the South Pacific against a Japanese assault and then collaborated with the marine corps in the attack on Guadalcanal in October 1942. Americal in Vietnam would reinforce the marines in the northern provinces.[41]

Americal Division infantrymen proudly called themselves "Jungle Warriors" and were under the leadership of a rising star within the army, Major General Samuel Koster. Critics such as Michael Bernhardt, however, called the division a troubled and mongrelized collection of hoodlums who ignored regulations and were so disgruntled with their station that they worsened its already dysfunctional chain of command. Serious command and control issues stemmed from inadequate training and no leadership from top to bottom, which encouraged a lack of regard for Vietnamese civilians and a poor field record that led to the division's deactivation in late 1971.[42]

Koster had his sights on becoming superintendent of West Point and felt it would help for him to have experience in commanding a division—even this one. Since he thought his tenure there would be temporary, he rarely talked with his staff and sought to avoid any questions about his leadership and promotional aspirations. Each day was preparation for his next step up the chain of command, in the tradition of MACV's commander, General William Westmoreland, and other four-star generals.[43]

Koster's stay with Americal proved especially problematic, because its headquarters were in South Vietnam's most northern reaches, which were under Marine command, requiring him to report to a Marine general. Westmoreland's vice-chief of staff, General Bruce Palmer, Jr., summed up Koster's situation in an oral interview for the U.S. Army Military Institute some years afterward. It was "terribly difficult," particularly in what was "perhaps the toughest part of Vietnam to fight in, 'Indian Country' that the Viet Cong had owned for generations." Without much troop experience, Palmer added, "we gave the toughest job in Vietnam to our most inexperienced commander, who was least qualified to be a division commander."[44]

III

Charlie Company's timing set it up for disaster. It had arrived in South Vietnam at a touchy time—as noted, just before the Tet Offensive—and in a highly sensitive area. By the time it made it to My Lai 4, the region had earned its reputation as a Viet Cong hotspot and one of the most dangerous parts of Vietnam. Quang Ngai Province appeared serene, a scenic haven graced with silky white beaches brilliantly contrasted by the warm, turquoise waters of the South China Sea. Yet beneath this outward calm lay a sense of foreboding, as recalled by those who were there, in large part because of the presence of the Viet Cong. In mid-1967, the U.S. Army had launched its initial operation in the area with Task Force Oregon, whose architects claimed to have killed more than three thousand Viet Cong and rounded up another five thousand suspects by the end of the year. But this effort, as ambitious as it was, hardly made a dent in the enemy's numbers, as Tet would show.[45]

Westmoreland had recognized soon after becoming MACV's head on June 20, 1964, that one key to success in the war was persuading the local farmers not to help the Viet Cong. But he also was aware of the great divide between theory and practice. For example, he knew he could not guarantee the friendly farmer's safety twenty-four hours a day. To win the war, Westmoreland insisted that he had to wear down the enemy and convince him of the impossibility of victory—which meant stepping up American firepower and leaving pacification of the countryside to the South Vietnamese. The injection of more firepower would of course result in more civilian casualties in the target areas and thereby interfere with pacification. By the end of 1967, in fact, U.S. soldiers had alienated the populace by destroying more than half of the province's homes, killing a great many civilians, and forcing large numbers of peasants to seek refuge in Quang Ngai City. American firepower drove many Vietnamese into either helping or joining the Viet Cong in a "people's war" against the outsider.[46]

Yet Washington's policymakers failed to grasp the implications of what had become a war of attrition. The Vietnamese suffered as much as the Americans in these harsh surroundings, but attrition worked to their advantage against an outsider unfamiliar with the terrain. According to a Vietnamese tradition that traced back to the thirteenth century—to the guerrilla tactics employed by the revered leader Tran Hung Dao in repeatedly repelling Kublai Khan's Mongol invaders—every Vietnamese would treat all intruders as the enemy.[47]

The American high command tried to reduce civilian casualties. Its aircraft dropped millions of leaflets on trouble spots, warning their inhabitants (most of whom could not read) of what was ahead, offering them the choice to leave and live as Vietnamese nationals or stay in their homes and die as Viet Cong supporters. Thus were the countryside and villages in the region turned into "free-fire zones" where, by definition, the only people remaining after an ordered evacuation had to be Viet Cong or their sympathizers and therefore legitimate targets. Yet in a battle of nomenclature, those who refused to leave and were injured or killed came to be called "collateral damage"—a euphemism perhaps indicating that the American military regarded the growing numbers of dead and wounded villagers as an acceptable cost of war. "No one has any feeling for the Vietnamese," reported one young soldier from Texas. "The trouble is, no one sees the Vietnamese as people. They're not people. Therefore, it doesn't matter what you do to them."[48]

Thus the deadly catch-22 of Vietnam faced Charlie Company and indeed all American soldiers in Vietnam: "collateral damage" was a phrase without meaning, since ultimately there was no way of distinguishing between innocent civilian and deadly foe.

The presence of children in war zones posed the most perplexing problem. Medina, for one, had been warned by an Australian adviser to be "extremely leery of children." As late as December 1967 when Charlie Company arrived, the Americans remained sympathetic toward young people, but that sentiment was rapidly disappearing with the escalating violence and with the realization that the enemy did not distinguish between children and adults. Intelligence experts asked a telling question: "If there are a hundred kids in a village, where are the men?" Calley thought he had the answer. Vietnamese men, he told Sack, were "getting ready to zap us while we're tied up talking to nice sweet kids." Calley remembered that "intelligence had a VC code saying this was a VC tactic now. Intelligence told us, 'Bust through. Get through to the goddamn village.' You know? Those kids had been following us right to where we would RON [remain overnight]. And been telling the VC, 'They're there.' "[49]

Calley's first encounter with the Vietnamese villagers led to what he remembered as a sharp disagreement with Medina, and it was over children. Calley expected his platoon to hate the children as much as he did. While he and his men guarded a bridge, hundreds of Vietnamese kids milled around, excitedly begging for gifts and offering to do laundry for pay. "All the men love them," Calley declared with disgust. "Gave the kids candy, cookies, chewing gum, everything. Not me: I hated them." OCS instructors had warned that kids put explosives in gasoline tanks or in GIs' hooches. "I was afraid of prostitutes too...but I was more afraid of Vietnamese kids."[50]

When Calley complained to Medina about the kids, the response came in the form of questions. Whether or not he shared Calley's concerns, he had more important matters to deal with than childish squabbles between an officer and his men.[51]

"Are you an officer of the United States Army?" Medina asked Calley during a confrontation.

"Yes sir."

"And can you control your men?"

"Yes sir."

Calley had taken away a PFC's stripe in an attempt to stop him from coddling the kids. Medina, however, refused to back him on this demotion. When Calley admitted that his tactics had not worked, Medina simply asked, "Why should I do the paperwork?" "And what do I do about those kids?" Calley asked Medina. "Well, you're a lieutenant, aren't you? And you can control your men?" The meeting was over. Calley rejoined his men, angrily telling them, "Someday, a little sonofabitch's going to grenade you." Seeing that his warning had no impact, he muttered to himself, as he told John Sack, "*Let them learn.*"[52]

Calley always maintained that he had learned a great deal in his first three months in Vietnam, both about his men and about himself, but little about the Vietnamese themselves. In an exchange recorded by Sack, Calley recalled a conversation with a prostitute he had befriended. "Susie"—employing pidgin English—had been trying to understand why Calley, and by extension all the Americans, were so against the Viet Cong.

"You no like VC. Why?"

They were bad, he responded.

"VC no hurt me, VC no hurt you. You nice to VC, he nice to you."

The VC hurt the Vietnamese people, Calley insisted.

"Same same!" Susie exclaimed. "VC Vietnamese. Vietnamese VC."

But the VC are Communists, he declared.

"*No bitt*," she replied, saying she did not understand. Calley remembered that he was determined to drive the lesson home. "Even the Good Book, the Bible, says, 'You shall destroy your enemy.' I just knew, *I must communicate with you. Or else you're dead.*"[53]

The Bible aside, the heart of the problem in Quang Ngai was the Viet Cong's 48th Local Force Battalion, which reportedly operated out of My Lai 1 and numbered more than 250 strong. Since the fall of 1965, the Local Force had become legendary, masterfully avoiding full-scale engagements while conducting highly effective harassment actions from deep within Pinkville. Nguyen Duc Te, chief of the Census Clearance Center and a resident of Quang Ngai Province, went so far as to declare My Lai 4 a "combat village of the Communists." When asked if the women and children were also Communists, a villager warned that all his relatives were Communists and that "if any friendly units from the government controlled area go to My Lai they would fight." Both men and women gathered information for the Viet Cong and laid mines and booby traps. My Lai 4, Te insisted, was a "VC stronghold."[54]

Nguyen Duc Te was part of MACV's Phoenix Program (known in Vietnam as Phung Hoang, the mythical "All Seeing Bird"), created in 1967 and financially supported by the CIA to gather intelligence and make arrests aimed at destroying the Viet Cong infrastructure by means of Provincial Reconnaissance Units (PRUs), or People's Action Teams. These PRUs became known for using any means necessary, including open-ended detentions, torture, and even assassination. Te's agents in the Communist-controlled areas supplied the program's American leaders with the names of many residents of My Lai 4, including women who worked with the Viet Cong and were on a "Black List" kept by the Quang Ngai Province Committee.[55] Phoenix strategists soon set monthly quotas for "neutralizing" the Viet Cong, a euphemism for gathering intelligence by whatever methods their agents deemed effective.

Ta Linh Vien of the Census Grievance Center (secretly funded by the CIA) dealt with intelligence for the entire province and also thought My Lai 4 was, as he put it, "under VC control." The center had officers working with the people in government-controlled areas, along with secret agents passing in and out of the Viet Cong–controlled areas or actually living there. The Viet Cong had planted a number of booby traps and mines around the settlement, which had inflicted horrific injuries on Vien's agents with explosives detonated by women and small children. "My Lai is a combat village," Vien claimed, where many ARVN had died. All people living there—women, children, the elderly—"have some weapon at home." All the younger men fight with the Viet Cong.[56]

Vien further asserted that the Viet Cong had kept constant pressure on Quang Ngai City, using My Lai 4 and the whole of Son My Village as bases for mounting attacks in the surrounding area. Most if not all civilians were VC sympathizers or had relatives who worked for the Viet Cong and refused to leave despite warnings of personal harm. Vien insisted that the blacklist was meaningless, because all the inhabitants in the My Lai area worked for the VC. And, he added, the VC support group included children.[57]

The Saigon government's intention—as everyone in Quang Ngai Province knew—was to launch a big "saturation area of operation," as Vien put it. In December 1967 a helicopter repeatedly broadcasted warnings as it loudly flew around My Lai 4. Government agents assured its residents and others living in surrounding areas that those not supporting the Viet Cong who moved out and waited until the government's forces had cleared the village before returning would receive assistance. Those who remained would be in "a free-fire zone." By this point, nearly everyone understood what that term meant.[58]

U.S. military personnel thus drew the conclusion from Vietnamese and American intelligence sources that My Lai 4 was essentially an enemy bastion. The head of the U.S. intelligence team, Captain Eugene Kotouc, drew on

Vietnamese contacts and other sources of information in declaring My Lai 4 a well-fortified bunker connected to a maze of tunnels. Medina's radio-telephone operator (RTO), Fred Widmer, thought that most of the villages in this area were Viet Cong because of the large number of Russian, Communist Chinese, and NVA flags. When asked whether My Lai 4's people sympathized with the Viet Cong, rifleman William Doherty spoke for many others in responding, "Yes, sir, definitely....a hundred per cent."[59]

Satisfied that My Lai 4 was a Viet Cong staging area, the U.S. Army command in Quang Ngai focused on destroying the village with a new outfit created on New Year's Day of 1968: Task Force Barker, a contingent of five hundred soldiers put together from several units under the command of an eighteen-year veteran, Lieutenant Colonel Frank Barker. His men soon dubbed themselves "Barker's Bastards" because of their alleged illegitimate status within the already bastardized American Division. The major components of this force were three companies—Alpha, Bravo, and Charlie—which would engage in search-and-destroy missions for the next ninety days in Pinkville as part of Operation Muscatine, named by Major General Koster after a town close to his home in Iowa. When Medina in turn announced the imminent offensive to his men, they cheered. They were finally going to destroy the Viet Cong's 48th Local Force Battalion.[60]

Charlie Company's initiation into guerrilla warfare proved so horrid that it dispelled any dreams of glory that Medina's men might have had. In mid-January 1968, he sent his forces on a series of patrols in the hills of Quang Ngai Province, a hundred miles or so west of the heart of Pinkville. Private Eusebio Santellana of Texas was among these young grunts and later provided a graphic first-hand account of their introduction to the Viet Cong. A patrol had worked its way up a hill held by the enemy but did not return by nightfall. No one in his platoon ate or talked much that night. "We hadn't had a loss. The hills were as quiet as a Texas desert."[61]

Late in the night, they were startled by blood-chilling screams—"the vomit cry," recalled Santellana. "Like death. But it didn't stop. Not after one time. It kept going. It got weaker and weaker, but it held out. And it did make you want to shit right there in your tracks. The bastards!" Calley remembered the agonizing, gut-wrenching sound, magnified in the darkness as if the Viet Cong were using some amplifying device. He and the others could do nothing except wait for morning. No one slept. Several of the young men cried, their bodies shaking.[62]

At daylight, the first patrol in that area found the body of a tortured American soldier, a bloody hulk hanging from a pole. "Dink shitheads had skinned him alive," asserted Santellana. The Viet Cong had peeled off most of his skin and then doused his wounds in salt water while forcing him to drink water to remain alive and scream even more. Calley noted that the Viet Cong had ripped the skin from all parts of his body except his face—even cutting off his penis. *"What in the hell's happening? What in the hell inhuman, crude, and—and God,"* thought Calley. Nothing but death, death, and more death.[63]

"We never did find the others," Santellana recalled. "God knows what the sonsofbitches did to them." After a pause, he announced his decision: "Goddam, you had to kill."[64]

This soldier's grisly death and the presumed similar fates of his missing comrades quickly combined with the growing numbers of casualties from mines, booby traps, and snipers, to fuel an enraged and frustrated cry for revenge. But just as Task Force Barker was gearing up for action, Viet Cong and NVA forces suddenly attacked South Vietnam in the Tet Offensive of late January 1968.

At four in the morning of January 31, 1968, Charlie Company was bunked in base quarters on the outskirts of Quang Ngai City when they were awakened by a thunderous barrage on the airfield, jail, fort, and ARVN headquarters and training area. The American Division responded with mortar and rocket fire, lighting up the sky. Tet had begun, leading to a major American and South Vietnamese counteroffensive that helped to make 1968 the bloodiest year of the war. As part of this return assault, Task Force Barker's mission took on added importance by going after the Viet Cong in Pinkville. Caught up in this vortex was Medina and his three platoon leaders, including Calley.[65]

Two

ALMOST TWO WEEKS INTO TET, Charlie Company had not yet experienced combat, but on the early afternoon of February 12, 1968, the 1st Platoon came under sniper fire while patrolling the bank of the Song Diem Diem, which was strategically important because it lay just a mile northwest of My Lai 1, or Pinkville. The men hit the ground, then crawled frantically through the mud while Calley radioed for artillery support. In moments American mortar fire blasted the area but failed to inflict any Viet Cong casualties.

When the firing stopped, Calley ordered his men back to the river. Quickly assessing the situation, he decided against walking them through its waters. Not only might they strike enemy mines, but they would be slow-moving targets for enemy guns. Instead, "like a fool," he later told John Sack, he moved them single-file along the top of a four-foot-high levee, exposing them to snipers. In a fiery exchange, Calley's forces managed to kill two enemy soldiers but suffered five casualties, including his radio operator, William Weber, a highly popular infantryman from Minnesota. "I been shot," Calley heard Weber gasp as he rolled off the levee and died in a pool of reddening water. He was Charlie Company's first KIA. Private Roy Wood went into shock, screaming uncontrollably before turning into "nothing but a zombie," as Calley recalled, "just a complete nothing," as his comrades lifted Weber's blood-soaked body onto a medevac helicopter. Many of the men blamed Calley for Weber's death. Calley agreed with them. "I admit it: I was stupid that day."[1]

Calley and his forces managed to escape, calling in the artillery and crawling nearly seven hundred feet to My Lai 3, which they used as a refuge until the approaching nighttime forced them to leave to avoid an encounter with returning Viet Cong. The next day, the joint U.S.-ARVN force swept the area without meeting resistance: The Viet Cong had again gone into a strategic retreat.[2]

The next day, February 13, American and ARVN forces took aim at My Lai 1 in an effort to destroy what they believed to be the headquarters of the entire Viet Cong stronghold. With Charlie Company acting as a blocking force above My Lai 4, Bravo Company approached My Lai 1 in a heavy fog. Suddenly, shots came from nearby My Lai 6, from behind the tree lines and hedgerows, pinning down the troops with a hail of small-arms fire. Reinforcements soon rushed into the hot area, enabling the trapped company to pull out at dark with one dead and five wounded.

For the next two days, Alpha Company made its way into the same territory, encountering snipers, mortars, and automatic weapons fire until, with the arrival of Bravo Company, they made a breakthrough into the small peninsular village of My Khe 4 below My Lai 1. But the Viet Cong had left My Lai 1 during the night. The American forces found the area outside the village so thick in mines and booby traps that moving forward proved impossible. They also discovered a large number of tunnels, spaced about fifty feet apart, and confiscated a huge cache of mortar rounds and small-arms ammunition. In the course of the three-day operation, the Americans claimed to have killed eighty Viet Cong without capturing any weapons, while themselves sustaining three dead and fifteen wounded.[3]

The Viet Cong had skillfully avoided a confrontation by staying in the shadows.[4]

The entire region was "an enemy base," according to Captain Patrick Trinkle of Alpha Company in his testimony before a congressional committee in 1970. Women were armed with carbine rifles, young boys and girls had set up local organizations of resistance and laid booby traps, and boys as young as fourteen threw grenades. Pinkville was an armed camp under Viet Cong control. "The neutrals," he insisted, "had long since gone to refugee centers." Not everyone there was Viet Cong, but all were "Viet Cong–controlled."[5]

I

Over the next several days, U.S. forces began to grasp the enormity of their problem in Pinkville while exploring a large and intricate tunnel network connected to rooms twenty feet below the surface. They discovered places of refuge as well as an entire underground medical dispensary. The enemy had bricked up the tunnels and rooms, creating a fully fortified subterranean headquarters. It was clear that the Viet Cong's 48th Local Force Battalion had been there for many years and intended to stay many more.[6]

Calley's men remained furious with his poor leadership. Not only did they feel he had exposed them to enemy attack, but they suspected him of putting them in high-risk situations to impress Medina. "No one in the company" liked Calley, asserted 3rd Platoon Squad leader Sergeant John Smail to the Peers commission almost two years later. More than once he heard rumors that men in Calley's platoon had collected money as a bounty to give to anyone who killed him.[7]

Calley was not a unique potential target of a practice that became known in Vietnam as "fragging." Other officers there as well as in every war America has fought were unprepared for combat leadership and alienated their men by focusing on advancing their own careers. But the notion of killing a superior officer became so widespread in Vietnam that it acquired a specific name—derived from the use of the fragmentation grenades carried by infantrymen. They were a weapon of choice because they left no fingerprints and killed or maimed everyone within thirty-three feet of an explosion that occurred five seconds after release of the pin and threw out nearly two thousand missile-like fragments.

Fragging was less frequent in 1968 than it became after 1969—when it appeared that the U.S. involvement in Vietnam was winding down: Nearly eight hundred fragging attempts from 1969 to 1971 resulted in eighty-six officers killed and 714 injured—the most common reason being the officer's lack of concern for his men. Calley fit that perception, although Smail came to his defense by declaring that it was "impossible" for Medina to control an entire company and that platoon leaders were in the position to make many crucial decisions and to impose discipline on their men.[8]

A few days later, a chaplain conducted a memorial service for Weber at Landing Zone Dottie, the U.S. base near Quang Ngai City named after Barker's wife. The ceremony brought dozens of his comrades to tears and left them even angrier over his death at the hands of an invisible enemy who had taken advantage of their platoon leader's incompetence.[9]

Morale continued to plummet, temporarily rising only when Alpha and Bravo Companies launched a second operation in Pinkville on February 23 and engaged the Viet Cong in an all-day firefight. The two companies lost twenty-one men, including three killed, in what turned out to be a two-day operation, while reportedly killing seventy-five Viet Cong and capturing six weapons. The enemy again disappeared.[10]

In the aftermath, Charlie Company was clearing the area on the morning of Sunday, February 25, when one of the men accidentally detonated a mine. At first Medina thought it was incoming artillery—until another mine went off, followed by another one. A string of explosions ripped the company apart as one soldier after another tripped more mines while trying to save his friends, leading to the deaths or injuries of more men. Medina somehow stayed calm while working with the medic and trying to get his men to safety by directing those soldiers with mine detectors to find a way out.

Charlie Company lost three dead and sixteen wounded, including one soldier whose death was so nightmarish that Medina later testified that he relived the experience over and over for years afterward. "I had never seen anything that looked so unreal in my entire life." The young soldier was "split as if somebody had taken a cleaver right up from his crotch all the way up to his chest cavity." When they laid out a poncho next to him and tried to put him on it, they set him down on another mine, hurling Medina and the others backward.[11]

Charlie Company had experienced war for the first time, according to Widmer. Bernhardt agreed. "When you have been through a mine field and put the remains of friends in body bags, nothing shocks you anymore."[12]

Later that same day, Calley returned from R & R (rest and recuperation) on the seaside, already reeling from an experience while away that underlined the reality of war. He had awakened early one morning to the sound of South Vietnamese police machine-gunning a half dozen women in the streets who had gone to market a few moments before curfew had ended. "For the first time," Calley later testified in court, "it dawned on me that we weren't playing games." Further proof came at the firebase landing strip at LZ Uptight, where he watched helicopters arrive from the clearing operation carrying more than a dozen dead and wounded soldiers, along with piles of blood-soaked clothing. For him, the "worst" sight was bloody boots with the soldiers' feet still inside.[13]

Pinkville was awash in mines. The army had tried to avoid the fate of Charlie Company by posting minefield warning maps—elaborately covered with circles of blue for friendly mines, red for enemy, and yellow for those that might be either one—but they proved ineffective. The Viet Cong immediately made these maps obsolete by periodically digging up and relocating the mines and "bouncing Betties" (land mines that exploded up to six feet in the air, spraying shrapnel capable of tearing a body in half) and making it virtually impossible to keep the maps up to date. Charlie Company once captured a ten-year-old boy clutching a bag containing four mines he had unearthed; he would have had a fifth, but it blew up and took off the right side of his face.[14]

By the last week in February, resentment and hostility had spread among the GIs, aimed primarily at the villagers, who they knew must have known of the minefields and said nothing. Sergeant Hodges noted that in the weeks after the Tet Offensive, the men's attitude had changed from hatred of the VC and North Vietnamese to hatred of all Vietnamese.[15]

In his discussions with Sack, Calley spoke of a "chronic fear" that set in, causing a "mild panic" that impelled him to find the Viet Cong. "If there are a hundred kids in a village," he recounted asking himself, "where are the men?" No longer were rice paddies dismissed as a scenic array of green adorning the landscape. His apprehension was rapidly turning into paranoia. Every village, tree, and bush could hide the Viet Cong. Every man, woman, and child could be VC. The hardening feelings his men felt against him they likewise projected onto the Vietnamese. They were becoming paranoid about the ghostlike Viet Cong, Calley told Sack, making this "a different company" from the one he had left behind for R & R less than a week earlier.[16]

At seven the next morning, February 26, Calley and his men resumed their daily routine of going through the villages, harassed by sporadic sniper fire. "We never knew who the snipers were," Calley declared to Sack, "and the Vietnamese told us, 'We don't know, either.'" The snipers had learned that it was more effective to disable rather than kill their targets, knowing that American soldiers refused to leave their wounded behind and that their attempts to rescue comrades put more targets in the line of fire. The ominous sense of threat from all directions continued to mount. They were there to protect the Vietnamese people from the Viet Cong yet could get no assistance from them in locating the enemy. "We had been in Vietnam three months: we were losing men, we were being nickel-and-dimed away, we were being picked off. We were in Vietnamese villages daily, and we still hadn't seen one VC."[17]

This brought on an identity crisis. Calley testified that he was starting to wrestle with a question that was on his mind and others' as well. "I didn't know why in the goddamn hell we were in Vietnam. Or even know who to ask about it. Captain Medina? Medina didn't know it. Colonel Barker? General Koster? President Johnson?" After nearly twenty ambush experiences, Calley had not seen the Viet Cong.[18]

To Calley, and to so many others, the absence provided the answer. The Viet Cong were nowhere because they were everywhere. *All* Vietnamese were Viet Cong. He had not come across a single Vietnamese villager who helped the Americans. So they all were the enemy. At his trial, he recalled starting to see wicker baskets everywhere, each one turned upside down. Thinking this unusual, he inquired about it and learned it was a Viet Cong signal that Americans were in the area. Once Calley realized this, he no longer felt frustrated. "I wasn't fooled anymore," he told Sack. Calley stopped asking

Vietnamese people where the VC were and instead threw out the question, "Everyone here is a VC, isn't he?" "No no," they replied. "We love the GIs. We give you water." Calley disgustedly remarked, "Hell, if I let them they'd poison the water, too. I didn't listen: I just walked on. I had no love for these people now. I did have a few weeks earlier, but it had been slowly driven out."[19]

Calley and many of his men in Charlie Company recalled a feeling of relief at seeing the enemy for the first time. This new "discovery" fit perfectly with what he had learned in basic training and OCS: Trust no one. There are no innocent civilians. Kill quickly and without emotion. His past had meshed with his present. "Everyone said eliminate them. I never met someone who didn't say it," he told Sack.[20]

All this was not unique to Calley, of course; it reflected the attitude of those who had undergone the same boot camp training and were now in Pinkville only a few weeks after the Tet Offensive.

Medina recalled that in the immediate aftermath of Tet in early February he and his men had set up a blocking position on a hill, where they observed VC forces in their black clothing, carrying weapons and bodies and accompanied by women and children as they withdrew from Quang Ngai City and headed for safety in the outlying area. They were spread out and vulnerable to attack, but Medina could not get permission to pursue them, principally because of the presence of civilians. He finally won clearance to open artillery fire, but by then they were gone.[21]

February had been a month of bloodshed and frustration, of recovering from the shock of Tet while reconciling oneself to an invisible enemy; in March, the mood changed when Task Force Barker secured approval for its first full-scale combat assault on Pinkville, a search-and-destroy operation set for the morning of March 16, 1968. "We were looking forward to going," Medina recalled. The two February operations proved that the Viet Cong's 48th Local Force Battalion was headquartered in Pinkville and that its outposts stretched as far west as My Lai 4 and north, south, and east to the ocean. Should anyone invade the area, the Viet Cong intended to hold on until their battalion leaders and the rest of the troops escaped to the Batangan Peninsula—known in Vietnamese as Ba Lang An, or the Three Villages of Peace. To prevent that, the assault force would strike hard and fast.[22]

On Thursday, March 14, a well-liked and respected sergeant from Charlie Company, George Cox, was blown to pieces by a booby trap that also inflicted terrible injuries on two soldiers with him—one losing his arms and legs, the other blinded by the blast. The rest of the squad loaded their comrades onto a helicopter and then began the slow trek back to LZ Dottie.

En route, they pulled a man off his bicycle and beat him until he managed to get away. They then shot a woman working in the distant fields when a soldier yelled that she was armed. When they reached her, she was alive and unarmed. They decided to kill her, first stealing her ring and then kicking her repeatedly before finally putting her out of her misery by shooting her in the head. By then they were close to headquarters, where they came face to face with a group of enraged villagers who had seen what had happened and burst into the camp, accusing the soldiers of murdering an innocent civilian. Medina stood up for his men, convincing his superiors that the woman had been holding a detonator. Calley supported this lie, later remarking that Medina rightfully refused to give up any of his men just because they had "kicked a Vietnamese kid or killed a damn innocent woman." The important thing was to keep the unit "combat-effective."[23]

On the eve of the March operation, Charlie Company had sustained twenty-eight casualties, including five dead—all due to an enemy still unseen.[24]

II

Both officers and their men were in an angry and aggressive mood at the briefings for the operation when, on Friday, March 15, Colonel Oran Henderson assumed command of the American Division's 11th Infantry Brigade and made his way to the officers' meeting. Tall and stoic-looking, Henderson was taking on his initial combat command assignment. He was nonetheless familiar with the men of that brigade, as he had earlier served as its commander at Schofield Barracks in Hawaii starting in July 1966 and, a little more than a year later, as its executive officer. This new appointment placed him in Vietnam. After a change-of-command ceremony at Duc Pho, Henderson flew to LZ Dottie for Barker's officer briefing on the Pinkville operation.[25]

Henderson arrived just before the meeting's start time of 1300 hours and asked Barker to brief him. Barker asked him, as the new brigadier general, to address the chain of command, a gathering of company commanders and battalion staff that included the head of operations, Major Charles Calhoun; the task force artillery liaison, Captain Dennis Vasquez; and Barker's chief intelligence officer and aide, Captain Eugene Kotouc.

Henderson looked surprised at the request, some who were there recalled, perhaps because like Major General Koster he was not familiar with the details of the plan. He and Koster knew its overall strategic objective, but Koster had not studied the finer tactical points. Henderson quickly collected himself, first lamenting the lack of military progress in Pinkville and proclaiming that he would accept nothing less than the enemy's destruction. As he testified more than once, the intelligence provided by Major David Gavin of the Son Tinh District (northeast of Quang Ngai City and encompassing Pinkville) indicated that the Viet Cong's 48th Battalion was "hurting the hell out of us with mines and booby-traps, primarily sniper fire and things of this nature." And he knew that Charlie Company had lost more than a dozen men in a recent minefield incident.[26]

The new operation, Henderson declared, would begin with a troop landing outside My Lai 4 at 0730 hours and without ARVN support, because of leaks regarding the previous action in that area. He told those assembled to make sure their men cleaned their weapons and to verify that everything worked. The artillery commander for the operation, Captain Stephen Gamble, termed this a "pep talk."[27]

After a few minutes of preparatory artillery fire launched from six miles away at LZ Uptight, the attack force would enter My Lai 4 on its western outskirts, under the protection of Huey helicopters hovering over the landing zone. My Lai 4 was not "a peaceful existing village," Henderson asserted in later testimony, but "a defended village, defended by a bunker system [of] communications, trenches running through it."[28]

Henderson urged the three company commanders—Medina, Captain Earl Michles of Bravo Company, and Captain William Riggs of Alpha Company—to close with the enemy as quickly as possible. In the two February operations, American forces had exposed themselves to counterattack by stopping to evacuate the wounded; the best way to protect an evacuation was to drive the enemy out of the area so that the medevac helicopters could enter safely. The entire area was dotted with mines and booby traps, and casualties had been high in a recent skirmish in which the enemy had pinned down a company fighting in coordination with ARVN forces. That operation had collapsed in less than twenty-four hours when the ARVN refused to accompany the Americans into the area. This time, Henderson asserted, they would carry out the mission on their own.[29]

In testimony more than a year later, Henderson elaborated on his thinking about combat by emphasizing that he saw no difference between search and destroy and search and clear. "Both operations are combat sweeps," he insisted, aimed at "finding and killing Viet Cong." However, he approved of the destruction of only those houses in which, as he put it, "there was very positive enemy in them or booby trapped to where it would endanger them or U.S. forces if they attempted to enter." The troops could return fire that came from a specific dwelling but were forbidden to open general fire on the village itself. Americans had shown remarkable restraint in comparison with the Viet Cong, who did not respect civilians. "They open fire on your forces usually from within and amongst a group of civilians, and it takes a hell of a lot of courage and strength on the part of your command and our soldiers not to immediately start returning fire, to be selective." He repeatedly emphasized, "We would never fire artillery on villages." He also made it clear that this was no ordinary village.[30]

As Henderson left the briefing a little after 1400 hours and returned to Duc Pho, Captain Kotouc felt great satisfaction with this new aggressive approach, a point he emphasized in later testimony: Americans would finally take the offensive. Kotouc prefaced his follow-up briefing of Barker with an assessment of the intelligence situation, asserting that the Viet Cong had about two hundred experienced fighters in the area who counted on help from civilians in My Lai 4. Yet one key factor worked in the Americans' favor, he argued: Many villagers would have heeded the warning to leave, while others would have gone to market by 0700 hours, a half hour before the attack. Nearly all Vietnamese remaining in My Lai 4 would therefore be Viet Cong and their supporters.[31]

Kotouc had in fact acquired his intelligence information from several sources, the most notable being the new coordinator of the Phoenix Program in Quang Ngai Province, Robert Ramsdell of the CIA, which sent him there in February 1968. A short and scruffy-looking man in his mid-forties, Ramsdell had worked for the army's Criminal Investigation Division before becoming a private investigator in Florida. He now carried an air of mystery about him while toting a submachine gun and wearing a beret, blue jeans, and an army combat jacket. He had arrived in Vietnam shortly after the Tet Offensive, anxious to upgrade the Phoenix Program. He immediately gathered information on Viet Cong activity throughout Pinkville, using it to compile blacklists containing the names of Viet Cong suspects, lists that he furnished to military units about to enter a village.[32]

This is partly speculation, though it seems inconceivable that the two principal intelligence specialists in the area—Ramsdell and Kotouc—would not have communicated on this pending assault, given its scale.

Ramsdell had never met Barker, but he knew both Kotouc and Major Gavin and provided Kotouc (and likely Gavin) with critical information on the two most important planning aspects of the operation: enemy strength and civilian presence. As Seymour Hersh and other writers reveal, Ramsdell insisted that the ghostly 48th Viet Cong Battalion would have about 450 soldiers in Pinkville on the day of the assault and that the civilians in My Lai 4 would have left for market by 0700 hours—again, meaning that the only Vietnamese staying behind would be the enemy. In an interview with Hersh in May 1971, Ramsdell made a remark that Hersh claimed was similar to one expressed earlier in secret testimony to the Peers commission: Americans considered any Vietnamese in the area Viet Cong suspects "because they couldn't survive in that area unless they were sympathizers." His information on the Viet Cong's numbers sharply differed from the assessments of all other U.S. intelligence officers at the various provincial headquarters, along with the intelligence summaries prepared separately by the Americal Division, the III Marine Amphibious Force, and MACV. They all agreed that the 48th had sustained such massive losses in the fighting in Quang Ngai City during the Tet Offensive weeks earlier that it had temporarily relocated to the mountains some distance away to recuperate and rebuild. Kotouc rejected the analyses of his associates and agreed with those from Ramsdell.[33]

Through Ramsdell, the CIA affected the My Lai events. Information crucial to Barker's planning came from Kotouc, who was his chief intelligence officer and who had accepted Ramsdell's assessment over the others. As the new head of the Phoenix Program, Ramsdell was anxious to make his mark and could not have resisted the opportunity to eliminate a Viet Cong staging area in My Lai 4, just six miles from his office in Quang Ngai City— confirming what the CIA-funded Census Grievance Center had recently reported. His list of Viet Cong suspects was never found, and there remains no direct evidence that Ramsdell's information directly shaped the intelligence Kotouc passed to Barker. Nonetheless, Ramsdell's thinking fit Kotouc's report rather more neatly than that of nearly all other American analysts did.[34]

In any case, only the playing out of events at My Lai would determine the accuracy of Kotouc's intelligence report: Barker planned the March 16 operation mainly on the basis of its conclusions. Barker briefed his three company commanders and at least five other officers in his usual informal manner: nothing in writing. But his message was clear: Charlie Company would take the lead in Pinkville by first targeting My Lai 4, where, according to Sergeant Lawrence LaCroix, a squad leader in the 2nd Platoon, they were—as he put it in later testimony—to "destroy everything that came in front of us with any resistance." They would then link up with Alpha and Bravo Companies in establishing a defense perimeter along the outer edges of the village that would trap any Viet Cong trying to escape. Barker wanted to neutralize the area by filling in the tunnels, knocking down the buildings, burning the hooches, and killing or running off livestock. He later consistently maintained that he had said nothing about either polluting the wells or how to deal with civilians who refused to leave the area.[35]

Barker's instructions were contradictory and incomplete. In previous operations, he had urged his men to exercise care in handling civilians; this time he called for no such caution. He did not specifically order his men to kill civilians, nor did he specifically order his men *not* to do so. He repeatedly emphasized that only Viet Cong and their followers would be present, even while admitting to the likelihood of a few noncombatants refusing to leave.[36]

Captain Kotouc's analysis emphasizing the absence of any civilians seems unfathomable in hindsight, as does Barker's ready acceptance of it. Sergeant Clinton Stephens was an S-2 officer in charge of the task force military intelligence division, who in later testimony noted that numerous civilians were always in the Son My area—including in My Lai 4. Every time American soldiers went through this area, he insisted, a number of civilians, accompanied by "some enemy," would evacuate down to Highway 521. Barker and everyone else knew that in every previous operation "the civilian personnel would start moving out; they didn't stay there." Americans "just let them go" without firing at them—even if VC cadres were running with the civilians.[37]

Moments after Barker's briefing, he took his three company commanders—Medina, Michles, and Riggs—along with Vasquez and perhaps Kotouc, on an aerial reconnaissance of the proposed helicopter landing zone, close enough to the initial target of My Lai 4 but far enough away to avoid tipping off anyone of something unusual.

Over the deafening *whop-whop-whop* of the blades, Barker shouted to Medina that "artillery would be placed onto the village" as well as its outer fringes. Barker knew that the rules of engagement prohibited firing on settlements except in retaliation, but he also viewed My Lai 4 as an operational base of the Viet Cong and no longer a mere settlement. He therefore told Medina (and presumably Michles and Riggs) that his men "had permission to destroy the village, to burn down the houses, to destroy the food crop that belonged to the Viet Cong, and to kill their livestock." Medina testified later that he understood Barker to mean they were to destroy everything useful to the enemy. My Lai 4 was therefore a free-fire zone. Medina was convinced that artillery and gunship fire—meaning from Huey helicopters—would reduce American casualties, even if the result was greater civilian casualties. The Viet Cong forces would no longer benefit from nestling among their people.[38]

Thus this operation was different than anything undertaken in Pinkville before. Villagers would go to market that morning, a Saturday, and My Lai 4 would receive a warning to evacuate, which meant that once the attack got underway, the assumption would be that the only Vietnamese left in the village would be Viet Cong and their sympathizers. But what truly marked the operation was the sense of vengeance.

The mood in the camp—among both the officers and the enlisted men—had markedly shifted. The operational planning had focused on standard military procedures, specific tactics, and rules of engagement—a clinical approach that had changed to something more feverish by the time Medina met to brief his men that evening on the operation.

Late that afternoon, the soldiers held a memorial service for Cox, one that focused on the impact of his death on his wife left behind in Hawaii and the horrifying injuries inflicted on the two men with him. Sergeant Charles West was Cox's assistant squad leader and was stunned by his death. "On the way back to camp I was crying," he recalled in a published interview. "Everybody was deeply hurt, right up to Captain Medina. Guys were going around kicking sand bags and saying, 'Those dirty dogs, those dirty bastards.'" A Catholic chaplain memorialized not just Cox but seventeen slain soldiers, including two more who had died earlier that same afternoon, the afternoon of the briefing.[39]

As Medina stood outside his tent that evening to address most of his officers and men—a dangerously depleted force of a little more than one hundred—he recognized the need to lift their spirits. Some of the men were standing while others sat in a semicircle on a bunker. "Everybody was pretty well down," Sergeant David Hein from the mortar group told the Peers commission. "Like me, I lost my best friend from Minneapolis [Weber] right outside the same village."[40]

After prayers, Medina reminded his men of the fighting that lay ahead. "We haven't time to cry about this. It's over with. It's done with. Forget it: especially since we are going to Pinkville tomorrow." His men bolted upright at hearing the word that had become synonymous with both vengeance and death. "We're going after the 48th battalion," Medina asserted. "The landing zone will be hot. And they outnumber us two to one." He told them to expect "heavy casualties tomorrow."[41]

Medina explained that the assault on My Lai 4 would begin with a two-headed sweep aimed at catching the enemy in a pincers operation while destroying fortifications and livestock. According to Kotouc, who was there as part of the briefing, there was no mention of killing civilians. He remembered sitting on a sandbag next to the company's Vietnamese interpreter as Medina pulled a shovel from a nearby Jeep and leaned against it while solemnly acknowledging that "they had been through quite a bit of hell lately." His men must have thought the same thing. Charlie Company had suffered more than twenty casualties from minefield explosions alone—and at the hands of a phantom enemy.[42]

Task Force Barker, Medina declared, would focus on Pinkville. It was once the responsibility of the ARVN, but its soldiers now refused to go there. The campaign would begin at My Lai 4, which had excellent natural defenses and was the immediate target. The terrain around the village was primarily flat and filled with rice paddies ready to harvest that provided countless hiding places for the enemy. Sugar cane fields ringed the village, along with trees and hedgerows furnishing additional cover running alongside ditches deep enough to serve as excellent passageways in and out of the settlement. They should expect "heavy combat" with the Viet Cong, who "would be in fortified positions." They must "engage the enemy to kill the enemy." Perhaps noting the concern on his men's faces, Medina contradicted Henderson by repeating what Barker had told him in the helicopter: that the LZ preparation fire would be "onto the village."[43]

Medina then outlined the plan of attack. Two platoons from Charlie Company would enter My Lai 4 on its western side and keep any captives in front of the advancing U.S. forces; a third platoon would follow about forty-five minutes later, searching for weapons and stragglers, and then meet up with the rest of the forces on the other side of the village to establish a defensive position. According to testimony, he told the men that they had to "destroy the village of My Lai 4 by burning it, destroying the crops, destroying the livestock and closing the wells." This operation would be "a pretty good combat engagement," Medina asserted while using the shovel to draw a map in the sand showing the key targets. The names left indelible marks in the soldiers' minds as he ticked them off in the order of attack from west to east: My Lai 4, My Lai 5, My Lai 6, and, finally, My Lai 1—all of them comprising Pinkville, the Viet Cong's chief haven abutting the South China Sea. Medina reportedly told his men to follow the "5 S's": "search, safeguard, silence, segregate, and speed the enemy to the rear." He emphasized the top priority again: "We mustn't let anyone get behind us." It was a lesson that Calley remembered clearly.[44]

Medina's instructions regarding the inhabitants of My Lai 4 were imprecise and therefore remain open to a range of interpretations. He admitted telling his men to burn the village after the search, but he denied ordering them to kill its people. In later testimony, Medina insisted that he knew it was standard operating procedure to send any civilians to provincial headquarters with instructions to report to the district adviser of the South Vietnamese Army. If so, according to others, he did not make this clear at the briefing. "It never entered my mind that there would be any civilians there," he later insisted. One soldier sought clarification. "What if we see a woman or something like this? Can we shoot then?" "No," Medina later attested that he had replied. "Only if they are engaging you or have a weapon. You have to be extremely careful and use common sense; if they are endangering you or have a weapon or are evading, then you can shoot at them." Medina later told the press that he did not issue instructions regarding women and children, because they were not expected to be there.[45]

Calley and a host of others had a radically different reading of Medina's response. "Our job," Calley remembered him declaring, "is to go in rapidly and to neutralize everything. To kill everything." When asked if this included "women and children, too," Medina replied—according to Calley and more than twenty other officers and men—"I mean everything."[46]

The men had different recollections of Medina's orders, but several of them later and repeatedly referred to either an order or an unmistakable implication from numerous statements that they were to kill everything that moved. Sergeant David Mitchell insisted that Medina had told the men to go after the Viet Cong forces and "wipe them out." Medina's radio operator, SP4 John Paul, maintained that he had heard Medina emphasize over and over that only Viet Cong or their sympathizers would be there, and, he said, "I understood them to be annihilated—killed." PFC Michael Bernhardt remembered that Medina "didn't specifically say to kill every man, woman, and child in My Lai. He stopped just short of that but he gave every other indication that is what he expected." SP5 Lenny Lagunoy noted that "the word at the time" was "Destroy the place, kill everything that moves." Squad leader L. G. Bacon concurred that they were to "kill anyone who is VC or VC-suspected or who you see helping a VC." In a discussion with his squad after the briefing, he testified, the men agreed they had instructions to kill civilians, whether VC suspects or sympathizers.[47]

PFC Charles Gruver from the 3rd Platoon later insisted that their objective was to destroy the village. They were "to load down with all the ammunition [they] could carry and ... to go in and destroy the whole thing—women, children, animals, throw bodies in wells, ruin their water supply, kill their work animals. Wipe it out; burn the village. Every living thing. Just kill it. Exterminate."[48]

According to Corporal Kenneth Schiel, Medina had proclaimed that only the Viet Cong would be there and that "this time we were going to kill everything that breathed ... including the women and children." SP4 Louis

Martin confirmed this assessment, testifying that, with no "innocent people" there, they were "to kill everything that moved." Mortar observer SP4 James Flynn recalled Medina telling the large group, "Kill everything that moves." When asked if this included "young kids," Flynn claimed that Medina replied, "Yes."[49]

To Private Dennis Conti of Calley's command group, Medina had "psyched up" the company for battle but did not match the fervor of Calley's speech afterward to his platoon. The children, according to Calley, were "future VC" and thus "the same as the mothers and fathers." Did that mean the troops were under orders to shoot men, women, and children? asked a member of the Peers panel. "I don't know," Conti responded. "I think, at the time, that's the way I interpreted it."[50]

Meanwhile, in another part of the camp, Captain Michles was briefing his platoon leaders in Bravo Company about a possible invasion of My Lai 1 and My Khe 4, located about a mile and a half east. His men were to destroy the enemy and villages, but, according to later testimony by Sergeant Wilhelm Dahner, they were to leave the women alone or face a court martial. Again, later accounts were in conflict. Lieutenant Kenneth Boatman asserted that Michles had quoted Barker saying "everything down there was VC or VC sympathizers." The captain declared that "we've had a lot of trouble there, not just a little," and they were to "clean the place out." Lieutenant Thomas Willingham, leader of the 1st Platoon, attested that Michles had ordered him to "burn all villages," and Boatman claimed in later testimony that he had received the same instructions. Everyone understood that they were engaging in a search-and-destroy operation and that, according to Sergeant Earl Rushin, anyone there would be the enemy. SP4 Lawrence Congleton came away from the briefing, he later said, convinced they were to destroy the village. Two men from the 1st Platoon believed they were to shoot everyone. One soldier recalled either Michles or his platoon leader declaring, "This is what you've been waiting for—'search and destroy'"[51]

To vengeful, scared, and young green troops, search and destroy meant search and *destroy*.

III

Captain Kotouc was perhaps closest to the truth in declaring that the mood in Charlie Company was such that the men did not need a specific order to kill everyone. Only the enemy would be in the village, as the innocent civilians would have left, either heeding the army's warnings or going to the Saturday market. Kotouc realized that in every operation some civilians would refuse to leave, no matter how many warnings they received. Nonetheless, in an attempt to defend Medina at the trial, Kotouc asserted that he did not remember Medina saying anything about shooting every person they saw. "I didn't have the impression that they were going in to shoot anybody other than the people who ought to be shot." Thus the GIs would shoot only those villagers who deserved it while moving the noncombatants remaining behind down Highway 1 to Quang Ngai City and the district of Son Tinh.[52]

The vast majority of the men heard one simple message in Medina's briefing: the Viet Cong numbered at least two hundred, and they would put up a fierce defense. The objective was clear, even if the means—in terms of both tactics and rules of engagement—were not. U.S. forces numbered one hundred or so—about half the enemy size—and, without massive artillery support and air cover, faced a well-fortified and more experienced force. Their emotions had led them to believe they could overcome these handicaps. "Charlie had been staying in this village and we better find him," declared Medina, challenging his men.[53]

A mixture of fear, grief, frustration, and anger gripped the men as they listened to Medina. One of Calley's two squad leaders, Sergeant Bacon, later asserted that the men were frightened because they had never engaged in a firefight against a battalion. "I was really scared," he remembered. Grenadier SP4 Andress Delgado of the 2nd Platoon likewise noted the fear among his men—new in Vietnam and about to face an enemy they had never seen. Everyone was "pretty well scared anyway of going into that place," asserted Sergeant Hein. When they learned they would enter the village with infantry alone, he said, "We were pretty well shaky."[54]

For his part, Kotouc thought the men were so "worked up" that they were capable of anything. They were not on drugs or smoking marijuana, he insisted in a later statement upheld by numerous testimonies. They were anxious, "sitting around and punching each other" as Medina described their appointment with the Viet Cong. "They were nervous and they anticipated a fight, and they were shaking their heads." They "were keyed up, anticipating something, and they did not know what they were anticipating." When Medina told them how many hand grenades to take, it was clear that he too was "somewhat nervous," recalled Kotouc. "I was [scared] myself," he admitted. For most of the young men, this would be their first combat.[55]

Now, nearly fifty years later, controversy still swirls over Medina's orders, which were, of course, the basis for what happened in My Lai 4. Did he believe what he said—that no innocent civilians would be in the village and that his men could do whatever was necessary to clean out the enemy? Had he, in the heat of the moment, ignored the possibility of an error—one that would make him and his men accomplices in murder? Like Barker, had he failed to recognize that in the fog of battle the absence of specific orders against killing noncombatants would be fatal to innocent people? We do not know whether Medina told the truth in later denying that he included women and children, and that those who said he had, such as Flynn, had been lying or were simply wrong. No one claimed to have heard Medina say what he later insisted he said: "You have to use common sense." Even if he had said those words, what meaning would they have in combat? Ten soldiers of perhaps a hundred in attendance later attested that no such directives were necessary, because Medina had left the impression that they were to kill everyone in the village.[56]

Ultimately, Medina felt the same as his men: He wanted to wreak vengeance on a vaporous and ruthless enemy who refused to fight in the open and yet in the past three months had inflicted dozens of casualties on his forces in Pinkville, primarily from mines, booby traps, and snipers.[57]

Most officers and men accepted Medina's invitation to avenge the recent losses of American comrades.[58]

A number of soldiers later noted that Medina's call for revenge had played to their emotions. James Bergthold, Gary Crossley, and Gary Garfolo thought so, as they later made clear, with Garfolo declaring, "What the hell, they're gooks, they caused Cox's death." Greg Olsen described his fellow soldiers' mood in a letter to his parents in Utah: "They slugged every little kid they came across." Herbert Carter of the 1st Platoon remembered Medina asserting, "When we go into My Lai 4, it's open season. When we leave, nothing will be living." Widmer agreed, he later admitted. We were going to have "one hell of a fight and we were going to kick some ass when we got down. And there wasn't going to be anybody left." Carter and Harry Stanley, also of the 1st Platoon, recalled predicting a "slaughter of civilians." Stanley told CID investigators that all members of his squad came away from the briefing convinced that "Medina meant that they were to kill every man, woman, and child in the village." The troops had never been in a firefight, and the coming assault, according to Martin, would be "the first mission I recall when we were in strictly offensive."[59]

Sergeant Hodges, squad leader of the 2nd Platoon, best summed up the prevailing mood of Charlie Company. The mission afforded the opportunity "to get even" and "settle the score" by getting "revenge for our fallen comrades."[60]

The absence of written orders, as we can see now, guaranteed considerable leeway in interpreting details of the operation. And we will always question the degree to which one can trust the memories of so many soldiers, hell-bent on revenge and knowing they must shoot first to avoid making the day of the assault their last. Survival meant carrying out what the drill sergeants in Basic Training had proclaimed as the central objective of any combat engagement in Vietnam: kill the enemy.

Add to this a breakdown in leadership from the division head at the top to squad leaders below. Commanders had not realized how far their emotionally charged orders could take a group of young and embittered soldiers, who feared (and even expected?) death in their first firefight against a seasoned VC battalion that had already killed or wounded nearly thirty Americans. They had perhaps failed to recognize what a veteran of both Korea and Vietnam once told Philip Caputo, then fighting in Vietnam himself: "Before you leave here, sir, you're going to learn that one of the most brutal things in the world is your average nineteen-year-old American boy."[61]

In retrospect one can read into Medina and Michles's instructions whatever one wants. On March 16, 1968, things would have been less clear, particularly in light of the recent casualties and the all-consuming thirst for revenge, combined with the nervous anticipation of engagement with an enemy they had not yet even seen and could only imagine. They were young men anxious to prove their manhood to comrades and, perhaps more important, to themselves. They were determined to avenge their buddies' deaths. Most of all, they were afraid to die. Basic Training had taught them the Vietnamese were merciless, a belief that justified equal mercilessness.

America's troops in Vietnam had in fact received little or no instruction on the treatment of noncombatants. Some might not even have been able to offer a definition of a noncombatant. How does one distinguish between a Viet Cong and a civilian, even between male and female, when the common apparel among peasants of all allegiances was black?

The March 16 operation would exceed in size and scope either February mission in Pinkville. Martin noted that the number of helicopters was more than double the usual four or five. They were outnumbered and needed greater fire power to eliminate anything useful to the Viet Cong.[62]

In his recollections Sergeant Bacon put his finger on the greatest problem confronting the platoons: the likely presence of civilians and how to distinguish between them and the Viet Cong and their supporters. In later testimony he said he had made his position clear to Calley after the briefing in a discussion with him and the other squad leader in the 1st Platoon, Sergeant Mitchell, who later told the Peers commission that he could not remember such a meeting. "We will round all the people up," Bacon declared to Calley, "and I will send my people to you, sir, because I don't know who is VC and who is not VC." Calley maintained that he had agreed to take responsibility for the villagers and told both of his squad leaders: "Move the civilians in front of you in case there are minefields and when you get to a certain area move them to me or send them to me." Calley asserted that he would follow the "usual" procedure, which Bacon understood to mean sending the villagers to Medina for interrogation. "You round them up and send them to me," Calley declared, "and I will take care of them."[63]

If what Bacon asserted is correct—that Calley would gather the villagers for interrogation—it is difficult to reconcile this procedure with Medina's alleged order to kill everyone.

Calley testified that he had been convinced that Medina had approved blanket destruction, and yet he had also emphasized the importance of keeping the villagers in front of the assault force to avoid taking fire from the rear. Before the briefing that day, Calley said that he had told Medina, "All right: I'm not going to play around. I'm not going to let anyone get behind us." If Calley considered these two directives contradictory, which they were, he did not lead Paul Meadlo of the 1st Platoon to think so. The young private from southern Indiana later declared that both Medina and Calley had told the men to kill all people in My Lai 4 because they would all be the enemy.[64]

In his testimony to CID more than two years later, Medina inadvertently admitted to awareness of the possible presence of noncombatants when explaining that he had issued no instructions regarding detainees or civilians, because the soldiers' previous training and briefings had already provided clear procedures. In effect, he was saying that an officer could assume that his men were familiar enough with the key aspects of combat that they did not need to go over them again. Yet if so, this was a risky assumption. Medina was keenly aware that he commanded a primarily green group of youths who had not experienced battle and indeed might not even recognize the enemy.

Medina had operated on the basis of Kotouc's intelligence, which asserted that a Viet Cong Battalion of about two hundred men would be in Pinkville and that the women and children in My Lai 4 would have gone to market by 0700 hours. He expected no evacuees on this mission—and hence issued no processing directives—and he saw no need to warn his men against harming civilians because none would be present.[65]

In retrospect, the key to understanding the meaning and impact of Medina's instructions lies in Calley's reaction to them. As noted earlier, theirs was both a strange and a strained relationship. Calley perceived Medina as a role model, someone he sought to impress. In return, Medina humiliated

Calley before his men. Now he was using Calley's fawning admiration of him to eliminate the enemy in My Lai 4.

Surely Medina knew Calley well enough to realize that he (and others) would follow orders, whatever they were, without questioning them. About half of the men in Calley's platoon thought their orders were to kill everyone, including women and children. Of fifty soldiers in the entire company who expressed specific views on what Medina had said in the briefing, thirty declared that he had ordered his men to kill everyone. Calley's blind faith in Medina's leadership led him to welcome the use of deadly force against an enemy he had already defined as every Vietnamese man, woman, and child. He was ready to carry out the will of his commanding officer, who had told the men to prepare for what could be the final day of their lives.[66]

During the briefing and at his trial three years later, Calley thought that Medina did not have to remind the men they were going to die. "*Everyone knew it:* Alpha and Bravo Companies had been there before. And men had their heads blown off or their balls blown off: I mean literally, or were vegetables now at Walter Reed, in Washington." Calley's grim thoughts were perhaps similar to those of others sitting on sandbags or leaning against the rusty oil drums as they listened to their commander. Calley walked the camp that night, checking on his men and telling them to double their ammunition. "Are you ready, troop?" "No sir." "I am not ready either," Calley said he replied. "I will never be."[67]

Death awaited them at Pinkville, he believed.

Three

WHATEVER HAD BEEN ORDERED OR NOT ORDERED, suggested or not suggested, implied or not implied at the pre-attack briefings on Pinkville, the day of the operation, March 16, arrived. Colonel Oran Henderson's late departure from LZ Dottie delayed his arrival at the combat zone—a distance of about six miles—until around the time Medina's forces began entering My Lai 4. At 0750 hours, the grim and leather-faced colonel swooped over the scene—about twenty minutes after the artillery barrage had ceased. Before the booming subsided, two Huey gunships (known as "Sharks" because of markings on the front of their craft depicting sharks with red mouths and white teeth) from the 174th Aviation Company went to work, safeguarding the troops' arrival by peppering the edges of the village and the nearby landing zone with machine-gun fire. To prevent the Viet Cong from escaping the trap, Alpha Company took a blocking position along the upper bank of the Song Diem Diem about a mile northwest of Pinkville, while Bravo Company did the same below My Lai 1 to the east. Bravo was under orders to invade that settlement and nearby My Khe 4 after Charlie Company had entered My Lai 4. According to testimony in the Peers Report, the first two of Medina's three platoons meanwhile prepared to assault the prime target of that morning. Bravo and Charlie Companies would link up that evening.[1]

A few minutes before Henderson's appearance, the two gunships killed three armed Viet Cong trying to escape in the open fields; the Hueys were also probably responsible for the deaths of several noncombatants who had tried to flee the subhamlet. As Henderson later testified, he had seen about three hundred Vietnamese leaving the area in "an orderly manner" along Highway 521 southwest. As the gunships fired on alleged Viet Cong below the highway, a large number of the Vietnamese evacuees—mostly elderly men, women, and children—squatted along its side. Lieutenant Colonel Barker had received word of this mass exodus and, according to Henderson, intended to "check out" the people on the road. Henderson had meanwhile investigated the matter and saw three Vietnamese dressed in what the American soldiers called black pajamas—the black trousers and shirt commonly worn by South Vietnamese peasants but regarded by GIs as the Viet Cong's uniform. In minutes his helicopter crew captured two of the three Viet Cong suspects as they tried to run away and took them to LZ Dottie for interrogation. Henderson had also seen two bodies with two weapons and web gear holding ammunition and other combat materials, along with the bodies of several civilians on the trail leading into the village who he assumed were victims of artillery or gunship fire.[2]

At 0755 hours, Barker notified the Tactical Operations Center (TOC) at LZ Dottie that Charlie Company was on the ground and had had no contact with the enemy. Yet TOC informed him of a report just received—apparently sent by Medina, according to the Peers commission—that Charlie's forces had killed fifteen Viet Cong without sustaining any casualties. Despite this glaring contradiction, there is no evidence that Barker questioned this report.[3]

Henderson saw the last stages of the artillery fire hit the edges of My Lai 4 along with its outlying districts but expressed no concern about whether stray shots or shrapnel had killed civilians. The subhamlet, after all, was a "heavily bunkered complex" housing the Viet Cong, and there was bound to be collateral damage. My Lai 4, he observed in testimony to Colonel William Wilson of the Inspector General's office, was not a village as usually defined and did not deserve an exemption from the bombardment. "Instead, it was a system of connecting tunnels, underground chambers, and fighting bunkers."[4]

Henderson was correct in saying some of the shells struck the village rim, but eyewitnesses sharply disagreed over whether this had been intentional. The commanding officer of the artillery battalion, Lieutenant Colonel Robert Luper, insisted that Barker had wanted the shells to hit outer parts of the village and, having watched the firing from his seat in the command helicopter with Henderson, maintained that "all the rounds landed exactly where they were supposed to." Barker's pilot, Dean Lind, testified in April 1970 that the artillery strayed off target to the south, hitting the western and southern sides of the village, along with the rice paddies near the landing zone. Also on Barker's helicopter was the artillery liaison officer for the task force, Captain Dennis Vasquez, who declared in his own testimony earlier in April 1970 that their objective had been to fire "in that area for the preparation"—the tree and bunker line along the west side of the village to take out any enemy positions, and part of the landing zone to protect the infantry, but *not* the village itself. He admitted, however, that as a result of shortening the first overshots of the target, "some did fall within the village." He nonetheless did not call for corrections, because the firing would last only five to six minutes, and changing the range would have virtually canceled the entire operation by extending the artillery barrage into the scheduled landing time.[5]

Lieutenant Colonel Luper, however, was correct: Barker had wanted some of the shelling to hit the edge of the village. Technically, he remained within the rules of engagement, but with the full knowledge of Luper, Calhoun, Vasquez, and Medina he had violated the spirit of these guidelines by subjecting civilians to U.S. firepower. Barker recognized the likelihood of a civilian presence based on past operations here and the large number of evacuees as this one began, but his priority, he later maintained consistently, was the safety of his men. He therefore had called for the artillery barrage to include parts of the landing zone, along with the western and southwestern sectors of My Lai 4—and without warning its inhabitants. Furthermore, he ordered suppressive fire into portions of the landing zone to protect the soldiers at their most vulnerable moment—when disembarking from the helicopters.[6]

Meanwhile, Task Force Barker's chief intelligence officer, Captain Kotouc, sat at LZ Dottie, monitoring the radio transmissions. In the Peers testimony he said he had been replaying the previous day's briefing in his mind. Once the 48th Battalion was taken care of, Henderson had said, "they won't give us any more trouble.... We're going to do them in once and for all." Henderson had made it clear that this was a search-and-destroy mission, making it unnecessary for him to specifically order his men to burn and destroy the village. Barker, however, left no doubt about its purpose. While his order omitted any reference to the few civilians expected to be there, he had to have known they could not escape harm resulting from a scorched-earth policy that would transform My Lai 4 into a free-fire zone.[7]

Kotouc likewise testified that he knew an artillery assault could lead to considerable collateral damage. A mere four-minute shelling would lob about a hundred rounds of fire from four 105 mm howitzers dispensing shells containing high explosives and white phosphorous, enough to kill everyone in their impact range of a little over a hundred feet—including those Vietnamese civilians who had failed to heed the repeated notices to leave. And no one had assigned a spotter to the siege area, to send warnings if the shelling strayed off target. In any case, as Vasquez emphasized, by the time any adjustment could take place, the brief barrage would be over.[8]

As we have seen, Kotouc had provided Captain Medina with two critical pieces of information that shaped the entire mission. He had taken the position advocated by CIA operative Robert Ramsdell: first, that the enemy would be in Pinkville and, second, that by 0700 hours the great mass of Vietnamese women and children in My Lai 4 would have followed their Saturday pattern of going to market in Quang Ngai City—meaning that nearly every person remaining in the targeted village would be Viet Cong or a sympathizer. Based on Kotouc's information, Medina expected all-out combat in Pinkville with a deadly enemy at least twice the size of Charlie Company.[9]

I

Calley had awakened a little before six that morning, like many others in the company, still pondering what lay ahead. The assault did not have the element of surprise. Ample warning to the enemy would come from the loud and rhythmic *whop-whop-whop* of nine unarmed Huey "Slicks," making the short trip twice from LZ Dottie and carrying eighty-two GIs from the three platoons along with about twenty-five other personnel and tons of military gear.[10] He and his men would be exposed to sniper fire the moment they jumped from the helicopters and hit the ground. And the danger would have just begun. The distance from the landing zone to My Lai was about a hundred yards, mainly open terrain except for patches of wild grasses and rice paddies.

After shaving and eating breakfast, Calley checked his weapons and ammunition, filled six canteens with water, jammed C-rations into his rucksack, and did anything he could to occupy the empty time before boarding. "It's weird," he later told John Sack. "I even combed my hair thinking, *Why in the hell am I doing this?*"[11]

A few minutes after 0700 hours, LZ Dottie burst into a frenzy of activity as eleven Huey helicopters began arriving—five troop carriers (the "Slicks," sometimes known as "Dolphins" because of their shape), two gunships ("Sharks") from the 174th Aviation Company, and four more troop-lift gunships ("Firebirds") from the 71st Assault Helicopter Company. Space limitations for the initial lift at 0715 hours only permitted the transportation of the twenty-eight soldiers of the 1st Platoon, some of the twenty-four members of the 2nd Platoon, and Medina with his seven-man command group; the second lift would carry the remainder of the 2nd Platoon's troops along with the thirty men from the 3rd Platoon. Additional forces included a mortar section of nine members, a three-man team of artillery forward observers, two demolition specialists, and an ARVN interpreter. Moreover, to gather material for press releases and take photos for both *Stars and Stripes* and other news outlets, two members of the media would be on board: a reporter from the army's Public Information Office, Jay Roberts, and army photographer

Ronald Haeberle, drafted in his final year of college and now in his first major military operation. Roberts and Haeberle would enter the embattled village with the command group and the 3rd Platoon during the mopping-up stage, meaning after the main event was over and most of the firing had stopped. To identify the expected small numbers of Viet Cong suspects rounded up for questioning, the South Vietnamese had provided two National Policemen to arrive at the proper time. Despite all these distractions, the mission hinged on the ability of the three platoons to reassemble quickly and efficiently just outside My Lai 4.[12]

As Haeberle waited, he noted the great excitement around headquarters over the possibility of generating great publicity for this much beleaguered Americal brigade. He had volunteered for this mission as the last before his discharge after two years of service because he heard it would be a "hot one" and the brigade's first "big contact" with the Viet Cong. This was his initial assignment as a still photographer carrying an army camera that, unfortunately, could accommodate only black-and-white film: Photographers had no means for processing color in that area, and the news media did not handle color. His only oral guideline, as he recalled in testimony, was to take pictures of "newsworthy events" for hometown release; never was he under any restrictions on the kind of pictures to take. Like other soldiers, he had permission to take a personal camera as well, which would use color film he had bought in Hawaii and intended to process after leaving Vietnam at the end of his tour about a month later.[13]

Eight minutes after the first lift's departure, at 0730 hours, base radio announced that the operation had begun with the arrival of the first wave of Slicks at the landing zone west of My Lai 4. The pilots of the troop carriers had flown in a southwesterly direction out of LZ Dottie for two reasons: to stay clear of the gun-target line between the artillery fire coming out of LZ Uptight and headed to My Lai 4, and to avoid alerting the Viet Cong with any kind of radio communications equipment. As part of what Medina later called a "feint," they followed a circuitous route down Highway 1 south until breaking out of their V formation and crossing the river before a brief touchdown in a small rice field about three hundred feet outside the village.[14]

The second lift departed at 0738 hours and arrived at the landing zone nine minutes later, completing the drop. Everything seemed to be going according to plan. U.S. Navy Swift Boats were patrolling the coastal waters east of Son My Village and off the Batangan cape; Alpha Company had taken its place north of My Lai 4; and Bravo Company had situated itself in the south, ready to help Charlie Company if necessary. Over the battle area were air spaces reserved for three command helicopters to circle in a counterclockwise direction while carrying Major General Koster (code name "Saber 6") at 2,000 feet, Colonel Henderson ("Rawhide 6") at 1,500 feet, and Lieutenant Colonel Barker ("Coyote 6") in his observation and command position at 1,000 feet. In addition, the "Warlords," an aero scout team of three helicopters from the 123rd Aviation Battalion—two of them Huey gunships to fly below Barker's craft and shoot fleeing Viet Cong—would soon be in position to help Charlie Company's 3rd Platoon protect the southern flank of its fellow two platoons preparing to invade My Lai 4.[15]

Already airborne from Chu Lai air base to the north and headed for the combat area twenty-five miles away was the third aero scout, known as "Skeeter," an OH 23 Raven (observation helicopter), a small bubble-like craft with a Plexiglas cockpit and two M-60 machine guns, one on each side of the craft, attached to bungee cords for flexibility. Its pilot, Warrant Officer Hugh Thompson—a lanky twenty-five-year-old from Georgia—sat between his two younger companions, a twenty-year-old crew chief SP4 named Glenn Andreotta from Missouri on his left, and gunner SP4 Lawrence Colburn, eighteen and from Washington State, on his right with his feet on the skid. Their primary task was to fly just above the treetops to draw enemy fire and thereby help the two accompanying gunships locate and destroy their targets. "We were bait," Colburn said in a 2013 interview, inviting the enemy to shoot at them to reveal their position.[16]

A little before 0800 hours, Thompson and crew arrived over the combat area and spotted "a draft-age male running south out of the village with a weapon." A Viet Cong "in uniform" and with a carbine and a pack, Thompson thought. "Who wants him?" he shouted. "I'll take him!" Colburn shouted back. But in his excitement Colburn fired off a flurry of fifty rounds that missed the suspect, allowing him to escape through a rice paddy and into the trees and earning Colburn the nickname "Deadeye" from Thompson.[17]

In the few minutes it had taken to reach the destination, Calley and the others experienced an adrenaline rush, a mixture of exhilaration and terror as the helicopters zipped closer to the landing zone and they could see as well as hear the artillery pummeling the area. Medina later recounted that he saw "the artillery rounds that appeared to be landing on to the village," causing the scattered air bursts followed by "the pounding and the dust coming up" from the edge of the homes. No one knew what to expect—a VC squad, a platoon, a company, the full battalion? All Calley knew was, whatever was there would be "*shooting at us.*"[18]

"When I get low, *unass!*" shouted the pilot to his passengers.

"Well, here we go," Calley remembered thinking as he prepared to jump from five feet—but suddenly could not move. Frozen in fear? "I tried, I just forced myself, I jumped a few meters into the paddies under me." And his men followed—into a hail of suppressive fire, he later recalled.[19]

Just ahead was the target, not much more than a football field away: My Lai 4. Calley hit the ground running alongside the others, all of them expecting to be hit at any moment. "I had always known it," he told Sack. "Ignored it: and knocked on the door of death today, and I couldn't ignore it. The fear now: I was saturated with it. I *felt* it. I kept running but it took extra effort to." He tried to find order in the chaos as wild thoughts raced through his mind. "A bullet: a pretty good way to go, I knew. No fuss. No muss, I wouldn't even know it was hitting me. A mine: that's worse, to wake up and think, *Now, what did I lose? My legs: I still have my arms, though,* I would try to think positively... and I kept running."[20]

"The fear: nearly everyone had it," Calley mused. "And everyone had to destroy it: My Lai, the source of it."[21]

Fear shadowed the follow-up move to the subhamlet. Its outlying rice fields were ribbed with dikes, which provided a wealth of hiding places for the enemy along with dense underbrush, trees, and thick hedgerows beside the village. The threat of mines, booby traps, and snipers in the outlying areas had necessitated the preparatory artillery fire, but that still could not guarantee safety for the ground forces. If the gunships drew fire or their shots set off mine explosions, they would continue to protect the advancing infantry by lingering overhead. The troops intended to seal off the tunnels with explosives at their entrances and toss in canisters of tear gas to drive the Viet Cong out of their refuge, linked to the outside by myriad passageways, some of them winding three to four stories below ground. They first had to reach the village.[22]

The soldiers rapidly disembarked into thick elephant grass and scurried to safety in an irrigation dike—all amid the deafening clatter of the engines and propellers, the last explosions of artillery shells a short distance away, and the friendly but all-too-close ground shots from the two gunships spraying the landing area around the troops in an effort to clear their way of mines and booby traps. Some men had jumped out while their lift was still several feet in the air and frantically led others running for cover. Calley's 1st Platoon had hit the ground first, moving quickly to a spot west of My Lai 4 to safeguard the second lift's arrival in the landing zone. Lieutenant Stephen Brooks's 2nd Platoon did the same in the northwest sector.[23]

The first lift's landing was surprisingly cold, suggesting that the enemy intended to attack as American forces neared the target. Medina saw no enemy as he and his men jumped off the helicopters and he marked the landing spot for the second lift with smoke. "I didn't feel the familiar crack of the bullet or whining beside you or cutting the air beside you," he told the Peers commission. "I didn't hear the familiar sound of somebody shooting at you."[24]

But trouble developed just after Medina reported a cold landing and finished guiding in the second lift. During its departure from the landing zone, the lead pilot broke in on the radio, excitedly informing Barker overhead, "Negative, negative, the landing zone is hot, we're receiving fire, you're receiving fire! We've engaged Viet Cong fleeing from the village with weapons!" Their helicopter had taken fire from a nearby village. The gunships immediately lurched forward, firing rockets and spraying the area with miniguns and 40 mm grenades. "From where I was," Medina asserted to the Peers panel, "it looked like they were firing into the village."[25]

At TOC in LZ Dottie, Kotouc heard the radio message stating the troops were under fire. He knew that in a combat situation, running from a Viet Cong hotspot automatically meant that that person was the enemy and was probably armed. Indeed, the reports of a hot landing and gunships killing an armed VC south of My Lai 4 could signal the beginning of an enemy counterattack. The accounts were mixed. Demolition expert Jerry Heming alleged in the Peers Inquiry that gunship fire had killed an armed VC, but curiously noted no additional resistance. The perspective was far different from the air. "He doesn't have a weapon," Thompson had shouted from his Skeeter. A search team found nothing.[26]

Medina was mistaken in insisting that Charlie Company had come under heavy enemy fire. Neither the Task Force Barker Journal nor the record of Barker's radio conversation with the leaders of the lift helicopters confirmed Medina's assertions of engagement with the enemy. Medina perhaps thought the company was under attack because of the radio exchanges between Barker and the gunship commanders ordering them to fire at a small number of armed Vietnamese fleeing the subhamlet or at the sources of small-arms fire coming from inside or close by. Medina's claims of a strong enemy presence in Pinkville helped set the tone for everything that followed in My Lai 4.[27]

The initial declaration of trouble caused a rush of activity at LZ Dottie. Major Charles Calhoun immediately radioed his ground commanders to take all cautionary measures before firing back. According to testimony given by Kotouc in December 1969, Calhoun told Medina and Captain Michles of Bravo Company, "Make sure we're not shooting anyone that's not necessary. Let's not be killing any civilians out there." Kotouc heard Medina "roger" the directive.[28]

Whether the heavy fire encountered by the platoons advancing on the subhamlets was perception or reality did not matter; they were indistinguishable. A number of soldiers from different sectors of the landing force reported sniper fire or other signs of an enemy presence. Sergeant Bacon from the 1st Platoon declared that the helicopter carrying him to the landing zone had come under fire. In the CID report, Sergeant Esequiel Torres, a machine gunner of the 2nd Platoon, likewise said he reported scattered resistance, as did SP4 James McBreen. Calley's radio and telephone operator, SP4 Charles Sledge, thought they might have taken sniper fire from Hill 85 while approaching in the air about a mile south of My Lai 4.[29]

PFC Harry Stanley of the 1st Platoon offered what seems to have been the most detailed and accurate description of the beginning of the operation. As the troops landed, helicopters were darting into and around the village, firing into any area that might have been hiding the enemy. The moment the infantry units hit the ground, they began shooting blindly as they neared their objective. Men, women, and children fled from the village—they had not left for the market in Quang Ngai City, apparently—but in their panic became targets of skittish and trigger-happy young soldiers. Refusing to stop when instructed (*"dung lai!"*), the frightened villagers marked themselves as the enemy under the rules of engagement. Yet even compliance with the warning did not matter. According to Stanley's testimony, one soldier shot and killed an elderly man at close range, though the man had not run and his hands were raised.[30]

And so it began.

II

The 2nd Platoon saw its first combat before entering the subhamlet, or so PFC Dennis Bunning from California thought. Soldiers from all three platoons immediately fired on a small group of male and female Vietnamese working in the fields. All the shooting took place spontaneously, causing pandemonium when the Vietnamese ran in panic amid the noise and confusion, making it impossible to determine who among the Americans fired first, but six Vietnamese went down without anyone having given the order to shoot. This was not the way battles began, he recalled thinking, at least not according to the training manuals he had read.[31]

The shooting stunned Bunning, freezing him on the spot. His squad commander was Sergeant Kenneth Hodges, who became infuriated with Bunning for cowering at the first sign of danger. Hodges yelled at him to open fire.

Bunning said he shouted back that he "wasn't going to shoot any of these women and kids." Hodges, having determined that Bunning could not be relied upon, angrily told him that when they entered the village, he wanted him out of the main stream of the advance—to the far left side, just outside the northern tree line and in the rice paddies.[32]

Bunning testified that he knew his banishment to the outer edge would make him look like a coward to his buddies, but he denied he was one. "I'm not a natural murderer, and to me it wasn't quite right." Besides, so many were shooting "that they didn't need me to shoot them." Hodges, he said, "gave me hell for not shooting. And I gave him hell because I wasn't going to."[33]

Members of the 3rd Platoon also reported sporadic hostile fire on their arrival. Sergeant Manuel Lopez characterized enemy action as "severe," he recalled, with his men ducking from sniper fire at the landing zone and quickly firing back and claiming to have captured five enemy weapons. Medic Abel Flores and PFC Rickey Neria confirmed the assault, as did PFC Charles Gruver, who declared that in a few moments they captured one enemy weapon. And PFC Gary Garfolo fleshed out Gruver's account by triumphantly asserting that they had shot a VC and seized his carbine. In what was perhaps not an isolated incident, SP4 Roger Murray in Medina's command group misread the two gunships' protective fire as hostile, convinced that he and others were under attack, as bullets zinged uncomfortably close to their feet. What seems clear from accumulated reports is that the gunships' suppressive fire pelting the landing zone created the illusion of an enemy attack.[34]

But at the time of the landing perception again overtook reality. Imagining the worst on that bright and clear Saturday morning, the last of the troops getting off the Dolphins hurried through the sharp-edged and almost impenetrable elephant grass, making it to their first point of safety, an irrigation dike. They then inched around trees and through dense hedgerows, in and out of dry irrigation trenches, and finally through the thick rice paddies of winter harvest time. Finally arriving at the edge of My Lai 4, they became especially wary of mines and booby traps while nervously scouring the area in expectation of a full-fledged counterattack. These intense conditions made it almost inevitable that the men would fire on the slightest impulse.[35]

The soldiers were on edge as they got closer to the village and, as SP4 Roy Wood of the 1st Platoon later testified, fired wildly in every direction. PFC Paul Meadlo and four others from the 1st Platoon found an elderly Vietnamese man curled up in a corner at the bottom of a shelter. "There's a gook over here!" shouted one of the GIs. "Shoot him!" yelled back Sergeant David Mitchell, according to Meadlo's account on *60 Minutes* in November 1969. The GI followed the order. Mitchell then led his squad east along the southern side of the village, in conjunction with other groups advancing on their left to the west, and with most of the men shooting at everything moving— or, as Calley called them, "targets of opportunity"—pigs, cows, chickens, ducks, water buffalo—and villagers.[36]

Much of the source of anxiety among the troops was imagined. They could not have known that the Viet Cong had decided against mining or booby trapping My Lai 4, to avoid harming its own people. In most instances, camouflaged mines and booby traps lay along the outskirts of the village, which meant that once they were inside, the advancing soldiers would become safe.[37]

The problem, of course, was that most of the nearly four hundred residents of the village had *not* left either for market or in compliance with the warning thought to be part of the plan. Most of them were at the breakfast table and did not seem to expect trouble, even with the artillery and gunship fire just moments earlier. One of the mysteries of the story is why they stayed.

In fact, a few witnesses later admitted that several Viet Cong fighters had spent the night in the subhamlet but left early that morning. Many families believed that the soldiers would call them outside and follow their usual pattern of talking to them in a "friendly way" before leaving. Seventy-one-year-old female Do Thi Don concurred, noting that the Americans had never hurt the villagers in previous roundups. Several men were working in the fields, seeing no danger in leaving their families at home and unprotected, and other family members had indeed gone to market. That many villagers readily complied with the Americans when ordered outside demonstrated that they believed cooperation was their best protection. Why should this visit be different?[38]

Despite all the talk by Calley and others about having warned village residents of an attack, later investigations showed no evidence that they had either received leaflets or heard loudspeaker broadcasts urging them to leave the area. Captain Donald Keshel from Psychological Operations, for one, maintained that he had not been aware of a leaflet drop or any other propaganda effort prior to the operation. And Medina later confirmed that no one had issued warnings. But the soldiers did not know this at the time. They thought the unexpectedly large numbers of Vietnamese reflected the strength of Viet Cong resistance, of which they had heard so much but seen so little. That explained why several villagers reacted to the surprise artillery shelling and gunfire by taking cover in their bunkers, refusing to come out of their hooches, or fleeing into the fields. They had received no warning of an attack, and they were not aware of the Americans' rules of engagement—that a running Vietnamese was automatically a Viet Cong.[39]

Whatever the distinction between combatant and noncombatant, Charlie Company's young and largely untried soldiers faced a task that even seasoned veterans of Vietnam had found impossible: distinguish immediately between enemy and innocent when both camps were Vietnamese. And the high number of Vietnamese on hand provided a logistical nightmare for those attempting to evacuate them from the village by driving them forward. They knew that above all they must not repeat Alpha and Bravo Companies' February mistake of allowing the enemy to get behind them.

Barker, for his part, at least according to testimony by Kotouc, had realized that not all civilians would pull out of the village before the attack and perhaps purposely left a gray area in his instructions that allowed his troops some discretion in determining what to do with the villagers. At issue was how to distinguish between combatants and noncombatants, given that the ghostly Viet Cong 48th Battalion was a local unit, having blood connections with families in the area. Barker had of course counted on many villagers leaving home around seven that morning, headed for Quang Ngai City to sell produce or to stock up on provisions. Yet according to Kotouc, Barker fully realized that not all the villagers would be at the market; often remaining behind were pregnant women, mothers and their babies, and the elderly.[40]

Therefore the question is whether Barker and other commanders thought that their troops were adequately prepared for dealing with noncombatants in a combat situation. Kotouc's careless attitude perhaps typified that of others in the military. After leaving Saigon, he had attended a five-day program in Chu Lai that highlighted directives on how to treat Vietnamese civilians. The movies the soldiers watched and the periodicals they read emphasized how to treat villagers humanely as a major part of establishing democracy. If anything, it was to counterbalance what their boot-camp sergeants had repeatedly drummed into their heads: kill or be killed.[41]

Barker had of course issued no written instructions, a normal approach in a military operation based on "standard operating procedures," though the My Lai mission was far more ambitious than the usual assault and was less subject to standard operational procedures. As related in the previous chapter, the lack of written instructions virtually assured differing views on what he had told his officers at the briefing. Calhoun remembered no specific directives; Kotouc later insisted that Barker had itemized several priorities fundamental to destroying anything beneficial to the enemy. Medina maintained that on a reconnaissance flight just after the March 15 briefing, Barker had ordered him—and possibly Michles as well—to destroy the village. But no one else on board heard the conversation because of the noise blasting through the open helicopter door, and neither Barker nor Michles could testify; soon after the assault they were both killed when their helicopter collided with an Air Force plane.[42] Whatever the case, the American forces were under no restraints.

Just outside the village, the soldiers believed they detected some light resistance and started firing into the general area of its origin. Medic George Garza of the 2nd Platoon later declared that they were taking intermittent sniper fire again. Torres agreed, as did SP4 Fernando Trevino, who maintained that their commanding officer, Lieutenant Brooks, had already ordered his squad to shoot any Vietnamese running from the village. So much firing took place, Trevino remembered, that he had thought a firefight was underway. SP4 Stephen Glimpse, radio telephone operator of the 3rd Platoon, remembered that fellow soldiers shot at three groups of Vietnamese males running from the village. At one point, he saw two piles of bodies and turned around just in time to see a soldier from the platoon shoot a wounded youth. Sergeant LaCroix of the 2nd Platoon provided the most detailed and yet unsubstantiated account when he declared that his squad encountered VC armed with automatic weapons and Chinese hand grenades. In one instance, he later insisted, he and his men had had to ward off an attack by villagers wielding hoes, shovels, and other garden tools.[43]

At 0750 hours, the fifty-two infantrymen comprising the 1st and 2nd Platoons prepared to enter My Lai 4 and gathered at its lower western corner.[44]

The temperature was in the mid-seventies and was expected to climb to the upper nineties by noon; the air was rich with floral smells and the view unhampered by morning fog or mist. As those up front peered into the dense foliage ahead, they saw the first of what had been a large number of thatch-roofed hooches and red brick houses with porches and manicured yards. Most had by this point been destroyed and were simply shells resting on top of bunkers or tunnels.

Calley's 1st Platoon, made up of two squads totaling twenty-eight men (down one squad and no longer forty-five in number) and led by sergeants Bacon and Mitchell, hurriedly collected on the right, ready to sweep eastward. Brooks just as quickly organized his slightly smaller 2nd Platoon, which consisted of three squads totaling twenty-four men on the left, under the lead of two sergeants, LaCroix and Hodges, and Corporal Kenneth Schiel. They would move northwest and then east through the upper half of the village, rendezvousing with Calley's forces on its eastern side.[45]

The 3rd Platoon, thirty soldiers under Lieutenant Jeffrey LaCross, in his first combat assignment, would wait outside the village, near the landing zone with Medina's command group. They were to work with the mortar section in providing a defense perimeter along the west side of the village and then in due course wind down the operation inside. The first platoons were to have finished the sweep in roughly forty-five minutes, and the 3rd Platoon would begin "mopping up," which meant conducting a broad sweep through the village center, disposing of any remaining enemy, counting bodies, killing livestock, and burning the hooches. Medina and his command team of seven men would accompany the 3rd Platoon on its entry into My Lai 4, continuing to coordinate all company movements by radio while trekking east and emerging at the other side, along with the first two platoons. Some soldiers recalled Medina entering the village shortly after the 3rd Platoon at 0845 hours; Medina nonetheless later insisted that he and his command group waited until more than an hour afterward.[46]

After searching and clearing the subhamlet of the enemy, Charlie Company would gather any detainees for relocation in refugee centers in Quang Ngai City, where the market was located, a six-mile journey down Highway 521.[47]

III

Every soldier entered the village prepared to shoot at anything that moved. Calley remembered that all he had in mind was Medina's order to "keep going," which he repeated to his men. "*Keep going! Keep going!*" Though hearing no VC rifle or mortar fire, he intended to push his men, refusing to let them slow down and allow the enemy to fan out and get behind them. Like a cross-country runner leading the pack, he knew that looking back or easing up could mean disaster.[48]

A little before 0800 hours, the first two platoons entered My Lai 4 on full alert. PFC Elmer Haywood of the 1st Platoon heard small-arms fire coming from the 2nd Platoon to his left and out of sight behind the greenery. He and his comrades started to follow Medina's orders as they understood them. The 1st Platoon tossed grenades into houses and bunkers and shot anyone trying to flee. Other villagers desperately pleaded "*No VC! No VC!*" as the soldiers quickly evacuated them to a clearing on the trail leading south out of the subhamlet. From his position at the rear of the platoon, Sergeant Isaiah Cowan saw "no unnecessary killing of civilians" but remembered that he heard a lot of gunfire ahead. He and his men fired into any place the enemy might hide, including bunkers and bushes. Meadlo likewise declared that the killings began as soon as the men entered the village and remained constant throughout the west-to-east sweep.[49]

The troops met no resistance, Sergeant Jay Buchanon later attested, yet in firing on everyone they came across, they built up an offensive momentum that was difficult to contain. Andress Delgado, Salvador LaMartina, and Diego Rodriguez shot at anything moving. Charles Hutto, Max Hutson, Thomas Partsch, and Dean Fields did the same, claiming they were following orders. Hutson and Partsch expressed surprise at finding villagers there, as did Garza, who would maintain that they were all certain they were killing Viet Cong forces. Tommy Moss noted that the operation began as a search but markedly changed when the first Americans shot civilians running from them. Bernhardt asserted that Buchanon had been one of the few officers to tell the men not to kill unarmed people, but he could also not stop what had already begun. According to Medina's radio telephone operator, Fred Widmer, "Once the first civilian was killed it was too late, period. Whoever killed the first civilian that was the end of the situation. It went out of control."[50]

Partsch was among the first to realize that the battle lines in the village were not as clear as Medina and others had anticipated. Only Viet Cong and their supporters were supposed to be there, but the American forces kept "finding people" in the houses, as he later reported. "What the hell is this? They're not supposed to be in here." No one said anything at first. "Then, a couple of crazy guys said, 'Hey, they must be VC.'" At that point, Partsch declared, "Some of the guys started shootin'." Haeberle was stunned. "It was just shoot, shoot, shoot at anything. I don't care what moved. I mean, it's just—the person would come out of a hut. Bang, shoot! It was just complete carnage there that day." LaCroix noted that when they saw bunkers, they started tossing grenades into the openings. "It was about that time that we started hearing the screaming from inside."[51]

By a few minutes after 0800 hours, My Lai 4 had become a free-fire zone.

Nineteen-year-old SP4 Varnado Simpson of Mississippi maintained that he had immediately noted something was wrong. For an effective sweep, the troops had to stay in a tight military line and act as a unit in putting down resistance from the beginning of the advance, but instead their organization began falling apart as they came across steadily growing numbers of villagers who were not supposed to be there. Within minutes the two platoons had rounded up close to fifty civilians at the trail—primarily women, children, and elderly men. And they kept coming.[52]

The killings had intensified within fifteen minutes of arrival. Wood and Stanley shot and wounded a woman who had startled them by suddenly emerging from a hooch carrying a baby and holding on to a toddler. After sending her to Calley, Wood stared in horror at an elderly woman desperately struggling down a path. She had apparently been shot by an M-79 grenade launcher; its missile had not exploded and was embedded in her stomach. Two of Calley's young privates, James Bergthold and Robert Maples, burst into a hooch and found three terrified children clinging to an elderly man and a woman, both wounded and helpless. Maples watched as Bergthold pulled out his .45 pistol, pronounced the man in agony and near death, and shot him in the head. Bergthold later insisted that he had seen this as a mercy killing.[53]

The killings continued almost nonstop. Sergeant Mitchell threw a grenade into a hooch in which there were several women and children. At the junction of the trail near the center of the village, a group of soldiers gunned down twenty women and children from behind as they knelt in prayer at a Buddhist temple with incense burning. And Stanley stood aghast as he saw Allen Boyce shove a Vietnamese farmer down the trail and, without warning or reason, stab him in the back. When the man fell to the ground, gasping for breath, Boyce finished him off, either with a bayonet or by shooting him. Stanley could not remember. "There were so many people killed that day, it is hard for me to recall exactly how some of the people died." He did remember, however, that Boyce then grabbed another man being held by some of the soldiers, picked him up, threw him down a well, then tossed in a hand grenade.[54]

"That's the way you gotta do it," Boyce remarked to Simpson, who was standing nearby. Maples said that he muttered to Stanley that Boyce had "gone crazy."[55]

But the clearest sign that everything was going horribly wrong came when Calley's platoon stopped moving forward, mired down by a group of Vietnamese far larger than expected—nearly forty men, women, and children his men had gathered, along with a few others the 2nd Platoon had brought to the trail leading to Highway 521.

From his command post outside the village, Medina said that he had become openly upset with the slow progress of the mission. The worst outcome would be a Viet Cong attack on the rear of the advancing American force. A few minutes after 0800 hours, he radioed Calley, asking why it had taken him so long to go through the settlement and position his men for the expected encounter with the Viet Cong.[56] The exchange, as recalled later, appears in Sack's book.

"Where are you?"[57]

"I'm on the eastern edge, and I'm checking the bunkers out."

"Well, damn it! I didn't tell you to check them out. Get your men in position."

"I have a lot of Vietnamese here."

"Get rid of 'em. Get your men in position now."

"Roger," responded Calley.[58]

Calley understood his commander's anger. Speed was of the essence in a sweep, and the 3rd Platoon's mopping-up operation would begin in about a half hour. Zippo squads—so called because they used Zippo cigarette lighters to start fires—would begin burning the village, part of Barker's strategy in destroying this Viet Cong haven, and everyone had to be out.[59]

In his interview with journalist Mike Wallace for *60 Minutes*, Meadlo said that Calley approached him while he was standing guard over close to fifty Vietnamese men, women, and children—including babies—all shivering with fear.

"You know what to do with them, don't you?"

"Yes," responded Meadlo, thinking Calley meant to continue guarding them.

Calley maintained a veneer of confident leadership but knew as well as did those under his command that he did not know what to do with the mounting number of villagers.[60]

But before Calley could say anything more, he noticed one of his soldiers, standing off the trail, his pants down to his boots as he clutched the hair of a young Vietnamese woman on her knees before him while she frantically held on to her child. PFC Dennis Conti had yanked this young mother aside for oral sex. And even worse, he was forcing her into it by pointing a gun at her four-year-old's head. In his court-martial testimony Calley said he sprinted over, yelling at Conti, "Get on your goddamn pants. Get over there where you're supposed to be!"[61]

Calley was not naïve about the frequency of sexual assaults in Vietnam. No one was. He knew that rapes were widespread, including a few committed by his own platoon—himself included, according to Bernhardt in an interview years afterward. Truong Quy of My Lai 4 was a forty-two-year-old Viet Cong security chief who had hidden when the artillery hit the rice fields but watched American soldiers kill several villagers. In Major General Karl Gustafson's report to the chief of staff, he recorded testimony alleging that among the bodies were those of three women who appeared to have been raped. Whether or not Calley was aware of it at the time, his men had already assaulted nine women and children. His radio operator, Private Dean Fields, was never far away from Calley and in testimony reported seeing an American soldier rape a nude Vietnamese girl.[62]

Calley insisted that he had not become "damn saintly," as he told Sack. But "if a GI is getting a blow job, he isn't doing his job. He isn't destroying communism…he isn't doing what we are paying him for. He isn't combat-effective." Better to hire a Vietnamese prostitute, as Calley admitted he had done on more than one occasion. Calley had taken on Medina's outlook toward the Vietnamese—making no secret that he loathed them—and embraced the culture of racism prevalent among American soldiers and officers. But this view did not include condoning rape in the midst of battle. Regarding the next GI he caught in the act, Calley says he exclaimed to a fellow officer, "I will court-martial him!"[63]

Racism was fundamental to Calley and Medina's perspective on the Vietnamese. Humanity was not a consideration. Now, under pressure from Medina, who had already blasted him for threatening the mission, Calley made the most momentous decision of his life. Everything in his training supported it. His superiors in both boot camp and OCS training had dehumanized and demonized the enemy. They had taught the art of killing and expected him to apply it in combat. Calley believed he could win the favor of Medina and by extension the army by accumulating a high number of kills. And surely nothing was either legally or morally wrong in adopting any action conducive to winning the war. Calley had interpreted Medina's briefing to mean that they were to kill everyone in the village to exact revenge for past deaths, achieve a signature victory, and live to fight again—and eventually to go home.[64] Since it was impossible to distinguish between friend and foe, the only conclusion was to presume that all Vietnamese were Viet Cong and kill them all.

If by this point Calley needed support for his decision, that came from a second radio call from Medina, just moments after the first one, and again related to Sack: "What are you doing now?" Medina asked Calley.

"I'm getting ready to go."

"*Now* damn it! I told you: Get your men in position *now*! Why did you disobey my damn order?"

"I have these bunkers here—"

"To hell with the bunkers!"

"And these people, and they aren't moving too swiftly."

"I don't want that crap! Now damn it, *waste* all those goddamn people! And get in the damn position!"

"Roger!"[65]

The idea of questioning orders never crossed Calley's mind, particularly during combat. As he recalled, he hated it when Medina upbraided him not once but twice over a radio frequency others had tuned in to as well. "I was sick of it. Medina was right behind me and pulling my string. And the colonel his?" The sheer number of villagers made it impossible to move them out of the village fast enough to satisfy Medina. He could not take them with him, and he could not leave them behind. "We mustn't let anyone get behind us," Medina testified that he had repeatedly told his men. "Our job is to go in rapidly and to neutralize everything. To kill everything."[66]

When Calley returned to the trail about fifteen minutes later, he saw Conti standing next to Meadlo, who had not moved from his original position, and all the villagers were sitting on the ground.

Meadlo reported that Calley scowled at him. "How come you ain't killed them yet?"

"I didn't think you wanted us to kill them, that you just wanted us to guard them."

"*No*," Calley sharply replied. "*I want them dead.*"

Meadlo and Conti stole a quick glance at each other and backed away to stand with two or three other GIs.

"Come here," Calley demanded, by now exasperated that his two subordinates had refused to obey a direct order. "Come on, we'll line them up; we'll kill them."

Conti maintained that he refused, that he was desperately searching for a reason to ignore this order. Doing no more than the minimum was a formula that had kept him alive as a soldier. Like so many others in the platoon, he had no respect for Calley as a leader. The incident involving the young Vietnamese woman he had assaulted only heightened his enmity. Finally, according to Meadlo and Conti's testimonies, Conti mumbled that he did not want to "waste" the ammunition for his weapon—a grenade launcher. "I figured that was a good excuse," he later told the Peers commission. He would instead pull back to the tree line and make sure no one escaped.[67]

Glaring first at Conti and then at Meadlo as if daring him to say no, Calley gruffly ordered, "When I say fire, fire at them!"[68]

Conti noted from his position under a nearby tree that Meadlo complied with Calley's order and joined him a bare ten feet from their terrified targets. Setting their M-16s on automatic, they raised the barrels and sprayed clip after clip of deadly fire into their screaming and defenseless victims as mothers frantically scrambled to shield their children.

A little more than a minute later, as the shrieking and sobbing echoed through the clearing, Meadlo stopped firing, breaking down in tears and stumbling away from the bloody site. Thrusting his rifle into Conti's hands, he later testified, he sobbed, "You shoot 'em."

Conti shoved the weapon back, according to his Peers testimony. "I'm not going to kill them." Turning toward Calley, Conti declared, "Let him do it. He looks like he's enjoying it."

At this point, a few children who had somehow escaped the torrent of gunfire struggled to their feet and stood in a daze, bewildered that their mothers and grandparents lay still before them. Calley coldly and methodically picked off the children one by one with his M-16, ignoring Conti's shouts until both his voice and the cries of the children had gone silent.

"OK, let's go," Calley asserted with an air of official finality.[69]

Yet it was not over. About a dozen women and children had managed to climb to their feet and were scurrying to the tree line for safety. "They're getting away!" yelled a soldier. "Get them, get them! Kill them!" bellowed Calley, looking to Conti, who was in their path. Conti trained his grenade launcher and fired four rounds at the Vietnamese running past him, missing high in the trees. He asked whether he should go after them. No, Calley declared, angrily muttering to himself, according to the CID report, that he knew Conti had missed on purpose.[70]

Calley's decision to shoot reflected no concern about killing children. "On babies," he later remarked to Sack, "everyone's really hung up." Those on the outside could not understand what was at stake and yet always cast the most severe judgment. "But babies!" they exclaim. "The little innocent babies!" Americans had been in Vietnam for ten years, Calley declared. "If we're in Vietnam another ten, if your son is killed by those babies you'll cry at me, 'Why didn't you kill those babies that day?' In fact, I didn't say, 'Kill babies,' but I simply knew, *It will happen*." This was a war against communism, and he was there to destroy it. "Personally, I didn't kill any Vietnamese that day: I mean personally. I represented the United States of America. My country."[71]

At 0840 hours, just moments before Calley ordered the execution of those Vietnamese on the trail, Medina informed Barker that the men had killed sixty-nine more Viet Cong, which, combined with the fifteen killed by gunships, brought the total to eighty-four. Medina did not submit a follow-up report of enemy casualties, nor did he mention civilian casualties until later that afternoon. Calley, however, later told Sack that Medina had asked him for a body count and that the number he gave him was not the same one passed on to

Barker. "*Six to nine bodies*," Calley says he had specifically told his company commander.[72]

There were still no American casualties.

IV

Second Platoon's PFC Bunning had meanwhile realized that distance could not insulate him from the killing. Almost everyone in Charlie Company had turned on the populace who lived and worked among the mines and booby traps but refused to divulge their location to save American lives. The resentment became evident early on. Just as his platoon entered the northwest corner of the village, three children, aged seven- to nine-years-old, suddenly darted toward the soldiers with their hands out, yelling "*chop chop*" to beg for food and candy as they had previously done when other GIs passed through. Bunning stared in horror as two or three soldiers near him shot and killed the youths from forty yards away.[73]

Bunning had no qualms about killing the enemy in battle, but the Vietnamese shot at both the outskirts of My Lai 4 and just inside the village were not combatants. He was not naïve, he said in his testimony, nor was he an ideologue who refused to hurt anyone on principle. That did not mean he blindly trusted the villagers. They were crafty. "I have never seen a Vietnamese over there yet make a hostile movement" when "within visible sight," he added. He never saw the villagers carrying weapons, and yet he considered them all VC "supporters or sympathizers." But to simply kill everyone led to mistakes. In an earlier mission he had recorded his sole kill in Vietnam—a girl of about twenty-one, he later found out—in the darkness and in the heat of a military operation in which all moving silhouettes had become the enemy, maneuvering to kill him and his buddies. She "definitely was an enemy," he insisted.[74]

Bunning had already separated himself in his mind from soldiers like Corporal Schiel, an ambitious twenty-year-old squad leader from Michigan, who had concluded that the fastest path to promotion was to amass an impressive body count—even if the figure included noncombatants. Medina's previous night's briefing, Bunning was convinced, had implicitly authorized blanket killings of Vietnamese, encouraging those like Schiel to shoot everyone. "I'm not going to do it," Bunning had decided.[75]

Bunning's relegation to the farthest point on the left flank of the sweep had put him on the outer edge of the subhamlet, away from most of the action and yet, ironically, in good position to see almost everything inside the tree line. Tall and dense hedgerows stood between him and Schiel, but he kept abreast of events by peering through scattered open spots in the greenery and seeing fellow soldiers creeping forward. Bunning had inched a little in front of the formation and inside the next hedgerow but hesitated to push too far ahead, because that would bend the military line and put him in a hot area.[76]

To prevent the enemy from getting behind the platoon, its men tried to maintain a tight and straight skirmish line, but, as Simpson had observed, the trees and hedgerows mixed with hooches broke up the order, making it impossible for the advancing forces to see each other except for occasional glances that made it unclear whether they were ahead of or behind the moving perimeter. As the men drifted apart and broke into smaller groups, Bunning noted that they were jumpy and continually wheeling around and shooting wildly to the rear. At one point he almost became a statistic. He had fallen a little behind the front line and caught a glimpse of its bulging center, causing him to panic on seeing the men swinging their guns back toward him. He ducked and scampered forward to safety.[77]

From his winding route no more than a hundred feet into the village and along the northern tree line, Bunning had seen the first of several random shootings. Less than a half hour into the operation, a small contingent of soldiers came upon a large brick house, where Bunning could see nine Vietnamese on its porch, all frantically clinging to one another—three men and three women, all elderly; two children he guessed between six and nine years of age; and a girl of about ten.[78]

He was curious why they were so scared. Surely they had already encountered American soldiers asking them about the Viet Cong. Cooperation followed by denials of any knowledge of the enemy had repeatedly assured their safety. But when he turned his head only slightly, he could see a dark portent of trouble. Standing a few yards in front of the Vietnamese were six squad members led by Schiel, who had gruffly ordered the family outside—"*Lai dai! Lai dai!*"—while instructing his men to keep their M-16s trained on their captives. Schiel said that he repeated over and over to himself in a monotone loud enough for Bunning and others close by to hear, "I don't want to do it, but I have to because we were ordered to do it." Whether his display of concern was real or reflexive, he was attempting to justify what he had already decided to do.[79]

Bunning remembered standing motionless and speechless a little more than ten yards away, peering at what was about to happen through the funneled opening of a hedgerow in a village thousands of miles from home.[80]

In that moment, Bunning testified, he tried to imagine Schiel's predicament, tried to understand—perhaps even rationalize—what he was about to

do. It was a moment of truth. His company commander had assured his men
that the only Vietnamese in My Lai 4 were Viet Cong or their supporters. If
he failed to kill the enemy in front of him, the soldiers under his command
would say, "Well, what the hell kind of guy is he, he won't even, you know, do
what he's supposed to do." Respect from his men, the satisfaction of following
orders, the chance for promotion, another small step toward victory in a long
and dirty war...all these were only seconds away.[81]

Five of the soldiers had set their M-16s on automatic, each assault rifle
packing a magazine of nineteen rounds. In the eerie silence came the sounds
of a sixth infantryman loading his M-60 machine gun with a hundred-round
cartridge, followed by the CLANK of the bolt closing just before the soldiers
opened fire.[82]

For less than a minute they shot from their waistlines, not bothering to
aim as they raked their targets with a withering stream of fire that, Bunning
noted, "almost literally tore up their bodies." After two rounds, he estimated,
the silence suddenly returned.[83]

Schiel later insisted that, "on the basis of the instructions the company
received," he had not shot anyone "considered an unarmed civilian." When
specifically asked whether he had shot unarmed civilians, he carefully replied,
"Not on the basis of what my orders were."[84]

The time was 0830 hours when Schiel and his squad turned away to catch
up with the rest of the 2nd Platoon making its trek through the village. When
later asked what the troops did after "this particular incident," Bunning insisted there was nothing "particular" about this "incident" and that "it was
going on all the time." He added, "We just kept on moving through the village, and more of the same. I mean they was shooting all the people that were
there to be shot, and the animals."[85]

Bunning's conclusion was bolstered by what was happening in another
part of the village, where SP4 Gary Roschevitz of Kansas was positioned. At
twenty-five, Roschevitz was older than most grunts. Nearly six feet tall, he
weighed 230 pounds, had blond hair and blue eyes, and was easily identifiable
by two long scars on his left hand and left forearm. But he was most memora-
ble for his perpetual anger. In one instance, Max Hutson admitted that he had
joined a dozen other platoon members, including Schiel and Roschevitz, in
using M-16s and an M-60 machine gun to kill ten unarmed villagers in front
of a hooch. Private Johnnie Tunstall attested that Roschevitz had boasted of
beating a child and then viciously killing a man who dared try to protect the
child. And Tom Makey and Curtis Fritts asserted that Roschevitz killed a
woman by shooting her in the back with the platoon's artillery piece, a M-79

grenade launcher—a single-shot, shoulder-fired weapon that propelled 40mm fragmentation missiles and was known as a "thump gun" because of its distinctive sound. James McBreen, Leonard Gonzalez, and 3rd Platoon squad leader John Smail confirmed this latter story and offered another one that was never verified—that Roschevitz had pulled out his bowie knife and brutally slashed and killed an unarmed Vietnamese man.[86]

It was the kind of story that in Roschevitz's case rang true. He had somehow managed to be at the heart of trouble if not always its cause. On the far right side of the 2nd Platoon, its forces sporadically came in contact with those on the left flank of the 1st Platoon as they made their way through the subhamlet. Roy Wood and others from the 1st Platoon had just burst into a hooch and forced an elderly Vietnamese man, his wife, and two daughters outside for questioning when Roschevitz and a small band of soldiers from the 2nd Platoon happened by. Roschevitz towered over those with him, leaving no doubt that he was in charge.

With Simpson at his side, Roschevitz denounced the soldiers of the 1st Platoon for bothering to interrogate the enemy. "Kill them all!" he stormed. "Don't turn them over to the company, kill them all!" Sensing hesitation, Roschevitz grabbed at Wood's rifle, apparently wanting a lighter weapon more suited to short-range killing than his unwieldy M-79. Wood was considerably smaller than Roschevitz but stood his ground and refused to give up his weapon. Roschevitz yanked Simpson's M-16 from his hands. Clicking it onto automatic, he shouted, "Don't let none of them live!" and shot the man, woman, and two girls in their heads, spraying blood and brain matter all over the ground. "These mothers are crazy," Wood remembered thinking to himself.[87]

Other witnesses confirmed the details in later testimony. Bergthold and Maples from the 1st Platoon had come on the scene just as the Vietnamese man emerged from his hut. Roschevitz shot the man in the head. When his wife and two children came outside, Roschevitz shot them in the same manner. Simpson affirmed what the other soldiers asserted—that Roschevitz had killed two adult Vietnamese and their two children, all unarmed and not one trying to escape.[88]

Gary Crossley from the 2nd Platoon had begun questioning the use of force after he and Partsch approached what was once a fairly large house, and an elderly man came to the door attired in black pajamas. Crossley saw him as a Viet Cong and immediately shot him in the left forearm. *"No VC! No VC!"* yelled the man, desperately trying to raise both hands. A woman, also in black pants but wearing a white blouse and holding a baby, appeared at the door, screaming as she pulled the man back inside. "Why didn't you finish the job?" asked Partsch twice. Crossley replied that he could not do it. All he wanted was to see what it felt like to shoot someone, he said.[89]

Suddenly Max Hutson and Floyd Wright burst on the scene with a machine gun and, thinking their two comrades had just had an encounter with Viet Cong, ran into the house and shot and killed the couple and their baby.[90]

Crossley was distraught by this experience and joined others in radioing Medina, asserting that they had seen only women and children. No Viet Cong. "Just keep going," came the sharp reply, Crossley said. Like Calley, Crossley read Medina's message as an order to get rid of anyone slowing the soldiers' passage through the village. But unlike Calley, Crossley quietly refused to obey that order. "It wasn't anything we wanted to do," he later asserted. "You can only kill so many women and children. The fact was that you can't go through and wipe out all of South Vietnam."[91]

Not everyone in the 2nd Platoon was killing indiscriminately. Somewhere near Bunning on the left wing was a group of men from the 2nd Platoon, led by Sergeant Buchanon, who had encountered no resistance but could hear what sounded like a firefight on the other side of a wall of thickets. His men, he told the Peers commission, were "tight, scared to move for fear they're gonna be blasted." The lack of an enemy presence had heightened their anxiety because of the Viet Cong's reputation for waiting until the "last minute" to attack. To prevent unnecessary killing, Buchanon claimed he repeatedly told his men "to fire when they're fired on, keep moving, keep moving, stay on line, just keep moving through the village. Don't shoot unless you're fired on."[92]

IF SO, BUCHANON and his men were among the few exceptions: The orders were to kill everything, Bunning declared in his testimony, "and that's what they were doing." His platoon moved quickly through the village, tossing grenades into bunkers and huts to make sure "there was nobody left to pop up and start shooting us from behind, or start shooting the other people." Using assault rifles and machine guns, the squads slaughtered villagers and livestock—anything that moved.

Like Crossley, Bunning was in shock at what was happening all around them. "As I walked east, I observed numerous Vietnamese, about fifteen to twenty men, women, and children, being shot at random. Everyone except a few of us were shooting." This indiscriminate killing of individuals or small gatherings of men, women, and children in their homes or outside continued throughout the platoon's advance to the eastern edge of the village. Bunning saw no huge piles of bodies, because there were none. Most soldiers in the 2nd Platoon found it more expeditious to shoot the villagers singly or in small groups on the spot rather than follow the pattern of the 1st Platoon— take them to the trail for a mass evacuation that turned out to be a mass execution.[93]

Four

FROM HIS VANTAGE POINT ACROSS THE HEDGE, PFC Dennis Bunning did not fully realize that the killings had picked up almost in sync with the rising number of villagers. As had been made clear, no one had expected to find civilians in the village, but when great numbers of them filed out of hooches and bunkers, the soldiers followed what they understood to be Medina's direct orders. Floyd Wright had said he argued that the company commander's directives were unclear and the men "did not know what else to do with them." Although not all soldiers joined in the killing, others excused their own participation by attesting that everyone took part. Sergeant Esequiel Torres nonetheless asserted in the CID report that "they had been under orders and there was not a man in the company who did not kill that day." Thomas Partsch concurred with this assessment, tying the killings to Medina's assurance that only Viet Cong would be in the village. When they came across increasing numbers of Vietnamese, he said, "the situation got out of hand" and "nobody took the initiative to stop the mass killing."[1]

I

Numerous soldiers in the 2nd Platoon admitted to witnessing or taking part in the killings, but no one claimed to have seen mass murders comparable to those committed by the 1st Platoon. The major difference between the two platoons' approaches appears to have stemmed from the relationship between Captain Medina and Lieutenant Calley. The soldiers in Calley's platoon had followed his instructions at the briefing to collect the villagers from individual hooches and deliver them to him, thinking he would send them to Quang Ngai City's refugee centers. But the process ground to a halt on the trail, largely because of the surprisingly large numbers of elderly men, women, and children involved. To placate his irate superior, Calley ordered his men to open fire on them.

Yet the killings by the 2nd Platoon were no different than those of the 1st and were perhaps even more personal, in that small numbers of soldiers shot or threw grenades inside homes and bunkers or killed them from up close when they came outside. And the manner of their killing allowed a quicker advance through the village. Kill them where they were and move on to the next hooch: that became the mantra of the 2nd Platoon as it inched toward the expected climactic confrontation with the Viet Cong, unencumbered by evacuees and leaving no one to attack from behind. In his testimony, Charles Hutto confirmed this approach, reporting that he and others killed every Vietnamese man, woman, and child they had encountered, not stopping until they finished the sweep.[2]

They were to kill everything living, Varnado Simpson asserted, speaking for many of his fellow GIs. "From women and children to dogs and cats, yes. Yes." He admitted to shooting and killing eight elderly men, women, and children trying to hide or run away from the onslaught, and he saw Gary Roschevitz, Max Hutson, Floyd Wright, Charles Hutto, Stephen Brooks, John Mower, and others likewise kill a large number of "defenseless women and children." Hutson later declared that he followed orders in machine-gunning women and children, adding that his squad was responsible for about a third of the seventy-five civilians killed by the platoon. Medic George Garza saw up to forty men, women, and children killed on the spot, and James McBreen saw about thirty men, women, and children shot in or near their huts. Numerous times Tommy Moss watched his buddies beat villagers before shooting them and leaving them where they lay.[3]

One of these deaths in particular had created Simpson's own special hell. Ordered to shoot a woman running and seemingly carrying a weapon, he turned her over and found a dead baby—her three-month-old son, killed by bullets that had passed through his mother. "The baby's face was half gone," he declared in an interview in 1989. "My mind just went." The first killing had made it easier to kill again and again without emotions. Lieutenant Brooks had ordered Simpson to shoot the woman because she appeared to be carrying a weapon. That act triggered a string of killings. Simpson confessed, "I was personally responsible for killing about twenty-five people. Personally. Men, women."[4]

Why didn't someone speak out?

To the Peers commission, Bunning offered two reasons, and the first was racism. Most of the men in his company despised the Vietnamese and would not turn in any soldier for killing them. "The fact is some of them…didn't even consider them human. I would rather see a Vietnamese die than me die if I have to make a choice," Bunning admitted, but he could never condone the actions of those soldiers who dismissed the Vietnamese as "plain nothing." Still, he added, anyone who reported what had happened could expect severe in-house retribution. "Nobody is going to squeal," Bunning asserted, "because you've got your own life to think about."[5] The second reason Bunning gave was fear.

Once the 2nd Platoon completed its sweep and arrived at the eastern side of the village, the men received a radio message that gunships had shot two armed villagers among some hedgerows or trees to the north and that someone needed to retrieve their weapons. Bunning drew the assignment of walking point in a small file formation through three-foot-high rice paddies outside My Lai 4, guided to the victims by radio and smoke grenades dropped from the gunships. About two hundred yards past the village, his small party located the bodies of two young men, both about twenty years of age and in black clothing. One of them was wearing a pistol belt holding clips of ammunition, and the other was carrying rice. The GIs also found a carbine and an M-1 rifle. The two Viet Cong cadres were from Binh Tay, a subhamlet immediately north. The rest of the platoon headed toward the settlement, determined to deliver a message to the Viet Cong.[6]

Bunning and his companions caught up with the others in Binh Tay a few moments later. The soldiers already there were standing around in no particular formation. Some of them were tearing up the hooches, looking for souvenirs, weapons, or anything helpful to the Viet Cong. Others had collected about twenty Vietnamese men, women, and children from two or three huts into a group.[7]

And Roschevitz was at its center. According to Gary Garfolo, Roschevitz was sneering that he needed more practice with his M-79—on the small number of Vietnamese squatting in a circle. Earlier that morning in My Lai 4, he had fired his rifle grenade launcher into some Vietnamese sitting on the ground. His first shot missed the mark, but the follow-up missile hit the middle of the group, ravaging its victims and yet leaving some alive for other soldiers to finish off. The M-79 was not really effective at point-blank range, so in this instance, as Bunning testified, Roschevitz backed up in preparation for test firing "a few rounds into this group of people, which would wound most of them, and kill a few of them."[8]

Onlookers watched Roschevitz climb a little hill about ten feet high— probably a bunker—and walk about a hundred feet. Within seconds of reaching the needed distance, he fired three rounds of grenades into the little band of Vietnamese. The muffled and airy *oomph* from each shot preceded the immediate successive explosions, leaving some of the victims barely alive until several other soldiers shot them with their M-16s. Lieutenant Brooks had already passed through this area but, like Sergeant Jay Buchanon, did not witness what had happened.[9]

In short, no non-commissioned officer (NCO) or sergeant was nearby to regulate the actions of the lower ranks.

Moments later, PFC Leonard Gonzalez spotted Roschevitz in another sector of the village standing next to the bloody remains of seven naked Vietnamese women ranging in age from their late teens to mid-thirties. Roschevitz was loudly boasting to those nearby that he had persuaded the women to strip by warning that he would shoot them if they refused. When he grabbed one and demanded "boom-boom," they all screamed in fright and clung to each other. Roschevitz had coolly backed away a few steps and killed them all with his M-79.[10]

Gonzalez later maintained that he had never seen anything so purely evil. Roschevitz had combined murder with attempted rape. Gonzalez had arrived on the gory scene and saw the seven women piled near a hooch, their bodies peppered with pellet-sized black holes. Roschevitz had loaded his grenades with buckshot—a special ingredient reserved for close-in jungle fighting.[11]

Yet Gonzalez should not have been so shocked. His 2nd Platoon had become a legend in its own time, the lair of the most prolific rapists in Charlie Company. Pham Day had hidden in the fields when the Americans approached but later saw them kill a number of Vietnamese civilians that day, including women they first raped. She noted what now appears to have been a widespread rite in Vietnam that many GIs considered a badge of manhood. More than a few men in Charlie Company had joined the ranks of other soldiers in-country who had earned the reputation of "double veterans" by first raping women and then killing them—sometimes after performing any number of sadistic acts. They often left the company's calling card with their victims—the likeness of an ace of spades cut into their chests as a portent of bad luck. Officers as well as grunts took part in the sexual assaults. According to Thomas Partsch's testimony to the Peers commission, Lieutenant Brooks regularly turned a blind eye to reports of his men's actions, but in at least one instance he took a place in line with his men waiting their turns with a woman a hunter team had found after searching the hooches.[12]

Gonzalez witnessed rapes every time his platoon entered a village on what several of the men regarded as a treasure hunt for eligible females. In one case, he tried to save a young woman from his own squad by urging her to run away; he had heard that thirteen soldiers had raped her and now more men wanted their turn. Gonzalez told them to leave her alone but realized he could do nothing to stop what was about to happen and that the woman could barely walk, much less run. Like Bunning, Gonzalez had refused to kill innocent Vietnamese, and, like Bunning, he had been exiled to the far left wing of the platoon.[13]

There were at least two gang rapes in Binh Tay among the estimated twenty rapes—according to CID findings and the Peers Report—recorded that day in Pinkville, at least one and perhaps both of them involving a sergeant, Kenneth Hodges, and eight subordinates: Andress Delgado, a twenty-three-year-old from Texas; Diego Rodriguez, a twenty-one-year-old also from Texas; and six other soldiers who were never identified.[14]

Bunning witnessed the first instance of gang rape, later declaring it one of seven rapes that occurred in less than an hour in Binh Tay, including one committed by three men of a girl he thought was "about eighteen years old."[15]

Bunning did not know the names of the three men, but thought two of them may have been Delgado and Rodriguez. "I saw three U.S. soldiers with her." Two others in the 2nd Platoon, Max Hutson and Dean Fields, confirmed Bunning's allegation, claiming they saw the GIs rape and sodomize the young and naked Vietnamese girl.[16]

Afterward, as Bunning continued to observe, the girl stood up, dressed quickly, and tried to get away, only to run into Hodges, who restrained her with a bear hug. At first she shrieked and tried to fight him off, but she "wasn't putting up that big of a fuss; she only yelled or screamed a very little bit right at first when he grabbed her but then she never did any more after that."[17]

According to Bunning's testimony, Hodges shoved her inside a small hut with no doors, and from thirty feet Bunning and four or five others could see that "she was just laying there" as he knelt over her on the floor. Hodges was in the hooch for no more than three minutes, Bunning declared, adding that only the sergeant's head and the top of his body were visible as he rocked back and forth. When she came outside a few moments later, McBreen claimed she had a "red face" and was clothed only in her blouse.[18]

The girl did not appear to have any bruises or cuts, and soon afterward joined a small group of other Vietnamese, Bunning remembered. As she walked with her people she had her arm around someone—a male Bunning could not identify. "She never resisted or tried to run or escape.... Could have been shock you know, of being grabbed, because she never really struggled or yelled.... Well, you know how a girl will scream sometime, you know, just a couple little screams or something."[19]

The victim of the other gang rape was thirty-eight-year-old Nguyen Thi Cuong, who was at home with her mother, husband, and twelve-year-old son when the soldiers burst through the door. They first took her family from the house, but six of them kept her inside. After stripping her, she later attested, three soldiers raped and sodomized her while the others held her down. They then took her outside, still naked, and pushed her into a group of fifteen villagers. Then, without warning, several soldiers began shooting them, one shot hitting her arm and causing her to lose consciousness. When she awoke, the soldiers were gone, but they had killed all the villagers, including her family, and destroyed her house and animals.[20]

In his testimony to the Peers commission, Bunning recalled how the rapes had started weeks before the assault on My Lai 4 and stated that when he criticized some of the soldiers for their actions, they threatened to kill him if he interfered. He was one of the biggest men in the battalion, perhaps only five or six pounds lighter than Roschevitz, and on one occasion warned two or three of his comrades to stop the rapes. "You leave that girl alone," he maintained that he repeatedly declared. But after a couple weeks of bitter exchanges, five soldiers came to him and threatened him. "Look Bunning, you leave us alone or we're going to kill you."[21]

What could he or anyone else do? All the perpetrators had to do was shoot anyone who objected and dump his body in the bush. "We had a pretty rough bunch in the company"—a group of "thugs," Bunning called them in his testimony. Hodges did nothing to stop the rapes, Bunning asserted. "He kind of liked it himself."[22]

As for Brooks, Bunning praised him as "a real good man" and remarked that the rapes "almost had to be done behind his back." Yet the very openness with which the GIs looked for women, making little or no effort to hide both individual and gang rapes, shows that they expected no one to report their actions higher up the chain of command. These so-called conquests were acts of violence aimed at proving their prowess and power, perhaps a rite of passage to manhood, which they enhanced by their boasting and, as Hodges and others made clear, by providing voyeurs with something to look at on the pathway, inside a doorless hooch, or in close quarters. Rapes were "an everyday affair," claimed John Smail from the 3rd Platoon to Hersh. "The guys are human, man." Word of gang rapes traveled like lightning through the informal news circuit of a company of soldiers already competing on the platoon level for the fiercest reputation. Bunning would surely have been surprised by the accusation that Lieutenant Brooks had looked the other way a few weeks before when hearing of a rape and cavalierly remarking about his men, "They've

got to get it someplace" and "might as well get it in the village." He would
have been floored had he seen his commanding officer lined up with his men
for that same reason, as later testimony stated he did.[23]

About halfway through Binh Tay, at 0915 hours, Captain Medina radioed Brooks "to quit killing people." It has never been clear in the nearly fifty
years since My Lai why he issued the ceasefire to only the 2nd Platoon, leaving the other two platoons to continue on their rampage for another hour or
so. Bunning thought the killings in Binh Tay stopped after the order arrived,
but he knew of one instance in which a villager ducked into a home bunker
and never came back out after a soldier threw in a grenade. The 2nd Platoon
soon released about sixty civilians before returning to My Lai 4. In less than
an hour, its forces had killed at least seventy men, women, and children in
Binh Tay.[24]

Bunning, for one, maintained that he thought the ceasefire made no sense.
Why did the killings have to stop, when Medina had said they were going to
sweep all the villages? "All I could ever figure out was, he figured he got away
with as much as he probably thought we were going to get away with."[25]

The ceasefire issued to the 2nd Platoon did nothing to deter the 1st and 3rd
Platoons, both of them now operating in My Lai 4. And yet there was still no
recognition by Medina that anything had gone awry—that his chief intelligence officer had been wrong and that his officer corps had either lost control
over its men or was leading them or even participating with them in conduct
not befitting their uniforms.

Despite all the testimony and paperwork, it has proven difficult to say
how many Vietnamese civilians the 2nd Platoon killed that day, particularly
because its men often intermingled with those of the 1st Platoon in My Lai 4,
making it impossible to determine which platoon was responsible for which
specific killings. The best estimates, consisting of victims from both My Lai 4
and Binh Tay, range between 120 and 170, based purely on the soldiers' observations.[26]

                                        II

The 1st Platoon's mass killings on the trail had meanwhile brought a stunned
silence that Lieutenant Calley broke around 0900 hours by ordering his men
to search for more Vietnamese to take to the irrigation ditch outside the
village's eastern edge. When a still-distraught Paul Meadlo arrived a few moments later with SP4 Ronald Grzesik, they saw ten soldiers standing guard
over close to a hundred Vietnamese, including a number of infants held by

their mothers or crawling on the ground. Nearby was a crude log bridge over a drainage ditch about six feet wide and four feet deep with a watery bottom. PFC Dennis Conti was already there, bragging to a soldier from Ohio, Charles Hall, that Calley had caught him having sex with one of the village women. Hall and the other soldiers close by would not have been surprised by Conti's behavior; they all knew him as one of a half dozen soldiers who had become a legend around camp by having to take penicillin shots before every mission to avoid contracting venereal disease. Calley had seated himself on the ground but looked up at Meadlo and Grzesik and groused, according to Meadlo's interview on *60 Minutes*, "Meadlo, we got another job to do."[27]

But Calley first wanted to question a Buddhist monk from the group about the location of the Viet Cong and their weapons. In a clearing near the temple, the monk, about fifty years of age and dressed in white robes and with a goatee, had been praying for a sick elderly woman lying on a makeshift bed when American soldiers pulled him aside.

"*VC Adai?*" demanded two interpreters, first Grzesik and then Stanley, asking where to find the Viet Cong.

"*No bitt*," responded the monk again and again.

Recognizing from their threatening demeanor that this was no usual interrogation, the monk started to cry and repeatedly bowed before his captors, trying to tell them he knew nothing. By this time Calley stood before him, angry and certain that he was lying. According to multiple accounts, Calley rifle-butted the man in the face, crumpling him to his knees just as a child about two years old crawled out of the ditch and toddled toward the village. "There's a kid!" yelled someone. Calley abruptly turned from his prisoner to hurry over and grab the young boy, sling him back into the muddy trough, and shoot him. Calley then calmly strolled back to the monk and, over the pleas of horrified villagers to spare his life, finally said, "You're a VC" and dragged him toward the rice paddy and shot him in the head at point-blank range with Meadlo's M-16. When the elderly woman cried out in anguish while trying to rise from her sickbed, "someone shot her," Stanley later testified.[28]

According to the CID Report, Calley told Meadlo and PFC Allen Boyce that he wanted all the Vietnamese killed as he shoved three standing near him into the ditch and shot them. SP4 Greg Olsen, a Mormon from Oregon who was barely out of high school, remembered that Calley ordered Meadlo to "waste 'em." Meadlo meanwhile had gathered his emotions and instantly pushed the closest Vietnamese into the ditch and then shot him as well. Again Conti turned away and, joined by Thomas Turner and Daniel Simone, went to sit in a dike about two hundred feet from the site. They watched Calley and others rifle-butt most of the remaining villagers into the ditch and kill them in a lengthy hail of gunfire. Meadlo later testified that they spared the lives of a few "gooks," as he called them, so they could take point in front of the advancing soldiers to shield them from mines and enemy fire.[29]

Turner and the others remained seated at the dike, numbed by the systematic killings. When the shooting finally ended about ten minutes later, Calley walked toward them just as a frightened young Vietnamese woman approached with her hands in the air. Turner claimed that Calley "shot her several times" before returning to the ditch.[30]

If Calley's purpose was to facilitate Charlie Company's rapid passage through the subhamlet, his strategy was not working as the soldiers kept bringing more and more villagers to the ditch. Frustrated that the captives were holding him back, he ordered his men to kill them. Sa Thi Qui tearfully recalled that she and other villagers "were chased into the ditch like ducks" and "fell head first." They were crying while pleading, "Oh God, have pity!" But the soldiers obeying his order shot everyone. Then came a brief silence, Qui testified, broken only by the faint scuffing sounds of "tiny children crawling along the edge of the ditch"—soon followed by more shots. Qui lay still, knowing any movement meant death. "I couldn't breathe."[31]

SP4 James Dursi and Herbert Carter had been playing with some children as this scene unfolded before them. Dursi stood in shock, helplessly watching as mothers scrambled to protect their babies and children from the automatic fire of M-16s amid the shrieks and screams of both the killers and the killed. "Why aren't you firing?" Meadlo yelled at Dursi, according to the CID Report. "Fire, why don't you fire?" Dursi could not move. "I think Calley wants them all killed," he said he muttered to Carter, who likewise stood motionless, mumbling in disbelief, "Oh no."[32]

Neither Carter nor Dursi were new to violence, but they reacted differently to what was happening. The previous month Carter and Calley had been interrogating an elderly peasant farmer when Carter—according to Stanley's testimony to CID—suddenly punched the man twice in the mouth and heaved him into a well. Four witnesses attested that Calley shot him and, according to James Bergthold in his testimony, radioed Medina that he had killed a suspect trying to escape. Dursi had actually killed someone. Earlier that same day he had shot a Vietnamese running from the scene while apparently carrying a weapon, only to find a woman clutching her baby. Still reeling from this incident, Dursi had made the decision, he said, not to kill again. Calley "can send me to jail but I am not going to kill anybody."[33]

Grzesik and Stanley also refused to obey Calley's order. Already repulsed by the large number of bodies on the trail and in the ditch, Grzesik could take no more. Calley ordered him back to the village. Stanley's refusal, however, led to a confrontation. An officer's rights were nowhere more clear, Calley knew, than in shooting a subordinate who refused to follow orders. In combat, as the officer in charge he became at one time the judge, the jury, and the executioner.

Calley threatened him with a court martial. "If you wanna court-martial me," Stanley declared, "you do that." Calley angrily turned his M-16 toward Stanley, who held his ground and shouted, "Go to Hell!" Calley finally turned away. As Stanley explained in an interview years afterward, "A soldier, he's taught not to disobey orders. But murder was totally against my nature. You can't order me to do this. It's craziness."[34]

PFC Robert Maples had just come to the site with his machine-gun crew and immediately took a stand against Calley's order to shoot the captives. He had recently seen fellow soldiers roll over the bodies of Vietnamese they had ambushed, lopping off ears to string as trophies. He had been with Bergthold when he shot and killed a defenseless man in front of three children. Like Turner, Dursi, Grzesik, and Stanley, Maples had seen enough.[35]

Calley, for his part, had also seen enough—of insubordination. He glared at Maples, standing next to a Vietnamese woman who had just shown him where she had been shot in the arm. Calley jerked her away and threw her into the ditch. "I wanna use your machine gun," Calley told Maples.

Maples refused to hand over his gun. Nor would he use it. "I'm not going to do that," he declared. "I'm not going to kill these people."

"I'll have you court-martialed," Calley yelled and pointed his M-16 at Maples.

"You can't order me to do that, lieutenant," Maples shouted back, according to Stanley's testimony to the Peers commission. Maples had seen women and children among dozens of victims he passed during the sweep, and now he was looking at more than a dozen other civilians forced into a ditch and shot. "I knew it was wrong," Maples told CID investigators and repeated in an interview some twenty years afterward. Those who killed civilians were "crazy."[36]

Calley angrily threatened to shoot Maples on the spot, just as he had Stanley. But the other GIs in Maples's group pulled their guns on Calley, causing him to back down and storm away as Maples and his men left the scene.[37]

Other groups of soldiers had meanwhile arrived at the ditch, including some from the 2nd Platoon, further stiffening Calley's determination to kill the remaining captives. He ordered Sergeant Mitchell to gather other men to help carry out the killings, and now, according to Meadlo, he led a group including himself, Boyce, Bergthold, Simone, and possibly Mitchell in shoving fifteen more Vietnamese into the ditch and methodically emptying their rifles again and again into the huge throng of elderly men, women, and children clinging to each other below.[38]

Not all died. Pham Thi Tuan and her children survived by lying still throughout the shooting and afterward. "Their dead bodies weighed down on me," she recalled. Another woman, a Mrs. Thieu, had earlier escaped with her children after her house was burned, but the Americans captured her and threw her into the ditch with the others. Pretending to be dead during the shooting, she lay face down as the pool of blood deepened and threatened to drown her. Ever so slightly, she turned her head until she could breathe through her nose.[39]

Stanley and others who had refused to follow Calley's order soon joined the small number of GIs gathered on the opposite side of the rice paddy.[40]

Olsen was haunted by what he saw while crossing the ditch afterward. Calley had been waving them out of the village and across a makeshift bridge when Olsen first gazed down into the ditch filled with bodies. "I don't know how I walked across that ditch," he declared in perhaps one of the most haunting pieces of testimony about My Lai. "I remember looking down and making eye contact with somebody in the ditch and it was like looking at a mannequin.... Some of the people appeared to be dead and others followed me with their eyes."[41]

Shortly after the guns went silent, Lieutenant Brian Livingston, the pilot of one of the two Huey gunships, flew over the targeted area. He had earlier seen a team of gunships firing into fifty or so Vietnamese civilians running southwest out of the village, and now he saw an even larger number of dead in the ditch and no signs of enemy fire in the village. "All of the killing was unnecessary," he later attested to CID investigators. Most of the bodies were women and children, and the "shallow water in the ditch appeared to be red with blood."[42]

Calley had called a halt to determine that everyone was dead, and in that quiet interval shortly after 0915 hours, a small helicopter noisily circled the area, preparing to land. It was Thompson and his two-man crew. Earlier they had seen a large group of primarily women and children heading down the road to market with their empty baskets and, seeing no military action, had returned to base for refueling. But when coming back to the combat scene some ten to fifteen minutes later, they saw large numbers of these same Vietnamese lying dead on the trail and now in a ditch. What had happened? In his testimony to the Peers panel, Thompson remembered that he had heard nothing unusual on the radio, no call for medevacs or more forces. And yet, "all heck had broken loose" in the short time he was gone.[43]

Thompson had begun tossing around alternative explanations in his mind. Had the Vietnamese panicked from the artillery barrage and run from their houses into the open? That made no sense, because of the greater safety provided by their bunkers inside. "Maybe," Thompson said he thought, the American soldiers "took the dead and put them in this big ditch as a mass burial, you know, a mass grave." But in looking closer at the ditch, he could see movement. "We don't put the living with the dead to bury them." He thought about the Nazis "marching everybody down into a ditch and blowing 'em away." Surely Americans had not done this. "We're supposed to be the good guys in the white hats."[44]

Thompson's teenage door gunner, Lawrence Colburn, was also sickened by what he saw. Moments before they had seen a number of bodies scattered in the rice paddies below the village and "bunched up" on the road—elderly men and women, as well as children. There did not seem to be any males of draft age. There were no signs of a battle having been fought. Merely bodies. The American soldiers were "just walking around in a real nonchalant sweep. No one was crouching, ducking, or hiding." "Like fish?" asked a member of the Peers commission. "Yes," Colburn replied. "I thought they had either been marched down into the ditch and shot or they had been shot and collected and thrown in the ditch." And there was no sign of an enemy threat, he added.[45]

So many casualties with no Americans taking fire, Thompson thought to himself as they got closer to the ground. "It didn't make sense." Something kept telling him that *Americans* had "marched these people down there and shot them." He remembered feeling complicit. Had he not marked the victims' locations for the troops on the ground?[46]

Just twenty minutes earlier, Thompson had spotted an unarmed young woman lying in the grass, "flailing around, waving back and forth," with "gushing chest wounds." Thompson dropped a smoke flare intended to mark her location for medical assistance from a squad a short distance away. He then wanted someone on the ground to help the woman. But he lacked radio communication with the ground command and had to send the message through the pilot of the nearby high gunship, who relayed the request to the ground command. The response came: "Yes, I will help her."[47]

Soon a soldier with captain's bars on his helmet came to the spot and pushed her with his foot, before turning and moving away. Curious about what the officer might do, Thompson lingered nearby in his helicopter, no more than twenty feet away and barely ten feet above ground. Suddenly, the captain wheeled around after about ten steps and for no apparent reason repeatedly shot her with his M-16 on automatic. "She's history," Thompson muttered, "and I'm sitting here. My God, he just killed her." His companion Colburn told an identical story. He and crew chief Glenn Andreotta watched the captain "look down at her, kick her with his foot, step back and just [blow] her away, right in front of us."[48]

"You son of a bitch!" they yelled in unison.

Only later did the three men in the helicopter learn that the officer was Medina.

Colburn remembered that this particular shooting clinched the case for guilt. Rather than just bodies, they had actually seen an American soldier—*an officer*—kill a Vietnamese civilian: *Americans* were responsible for the bodies on the trail and in the ditch. Thompson, Colburn told the Peers panel, "was just beside himself." He told his crew, "This isn't right, these are civilians, there's people killing civilians down here." Turning to Colburn and Andreotta, he angrily asked, "We've got to do something about this. Are you with me?"

"Yeah!" they replied.[49]

As they flew closer to the ditch, Thompson estimated that he saw 150 dead and dying Vietnamese "babies, women and children and old men" before suddenly seeing soldiers shooting survivors trying to crawl out. Thompson asserted in disbelief that it's "our people doing the killing! This is going to stop right now!" Lacking air-to-ground radio communication, he broke a cardinal rule of safety and landed his helicopter in a combat zone. Colburn recalled that they could see the Vietnamese "begging for mercy," but, he added in an interview, "there was no mercy until Thompson arrived."[50]

The shooting came to an end as Thompson eased the helicopter down next to the ditch and jumped out, demanding to know who was in charge. SP5 Lenny Lagunoy was the first person Thompson saw, and he called him over to his helicopter, though neither Lagunoy nor the four other GIs nearby could hear a word because of the propellers. The pilot was "kind of upset," Lagunoy remembered. Sergeant Mitchell immediately approached Thompson, who shouted above the din, asking whether he could do anything for those in the ditch. No, Mitchell sharply replied, adding that "the only way to help them was to put them out of their misery." "Come on man!" Thompson said he yelled, thinking this a morbid attempt at humor. "Quit joking around. Help them out." "OK, Chief, we'll take care of it."

Thompson recalled that he thought he had resolved the matter when a lieutenant (later determined to be Calley) joined the conversation, and it soon became clear that something was wrong—really wrong.[51]

"There's lots of wounded here," Thompson declared, angrily shaking his finger at an officer who outranked him.

"Yes," Calley crisply replied.

"So what will you do about it?"

"Nothing. Relay it to higher."

"I already did," Thompson testily asserted, referring to the only radio communication he had—with a nearby gunship. "Can you call for a dust-off?"[52]

"Can *you*?" asked Calley, visibly irate over Thompson's interference in infantry business and making it clear this was not his concern.

"I already did. But they don't respond," declared Thompson.

"If they don't respond to you," Calley asserted, "they won't respond to me."

Thompson knew he could not win this argument and, still thinking he had put a halt to the killing, abruptly wheeled around in anger and headed back to his helicopter.

"He don't like the way I'm running the show," Calley remarked to Sledge, standing nearby, "but I'm the boss here."[53]

As soon as the helicopter was off the ground, Calley radioed Medina about the pilot's complaint. "Get in the goddamn position," Medina shot back for at least the fifth time. "And don't worry about the casualties." Calley immediately ordered Mitchell to "finish off" the wounded. Thompson's helicopter was still taking off when Mitchell resumed the killing. "My God, he's firing into the ditch again," shouted Andreotta over the intercom.[54]

Calley and his soldiers were leaving the scene. He had left Mitchell behind to kill the wounded.[55]

"My God, what's happening here," Thompson said to the others in stunned disbelief, according to his testimony in the Hébert Hearings.[56]

"That did it for me," Thompson hotly declared after swinging the Scout around so his crewmates could see what was happening in the ditch. He was determined to stop the killing, but he could not figure out how. He was unable to speak with the commander in the air (Colonel Henderson) because they were on a different radio frequency. Thompson radioed the Huey pilot in the high gunship, urging him to contact the commander on the ground and persuade him to stop the shooting. No response. He could return to LZ Dottie and report the killings. But so much time would pass and so many more lives would be lost.[57]

Thompson's radio messages had not gone unheard—but they did not lead
to any corrective action. Thelmer Moe of Texas was in a field operations van a
little after 0930 hours when he heard Thompson radio his allegations that
American soldiers had indiscriminately killed many civilians and that he got
no help from ground forces when trying to rescue some women and children.[58]

III

Attention then and later remained on My Lai 4, which meant that another
part of the assault on Pinkville went largely unnoticed. Task Force Barker had
instructed Bravo Company to attack the eastern sector of this hot zone lying
between enemy-controlled area and that parcel still held by the South
Vietnamese Army (or ARVN). First reports (unconfirmed) indicated that
American troops had sustained mild losses while killing a moderate number
of Viet Cong in My Khe 4 (known to the Vietnamese as Khe Hoi or My
Hoi). But the U.S. Army remained silent about this second and concurrent
assault a little more than a mile to the east, helping to explain why it attracted
little interest until many months afterward.

Bravo Company had begun its operations not only in My Khe 4 but in the
central target of My Lai 1, located less than two miles from My Lai 4. In accordance with Barker's operational plan, this American contingent held its
blocking position below My Lai 4 until Charlie Company's first two platoons
had safely entered the village. Then Bravo's forces relocated at LZ Uptight to
await a lift to the landing zone just below Route 521 and southwest of My Lai 1.
In preparing for the assault, the army followed the approach used at My Lai 4:
an artillery barrage near the targeted area, this one at 0808 hours—about the
time the lift got underway. The helicopters took a southeast route over the
South China Sea before veering inland and north toward the eastern sector of
Pinkville. After a brief delay caused by the unexpected length of the artillery
preparation, the first lift of helicopters reached its destination at 0815 hours,
followed by the second lift twelve minutes later. Both landings were cold,
meaning they experienced no resistance.[59]

Bravo prepared to launch a two-pronged assault, one on the suspected
Viet Cong Battalion headquarters at My Lai 1, the other on My Khe 4. The
2nd Platoon, under the command of Lieutenant Roy Cochran, moved north-
ward to My Lai 1, crossing Route 521 toward its target, while to the west the
3rd Platoon, along with the weapons platoon and the command group, moved
in the same direction to secure the area just above the trail. Some of the men
heard rifle shots and thought they were under attack. It seems likely, however,

that these were the rounds fired by Charlie Company advancing east through My Lai 4. In the meantime, the 1st Platoon, led by Lieutenant Thomas Willingham, made its way north to Route 521 and then turned east to follow the road to the narrow bamboo bridge over the Song My Khe just outside My Khe 4. At that point the platoon operated on its own, although maintaining radio contact with Captain Michles and the others in his company. The troops almost immediately encountered trouble: someone allegedly threw a couple of grenades at them that failed to explode. No one found either a culprit or a grenade.[60]

The 2nd Platoon's attempt to enter My Lai 1 resulted in a number of American casualties that ultimately caused it to abort its mission. One of the GIs tripped a land mine, killing Lieutenant Cochran and critically injuring four members of his platoon as they crossed a hedgerow just outside the village. The advance came to a halt until a dust-off evacuated the victims at 0915 hours. But as soon as the helicopter left, the 2nd Platoon tried again to enter My Lai 1. And again, someone stepped on a mine, which wounded three more men. Barker was overhead at the time of the second explosion and notified Michles that he would pick up the wounded and carry them back to LZ Dottie. The heavy losses demoralized not only the remaining members of the 2nd Platoon but also those men in the 3rd Platoon, weapons platoon, and command group, who had twice watched the shattered victims carried away, five on the medevac and three on the command helicopter. The concern etched on these soldiers' faces must have convinced Barker to terminate the My Lai 1 operation, because Michles ordered his men to pull back.[61]

There still had been no evidence of the Viet Cong's 48th Battalion.

The 1st Platoon had meanwhile made it to the My Hoi bridge leading into My Khe 4—and without casualties. Shortly after 0900 hours, Willingham organized his men into two rifle squads, each accompanied by a machine-gun crew and all following a four-man point team whose assignment was to locate mines and booby traps along the way. When they reached the western approach to the bridge, Willingham requested gunship support as his men prepared to cross a bridge about a hundred feet long and only three feet wide. But the gunships were reloading in camp and unavailable, and Barker recommended that the platoon clear any potential resistance by firing mortar rounds into the area east of the bridge. More bad news. Most of the four or five rounds fired were duds that hit the beach beyond the target. Michles then directed Willingham to spray the area on the other side of the bridge with machine-gun fire before moving forward. By this time, the captain had doubtless informed

Willingham of what had happened to Cochran and his platoon—the land mines—news that probably made the men jumpy. Willingham believed they were taking heavy sniper fire, which drove them back in their first attempt to cross; several others claimed the sniper fire was light; still others reported no shots at all. Whatever the case, the platoon kept moving forward.[62]

About 0930 hours, the 1st Platoon began inching across the Song My Khe in a widely spaced single-file formation while three men remained behind at the western entrance of the bridge to protect the rear. The platoon followed its point team and, to dodge booby traps, remained on a trail leading directly into the narrow village. Between the upper part of the trail and the South China Sea was a ridge that blocked a view of the beach only a hundred yards away and on both sides of the trail sat the tiny village of My Khe 4—fifteen to twenty mud and straw huts still standing amid the rubble of dwellings that at one time housed about 200 villagers. The GIs could see a few villagers through the brush, "washing or something," said one soldier, "just their household chores."[63]

The American troops did not know this, but watching them cross the bridge was a young man not quite sixteen years of age, Vo Cao Loi, who was among about ten males of fighting age who had fled their homes to hide in the huge swamp-like area along the riverbank known as the Rung Dua Nuoc ("water coconut forest"). Loi must have wondered how much more damage his village could take. Most houses had already been bombed or burned, forcing nearly everyone to live in shelters. Now here he was, more than 600 feet from the bridge and hiding under one of many widely spaced floating shelters made of water coconuts covered by bamboo.[64]

Despite the artillery barrage and two helicopters guarding against a Viet Cong attack, Loi initially thought it a normal military operation. The continual passing of Viet Cong regulars through the village, some of them staying the night, had led to ARVN raids every ten days or so. The area had long been a problem for both the Saigon government and its U.S. ally, particularly after the military arm of the National Liberation Front (NLF) in South Vietnam, the People's Liberation Armed Forces (PLAF, known to the West as Viet Cong), claimed to have liberated it in 1964.[65]

In interviews with the author, Loi emphasized that most if not all the people in the village supported the Revolution rather than the ARVN and its American ally. Some of the villagers in both My Lai 4 and My Khe 4 worked for the Viet Cong as "undercover guerrillas"—as Loi put it—in promoting the "political struggle." The night before the American assault, a Viet Cong unit of about nine cadres had stayed there until learning an attack was coming and left before dawn. His two brothers had joined the Viet Cong, as did his two sisters. His father was away, fighting for the Viet Cong.[66]

American and ARVN forces had entered My Khe 4 a number of times during the preceding months, sometimes beating and robbing villagers while shooting animals and burning houses, but never killing people. If the invading force was strong, Loi declared, the NLF troops avoided a confrontation by hiding in the tunnels beneath My Lai 1, a sector with few if any civilians that had become a battlefield. U.S. forces usually asked questions about the Viet Cong before moving on, but the ARVN—sometimes accompanied by a squad of Americans—stayed longer and came more often, looking for males sixteen to fifty years of age to force into joining its army. The NLF did not recruit by force, Loi declared; the ARVN did. The Saigon government had passed a law ostensibly intended to prevent enemy conscription of these males by prohibiting them from living in Viet Cong-controlled areas and thereby forcing them into the ARVN. Village priority was to evacuate eligible males when either American or ARVN forces approached. All others remained behind—in the shelters, where they had always been safe.[67]

Loi was a month away from turning sixteen but close enough to fighting age for his mother to want him out of the village. "Now you are already a grown-up, you need to hide away," he said she told him. She rushed him and other family members into their shelter, where in preparation for his escape she hurriedly filled a cloth bag with two cans of rice and another set of clothes. Knowing her son could not go far—the village was a veritable island sitting between the river and the sea—she told him to go with Uncle Bay (Vo Cao Tai) next door. Tai's wife was away at market, leaving him in charge of their four children. Thinking the Americans would not harm them and knowing they were little and he could not carry them all, he left his three young daughters under the care of his twelve-year-old son Duc and told them to go into the shelter. Tai took Loi with him to join others already in the water, none under fifteen and a few farmers in their early forties, all hiding along the riverbank and out of reach of the Americans.[68]

Loi left the shelter around eight that morning, but to avoid being seen with his uncle they had to dodge the two American helicopters circling over-head. He had earlier watched the pilots periodically rotate their positions by changing their height so that one was always flying higher than the other. These short periods of adjustment required undivided attention on the part of the pilots and afforded the only opportunities for Loi and his uncle to move from one shelter to the next. It took them more than a half hour of har-rowing starts and stops to reach the riverbank, which was less than a mile from the village.[69]

From their secluded site Loi and his uncle could see the U.S. troops crossing the bridge—eighteen, Loi counted, all of whom he knew to be Americans
"because they were big."[70]

At 9:35 a.m., Loi and the others watched the soldiers regroup in a horizon-
tal formation less than 250 feet from the village and throw grenades before
opening fire. M-16 rifles and M-60 machine guns raked the hooches and dirt
paths for nearly five minutes, the firing so intense that the radio operator on a
navy Swift Boat nearby reported "a lot of small arms fire coming from that
direction on the beach." The platoon's fire killed or wounded large numbers of
the nearly 150 villagers inside—mostly women and children. Less than a
dozen others had been fishing at the ocean, and perhaps as many as forty more
were not there, including the ten hiding in the swamp.[71]

Willingham ordered a ceasefire at this point and the invasion began. Ten
soldiers comprised of the point team and six members of the 1st Squad followed the trail south into the village, one machine gunner ignoring the cease-
fire order and firing from the hip while "everybody," according to another
participant, shot at anyone who ran. As one GI attested, "We engaged upon
them whenever they would run like that." Still another soldier cynically recalled that they "were out there…having a good time. It was sort of like being
in a shooting gallery." From the swamp, Loi remembered that he could hear
the nearly unbroken sounds of small-arms fire but even more the grenades
exploding and destroying the shelters filled with people—including his
family. Moments into My Khe 4, one soldier not identified by Hersh declared, "the word was out…you more or less can do anything you like."
Captain Michles encouraged this attitude, according to this soldier. He may
have stressed the importance of "treating the people right. 'Now remember
they're human,' he'd say—and then he'd sort of snicker."[72]

The small American force slaughtered a large number of civilians in the
village. In addition to searching through and then burning down their huts,
they destroyed bunkers and shelters with TNT, usually without checking to
see if anyone was inside and under orders to "shoot them as they came out,"
according to another GI Hersh also did not identify. Most of the deaths came
from grenades tossed into shelters, Loi asserted. Of three villagers in one shelter, one died, and his eleven-year-old cousin Vo Thi Lien and a Mr. Tam survived two grenades, one collapsing part of the shelter, the other destroying the
opposite side, but neither hitting the middle where they had huddled together. According to Hersh, one unnamed soldier remembered, "We got sixty
women, kids, and some old men." Another soldier, SP4 Homer Hall, told the
Peers commission, "We just flattened that village."[73]

Just before 1000 hours, fifteen minutes after the entry into My Khe 4, Willingham began reporting casualty figures. Michles passed on the message to Barker, telling him the 1st Platoon had killed twelve Viet Cong fitted with web gear holding ammunition and supplies. A half hour later, Willingham informed Michles that his men had killed eighteen more Viet Cong and by 1420 hours that afternoon another eight, meaning they had killed thirty-eight enemy forces that day. The American troops suffered no casualties, never needed fire support, and, perhaps most surprising, seized no weapons.[74]

Furthermore, according to the Peers Report, Willingham reported no civilian casualties, despite his radio operator's claim to have walked with him through the village in the late morning and counted twenty dead civilians— all women and children.[75]

By one that afternoon, the gunshots had sharply diminished and the helicopters had left. Two hours later, the firing had ended and the Americans withdrew. In the silence Loi heard someone in the village scream, "They killed everyone!"[76]

Loi and his uncle waited with the others until they were certain all the U.S. troops had gone before returning to their homes. All the men's wives except Tai's and most of their children were dead. Loi found his mother shot in the head and lying near the gate of their collapsed shelter. Amid the debris were his sister-in-law and his nephew and niece, all dead. Three siblings had died, one sister burned to death along with her year-old son. He frantically searched through other shelters nearby, finding in one of them his sister-in-law and her five-year-old son, both dead, along with sixteen others. During the course of the day Loi had lost eighteen family members, and Tai found all three of his daughters dead—including his five-year-old, who had gotten on top of the shelter to play, where a soldier shot her. The other two girls burned to death under the shelter. His son Duc survived but lost his arm when the shelter fell on him.[77]

Neither Tai nor Loi returned to My Khe 4. Tai and his wife and son moved to Hué; Loi joined other youths in following VC Battalion 48 to the mountain location of the NLF's armed forces (PLAF), where they became active supporters of the revolution. "It's either being a soldier for the ARVN, or the NLF," Loi explained. "I lived with the NLF and then joined the Army," where he often whipped up emotions by telling his story to troops.[78]

Several Vietnamese sources soon accused U.S. forces of killing up to ninety noncombatants in My Khe 4. Two days after the assault, the Census Grievance Center in Quang Ngai City filed a report alleging that Americans had killed eighty Vietnamese people, both "young and old." Less than a week later, Son

My's village chief submitted a report to the district chief of Son Tinh that raised the number to ninety. The chief of Co Luy Hamlet had talked with survivors in Quang Ngai City and declared that the Americans killed eighty-seven. The National Liberation Front Committee charged the Americans with killing ninety-two civilians.[79]

The most detailed account of the My Khe 4 massacre came from a survivor—Nguyen Thi Bay, who told CID investigators that she witnessed the killings and was raped by two American soldiers. U.S. troops entered the village between nine and ten o'clock in the morning and, despite encountering no opposition, shot and killed ninety Vietnamese civilians, many of them as they came out of their shelters. She had hidden in a shelter with two women and three children, but three soldiers found them and took them to a hooch, where two of them raped her after hitting the other two women with a rifle butt when she at first refused their advances. Bay was two months pregnant at the time and lost her baby the following day.[80]

It remains impossible to be certain about the number of Vietnamese casualties at My Khe 4. Of the ten participants in this search-and-destroy operation, two were dead by the time the Peers commission learned of possible atrocities in that village, and all the others refused to talk about what happened or claimed not to remember.[81]

According to Loi, ninety-seven elderly men, women, and children died that day in My Khe 4.[82]

THE OVERWHELMING CONSENSUS is that American forces encountered no organized resistance on the morning of March 16, either in My Lai 4 or My Khe 4 because, as one villager in each targeted area explained, a contingent of Viet Cong regulars had stayed in both villages the night before but followed their usual pattern of leaving early in the morning.[83]

Four Viet Cong cadres had been in My Lai 4 earlier that morning but none from the 48th Battalion, the target of the attack. Truong Quy, as security chief, had been in the field and declared the attack a surprise. Do Vien, a thirty-four-year-old man who worked for the Viet Cong, asserted that about ten active supporters had been in the village when the shooting began. All but one of them—a local VC guerrilla—worked in propaganda, civilian labor management, education and youth guidance, or security matters. American gunships killed two Viet Cong as they fled the village. Vien was in the fields but escaped. Dang Thi was a twenty-three-year-old medical corpsman for the Viet Cong in My Lai 4 who, when captured, insisted that no fighters were there. And Nguyen Co was a subhamlet chief for the Viet Cong, who had hidden with his family in their bunker when the Americans ordered them out. He ignored the order and remained inside the bunker until noon, when he emerged to look for his family. His wife and children had escaped by pretending to be dead, but he found the bodies of his mother and grandmother on the trail.[84]

All this death and destruction had been for the sake of attacking an enemy who was not there.

Five

DESPITE CAREFUL PLANNING, the My Lai 4 operation rapidly descended into chaos and depravity. During the morning of March 16, the first two platoons of Charlie Company had made their way east, followed shortly before 0900 hours by Captain Medina, who led his command group into the village from the trail in the south, along with the 3rd Platoon assigned to carry out the mopping-up operations. Gary Garfolo immediately noted the confusion, he told Hersh. "I could hear heavy shooting all the time. Medina was running back and forth everywhere. This wasn't no organized deal."[1] Without guidance, Garfolo and several other GIs acted on their own—in the midst of terrified villagers. Caught in the violence, the villagers ran in every direction, grasping wicker baskets containing hastily grabbed possessions while frantically trying to find a way out. The GIs, however, thought they were confronting their first Viet Cong forces trying to escape and fired at them. And even if the Vietnamese dodged soldiers on the ground, they could not hide from the gunships, whose marksmen saw the peasants running from the American ground force and likewise assumed they were Viet Cong.

Twenty-two-year-old Sergeant Charles West stood at the rim of the village and shot six villagers fleeing their homes. As he told Hersh, "These people were running into us, away from us, running every which way. It's hard to distinguish a *mama-san* from a *papa-san* when everybody has on black pajamas." He and his men were stunned by the large numbers of villagers darting all around them and thought their own survival depended on shooting everything that moved. "I knew that everyone was being killed."[2]

I

PFC Michael Bernhardt was assigned to the command group, from which he witnessed numerous killings while slowly making his way through the village next to Medina. The young soldier from the 2nd Platoon had not entered My Lai 4 along with his company commander; Medina ordered him to inspect a suspicious-looking wooden box just outside the subhamlet to determine whether it was a booby trap. After finding it harmless, Bernhardt caught up with the command group inside My Lai 4 and was shocked to see the 3rd Platoon setting the huts on fire and shooting their inhabitants as they ran outside, or breaking into them and shooting everyone inside. Other GIs assembled the villagers in small groups outside their homes and shot them on the spot. "The whole thing was so deliberate," he told Hersh. "It was point-blank murder and I was standing there watching it. It's kind of made me wonder if I could trust people anymore."[3]

The 3rd Platoon, led by Lieutenant Jeffrey LaCross, began the final phase of the operation before the other two platoons had made it through the village, but its so-called "mop-up mission" quickly became a euphemism for killing anyone still alive. Photographer and Sergeant Ronald Haeberle took picture after picture of civilians scattered everywhere, some already dead and the others now slain by the 3rd Platoon. No doubt out of concern for his own safety, he decided against photographing soldiers shooting villagers, but his camera recorded a great number of bodies spread out or together, depending on where the victims had been when they were murdered. It also showed bunkers, sometimes filled with villagers, ripped apart by grenades; domestic structures damaged or destroyed by what he at first assumed was errant artillery fire; hooches burned to the ground by Zippo squads; pigs and water buffaloes killed; wells contaminated by animal remains.

"I knew it was something that shouldn't be happening but yet I was part of it," Haeberle recounted in an interview years later. "I think I was in a kind of daze from seeing all these shootings and not seeing any return fire. Yet the killing kept going on." Several soldiers rounded up the civilians and shot them, while others killed them individually or in small groups on the spot. Everyone in Haeberle's mind bore responsibility, including Major General Koster and Lieutenant Colonel Barker for failing to monitor and control their troops. All refused to take prisoners. "It was completely different to my concept of what war is all about."[4]

Numerous soldiers' accounts confirmed the continuing slaughter. In the CID Report, Sergeant West admitted that they had killed women and children. PFC Richard Pendleton and his men shot a half dozen men and women running from the village, killing three of them. Fred Dustin watched his fellow grunts kill a group of Vietnamese that included children. Stephen Glimpse saw a soldier behind him shoot a wounded youth.[5]

One of the 3rd Platoon's most flagrant killers was PFC Robert T'Souvas, who later explained that in accordance with their search-and-destroy orders he and fellow GIs had burned everything and killed about eighty unarmed Vietnamese men, women, and children. Among his victims were two teenaged boys, one of them already wounded. Larry Polston saw T'Souvas mow down two wounded and sobbing children with his machine gun, afterward declaring, "they were already half dead." The killings were "senseless," Polston concluded.[6]

At the time and later, a number of soldiers who were there did not want to believe the worst of each other and held fast to the idea that the civilians were victims of collateral damage. Sergeant Manuel Lopez saw Vietnamese bodies in stacks but attributed their deaths to air strikes, artillery fire, and napalm. Medic Abel Flores blamed gunship fire or accidents. PFC Gene Oliver figured that Medina had issued the cease-fire order because the platoon sergeants had lost control over their men, but Oliver thought it likely that artillery or mortar fire was responsible for the bodies he saw.[7]

There were several instances of alleged mercy killings. In testimony for the CID Report, T'Souvas said he had killed a young girl, a woman, and three elderly men because they had been badly wounded and would get no medical assistance. Pendleton asserted that when he and his men came upon a ditch containing about forty dead and wounded men, women, and children, they saw two young privates, twenty-one-year-old Michael Terry from Utah and twenty-year-old William Doherty from Massachusetts, agonizing over the plight of the victims. "They were pretty badly shot up," Terry told Hersh. "They weren't going to get any medical help, and so we shot them. Shot maybe five of them." Both men had wrestled with their consciences about what to do and clearly had doubts about what they did. Doherty blotted the killings out of his mind by later insisting that he could not remember the attack and the events associated with it—that the whole affair was a "blank."[8]

There are conflicting reports on Medina's location at the time of the slayings and whether or not he had participated in them. Some observers have argued that Medina not only knew of the killings but personally shot several civilians, including two women and a child. Medina adamantly denied these allegations in the Hébert Hearings and to CID, maintaining that he did not enter the subhamlet until after ten o'clock for the "mop-up." But news correspondent Jay Roberts from the army's Public Information Office remembered Medina and his command group coming in immediately after the 3rd Platoon and "directing the operations in the village." Medina "was in the village the whole time I was—from nine o'clock to eleven o'clock," Roberts told Hersh. West concurred with Roberts, asserting that "Medina was right behind us."[9]

It seems inconceivable that Medina could have been oblivious to what was going on all around him—particularly when several members of the 3rd Platoon and his command group spoke of seeing numerous bodies as they accompanied him through the village. Flores thought that Medina had to have seen one of his radio operators, Fred Widmer, just twenty-five yards behind at the trail junction, killing a five-year-old boy who had head wounds. Thomas Kinch and Jerry Heming had followed Medina and saw "numerous dead women and children along their route." On one occasion, Kinch noted to the CID investigators, "Medina stepped over the body of a youth." SP4 James Flynn saw a large group of bodies on the trail close to where the captain ordered an unidentified soldier to shoot a wounded child. According to Heming, Medina appeared "saddened" by the bodies of six women and eight children in a rice paddy. Sergeant Martin Fagan made a similar observation to CID, remarking that Medina seemed "distressed" at the extent of the massacre. Louis Martin and the company's forward artillery observer, Roger Alaux, were with Medina most of the time and insisted that he was fully aware of the "slaughter." Martin had no doubt: "Captain Medina knew."[10]

Furthermore, according to at least four witnesses, Medina joined in the killing. Pendleton recalled that as they reached the southern perimeter near the center of the village, he saw Medina raise his M-16 and shoot a small child standing among a dozen bodies of men, women, and children. Flynn and one of Medina's RTOs, SP4 John Paul, reported seeing Medina shoot and kill a wounded woman sprawled face down among a number of bodies, with Medina claiming that she suddenly moved, drawing what Paul termed an "instinctive" fatal shot. And Bernhardt stood close by as Medina shot a woman bending over in a field, picking rice. "Medina," Bernhardt asserted, "lifted the rifle to his shoulder, looked down the barrel and pulled the trigger." The woman dropped to the ground. Medina then walked to within six feet of her "and finished her off." Bernhardt remembered that her clothing moved and her body twitched when the bullets struck. "I couldn't see any holes," he declared on approaching the body, meaning that Medina had not shot her in the head. A moment later, Bernhardt told Hersh, he "gave me a look, a dumb shit-eating grin."[11]

Herbert Carter of the 1st Platoon provided the most detailed first-hand account of Medina's either killing civilians or ordering his men to do so. Soon after the initial landing that morning, the advancing forces spotted an elderly man in the field, waving his arms while giving some sort of greeting in Vietnamese. Either Medina or Calley, according to Carter, ordered someone to kill the villager, and "a big heavy-set" soldier shot him. "This was the first murder." As they got to the edge of the village, a woman came out, and after a soldier knocked her to the ground, Medina shot her with his M-16. "I was fifty or sixty feet from him and saw this. There was no reason to shoot this girl." It was "a pure out and out murder," Carter testified for the CID Report. A few minutes later Medina ordered a teenaged boy leading a water buffalo to stop and then told him to "make a run for it." But the boy refused to run, Carter declared, "so Medina shot him with his M-16 rifle and killed him." Carter was less than eighty feet away and, along with the command group, demolition crew, and other soldiers, "saw it plainly." He insisted that "Medina both personally shot a woman and a youth and personally directed the killings of several other noncombatants."[12]

Carter detected little or no remorse on the part of either Medina or the men. One of the company's two ARVN interpreters, Sergeant Nguyen Dinh Phu, killed a large number of villagers in My Lai 4, including in one incident in which he and Medina "fired on the same group at the same time" and laughed about it, according to Carter. Most of the troops felt the same about killing Vietnamese, Carter declared. "The boys enjoyed it." Those who objected were small in number or simply said nothing. Carter even thought at the time that Medina liked the killings. "You can tell when someone enjoys their work." Warned of the seriousness of his charges, Carter staunchly responded to the CID investigator, "What I'm telling is the truth, and I'll face Medina in court and swear to it."[13]

Confirmation of many of Carter's allegations came from other soldiers in the 3rd Platoon. Bernhardt saw them shoot twenty villagers, mostly women and children, and he witnessed numerous other killings that left bodies strewn throughout the village. He and his companions counted more than a hundred bodies—women, children (including infants), and old men, all "in very large heaps." He also saw fellow GIs mistreat civilians, including elderly men, by beating them and, in a major insult, cutting off their beards. Garfolo watched one soldier go "wild" while joining others in scalping their victims.[14]

Haeberle also declared that the soldiers killed a large number of Vietnamese men, women, and children; systematically destroyed the village; and claimed to be acting under orders to kill everyone. When a woman peered out from behind the vegetation, they fired on her without attempting to determine whether or not she was Viet Cong. As she fell into the rice paddies, her head lay propped up against a stalk and provided a target. "They just kept shooting at her," Haeberle asserted. "You could see the bones flying in the air chip by chip." He looked at Jay Roberts and, as he later remarked, "We just shook our heads."[15]

Haeberle took a picture of the woman afterward, along with many others, including nearly a hundred Vietnamese civilians killed by about thirty soldiers. He remembered a man and two children aged five to ten walking out of the ditch and toward the troops while the little girl pleaded for their lives, saying over and over, "'No, no'. ... All of a sudden the GIs opened up and cut them down." A machine gunner riddled a group of women running away with their children and babies. Another soldier fired his M-16 at two young boys walking down the road. The older boy—perhaps eight years old—tried to protect the other one by falling on him. But the shooter kept firing until he had killed both of the children.[16]

Roberts saw Charlie Company deliberately kill "defenseless men, women and children" while destroying their homes, livestock, and crops. He also saw a soldier shoot a child digging through a pile of dead men, women, and children, apparently searching for a relative. Another boy, already wounded, was shot in the same area at the same time. In another instance, the soldiers pulled an elderly man out of hiding for questioning by Medina. It was clear, Roberts noted, that the man knew nothing about the Viet Cong and that his chief concern was holding up his pants. But when the GIs asked Medina what to do with them, he coldly replied, according to Roberts's testimony to the Peers panel, "I don't care." As Roberts walked away, he heard a shot and turned around to see the man lying dead. Medina, Roberts thought, tried to avoid seeing the killings but had to have known they were taking place.[17]

Medina stayed on the trail that ran along the village's southern outskirts until moving toward its center around 10:30 a.m., but not before being in a position to see dozens of bodies of men, women, and children along the way. Haeberle was with Medina and the command group at the time and saw the captives kneeling as American soldiers slaughtered them in torrents of machine-gun fire. Yet Medina asserted to the Peers commission that in response to Major Calhoun's direct radio call at 10:25 a.m. citing a report that "innocent civilians had been shot or killed," he admitted to seeing up to twenty-five civilian bodies along the trail—probably killed by small arms, artillery, or gunships.[18]

Additional suspicion of Medina's behavior came from the other ARVN interpreter, Sergeant Duong Minh, who had arrived by helicopter and entered the village a little before nine o'clock with Lieutenant Dennis Johnson, the military intelligence officer for whom he worked. Minh expressed shock at the number of civilians killed by the Americans and immediately demanded an explanation. When Johnson finally conceded that he had no answer, Minh stalked away and found Medina at the village school, near a stack of bodies.

Why have the Americans killed so many Vietnamese? Orders, Medina sternly replied, according to Minh's testimony to CID—orders to destroy the village. "Sergeant Minh, don't ask anything—those were orders."[19]

If Medina ever had control over his men, that control was gone by mid-morning. Within the first hour of the assault, it was clear there was no enemy in My Lai 4. Calley, Minh, and others had informed Medina of the surprisingly high numbers of villagers without tying them to the Viet Cong. Medina saw bodies along the southern edge of the village before nine o'clock but ignored these signs of trouble. Kinch claimed to be ten to fifteen feet behind Medina "all the time" in the operation, even when they later crossed the ditch and could see dozens of bodies of women and children below. Olsen remarked years afterward on PBS-TV's *American Experience*, "I don't think Medina had any interest in knowing all the details on what's going on out there." The young soldier had already seen enough of the war to become disenchanted before the assault. In a letter to his father after My Lai, he wrote: "My faith in my fellow man is all shot to hell. I just want the time to pass and I just want to come home."[20]

When an investigator from the Peers Inquiry later asked Medina whether he had made any effort to determine what killed these people, he replied, "No sir. I did not. I did not go over near the bodies and I did not try to determine how they died."

"Why not?"

"I had never seen anything in my previous combat experience of this nature. The pile of bodies—well, the twenty to twenty-eight bodies I saw on the trail were on the southern portions of the village in the direction that Lieutenant Calley's platoon had passed through."

When asked if it was possible that Calley's men had killed numerous noncombatants without his knowing, Medina responded, "I don't know, sir."

"You were there in the area. The men were dispersed. In your judgment is it possible that this could have happened and you would not have seen it or heard about it at the time?"

Medina responded that Calley's forces appeared to be out of control and "not functioning properly under him.... It is possible that it could have happened. I did not see it. I did not hear about it."[21]

No organized Vietnamese resistance, an inordinate number of bodies, no American casualties, only three weapons confiscated (all American manufactured, according to Peers, and probably captured in another ARVN or U.S. operation)—and yet Medina as company commander did not pause to reassess strategy.[22] His inaction seems almost impossible to understand, even fifty years later—after other atrocities that have taken place since My Lai.

What was true then about leadership remains the case. A leader provides detailed instructions intended to cover every possible contingency, including efforts to minimize collateral damage. He adapts to changing circumstances by either being on the combat scene to recognize altered conditions or having advisers there to keep him apprised. He examines any reports of civilian casualties. And he must be flexible enough to revise his troops' actions if the situation calls for a change and not simply adhere to a plan that no longer is applicable or is clearly wrong. Medina ignored the evidence all around him as well as his own humanity.

II

Hugh Thompson remained furious about his encounter with the officer at the ditch, an officer who he later learned was Calley, but before he could decide what to do, he saw something that compelled him to take immediate action: a small group of what looked like women and children scurrying toward a bunker just outside My Lai 4 to its east and about ten soldiers in pursuit.[23]

Thompson radioed his friend and the pilot of the lower gunship, Danny Millians, that he had spotted some Vietnamese in a bunker and wanted to land and investigate. As Thompson's helicopter closed in on a small horseshoe-shaped open field, Andreotta saw the faces of three, perhaps four Vietnamese in an earthen shelter at the end of the rice paddy and close to the drainage ditch. Advancing toward them was a contingent of the 2nd Platoon returning to My Lai 4 from Binh Tay a few minutes after the 9:30 ceasefire—and, Thompson feared, looking to kill more innocent civilians. He had less than thirty seconds to save them.[24]

"Those people are going to die," he told crewmates Colburn and Andreotta, Colburn recalled in an interview in 2011. "I'm not going to let this happen. We've got to do something. Are you guys with me?"

No hesitation from either man. "If we're going to do something," Andreotta warned, "we better do it right now!"[25]

Colburn concurred while muttering to himself, "How did we get into this?"[26]

Thompson eased down the helicopter in the middle of the field while keeping an anxious eye on the spectacle unfolding before him—the chance of being killed in a crossfire between U.S. troops and Viet Cong forces or a possible firefight with American GIs preparing to shoot defenseless Vietnamese civilians huddled in a makeshift bunker. He thought about what he might have to do and how it could mean going to jail for life—and taking his two crew members with him.[27]

But overriding every other consideration was Thompson's refusal to permit another slaughter of unarmed civilians. As he set down his small craft between the soldiers and their prey, he left the engine running in flight idle to discourage their approach and ordered his crewmates to cover him "real close" while he talked with the infantry commander. While Millians's gunship circled lower to observe, Colburn and Andreotta hurriedly packed extra ammunition and backup weapons and, after grabbing the machine guns attached to the bungee cords, climbed down and set up a defense perimeter around the helicopter not only against the American soldiers but for protection from Viet Cong possibly hiding in the nearby tree line. Thompson went to the village edge and quickly determined who was in charge, a lieutenant later identified as Stephen Brooks of the 2nd Platoon. Just as a few moments earlier, Thompson confronted another officer who outranked him and commanded a much larger force unit than he had.[28]

"Hey, there's some civilians over here in this bunker," Thompson said he yelled. "Can you get them out?"[29]

"Yeah," came the curt reply. "We can get them out with a hand grenade!"

Thompson had heard the same dark humor at the ditch. He later publicly claimed he angrily responded, "Just hold your men right here please. I think I can do better."[30]

Colburn could not hear all their conversation, but he could see they were screaming at each other. "Keep your people in place," shouted Thompson as he turned back toward the helicopter after almost five minutes of arguing.[31]

Like Calley, Brooks was livid that a soldier beneath his rank was telling him what to do—and in front of his men. Perhaps he (again, like Calley) resented someone from the air corps trying to tell the real warriors what to do on the battlefield. But Brooks restrained himself, warily eying Colburn and Andreotta, each wielding a machine gun.[32]

Thompson knew what he had to do but did not look forward to doing it. Years later, at a question-and-answer session at the Naval Academy, he said, "I felt I was in a cage. Innocent people were getting harmed. This was not combat. This was not war. I had tried talking. I had tried asking. I had tried screaming. None of that was working."[33]

On returning to the small craft, Colburn recalled Thompson telling him and Andreotta to prepare for a confrontation with the soldiers. "They're coming this way. I'm going to go over to the bunker myself and get these people out. If they fire on these people or fire on me while I'm doing that, shoot 'em!"[34]

Colburn and Andreotta gazed wide-eyed at each other and then looked at the soldiers less than fifty yards away, probably just as bewildered over how they had gotten into a potentially deadly showdown with three American airmen. Colburn maintained that he never feared that one of the soldiers would purposely shoot him and Andreotta, but he thought the officer might use a grenade on the people in the bunker and force them out. Sweat trickled down the brows of the two young crew members as they tried to stare down their new adversaries while carefully pointing their guns to the ground in case one of them accidentally went off. Each stood stern-faced and motionless as the rotor blades whirled loudly above.[35]

As Brooks's soldiers looked at the two machine guns, one of them years afterward remembered thinking, "Oh my God, what are they gonna do?"[36]

Brooks chose discretion and sat down on the ground with his men, some of them breaking out cigarettes or opening their rucksacks for an early lunch.[37]

Thompson, meanwhile, made his way to the bunker, keeping his gun holstered to avoid frightening the Vietnamese. At first uneasy about walking into an enemy trap, he soon realized there was no danger and that his major problem was winning their trust and coaxing them out of the bunker. Although they were at first hesitant, he kept motioning for them to come out until, one by one, they did. There were more people in there than he had thought. Nine Vietnamese civilians emerged slowly and hesitantly from the bunker, five of them children, along with two men and two women, one of the men elderly and feeble with a white beard and one of the women older and in black pajamas with a frightened child clinging to her leg. "Oh, my God," Thompson said to himself, as he recounted at Annapolis. "I got a problem."[38]

Thompson gathered the Vietnamese close behind him while herding them toward his helicopter and glancing nervously at the soldiers across the way. How could he get these nine people out of the area? His small craft barely held him and his two-man crew. And it was "overgrossed," Colburn later noted—the small leftover spaces jammed with ammo boxes, weapons, and grenades. Thompson knew that if he left the Vietnamese behind, they would all be dead in minutes. To defend them against fellow Americans could lead to a gunfight resulting in casualties—perhaps deaths—on both sides, as he related to an audience at Tulane University in December 1994, and which Colburn corroborated in an interview with the author.[39]

Now back at the helicopter, Thompson radioed for assistance from the pilots of the two gunships nearby, Millians and Brian Livingston. "Danny, I need a favor." Thompson realized that what he was about to ask would put everyone in danger, but he felt that he had no choice. "Hey, I got these people down here on the ground." Women, kids, and a couple of elderly men, he added. "How about the landing? I got about nine or ten people here and I can't haul them. You all land and get them out of here."[40]

"Where do you want me to take them?"

"Away from this place," Thompson replied.

Thompson had asked Millians and Livingston to join him in violating protocol by landing in a free-fire zone reportedly infested with Viet Cong to pick up Vietnamese civilians threatened by American soldiers. But he and the others in the helicopters were flying low enough to have the same overall view Thompson had of what was happening on the ground. The rescue operation set a precedent in another way as well. As Colburn later remarked about Millians in an interview, "You don't land a gunship to use it as a medevac, but he did." How more surreal could these actions be in a war that had already proved unconventional and unpredictable?[41]

While waiting for the Hueys to land, Colburn noted that Thompson "stood between our troops and the bunker. He was shielding the people with his body. He just wanted to get those people out of there." Colburn knew what he was supposed to do if fellow Americans fired on the villagers. But in a quiet confession to himself, he admitted he was not certain he could do it. As he told Hersh, "I wasn't pointing my guns right at them, but more or less toward the ground. But I was looking their way."[42]

Most of the soldiers, Colburn thought with some relief, were "just watching." Some remained standing, while others were either sitting or lying on the ground. To relieve the tension, Colburn at one point waved at them with his palm open to signify that he and Andreotta meant them no harm. One of them waved back.[43]

In a few moments, Millians set down his craft while Livingston remained airborne, circling four to five hundred feet overhead to provide protective cover. "A helicopter on the ground in enemy territory," Colburn found himself thinking, as he told the author—a "sitting duck." Millians agreed. "A gunship just never landed out in the boonies like that to pick up somebody," he later declared on *American Experience*. "It was just not done. I don't know why we did it, other than the fact that those people needed to be out of there."[44]

Millians and Thompson quickly discovered that even the larger gunship could not hold all nine Vietnamese; the evacuation required two trips. As the GIs continued to sit not much more than a hundred feet from the gunship,

Thompson tried over the thunderous din of its huge propeller to convince the terrified Vietnamese to climb aboard individually and not all at one time. "We were dead scared," remembered Phan Thi Nhanh in an interview forty years later. "Were they going to drop us into the sea?" Over the course of twenty anxious minutes, Millians made two round-trip flights to a spot a couple miles down the road, transporting all nine Vietnamese civilians to safety while Livingston stayed over the crisis site.[45]

In testimony before the Hébert subcommittee, Millians's co-pilot Jerry Culverhouse insisted that he never felt in danger while there, from either the Viet Cong or the American soldiers. Both gunships had earlier flown over the village for close to an hour and had taken no fire. Nor had Thompson reported any enemy fire. Neither the ground soldiers nor Thompson's crew appeared to threaten each other, Culverhouse added. On only one occasion did he hear a weapon fire, and that came earlier when Thompson had landed at a ditch and Culverhouse heard the "burst" of an automatic weapon, which caused Millians to take evasive action and prepare to launch suppressive fire. But Culverhouse saw the firing coming from a soldier—later identified as Sergeant David Mitchell from the 1st Platoon—standing at the eastern edge of the ditch, holding his gun at his shoulder and shooting toward the bodies below him.[46]

Despite a half hour of noise and confusion outside the village—where Medina later claimed he had remained—he insisted, "I did not see a gunship land."[47] In telling the truth, he undermined his assertion that he had stayed outside My Lai 4 until after ten o'clock. Thompson had confronted a few GIs from the 2nd Platoon at the bunker after Medina had declared a ceasefire in Binh Tay a half hour earlier, and not only had he landed his helicopter, he had called in two gunships—all making such a deafening racket a short distance from the eastern side of the village that a number of villagers had gathered a hundred feet away to watch.[48] One gunship made two evacuation trips east to west and along the entire southern rim of the village, roaring back and forth four times. If Medina and his command group were still below and outside the village until after ten o'clock, as he later asserted, it is likely he would have seen and heard two gunships approaching and hovering over the bunker and even more likely he would have seen and heard at least one of them passing by four times over the course of twenty minutes beginning shortly after ten o'clock.

Medina did not see a gunship land outside the village, it seems safe to conclude, because he was already inside and had been there since before nine o'clock.

Thompson continued to agonize over the large numbers of dead. "Everywhere we looked, we saw bodies." Infants and children between two and five years old, along with women and elderly men, but, tellingly, "no draft-age people whatsoever" and not a single weapon among hundreds of bodies. Where was the enemy? He and his crew had seen only one suspected VC, and that was before the battle had even started. Had the Viet Cong pulled out before the assault, leaving the villagers unarmed and on their own?

An earlier experience that day encapsulated for Thompson what had gone terribly wrong. They had seen a woman from less than eight feet above hiding in the tall grass in the fetal position on the side of a road. Colburn motioned for her to stay there and keep quiet while they finished their recon. "I was hoping she wouldn't be detected," Thompson remembered, but when they returned a few moments later, she lay dead, eyes and mouth wide open and next to her hat. As they moved in closer, they saw something else—her brains splattered on the ground. "I'll never forget that look of bewilderment on her face," Colburn declared, not knowing why they did not pick her up at that moment and realizing instantly that this experience would haunt him for the rest of his life.[49]

Thompson still wrestled with the question of how so many civilians had died in the ditch. By now he had dismissed artillery as the culprit. Every dwelling in Vietnam had a bunker, and the villagers would have sought safety inside their homes or bunkers rather than in the open areas or in a ditch. "Then it sunk into me that these people were marched into that ditch and murdered," he told his listeners at Tulane. "That was the only explanation that I could come up with."[50]

Images of their nightmarish experience flashed through Thompson's mind, he said: men, women, and children ordered out of their homes and into a ditch under a hot mid-morning sun. Forced to kneel or squat while facing their captors armed with machine guns and assault rifles. Hearing the deadly clinks and clanks of ammo loading and bolts closing, mixed with low-level and undecipherable yet eerie conversations and ghost-like movements of soldiers clicking their M-16s on automatic or setting up machine guns. Directed to stand up and turn around so they could not look their executioners in the eye. That split second of silence suddenly shattered by the thunder of gunfire. The lucky ones died instantly, while the others fell, some living long enough to see others die—or, perhaps, pretended being dead as they lay still among or under the bodies, waiting for the soldiers to leave. A river of blood, Livingston later described the macabre scene from above. "These were animals, not soldiers," Thompson declared in an interview, adding that he thought of them with disgust and considered them guilty of "pure, premeditated murder." A "lot of evil going on," as he put it in that question-and-answer session in Annapolis years later.[51]

And worse, Thompson knew, the killing had not come to an end. How could he forget what Andreotta had shouted as they ascended from their first confrontation with Calley at the ditch earlier that day—that a soldier had resumed firing on the few Vietnamese survivors desperately hanging on to life while trying to escape their hell.

Thompson said that he resolved then and there to charge these American ground troops and others with war crimes.[52]

III

In the meantime, the 3rd Platoon completed the final phase of Charlie Company's trek through My Lai 4, searching the hooches for the last villagers, burning and destroying what remained of their homes, killing most of the livestock, and disposing of any other possessions deemed helpful to the enemy.[53]

Shortly before ten o'clock, two young soldiers, Sergeant West and twenty-year-old PFC Gerald Smith, burst into Le Thi Huynh's home near the plaza and forced her and eight others outside. Filing out with her were her twenty-four-year-old sister-in-law Do Thi Can; Do Hoi, a guest; Ba So, a merchant from the nearby village of Tan Hai, and her teenage daughter Ba Moi; an older woman, Ba Phu; and three children—Huynh's six-year-old son Do Hut; Do Thi Be, the seven-year-old daughter of a former chief of the sub-hamlet; and a young girl, Do Thi Nhut. Unknown to their captors, Huynh's husband was a fairly prominent Viet Cong figure, Do Vien, who helped to administer the settlement and as the director of information disseminated propaganda.

"VC! VC!" shouted both West and Smith, proudly escorting their captives out the door and joining four other excited GIs in front of the hooch making the same loud accusations. Roberts and Haeberle had arrived after hearing the ruckus and quietly took a place off to the side of the group, one already scribbling notes, the other taking photos as villagers gathered around to watch. In the noise and confusion, Huynh and Do Hoi slipped away and fled the village.[54]

As recorded in a number of sources and testimonies, a brawl erupted when one of the soldiers yanked Do Thi Can from the group and sneeringly asked if she were a "VC whore."

"VC Boom, Boom," mocked another GI.

"Jesus, I'm horny," moaned one of them in her face.

"Let's see what she's made of," shouted the GI while pulling at her clothing.[55]

Seeing that her teenage daughter Ba Moi was in danger along with Do Thi Can, Ba So screamed as she thrust herself between the soldiers and the girls, biting, kicking, scratching, and clawing the men. Her actions shocked everyone—especially the soldiers. Rarely had any Vietnamese dared to physically resist them. Indeed, the villagers' strategy for survival was to quietly comply with the search and follow-up interrogations. Roberts recalled that he was surprised by the resistance, praising this small woman in a red blouse trying to protect the girls by "fighting off two or three guys at once. She was fantastic. Usually they are pretty passive." The melee spread when the other three women and the two children jumped into the fray and one of the GIs smacked Ba So with his rifle butt and another kicked her in the rear. Punching her again and again, they finally pushed her aside to get at the two girls, tearing Can's blouse partly off as all six rushed in to grab their breasts.[56]

Ronald Grzesik from the 1st Platoon happened by with his fire team at this instant, not expecting to see anyone alive in the village as they passed from the ditch to the plaza. Instead, they found themselves gawking at a wild scene: three Vietnamese women and two children in a shoving match with a half dozen soldiers, trying to protect two young girls—one of them from a GI struggling to rip off her blouse. Grzesik had just left that humiliating experience with Calley, who had ordered him back to the center of the village because of his refusal to kill anyone at the ditch. Grzesik wanted only to avoid trouble, but the same impulse that had governed his actions at the ditch left him with no choice, he felt, but to intervene here. He said he realized that the soldiers would kill these Vietnamese if the situation continued to escalate. They might, in fact, kill them anyway. Grzesik jumped in to separate the two groups.[57]

At this point, Haeberle stepped up to take a picture when one of the soldiers spotted him. "Watch it! He's got a camera!" he yelled, as Haeberle remembered. Not wanting to be on film, they turned away from Haeberle and backed off from the girls. Grzesik likewise did not want his picture taken in an encounter with fellow American soldiers and eased away with his men.[58]

Haeberle prepared to take a picture of the Vietnamese clinging to one another as the six soldiers hurriedly discussed what to do with them. Take them to a collecting area? No one knew whether there was one. And how would they get them there without more trouble? This was their first experience with resistance, and they did not know what to do. The Vietnamese were usually reticent and never so brazenly hostile.[59]

The soldiers could not take them, nor could they leave them. Roberts remembered the exchange.

"What do we do with them?" one GI asked in exasperation.

"Kill 'em," someone groused.[60]

"Waste 'em!" shouted West.[61]

Like Calley, West was a young officer in charge of even younger soldiers and was now forced to make a life-or-death decision in what was effectively his first combat situation. He was surprised and frustrated with the unexpected opposition and, also like Calley, decided to rely on Medina's orders to justify any actions to remove this hindrance to their advance through the village. These people were either Viet Cong or their sympathizers—and subhuman at best.

Roberts realized the soldiers were going to kill the villagers and turned away and started walking from the scene just as the gunfire began. He could not look back as the thunderous clatter of M-16 automatic fire broke the silence.[62]

Multiple sources indicate that West and Smith gunned down all seven Vietnamese. Haeberle recalled that he had just taken their picture when he saw all but one of them fall to the ground, hit by two M-16s firing on automatic. Only a child about five years of age remained standing. When he turned around, he saw the muzzles smoking. Before anyone could speak, one of the two GIs shot and killed the child as well. Roberts finally looked back from thirty feet and saw the victims lying dead on the path.[63]

Haeberle years later remarked about the picture while on the PBS-TV's *American Experience* program, "You can see the fear in the faces on especially the small children, and the older woman trying to protect the daughter. Then, all of a sudden, the next instant, automatic fire. They were all shot. I saw them drop to the ground."[64]

The six soldiers coolly filed past the bodies to resume their passage through the village.

It seems beyond understanding why the soldiers killed these people, particularly while Haeberle stood by with his camera. Roberts later offered the simplest and perhaps most convincing explanation. "It's just that they didn't know what they were supposed to do; killing them seemed like a good idea, so they did it." Roberts struggled with the possible reasoning behind it all. "The old lady who fought so hard was probably a VC," he concluded. Or it might have been purely personal. "Maybe it was just her daughter." West likewise struggled to explain what had happened. They had simply followed orders, he insisted to Hersh, adding that he personally criticized Haeberle for photographing soldiers who had performed their duty of killing VC. "I thought it was wrong for him to stand up and take pictures of this thing. Even though we had to do it, I thought, we didn't have to take pictures of it."[65]

Roberts's reaction seems indicative of a general attitude among those who were there and who sought to dismiss what they had seen as what happens in war. When asked by the Peers commission who made the decision to kill these people, Roberts responded numbly that he could not remember. "I don't recall any specifics, whether it was an order, or whether it was a suggestion that happened to be acceptable to the group of people."

The Peers questioner found this response difficult to understand—that Roberts so "nonchalantly accepted," as he put it, such a decision. Roberts reflected that he had become jaded to war and killing, perhaps because he had seen so much of it that he had built an internal defense mechanism. "I tried to forget this whole thing, and thought as little as possible about it after that, and pretty effectively forgot it in about three months. At the time, I don't recall that this was a particularly unusual thing."[66] Among all the statements made to the Peers commission, this was perhaps the most chilling.

Roberts was not the only American soldier who had lost his moral compass. This was not combat. The only physical resistance they had encountered had come from a mother defending her daughter and a young woman against lewd advances joined by a small group of women and children defending the mother and the girls. Charlie Company had not seen the enemy, though during its deployment it had lost a number of men to land mines, booby traps, and snipers. The primary assignment of these short-term enlistees and conscripts was to kill the Viet Cong without worrying about any gray zones between right and wrong. These people helped the enemy. Perhaps Roberts would have agreed with Olsen, who argued that he did not believe the war had destroyed his sense of "right or wrong" but had narrowed the "degree of wrong" to allow for many acts not normally acceptable.[67] Like so many soldiers in this alien setting, in which they were both powerful and completely helpless, knew nothing about the language or the customs, and lacked any sense of connection to bind them to these people, Roberts became utterly detached from his situation. The Vietnamese were not human beings, and morality had no place in war.

Whatever the truth, Roberts dealt with the matter by not dealing with it in the moment. Later would be another matter. His father noted that his son had written him just after the My Lai incident and that in his letter he had been "disturbed" and "very much upset" but would not go into details. He assumed that his son, like others, "just tried to get it off their minds when they left there, and they didn't bring it back with them."[68] Roberts blotted out anything he could remember about the soldiers—names, distinguishing characteristics, whether he had seen them before or after—perhaps hoping he could come to believe that My Lai never happened.

Yet Roberts did not succeed: he looked back.

This one incident among so many other terrible and tragic incidents took root in him. Part of this was due to Haeberle, whose single snapshot appeared with other photos nearly two years afterward in *Life* magazine and has since become the enduring image of that long conflict: Ba So at the front in a red shirt, sobbing in anguish and disbelief over what was to come while being consoled and held from behind by her daughter Ba Moi; the terrified young girl Do Thi Nhut in a white shirt and black pants, clinging to the ashen faced and balding Ba Phu; Do Thi Can in a black shirt and pants, feverishly struggling to button her blouse after the sexual assault while holding her bewildered nephew Do Hat; and Do Thi Be, thin as a rail and barely visible below Do Hat—all just seconds before the fatal shots. No picture has better captured the nightmare of Vietnam.[69]

In the meantime, Huynh and her two-year-old boy spent the day hiding in a portable rice bin in the field and returned to the village the following morning, only to find her thirty-four-year-old husband and Viet Cong cadre, Do Vien, burying their son Do Hut and the little girl Do Thi Nhut. Do Vien had been at work in the rice fields when the artillery struck west of the village in the paddies and helicopters fired into the edge of the village and along the road. After eluding shots from a helicopter, he hid in nearby Ba Lang subhamlet and returned home at noon after the Americans left. In a "pile of corpses" near his house, as he later told the Peers panel, he found his sister Do Thi Can and son Do Hut along with Do Thi Nhut. All around him was devastation and death: his home burned; his banana and papaya trees cut down; his chickens, hogs, and buffalo slaughtered.[70]

Do Vien's loss of his son, his sister, the little girl, and all the others had strengthened his resolve to support the Viet Cong. He had already seen the widespread destruction and the raped and murdered women and girls, including the body of ten-year-old Do Thi Nguyen, found by her widowed mother, Pham Thi Day. The young girl's clothing had been ripped off, exposing a single but horrific injury—her vagina torn open and covered in blood. Vien was later captured and put in a POW camp at Chu Lai, the American air base twenty-five miles north of My Lai 4. There, from Haeberle's color photograph provided by

CID investigators, he identified his sister Do Thi Can, his son Do Hut, and Ba So, a merchant from nearby Tan Hai, who had been in My Lai 4, he asserted, selling a fish sauce called *nuoc nam*. Vien said he had counted 211 dead in and around the village and helped bury many of them.[71]

IV

It should have been clear to the high command, even before nine o'clock, that no Viet Cong forces were in My Lai 4, where American soldiers incurred only a single casualty in a campaign heralded by Henderson and Barker as the final showdown with the enemy. Yet this casualty figure of exactly one—Herbert Carter of the 1st Platoon—raised few eyebrows among those leaders who wished to keep details of the operation quiet. Indeed, the Task Force report attributed Carter's wound to enemy fire despite considerable evidence to the contrary. That there was only one casualty in Charlie Company again suggests the absence of an enemy and raises serious questions about why Medina did not revise the combat plans early in the morning of that day in My Lai 4.

A brief account of this incident makes it clear that no one at the scene thought Carter had been the victim of enemy gunfire and that his injury resulted from a cause far different in origin.

A little before 10:20 a.m., he and Harry Stanley were standing at the command post, gazing at the fires in the village while knowing that its inhabitants lay dead all over. Among a stack of bodies was that of a Vietnamese boy no more than five years old who had been shot in the stomach and was crying. According to the CID Report, Fred Widmer walked up to Carter and said, "Let me see your pistol." Carter handed it over, fully aware of Widmer's reputation among the ranks as "Mr. Homicide."[72]

Widmer moved to within two feet of the boy and shot him in the neck. Blood rushed from the wound as the child struggled to his feet and in a daze tried to walk but could take only two or three steps before falling to the ground. He lay there, gasping for air before he finally stopped breathing. Widmer had stood by the boy to the end, ready to shoot him again when the trigger locked. "The damn thing jammed," he complained, handing the gun back to Carter.[73]

Widmer looked at Stanley and proudly asked, "Did you see that fucker die?" Stanley said he responded, "I don't see how anyone can just kill a kid." Widmer laughed.[74]

Stanley also recalled that Carter remarked to him, "I can't take this no more" and then wandered away. A few moments later, a gun went off followed by Carter's scream. "I went to Carter," Stanley explained, "and saw he had shot himself in the foot. I think Carter shot himself on purpose." Stanley did not remember the pistol jamming. "All I remember is [Widmer] shooting the kid and giving it back to Carter." When the shot rang out, Stanley asserted that he and others thought the Viet Cong had finally come into the open. Seeing no enemy, however, he turned to Carter and saw a "nice little hole" in his foot. He cut off Carter's boot and sock and bandaged the wound before a medic arrived.[75]

Controversy soon developed over the cause of Carter's injury. In less than a month, the Task Force casualty report indicated that during the combat mission Carter took a "hostile" gunshot in the left foot; but CID investigators in September 1970 affirmed Stanley's earlier contention that Carter shot himself on purpose. Some soldiers thought Carter had shot himself accidentally while trying to clean the pistol; others insisted that he had become sick of the war and deliberately shot himself in the foot. His friend Michael Bernhardt testified that it was "ridiculous" to think that Carter would shoot himself with a .45 when there were "much better ways" to escape the service. Carter insisted that the wound had resulted from the accidental discharge of his pistol, a conclusion substantiated by Medina at the time before calling for a medevac.[76]

As Charlie Company's sole casualty at My Lai 4, Carter was on his way home by 10:30 a.m., the wound wrapped in a field dressing, a joint in his mouth from Widmer to lessen the pain, and the letter "M" scrawled on his forehead to signify that he had had an injection of morphine.[77]

At eleven o'clock, Captain Medina informed Lieutenant Colonel Barker that the men had killed ninety Viet Cong. The platoon leaders had provided this estimate, a figure that they claimed included no civilians. As we have seen, Medina and his command group had passed by the southern rim of the village earlier, within eyesight of the great number of villagers slain by the 1st Platoon, en route to the eastern edge. He counted perhaps two dozen bodies. They then moved along the trail into the village, where several soldiers in his command group saw up to eighteen more bodies. Medina, somehow, saw none. When he received his platoons' report on the number of dead VC, he and his contingent were less than three hundred feet from the ditch where many Vietnamese lay dead. Again they seemed to be outside his field of vision.[78]

Of the ninety reported enemy dead in My Lai 4, only three had been killed in action—by the gunships—and each victim had been armed with an American weapon, probably seized during earlier encounters with ARVN or U.S. troops. This finding led to immediate speculation that the enemy had used captured American guns, which explained the apparent lack of resistance to the assault: the sounds emitted by the guns would have been the same on both sides, meaning that the absence of either Russian or Chinese weapons did not rule out an enemy presence. But this argument had no credibility, argued Lieutenant General William R. Peers, head of the army's inquiry into the My Lai massacre. "When one is being *shot at*," he explained, "one hears a sharp cracking sound that is clearly different from the sound of one's fellow soldiers shooting at the enemy, regardless of the origin of the weapons being used."[79]

The only resistance to the American assault on My Lai 4 came from scattered small-arms fire that occurred in the last stages of the landing. No evidence supports the claim that any of the other eighty-seven killed were Viet Cong. Nor does any testimony show that Charlie Company took enemy fire after hitting the ground. In only one instance did the expedition appear to come under enemy attack, and that was when the pilots of the second lift claimed the landing zone had become hot. Even then, the claim seems dubious, given that no helicopter took a hit and the gunships at that time were spraying the ground to protect the soldiers. Most important, several members of Charlie Company's three platoons, along with the command group led by Medina, asserted that they never encountered any opposition from the Vietnamese. There was no enemy either at the beginning of the assault or throughout the rest of the operation.[80]

Yet the high command remained oblivious to these realities. Henderson, who arrived at My Lai at 7:50 a.m., later claimed he had not seen more than eight Vietnamese killed during the operation and did not know whether they were VC. He remembered seeing among the dead one woman, a couple of children, and two cows, all apparently hit by artillery or gunship fire judging from the way their bodies had been torn apart. He maintained that he saw no stacks of bodies and heard no radio transmissions relating to soldiers killing civilians. Barker attributed the deaths of about twenty women and children to either artillery or gunship fire. As for the low number of weapons seized, Henderson declared that the Viet Cong had run off with their weapons and, after hiding them, pretended to be innocent civilians.[81]

Thus during the morning of March 16, Henderson learned that civilians had been killed, and by the evening he knew that the number was around twenty, yet the situation report made by the 11th Brigade to the Americal Division contained no reference to civilian deaths, whether by artillery, gunship, or small-arms fire.[82]

Thompson wanted to make one more flyover before returning to base and filing a report. He and his two crew members hovered low over the ditch, searching for signs of life while flinching at the sight of headless children. Andreotta thought he spotted movement in a large pile of bodies and urged Thompson to land. For a third time he did so. Andreotta and Colburn solemnly walked to the ditch while Thompson remained at the controls with an M-16. "Nobody said anything," Colburn later asserted to Hersh. "We just got out."[83]

Andreotta made his way down into the trough, slick on its sides with blood and already stench-filled, while Colburn stood at the edge. "I didn't want to look into the ditch," he recalled. Andreotta quickly sank "knee-deep in people and blood" but saw a young kid a short distance away. Andreotta struggled to the child through dead and dying human beings, some grasping at his legs and pleading for help. "I can't help you," he mumbled over and over again. "You're too bad off." Finally, Andreotta found what he thought was a boy of about three years of age, alive and pinned under several bodies, covered with blood and clutching a corpse riddled with bullet holes. "He was still holding onto his mother," Colburn told Hersh. "But she was dead." As Andreotta pried him loose, the boy made no sound and stared blankly ahead. Thompson later explained to the Peers commission, "I don't think this child was even wounded at all, just down there among all the other bodies, and he was terrified."[84]

Andreotta picked up the boy by the back of his clothing and, after setting him down numerous times to check for other survivors, made it again through the carnage to the wall of the ditch. He hoisted the limp boy to Colburn, who grabbed him by the shirt with his left hand, thinking, as he declared on PBS-TV's *American Experience* program, "I hope these buttons are sewn on, or if the shirt lets go I'm going to lose the boy." Using his rifle butt with his right hand (the safety off and the weapon pointed at his own stomach, he later realized), Colburn pulled Andreotta up the slippery wall, his boots filled with blood spurting out the tops and down their sides. Colburn laid the child on the ground. Thompson remembered that the sight of this boy made him think about his young son back home.[85]

Do Hoa was that boy in the ditch, and more than forty years afterward remembered that day; he was eight years old at the time and tiny for his age. "I lifted my head up and saw a helicopter landing in the rice fields," he explained on *American Experience*. "I was really scared, wasn't sure if they would shoot again. But when I lifted my head, I saw three American soldiers approach, so I pretended to be dead.... I looked up a second time and they came and pulled me out."[86]

All three men were overcome by emotions that quickly swelled into rage as they laid the boy across their laps and began what Thompson termed "a very sober flight" to the hospital in Quang Ngai City. Following behind them for protection was his hoochmate and close friend Charles Mansell, co-pilot of a UH-1 Bravo then covering the infantry. Thompson had contacted him about rescuing a wounded child, saying something about his own son. "There was something going on that day," Thompson said over the radio, and "it wasn't right." Mansell must have agreed. Never had he seen so many bodies—along the trail, throughout the village, and in the ditch. On their arrival at the hospital, a nun took the boy inside. "I don't know what you're going to do with him," Thompson said he told her, "but I don't think he's got any family left." She arranged for his stay at the orphanage next door. He and his crew then made the short trip to LZ Dottie to report what they had seen at My Lai 4.[87]

By late morning, the last of the three platoons of Charlie Company had completed the mission in My Lai 4, shooting the remaining Vietnamese villagers either inside their huts or at the doorways. Other civilians had taken refuge in bunkers all over the village and were killed where they were or driven out by grenades—running and thereby drawing fire. There seemed to be no escape.[88]

Most of the killing in My Lai 4 ended a little after eleven o'clock, when the final contingent of U.S. forces joined the other two platoons at the eastern edge of the village and Medina declared a lunch break—somewhat grotesquely, alongside the dead and dying Vietnamese in the ditch that he pretended did not exist. Bunning remembered the location because of the pungent odor of burning bodies in a hooch on fire nearby.[89]

A few moments later, around 11:40 a.m. and with no explanation, Medina ordered a ceasefire for the entire company.

Just as the soldiers had disagreed over the meaning of Medina's instructions at the briefing, they differed over whether he had issued a ceasefire. Some said that Barker had received a report that aviators had seen a large number of civilian casualties and demanded guarantees that the soldiers were not killing noncombatants. Others thought it had nothing to do with the aviators. Bernhardt testified that the ceasefire had come only after the lead elements had completed their sweep of the subhamlet. The order had come from base headquarters, Thomas Partsch declared—"Cease-fire, cease-fire!" After a couple more shots, "Cease-fire!" rang out again. "And then," Partsch said, "it was quiet."[90]

Coda: The cease-fire order had not prevented the death of perhaps the final victim that day of American fire—a child. In the late morning, West saw a Vietnamese boy about seven years old standing alone in a path, shot in the leg and in a daze. "He was just standing there staring; I don't think he was crying." Someone asked, "What do we do with him?" West did not know, for

Medina had just stopped the killing. "I just shrugged my shoulders, and said, 'I don't know,' and just kept walking."

In the meantime Haeberle and Roberts also came upon the child. Haeberle moved in close to take a picture. As he adjusted the focus, a GI approached just to the side of the boy. Perhaps this soldier was one of many not aware of the ceasefire, or he might have been among those who had gone out of control at the beginning of the operation and remained in that black space outside civilization. In any case, he knelt down beside Haeberle, raised his rifle, and shot the boy three times. He then gave Haeberle what he described to the Hébert subcommittee as "the coldest, hardest look" before standing and continuing down the path. Haeberle had seen the shooting through his camera lens. "He looked up in shock," Roberts recalled. Haeberle "just turned around and stared. I think that was the thing that stayed in our mind. It was so close, so real, we just saw some kid blown away." West had also turned around on hearing the shots and no longer saw the boy.[91]

Charlie Company left My Lai 4 about 1:30 p.m. to meet up with Bravo Company and prepare for encampment that night in a graveyard about nine hundred yards southeast. Lieutenant Brooks had retained about eighty-five villagers and, after holding those of military age for interrogation, told the others to relocate south. Medina directed close to 140 Vietnamese civilians to Quang Ngai City. He then ordered his company northeast through the largely abandoned subhamlets of My Lai 5 and My Lai 6, telling his men to destroy everything of value on the way. As for those villagers who remained in one of the settlements, he told the interpreter, Sergeant Phu, to warn them "to go away or something will happen to them—just like what happened at My Lai 4."[92]

By dinnertime that evening, the two companies had set up bivouac in the little graveyard, where a few Vietnamese survivors of the massacre had gathered—children and elderly men who had no place else to go. The GIs shared their C-rations with them.[93]

THE OFFICIAL STORY had already begun to take shape—that U.S. forces had grappled with the enemy in Pinkville and by eleven o'clock had killed 128 Viet Cong while incurring only one casualty.[94]

Medina's chief concern was to defend that story...and himself. That evening, he met with his three platoon leaders and asked if their men had killed any civilians. "I received negative indications," he told Hersh. According to Bernhardt, Medina assured his men that he would tell any investigators "there was a gunfight and that we did a lot of shooting." Everything would be alright. "The guys weren't worried," Bernhardt asserted. "They had absolute faith in him."[95]

Not everyone had that level of faith. Sergeant Thomas Kinch, a three-and-a-half-year veteran, told the Peers commission that as he followed the command group through My Lai 4 that day, he overheard Medina tell Lieutenant Colonel Barker over the radio speaker around lunchtime that the body count was 310. And he did not specify that they were VC. "What's happening?" Kinch remembers asking himself. The number of Viet Cong casualties was nowhere near that large, nor was the number of bodies of villagers he had seen. "It just scared the hell out of me."[96]

Rumors of an army cover-up nonetheless spread throughout the company. Michael Terry recalled: "We talked about the way the Army was going to cover it by saying it was such a good thing…a big victory." Terry, Greg Olsen, and Michael Bernhardt agreed that the field officers must have been aware of the mass killing. Bernhardt had heard that the body count was much higher than the official figure of 128—more than three hundred, he asserted, and that number did not include infants and children too young to walk.[97]

Yet the army's battlefield reports highlighted a strong VC presence that Barker expected Roberts to portray in his press coverage. Roberts realized, however, that civilians constituted most of the dead. "How do you write a story when you have 128 bodies and only three captured weapons?" When he asked Barker about the wide disparity between body count and weapons, the commander, Haeberle declared, "said something to the effect that I could make a good story without that fact." The guidelines for Roberts's story became clear that same day, when MACV released a news communiqué datelined Saigon that praised the operation for killing 128 Viet Cong.[98]

With Haeberle's concurrence, Roberts fabricated a news release claiming the soldiers had faced hostile fire and emerged with a stunning victory. Haeberle attempted to justify their decision. "We felt we were not going to break this story because we were part of it." They would wait until someone exposed the truth and then provide supporting evidence for the allegations. Roberts had witnessed many killings of defenseless elderly men, women, and children, and Haeberle had eighteen color slides and thirty-nine black-and-white photographs of the victims.[99]

"Everyone was afraid to tell the truth," Haeberle admitted—"including us." He had only a couple of weeks to serve before going home, but Roberts had another year. "Their lives would be in danger." In adopting this approach, both Roberts and Haeberle broke the law—Roberts in writing a phony news story and Haeberle in withholding photographic evidence of a massacre— and thus became integral figures in a cover-up already in the making.[100]

PART II

Aftermath and Cover-Up

Brigadier General George Young on the left in a discussion with Lieutenant Colonel Frank Barker (Ronald Haeberle photo). *Courtesy Library of Congress.*

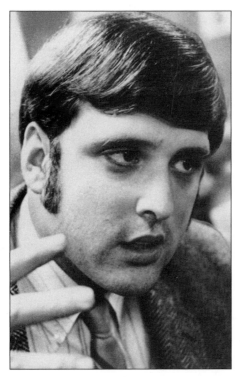

Ronald L. Haeberle was a sergeant and army photographer in March 1968, who showed that a massacre had occurred at My Lai by taking numerous photos during the operation that appeared in *Life* magazine and other news outlets. *AP Photo.*

American helicopters offloading soldiers at the landing zone near My Lai 4 (Ronald Haeberle photo). *Courtesy Library of Congress.*

Unidentified U.S. soldiers moving toward My Lai 4 (Ronald Haeberle photo). *Courtesy Library of Congress.*

A soldier's view as he approached My Lai 4 (Ronald Haeberle photo). *Courtesy Library of Congress.*

Pham Mot Lai pulled out of hut to the road through My Lai 4, just moments before American soldiers shot him (Ronald Haeberle photo). *Courtesy Library of Congress.*

The body of Nguyen Thi Tau, whose son, Tran Van Duc, survived the massacre (Ronald Haeberle photo). *Courtesy Library of Congress.*

Truong Bon and Truong Nam, two of Truong Nhi's four sons shot and killed that day. Their uncle identified his nephews and buried them (Ronald Haeberle photo). *Courtesy Library of Congress.*

Truong Nhi and his nine-year-old son Truong Cu Ba, along with a woman above Nhi's head identified by CID as Phong Thi Chan (Ronald Haeberle photo). *Courtesy Library of Congress.*

Unidentified bodies on the trail (Ronald Haeberle photo). *Courtesy Library of Congress.*

This photo of unidentified bodies of women, elderly men, and children provided the basis for an antiwar poster containing the words "And babies," repeatedly used by Mike Wallace in his TV interview of Paul Meadlo on *60 Minutes* on November 24, 1969 (Ronald Haeberle photo). *Courtesy Library of Congress.*

The ditch along the eastern edge of My Lai 4 that contained at least one hundred bodies seen by helicopter pilots, including Warrant Officer Hugh Thompson and his two crew members, door gunner Lawrence Colburn and crew chief Glenn Andreotta. (Ronald Haeberle photo). *Courtesy Library of Congress.*

The moment before death for a small group of Vietnamese women and children (identified in chapter 5 of this work) gathered in front of a hooch in My Lai 4 (Ronald Haeberle photo). *Courtesy Library of Congress.*

An example of the widespread destruction in My Lai 4 (Ronald Haeberle photo). *Courtesy Library of Congress.*

Charlie Company's only casualty at My Lai 4—PFC Herbert Carter, tended by medic Nicholas Capezza with Captain Ernest Medina standing in the background with his handset. To Medina's left is Sergeant Duong Minh, and to his right from right to left are SP4 Roger Murray, SP4 Jerry Heming, and SP4 Louis Martin (Ronald Haeberle photo). *Courtesy Library of Congress.*

Captain Ernest Medina stands among his men, pointing in the distance while his RTO, SP4 Fred Widmer, is behind him on the porch. To Medina's left and on the ground: Sergeant Nguyen Dinh Phu, Sergeant Leo Maroney, and Lieutenant Roger Alaux (Ronald Haeberle photo). *Courtesy Library of Congress.*

Captain Ernest Medina and his men exiting My Lai 4 at its eastern border near the ditch (Ronald Haeberle photo). *Courtesy Library of Congress.*

Lunch break a few feet from a pile of bodies. From right to left: Lieutenant Roger Alaux, Sergeant Leo Maroney, Sergeant Nguyen Dinh Phu, Sergeant James Flynn, and Sergeant Martin Fagan in the rear, with the Plotting Board (Ronald Haeberle photo). *Courtesy Library of Congress.*

Retired Colonel Ngo Duc Tan, who commanded the 48th Viet Cong Battalion in March 1968, and Vo Cao Loi, a survivor of the massacre at My Khe 4 who later joined the North Vietnamese Army. *Courtesy Ngo Duc Tan and Vo Cao Loi.*

Twenty-five-year-old Warrant Officer Hugh C. Thompson in 1968 reported his firsthand observations of the My Lai massacre to his superiors and brought about a cease-fire that ended the killings. *AP Photo.*

Seventeen-year-old Private E-1 Lawrence M. Colburn in basic training at Fort Lewis, Washington, in 1966. *Courtesy Lawrence Colburn.*

Twenty-year-old Glenn W. Andreotta, beginning his second tour in Vietnam in late 1967. Photograph taken by his father. *Courtesy Jim Andreotta (Glenn's cousin).*

Antiwar poster of 1971. *Unknown origin.*

Ronald L. Ridenhour at Claremont Men's College on November 26, 1969, about eight months after writing a letter to the president and other high officials in Washington, DC, urging them to investigate what happened at My Lai 4. *AP Photo*.

New York Times reporter Seymour Hersh at his Washington Bureau desk in 1972, less than three years after he exposed the My Lai 4 story in the press and won the Pulitzer Prize for *My Lai 4: A Report on the Massacre and Its Aftermath. Bettmann/Corbis.*

Ex-serviceman Paul Meadlo with his parents, Tony and Myrtle Meadlo, at their home in New Goshen, Indiana, on November 25, 1969, the day after he appeared on CBS-TV's *60 Minutes* and admitted to killing Vietnamese civilians at My Lai 4. *AP Photo/EDR.*

Lieutenant General William R. Peers in his Pentagon office after his appointment in November 1969 to head a special army investigation into whether there had been a cover-up of the My Lai massacre. *Bettmann/Corbis.*

Pentagon news conference on March 17, 1970, with Secretary of the Army Stanley Resor at the microphone, General William C. Westmoreland standing to his left, and Lieutenant General William R. Peers and attorney Robert MacCrate seated. *Bettmann/Corbis.*

Major General Samuel W. Koster, who resigned as superintendent of the U.S. Military Academy at West Point, New York, after the Peers commission accused him of covering up the My Lai massacre. *AP Photo*.

William Calley surrounded by four unidentified Vietnamese children on the cover of the November 1970 issue of *Esquire* magazine. *Courtesy* Esquire.

Lieutenant William Calley leaving court on February 12, 1970, with his defense team led by civilian attorney George Latimer and, behind him, Major Kenneth Raby. *Bettmann/Corbis.*

Captain Aubrey Daniel headed the prosecution in the trial of Lieutenant William Calley and later wrote a letter appearing in the *New York Times* in early April 1971 that criticized President Richard Nixon's intervention in the affair. *AP Photo/Joe Holloway, Jr.*

The My Lai ditch claims another victim

Cartoon in the *Los Angeles Times* in 1971 that ran nationwide in its criticism of American popular support for Lieutenant William Calley, despite his conviction for murder in the My Lai massacre. *Courtesy Dave Conrad Estate.*

President Richard Nixon meeting with advisers in the Oval Office. From left to right: advisers H. R. Haldeman and John Ehrlichman, and White House Press Secretary Ronald Ziegler. *Courtesy Richard Nixon Library.*

John Dean III, President Richard Nixon's legal counsel, who virtually stood alone in opposing a White House intervention in the Calley case until it entered the appeals process. *Courtesy Richard Nixon Library.*

Captain Ernest Medina and his attorney, F. Lee Bailey, hold a press conference at the Pentagon on December 4, 1969, soon after Medina's appearance before the Peers commission that day. *Bettmann/Corbis.*

Pencil sketch by Preston Russell of the principal figures in the Captain Ernest Medina trial from August to September 1971. *Courtesy William G. Eckhardt.*

Colonel Oran Henderson talking with his chief defense attorney, Henry Rothblatt (Lieutenant Colonel Frank Dorsey in background), on the morning of August 4, 1971, the opening day of Henderson's court-martial for the charges of failing to thoroughly investigate the My Lai massacre and lying to the Peers commission about his handling of reports on the matter. *Bettmann/Corbis.*

On March 6, 1998, just after the Pentagon awarded the Soldier's Medal to all three men, Hugh Thompson and Lawrence Colburn react to memories of Glenn Andreotta as they hold a piece of paper containing a pencil-traced copy of his name on the wall at the Vietnam Veterans Memorial in Washington, DC. *Courtesy Getty Images.*

My Lai monument at the Son My War Remnant Site. *Courtesy Nissa Rhee (nissarhee. com).*

Memorial plaque in My Lai museum containing the name, age, and gender of each of the 504 Vietnamese killed in the My Lai massacre. *Courtesy Nissa Rhee (nissarhee.com).*

Pham Thanh Cong, survivor of the My Lai massacre and director of the Son My War Remnant Site. *Courtesy Derek Frisby.*

Six

FOR ALMOST A WEEK FOLLOWING the Pinkville operation, Jay Roberts's news release from the army's Public Information Office provided the story behind the front-page headlines of the *Trident*, the 11th Infantry Brigade's journal (edited by Roberts); the Pacific issue of *Stars and Stripes*; the Americal News Sheet (datelined San Francisco and written by Roberts); and the *New York Times*, all heralding the army's successful assault on March 16, 1968. In a "bloody day-long battle," read one account, American troops "mauled" the enemy, making up for their two previous setbacks in the Viet Cong strong-hold of Pinkville. Following a brief artillery barrage, the "Jungle Warriors" launched their search-and-destroy mission in My Lai a little after eight in the morning, supported by Huey gunships, while encountering "heavy contact" with the enemy outside the village.[1]

The coverage continued, describing how the commander of Charlie Company, Captain Ernest Medina, led his infantrymen to the target, killing four-teen Viet Cong within minutes of landing and capturing two M-1 rifles, a carbine, a radio, and several enemy documents. His troops also detained ten suspects, one of them asserting that at least thirty-five Viet Cong had arrived in My Lai on the morning of the assault. The Jungle Warriors had anticipated massive counter fire as they made their way across the open field and through the elephant grass, marshes, and rice paddies, their anxieties rising when they discovered sixty-nine Viet Cong bodies west of the village, the victims of American artillery and gunship fire.[2]

The 1st and 2nd Platoons of Medina's Warriors burst into My Lai after the artillery pummeling and quickly became "locked in heavy fighting with the unknown size Communist force." In the meantime, another battery of sol-diers under the command of Captain Stephen Gamble fired on the enemy from three miles to the north and then moved toward the first contingent to entrap the enemy while "encountering sporadic enemy contact throughout the day." In the third and final stage of the battle inside My Lai, the 3rd Platoon began mopping up less than an hour after the other troops' initial entry by searching every hut, tunnel, and bunker for Viet Cong and weapons while rounding up and interrogating villagers about enemy location and activity. The Viet Cong had put up four hours of resistance before slipping away by late afternoon, leaving Americans in control of the village.[3]

"The combat assault went like clockwork," reported the head of the operation, Lieutenant Colonel Frank Barker. "We had two entire companies on the ground in less than an hour," both closing on Son My Village from opposite directions. By noon American forces had seized control of My Lai and surrounding settlements while incurring only two dead and a dozen wounded and, "in a running battle," killed 128 Viet Cong, captured thirteen suspects for questioning, and seized three weapons. The operation was a huge success, capped by the largest body count ever recorded by the Jungle Warriors in a single day's fighting.[4]

The press on both sides of the Pacific hailed the triumphant assault on My Lai as a signature campaign of several attempts to roll back the Tet Offensive of late January. Among the enemy dead in the early stages of the offensive were one shot by soldiers while fleeing the landing zone below the village, along with four others killed by the gunships. The "War Lords" from the 123rd aero-scout reconnaissance helicopter team meanwhile killed two Viet Cong and seized forty 60mm mortar rounds.[5]

In the meantime Hueys had brought in another platoon of "Barker's Bastards," led by Lieutenant Thomas Willingham of Bravo Company, who seized a point a half mile south of My Lai and quickly got into a firefight that killed another thirty Viet Cong. That same afternoon, his troops moved beyond the village and up the beach to the east, where they spotted an enemy soldier scrambling into a tunnel. In exploring the entrance, they found that it opened into an underground maze, where after a brief pursuit in its dark and winding caverns American "tunnel rats" killed eight more Viet Cong. The subterranean complex housed a hospital and storage area containing web gear, hand grenades, and small-arms ammunition, all confiscated by American forces.[6]

Task Force Barker, Roberts summed up, had killed 276 Viet Cong in the three Pinkville operations that began in February and now climaxed in mid-March. Almost half of the enemy dead had come in the final campaign at My Lai. "American and South Vietnamese troops would remain in this area to keep the village free of Viet Cong."

Roberts's account of a heroic battle inside My Lai became part of the official record. Soon afterward, General William Westmoreland officially congratulated his officers and men on their "outstanding action."[7]

All these stories stemmed from Roberts's first-hand reporting of events, an account that he later admitted to CID investigators had grown out of his "false news release."[8]

I

Suspicions of unusual behavior in My Lai 4 had nonetheless begun to spread as early as the late morning of the assault, when Warrant Officer Hugh Thompson returned to base from the battle site in his OH-23. On landing at LZ Dottie, he jumped out of his helicopter and slammed his helmet on the ground, shouting to his section leader, Captain Barry Lloyd, that American infantry forces were no different than the Nazis in slaughtering innocent civilians. "I was very upset. I was very mad.…I was not going to be a part of this." Lloyd tried to calm his pilot. "It's mass murder out there," Thompson angrily continued, according to his account given years later at Tulane University. "They're rounding them up and herding them in ditches and then just shooting them." He intended to make good on his threat and charge the infantry with war crimes.[9]

When Danny Millians and Brian Livingston landed their Hueys and confirmed Thompson's story, Lloyd realized this was more than a fit of anger and recommended that they take the matter to their commander, Major Frederic Watke, who was in the aviation operations van.[10]

In moments, Thompson arrived at the van, accompanied by two other pilots Watke could not identify later except as possibly Millians and another warrant officer. Watke expressed shock at the accusations made by Thompson and supported by his two companions. The major had attended the March 15 briefing and remembered that no one said anything about American soldiers killing civilians. He had regarded the My Lai 4 operation as no different from other combat assaults and, in fact, had watched the initial proceedings from three hundred feet above while co-piloting the low-flying gunship. He saw the artillery fire along with hundreds of Vietnamese migrating unmolested south to Highway 521 and then toward Quang Ngai City. A little less than two hours later, he returned to LZ Dottie, saying he had seen no bodies. He had heard various claims that the artillery had caused a few civilian casualties and that Thompson's aero-scout team had gotten into a dispute with infantrymen. But now Thompson had burst into his office, accusing the infantry of indiscriminately killing civilians. In a statement that he later admitted to his Tulane audience came "real close to insubordination," he proclaimed, "If this damn stuff is what's happening here, you can take these wings right now 'cause they're only sewn on with thread. I ain't taking part in this."[11]

The substance of Thompson's charges almost instantly came into dispute, with Watke and others in the van later insisting they did not remember hearing much of what he claimed he had said—that fellow soldiers shot unarmed civilians forced into a ditch, that he had a heated exchange with a lieutenant over the killings, and that he saw a captain shoot a wounded woman lying helpless on the ground. Both Captain Lloyd and Sergeant Lawrence Kubert were at the meeting and, like Watke, did not remember Thompson mentioning either the shooting of a wounded woman or a ditch filled with bodies; but Kubert testified that someone in the group used the word "murder" and that they all heard Thompson complain of "unnecessary" and "needless" killings of "primarily women, children, and older men." Watke's main concerns were Thompson's references to indiscriminate firing and a confrontation with fellow soldiers.[12]

Watke told the Peers panel that he was more concerned about the alleged confrontation between American soldiers than he was about civilian casualties. He was not convinced that Thompson and the other pilots "really had seen what they had thought they had seen." Nor was he certain that there were as many casualties as claimed. Reports over the radio did not suggest a battle taking place.[13]

It seems inconceivable that Thompson would have attested to war crimes without specifying what he meant. He himself later insisted that he had told Watke "everything and possibly more." Thompson demanded a full-scale investigation and immediately began preparing an after action report.[14]

Watke was dubious about Thompson's charges even though other witnesses that same day confirmed much of what he had said. Watke spoke with a number of crewmembers, none of whom said anything that conflicted with Thompson's account. To the Peers commission, Watke allowed that thirty or more noncombatants had inadvertently been killed in the onslaught, but he asserted that Thompson's emotional state had resulted from his limited combat experience and that this had led him into "over-portraying" what happened.[15]

Still, the charge of war crimes should have led Watke to seek an impartial inquiry at the highest level. The regulations were clear on war crimes. MACV Directive 20-4 stipulated that military personnel knowing or hearing "a report of an incident or an act thought to be a war crime" must report it to the commanding officer "as soon as practicable." First laid out in 1967 and then updated in February 1968, MACV reiterated its requirement in a "message" that field unit commanders must investigate "all known, suspected or alleged war crimes or atrocities committed by or against US personnel." Failure to report "an alleged war crime" was a "punishable offense."[16]

But MACV Directive 20-4 had left an opening for those not anxious to report an incident suggesting a war crime. According to Section 5a, "all military personnel" were to report any act *"thought to be a war crime"* [emphasis mine] to the commanding officer.[17]

Unsure what to make of Thompson's accusations, Watke later claimed that he "thought the matter over" for about fifteen minutes before going to the Tactical Operations Center (TOC) and informing Lieutenant Colonel Barker of the charges. Watke had followed correct procedure by reporting the allegations to his superior officer, a move that he knew had serious ramifications. Barker commanded the men accused of war crimes, and it was what he thought that therefore counted. When Barker immediately hopped into his helicopter to investigate first-hand, Watke felt confident that he had met his responsibilities as an officer by putting the matter "in the hands of the men who could do something about it."[18]

But Watke knew more than he had revealed to Barker. Sergeant Clinton Stephens was an intelligence officer with the task force who was in the TOC the day of the My Lai 4 assault and had heard the radio calls from the field. He stayed at the center until around ten in the morning, joining others in listening to the exchanges over an open speaker hooked up to about five radios on the table. Amid the noise and confusion of battle, Stephens later told the Peers panel, he was certain he heard Watke, the commander of the so-called Warlord aero-scout helicopters, tell the operations officer at TOC, Major Charles Calhoun, that "they were killing innocent civilians." Stephens could hear shooting and yelling, much like "a John Wayne–type movie," he asserted in the Hébert Hearings. Yet Watke left no indication of something big going on.[19]

After receiving the transmission, Calhoun assured Watke that he would take care of the matter. Calhoun "more or less cut it off," Stephens later asserted, and then ordered Barker to check into the claim. This directive did not seem to surprise Barker, who apparently had monitored Watke's conversation with Calhoun. Watke soon arrived at TOC to see Calhoun, who met him at the door, and together they left for a private conversation.[20]

Soon afterward, according to Calhoun's testimony, he radioed Medina, instructing him to take precautions against killing civilians. Like Watke, Medina estimated that about thirty civilians had died from artillery fire. Calhoun declared that at one point that morning of March 16, Medina appeared upset about the killings when he radioed the task force command, asking permission to change the operation from search and destroy to search and clear. The enemy had withdrawn, Medina insisted, and only women and children remained in the village. His request had at first been denied, then received approval a short time later.[21]

Thompson's allegations—conveyed by Watke—led Calhoun to order a ceasefire a few moments after the warning. Some of the troops noted that Medina ran "madly" around the grounds, ordering them not to kill anyone else. According to several soldiers, it appeared that Medina had lost control over his company. A number of them also heard some variation of these tell-tale words crackling over the radio: "Stop killing civilians" or "Stop the killing." "Knock off the killing," was what Brooks had shouted to his men in the 2nd Platoon, according to testimony before the Peers Inquiry.[22]

Thompson later maintained that he had felt no relief, despite reporting what he had seen and knowing that a cease-fire order had gone out. He wondered what the chances for an objective investigation would be after Watke had forwarded the matter to the officer in charge of the operation. He was still in a rage as he and his two crew mates headed back to My Lai 4 around noon on March 16. As they approached the eastern edge of the village, Thompson later said he had been appalled at seeing a group of soldiers sitting in the shade of a tree, eating lunch near the ditch filled with bodies. Colburn recalled how angry Thompson had been, so angry that he put the helicopter into a forty-five-degree dive at ninety miles an hour and flew directly toward the men to scare them. But he buzzed them so closely that the propeller sheared the tree above them, and he had to land after its branches lopped off a piece of the craft's rotor blade.[23]

According to his testimony in the Peers Inquiry, Medina remembered a small helicopter on the ground near the eastern edge of the village and the pilot and one of his men checking the rotor blade before boarding and taking off again. Ironically, Calley had arrived a few moments earlier from his sweep of the village, and Medina ordered him to set up security around that helicopter until its departure.[24]

Thompson was still livid when he returned to base in the late afternoon on the sixteenth and privately told Episcopalian priest Carl Creswell, his chaplain friend and confidant, that American soldiers had killed about 160 civilians at My Lai 4, most of them women and children. Furthermore, as Creswell testified at the Hébert Hearings, "some sawed-off lieutenant" (Stephen Brooks) had opposed his rescue attempt and shouted at him to leave and let him run his own operation.[25]

Creswell thought Thompson was "terribly upset" and recommended that he take his protest to the next highest commander while he, Creswell, did the same through "Chaplain Channels." Thompson had already presented his case to Watke, and Creswell took the matter to the senior chaplain, Lieutenant Colonel Francis Lewis, who in turn talked with several officers about what had happened at My Lai. Two lieutenant colonels from the division, Tommy Trexler of Intelligence and Jesmond Balmer in Operations, had by this point heard similar charges and assured him of an investigation. On two occasions, according to the Peers Report, Lewis discussed the matter with Major General Samuel Koster's chief of staff, Colonel Nels Parson, who declared an investigation was already under way and urged the chaplain not to talk about it. If something of this magnitude had happened, Lewis asserted, "it would have been common knowledge throughout the division, but it didn't come out." And since nothing did come out, he attributed it to "an operational mistake" that resulted in civilians being killed by artillery, gunships, and crossfire, as reported in the briefing. He later claimed he had suspected nothing more than that.[26]

Lewis assured Creswell of an investigation but ultimately accepted Barker's explanation: "It was tragic that we killed these women and children, but it was in a combat operation. That is what I will report back to Colonel Henderson."[27]

Later that same day, Captain Lloyd followed up on Thompson's allegations by inspecting the area first-hand. Around 12:30 p.m., he took over his regularly scheduled relief duties for Thompson and flew over the areas north and east of My Lai 4 at a height of about a thousand feet. Thus Lloyd's only view of the village was a series of smoke columns billowing upward from burning buildings. In his hour in the air, he did not fly directly over the village and hence did not see any bodies on the ground or in the ditches. "Everything was quiet during my mission."[28]

Thompson had left the impression that everyone in the village was dead, Lloyd declared to CID investigators, but he "saw nothing of this." Yet based on what Thompson had told him, he and Lloyd had complained to Watke earlier that day, followed by Lloyd's filing a "written complaint." About noon, Watke forwarded both complaints to Barker along with reports from air crews of large numbers of other dead and wounded civilians, probably from artillery fire. Lloyd highlighted Thompson's after action report and marked it with the word "NOTICE" in capital letters, to draw the attention of the officers; but when he checked on the status of his written report a week later, the intelligence specialist in that office told him he had seen nothing. "I don't know what happened to this report," Lloyd asserted.[29]

Colonel Henderson meanwhile remained uncertain about the number of Viet Cong dead and weapons captured, and late in the afternoon of March 16 decided to secure a "dead count" by sex and age. Lieutenant Colonel Barker's investigation had led him to declare that about twenty women and children had died as a result of artillery and gunship fire. Henderson was more suspicious of the 128 Viet Cong reportedly killed. Where were the bodies? Medina explained that he had compiled these figures after asking each platoon leader to estimate the number of Viet Cong his men had killed and the number of civilians dead. Unhappy with this method, Henderson testified to CID and the Peers commission that he had wanted Medina to "make a more positive count," because he doubted that in the heat of battle the Viet Cong could have removed that many bodies. Henderson wanted a detailed report on the number of men, women, and children killed and how they died, along with another search for weapons in the rice paddies. Around 3:50 p.m., Henderson ordered Barker to send Medina back to My Lai 4.[30]

Medina strongly objected to an immediate return, declaring that he had almost reached his night-time defensive position and was waiting for supplies. To go back to the village so late in the day meant that his men would have to move in the dark through a heavily mined and booby-trapped area. Most alarming, Medina noted, a Vietnamese villager under interrogation had asserted that the Viet Cong forces had scattered into the rice paddies, where they could easily hide among them and launch a surprise attack. Medina knew that one of the Viet Cong's tactics was to let the Americans enter an area and come in behind them. According to his testimony, Medina had told Henderson, "I am concerned about the safety of the troops for the evening and for overnight stay in this area, because we know there are a lot of them out there. We ran out a lot of them. We did not get those."[31]

Medina's warnings had an almost instant impact, for later that same afternoon of March 16, Henderson received a radio message from headquarters informing him that Major General Koster, for safety reasons, had countermanded the order to return to the battlefield for another casualty count. Koster had monitored Barker's radioed directive to Medina and broke in to ask why he opposed the return. Medina explained his reasons and informed him of twenty to twenty-eight civilians killed. Koster saw no need to "go look at that mess" and thought that number "about right." Although unable to reach Henderson by phone, Koster made his feelings clear to him in a radio message that Captain Kotouc overheard and related to the Peers commission. "I just don't want you to go back through there," Koster told Henderson. "You have done a fine job so far. I don't want you to go back down there and subject yourselves to more danger for apparently no reason whatsoever, or very, very minor reasons." Not only would the move put American troops in danger, but they would not have the protection of the gunships, which had prior commitments elsewhere and would not be available for the next two or three days.[32]

Medina was concerned that the disclosure of a large number of dead civilians would raise questions about his claims to have seen no more than thirty bodies as collateral damage. He knew by now that no Viet Cong had been in My Lai 4, making his claimed fear of an attack from the rice paddies part of an effort to cover up the truth. What he did *not* know was that the Viet Cong threat would have been real. Had he and his men gone back to the village for a recount, they would have confronted one if not two contingents of Viet Cong from the 48th Battalion—one in My Lai 4, and perhaps another in nearby My Khe 4—both sent to the subhamlets in the early evening of March 16 to help the survivors bury their dead.

A little before six that evening, news of the massacres had reached the commander of the 48th Viet Cong Battalion, Lieutenant Ngo Duc Tan, who was about three miles away with a larger force than U.S. intelligence had anticipated: three companies, comprising four hundred regulars and one hundred support personnel.[33]

That night, according to survivor interviews, an unknown number of VC regulars arrived in My Lai 4 (and likely My Khe 4), working into the night and the next day alongside the survivors, providing medical assistance and helping to identify and bury their family members. Only then did the Viet Cong units pull out of both villages, leaving the local guerrillas in charge.[34]

Years afterward, Tan, now a retired colonel, explained that at the time of the American assault the 48th was in the mountainous region north in Tinh Hoa commune. From there, he and his men could "observe clearly." But, he added, "we couldn't predict" what the U.S. soldiers would do. "I thought they came in to search for the revolution's troops. I couldn't believe they would kill the people." Had he known that the Americans "would turn this into a massacre" by killing children, women, and old people, he and his battalion would have returned "to face the enemy," and there would have been "no American soldiers to return home that day."[35]

Tan and his men followed the Central Party's directive to create what was known as a "mourning flag" for the dead to show their intention to avenge the massacre. To underscore his promise, he signed his full name in blood on the flag. In the meantime, the villagers continued to serve as his eyes and ears, reporting anything they heard about American troop movements. The battalion soon began monthly attacks on enemy checkpoints, towns, and strategic hamlets, always ready to return in full force if the Americans launched another attack into Pinkville.[36]

In those interviews in 2014, Tan insisted that the fundamental premise of America's intelligence network in March 1968 had been wrong: Battalion 48 had no headquarters and was constantly on the move, never staying for more than one or two days in one spot. Local people welcomed his troops throughout the "liberated zone"—in the communes of the Binh Son district in the northwest and in the Son Tinh district, including Tinh Ky in the northeast, Tinh Hoa in the north, and Tinh Khe in the south. Each commune had three squads of three people from Tan's forces in each so-called group, and each group stayed in a household. They worked alongside the villagers in the fields, provided medical aid, and trained them in firing guns and throwing grenades. "We scattered to different places, never to be in one place" to avoid exposure and attack. There were "bad people" who came from other areas to trade or sell and would report them. Many times, Tan recalled, he had tricked Americans into believing his forces were in one locale when they were in another.[37]

Americans were not aware of all aspects of this intricate network, but they were highly dubious about using the term *non*combatants in referring to innocent villagers. Their skepticism was warranted. In a "people's war," an untold number of civilians became virtual allies of the Viet Cong and North Vietnamese forces who were fighting an enemy that had brought death and destruction to their land. They were as integral to eventual victory as the Main Force regulars and the Local Force guerrillas were. Villagers did not wear uniforms or regularly carry weapons, but they helped in numerous ways: furnishing military intelligence to both local and main Viet Cong units; setting mines, booby traps, and punji stakes; engaging in sabotage and terrorist missions; harassing American patrols and convoys; quartering VC regulars; and supporting local guerrilla units and self-defense forces—all critical tasks that elderly men, women, and even children could perform.[38]

Thus from the Vietnamese perspective, the so-called noncombatants were loyalists defending themselves against outsiders—the Americans, but from the American perspective, they were spies and liable for their actions.

Vietnam veteran and bestselling author Tim O'Brien wrote memorably of his first-hand experiences with soldiers who feared the unknown and the unexpected—an unseen enemy that surrounded them in the villages and while on patrol. Their greatest fear was the Viet Cong's greatest ally: the noncombatants who produced the wide range of explosive devices hidden in the earth, sand, fields, rocks, water, dikes, rice paddies, trees, bushes, hedgerows, shrubbery, grass, and mud floors of hooches. "It is not easy to fight this sort of war," O'Brien writes. "You try to second-guess the mine" by walking "with your eyes pinned to the dirt, spine arched" while "shivering" in fear. "We walk through the mines," trying to find "the mythical, phantom like Forty-eighth Battalion," much "like inexperienced hunters after a hummingbird."[39]

A high percentage of American casualties in this war came at the hands of these noncombatants, an enemy they could not see and yet was all around them in plain sight. Thus the most frustrating enigma of the war: how to operate among an unarmed but hostile populace.[40]

II

Colonel Henderson was not the only officer dubious about the low number of casualties; at the five o'clock briefing at Americal Division headquarters in Chu Lai on the evening of March 16, others in the army command were openly skeptical about the initial reports praising the assault. Major General Koster sat in the front row, with Chaplain Lewis sitting a few feet behind and overhearing officers murmuring in disbelief that their forces had killed 128 Viet Cong at My Lai 4 without capturing more than three weapons. Usually the men celebrated a victory with a rousing cheer, but this time they were subdued and asking questions. VC bodies usually carried some form of documentation, whether diaries, letters, or official papers. Where were the documents? Given that Americans had killed so many enemy forces and captured so few weapons, did this mean they were killing unarmed civilians? Something was not right. Lewis noted in the Hébert Hearings that the "undercurrent of uncertainty" quickly grew into "restlessness" and "rumbling" when he thought he heard the civil affairs officer, Lieutenant Colonel Charles Anistranski, sarcastically remark under his breath that only four males of military age were among the 128 enemy dead and that the rest "were all women and children."[41]

Lewis was not naïve. He had long realized that the term Viet Cong covered "a multitude of people"—which meant "anyone who was in a Viet Cong area that might be either fighting in the force, or assisting with rice or whatever." In one case he remembered that the dead had included twelve-year-old girls wielding rifles. Anyone between seven and ninety years old—all were listed on the board as Viet Cong. "That's why we have the 128 count there," Lewis claimed in the Hébert Hearings to have thought at that time. As the American officers had previously told their men, all Vietnamese killed in this hot area had to be Viet Cong.[42]

Koster, for his part, was furious but, according to Anistranski's testimony, less about the civilian deaths than the realization that the battle figures reflected poorly on his leadership. Turning to his briefing officer, Koster ordered him to find the weapons. So many kills and so few weapons seized could leave the appearance that these were innocent bystanders.[43]

Koster's concern did not surprise Anistranski, who had worked with his commanding officer long enough to know that he "always equated kills with the number of weapons, because if you kill an enemy, he has a weapon." Koster demanded that his soldiers adhere to the rules of engagement prohibiting any firing on civilians. Countless times he asked, according to testimony given to the Peers commission by Watke's executive officer, Captain Clyde Wilson, "Are we sticking to the rules of engagement?" Indeed, he brought the guidelines to staff meetings when discussing civilian casualties. "Don't go in and shoot up the villages and get all these kills without any weapons," he had repeatedly admonished his men. It was "incumbent" on them to establish legitimate kills by finding the weapons after a battle. And in this instance the numbers were wildly out of proportion and magnified the need to act quickly. It was highly unusual to have ten or so civilian casualties in a battle, Anistranski noted. But 128 deaths and only three weapons found? "It could be suspected," he wryly commented, that these were civilians.[44]

Thompson's allegations meanwhile began to spread throughout the base and up the command chain, generating indignation and anger. On that same evening of March 16, Watke came to realize that he had not acted forcefully enough. Barker had earlier assured him that Thompson's charges were baseless; Watke thought Barker was lying. Now, in the mess hall, he had gathered his pilots for a briefing when one of the young aero scouts brusquely interrupted an intelligence officer coldly reporting the enemy body count at Pinkville. "Yeah, what about killing women and kids?" A ruckus broke out in which Watke restored order only by jumping up and proclaiming, "That's enough of that kind of talk!"[45]

Around ten that night, Watke contacted his battalion commander at Chu Lai, Lieutenant Colonel John Holladay, and appeared to adhere to MACV regulations requiring a report to superiors on alleged atrocities by giving him a synopsis of Thompson's story. According to Holladay's testimony at the Hébert Hearings, Watke emphasized Thompson's claim that American ground troops killed "a great many civilians" that day. What "sticks to my memory," Holladay declared, was that a sergeant with either an M-16 rifle or an M-60 machine gun stood on the side of a ditch and fired into a group of civilians "hiding, crouching, somehow being in that ditch." But he also learned that a group of civilian men, women, and children were in a bunker, terrified as American forces led by an officer advanced toward the spot until Thompson landed and threatened to fire on his countrymen. Thompson also evacuated a child from the ditch to the hospital in Quang Ngai City. Watke did not recall providing Holladay some of the details he mentioned—particularly about a sergeant shooting into the ditch—but he had told enough to meet the regulations for notifying his superior of war crimes.[46]

"Do you know what you're saying, Fred?" he says he asked Watke.

"Yes, sir, I know what I'm saying," Watke had replied.

Thompson had to be "emotionally overwhelmed to do such a thing," Holladay quietly observed. He had never heard of such an "unbelievable" event, one in which an American serviceman had threatened to shoot other Americans in uniform. The massacre was the most devastating charge, Holladay asserted, but, he added, "I consider the confrontation, if that's what it was, as an outgrowth of that product of it." The term "war crime" did not enter his mind. "I thought of it in terms of murder," as if that were a distinction that offered some logic. He claimed he was "overwhelmed at the magnitude of the killing that took place down there that day."

After a conversation lasting into the night, Watke and Holladay decided to wait until morning to take the matter to the next level—the division's assistant commander, Brigadier General George Young. They expected him to forward the allegations to his superior, Major General Koster.[47]

A pattern of ineptitude—if not outright deception—had quickly developed. Watke had only belatedly taken proper if informal action, and Holladay made no effort to confirm Thompson's allegations by talking with him or any number of pilots or crew members stationed at Chu Lai. Thus nothing changed. Only Watke had talked directly with Thompson. Watke's attempt to downplay the accusations had kept them fairly quiet, and Holladay's lapse in judgment—not seeing what happened as rising to the level of a war crime—had kept Thompson's full story from reaching the high command.[48]

Early on the morning of Sunday, March 17, Watke and Holladay went to Brigadier General Young's office in Chu Lai, where Holladay asked Watke to relate Thompson's accusations. According to Watke, as Holladay later testified, there had been "lots of unnecessary killing...mostly women, children and old men," and a confrontation had taken place between GIs and helicopter pilots. Other aviation personnel had confirmed Thompson's allegations. Young expressed alarm about the killing of civilians as "murder," but he appeared "much more concerned" about the "so-called confrontation." This "surprised me a little bit," Holladay later asserted, because he considered his priority "just the other way around"—the slaughter of defenseless civilians.[49]

Young's account of the exchange was vastly different. After the evening briefing of March 16, he had walked back to the command building with

Koster and expressed surprise that their forces had engaged the 48th Viet Cong Battalion while capturing so few weapons in relation to the number of enemy killed. Koster could offer no explanation for the figures. But perhaps now, after this discussion with his two colleagues, Young had discovered part of the answer. Although disturbed by Watke's account of unintentional noncombatant deaths, Young testified at the Hébert Hearings that he remembered no reference to indiscriminate killings. As he read the situation, Thompson had seen civilians caught in a crossfire between American ground troops and the enemy and had taken two actions: first, landing his helicopter close to the villagers in an effort to protect them, and second, warning the infantry commander that if he shot at these people, he would order his crew to fire on the GIs. It was possible, Young conceded, that some of the Viet Cong reported killed were civilians. Yet in his testimony he continued to express greater concern about "a serious confrontation between friendly forces." After that forty-five minute conversation, Young conferred with Barker and Henderson before going to Major General Koster's office around noon.[50]

Koster was of course already aware of the issue. He had been airborne on March 16 from 8:00 to 9:30 a.m., observing one of the platoons in action and seeing "nothing untoward." While flying above the other commanders at two thousand feet, he declared, "I heard no unusual transmissions." On his return to division headquarters later that morning, Henderson informed him of six to eight civilian casualties. But then, around noon, stories spread throughout the base that Thompson had reported hundreds of civilians killed by American soldiers. And that evening at the briefing, Koster learned that the number of civilian dead—men, women, and children—had grown to twenty, all victims from artillery and gunship fire, and that his forces had killed 128 Viet Cong. At the Hébert Hearings, he admitted that at the time he had wondered how the two assessments and the two sets of figures could be so far apart.[51]

These contradictory casualty figures must have run through Koster's mind when Young told him around noon of March 17 that Holladay and Watke had asserted that a helicopter pilot had made several charges against American soldiers. Koster later claimed that Young had told him of the pilot's claim of "indiscriminate firing" but said "nothing about unnecessary killings" or civilian casualties. Koster called for an investigation into two issues: the confrontation between American forces and the assertion that the GIs had fired more times than necessary. He understood why Young had found it "hard to believe" that a confrontation had developed over Vietnamese civilians caught in the crossfire between American troops and the enemy.[52]

It seems odd that Watke and Holladay would have focused solely on the confrontation without tying it to the uncontrolled killings of civilians. Fully expecting an inquiry into Thompson's charges, the two officers would certainly have highlighted the mass killing of civilians. If for no other reason than to protect themselves from legal action, they would have told Young the whole story, so he could pass it on to Koster. Later in the afternoon of the seventeenth, Holladay told the same story to Koster's chief of staff, Colonel Nels Parson. According to Holladay, Parson was "very much shaken by the news." Grabbing the sides of a chair, he declared, "That is murder. We are trying to win these people over, and we do things like this."[53]

Koster was not oblivious to the possibility that this was more than murder. When asked later about Holladay's assertion that the pilot had wanted to prevent American forces from killing Vietnamese civilians clinging to each other in a bunker, Koster blandly replied, "There was some indication that there had been something of this during the course of the confrontation, but I can't say what it concerned, or what it was about." But he was certain about one point: "There were no comments about any killings going on." Yet, he concluded, "This was enough to cause me to direct General Young to investigate the matter."[54]

Young had recommended a full investigation of this confrontation in line with Army Regulation 15-6. Koster preferred that Colonel Henderson— going down rather than up the chain of command—merely look into the matter on an informal basis and report back to divisional headquarters. A formal investigation under army rules, as Koster knew, would mean publishing the official order that appointed the investigating officer, requiring sworn testimony, and filing the final report through army channels. It was, as he also knew, much simpler to keep the process informal and quiet—particularly since Young had already concluded that the subject of the inquiry did *not* rise to the level of war crimes. But Koster had cast a cloud of suspicion over his actions by asking his brigade commander to investigate his own command decisions. At the Hébert Hearings, Koster defended his decision as constituting standard army practice of assigning a unit commander to inquire into the actions of his men.[55]

Young told Holladay and Watke to fly down to LZ Dottie, where, at nine on the morning of March 18, they gathered with Barker and Henderson in an emergency meeting in Barker's command post van. "Nobody knows about this except the five people in this room," Young declared, according to Holladay's testimony in the Hébert Hearings, setting the tone of the session. Watke maintained that he interpreted this opening statement as a reminder to say nothing to anyone because of what he suspected was an oncoming investigation of the charges. Holladay had, he later said, a different take, thinking Young wanted to keep the meeting itself secret, because "a great many people knew about the affair." But Young's central concern remained the confrontation rather than the Vietnamese deaths. "We don't want Americans shooting Americans," he emphasized. Holladay recalled Watke earlier recounting the confrontation as well as seeing a ditch filled with bodies and a sergeant standing on its edge, shooting those Vietnamese still alive; Watke remembered telling him that Thompson had spoken primarily about his confrontation with fellow soldiers and only mentioned a few civilians dying in a crossfire. Holladay, for his part, thought the two issues were inseparable—the confrontation "as a result of the killing."[56]

Young's caution (and that of Koster) was understandable—assuming he ordered a comprehensive and thorough inquiry; but according to Henderson, Young focused on the standoff between Thompson and the U.S. troops, asserting that he was "very unhappy" over the incident and that "under no circumstances was this to occur." In a suggestion that must have astounded the others in the van, he "wondered why charges shouldn't be preferred against the warrant officer"—meaning Thompson. Young later claimed that he had not felt confident he had the full story about what had happened between Thompson and, as Henderson put it, an "unidentified soldier who apparently was shooting into some civilians in the bushes or trees." Consequently, Henderson remained silent as Young criticized Thompson. The five officers agreed on the need to gather more information in defense of the ground soldiers. But as Henderson recalled, they also began to pick apart Thompson's story. How could he have had direct communication with the ground forces? From his vantage point in the air, could he have seen what he alleged had happened? What kind of person was he?[57]

Under III Marine Amphibious Force of MACV regulations, the charges of atrocity merited a full-scale investigation by the divisional command that, if substantiated as "probable war crimes," went upward to the staff judge advocate of MACV. But Koster and Young had discerned no war crimes and opted for a quiet inquiry set out by Watke and Henderson, focusing on the confrontation and therefore seeing no need to file a formal report under MACV Directive 20-4. "One must be aware that a war crime has been committed before it can be reported," Young emphasized to CID investigators, a debatable interpretation of the directive's call for a report on any act alleged to be a war crime. Privately, Watke had shifted from his original position of thinking that Thompson had overstated the situation to believing there had been a large number of civilians killed, and thus to suspect a cover-up in the making. The top two divisional leaders knew that every officer in the van had everything to lose from even the suspicion of a mass killing, and, according to Koster, Young was to supervise (a claim Young did not recall in his testimony) a special arrangement: Henderson was to question all personnel on the ground and in the air at My Lai 4 on an informal basis and report back within seventy-two hours.[58]

Such an approach appealed to all six officers involved in the early stages of the investigation. The first indication that this would skew results came when Henderson made an effort to secure an accurate count of victims at My Lai 4 on the evening of March 16, only to have Koster countermand the order because Medina had objected to the idea, warning that re-entering the village so late in the day would imperil his men. It seems likely, however, that Koster also suspected something was amiss because of the low number of civilian casualties. He therefore sought to confine his investigation to the confrontation between Thompson and the other Americans and the matter of excessive shooting. Medina was undoubtedly also concerned that a recount would uncover the mass deaths.

At this point, the issue became mired in a transparently phony investigation. Whether a conspiracy of action or a conspiracy of silence, everyone in that van on the evening of March 16 was arguably as complicit in the war crimes as were the soldiers who either committed them, observed them, or walked away and did nothing to stop them. Every soldier and every officer either directly or indirectly involved in this story had a single purpose arising from self-interest: covering up what happened at My Lai 4.

Colonel Henderson had changed his mind about asking for the recount but, as he testified, decided not to object to Koster's order or to call for implementing the recount on the following day. Barker then requested that Jay Roberts draft a news release about the "battle" that effectively whitewashed what had happened at My Lai 4. Watke, for his part, initially failed to report Thompson's charges to superiors and instead turned them over to Barker, who declared them unfounded. After the blowup in the evening briefing, Watke finally realized the gravity of the situation and took the matter to his superior, Holladay, who joined him in taking the proper step of informing Young and counting on him to forward the charges to his commander, Major General Koster.

It was no coincidence that all these officers—Watke, Young, Holladay, Henderson, and Barker—had professional interests at stake in exonerating their soldiers of atrocity charges. Watke and Holladay understood the costs to their careers of an indictment of pilots under their command for threatening to shoot fellow soldiers. The other four officers were equally concerned about the fallout from their ground troops intentionally killing Vietnamese non-combatants. Barker had been heading toward a promotion to full colonel and knew that such charges would very likely end his career. Henderson had wanted to be a general from the moment he joined the Indiana National Guard at eighteen. Young also aspired to something higher—a second star signifying a promotion to divisional commander. He had been on the fast track up the military ladder, leading his infantry platoon into Sicily and later at Salerno during World War II, and then rising to battalion commander in the Korean War. Consequently, he attempted to discredit Thompson's atrocity claims by charging him with threatening American ground troops. Koster wanted to follow Westmoreland's path to the top. Like the commander of American forces in Vietnam, Koster was about to become superintendent of West Point, which would carry him to the rank of three-star general, followed by a seat on the General Staff and ultimately to his becoming chief of staff. All these lofty dreams would have been blown away in the stormy revelations about what U.S. troops did at My Lai 4.[59]

The six officers—the five plus Koster, who directed the investigation, such as it was, back down the chain of command—were taking a huge risk by failing to report atrocities, whether suspected or actual.

The purpose of Koster's informal inquiry immediately became blurred. Watke noted that the major objective was to determine whether there had been "unnecessary shooting and wounding and killing of civilians." Young, however, remained riveted on the confrontation between American soldiers. Henderson left the meeting, he said, "with the understanding that I was going to look into it," but was uncertain what "it" meant. He finally concluded that the two issues were inseparable and decided to examine both.[60]

Later that same morning of March 18, Henderson began his special assignment by meeting with Thompson for about a half hour, again in Barker's van. Henderson also noted the presence of Watke's executive officer, Captain Clyde Wilson, although Thompson indicated in his testimony that no one else was in the van and Wilson himself strongly denied being there or ever meeting Henderson. Thompson was emotional and, according to Henderson, insisted on standing. He first expressed reluctance to make this report but, as he later said, felt obligated to do so. He had witnessed "extremely wild shooting by troops on the ground," where "everything was out of control." In addition, the aircraft gunners, particularly the Sharks of the 174th Aviation Company, "were like a bunch of wild people" in "shooting wildly all over the area."[61]

It did not matter that Thompson and Henderson disagreed on whether the women and children listed as casualties were Viet Cong sympathizers; as unarmed and non-resisting Vietnamese civilians, they were not subject to summary execution. Thompson declared that he saw more than a hundred dead civilians; Henderson informed him the infantry units had reportedly killed 128 VC. Thompson later said he wondered if Henderson was trying to suggest that they were referring to the same groups of dead. Thompson was not aware of these reports of enemy dead and insisted that the bodies he saw were not VC but "old men, old women, and children" who lay scattered all over the village and in a ditch containing nearly a hundred victims. When he landed and protested the killings, a sergeant on the scene refused to listen, remarking that the only way to help these people was to shoot them. While in the air, Thompson continued, he saw an officer with captain's bars on his helmet—soon determined to be Medina, because he was the only captain involved in the My Lai 4 assault—shoot and kill a badly wounded woman. And, Thompson continued, he and his crew rescued a young boy in the ditch. Finally, Thompson testified later that he explained that he had intervened on behalf of a small group of defenseless Vietnamese men, women, and children in a bunker and about to be shot by American soldiers. He reported that he landed between them and the Vietnamese and stopped another slaughter by threatening to shoot the Americans. Henderson, Thompson remembered, took a few notes and did not place him under oath or ask him for a signed statement.[62]

Henderson told the Peers commission that he first heard of this confrontation between American troops at the meeting with Thompson in Barker's van. Yet moments afterward, he contradicted this claim, declaring he did not believe Thompson had mentioned the confrontation in this meeting. This seems strange, given that Thompson specifically requested a meeting with the commander to talk about Americans killing civilians. More likely, Henderson recognized his precarious situation as commander of the 11th Infantry Brigade (and hence of Task Force Barker) and tried to distance himself from the issue. He succeeded only in arousing suspicions about his motives. Furthermore, Henderson declared on March 17 that he was at a meeting in which Young expressed great concern about Thompson's threatening to shoot U.S. soldiers. Finally, Henderson further muddled the matter by asserting that on the same day he met with Thompson, March 18, he attended a meeting with other officers in a small tent at LZ Dottie, where he first learned of the face-off between the pilots and the American infantrymen.[63]

Only later did it become clear that on March 18 both door gunner Lawrence Colburn from Thompson's crew and Warrant Officer Jerry Culverhouse, co-pilot with Danny Millians at the bunker, also discussed the matter with Henderson in the operations van. Henderson claimed to recall talking only with Thompson, who had said nothing about women and children shot in a ditch or about his intervention aimed at preventing American ground troops from killing more civilians. The record shows that Henderson talked with all three airmen and that their stories confirmed mass civilian deaths, which was why Watke had urged Henderson to talk with them. From this time on, the Peers Report concluded, Henderson engaged in a "pretense of an investigation" aimed at suppressing the truth.[64]

Thompson had convinced Colburn to meet with Henderson, even accompanying him into the van and then leaving a few moments later—to avoid possible charges of tainting his crew member's testimony. Colburn was still wearing the blood-stained fatigues he had worn while helping to rescue the child from the ditch and carrying him on his lap en route to the hospital. He later testified that in a ten-minute conversation while no one else was in the van, he told Henderson that the ditch was filled with bodies, that a captain had shot a wounded Vietnamese woman, that he and his two crew members had rescued some Vietnamese at a bunker and a child from a ditch, and that Americans had unnecessarily killed "innocent people." Henderson took notes on a pad with a pencil. Colburn nonetheless remembered feeling perplexed that the colonel appeared "nonchalant" about what had happened. "I am sure he didn't really feel that way." Yet in the most emotion-laden part of the My Lai investigation, Henderson showed no emotions. "I don't know what his reaction was," Colburn declared.[65]

Thompson had also wanted the other member of his crew, Glenn Andreotta, to talk with Henderson, but Andreotta declined, because, according to Colburn years afterward, he was still in shock after wading through the bloodied ditch to save the small boy just moments earlier and as a "quiet guy" believed actions were more important than words. Andreotta died in battle just three weeks later and was never able to provide his perspective.[66]

Thompson also suggested to Culverhouse that he talk with Henderson, and Culverhouse willingly did so. As Millians's co-pilot, he had helped provide air cover for Thompson and evacuate the Vietnamese. Culverhouse testified in the Hébert Hearings that he told Henderson of repeatedly circling slowly over the village and seeing almost a hundred dead civilians, including several elderly men, along with numerous women and small children, many of them babies. He saw no males of draft age. As many as seventy-five of these bodies lay four or five deep, some face up and the bodies "all jumbled together" in about a thirty-yard section of shallow water in a ditch about eight feet wide and nearly five feet deep. He also saw bodies all over the village. Henderson took no notes and asked for no written statement, but he looked "uneasy," Culverhouse recalled to the Peers panel, particularly when he reported a sergeant shooting survivors with the "blood actually running off from the bodies down into the ditch."[67]

Henderson sought to comply with Koster's directives by keeping the focus on Thompson for turning against fellow American soldiers. In his later testimony, he made no reference to talking with Colburn and Culverhouse and clearly hoped to plead ignorance of the full extent of what happened.[68]

It was in Henderson's interests (as well as the others') to undermine the charges of atrocity by ignoring the testimony of the two other witnesses and joining Koster in creating a trio of defenders who kept attention on the accuser. Henderson therefore prepared a short and simple account aimed at destroying Thompson's credibility.

III

Henderson concluded his meeting with Thompson on March 18 and flew back to the embattled area to talk with Medina, who was still on patrol near My Lai 1. Just the day before, he had led his company south of My Lai 4, hoping to establish an observation post on Hill 85, locally known as Elephant Hill because of its shape. South Korean marines and ARVN forces had heavily mined the hill, making it dangerous. Medina sent Lieutenant Calley and the 1st Platoon up the hill but warned against going to the top. Calley ignored the order and indignantly dismissed a similar warning from Sergeant Isaiah Cowan. Calley had had run-ins with Cowan before and was not about to let a sergeant tell a lieutenant what to do with *his* platoon. With PFC Paul Meadlo working the minesweeper, Calley led a squad all the way up the hill. Cowan and the rest of men stayed behind.[69]

Trouble began as the squad came back down. Meadlo had cleared a path on the way up, but Calley chose to use a different return route to avoid rough terrain and had Meadlo walking in front of him with the minesweeper. Meadlo was uneasy about the new route but complied. A few moments later he stepped on a mine that exploded and threw him and the minesweeper into the air. Calley took pieces of shrapnel in the face, and Meadlo lost a foot and sustained injuries to a hand and his forehead. Amid the ensuing chaos and Meadlo's screams of agony, other platoon members gathered around while the medic bandaged his leg and gave him a shot of morphine. Less than a half hour later, according to an interview Meadlo later gave Mike Wallace on *60*

Minutes, the medevac arrived, and as the men lifted him onto the stretcher, he yelled at Calley, referring to My Lai 4, "Why did you do it? Why did you do it? This is God's punishment to me, Calley, but you'll get yours! God will punish you, Calley!" With blood running down Calley's face, he shouted to his men, "Get him on the helicopter!"[70]

Medina abandoned the observation project and moved south again, burning the hooches in the villages of My Khe 1 (where they found fifty "bouncing Betty" mines), 2, and 3 and killing two alleged Viet Cong but capturing four other suspected VC near My Khe 2 as they fled their burning hooch in mid-afternoon. Greg Olsen told Seymour Hersh that one of the GIs (later determined to be PFC Dennis Conti) pulled one of the captives from the hooch—a young woman whose blouse had been ripped away in the fracas—threw her over his shoulder, and began to strut around the area, proudly announcing that he "was going to 'put it' to her." But after examining between her legs, he threw her down and warned the men milling around waiting for their turn that "she was too dirty." He instead took her to Medina, where she suddenly began frothing at the mouth in what he called "child bubbles." He and the medic knew she was faking illness and snapped her out of it by putting an ammonia tablet in her nose. Medina yanked the shirt off one of the male suspects and gave it to her, later insisting he knew nothing about why she had lacked a blouse. The twenty-one-year-old girl, Nguyen Thiu May, was carrying medicine and was probably a nurse for the Viet Cong. Other GIs told Hersh that several men from the 2nd Platoon ignored Conti's warning and raped her.[71]

Medina welcomed the opportunity to interrogate the three male captives. He thought they were Viet Cong: two from the 48th Battalion—one a lieutenant carrying a small cloth pledging loyalty to the Viet Cong, the other a fifteen-year-old cadre—and the third a bit older and possibly a high-ranking member. Medina had experience in interrogating prisoners and was a bit of a showman, as Calley attested. Medina (and other interrogators) knew that the Vietnamese considered being touched on the head degrading, but this did not stop him. In one instance, Calley told Sack, he "scared the living hell" out of a detainee by jumping on him and wrestling him to the ground.

But this time Medina went farther, according to Calley, whose account focused on how unhinged Medina had become.[72]

When the captive refused to talk and instead shouted out a command in Vietnamese, Medina struck him on the head with the back of his hand hard enough to draw blood. He then took the advice of his interpreter, Sergeant Phu, who remarked, "If you shoot at him very closely he might talk." Medina took out his .38 revolver and threatened to use it unless he got answers. First secretly removing the ammunition, Medina played a game of Russian roulette, spinning the chamber and pulling the trigger at the back of the prisoner's head. Again this did not have the desired effect.

Medina picked up his M-16, grabbed the captive by his hair, threw him against a coconut tree, and backed up about forty feet. At this point, Phu warned the captive to talk or face execution. He remained silent, leading Medina to raise his rifle, take aim, and fire. The bullet passed eight inches above the man's head and burrowed into the tree. Medina returned to the prisoner and Phu asked if he was ready to talk. Still nothing.

According to multiple accounts, Medina returned to his shooting spot, took aim again, and fired a second time, two or three inches lower—again with no results. Medina walked back to the prisoner once more. "I showed him where the two rounds were with my fingers. I put my finger in the last hole and then I put him up against it and somehow or other, it came almost between his eyes, indicating that the next round, the third round, was going to go right between his eyes." By the time Medina got back to his shooting position and began to take aim (with the M-16 apparently set on safety), the man, according to Sergeant Thomas Kinch, who was there and later told *Life* magazine about it, was "very scared" and "rapping like hell."

Medina later insisted to the Peers commission that he would never have shot the prisoner, but he celebrated his achievement by posing for a picture while drinking from a coconut and holding a Bowie knife tightly against the captive's throat while he was gagged and tied to a bamboo tree.[73]

The prisoner, Tran Van Quyet, was then in his mid-forties and had been a member of the Communist Party for thirteen years. He was posing as a South Vietnamese official on the level of a district chief while heading the food supply effort for the Viet Cong in Quang Ngai Province. He had moved freely among the villages, wearing a belt outside his shirt to identify him as a leader of the Viet Cong infrastructure but keeping it underneath when Americans were around. Especially noteworthy was his insistence that the 48th Battalion was far away in the mountains—which meant he was telling the truth. As Colonel Tan had recently declared in an interview, the 48th had not been in or around My Lai 4 on the morning of March 16.[74]

By the time Medina met with Henderson on March 18, he must have had doubts about the enemy presence as well as a growing awareness of his men's concern about what they had done.

Medina had expected the visit. While searching for mines in the operations area southeast of My Lai 4, he had received a radio call informing him that Henderson was en route and asking him to secure a landing spot. This proved impossible on such short notice, and when Henderson's craft arrived about three in the afternoon, the landing took place in a relatively open area that exposed him and the others to sniper fire. The moment he jumped out, accompanied by Lieutenant Colonel Richard Blackledge, his intelligence officer, and Lieutenant Colonel Robert Luper, the commanding officer of the artillery battalion, the pilot went airborne to avoid possible fire while they crouched close to the ground until Medina ran up and unwisely saluted before shouting, "Let's get the hell out."[75]

The four men quickly ducked into a safe place near an old cemetery and lay prone in what Blackledge remembered as "a potato patch" behind a burial mound. Henderson and Medina talked about fifteen minutes. As the helicopter circled loudly overhead, they made Blackledge and Luper privy to their conversation, as they had to shout to be heard. Henderson adhered to his informal approach, administering no oath, taking no written testimony, and neither warning Medina of his rights before questioning nor asking him to sign any document attesting to anything said at this meeting. Henderson later testified that he found none of these legal procedures necessary, insisting that he had followed orders in making an informal attempt to collect information. "I did not at the time, nor do I now consider it as an investigation."[76]

On the short trip back to this area, Henderson noted to Medina that he had scanned My Lai 4 with his field glasses and spotted no bodies or buildings destroyed. By this time the VC regulars and villagers had buried all victims, and nearly every building had been burned or destroyed. Yet in his testimony to the Peers commission, Henderson claimed that on the morning of the attack he had seen only two VC with weapons and in uniform north of the village and perhaps eight civilians—some of military age—to the south along the trail. It was therefore unlikely, as he later admitted in testimony, that any bodies would be there two days afterward. Nonetheless, he had been "highly suspicious" about the report of 128 VC killed. Where were the bodies? A lot of them, Medina surmised, were spread out in bushes and among the trees sprayed by the gunships. Others were in the bunkers around and in the village. And, he noted, it was difficult to see bodies from the air, particularly those torn apart by heavy fire. Henderson asked Medina, "Were all those you reported as casualties military-aged males?" In the fog of battle, Medina explained, it was difficult to discern noncombatants from the enemy, and sometimes they got caught in the crossfire.[77]

Henderson still wanted to see bodies. "Are there any bodies near here that I can look at myself?"

"No, sir, there are not," Medina replied, apparently basing his answer on radio information and not first-hand observation. To search for bodies, he knew, would require moving the entire command post to provide Henderson with protection, perhaps even bringing in more troops.[78]

Henderson asked Medina two questions, both of which cut to the heart of the matter but whose answers were predictable. Do you know of any murders of civilians by your company? Did you order your men to kill civilians? Medina emphatically responded no in both instances, insisting that the twenty civilian deaths had come from artillery or gunship fire. As for Calley, Medina asserted that he was at his command station outside the village during the assault and did not see his second lieutenant until all the American forces were on the other side of the settlement—*after* the operation was over.[79] Medina did not volunteer any information relating to the contents of two alleged radio conversations with Calley, which had resulted in directives he interpreted as authorization to shoot the Vietnamese as obstacles to the operation. More to the point, Henderson did not ask what if any radio communications Medina had with Calley.

"Captain Medina," Henderson stated, "I'm out here to investigate informally if there were any war crimes committed by your people in My Lai 4." After a pause, "Do you have any knowledge of this?"

"No sir," replied Medina. "I do not."[80]

According to Henderson's testimony to the Peers commission, he pushed the matter.

"Captain Medina, the helicopter pilot has stated you killed a South Vietnamese woman. Is this true? Dammit Ernie, I want the truth from this, was that you?"[81]

Medina knew that Henderson had come to the field to investigate the atrocity charges made by the pilot and had been prepared to explain what he believed had happened. He also knew that the gunship pilots had been reporting the locations of dead Viet Cong so his soldiers could seize their weapons before the Vietnamese women hid them. He mistakenly assumed that the light helicopters—the OH-23s—had had the same mission. Medina explained that he had acted in accordance with the gunship pilots' attempts to locate enemy dead or weapons on the ground—which meant that he and his troops had been extremely cautious in approaching any areas marked with smoke, ready to shoot any surviving Viet Cong. Not until afterward did he learn that the small helicopter had been locating the civilian wounded so they could receive medical assistance—and that the woman had been one of those designated for help.[82]

The problem, as Medina later claimed, was that he had never received instructions regarding the meaning of differently colored smoke grenades and acted predictably. Captain Eugene Kotouc of Intelligence explained in later testimony that red smoke indicated real danger and green meant a safe area. This was all part of a "standard color scheme" that everyone was supposed to know. Captain William Riggs, commander of Alpha Company, noted that helicopter pilots mainly used red to signify an emergency. Colburn, however, insisted that the matter of color had never come up during discussions with either Thompson or Andreotta. Their helicopter had simply carried smoke canisters for marking locations of anything considered important. To Medina, however, all smoke marked the presence of armed Viet Cong.[83]

Medina had inadvertently highlighted the greatest problem confronting the soldiers combing the area for weapons and Viet Cong: American soldiers could not be certain what lay ahead in light of the difficulty of distinguishing innocent from enemy. In a war lacking distinctive uniforms and in which both combatants and noncombatants were Vietnamese, a soldier could not be too careful in a combat area—particularly one reputedly controlled by a deadly Viet Cong battalion. The victims of the battle might be enemies pretending to be dead while armed.

In his testimony to Colonel William Wilson of the inspector general's office, Medina explained what Major Calhoun had sensed from the base—the soldiers' fear of encountering live and armed Viet Cong—and finally shouted over the radio, "Damn it, Ernie! Get somebody over to get the weapons!" "OK," Medina replied, at that time about 150 yards from the smoke flares. As he neared the area, he noted red smoke hanging in the thick and humid air—the color that universally signaled danger—and knew what he might have to do. He first came upon a Vietnamese male, perhaps two, and a woman, all "mangled pretty badly" by artillery or gunship fire. Finding no weapons, he moved to a spot where a small helicopter (Thompson's) was hovering about twenty feet over another body, apparently the victim of small-arms fire or shrapnel.[84]

Inching closer, Medina testified, "I seen it was a woman," perhaps in her early twenties. The helicopter meanwhile pulled back from the spot. "I seen it didn't have any weapon laying around it, and she appeared to be dead. She wasn't moving." He nudged her and she still didn't move. "I didn't turn her over or anything like that. The helicopter, they could have seen it was a woman with no weapon, so as I turned around to walk away I caught a glimpse out of the corner of my eye of something in her hand underneath her and she started to move and the first thing that went through my mind was, 'You dumb bastard, you're dead.' She had got a hold of something." A hand grenade from the basket she had carried? Wielding his M-16, he "spun around and fired two or three times." Medina testified that by this time he was standing over Henderson, animatedly twisting his body around to illustrate how he had shot from the hip. "I killed her and he [the helicopter pilot], I know, reported this."[85]

Medina's detailed explanation concurred with Thompson's statements in all particulars except one. From his helicopter, Thompson never saw the girl move, if indeed she had. It was the word of someone on the ground, against the word of someone in the air and no longer over the spot. Medina insisted he shot her only after detecting a hand movement; Thompson reported no such movement—either because he could not see it from his vantage point or because it never happened. And yet, according to Henderson's testimony to the Peers panel, Medina would surely *not* have risked his life by walking away without feeling certain she was dead, and then, for no reason, suddenly wheel around to shoot her—especially when he knew a pilot was watching overhead. He must have thought he saw movement and suspected she was an enemy pretending to be dead.[86]

Henderson pursued the matter, confirming that the girl had *not* been armed.

"How do you account for the woman you just admitted shooting?"

"Sir, after I had shot her, I went and checked around her body for any equipment she may have had. And I found in her vicinity a basket which had some medical supplies in it, and I chalked her off as a VC nurse."[87]

Henderson concluded that Medina had thought his life was in danger and instinctively acted in self-defense. He nonetheless later wondered whether he had been correct in accepting Barker and Medina's conclusion that she had been a Viet Cong nurse and hence one of the 128 enemy dead, rather than one of the twenty civilians killed accidentally by artillery or gunships. But at the time— lying in a cemetery, shouting to be heard over the sound of the helicopter blades—he said he had thought Medina's explanation "appeared plausible." Besides, he found it difficult to believe that Medina would order the destruction of everything and everyone in My Lai 4. Admittedly, critics called Medina "Mad Dog," because he was so driven to report high body counts. Yet Henderson rejected this crude characterization, insisting in testimony that Medina was a "very aggressive commander" who ran his company "by the book," strict but "always fair." He felt comfortable with Medina's explanation on both counts.[88]

"OK, I understand that," Medina testified that Henderson said as he rose to leave. "That's understandable that something like that would happen. OK, continue with your operation."[89]

Henderson never launched an in-depth investigation of Thompson's charges.[90]

Henderson maintained that he attributed Thompson's "general statement that he had seen a lot of civilians dead" to his inability to distinguish between noncombatants and enemy supporters and was actually referring to the bodies of what turned out to be 128 Viet Cong and twenty civilians. Medina and Barker testified that they had felt confident that non-VC in the villages had left before the battle and claimed they had not seen any innocent civilians shot. Henderson later conceded that there should have been a major inquiry into such a serious charge, including whether the twenty civilians perished in a firefight rather than from gunship and artillery fire. He remained certain that neither Medina nor Barker had seen an extraordinary amount of bodies, but later also conceded that he "did not give enough credit to Warrant Officer Thompson's statement." Barker, Henderson found out, had learned of a high number of civilian casualties perhaps as early as the day of the assault. Henderson said that he had made this discovery too late to question Barker, who died in a helicopter crash in June 1968.[91]

Henderson found what he had wanted to find—that neither Medina nor Barker had seen atrocities. Medina, he said, was "an outstanding young officer, and I know his family, and I know he is not the type of an individual who would have knowingly permitted any atrocities to have taken place up in that area. I have all of the confidence in the world in this young man." He acknowledged that Medina had situated himself a short distance west of My Lai 4, where he could maintain control over his platoons by radio. Yet in his testimony Henderson said he thought it conceivable that Medina would not have known what was going on. On the ground, it was difficult to see more than a few feet. "These rice paddy dikes which look from the air like flat rolling terrain, and when you get down on the damn ground you are blinded by a hundred meters or even a little hedgerow which looks from the air like a pool table." Henderson likewise insisted that Barker would not have knowingly condoned atrocities. He was the type of commander who went to the battleground to keep abreast of what was going on. "I cannot believe that any of these officers either issued the order or stood by while atrocities were being committed."[92]

AND SO CONCLUDED the first investigation into what happened in My Lai 4, an investigation that effectively tried to dispel the atrocity accusations either by ignoring them or by taking explanations for what had happened at face value. In any case, it had little chance for success in view of the U.S. military's code of conduct for officers. Even if an officer did not see his subordinates engaging in illegal actions, he was responsible for their behavior if he did nothing to stop it once he was aware of it. As even Henderson's short-shrift and casual investigation had proved, officers had known more than they said, and that would open the door for more investigations. In the end it came down to what was known, and what should have been known. The U.S. Army Field Manual, *The Law of Land Warfare* in 1956, made clear that there was more to a commander's responsibility than knowing a war crime had occurred. If reports showed that he should have known of the illegal act, he remained responsible for stopping it. As one legal scholar put it five years after My Lai, "The actual knowledge test, in a context like My Lai, is an invitation to the commander to see and hear no evil."[93]

To anyone seeking to cover up a war crime, this narrow interpretation of *The Law of Land Warfare* offered a way to hide the very crime that the law intended to expose. But some crimes simply will not remain hidden forever, or even for very long.

Seven

COLONEL HENDERSON RETURNED TO LZ DOTTIE on March 18 and, as he later testified to the Peers commission, briefly reported his initial findings to Brigadier General George Young. Thompson appeared to be a "new and inexperienced" officer who had confused "a fierce firefight" on the ground with "an act of savagery." He had dropped flares to signify wounded civilians in need of medical treatment; Medina and his men, however, interpreted the smoke as denoting injured and possibly armed Viet Cong and approached the areas with firepower ready. Thompson's accusations were "possibly exaggerated because he was not on the ground knowing what the hell was really occurring." Indeed, he may have been responsible for some civilian deaths when the smoke told the enemy where the Americans were, drawing them to it. Thompson, Henderson emphasized, "had been unknowingly marking people for death."[1]

The accuser had become the accused.

I

After talking with Thompson and Medina, Henderson turned to the third and final part of his assignment: questioning the soldiers returning from their three-day mission. On that same day of March 18, he met them on their arrival at LZ Dottie, determined, he said, not to scare them into silence by asking whether or not they had committed war crimes. He was no more than a hundred feet from the helipad when a twin-engine CH-47 Chinook helicopter landed and thirty or so troops disembarked amid near-deafening noise. Henderson found out this was part of Charlie Company. "Just hold up the men here a minute, if you will, sergeant. I want to talk to your people," he recalled asking an NCO. Henderson waited until the helicopter was airborne and its sound abated before he spoke to the soldiers now milling around, anxious to reach their quarters.[2]

Many of these GIs were from the first two platoons to enter the subhamlet on March 16. Four of the men, he later realized, were from Lieutenant Calley's 1st Platoon. After praising their valor, Henderson informed them of an unconfirmed report of indiscriminate killing of civilians. This was not our policy, he emphasized, making it clear (as he had done with Medina) that he simply wanted to gather information on an informal basis and did not require either an oath or a signed testimony. "Was there anything with this operation different from any other operation or were you ordered to shoot innocent civilians?"[3]

He received, he recalled, a strong negative response.[4]

"Did anybody here, did any individual, any of you observe any acts against noncombatants, any wild shooting? Did any of you, or do you have knowledge of anybody killing any civilians during this operation?"

Silence.

Henderson changed his approach. Pointing to three or four soldiers in a group, he later said he asked each one, "You, young man, did you see any killing of civilians, or did you get any reports, or did you hear anything about it?"

"*No, sir,*" replied each soldier, looking Henderson in the eyes.

Turning to a sergeant standing nearby, Henderson asked "What about you?"[5]

"I would rather not answer that, sir."[6] The responder was Jay Buchanon of Lieutenant Brooks's 2nd Platoon.

It was a highly suggestive response from a seasoned veteran that should have led to follow-up questions.

Instead, Henderson abruptly moved on to other GIs. "Did you participate in, did you observe, or did you hear of any reports of civilians being killed at this operation?"

"No sir" came the same reply, all soldiers holding their heads high and looking directly at him.

Henderson recalled that he believed he had as much of the story as he needed—or wanted—to know. "They didn't appear to me to be a bunch of soldiers who had just gone out and shot up the countryside and killed a bunch of women and children." He thought they were telling the truth. "I think you have done a damn fine job, and again I deeply appreciate everything."[7]

Henderson expressed relief at the responses. "I know that I personally felt a hell of a lot better after talking to these men—that maybe something didn't happen," he testified. He admitted that he had not expected anyone to say, "Yes, I killed a bunch of people," but he had studied their physical reactions to his questions and judged them innocent. "Their heads were held high and there wasn't any 'dogtail' look about them." No one failed to look him in the eyes.[8]

In his testimony, Henderson suggested that Thompson had been mistaken. "I know that a guy in the air doesn't see the same thing that an individual on the ground sees." Lieutenant Colonel Barker supported Henderson's assessment, insisting that his company was not guilty of "wild shooting" and had instead been deeply engaged with the VC. This was the action Thompson saw from the air. Based on this small sampling, Henderson concluded that not a single soldier in Charlie Company saw any unnecessary killing of civilians.[9]

Medina had meanwhile arrived back at LZ Dottie in the last helicopter from Pinkville, where, according to his testimony in the Hébert Hearings, Barker told him that Henderson had been questioning the soldiers about alleged atrocities. Barker asked Medina to carry out an informal investigation and to tell his men not to discuss the matter among themselves. According to Sergeant Stephens, Medina made a surprise visit to the Tactical Operations Center, where one of the two or three people there asked if the story was true that artillery had killed some civilians. "Is that where you get all this body count?" No, Medina replied, declaring that "none of them were counted in the body count." The story must have come from the helicopter pilot who watched him shoot a woman. Medina claimed he had not wanted to do this, but "had no other choice." In speaking of the pilot, he added, "I don't see how he can come in here and say we are killing civilians [based] on an incident like this."[10]

Medina's story eased Stephens's concerns about My Lai 4. He testified that he continued to hear some of the men around brigade headquarters talk about a large number of civilians being killed, and he also overheard soldiers of the 11th Infantry Brigade at Duc Pho discussing whether the task force had killed civilians. Yet in any major operation "someone is going to get hurt." After hearing Medina's explanation, he said, "I was perfectly satisfied that nothing happened."[11]

That same day, Henderson thought he had clinched his case for the infantry's innocence after asking Major Glenn Gibson, the commanding officer of the 174th Assault Helicopter Company at Duc Pho, to question his Huey pilots about Thompson's charges. If any killing of this sort had taken place, they would surely have seen it and perhaps had been involved. According to Henderson, Gibson assured him the following morning that he had talked with every pilot, and not one had seen any "indiscriminate firing."[12]

In his testimony, however, Gibson said he did not remember any conversation with Henderson about the matter. Henderson angrily retorted that

Gibson had either "completely forgotten" or "just refuse[d] to stand up and be counted." He insisted that he met with the major either at the back of the brigade briefing room or just outside and recalled "very distinctly eyeballing that young man" and "asking him to query his pilots."[13]

Whatever the truth, Henderson's questions had reverberated throughout LZ Dottie, causing Medina to gather his company around him and issue a direct order, as Sergeant L. G. Bacon recounted in the Peers Inquiry: "Don't repeat anything—say anything about what happened in My Lai because there was an investigation going on."[14]

Medina's directive was perhaps justified in view of the ongoing inquiry, but it was also a self-serving way to prevent anyone from coming forward to provide an eyewitness report that might belie his own claims. He assured his men he would accept responsibility for their actions and do all the talking with investigators. Sergeant Thomas Finch told the Peers commission that he remembered Medina's instructions. If any investigators ask questions about Pinkville, he declared, "Tell them that we were in the village, we caught hostile fire, and we returned fire."[15]

Medina carried a special message to PFC Michael Bernhardt, who had recently complained to his congressman about other army matters. In front of the platoon leaders and other soldiers, Medina told him not to write his congressman. It would not help anyone, Medina insisted, and could get "a lot of people in trouble." Bernhardt later declared that if he said anything, "I might get killed by my own people."[16]

Medina soon sent Bernhardt on a detail away from the company—probably, the young sergeant thought, as Ronald Ridenhour testified to the Peers panel, to keep him away from Henderson.[17]

But despite Medina's direct order, what had taken place in Son My Village could not be kept quiet. On that same day, March 18, the Census Grievance Committee in Quang Ngai City released a one-page report alleging a massacre. According to a number of oral reports, "allied forces" had killed 427 "civilians and guerrillas," both "young and old," in a "fierce battle" against "District VC and local guerrillas." Casualty figures included 347 at My Lai 4, with the remaining eighty from My Khe 4. The committee's head, Nguyen Tuc Te, had been unable to launch a first-hand investigation in the Viet Cong–controlled area.[18]

Henderson discussed his findings privately with Major General Koster on March 20 after having shown them to Brigadier General Young the previous day. Henderson and Koster maintained their informality at several meetings, sometimes including Young in what both senior officers later termed "conversations."

Henderson told them what they had hoped to hear: Although he had not taken any sworn statements, he had followed Koster's instructions to interrogate all pilots of that day, along with platoon leaders, sergeants, GIs, Lieutenant Colonel Barker, and Major Calhoun. Henderson concluded that Thompson was an "excitable young man" who had imagined seeing atrocities. The truth was indisputable: twenty civilians had been killed by artillery and gunship fire; Medina had indeed killed a woman but in self-defense; American ground troops did not indiscriminately kill civilians; and the "machine gun confrontation problem had apparently been whipped or had been put to bed." Finally, according to Koster, Henderson dismissed any problems over the small number of weapons captured in relation to the 128 enemy killed: Charlie Company's competition among its platoons over body counts had led to their counting some victims more than once. He found no evidence of war crimes. Koster thought Henderson's report thorough.[19]

Koster recalled that he expressed concern about the twenty civilians accidentally killed in the operation. Henderson had specifically asked Barker about this matter, and the lieutenant colonel listed these fatalities on a three-by-five-inch card, along with their sexes and ages, followed by an explanation attributing their deaths to artillery or gunship fire. This move did not mollify Koster. Henderson later recalled that Koster "let [him] know in no uncertain terms that this number of civilians [killed] in an operation like this, regardless of the intensity of fire, was unacceptable." How could so many civilians have died from artillery and gunship fire and none from small arms? "Damn it! This is just thoroughly unacceptable," Koster exclaimed. "We've got to provide in our plans so this doesn't happen anymore."[20]

Henderson knew the actual number was much higher and not the result of stray artillery and gunship fire. He said he warned Koster that blaming these deaths on errant cover fire made for a "fictitious report from that aspect." Commanders did not like to report small-arms killings of civilians when they could easily link them to artillery or gunships. What troubled Henderson was his own finding that the artillery barrage did not hit the village. "Our artillery or prep fire was in an LZ in which there should have been no civilians."[21]

Henderson failed to realize that the artillery preparation did hit areas alongside My Lai 4—and not all by accident. The artillery commander, Lieutenant Colonel Robert Luper, asserted in the Peers Inquiry that Barker had *wanted* the shells to hit the western and southern rims of the village to take out possible enemy positions in the tree lines and hedgerows and thus protect his men jumping from the helicopters and advancing toward the target.[22]

By dismissing artillery fire as a cause of civilian deaths, Henderson realized that he was left with only one conclusion. They had to be the result of small arms, which suggested purposeful killing. If U.S. soldiers had intentionally killed these civilians, he later explained to the Peers commission, it was the result of "rash acts" stemming from the fear of combat that Medina had seen among his men.[23]

Henderson admitted that the March 15 pre-invasion briefing might have stirred up the soldiers so much about the danger that they went out of control during the assault and fired at anything that moved. If so, he felt partly responsible, because he had instructed his officers to challenge their men to end the Viet Cong threat once and for all. The enemy, he angrily asserted, "had been hurting the hell out of us with mines and booby traps, primarily sniper fire and things of this nature."[24]

In a final effort to exonerate his men, Henderson left Koster and others with the impression that Thompson was the only person who claimed to have observed unnecessary killings.[25]

II

After undermining Thompson's credibility, Henderson hoped to quiet further talk about the charges by never mentioning meetings with Lawrence Colburn and Jerry Culverhouse, both of whom had corroborated Thompson's account. Indeed, Henderson later told the Peers panel that the name Culverhouse "doesn't ring a bell."[26] As was the case with Medina, Henderson kept no formal record of their discussions, and there was therefore no written evidence. The colonel also did not take Colburn and Culverhouse's statements under oath, nor did he compile extensive notes or probe any deeper into what they said. He simply dismissed Thompson's allegations as the emotional ranting of a young and inexperienced soldier.

Henderson instead accepted the verbal denials of officers and men who had a great deal to lose if found complicit in killing civilians—Medina, Barker, Calhoun, Charlie Company, and the Huey pilots from the 174th Company. Henderson pronounced them all innocent on the basis of their word that they had not seen or done anything wrong. All three company commanders in the combat assault denied killing civilians, except for Medina, who admitted to shooting the girl in self-defense.[27]

But despite his efforts, Henderson could not make Thompson's charges go away. He insisted that Thompson had no communications with anyone on the ground and could have known no more than anyone else, yet evidence from other pilots showed that Thompson had maintained radio contact with the lower gunship commander and had repeatedly identified the locations of the wounded. Henderson simply reported what Medina had told him—that the pilot was marking the locations of VC so the American soldiers could capture or kill them. He did not take into consideration that Thompson's OH-23 was an older helicopter with only one radio that he regularly used to communicate with his protective escorts—two Huey pilots who *were* aware of events on the ground. The gunships were flying behind Thompson and a little to the side, which allowed those on board to see everything and forward information to the ground command.[28]

Henderson's own radio operator, Sergeant Michael Adcock, had seen numerous dead civilians while sitting next to him in the cramped confines of their helicopter. Adcock testified that he had squeezed between Henderson and Luper in the back, while four others crowded into the front, including the pilot, co-pilot, and two gunners. As they hovered over My Lai 4 for about an hour following the artillery preparation, everyone aboard was in position in the early morning light to see what was on the ground. No artillery had hit inside the village, Adcock noted as they repeatedly banked or made turns overhead, but shrapnel had struck its western and adjacent sides while gunships strafed the tree lines. Their flight north followed the road to the village, where they saw what Adcock called "a few" bodies on a small access road.[29]

Adcock hesitated to say anything about the bodies, because this was his first combat experience and he hoped what he saw was normal. But he soon realized he was witnessing something unusual. Up to thirty dead Vietnamese civilians lay in small piles along the trails, one of them a group of about fifteen men, women, and perhaps children he could see from just fifty feet in the air, scattered along the tree line in the paddies and next to the road running south and on both sides of an irrigation ditch. "The only odd thing about it," he noted in his testimony at the Hébert Hearings, was that "they were all facing the same direction." It appeared "they were killed and all fell in the same direction."[30]

Neither artillery nor gunship fire could account for anything resembling a pattern. Either type of assault would have shattered its victims and spread their remains in every direction. Only a systematic execution of lined-up victims by rapid-firing M-16 rifles could drop them on the spot and explain the orderly fall of bodies Adcock described. Henderson could not have missed what both Adcock and Luper had seen. Luper also saw about twenty bodies off the side of the road, but in his testimony dismissed them as instances of collateral damage. "I rather resent the use of the term civilian," he asserted.

Henderson managed to keep quiet about the high number of bodies. Despite two witnesses in the same helicopter, he reported only eight dead civilians just south of the village along with two Viet Cong to its north.[31]

Why Henderson did not question any of the others aboard the helicopter paralleled his other efforts to follow his narrowly conceived orders. In accordance with Koster and Young's guidelines, Henderson had hurriedly investigated only a few selected members of his command within his seventy-two-hour window. Knowing what his two superiors wanted from the inquiry, and aware of what was best for his own career, Henderson had found what he needed and what they wanted to hear.

He had carried out no more than a perfunctory inquiry in asking a few soldiers from Charlie Company—in front of others in the same company—whether they had seen Americans killing Vietnamese civilians. What answer other than no could he have expected? For a soldier (publicly or privately) to turn on fellow comrades in arms was highly unlikely—particularly when the platoon would soon join other patrols in the remote bush, where informants risked severe reprisals—including death—from vengeful fellow GIs.

Henderson predictably uncovered no war crimes and, in so doing, violated army regulations requiring a report on any suspicions of such conduct.[32]

The cover-up became even more evident after a series of events connected with General William Westmoreland's message of March 20 congratulating Task Force Barker's success in Pinkville.[33]

Shortly after Westmoreland's commendation appeared in the army press, Lieutenant Colonel John Holladay called Major Frederic Watke into his office. They noted something suspicious: division headquarters had reissued the message for circulation throughout the service area a week later but with an additional paragraph that heaped more praise on Charlie Company—"a little bone" intended to "keep us quiet," Holladay remarked in the Hébert Hearings. Major General Koster had inserted a personal acknowledgment of his men's outstanding success, but Henderson followed with glowing words addressed to Medina and copied to Barker: "The success of this operation and the praiseworthy role of units of the 11th Infantry Brigade directly reflect your expert guidance, leadership and devotion to duty. The quick response and professionalism displayed during this action has again enhanced the Brigade's image in the eyes of higher commands. Please convey my sincere appreciation to those personnel responsible for a job well done." Captain Donald Keshel would have found Henderson's praise out of character. Keshel testified that he had worked under Henderson's command for eighteen months and had been "scared to death" of him. Never did he compliment his staff.[34]

Holladay later said he had found it difficult to believe that Koster was among those wanting to bury the charges of atrocity. It was "everybody else except him." But, as he later continued, he could only conclude that the additional paragraph commending the company had "originated in the American Division headquarters" as an attempt to silence the issue.[35]

Holladay's suspicions appear justified. The timing could not have been co-incidental: Koster and Henderson's preparation of this new material took place in the midst of their efforts to undermine Thompson's accusations of war crimes. The expanded release was for large-scale distribution—to a list of recipients that included not only soldiers but the commanding officers of the 11th Brigade and the 123rd Aviation Battalion, both under Koster's command. Endorsed by division headquarters, the message went out under his name.[36]

Holladay remembered that he had the "impression" that "a great many people" in division headquarters and around the area were aware of the massacre at My Lai 4. "And I think they knew it in the context that there were a lot of civilians killed down there that day, indiscriminately, or excessively, or whatever term was applicable. That they were not enemy." How could anyone question what happened at My Lai 4 when the head of MACV, the division commander, and the brigade commander praised the GIs?[37]

Yet the massacre stories persisted. Within a week of the assault, Lieutenant Colonel William Guinn, deputy adviser in Quang Ngai Province, claimed he gave Henderson the report of a massacre, a handwritten and barely readable translation into English prepared by the Census Grievance Committee. The document asserted that "over a thousand civilians had been killed in the My Lai area...by bombing and artillery" with "no indication in there that they had been killed by small arms or ground action." Had the casualties been Viet Cong, the Americal Division would have tallied the numbers because of, as Guinn put it, "the body count business." Even though Guinn remained un-convinced about the murder charges, he noted that Henderson "seemed sur-prised and somewhat taken aback by the allegations."[38]

Guinn had concluded that the report was Viet Cong propaganda, unsub-stantiated by the province chief and therefore not to go forward to MACV. The civilian casualties were the result of "an act of war" in a "free-fire zone" and hence no "war crime." And yet he thought the allegation serious enough that he flew to Duc Pho and handed the report to Henderson as he prepared to board a helicopter.[39]

Guinn testified at the Hébert Hearings that Henderson agreed to check out the report; Henderson denied any knowledge of the report. In late November 1969, Peter Braestrup of the *Washington Post* published an article on the army's probe into the allegations of killings and asked Henderson, now back in the United States, to verify the high numbers cited in that report. In the article, Braestrup declared that "reliable Pentagon sources" called Guinn's report brief and incomplete and claimed it did not reach Henderson until after his investigation. According to these sources, Henderson discussed the matter with South Vietnamese provincial authorities, who, according to his own investigation, had seen nothing to indicate a mass killing. But in June they changed their position after seeing this report. Henderson, the sources said, offered to help and then dropped the matter. Henderson again denied seeing any such document and immediately arranged to meet Guinn in Norfolk, Virginia. Henderson claimed he did not remember receiving a piece of paper containing any allegations. "Oh yes, sir," Guinn responded. "I carried that down to Duc Pho and handed it to you." Henderson again denied seeing the report.[40]

Just days after this atrocity report, South Vietnamese officials in the outlying areas of Quang Ngai Province received five more accounts of a massacre of five hundred unarmed men, women, and children in the two villages of My Lai 4 and My Khe 4 and passed translations of them on to Henderson and other U.S. military and civilian leaders. The charges were similar to those filed by the Census Grievance Committee, except that they accused Charlie Company of killing four hundred civilians at My Lai 4 and Bravo Company of killing almost a hundred more in nearby My Khe 4.[41]

Colonel Nguyen Van Toan, commander of the Second ARVN Division in Quang Ngai Province, told Henderson he had already heard about the charges and ordered an investigation by the provincial chief, Lieutenant Colonel Ton That Khien. Toan had received a copy of the allegations from Lieutenant General Hoang Xuan Lam, ARVN commander in the northern provinces of South Vietnam, who asked him to look into the matter. Toan quickly dismissed the paper as "VC propaganda" and joined Khien in deciding not to report the alleged atrocities for fear of damaging his country's relationship with its U.S. ally. Khien meanwhile ordered Son Tinh's district chief, Lieutenant Tran Ngoc Tan, to conduct an inquiry. Tan soon confirmed his superiors' belief that the VC charge "was not true." Hundreds of civilians had been caught in a firefight probably set off by sniper fire, and the Viet Cong had attempted to exploit the incident as propaganda.[42]

III

Whether credible or not, these Vietnamese reports kept the story alive, leading Major General Koster to deflect responsibility by showing that he had made every effort to protect the rights of Vietnamese civilians. Beginning on March 18 or 19, according to his testimony to both CID and the Peers panel, he repeatedly emphasized to his forces the importance of complying with *The Law of Land Warfare*. In the Combat Orientation Course during early training, he insisted that he had briefed 98 percent of the soldiers entering the division and every member of the 11th Brigade on the importance of realizing "the Vietnamese were not only our allies, but we were guests in their country." Just before the Pinkville operation, he warned his brigade commanders not to hit the villages with artillery fire or to burn any huts without specific approval of division headquarters. He then had this policy printed and distributed throughout the division. In his testimony, Koster expressed confidence that his soldiers had always conducted themselves appropriately—including the claim that they had evacuated the wounded and treated them at American medical facilities.[43]

Koster had defenders. Captain William Riggs of Alpha Company maintained that the army's orders regarding humane treatment of noncombatants had been standard policy long before the March 15 briefing—that civilians were not to be "intimidated or coerced, threatened, tortured, anything like that." Assistant Chief of Staff Jesmond Balmer noted at the Hébert Hearings that every replacement in the Americal Division went through a four- or five-day combat course at Chu Lai on the proper treatment of civilians and POWs, and Koster repeatedly stressed these points through command channels as a "very important part of his entire philosophy."[44]

Problems in Koster's leadership became evident before, during, and after the My Lai operation. We have seen that he showed no intimate knowledge of Barker's combat plan and that he did not closely follow up on that day's events. Although he repeatedly urged his officers and troops to adhere to humanitarian principles in their treatment of civilians, Balmer himself admitted that he never saw Koster focus on these issues in face-to-face meetings with subordinates. Lieutenant General Peers later expressed skepticism about Koster's testimony that his forces had the "Combat Operation, Rules of Engagement" in draft form prior to March 16, 1968, and that its publication on the day of the assault was a "coincidence." If Koster made these and other guidelines clear from on top, he failed to communicate them effectively to his officers and men on the ground.[45]

Koster also had not grasped the importance of specifying what soldiers could and could not do during an operation—that not prohibiting an action was tantamount to approving it. In his witness statement to CID, Koster rejected the claim by numerous soldiers that they were under orders to destroy the village and its inhabitants. "Absolutely not," he added for emphasis.[46]

On March 24, just eight days after the assault on My Lai 4, Koster issued a directive to all commanders that should have gone out before the operation: a strongly worded but toothless memo entitled "The Safeguarding of Noncombatants." He admitted that it was "a direct result of the My Lai (4) allegations." To protect civilians, military commanders were to remind all soldiers of their responsibility to treat noncombatants in a humane way: exercise great care in using firepower in settled areas; avoid unnecessary destruction of private property; warn civilians of coming operations; facilitate their withdrawal in instances where a prior warning would endanger the mission; institute evacuation procedures; and provide medical treatment for injured civilians. But he added a major exception that could undermine the entire program: make every effort to avoid civilian casualties—"short of endangering U.S. lives."[47]

In the best of worlds, these guidelines made for a laudable policy; in the fog of war, they were virtually impossible to follow. Koster did not give blanket approval to destroy anything useful to the enemy. He found it acceptable to destroy tunnel fortifications as integral to the enemy's military effort, for instance, but not hooches, livestock, and crops without his or a brigade officer's approval. He left to the discretion of ground commanders whether confiscation of foodstuffs and animals was justifiable if it was determined to be more than villagers needed. In some instances they could evacuate the village and turn it over to South Vietnamese authorities. "We did not destroy it, particularly in a populated area such as this [Son My]." But materials were subject to destruction if they were found in remote areas and "obviously just for military alone." If such military goods were in a populated area, the American officer in charge could ask ARVN forces to destroy them. "I know of no instance where we did this."[48]

But at My Lai 4 and My Khe 4, U.S. troops broadly interpreted Koster's strictures to mean that they could destroy everything deemed valuable to the enemy and therefore a threat to their survival.

Even if the rules of engagement had made their way into the soldiers' hands and they actually read them, it was doubtful that in the heat of battle they would have acted in accordance with humanitarian principles. Henderson admitted that officers did not regularly review the rules with the troops, but he emphasized that soldiers shipped to Vietnam had read them in Schofield Barracks in Hawaii and that the Americal Division had instituted a class on the subject in its training program for replacements. On occasion, Koster went over the rules at a brigade commanders' meeting, and Henderson then reviewed them with his battalion commanders, who passed them down the chain of command to company commanders. When the troops had a stand-down, which seldom happened, unit commanders often went over the rules with them. Henderson thought he had amassed enough post facto evidence to quash all talk of atrocities.[49]

On March 28, Lieutenant Colonel Barker submitted his after action report on the My Lai 4 campaign and addressed it to Henderson. The report confirmed the stories in the press by trumpeting the fiction of victory in a hard-fought battle, and it implicitly disclaimed all charges of a massacre by making no reference to civilian deaths. In five pages, Barker argued that the operation had aimed to destroy a "VC base camp" and was ultimately "well planned, well executed, and successful." Intelligence forces had warned of a Viet Cong battalion in My Lai 4, but the enemy instead had been two local companies of Viet Cong, along with perhaps three guerrilla platoons, all to-taling nearly two hundred fighters but still almost twice as large as the American attack force.[50]

The only recommendations Barker made in his report involved the treat-ment of civilian refugees. In areas where there might be numerous noncom-batants, military operations "should provide for civil affairs, psy-ops, medical, intelligence and police teams" soon after the combat troops arrive. This ap-proach "would facilitate population control and medical care, and would permit the sorting out of VC which have mingled among the population for cover." Finally, "these teams would free infantry personnel for combat opera-tions." Yet no evidence suggests any effort to employ these teams in either My Lai 4 or My Khe 4. According to Sergeant Stephens of task force military intelligence, "There was none that went out that I knew of."[51]

Like Roberts's news release, Barker mixed facts with falsehoods, both in coaching Roberts in drafting his story and in preparing this combat ac-count. Americans, Barker continued to claim, had killed 128 Viet Cong, incurred thirteen casualties that included two dead, and seized those three weapons along with hand grenades and ammunition. The report did not mention the hundreds of slaughtered men, women, and children on the trail, in the ditch, and scattered throughout the village—most of them in plain sight.[52]

Reaction to Barker's account varied. Henderson tried to distance himself from it by later insisting that he never saw the document and had no explana-tion for its covering only the first day of the operation. He had not raised the matter of 128 dead Viet Cong and focused instead on the twenty civilians, which Barker did not mention—despite his having sent Koster three-by-five-inch cards explaining how they had died. Nor did Henderson refer to the alleged thirteen American casualties as well as hundreds of civilian and Viet Cong evacuees. Lieutenant Jesse Frosch of military intelligence in Quang Ngai Province scoffed at Barker's claim to have killed that many Viet Cong at My Lai 4. Only a handful of enemy were in the area, and to say that American soldiers killed such a large number while capturing so few weapons was an obvious attempt to inflate battle figures.[53]

Not a single soldier in Charlie Company claimed to have encountered enemy resistance in the village. No one saw more than a few males of draft age.[54] Moreover, Barker had not referred to follow-up battles in the next two days for one reason: the ceasefire in My Lai 4 had effectively ended the Pinkville operation two and a half days before its planned conclusion.

Had Barker and Henderson issued a truthful report, they would have sought first-hand information by either filing a report that could have led to a CID investigation or posing hard questions to officers and soldiers. On the afternoon of the assault, they might have conducted either an immediate aerial observation by low-flying OH-23 helicopters or a physical inspection on the ground (or both), which surely would have revealed hundreds of Vietnamese bodies on the trail, in the ditch, and throughout the village. By no means could Barker and Henderson have dismissed all slain villagers as Viet Cong or their supporters; nearly half of the victims were teenaged children and younger, and many of these were toddlers holding on to their parents or babies killed while in their mothers' arms.

The vast differences between Henderson and Barker's reports reaffirmed the impression that in the days after the killing, a loosely conceived cover-up was initiated by Major General Koster and followed by the five officers gathered in the command post van. A well-planned attempt to hide the massacre would have led to investigatory reports by Barker and Henderson that corroborated one another. The only similarity between the accounts lay in their effort to conceal what had happened at My Lai 4. Barker fabricated key elements in the story; Henderson left them out.

Koster proved more receptive to Barker's positive assessment than to Henderson's summation. Barker gave credence to Koster's later claim that he never received an official report of civilian casualties, whether twenty or hundreds. A three-by-five-inch card did not constitute an official report. And Barker's report did not mention the noncombatants wounded and killed at either My Lai 4 or My Khe 4. Koster had heard unofficially that some thirty civilians had died at My Lai 4. Brigadier General Young had told him about the excessive shooting by the GIs and of Thompson's confrontation with American ground forces. But again, this was anecdotal.[55]

Henderson's oral report of March 20 was more problematic. At first pleased with its conclusions, Koster came to realize it was impossible to shut down atrocity claims by attributing the twenty civilian deaths to artillery and gunships.[56]

Henderson made no effort to speak directly with Koster about his revoking the recount order. Had Henderson wanted to offer his superior an accurate story, he could have either discussed the matter directly with Koster or launched a recount the following day; Koster had not prohibited him from sending back troops at another time.[57]

In any case, whichever report he favored, Koster insisted that nothing out of the ordinary had happened in Pinkville. Both Henderson and Barker had led Koster to believe no war crimes had occurred. MACV Directive 20-4 required him to report only "probable war crimes." Koster seems to have suspected there had been more civilian deaths than those reported by either Henderson or Barker. Koster later insisted in testimony that he had informed someone in command headquarters—either Lieutenant General Robert Cushman or another officer of the 3rd Marine Amphibious Force—of both the Viet Cong's charges of mass murder and Henderson's report, and that he shared this information with Lieutenant General Lam. Yet neither Cushman nor Lam, nor any other officer, remembered such a conversation.[58]

Not until much later, during the CID investigation, did Koster attempt to deal with one of the most important questions raised about the Barker report: the dramatically uneven ratio between the high number of enemy dead and the low number of enemy weapons captured. Doubtless influenced by the growing charges of a massacre at the time he presided over the military campaign, he admitted that the report appeared "peculiar" but tried to explain the discrepancy. On any other occasion, he would have attributed the disproportionate numbers to poor reporting procedures, but, he said, by this time it had become commonplace in Vietnam to see such figures so far out of balance. The enemy very often hid their weapons when confronting a superior force. "The rearguard puts up a fight while the rest try to escape and when the fight is over there are a number of bodies and very few weapons," he testified. This happened numerous times around Quang Ngai. "We would think they [the Viet Cong] were destroyed and they would recover their cached weapons and come back again."[59]

By late March, division headquarters had heard more reports from provincial authorities that something horrific had happened at My Lai 4. In Chu Lai, Lieutenant Colonel Anistranski told Captain Keshel of the 11th Brigade, as Keshel later testified, "Task Force Barker is in big trouble, and in fact the entire 11th Infantry Brigade might be in big trouble." Quang Ngai officials were "up in the air about this" and had started an investigation "to get to the bottom of what ever happened in the Barker area." What happened? asked Keshel. "Don't you worry about it," Anistranski replied, according to Keshel. "It's being taken care of." Tapping a manila folder on his desk, he asserted, "I got it all in here."[60]

One can only speculate about what was in the folder. The village chief's atrocity claims? Lieutenant Tan's initial conclusion that the war crimes charges were VC propaganda? The Census Grievance Committee's report alleging a massacre by American soldiers?[61]

Keshel testified that he later asked Barker about this conversation and that Barker shot back, "Anistranski's nuts. He is nuts." There had been no civilian killings as far as he knew. That was not "the American way."[62]

In early April 1968, according to Henderson, Koster asked him to put his March 20 oral report in written form for the division files. Again to circumvent the army's regulations on reporting atrocities, he instructed Henderson not to treat the written version as a formal report. Koster later explained that in addition to Thompson's charges, he had learned of those made by villagers and now needed a written record of both issues.[63]

Henderson later maintained that he had been puzzled when Young notified him of Koster's request. "Does he want this opened again and an informal investigation conducted?" "No," replied Young. "This paper you sent up, this VC propaganda message, has tripped his memory here a little bit, and he just wants some backup in the files here if anything further should develop on the matter. So provide him with a written report."[64]

Henderson claimed that he quickly put together a preliminary three-to-five-page document based on his notes, that he hand-delivered it to the Americal Division between April 4 and 6, and that he briefly discussed it with Colonel Nels Parson, the chief of staff. Parson, Henderson remembered, expressed regret for the twenty civilian casualties but called them a "hazard of war." In his written account, Henderson asserted that he had summarized Thompson's allegations before dismissing them and offered some suggestions regarding the treatment of civilians in wartime. Before turning in his interim report, Henderson declared, he showed it to Barker and the brigade operations officer, Major Robert McKnight, and then, without remembering whether he logged it into the record of deposits, put a copy in the safe in the operations office. Young, Henderson claimed, told him a few days later that Koster was "satisfied" with the report and that "the incident was closed."[65]

IV

Within days, however, the massacre charges erupted yet again. On April 11, Lieutenant Tan sent a note to Quang Ngai's provincial chief, Lieutenant Colonel Khien, declaring that he had reversed his original stand on the atrocity charges made by the Viet Cong: U.S. soldiers, Tan now argued, had killed nearly five hundred villagers in My Lai 4 and My Khe 4. New information supporting a dual massacre had come from Son My's village chief and included a list (never found) of four hundred civilians killed. Tan had already submitted this report to ARVN superiors and MACV advisers in the office of Lieutenant Colonel Guinn, who was acting senior adviser in Quang Ngai Province.[66]

Henderson received a copy of Tan's letter in mid-April and forwarded it to Colonel Toan with a note saying how "very much disturbed" he was about its subject line: "Allied Forces Gathered People of My Lai Village for Killing." The village chief had revised his initial account of events in My Lai 4 to claim that in retaliation for a Viet Cong mine killing one American soldier and sniper fire wounding several others, U.S. forces had "assembled the people and shot and killed more than 400 people at Tu Cung [My Lai 4], and ninety more people in Co Luy [My Khe 4] hamlet of Son My Village." The allies, Tan now declared, had killed nearly five hundred civilians in "an act of insane violence."[67]

Henderson offered Toan a few American troops to help look into the matter, but Toan dismissed the accusations as Viet Cong propaganda. "There is no truth to this, absolutely no truth to this," Toan insisted. "But you are investigating?" Henderson testified that he had asked. "No. I've told [Lieutenant] Colonel Khien of the Quang Ngai Province to handle it." Henderson, accompanied by Guinn, soon met with Khien, who questioned the village chief's credibility after learning that he no longer lived in Son My and had relied on hearsay. Khien planned to orchestrate a counter-propaganda operation rather than open an investigation. Toan meanwhile referred the report to the Americal Division in early April 1968 and on April 14 asked Koster to investigate the charges—but expected no reply.[68]

Koster, however, responded to Toan's request, but not to him personally. Koster took advantage of the letter to switch positions again on the massacre issue. Tan's charges were detailed and based on numerous eyewitness accounts, making it impossible to dismiss their stories as Viet Cong propaganda. If an investigation upheld his accusations, Koster would be in the position of having approved and put into written form Henderson's oral conclusion that the Americans had not engaged in unnecessary killing. Koster now disputed both Young and Henderson's accounts regarding the preparation of a written report after instructing Henderson to investigate the Viet Cong's allegations of a massacre that Tan had supported in his letter of April 11—days *after* the so-called interim report.[69]

Henderson soon completed his second report for Koster and, after showing it to Barker and McKnight, delivered the package of materials to Colonel Parson in the Americal Division office on April 24. In an envelope labeled "Report of Investigation" and bearing his initials on the seal, he inserted a two-page typed letter and two new pieces of evidence: an unsigned "Statement" dated April 14, 1968, and seemingly from a Vietnamese source, and an English translation of a Viet Cong broadcast script titled "American Evil Appears." Henderson did not remember logging in his report, but he put a copy in another sealed envelope marked "for his eyes only" and placed it in a safe in the operations office of the 11th Infantry Brigade. He also left a file copy with Sergeant Robert Gerberding from Brigade Intelligence, who later told the Peers commission that he put it in his safe along with other classified documents. Henderson revealed his concern over the army regulations on reporting war crimes, when he later declared, "I prepared what I termed a report of investigation which I acknowledge loud and clear is *not* a report of investigation."[70]

In his new report, Henderson repeated some of the information contained in his oral report of March 20, explained the causes of American casualties, and presented new evidence he thought further dispelled the charge of mass killing. Enemy resistance, he claimed, did not stop until three in the afternoon when all its forces had pulled out of Son My Village. As stated in his earlier report, Americans killed 128 Viet Cong, but twenty noncombatants also died as collateral damage. Americans suffered thirteen casualties, including two killed in action and eleven wounded, ten by booby traps and the other one shot in the foot by small-arms fire. In a series of interviews Henderson claimed he conducted on March 16 or 17, Barker, Medina, Calhoun, and Michles all assured him that American soldiers had not killed civilians gathered in groups. Thus the charges of a massacre made by the Viet Cong and supported by Lieutenant Tan were unfounded. It would not have been possible for such large-scale killings to occur, Henderson insisted; within the first hour and a half of the assault, all civilians had evacuated the area.[71]

Henderson's conclusions rivaled the Barker report in the level of fabrication in an official document. The chief purpose of his initial investigation had been to test the validity of Thompson's allegations; in this second report he did not mention Thompson. According to testimony from Holladay, Parson invited him to read the document a few days later, and he immediately called it a cover-up. The chief of staff "sort of smiled at me," Holladay remembered, leaving "the impression that he agreed." The only reference to the Viet Cong accusations appeared in the enclosed piece of Viet Cong propaganda urging the ARVN to shoot Americans as payback for their atrocities. Nor was there documentation of either Henderson's findings or the interrogations central to his oral report. Henderson relied on the "Statement" in disproving the massacre charges. It showed that despite the accusations found in Lieutenant Tan's April 11 letter, he had changed his mind again on the atrocity charges. Tan "does not give the allegations any importance."[72]

Young later told Henderson he had read the report and recommended that Koster approve it. Henderson declared that soon after April 24, Young asserted that Koster sent him the written report with a note calling it a good piece of work.[73]

But how valid was Henderson's new evidence? Lieutenant Colonel Khien's files included a copy of the statement found in the report. Rather than coming from a Vietnamese source, however, it bore the signature of Captain Angel Rodriguez, a deputy senior adviser to Major David Gavin at Son Tinh District headquarters. While Gavin was out of the office, a letter had come from Lieutenant Colonel Guinn in the provincial office (doubtless at Koster's behest) asking that someone investigate the charges in Tan's April 11 letter and prepare an official reply. Rodriguez first talked with an intelligence adviser of Son Tinh district, Captain Clarence Dawkins, before taking the matter to Tan. "If I recall," Rodriguez told Hersh, Tan "didn't pay much attention to this, because of the fact that he said this was just plain propaganda."[74]

Thus the unidentified writer of the statement was Rodriguez, a finding confirmed by the Peers Inquiry when it secured the signed copy from Khien. Rodriguez alleged that Lieutenant Tan no longer attached any importance to the charges he made in his April 11 letter, because he was "not certain of the information received and he has to depend on the word of the village chief and other people living in the area." Furthermore, Tan had no troops at his disposal and did not want to risk lives checking out the story by returning to an area he thought in danger of imminent attack. Rodriguez testified in the Hébert Hearings that he had agreed with Tan. The lieutenant would have needed two or three battalions to enter that reputedly hot zone, and Rodriguez had only Popular Forces at his command who were not dependable—"platoons of fifteen or twenty civilians dressed as soldiers."[75]

According to Rodriguez's testimony, he sat side by side with Tan while typing the official American response to his letter of April 11. Rodriguez then sent the "Statement," dated April 14, to provincial headquarters. Nearly a week later, according to Rodriguez, he and Dawkins talked with Major Gavin about the charges, and all three agreed that they were VC propaganda. Yet according to Dawkins, the statement rested on Rodriguez's personal judgment of the village chief's charges, and not on Tan's conclusions. Rodriguez did not hide his sentiments: "I never actually figured that an American soldier, the way we are trained, would do something like this.... It never came into my mind."[76]

Lieutenant Tan maintained that he had not changed his position on the massacre charge, despite what Rodriguez claimed. More pressing matters had arisen, Tan later told members of the Peers panel then in Vietnam. "I didn't see it very high on my list of priorities. At that time I was really concerned about saving outposts and keeping the VC from coming in our front door." Rodriguez's assessment, Tan added, "undoubtedly came from the fact that [the allegation] was a low priority, and not that I did not believe it was a correct report." More likely, the statement was a calculated but clumsy effort by either Rodriguez or someone higher in authority to undermine Tan's April 11 letter accusing the Americans of atrocities.[77]

In the story of My Lai, Tan's April 11 letter has had an unusual odyssey, but it is not alone in creating the impression that a cover-up was already in full swing. He remembered seeing the letter before it went to U.S. advisers at Quang Ngai provincial headquarters. But neither Tan's April 11 letter nor the signed statement of April 14 was in the advisory files, raising suspicions that either someone had purged these items or they never existed. So many important files had disappeared that, according to the Peers Inquiry, there appeared to be "a conscious effort to deceive."[78]

And who deleted the signature from the statement enclosed in Henderson's April 24 report? This was no small matter: that document would have carried more weight in debunking Tan's April 11 letter had it appeared to be of Vietnamese origin—as Henderson had implied by attaching it to his report with no signature or identification of its source. In late November or early December of 1968, according to Master Sergeant Kenneth Camell of Brigade Intelligence, Henderson's file consisted of a large brown envelope containing a number of documents, including the statement *with* Rodriguez's signature; but after Camell reorganized the files in January 1969 and deposited the envelope in a secure file labeled "Quang Ngai," the signed copy of the statement and other documents were missing in April or May after a personnel officer took the file to make copies of Henderson's report. The following September Camell once more turned over the file after another request, and he never saw it again. It is unlikely that its disappearance was an accident. Lieutenant General Peers spoke for the commission in declaring that the statement containing Rodriguez's signature could have disappeared "only with malice aforethought."[79]

Confusion remains to this day over how Henderson acquired the statement, as Hersh has noted, but the Peers Inquiry offered a likely explanation of its origin. According to the commission's final report, "The surrounding circumstances and the testimony of various witnesses place Lieutenant Colonel Guinn squarely in the central position at Quang Ngai both in handling Tan's 11 April letter—of which he was an addressee—and in arranging for the preparation and subsequent distribution of Rodriguez's 14 April statement concerning Tan's letter." The Peers commission could go no farther in this investigation, because Guinn refused to testify.[80]

The maneuvering did not stop with Henderson's submission of his April 24 report. Less than two weeks later, according to Henderson's testimony, Young informed him that Koster had reversed his earlier position and wanted either Young or Parson to conduct a "formal investigation and report"— which for the first time meant an adherence to army Regulation 15-6. Koster now expressed dissatisfaction with Henderson's April 24 report for dealing only with propaganda claims and failing to mention the original investigation's findings relating to Thompson's charges. But he was more likely concerned that if the atrocity charges proved true, he would have violated army regulations in not calling for an official investigation. Henderson claimed that Young had told him to launch another inquiry and "tacitly approved Barker as the investigating officer." Barker, Henderson insisted, was the "logical individual."[81]

Again, this created a conflict of interests—the accused investigating his own actions. Henderson offered an explanation to the Peers panel. "At no point at this time had I been led to believe or had any information, nor do I know at this date, that [Lieutenant] Colonel Barker was personally involved in this." Even though it was Barker's unit under investigation in his second report, Henderson insisted that the thought of a conflict of interest "did not enter my mind." Young approved the selection. Henderson told Barker that Koster had "wanted a formal investigation and that he was to take statements from anybody and everybody who was directly or indirectly related to this incident," and he "wanted the statements taken in adequate detail to prove or disprove that anything had taken place."[82]

Henderson assigned "top priority" to Barker's new report and in about a week received and endorsed the document before submitting it to Parson on either May 15 or 16. Henderson and Koster attested that the "Report of Investigation" consisted of three or four pages of summary accompanied by about twenty sworn statements from witnesses—pilots, soldiers, and all three company commanders. Henderson did not specifically remember statements from either Thompson or Calley, but he recalled ones from enlisted personnel within both Charlie and Bravo companies along with those in the battalion's Tactical Operations Center. Henderson's new conclusion was almost identical with that in his April 24 report: "There was no evidence to support that any soldiers had willfully or negligently wounded or killed civilians during this operation."[83]

Koster confirmed that Henderson delivered a second report to division headquarters that included statements from Barker and Medina. Essentially, it included all the information that had been gathered, formally and informally, after the killings. Based on Henderson's findings along with his personal interviews with Vietnamese authorities—Colonel Toan, Lieutenant Colonel Khien, and, he thought, Lieutenant General Lam—Koster concluded there was not enough evidence to prove wrongdoing by American soldiers. Furthermore, he explained, this was not a war crime, which meant, he maintained, that MACV Directive 20-4 did not apply and the matter remained at the division level.[84]

Problems immediately arose, however, over the mid-May report, just as they had over the earlier reports. Only Koster and Henderson claimed that the May report had existed; neither Young nor Parson had any recollection of it. Not one of those Americans questioned about their signed statements could remember giving such a statement. And no other brigade and division staff officers knew of the report, including those who would handle the documents—the inspector general and the judge advocate general, along with their officers and clerks. The S-2 in charge of military intelligence in the 11th Brigade allegedly received a copy of the report, but no one could find the original, nor could anyone confirm that Koster received it. In mid-June, Barker died in a helicopter crash, taking his story with him. When asked about Henderson's report of May 1968, Koster suddenly switched positions again and now declared, "I do not recall a written report."[85]

Henderson remained adamant about this report in his testimony, asserting, "If I had an opportunity to line up my brigade staff at this point or in the near future, I'm sure I could get the truth of this one out in a hurry. I don't think these boys would eyeball me and deny that such a report was prepared.

I can't think now who would have been involved or even on the fringes of this thing, but I know there must be somebody in my brigade headquarters aware that this formal investigation was going on and that [Lieutenant] Colonel Barker was conducting it, and either saw it, typed it, read it, or dispatched it."[86]

Henderson told the Peers commission that he could not understand why neither the early April report nor the May report was in the file. "I know there was no effort on my part to cover up any phase of this thing."[87]

Yet the central issue was not the location of these documents; rather, it was whether Henderson had violated army regulations in failing to report actual or suspected war crimes. He claimed he had never seen the MACV regulations regarding reporting and investigating wartime atrocities, but he admitted, "This does not negate my responsibilities as a commander for having knowledge of any atrocities committed." Henderson as investigating officer could not escape the strict wording of MACV Directive 20-4 of April 1967 and recently underlined in a MACV message for general distribution in February 1968: anyone knowing or hearing of a war crime—"known, suspected or alleged"—was to report this to his commanding officer.[88]

For this failure to act, Henderson appeared culpable.

A CONSPIRACY INVOLVING many people seems certain, and yet no one has uncovered proof of its existence. Over the fifty years since My Lai happened, serious questions remain. How could there have been collusion among so many participants without the truth leaking out? Who could have masterminded such a gigantic, far-reaching, and detailed cover-up that stretched from the division level down to the soldier? Where is the paper trail? Where are the eyewitnesses?

If there is an explanation, it is one that would not stand up in court, where the laws of evidence apply. And it runs as follows.

The cover-up began with Koster's countermanding the order for a body recount on March 16 and became a conspiracy when he met with Young on the following day and directed him to gather information by an informal investigation. Although these actions appear to fit the fundamental definition of a conspiracy—two or more persons secretly agreeing to commit an illegal act—this allegation is virtually impossible to prove, primarily because they never put anything on paper, or, if they did, that paper had disappeared. Koster had carefully skirted the army regulations calling for an official investigation into either a suspected or actual act of atrocity by directing an informal inquiry into accusations that Young had argued were, in fact, *not* war crimes: the confrontation between two groups of American servicemen and whether his soldiers had used excessive firepower during the assault. It was an act of misdirection, of investigating the lesser crime, though one that would have captured the attention of everyone concerned. Mutiny was far more interesting than murder.

Under the pretense of investigating the Thompson accusation, Koster and his five other officers fostered a cover-up of atrocities fueled by the specter of failed careers or, worse, convictions for murder, and needed no organized conspiracy to work. Most of those involved in the massacres, whether actively or passively, refused to talk about that day in an effort to protect themselves.

All this was not thought out, and arguably a cover-up is not the same as a conspiracy. If a well-thought-out plan had existed, there would have been no glaring contradictions between those original Barker and Henderson reports. Without such a plan, nearly every deceptive move was an independent knee-jerk reaction to each bit of news supporting the massacre charges. Thus the attempt was inherently flawed from beginning to end, based upon unspoken codes of silence and presumptions of innocence. In that respect it was, perhaps, an apt reflection of the war itself—messy, uncoordinated, and inherently self-deceiving. By March 1968 the war in Vietnam was going badly, and nobody wanted further proof of just how badly.

Eight

WHAT HAPPENED AT MY LAI 4 AND MY KHE 4 might have officially remained hidden had helicopter gunner Ronald Ridenhour from the 11th Light Infantry Brigade not run into an acquaintance from training days in Hawaii—PFC Charles "Butch" Gruver from Charlie Company. In late April, Ridenhour and Gruver had a catch-up conversation over beers in Chu Lai.

I

During the Peers Inquiry, Ridenhour described the scene for investigators.

Only a few moments into their chat, Ridenhour recalled, Gruver set down his beer and looked at him. "Wow! Did you hear what we did at Pinkville?"

Ridenhour professed he had not.

"We just went in there and killed all those civilians. Killed everybody in the village."

"Killed everybody! What do you mean?"

"We just shot 'em. Lined 'em up and shot 'em down. Three, four, five hundred people —I don't know how many."

Ridenhour testified that what Gruver said had stunned him. At twenty-two years old, Ridenhour had already become disenchanted with the war, he declared, particularly after a commander boasted about "killing dinks" in Vietnam. And he had seen fellow soldiers shoot noncombatants. But never had he heard of anything of this scope. Ridenhour was skeptical of a massacre—especially by American troops. Perhaps he was aware of Gruver's questionable reputation in the army—known by his squad leader as "immature" and "a misfit, a wild kid" who ignored orders and had spent time in Long Binh jail—the army's detention center—for marijuana possession, stealing a truck, and desertion. Yet he knew Gruver had been on the scene as part of Charlie Company's 3rd Platoon.[1]

Ridenhour barraged Gruver with questions, drawing a detailed and consistent description of what he and fellow soldiers had seen and done in Pinkville. Gruver asserted that Captain Medina's radio telephone operator (RTO) had spotted a young boy in shock standing by the trail and holding his arm as blood from a gunshot wound ran down his fingers. The RTO raised his M-16 and "blew him away." Another soldier had shot himself in the foot to avoid the orders to kill everyone. Gruver heard from "trustworthy"— Ridenhour's term—people that they had seen Lieutenant Calley round up several groups of civilians and machine-gun them. Nearly four hundred villagers had been killed. Gruver admitted to firing a few rounds at people running but insisted he did nothing more. Ridenhour repeatedly asked whether he was certain they had killed everyone. Each time, according to Ridenhour, Gruver replied with an emphatic yes—men, women, and children.[2]

Gruver also told Ridenhour that rape was common and that the officers said nothing as long as it did not take place in front of them. Gruver admitted to committing rape more than once. Indeed, Ridenhour observed, Gruver "almost boasted about it—if he got horny, he wanted a little, he just picked out a likely little girl in the village and raped her." His "attitude," Ridenhour declared, exemplified the "general feeling" of his company.[3]

Ridenhour instantly realized that his knowing about these revelations made *him* part of the story. "These no-good sons-of-bitches," he told himself in anger. "Look what they've gotten me into. Look at what they've gotten us all into." He had to expose what had happened "and let the chips fall where they land."[4]

Gruver had confessed to the wrong person. Years later Ridenhour became an investigative reporter in New Orleans and received the prestigious Polk Award for exposing graft in that city's government. But, he said, no story touched him as deeply as the one Gruver had told him. Ridenhour remembered that during his time as a door gunner on a small helicopter, he had passed over that site a few days after the combat assault and saw evidence supporting Gruver's charges—most hauntingly, a nude woman lying face up with an 11th Brigade patch across her crotch. His conscience might have compelled him to reveal what Gruver told him had happened in that village, but fear of retribution from the men led him to wait until he had left the service.[5]

In late April, Ridenhour transferred to a different assignment and met up with several soldiers who had been with Charlie Company on the day of the massacre. When he joined E Company, 51st Infantry, Long Range Reconnaissance Patrol (LRRP) at Chu Lai on May 1, he soon learned that Gruver was in that company as well, along with others from Charlie Company, including Michael Terry, William Doherty, Henry Pedrick, and Gary Garfolo. From them he learned details that substantiated Gruver's claims.[6]

Ridenhour recalled that he talked first with Terry, who, like Gruver, had been part of the 3rd Platoon in Pinkville. Ridenhour considered Terry "an old friend" since basic training and a course in leadership they both took at Fort Bliss in Texas. Together, they had gone through advanced infantry training at Fort Ord in California, jump school at Fort Benning in Georgia, and jungle warfare training at Schofield Barracks in Hawaii. Terry then spent four months in the 3rd Platoon before transferring to LRRP. Ridenhour and Terry stayed in touch after separate assignments. Terry was a "strict Mormon" and "like a brother to me," Ridenhour declared.[7]

One night while on an LRRP mission, Terry opened up to Ridenhour about Pinkville. Around noon on March 16, 1968, he recounted, the company took a lunch break, and he and Doherty sat down near a ditch filled with dead or dying civilians. The "wounded groaned and their arms flopped and they kicked," Ridenhour remembered Terry telling him, and after a while he and Doherty put their food down, picked up their M-16s, and walked toward them. Nearly two dozen Vietnamese were still alive but critically wounded and would get no medical care, Terry declared. "I guess we sort of finished them off." After a long silence in the darkness, Ridenhour told the Peers panel that he had whispered, "Mike, Mike. Didn't you know that was wrong?" "I dunno man," Terry replied. It was, in his words as reported by Ridenhour, "this Nazi kind of thing."[8]

Ridenhour realized that Gruver had told him the truth: A massacre had occurred in Pinkville. Terry—strict Mormon that he was—would never fabricate such a tale. Further confirmation of a mass murder came from brief exchanges with three others in the village on that day. "That's what happened, that's what we did," Doherty remarked, according to Ridenhour. "Yeah, it was terrible," Pedrick added. They wiped out a village and everyone in it, Garfolo declared.[9]

In late June 1968, Ridenhour talked with 2nd Platoon Sergeant Lawrence LaCroix in Chu Lai, who confirmed Lieutenant Calley's role in the massacre. LaCroix saw soldiers from Calley's 1st Platoon drag men, women, and children out of bunkers and hooches and assemble them on a trail in three groups of twenty, thirty, or forty people before killing them. LaCroix then mistakenly identified Sergeant Esequiel Torres rather than PFC Paul Meadlo as the soldier whom Calley ordered to machine-gun the first group and who had refused to do it. "It was terrible," LaCroix declared. "They were slaughtering the villagers like so many sheep."[10]

In mid-November, Ridenhour talked with PFC Michael Bernhardt, who was in Chu Lai and who, having been in Vietnam for a year, would soon be eligible to go home. Bernhardt had accompanied the command group and, according to Ridenhour's testimony, told the same story as the others, including the rape claims made by Gruver. Ridenhour testified that Bernhardt had maintained that he had refused to take part in the killings and thought it "rather strange" that the company's officers had made no issue out of his refusal. Someone should do something about what had happened, he declared. Ridenhour said that Bernhardt jokingly proposed that they meet back in the United States and eliminate all those responsible for this tragedy.[11]

At Ridenhour's urging, Bernhardt agreed to tell his story to investigators but expected a whitewash. Medina, as we have seen, had warned him not to write his congressman about that day and even sent him away from the base on detail duty so he could not talk to investigators. "I was a little paranoid," Bernhardt admitted, according to Ridenhour. "I had to go out on patrols with these people. I was just keeping my mouth shut and my ears open."[12]

Those soldiers Ridenhour talked with about Pinkville insisted they had acted under orders from higher authority than Medina and that he had implemented those orders. Neither Bernhardt nor Terry heard Medina declare at the briefing to kill everyone, but they did hear him say, "Destroy the village and everything in it." Some of his language was ambiguous and perhaps carried a "double meaning," Ridenhour speculated—which was especially volatile during a "pep talk" challenging them to avenge the recent deaths of fellow soldiers by mines and booby traps. He found it "difficult to see how it could be interpreted differently or how a man could expect it to be interpreted differently."[13]

Ridenhour testified that he wrestled with two questions: How could American soldiers have committed such a crime? And how could their officers have allowed the mass murders to take place—and even participated in them?

Terry was "exactly right," Ridenhour concluded. "It was this Nazi kind of thing, and we didn't go there to be Nazis. At least none of the people I knew went there to be Nazis. I didn't go there to be a Nazi."[14]

On March 29, 1969, more than a year after My Lai, Ridenhour sent a five-page registered letter to thirty military, administrative, and congressional leaders, in which he revealed what he thought had happened in Pinkville, as told to him by Gruver and four other participants. Late in April 1968, Ridenhour explained in his letter, he had heard about something horrific that had occurred the previous month in Pinkville and that U.S. Army officers had ordered this "act of barbarism." In the months that followed, he continued, he heard the same story from a range of people and became convinced that "something rather dark and bloody" had taken place. Michael Terry and William Doherty had been there during the massacre and corroborated a story about mass murders that he had first heard from PFC Charles Gruver, including an RTO using his M-16 to kill a wounded boy no more than four years old who "just stood there with big eyes staring around like he didn't understand." Terry and Doherty, according to Ridenhour's letter, believed that Medina had opposed killing everyone in the village but had to follow orders from above.[15]

Not until he had talked with Sergeant Lawrence LaCroix did he become convinced that the vague suspicions of atrocities were valid. Ridenhour wrote that LaCroix had witnessed Calley order and take part in the slaughter of at least ninety men, women, and children of all ages. Further support for these allegations, he wrote, came from PFC Michael Bernhardt, who had refused to take part in the massacre and did not see Calley participate in the killings. But Bernhardt, like Terry and Doherty, saw many bodies and thought the company officers had followed orders from their commanders to kill everyone in Pinkville.[16]

In his letter, Ridenhour called for Congress to launch "a widespread and public investigation" of these claims and to implement "constructive actions." He appealed to his recipients' patriotism by quoting former British prime minister Winston Churchill: "A country without a conscience is a country without a soul, and a country without a soul is a country that cannot survive." President Richard Nixon—who had replaced Lyndon Johnson in January 1969—Secretary of State William Rogers, and the chair of the Joint Chiefs of Staff, General Earl Wheeler, each received a letter. Other copies went to select members of Congress, including Senators Everett Dirksen of Illinois, J. William Fulbright of Arkansas, Edward Kennedy of Massachusetts, Eugene McCarthy of Minnesota, George McGovern of South Dakota, and Barry Goldwater from Ridenhour's home state of Arizona, along with Morris Udall, an Arizona congressman.

The first response came two days after the mailing, when Udall, an outspoken opponent of the war, asked Ridenhour for a list of weaknesses in the army's investigation of the My Lai incident that he could send to his colleagues on the House Armed Services Committee. Udall intended to press its chair, Democratic representative L. Mendel Rivers of South Carolina, to conduct a separate investigation.[17]

Ridenhour's letter could not have been a big surprise to the Pentagon. Just four months earlier the army had confronted another series of atrocity accusations that it could not pass off as merely Viet Cong propaganda. In late November 1968, a young mortar man from the 11th Brigade, Tom Glen, had sent a long letter to General Creighton Abrams, recently appointed as General William Westmoreland's successor as commander of MACV, expressing great concern over what appeared to be a pattern of sadistic and inhumane behavior by U.S. troops. How can we win popular support, Glen wrote, when American soldiers "apparently for mere pleasure, fire indiscriminately into Vietnamese homes and without provocation or justification shoot at the people themselves?"[18]

Major Colin Powell, a young officer in the Americal Division, received orders to investigate Glen's charges and forward his findings to the adjutant general. Powell appeared to follow a scripted procedure in handling the case, one that an experienced military intelligence officer noted had permeated throughout the military establishment in Vietnam: ignore, deny, or call whatever had happened a "field expedient" and, if necessary, exonerate the army by finding a scapegoat. Powell did not talk with Glen and instead interviewed only the officers in his unit along with the battalion commander, who termed him a "rearguard type" of soldier and in no position to see the alleged capture and torturing of prisoners.

Powell found no evidence substantiating Glen's accusations. "In direct refutation of this portrayal," he wrote in his report, "is the fact that relations between Americal soldiers and the Vietnamese people are excellent." The army dismissed Glen's complaint.[19]

Ridenhour's efforts to convince the army to investigate what happened in Pinkville would therefore have to be extraordinary. And they were.

His letter mentioned names of eyewitnesses and specific details rather than generalized complaints about the behavior of American soldiers. On April 12, Colonel John Hill in the chief of staff's office, now headed by General Westmoreland, privately assured Ridenhour that an inquiry was already underway. The House Armed Services Committee had meanwhile drafted a response for its chair, L. Mendel Rivers, to sign, calling on the army to investigate the charges. Secretary of Defense Melvin Laird likewise sent the army a copy of the letter, meaning that by early April the Department of the Army had received more than a half dozen copies.[20]

The investigation referred to by Hill had originated from Westmoreland's order. Ridenhour's letter, Westmoreland later declared in the Hébert Hearings, had left him in a state of "disbelief." The accusations were "so out of character for American forces in Vietnam that I was quite skeptical." Westmoreland denied having any suspicions about the high number of enemy casualties in relation to the small number of arms captured. During the Tet Offensive, he explained, the Viet Cong stretched their resources so thin that many of their forces were armed only with explosives and grenades rather than guns. In addition, they took any measure necessary to hold on to their weapons, even throwing them into the canals or rice paddies for later recovery. Westmoreland nonetheless ordered an investigation—the importance of which he emphasized by using a back-channel communication network operating under the auspices of the National Security Agency.[21] Everyone knew instantly that such allegations, if proved true, would have a major impact on America's involvement in Vietnam. By early 1969, America, having gone through a brutal presidential election year marked by assassinations and urban riots, was now deeply divided over the war in Vietnam. According to polls taken in late January, the majority of Americans continued the previous year's trend of opposing the war and mistrusting the official reports of military success. Ridenhour's accusations could be devastating, at a moment when the scales were tilting heavily toward getting out of Vietnam. The public did not know this, of course, but the new president was attempting to begin secret peace negotiations with the North Vietnamese government; the exposure of a massacre at My Lai could undermine this effort.[22]

In ten days the investigatory team reported that it had found nothing supporting Ridenhour's charges. Colonel Howard Whitaker, the deputy inspector general in U.S. Army headquarters at Long Binh, had reviewed the records at Chu Lai and on April 17 reported no evidence of either an atrocity or an inquiry into such an allegation. Neither the daily journals, Barker's Combat Action Report nor any other files suggested mass killings of civilians or mentioned "a 2LT Kally" referred to in Ridenhour's letter.

Colonel Whitaker insisted that an atrocity would have required a conspiracy so immense that it could not have escaped notice somewhere along the command chain. "An examination of all available documents concerning the alleged incident reveals that the complainant has grossly exaggerated the military action in question." To be certain, however, Whitaker recommended an interrogation of every person mentioned in Ridenhour's letter who made the allegations.[23]

Westmoreland agreed with Whitaker's recommendation—which meant a full investigation by the inspector general's office of the army in Washington.[24]

II

Colonel William Wilson was a former Special Forces officer who had recently (and unhappily) taken a desk job in the inspector general's office in Washington shortly before Ridenhour's letter arrived one morning in late March 1969. He read it four times, he recalled in later testimony, in "shocked disbelief and disgust." Particularly appalling, he thought, was the killing of the young boy. Wilson was a decorated World War II veteran who had been part of the Normandy invasion and had seen numerous civilians accidentally killed in combat. But never had he heard of anything comparable to the alleged Pinkville atrocities. He remembered that he had tried to convince himself the charges were unfounded. But if substantiated, he also told himself, that would establish what happened there as "cold-blooded murder."[25]

Wilson phoned the inspector general, Major General William Enemark, asking to see him immediately. At their meeting later that morning, according to Wilson's article in *American Heritage* magazine, the major general expressed concern about this portrait of the nation's soldiers and noted that Westmoreland and numerous congressional members demanded a full investigation. Wilson asked to head the inquiry, citing his wartime experience. Enemark granted the assignment, urging quick action before the story leaked to the public but also cautioning Wilson to remember that the charges rested on hearsay. Wilson's objective was to determine the facts, not to conduct a criminal investigation. To ensure an accurate and complete record, a veteran court reporter, Albert "Smitty" Smith, would take down sworn testimony verbatim.[26]

Wilson thought this "a particularly tricky case," as he later termed it, in which pre-interrogation warnings of legal rights did not seem advisable. If he warned a witness of liability for anything he said, it would undermine the fact-finding mission. Wilson discussed this matter with the division chief and Colonel Clement Carney, the JAG (judge advocate general) lawyer assigned to the inspector general's office. They agreed that he should not issue such warnings.[27]

The critical information in Ridenhour's letter involved the five soldiers he had interviewed before writing the letter. Wilson knew that he must first talk with Ridenhour, who now lived in Phoenix. He later admitted that he had hoped Ridenhour "would turn out to be crazy." Instead, at their meeting in a downtown Phoenix hotel on April 29, Wilson found him "extremely impressive" and his allegations "depressingly convincing." Ridenhour informed him that Charles Gruver and Michael Terry were now private citizens, the former living in Oklahoma City and the latter in Orem, Utah, and that the other three were still in the army—William Doherty at Fort Hood, Texas; Michael Bernhardt at Fort Dix, New Jersey; and Lawrence LaCroix at Fort Carson, Colorado. As an investigator from the army's inspector general's office, Wilson could order those in the military to appear, but he could not compel those out of the service to testify. To encourage cooperation from everyone, he decided to tell them that Westmoreland had ordered the inquiry. Wilson also decided to conduct the sessions while wearing his uniform bearing the combat infantry badge and the Purple Heart resulting from his wounds at Normandy. No one turned down his request to testify.[28]

The following morning Wilson and Smith left Phoenix for Utah to begin the interview process with Terry on May 1. At their meeting with Terry, he admitted to his part in the massacre but alleged that he had engaged only in mercy killings. This was, Wilson thought, "an ugly incident and grievous error," but he believed Terry's claim to have acted only to relieve the wounded Vietnamese of their misery.[29]

The following day in Colorado, Wilson interviewed LaCroix, who attested to Ridenhour's accuracy on some matters but not on others—most notably Lieutenant Calley's actions. LaCroix had told Ridenhour of watching Calley order his men to machine-gun three separate groups of close to one hundred men, women, and children.[30]

LaCroix, however, undermined his own testimony. In all three of his separate statements (Ridenhour's letter, Wilson's article, and the official transcript), he asserted that Calley had ordered his men to round up the groups of men, women, and children and move them to the easternmost side of the village. Yet whereas Ridenhour had declared (and Wilson concurred in his article) that LaCroix stated that he had witnessed "Kally" "gunning down ... at least three separate groups of villagers," Wilson's transcript reveals that LaCroix could not be sure about Calley's role in the killings.[31]

"You don't know who it was?"

"No, sir," he answered, explaining to Wilson that Calley "was not his platoon leader" and he was "nowhere near him."

"Did LT Kallai [sic] machine-gun these civilians?"

"Not to my knowledge, sir."[32]

LaCroix had now taken back his claim made to Ridenhour that a massacre had occurred. He told Wilson that the men had "no choice" in the first part of the operation "but to kill most of the people we found." LaCroix further insisted that the villagers were "extremely hostile" and "fought back" by "diving into tunnels, trying to get away, picking up grenades, ammo cans, and weapons." In the mayhem, according to LaCroix, he had shot three Vietnamese civilians: a thirteen-year-old boy holding a grenade, and two men, one running away and the other armed with a pick or shovel who joined others in "running toward my flank." About 150 people died in the village, and others disappeared into the tunnels, but "all 150 were VC"—perhaps forty of them armed and the rest "strong VC believers."[33]

Yet LaCroix added something that Wilson said caught his attention: Someone in a helicopter shouted over the radio, "From up here it looks like a blood bath. What the hell are you doing down there?" If this did not stop, warned the pilot, he would go get the division commander and bring him to the site. "I imagine from the air," LaCroix conceded, "it did look like a blood bath at that time—people running around crazy, running all over the place, and every few minutes machine guns were opening up." Wilson wrote that when he had asked, "Did you consider this a blood bath?" LaCroix admitted, "In some ways it was, yes, I mean, we weren't having that much return fire and most of the people we shot didn't have an actual weapon with them." In short, it was not a bloodbath because the Vietnamese civilians "were still offering resistance either in the form of trying to help other VC" with grenades and ammunition or "throwing grenades" at the soldiers. LaCroix could not identify the pilot, but Wilson realized that locating him could help determine whether a massacre had occurred.[34]

LaCroix's self-serving account did not persuade Wilson, who knew from others that American soldiers had met no major civilian opposition in assaulting the village and that their capture of such a small number of weapons meant that the so-called civilian supporters of the Viet Cong could not have been armed. Sensing this, during the course of the meeting, LaCroix admitted that he and others had unnecessarily killed a few civilians, but he then introduced a new element intended to minimize even that misstep—that the half dozen ARVN forces accompanying the Americans had engaged in "quite a bit of unnecessary killing." In fact, of course, no ARVN soldiers were in the village. LaCroix further claimed that the Americans had provided a great amount of medical help to the Vietnamese. Yet several accounts belie this assertion. Wilson did not follow up on these claims; his task was to determine facts, not to dispute testimony. He relied instead on LaCroix's initial allegations made to Ridenhour.[35]

The next two interviews appeared at first to substantiate Ridenhour's charges. The day after LaCroix's testimony, Wilson went to Oklahoma City to interview Charles Gruver, who affirmed the story of the young boy's murder while emphasizing that he trusted the people who made the charges against Lieutenant Calley, even if they were based on hearsay. Four days later, on May 5, Wilson interviewed William Doherty at Fort Hood, though first informing him he was under suspicion of committing a war crime—"wrongful destruction of a village and murder of Vietnamese civilians"—and then advising him he could exercise his right to counsel at any time during the proceedings. "Unless it sounds like it is going to commit me to something," Doherty declared, according to Wilson, "I will answer your questions, sir."[36]

Doherty explained that their squad leader had declared the area "completely NVA" and that the troops were under orders to "kill everything." However, he added, "a lot of the people I don't think should have been killed." In one instance, a young Vietnamese boy jumped up from "a pile of people" and ran until someone yelled that he had a gun and three or four soldiers shot him. Doherty noted, according to Wilson, that he was part of the 3rd Platoon, which entered the village last, when combat had already come to a close. "We didn't get shot at that much." Doherty never saw Lieutenant Calley but overheard others say his 1st Platoon had machine-gunned many men, women, and children gathered in groups. Doherty declared that he had been with Michael Terry most of the way through the village. "Did he fire on wounded civilians?" asked Wilson. Doherty deferred answering, not wanting to "get him involved." Asked if he knew who did the killing, Doherty replied, "No, sir."[37]

Three days later, Wilson talked with Michael Bernhardt in Washington. Bernhardt confirmed the massacre by calling the deaths "point-blank murder" and saying he "was standing there watching it." When entering My Lai 4, Bernhardt told Wilson, he had been with the command group behind the 3rd Platoon, and they saw "a lot of dead civilians, apparently civilians—women, children, old men, some of the children apparently not old enough to walk yet, who were dead, in very large heaps in areas." He looked ahead and saw that "our American forces were gathering Vietnamese villagers in a large group and making a circle around them and killing all the people." When he estimated more than one hundred victims, Wilson exclaimed, "You saw what?" "Over 100 dead people," Bernhardt replied. "Very few that I saw were men of military age. I believe that the company encountered very little resistance." They killed more than one hundred civilians "for apparently no reason."[38]

Bernhardt declared to Wilson that the order had gone out the night before the operation to destroy the village as "a supply point and a hideout" for the Viet Cong. In My Lai 4, "the people were killed, most of them, practically all of them, I believe all of them. I didn't see anybody alive. The houses were burned, trampled. The livestock was all killed." He acknowledged that stories had circulated of Calley's machine-gunning Vietnamese civilians, but Bernhardt never saw him do it. "I believe the whole company was involved in this."[39]

To learn the full story, Wilson expanded his interviews to include Captain Medina, who was then enrolled in Fort Benning's Infantry Advanced Officers

School. Realizing by this point that he was under suspicion of war crimes—wrongful destruction of the village and the murder of Vietnamese civilians—Medina secured a JAG attorney before consenting to an interview, which lasted almost five hours.[40]

During the course of it, Medina vehemently denied the charge of massacre. He insisted that Lieutenant Colonel Barker had approved the burning of My Lai 4, and he admitted to seeing "a group" of bodies from a distance but attributed some of their deaths to artillery fire. When asked whether any bodies were piled up near where the soldiers had eaten their lunch that day, Medina responded, "No, sir, I did not see any piles of bodies where we ate chow, sir." "Did you order the destruction of the inhabitants?" "No, sir, I did not. That is, if there was any, sir, I did not." He noted that Colonel Henderson had conducted an investigation and "rendered his report" showing no mass murders. Medina emphasized that Henderson had found him justified in shooting a young woman he had thought was about to throw a grenade at him.[41]

Piqued by the existence of an investigation and the possibility of picking up a paper trail, Wilson asked Medina whether Colonel Henderson had submitted a written report. Medina did not know, but he did say Henderson had been "conducting the investigation at the direction of the division commander."[42]

Wilson must have wondered why the division command had not reported the possibility of war crimes. If so, he said nothing at the time.

Medina then made a number of claims to defend himself against the atrocity allegations. He maintained that he had not seen Lieutenant Calley until after they had swept the village and were on its eastern side, failing to mention their repeated contacts by radio. Medina had not heard that Calley had rounded up civilians and machine-gunned them. He also denied seeing his RTO, SP4 Fred Widmer, shoot a Vietnamese boy and, as proof, declared, "He would have been with me" throughout the village. "By gosh, I would sleep next to him." Widmer later assured Wilson that he had not carried a radio in this operation because he had just gotten out of the hospital. He had entered the village with the demolition man assigned to the unit—not with Medina and the command group.[43]

Despite his misgivings, Wilson saw no evidence of Medina's complicity in a massacre and even years later described him as "a pretty sharp officer" and "very far from a monster."[44]

Instead, he focused on Medina's remark that Henderson's investigation had come at Major General Koster's behest. Had the divisional commander ordered an inquiry into these charges without filing a report in the inspector general's office? Wilson arranged for that office to summon both the operations officer, Major Charles Calhoun, and Colonel Henderson, for questioning in Washington.[45]

On May 19, Calhoun asserted to Wilson that he had never heard anything about atrocities and had witnessed no unnecessary killing of civilians. Headquarters, he explained, had received a complaint from a helicopter pilot hovering above the battle scene that ground troops were shooting civilians and Lieutenant Colonel Barker ordered Calhoun to fly to the site and check out this claim. He had found nothing to suggest purposeful killing of non-combatants. Calhoun affirmed an investigation led by Henderson at the direction of division headquarters but knew nothing about a written report. Calhoun admitted to Wilson that he had heard "through the grapevine" that a helicopter pilot had seen soldiers killing civilians unnecessarily, but he remained confident that the men would not intentionally harm civilians.[46]

By this point, Wilson had learned that the helicopter pilot referred to by LaCroix and others was Warrant Officer Hugh Thompson and that he was now a first lieutenant and assigned to Fort Rucker in Alabama. The army ordered him to Washington for an interview in June.

In the meantime, a week after Calhoun's testimony, Wilson met with Colonel Henderson, who emphatically denied both the existence of a massacre and Thompson's alleged machine-gun confrontation with American ground troops. Thompson, Henderson declared, had come to him "in tears," accusing U.S. soldiers of acting "like a bunch of wild men" who "were wildly shooting" elderly men and women and children "throughout My Lai." Henderson repeated what he had told Thompson at the time—that American troops had killed 128 Viet Cong, while another twenty civilians had been killed accidentally. He also denied hearing of mass civilian killings and produced an unsigned carbon copy of his April investigation, one that he at least considered thorough. Koster, Henderson declared, had asked him to conduct an "informal investigation" of the number of enemy killed and to determine whether that figure included civilians. He told Wilson that he had put a copy of the report in the brigade's office safe but failed to file a written report in the inspector general's office. It was not a "formal investigation where anybody was being charged with anything," he declared. The atrocity charges had come from propaganda and from the "young warrant officer"—Thompson—who was "new and inexperienced."[47]

III

During the course of Wilson's inquiries, the army had identified the "Kalli" (a third variant of Calley's name) accused of murder in Ridenhour's letter as

Lieutenant William Calley and ordered his return to Washington from Vietnam. He was to report to the inspector general's office for an interview with Colonel Norman Stanfield on June 9, 1969, less than three months before his scheduled discharge from the army on September 6.[48]

The timing was important, because if the army wished to charge Calley with murder, a Supreme Court ruling made it imperative to do so before his discharge. In the *United States ex rel. Toth v. Quarles* case (1955), the court had ruled that the military had no jurisdiction over civilians who had committed a crime while in the service. The defendant in this case, Robert Toth, had been in the air force when he allegedly murdered a Korean national. Although honorably discharged, he was arrested by air force police five months later at his home in Pittsburgh and flown back to Korea for a court martial.

In Justice Hugo Black's majority opinion, the court found that the secretary of the air force, Donald Quarles, had acted unconstitutionally in implementing Article 3(a) of the Uniform Code of Military Justice Act of 1950 to put a former serviceman on military trial for a crime committed while in uniform. Article 3 of the U.S. Constitution blocked "encroaches on the jurisdiction of federal courts" and thereby guaranteed the right of every citizen to a jury trial. Yet no American civil court had the power to try someone for crimes committed in a foreign country. Toth could therefore not stand trial in either the military or civilian courts. Black urged Congress to rectify this situation by considering the recommendation of the army's judge advocate general to enact legislation giving the federal courts the power to try these types of crimes. JAG took no action.[49]

No evidence has been found to suggest that William Calley was ever aware of either the crimes he may have committed or the legal arguments relating to them. He would never stand trial once out of the army.

Soon after March 16, 1968, Calley received a promotion to first lieutenant. Not long after that he had gotten into a long series of scrapes with one of his sergeants, Isaiah Cowan. Medina had decided to make a choice between them. He transferred Calley to the weapons platoon.[50]

According to Sack's book, three months after the My Lai 4 assault, Calley asked his commanding colonel for a transfer from field duties to an S-5 position in civil affairs, one that entailed helping the Vietnamese implement social and economic reforms. His intention, he explained, was to "win over their hearts and minds." The colonel was taken aback. "I'm tired of killing them," Calley told his commander. He had moved from search-and-destroy to locate-and-heal, hoping to provide the Vietnamese with what he called "the comforts that a democracy offered them." The colonel granted his request, and Calley initially found the new job so satisfying that he extended his time in Vietnam another six months. But he soon felt that the Vietnamese were unappreciative of his goodwill and wanted only to be left alone. Calley told the colonel of his intention to resign this position.[51]

After a year as an S-5, Calley had taken a new assignment when he received orders to fly to Washington.[52]

Colonel Stanfield first had to deal with Calley's sense of bewilderment. Calley had assumed his appearance was part of an investigation about whether the U.S. involvement in Vietnam was "right or wrong." Realizing this might not be the case, he confessed to Stanfield to being "kind of leery on what actually is going on." Stanfield declared his intention to focus on a military operation in My Lai 4 on March 16, 1968. "At the conclusion of this investigation," he asserted, you "will possibly be charged with murder." Stunned, Calley replied that he thought this "the silliest thing [he] had heard of." As a result of the assault, Stanfield explained to Calley, he was under suspicion of wrongfully destroying a village and murdering civilians in violation of articles 109 and 118 of the Uniform Code of Military Justice. The transcript of their conversation goes as follows.

"This is kind of a kick in the deck. I don't even know what I'm up against, to tell you the truth. I mean it sounds serious as hell that I am going up for a war crime. Can you advise me?"

Stanfield recommended a lawyer and offered help from the inspector general's office in arranging one for him.

"In other words, I am being investigated for a war crime?"

"That is correct."

"I guess I should get counsel."[53]

Calley secured an attorney from JAG and then offered a deal: he would disclose everything that happened in My Lai 4 if the army chief of staff granted him immunity in writing from criminal prosecution, whether in a military tribunal or a civilian court. Stanfield rejected any deal. "I can be certain that there can be no grant of immunity given." Calley insisted he had no desire to obstruct an investigation. "I myself, hell I have nothing to hold back on." But he had decided "to remain silent because there are just too many people involved that didn't want to be over there but did a damn good military job, to be pulled in and taken down in something like this, and probably take the rest of their life to forget about." Denied immunity, Calley exercised his right to silence in what turned out to be an abbreviated session. The army ordered Calley to new duties tying him to Fort Benning while it conducted an investigation.[54]

By September 6, Calley would either have an honorable discharge from the army or face murder charges in a court martial. And if the army failed to file charges before he mustered out of the service, as noted, he could not stand trial in either the military or the civilian courts.

Two days after Calley's encounter with Stanfield, Colonel Wilson met with Hugh Thompson in Washington, a meeting during which Thompson confirmed that a massacre had taken place on March 16. Essentially, he repeated what he had told Henderson and others. While flying over My Lai 4 in his helicopter that day, he told Wilson, he had seen many dead and wounded Vietnamese civilians scattered throughout the village and dropped smoke canisters to signify the locations of those in need of medical care. "The first one I marked was a girl that was wounded," Thompson asserted, but the soldiers "came over to her, with their weapons on automatic and let her have it." Thompson also saw a captain (Medina) shoot a wounded woman close up and on the ground. Thompson then landed near a drainage ditch filled with up to one hundred Vietnamese bodies and, according to Thompson, encountered an officer (Calley) overseeing the killing, who became upset over the intrusion.

Shortly after a bitter exchange, Thompson left, but he landed his helicopter again when he saw another American lieutenant and a few troops advancing toward a small group of frightened women and children clinging to each other in a bunker. Thompson offered to help the Vietnamese out of the bunker, but the officer (Lieutenant Stephen Brooks of the 2nd Platoon) had remarked, "The only way you'll get them out is with a hand grenade." Thompson decided to evacuate the Vietnamese and ordered his two crew members to fire on the American soldiers if they interfered.[55]

Two days after the March 16 assault, Thompson told Wilson, he had reported what he had seen to Henderson in a half-hour meeting. "I told him I had seen the captain shoot the Vietnamese girl. I told him about the ditches and the bodies in the ditch....I told him how I had gotten the people out of the bunker. I told him what I said to the lieutenant."[56]

Wilson considered Thompson "immensely impressive" and "the only hero of that awful day." He had provided "damning" testimony. "The trick would be to corroborate it."[57]

On the third and last day of the interview, June 13, Thompson identified Calley from a lineup arranged by Wilson. This put the lieutenant at the scene of the killings—the ditch filled with the bodies of Vietnamese men, women, and children.[58]

Less than a week after talking with Thompson, Wilson received confirmation of the pilot's account of a massacre from interviews with one of the gunship

pilots who had helped rescue the Vietnamese in the bunker—Dan Millians—
and with the door gunner on Thompson's helicopter, Lawrence Colburn.
Millians witnessed a great number of civilians killed by "needless" ground
fire—more than one hundred casualties, about seventy-five of them in the
ditch and the rest spread throughout the village. "No one in the ditch was
standing," he told Wilson. Colburn saw at least a hundred people "piled up
upon one another" in the ditch.[59]

On July 15 Wilson interviewed Medina's RTO, Fred Widmer, who also
attested to a massacre. Wilson did not advise him of his rights, because there
was no civil law that could hold him responsible for war crimes. Once assured
that military law did not apply to him because he was now a civilian, Widmer
went into considerable detail, describing groups of bodies on the ground. He
admitted to two mercy killings after borrowing a .45 pistol from Carter "to
finish off a couple of people that were not yet dead." The "dinks," he explained
to Wilson, were wounded and in "pretty bad shape" and "would have died
eventually." Asked how he could be so certain, he simply replied, "Because I
was standing beside them." Widmer also admitted to borrowing an M-16 and
shooting a small boy about three or four years old standing along the trail and
with a gunshot wound in his arm. This was not a mercy killing, he insisted,
but what it was he could not articulate. "At the time I would say [pause] I
couldn't tell you exactly how I felt, except to prove to myself I could kill someone because that was the first time I had ever killed anyone."[60]

Widmer asserted that at the time of the operation almost all the men felt
justified in their actions, but afterward most of them had realized they should
not have killed these people. "What it amounted to was mass murder."[61]

On July 16, a day about which Wilson remarked, "I would like to block
[it] from my memory," he interviewed Paul Meadlo in a motel in Terre Haute,
Indiana, a short distance from his home in New Goshen. The former soldier
presented a pathetic sight, Wilson recalled, with "his right foot and self-
respect gone" from a mine explosion and a string of accusations that he had
committed war crimes. Yet he was "determined to relieve his conscience and
describe the horrors of My Lai."[62]

Meadlo asserted that at the briefing the night before the operation,
Medina had left the impression "that we were supposed to move in and kill
the people." Calley was specific in his order to the 1st Platoon: "Kill all the
people in the village." The next day, Meadlo declared to Wilson, "We just
started wiping out the whole village. That is it. We burnt the village and killed
all the people and just one mass slaughter, just like you do a bunch of cows,
you know, just killed them all."[63]

Calley's platoon removed about eighty Vietnamese civilians from their homes and grouped them on the trail in a big circle in a cleared area inside the village. Looking at Meadlo, Calley had asked, "You know what to do with them, don't you?" Wilson recorded the conversation as Meadlo recalled it.

"No."

Calley walked away and soon returned. "Well, why haven't you killed them yet?"

"I didn't know we was supposed to kill the people."

"Let's kill them."

And "so we killed them," Meadlo told Wilson. "Lieutenant Calley opened up on the first and then I joined in." Wilson reported that Meadlo looked up at the ceiling in the motel room and cried. His body, Wilson noted, "shook with sobs" as he resumed his story. "We stood about ten to fifteen feet away from them," and Calley "started shooting." He then "told me to start shooting them," Meadlo asserted. "I used more than a whole clip—used four or five clips."[64]

Meadlo's admission shocked Wilson, who had found credible the denials by Henderson and others that a massacre had taken place. No one until now had admitted to taking orders from Calley and participating with him in massacring large groups of villagers. Wilson had simply asked Meadlo to relate what happened in My Lai 4 and had not expected a confession to murder.

"Wait, before you say anything else."

"O.K."

"I want to go over something before you say anything else now, Meadlo."

Wilson explained to him that this was a "formal investigation," but that he had not given Meadlo the standard warning against saying anything that could be used against him in court. He had already told Meadlo that he was no longer subject to army law and could not be tried in an American civil or criminal court because it did not recognize Vietnamese law, but he had not warned Meadlo that whatever he said might incriminate him and therefore could not be used as evidence. "Now on the basis of what you have said, and without a warning, your testimony cannot be held in evidence because you have incriminated yourself."[65]

Meadlo was puzzled, according to Wilson. "How did I do that by just following orders? Who am I to question orders when the rank is higher than me?"[66]

"An execution is not a legal order," Wilson says that he explained, "but the main thing that I am telling you is this, that until you receive a warning which gives you exactly what your rights are your testimony cannot be used as evidence against you."[67]

Meadlo had never felt personally responsible for killing the Vietnamese, because he had acted under orders. "I'd like to ask you a question," Meadlo said. "Can you really get me for anything like that or for killing people when I was just following orders?"[68]

"I just said there is no civil court that can try you for a crime, if it is concluded to be a crime, in a foreign country." Wilson went on to explain that he wanted to call Washington before giving him that legal warning, "because we have got to be right in this and you have to know your rights."[69]

Wilson stopped the testimony and told Meadlo to join Smith outside the room. He then called Colonel Carney at his home in Washington, explaining what happened and asking what to do, since he had not advised the witness of his rights prior to the interview. Carney told him to issue the warning and ask the witness to repeat his confession.[70]

Twenty minutes later, Wilson resumed the proceeding. He informed Meadlo that he was under suspicion of committing a war crime—"wrongful destruction of a village and murder of Vietnamese civilians." Wilson emphasized to Meadlo that he had the constitutional right to remain silent and warned him that any statement he made could be used against him in a potential criminal trial. "Do you desire to give any testimony?"[71]

"Anything that you want to ask me I will give what I can give you and that's it."

"Then you will consent to the questions and answer them if you desire?"

"If I can answer them I will answer them."

According to Wilson, Meadlo stated that his platoon rounded up close to fifty Vietnamese civilians, about a third of them men, and, in compliance with Calley's instructions, moved them into "a clearing in the center of the village." This time, however, when asked again if Calley "opened fire on these people," Meadlo responded, "I don't think I will answer that question."

"Did you ever see a ditch with a lot of bodies in it?"

"Yes, I did."

"Do you have any idea what happened to this group of bodies that were in the ditch—how they got there?"

"How they got there? Yes, they was pushed in there and told to get off in the ditch and then they was started to getting killed."

"Who did that?"

"I am not answering."

Meadlo told Wilson that he considered this a different type of operation in that usually the soldiers "never went through a village and just slaughtered the people." In this case, "We just rounded up the people and put them all in one location and then they were slaughtered." Wilson noted his use of the passive voice. There were two large groups and three or four smaller ones.

"Did Lieutenant Calley open fire on this group of Vietnamese?"

"I am not going to answer that."[72]

Wilson remembered his earlier interview with Ronald Grzesik, the fire team leader in Calley's platoon, who claimed that he had refused to obey Calley's order to "finish off the people" in a ditch. Calley, Grzesik told Wilson, had angrily ordered him and his team back into the village to burn it. In the process of doing so, he came upon Meadlo, bent over with his head in his hands and weeping like a child because, he explained, Calley had ordered him to shoot the Vietnamese people.[73]

Wilson knew that Meadlo had left the army immediately after sustaining his injury and that he was unlikely to be offering a version of events influenced by post-combat discussions in the barracks. "I was struck by the picture of this man Meadlo, crying by the bodies of the dead; he was possibly the crucial witness, the last man I needed to present the truth of My Lai."[74]

"I decided that the case was closed," Wilson concluded. A massacre had occurred at My Lai 4 that the army's Criminal Investigation Division of the Office of the Provost Marshal General would have to examine. Thompson had identified Calley in a lineup as the "Kally" referred to in Ridenhour's letter. After the legal warning, Meadlo had refused to repeat his accusations against Calley, but he also had not retracted them, and that was good enough for Wilson. "Something in me had died," he said, while listening to Meadlo's first-hand description of the atrocities committed in My Lai 4. "I had prayed to God that this thing was fiction, and I knew now it was fact."[75]

IV

Wilson returned to Washington and submitted his written report on July 17, confirming the charges made in Ridenhour's letter. His fact-finding mission rested on three months of testimonies from thirty-six witnesses and comprised a thousand pages of transcripts. A month later, he flew to Fort Benning to share his information with the legal officers there, who had the responsibility of deciding whether to charge Lieutenant Calley (and others) with war crimes.[76]

Wilson's report convinced Westmoreland that there was sufficient evidence to direct Chief Warrant Officer André Feher of the army's Criminal Investigation Division to conduct an inquiry into what happened in My Lai 4.

Feher would head a CID team of three agents, which soon grew to seven. In addition to investigatory work that would take him all over the United States for much of August and September 1969, he would later travel to South Vietnam to interview Vietnamese witnesses, making him among the first American soldiers to enter My Lai 4 after March 16, 1968. Wilson had compiled enough information for Feher to use in securing sworn statements from those involved in the operation and thereby build a legal case for prosecution. Feher's chief concern, he declared years afterward, was that his findings "would make the Army's conduct of the Vietnam War look very bad in the eyes of the public and that many mothers would feel that this was not the place for their sons to be."[77]

The pivotal moment in Feher's interviews came in Ohio on August 25, when he met with Ronald Haeberle, the photographer who had taken more than fifty black-and-white pictures with two army cameras at My Lai 4. Feher had not seen the pictures, because Haeberle had turned them in to the army after the operation and they were on file in the brigade's public information office at Duc Pho. But Haeberle provided long and graphic descriptions of numerous photographs that provided the first concrete evidence of a massacre— and of mostly women and children. Asked who had ordered the killing, he said he knew no names but "figured out it must have come from higher up, since the soldiers just do not start killing civilians in the mass they were doing."[78]

More startling, however, was his sudden declaration to Feher that he had also taken about twenty color shots of the village with his own camera. No one had instructed him what to do with these color slides, and he was never aware of any directive that made the pictures official and military property. He had kept them when discharged from the army on March 27, 1968, and in fact "put together a slide show" for public and non-profit presentations to hundreds of people in various civic, church, and educational groups. Some of them, Haeberle later explained, "couldn't believe this actually happened" and asked in astonishment, "Why would American GIs do this, especially to old men, women, and children?" Surely Hollywood had made this up, he recalled that someone had remarked. "What about the children?" Haeberle explained that the Viet Cong sometimes booby-trapped the children with hand grenades. This answer never satisfied his audiences. "I really couldn't come up with a here we go, the good solid answer. I never have been able to." Haeberle told Feher that he had once asked a group of GIs who had just shot some kids, "Why?" And one of them responded, "We had to."[79]

That night in Feher's motel room, Haeberle showed his color slides on a sheet hung up on the wall and with a projector Feher had gotten that afternoon from the CID office in Cleveland a short distance away. Haeberle promised to bring copies the next day. Feher took no chances, however. That night he used a borrowed Polaroid camera to produce his own color images of the slides, which he could use when interviewing other soldiers. Haeberle kept his word and showed up with his own copies the following day.[80]

Feher's interviews focused on members of the 1st Platoon and at the outset did not seem nearly as promising as the discussion with Haeberle. In New Jersey, Daniel Simone criticized Calley as a leader but denied seeing anyone kill women and children. When shown the color pictures of the dead, he declared that he "might have protested" had he known what others had done, but he refused to sign a statement or testify in court. "I did not do anything wrong," he asserted. "I did not see anybody firing on women and children. All I heard was that women and children were shot. But I did not like to listen to it."[81]

Allen Boyce, however, confirmed there had been a massacre and at a meeting at Bradley Beach on the Jersey shore asserted to Feher that he had seen Calley and Meadlo shoot civilians, and that Meadlo told him he had acted under Calley's orders. Boyce thought Meadlo had been reluctant to do the killing, but he was "a farm boy" who had learned to follow orders. Boyce estimated that a hundred villagers had been killed, eighty of them women and children. "I myself did not shoot any women or children." Boyce appeared to be a soft-spoken family man, Feher thought, not yet aware that Boyce's friend Harry Stanley had testified that he had seen him stab an elderly man in the back and throw another man into a well. Boyce agreed to testify in court and told Feher, "I hope that they get to the bottom of this and find out what the cause was, to prevent any other incidents. Incidents like this are the reason why we cannot win the war." Civilians "will help the Viet Cong."[82]

Greg Olsen in Seattle also attested to a massacre during his interview with Feher. He said that he had seen the drainage ditch filled with bodies of elderly men, women, young children, and babies. He watched Calley engage in a heated discussion with a helicopter pilot "shaking his arms" in anger. He also witnessed Sergeant Mitchell fire his M-16 into the ditch and Boyce throw a prisoner into a bomb crater and shoot him twice. "The prisoner was not trying to escape. Why Boyce shot him is anybody's guess." Olsen insisted that he never would have followed an order from Calley to kill civilians. "Even if General Westmoreland would have ordered me to shoot women and children I would have refused." Yet he felt guilty for not stopping the shooting or reporting it to Lieutenant Colonel Barker. "I did not want to get Captain Medina in trouble and I felt he was not responsible even though it was his company." All the men should have refused the order to kill. "To this day I do not know what came over them by not refusing." Olsen agreed to testify in court.[83]

Feher's final interview in that busy first week was with Calley's RTO, Charles Sledge, which took place in a Holiday Inn motel room in the small town of Sardis in rural Mississippi. Sledge declared that he saw Calley order and participate in the killing of villagers on the trail, and he was at the ditch when Calley told Mitchell to finish off those civilians still alive. Sledge also witnessed Calley shoot a Buddhist monk and toss a baby back into the ditch before shooting it with his M-16. Sledge's testimony was highly credible, because as the RTO he had been with Calley the entire day.[84]

In one week, Feher had amassed enough evidence to charge William Calley with the murder of more than one hundred Vietnamese civilians in My Lai 4.[85]

The problem, however, was the time constraint: Feher had concluded his final interview with Sledge on September 1, and Calley's discharge from the army was scheduled for September 6. After considerable scrambling to beat the clock, on September 5, just one day before the deadline, the United States Army charged Calley with killing at least 107 inhabitants of My Lai 4 by "shooting them with a rifle."[86]

Calley had stood at attention before the colonel's desk as he read the charges from a sheet of paper. Afterward, the colonel asked, "Do you understand these charges, Lieutenant Calley?"

"Yes, sir. I understand, sir."

Calley saluted and left the office.

Outside, according to a credible source, another colonel took Calley to his office. "There is no need to publicize this thing," this colonel declared, "The U.S. Army won't publicize it if you won't."

According to a Montgomery report, Calley concurred.[87]

In accordance with the Uniform Code of Military Justice, General Orwin Talbott, Fort Benning's new commander as of September 10, would set up an Article 32 hearing to review the evidence and determine if it justified a court martial.[88]

The army made every effort to keep this investigation secret, but the nature of the story made it impossible to prevent leaks to the public. Just four miles from Fort Benning, the *Ledger-Enquirer* of Columbus, Georgia, sent one of its reporters, David Leonard, to check out a tip that the army had charged a soldier with multiple murders. After a little digging, he learned that the accused was Lieutenant William Calley, and on September 6 the paper ran

Leonard's story on the front page under a two-column headline. Charles Black, associate editor of the paper, mined his longtime contacts in the army to find Calley and interview him. He soon discovered that Calley was living in the Senior Bachelor Officers' Quarters at Fort Benning and went to his door. But Calley claimed he could not grant an interview. Black, however, noticed the insignia of the Americal Division on Calley's uniform and after talking with soldiers who had returned from Vietnam and researching army newspapers and other files, he learned of a military operation at a place called Pinkville and prepared to dig deeper.[89]

Black was acting virtually alone on a story that at this point had aroused little interest. Other reporters had been unable to convince their news outlets to look into the matter. Their priority was the army's recent arrest of a small contingent of Green Berets for executing a Viet Cong spy. To keep the Calley story low-profile, Fort Benning's information office released a brief statement that the *New York Times* ran deep inside its September 7, 1969 issue. Headlined "Army Accuses Lieutenant in Vietnam Deaths in 1968," the news release identified Calley as the officer charged with murder following an "incident" in March 1968, but did not mention the killing of more than a hundred civilians. Rather, the murder charge was for "an unspecified number of civilians," or, as the chief information officer, Lieutenant Colonel Douglas Tucker, put it, "the deaths of more than one civilian."[90]

RONALD RIDENHOUR HAD meanwhile become unhappy about what he considered to be a whitewashed investigation and for months had tried to publish the story. Then, on that same day the *New York Times* piece had appeared, September 7, an anonymous military official in Washington notified him by phone that the army had brought charges against Calley. Ridenhour said that he was immediately convinced that the army intended to make Calley a scapegoat for My Lai 4. He knew that Calley was not the only one responsible for the massacre, and he was certain that authorities higher than Captain Medina had ordered him to destroy the village. Ridenhour phoned the Phoenix newspaper, the *Arizona Republic*, but he failed to convince anyone to run the story, and it remained—for the moment—off the national stage.[91]

PART III

My Lai on Trial

Nine

IN LATE OCTOBER THE MY LAI STORY took a national turn when a lawyer and part-time Washington journalist named Geoffrey Cowan called Seymour Hersh, whom he had never met. An anonymous source in the military had informed him that the army had charged an officer at Fort Benning with killing nearly eighty Vietnamese civilians. Concerned that the army would bury the story, he took the advice of an attorney friend and called Hersh, then a freelance investigative journalist. Cowan had heard of Hersh's reputation as a "tenacious reporter" and hoped the stories were true.[1]

At the time, Hersh was writing a book on the Pentagon, but he realized this new story was too big to pass up. Like the majority of Americans in 1969, his opposition to the Vietnam War had grown, as had his interest in helping bring that conflict to a close through reportage. Less than a week before Cowan made his telephone call to Hersh, 250,000 people had descended upon Washington to protest the war, while antiwar demonstrations spread to numerous other cities as well. "I stopped all other work and began chasing down the story of the My Lai massacre."[2]

I

The day after receiving Cowan's tip, Hersh called Fort Benning's information office and asked Lieutenant Colonel Douglas Tucker about an impending trial. Tucker denied that any such trial was underway. He provided no further information other than reading him a short piece on the matter in the *New York Times* of September 7 that mentioned Lieutenant William Calley. The next day Hersh began searching for him. He soon discovered that Calley did not live in Miami but in Waynesville, North Carolina, and, with Cowan's help, learned that a former judge of the U.S. Court of Military Appeals in Washington, George Latimer of Utah, headed his defense. Hersh then contacted a source in the Pentagon who indicated that the charge was first-degree murder for an incident in a place called My Lai on March 16, 1968. Latimer had served as defense counsel for one of the accused in the Green Berets case, but the government had recently declared that a fair trial was impossible and dropped the charges after the CIA barred its people from testifying on the grounds of national security. Hersh could not have known that Latimer had already considered asking the army to drop its charges against Calley. The so-called evidence, Latimer insisted, was hearsay.[3]

Hersh was in the Pentagon, checking out his tip, when he ran into an acquaintance, a colonel now working for General Westmoreland's chief of staff. "Tell me," Hersh asked, according to an interview he gave in 2012, "what's this about some guy shooting up a bunch of people?" His friend abruptly stopped in the hallway and, in what Hersh called "one of those magic moments," declared, "Let me tell you, Hersh, that guy Calley, he didn't shoot anybody higher than this high," holding his hand at his knees. "He just shot little kids. He deserves everything he gets." Hersh believed this story, because, he later remarked, "You can't make it up."[4]

Hersh wanted to discuss the matter with Latimer in Salt Lake City and called him: "I want to talk about this fellow Calley," Hersh declared, according to an interview cited in Robert Miraldi's book. "Oh, what a tragedy," Latimer replied. "The government is making a tragic mistake." Hersh made up the story that he was going to California but could stop in Salt Lake City if acceptable. Latimer agreed to a meeting.

Hersh planned first to win over Latimer by discussing some of his past cases and showing his familiarity with them. Before departing Washington, he went to the Army Military Library to print out some of these cases to read on the plane. The strategy worked. Not only did Latimer talk freely about his earlier experiences in court with Hersh, he brought up the subject of Calley and vehemently emphasized his innocence. Hersh wanted to know how many Vietnamese Calley allegedly killed in the village and doubled the number he had heard—in an effort to prod Latimer into correcting him. "I understand he was accused of killing 150 people." Latimer became so upset that he pulled out a piece of paper on the case and began reading aloud from it, while Hersh copied the first ten or twelve lines upside down. The army had charged Calley with the premeditated murder of 111 "Oriental human beings"—three words "I'll never forget," Hersh later asserted.[5]

Latimer told Hersh that Calley was at Fort Benning, and Hersh went looking for him there on November 11. Not finding him at the army barracks, he went to the office of the judge advocate general who would prosecute the case, identified himself as a reporter to a sergeant at the desk, and asked to speak with William Calley. The officer reached for a phone, explaining that he was under orders to call the colonel if anyone inquired about Calley. Hersh, however, slipped away before the colonel arrived but continued his search on the base.

Hersh soon found a soldier asleep in a bunk and, hoping to get lucky, kicked it while shouting, "Wake up, Calley." It was not him.

"Ever hear of the name Calley?" Hersh said he asked.

"William Calley? Oh, you mean the guy that shot up everybody?"

"Yeah."

The soldier put Hersh in touch with a friend in the mailroom, who checked the personnel files for Calley's address off base. But on arriving there, Hersh learned that Calley had recently moved. Disheartened, Hersh returned to the base, where a group of soldiers milling around told him Calley lived in the Senior Bachelor Officers' Quarters—complete with tennis court and swimming pool. Hersh remembered thinking at the time that the army had hidden Calley in the least likely place for anyone to look.[6]

At around seven in the evening Hersh began knocking on the first of fifty doors to find Calley, without success. He did, however, run into an officer, who invited him to a party where Calley would likely be. Near midnight Calley showed up, and the officer introduced him to Hersh. Calley maintained that he was not surprised by the visit; Latimer had told him that Hersh would show up sometime soon. They went to Calley's room, where, according to Hersh, he "pretended to be very cocky and calm" while relating his experiences in Vietnam. The war was "cool," Calley remarked—"really a fight, really a war." But somewhere around four or five in the morning they were still talking and drinking beers when Calley suddenly went to the bathroom and vomited blood—the result of an ulcer, Hersh thought, while gazing through the open door.[7]

Calley then turned to My Lai. Murders took place there, he declared, but all under orders. "Call Medina. He will tell you. He's on the base." Hersh did not know who Medina was until Calley explained that he was the company captain. At five-thirty in the morning, Hersh awakened Medina with a phone call and identified himself as a reporter following up on the killings at My Lai. Medina, Hersh recalled, went "wild."

"What? Where did you get this number? How do you know about this?"

"Captain," Hersh explained, "Calley said he was under orders."

"I never gave any such order! Calley's an unmitigated liar."

Calley was standing, listening to Medina's response as Hersh held out the phone. "After that," Hersh remembered telling himself, "Calley knew he was gone."[8]

This five-hour conversation with Calley provided the material for Hersh to write the first national exposé of the events at what he called "a Viet Cong stronghold known as 'Pinkville,'" an article he quickly realized no mainstream U.S. news outlet would print. He had originally sold the story to the *Washington Post*, but after editor Ben Bradlee and his staff had met with Hersh to discuss publishing it, they decided against doing so, opting instead to have one of their own journalists, Peter Braestrup, write a separate piece. After failing at both *Life* and *Look* magazines, Hersh placed the article with his friend (and tennis rival), David Obst, who had recently founded the Dispatch News Service—what he called "an antiwar news service devoted to telling the 'truth' about Vietnam." It proved to be a wise move. Obst persuaded thirty-five American and Canadian newspapers—including the *Boston Globe*, *Chicago Sun-Times*, *Miami Herald*, *Milwaukee Journal*, and *St. Louis Post-Dispatch*—to publish the article on November 13 under the title, "Lieutenant Accused of Murdering 109 Civilians." That same day the *Washington Post* ran Braestrup's story with appropriate references to Hersh's work, and the *New York Times* published its own account of the charge against Calley of the premeditated murder of more than one hundred Vietnamese civilians at Pinkville—but without the intimate details Hersh had mined from the accused.[9]

Hersh's article was not a complete scoop. The day before it appeared, Alabama journalist Wayne Greenhaw published a story of Calley's possible involvement in killing more than ninety Vietnamese civilians in March 1968. On the front page of the November 12, 1969, issue of the *Alabama Journal*, Greenhaw wrote an article headlined "Ft. Benning Probes Vietnam Slayings" and followed by the subhead, "Officer Suspect in 91 Deaths of Civilians."[10]

About two months earlier, Greenhaw had received an anonymous tip from the Pentagon that the army was holding a lieutenant for killing a number of South Vietnamese civilians. The newspaper's editor, Ray Jenkins, knew from a private source that the story was on the edge of breaking, and since the *Journal* was located just ninety miles from Fort Benning, he sent Greenhaw to investigate. Finding most of his contacts on the base reluctant to talk, Greenhaw returned with what Jenkins called "the barebones story," which appeared in the *Journal*'s afternoon issue the day before Hersh's more detailed account.[11]

Greenhaw reported that Lieutenant William Calley was under investigation for "the multiple murder of civilians in South Vietnam." Calley, according to "informed sources," was suspected of "wiping out an entire South Vietnamese village by killing 91 people—men, women and children." Lieutenant Colonel Tucker explained that his Office of Information at Fort Benning got the case for investigation at the end of August and that if an Article 32 investigation determined that the evidence justified the suspicion of a war crime, army authorities there would hold a court martial on the base. The judge advocate general would lead the prosecution against Calley's civilian defense attorney, George Latimer of Salt Lake City, a retired judge on the Military Court of Appeals.[12]

Hersh's more detailed story attracted more attention than others, because it appeared in a host of national newspapers and drew from his interview with Calley himself. Hersh provided the accused officer's first-hand account of the multiple killings committed in the "Viet Cong fortress" of "Pinkville" on March 16, 1968. Readers learned that this was the army's third attempt to breach this enemy-infested area after the Tet offensive of the previous January and that it claimed 128 Viet Cong killed in action by U.S. forces. But also slain in the operation, Hersh declared, were a large number of civilians who found themselves in a free-fire zone. The army's report, Hersh's piece noted, did not mention these casualties.[13]

Hersh had suddenly become part of a raging debate both inside and outside the army that started right after it had formally charged Calley on September 6 with the premeditated murder of "at least 109 Vietnamese civilians" in Pinkville. Hersh noted in his article that Latimer claimed his defendant was following orders, quoting him as saying, "You can't afford to guess whether a civilian is a Viet Cong or not. Either they shoot you or you shoot them." A soldier who accompanied Calley on the mission insisted, "There are always some civilian casualties in a combat operation. He isn't guilty of murder." An anonymous officer remarked, "It could happen to any of us. He has killed and has seen a lot of killing....Killing becomes nothing in Vietnam." Yet another anonymous officer blasted high-up army authorities for "using this as a Goddamned example." Calley was "a good soldier. He followed orders."[14]

But Hersh's piece asserted that an anonymous source in Washington had rejected this argument and considered Calley a cold-blooded murderer. His platoon "simply shot up this village and he was the leader of it. When one guy refused to do it, Calley took the rifle away and did the shooting himself." Hersh told of his talking with a Pentagon official who tapped his knee with his hand while glaring at him and angrily remarking, "Some of those kids he shot were this high. I don't think they were Viet Cong. Do you?"[15]

"With expressionless gray eyes and thinning brown hair," Calley appeared, according to Hersh, "slightly bewildered and hurt by the charges." In an interview, the young lieutenant insisted, "I like the Army...and I don't want to do anything to hurt it."[16]

Unknown to anyone outside of the Pentagon's inner recesses, on the same day Hersh's article appeared, the ongoing CID investigation led to a series of preliminary conclusions that not only substantiated Hersh's story but expanded it. CID sent a progress report to General Westmoreland affirming Hersh's public charge of massacre by American soldiers and adding three more explosive findings: Lieutenant William Calley "ordered and took part in the summary execution of unresisting noncombatant civilians"; Sergeant David Mitchell committed an "assault with intent to murder about thirty Vietnamese civilian noncombatants"; and Captain Ernest Medina either ordered his men to "wipe out" the village or left the "inference" that they should "kill everyone" in it. The company captain "was controlling the action by moving about the area, yet no one could remember Medina doing anything to stop the shooting of noncombatants as it was taking place."[17]

CID showed that Lieutenant Colonel Barker's after action report had not told the truth. The testimonies of seventy-five witnesses to date—twenty-eight still in the military and the others now discharged—had combined with numerous photographs of the scene to demonstrate that American forces had encountered no resistance. The victims were either seeking refuge from small-arms fire or were in "sizable controlled groups" of mainly women and children, "including infants."[18]

The CID report remained confidential, of course, but the army's past efforts to keep this story silent suggested that it was only a matter of time before these allegations leaked and reinforced those made publicly by Hersh.

Other reporters were already at work fleshing out more details of the story. The day after Hersh's article appeared, three members of the press corps covering the Vietnam War visited My Lai and confirmed there had been a massacre. Americal Division forces provided protection for Don Baker of ABC-TV, Paul Brinkley-Jones of *Newsweek*, and Henry Kamm of the *New York Times*, who found a destroyed and desolate village. The proof of life once there was, ironically, the evidence of death now everywhere—human bones, earthen mounds covering mass graves, shattered remains of bunkers, charcoal remnants of thatch and mud hooches, and burned out, skeletal foundations and framework of brick homes at times barely discernible because of the uncontrolled growth of vegetation. Those few Vietnamese who survived the assault had relocated to a refugee camp.[19]

Yet the immediate public reaction to Hersh's article was not the widespread outrage he had hoped for. Other stories attracted more interest, including the second moon landing and—ironically enough—the Nixon administration's attacks on the American press for its coverage of the war in Vietnam. More important, however, was the skepticism of many if not most Americans, who refused to believe that one of their young soldiers (and, as Hersh reported, perhaps at least six others under consideration for similar charges by the army) could deliberately murder more than a hundred Vietnamese men, women, and children. How could the army accuse a war hero like Calley of premeditated murder after awarding him the Purple Heart for a combat wound and recommending him for the Bronze Star with Oak Leaf Cluster for meritorious service in combat?[20]

To its critics, Hersh's article appeared to be part of the leftist antiwar movement in the country—a concern he had when going to press. He had, after all, released the article through a reputedly leftist, antiwar media outlet. The night before its publication, thousands of antiwar demonstrators in Washington grabbed both national and international attention when they began a long and single file "March against Death" in the freezing rain that started close to the gates of the Arlington National Cemetery, wound around the Lincoln Memorial, and moved past the White House toward Union Square Park. Six drummers playing a death-march beat led a long procession of participants from nearly every state in the nation, carrying candles and wearing placards bearing the names of those who had died in Vietnam. As they passed the White House, each person called out the name on the placard before putting it in one of the forty black wooden coffins at the end of the march near the Capitol. "There is no light at the end of the tunnel, only the darkness that came over my husband," said a widow just before the march began.[21]

To opponents of the war in Vietnam, the massacre charges confirmed their antiwar position; to the war's supporters, they were communist lies.

Yet the stories kept coming and, together with Hersh's article, began to raise nationwide concern about what had happened in Pinkville. The day after Hersh's article appeared, the public learned that the army had charged one of Calley's squad leaders, Sergeant Mitchell, with assault with intent to murder thirty Vietnamese civilians. Braestrup's November 13 article in the *Washington Post* had aroused great interest when he referred to an unnamed Vietnam veteran who wrote a letter to the Pentagon that brought about an in-house army investigation. And on the following day, Ronald Ridenhour, now a student at Claremont Men's College in California, told the *New York Times* that he was the ex-GI who had learned from friends about the massacre and sent the letters to various government officials that put pressure on the army to investigate. Calley and Mitchell were not the only perpetrators of this war crime, Ridenhour insisted. "The important thing is there are a lot of bigger fish in this kettle and they aren't being caught."[22]

The next day, November 17, a front-page story in the *New York Times* reported that more than a hundred Vietnamese had survived the massacre by playing dead under the bodies of victims and that one of them, Do Hoai, claimed that American soldiers destroyed their village and killed all the others who lived there. This amounted to 567 unarmed men, women, and children.[23]

II

The furor was already beginning when three days later, November 20, Hersh published a second article titled "Hamlet Attack Called 'Point-Blank Murder,'" which focused on three other GIs who had participated in the Pinkville assault. Hersh and Obst had gotten the idea for this article from Braestrup's reference to the unnamed soldier who wrote the original letter of exposé, followed by Ridenhour's coming forth in the *New York Times*. Hersh had immediately booked a flight to the West Coast to become the first reporter to talk with him. As they had lunch, Ridenhour provided dozens of addresses and phone numbers of soldiers who had been in Charlie Company, including three he had interviewed for his letter to leaders in Washington: Michael Terry, now at Brigham Young University in Utah, and two others still in the army—Michael Bernhardt at Fort Dix in New Jersey and William Doherty at Fort Hood in Texas. Hersh convinced all three participants to discuss the massacre with him by reading them key selections over the phone from Ridenhour's letter describing what happened at Pinkville and then emphasizing the letter's importance in leading the army to launch an investigation the previous April. Ridenhour agreed to wait three days until Hersh's article appeared before sharing the story with anyone else. "I was glad to," Ridenhour later declared. "He was the first person to respond."[24]

Hersh's second article attracted even more national attention than the first, as it contained the first eyewitness accounts of the massacre and testimony against Calley. It was "point-blank murder and I was standing there watching it," said Bernhardt, who honored his earlier commitment to Ridenhour to tell the story even though he was now a sergeant completing his time in the army. Calley's forces "were gathering people in groups and shooting them"—women and children as well as men—many of them with an M-79 grenade launcher and a machine gun. "You're surprised?" Bernhardt exclaimed to Hersh in the piece. "I wouldn't be surprised at anything these dudes did." U.S. forces encountered no resistance and incurred no casualties. The estimated death toll ranged from 170 to more than 700, many of the victims piled throughout the village. An army photographer had taken pictures of the bodies, Bernhardt asserted, photographs he saw during his late-October testimony during the ongoing Article 32 proceeding regarding whether to charge Calley with murder. In fact, the orders to destroy Pinkville undoubtedly came from higher up the command chain. "Calley's just a small fry."[25]

As we have seen, Bernhardt had sensed a cover-up as soon as the mission had ended, and he recounted what Medina had said to him—not to write his congressman because an investigation was underway. But nothing came of the inquiry, Bernhardt noted.[26]

Asked the reason for the mass killings, Bernhardt declared that "the company was conditioned to do this. The treatment was lousy....We were always out in the bushes. I think they were expecting us to run into resistance at Pinkville and also expecting them [the Viet Cong] to use the people as hostages." Another chief factor, he added, was the widespread hatred for Vietnamese civilians after a land mine blew up and killed or wounded more than twenty GIs. About 90 percent of the company took part in the shootings. He, however, refused to follow orders, asserting, "I only shoot at people who shoot at me."[27]

Terry, then in his second year in college, declared that American forces "just marched through shooting everybody....Seems like no one said anything....They just started pulling people out and shooting them." He maintained that he then saw them shuffle more than twenty villagers toward a large number of others "in a group standing over a ditch—just like a Nazi-type thing....One officer ordered a kid to machine-gun everybody down, but the kid just couldn't do it. He threw the machine gun down and the officer picked it up....I don't remember seeing any men in the ditch. Mostly women and kids." At a lunch break later near the ditch, Terry saw that "some of them were still breathing....They were pretty badly shot up. They weren't going to get any medical help, and so we shot them. Shot maybe five of them."[28]

The third witness to the shootings remained unidentified in Hersh's article, because he was concerned about his active-duty status in the army. But that soldier—Doherty—detailed what both Bernhardt and Terry had claimed. "I was shooting pigs and a chicken while the others were shooting people," he said. "It isn't just a nightmare; I'm completely aware of how real this was."[29]

Hersh's second article received a major boost when the *Cleveland Plain Dealer* ran it after a front-page story and the publication of the first of eight color photographs (although reproduced in black and white) taken by Ronald Haeberle that depicted the victims of the massacre and much of the village on fire. Haeberle was a hometown graduate of Fairview High School who had returned to Cleveland after leaving the army. After reading about Calley in the newspaper, he called a college friend at Ohio University in Athens who was now a reporter at the *Plain Dealer*, Joseph Eszterhas, and told him, "Joe, I have some photographs which might be this, what they are talking about, this massacre in Vietnam." Without hesitation, Eszterhas replied, according to an interview he gave, "Get down here."[30]

The paper's photographer, Richard Conway, was at his desk that night when Haeberle brought in the pictures. "I took a look at them and it was shocking," he remembered saying in a Cleveland *Plain Dealer* article published in 2009. "They were in color. They showed the terror on people's faces right before they were shot."[31]

The editors at first expressed concern about switching the news emphasis from the ongoing Apollo 12 moon mission, but they quickly changed their minds. Everyone was "shocked" by the photos of a "clump of bodies on a road" that included women and children and realized that the pictures fit with Hersh's article based on his interviews of three eyewitnesses. Eszterhas would write the story accompanying the photographs, which rested on an interview with Haeberle.[32]

According to Mike Roberts, at the time a *Plain Dealer* reporter in the Washington bureau, no one in the National Press Building believed Hersh's massacre story, and the executive editor of the newspaper in Cleveland, Bill Ware, had serious doubts. "Almost simultaneously," Roberts declared, "this kid comes forward with these pictures—Haeberle's photographs legitimized the story."[33]

This was not the first time the *Plain Dealer* had taken on a risky subject. It had established a reputation for boldness a year earlier by endorsing Carl Stokes for mayor of Cleveland and helping him become the first black mayor of a major American city. Soon afterward, the *Plain Dealer* became the state's largest daily newspaper, with a circulation of about four hundred thousand readers. The U.S. Army urged the paper's editors not to publish the photos as "prejudicial to the rights of individuals either charged or to be charged with illegal conduct in connection with the alleged murders." But the editors disagreed, arguing that their readers were "entitled to see them for what they are purported to be."[34]

Thus Calley and perhaps six others were not the only perpetrators of this massacre: as many as thirty soldiers, Haeberle declared in his interview for the paper, "indiscriminately and wantonly mowed down" about one hundred Vietnamese civilians—including women and babies. He vividly remembered a Vietnamese man holding a small boy in one arm and a little girl in the other, walking toward the Americans as the girl pleaded in English, "No, no." From twenty feet away a machine gunner coldly cut down all three with a burst of fire.[35]

There was no firefight, Haeberle emphasized, because no Viet Cong forces had been in the village. "They were just poor, innocent illiterate peasants." The soldiers were "intent on what they were trying to accomplish. There was no feeling, nothing human about it." He did not know whether the men acted under orders in killing the civilians. "I was shocked. I've never been able to forget what I saw there. I never saw U.S. GIs act like that before."[36]

Haeberle later declared in the Hébert Hearings of 1970 that he did not remember photographing the soldiers doing the shooting. Asked by a committee member why someone so close to the operation would not take such photographs, he replied that he had asked himself that question. "I can't come up with an answer." More than four decades later, however, he admitted to a reporter that he had taken pictures of American GIs shooting the villagers but destroyed the photos without showing them to anyone. "I was there in the operation," he explained. "I'm not gonna point a finger at some soldier out there and have him, you know, put up. No. We were all guilty. So I'm just as guilty as anyone else in the cover-up. I'll admit to that."[37]

The evening of the second Hersh article, CBS news anchor Walter Cronkite—the "most trusted man in America," according to some—displayed the *Plain Dealer*'s front page and the eight photographs in his lead story on his widely watched nightly news show. He first warned viewers of a gruesome sight before the cameras zoomed in on the photos. The images stunned Americans in staccato-like fashion: the bodies of men, women, and children shot to death by U.S. soldiers and left lying on top of each other in a ditch or along the road; the terrified expressions of nine women and children caught in the camera's eye just before American GIs raised their M-16s and killed them; and the fiery destruction of most of the village by the so-called Zippo squads.[38]

On that same night, Bernhardt appeared on both the CBS and NBC television news programs to tell his story to thirty million Americans.[39]

Haeberle's photos, coupled with Hersh's second article and Bernhardt's appearance on two major news networks, caused a national and worldwide sensation. *Newsweek* magazine referred to the Calley case as "only one of a string of related incidents" in which forty to fifty American GIs were "implicated" in the killing of 567 South Vietnamese. A *New York Times* editorial was more outspoken, declaring that the reports of "deliberative, methodical killing of hundreds of civilians—men, women and children—by American troops" were "so shocking, so contrary to principles for which this country has always stood, as to be beyond belief. Yet the evidence mounts daily that something horrible did take place." This story, combined with the "aborted Green Beret murder trial" and reporter Daniel Lang's recent account in the *New Yorker* of "the kidnapping, rape and murder of a Vietnamese girl by an American patrol," had helped make the war in Vietnam "an American nightmare." The *Times* called for a congressional investigation, insisting that the "barbaric conduct" by the Viet Cong and the North Vietnamese must not be used as an "excuse for any foot-dragging or cover-up by American authorities."[40]

Obst had meanwhile syndicated the story overseas. The *London Times* preceded Hersh's article on the front page with a story headlined "We Saw Women and Children Killed, Say US Soldiers." Inside the same edition were two related stories, one arguing that if the allegations were true, the My Lai massacre was worse than other cases of civilian deaths in that "American soldiers lined up unarmed civilians and mowed them down." Why had it taken so long for there to be an American investigation? Why hadn't Saigon's leaders shown greater concern? Why hadn't the Viet Cong more actively exploited the story? In the second story, an editorial, the writer called for a quick and open inquiry; otherwise the American military would continue burying accounts such as this one. Why had it taken twenty months for news of this alleged massacre "to filter out?" A front-page editorial in the sensationalist *Daily Sketch* of London made a pronouncement: "From today the war is over.... The president will have to pull out."[41]

In fact, President Nixon had become aware of My Lai about two months before Hersh's news stories appeared. On September 3, Secretary of Defense Melvin Laird sent him a memo warning that the publicity from the "My Lai Atrocity" could embarrass the United States and hurt popular support for the war by encouraging the antiwar movement and undermining the ongoing peace efforts in Paris. An attachment to the memo made clear that a soldier named Paul Meadlo had identified Lieutenant Calley as the chief director and participant in the small-arms killings of a large number of defenseless Vietnamese noncombatants who put up no resistance. Other witnesses corroborated the mass of bodies in the village, and an army photographer had provided color slides that helped launch a criminal investigation. "The known facts leave no doubt about the necessity of prosecution." When pressure grew on the White House to appoint a special commission to investigate the incident, National Security Affairs Adviser Henry Kissinger assured Nixon in a memo that such a move was unnecessary at this time for what appeared to be an "isolated incident." But if another atrocity occurred, a presidential commission would be advisable.[42]

Kissinger phoned Laird on November 21, warning that the "atrocity case" would become a "terrible mess" and informing him of the president's call for a "game plan." Laird thought Calley would plead insanity and probably escape conviction. "Only someone who had lost his sanity could carry out such an act." Kissinger had not seen the pictures, and Laird saw no reason for him to do so. "There are so many kids just laying there; these pictures are authentic." Laird remarked that he would "like to sweep the whole thing under the rug, but you can't do that." Laird convinced White House communications director Herbert Klein to warn the president's chief of staff, H. R. Haldeman, that the My Lai "incident" could "develop into a major trial almost of the Nuremberg scope and could have a major effect on public opinion."[43]

The White House, Laird insisted, must emphasize to Congress and the American public that these mass killings "didn't happen in our watch." They needed "some unified line," Kissinger declared. Laird intended to announce that he had discovered the atrocities in March and was so "shocked" that he ordered "a full investigation." He conceded that "those boys had been suffering terribly" and that one of them "had been killed just twenty-four hours before." As for killing civilians, "You can understand a little bit of this, but you shouldn't kill that many."[44]

In the meantime, the number of suspects of war crimes in the massacre continued to grow. On that same day of November 21, Robert Jordan, the army's general counsel, held an hour-long news conference in the Pentagon in which he announced that twenty-six persons were under investigation in connection with the alleged massacre, fifteen of them no longer in the service. Criminal investigators in both the United States and Vietnam were conducting interviews and gathering information on the case.[45]

Asked whether the army could try former soldiers for war crimes committed while in the service, Jordan remarked that the Supreme Court—referring to *Toth v. Quarles*—"has not been favorably disposed" to the military bringing charges against civilians, even if they had once been soldiers. But, he added, the situation might be different in this case, because the issue here was war crimes. "That avenue is a potential avenue against the civilians," but it involved "uncharted legal waters." This was a profoundly important issue, because "in military law a guy who orders somebody to kill someone unlawfully is considered as guilty of the murder as the guy who pulls the trigger." In an indirect reference to Calley, Jordan declared that "the charge against the two would be identical."[46]

III

The public exposure of the massacre continued to grow, as domestic and international news outlets sought the rights to reproduce the pictures. Haeberle and Eszterhas met with the corporate managers of *Life* magazine in New York to market their publication in color. The magazine agreed to pay Haeberle

$17,500 for the photos, considerably less than the $125,000 he asked for at first, but much more than the $500 he had received as a "gift" from the *Cleveland Plain Dealer* for showing eight of them. But he also sold reproduction rights outside the United States, receiving $5,400 from the *London Times*, $6,400 from *Stern Magazine* in West Germany, $500 from a Canadian newspaper, and $1,000 from an Australian paper. Eszterhas received $5,000 from *Life* magazine for helping to write an accompanying article.[47]

Hersh had meanwhile interviewed Paul Meadlo at his home in New Goshen, Indiana, on November 23 and convinced him to tell his story to the public. It had been almost as difficult for Hersh to find Meadlo as it had been to find Calley. While Hersh was on the West Coast, a soldier told him about Meadlo and thought he lived "somewhere in Indiana." Hersh found Meadlo's phone number, and his mother answered the call. "I don't know if he'll talk to you," Myrtle Meadlo warned. "Just come, but I can't promise." Two plane flights and a car drive later, Hersh finally located Meadlo's home—a shack housing him and his family and parents on a broken-down chicken farm about eighty miles from Indianapolis. His mother greeted Hersh unsmilingly on his arrival. "He's in there," she declared.[48]

Hersh first warmed Meadlo up by inquiring about his wounded leg, before asking what happened in Pinkville. "I just began to kill people," Meadlo asserted. Hersh managed to maintain an outer demeanor of calm as he asked how many civilians the GIs killed. Perhaps three hundred, Meadlo estimated, including women and children. He had followed Calley's orders, and together they had shot dozens of people on a trail and in a ditch. Meadlo showed some remorse. "The kids and the women, they didn't have any right to die."[49]

Hersh realized in the first moments of this interview that Meadlo had provided information crucial to convincing the public that its soldiers had acted under orders in massacring hundreds of Vietnamese civilians. He had gotten the first eyewitness account of Calley's actions, the first confession to murder (by Meadlo), and the first statement by a witness that Calley had not only participated in the group killings but in fact had ordered them. Hersh nonetheless professed afterward that he was not shocked by these revelations. Meadlo had exposed "the cancerous fingernail of what's going on in Vietnam," Hersh asserted in Miraldi's account. "This is what we do in Vietnam."[50]

Hersh immediately called Obst after the interview, exclaiming triumphantly, "We [have] the front page story of the world." Obst knew the press would run Hersh's third article, but he and Hersh now opted for something bigger—a television interview of Meadlo by Mike Wallace, co-host of the new program *60 Minutes*.[51]

But would Meadlo repeat his story to the American people? Hersh approached him with the idea, warning that he could be held responsible for anything he said. Meadlo consented to the TV interview.[52]

Hersh quickly brokered a deal whereby CBS paid the Dispatch News Service ten thousand dollars for facilitating Meadlo's arrival in New York. Hersh had kept the army apprised of his discoveries, including this one, but it expressed concern that the publicity generated by a TV interview might lead to a mistrial in the event of Calley's court martial, pending the ongoing Article 32 investigation stipulated by the Uniform Code of Military Justice. Hersh nonetheless convinced CBS of the overwhelming importance of broadcasting a first-hand report of what happened. The news network agreed to pay Meadlo's travel expenses but nothing more.[53]

On November 24, just four nights after Haeberle's photos appeared in the Cleveland press and on CBS-TV, Wallace interviewed twenty-two-year-old Paul Meadlo on national television. The night before, Hersh had stayed with him, sleeping on the couch. "I remember he cried out a lot that night." Early in the morning, he accompanied Meadlo and his wife on the plane to New York. Meadlo had admitted more than once in private testimony to his involvement in the killings, but never had he done so in a public venue and before millions of viewers, nor had he ever confronted an interviewer with such a bulldog approach as Mike Wallace.[54]

This was the American public's first introduction to an actual participant in the massacre, and to understand the reaction to his disclosures, one needs to know exactly what the viewers learned from Meadlo's interview that night.

After a general discussion of the mission's make-up and purpose in the assault on what was called Pinkville, Meadlo explained that his company's first combat action came during its advance toward the village when someone spotted a "gook"—a scared elderly Vietnamese man hiding in a shelter. Sergeant David Mitchell ordered him shot. On entering the village, the platoon began ordering everyone out of their hooches and gathered them near the village center in a circle. The number soon grew to nearly fifty people.

"What kind of people—men, women, children?" asked Wallace.

"Men, women, children," responded Meadlo.

"Babies?"

"Babies," Meadlo replied. "And we all huddled them up. We made them squat down, and Lieutenant Calley came over and said, 'You know what to do with them don't you?' And I said yes. So I took it for granted that he just wanted us to watch them."

But when Calley left and returned about fifteen minutes later, he asked, "How come you ain't killed them yet?" Meadlo tried to explain that he thought his job was to guard the captives, not kill them, but Calley told him in the presence of three or four other soldiers, "No, I want them dead."

Without saying another word, Meadlo said, Calley backed up about fifteen feet and began shooting the Vietnamese with his M-16.

"And he told me to start shooting," asserted Meadlo. "So I started shooting, I poured about four clips into the group." Asked how many shots were in a clip, Meadlo explained that each clip carried seventeen rounds.

Meadlo was uncertain about how many he killed. He was firing on automatic, which meant "you just spray the area," and he could not tell how many died because they were falling so quickly. "So I might have killed ten or fifteen of them."

"Men, women and children?"

"Men, women and children."

"And babies?"

"And babies."

"Okay, then what?"

Meadlo explained that they moved on to collect about eight more people and order them into a hooch before tossing in a hand grenade. But someone told them to take the captives to a ditch instead, where more than seventy other villagers were already squatting or standing along its edge. "Meadlo, we got another job to do," Calley declared while shoving them into the ditch. "And so we started pushing them off and we started shooting them," Meadlo asserted. "So altogether we just pushed them all off, and just started using automatics on them. And then—"

"Again—men, women and children?"

"Men, women and children."

"And babies?"

"And babies," Meadlo replied. "And so we started shooting them, and somebody told us to switch off to single shot so that we could save ammo. So we switched off to single shot, and shot a few more rounds" before leaving to gather more villagers.

Meadlo explained that the next morning he stepped on a land mine in a field that blew off his foot. "I feel cheated," he asserted, "because the V.A. [Veterans Administration] cut my disability like they did, and they said that my stump is well healed, well padded, without tenderness." Meadlo angrily denied their claim. "It hurts all the time. I got to work eight hours a day up on my foot, and at the end of the day I can't hardly stand it. But I gotta work because I gotta make a living. And the V.A. don't give me enough money to live on as it is."

"Did you feel any sense of retribution to yourself the day after?"

"Well, I felt that I was punished for what I'd done, the next morning. Later on in that day, I felt like I was being punished."

Wallace finally asked the question the answer to which everyone wanted to hear: "Why did you do it?"

"Why did I do it? Because I felt like I was ordered to do it, and it seemed like that, at the time I felt like I was doing the right thing, because like I said I lost buddies. I lost a damn good buddy, Bobby Wilson, and it was on my conscience. So after I done it, I felt good, but later on that day, it was gettin' to me."

Asked whether he was married and had children, Meadlo said yes and that he and his wife had a two-and-a-half-year-old boy and a year-and-a-half-old girl. "Obviously," Wallace noted, "the question comes to my mind…the father of two little kids like that…how do you shoot babies?"

"I don't know. It's just one of them things."

"How many people would you imagine were killed that day?"

"I'd say about 370."

When asked again how many he killed, Meadlo replied, "I couldn't say…just too many."

"And how many men did the actual shooting?"

"Well, I really couldn't say that, either. There was other…there was another platoon in there and…but I just couldn't say how many."

"But these civilians were lined up and shot? They weren't killed by crossfire?"

"They weren't lined up…they [were] just pushed in a ravine or just sitting, squatting…and shot."

"What did these civilians—particularly the women and children, the old men—what did they do? What did they say to you?"

"They weren't much saying to them," Meadlo declared. "They [were] just being pushed and they were doing what they was told to do."

"They weren't begging or saying, 'No…no,' or—"

"Right," Meadlo interjected. "They was begging and saying, 'No, no.' And the mothers was hugging their children and, but they kept right on firing. Well, we kept right on firing. They was waving their arms and begging…"

"Was that your most vivid memory of what you saw?"

"Right."

"And nothing went through your mind or heart?"

"Not while I was doing it. It just seemed like it was the natural thing to do at the time.... I was getting relieved from what I'd seen earlier over there... my buddies getting killed or wounded.... It was just mostly revenge."

"We've raised such a dickens about what the Nazis did, or what the Japanese did," Wallace observed, "but particularly what the Nazis did in the Second World War, the brutalization.... It's hard for a good many Americans to understand that young, capable, American boys could line up old men, women and children and babies and shoot them down in cold blood. How do you explain that?"

"I wouldn't know."

"Did you ever dream about all of this that went on in Pinkville?"

"Yes, I did... and I still dream about it."

"What kind of dreams?"

"I see the women and children in my sleep. Some days... some nights, I can't even sleep. I just lay there thinking about it."[55]

Meadlo had stunned a national television audience by confessing to murder, accusing Calley of murder, and claiming he had followed Calley's orders in gathering and shooting groups of Vietnamese civilians, including, as Wallace repeatedly emphasized, old men, women, children—and babies. And Meadlo aroused more outrage than sympathy when he complained about his injury and the problems he had with the Veterans Administration.[56]

The next night, Meadlo's parents lashed out at both the army and Calley for putting their son in this position. In a *CBS Evening News* interview, his mother bitterly remarked, "I raised him to be a good boy," and the army "made a murderer out of him." Meadlo's father, Tony, a retired coal miner who had lost a leg in a mining accident, was more direct: "If it had been me out there," he remarked in his Polish accent, "I would have swung my rifle around and shot Calley instead—right between the God-damned eyes. Then there would have been only one death."[57]

Meadlo made no money from his TV appearance and thought this unfair. When someone asked an employee of the Dispatch News Service in Washington how much CBS paid for the interview rights, he replied that it was an amount "in five figures." How much had Meadlo received? "The kid is getting absolutely zero," replied a spokesman for Hersh. Meadlo told a reporter that he knew nothing about any financial arrangements made by Hersh. "I've already told my story. I feel I should be getting something out of it."[58]

Meadlo's TV interview did of course far more than any newspaper article or photograph to convince the American people that what had taken place was a war crime. "It was the CBS interview," declared Hersh. And for those who missed the TV show, the *New York Times* ran a story the following day on the spectacle and reprinted the entire transcript of the exchanges between Wallace and Meadlo. This "incredible interview," Hersh concluded, "turned the corner" on showing the public that its boys in uniform had murdered hundreds of helpless human beings. Ridenhour likewise praised the media. The interviews with Meadlo, Terry, and other soldiers appearing on national TV over the next few days made it clear that "these young men were painfully telling the truth" about what they had seen.[59]

Two senators, however, publicly blasted CBS for televising such an interview. The day afterward, Republican Peter Dominick of Colorado upbraided the news network for hosting a soldier suspected of shooting defenseless people during a combat assault. Meadlo had endangered the legal rights of both himself and Calley by alleging that they had participated in killing hundreds of Vietnamese civilians—including women and children. "What kind of country have we got when this kind of garbage is put around?" Democrat Ernest Hollings of South Carolina asked what would happen if every soldier who made "a mistake in judgment" while in combat went to trial "as common criminals, as murderers?" Meadlo, he angrily declared, "was obviously sick" and "ought not to be exposed to the entire public."[60]

The Nixon administration immediately proclaimed that it had nothing to do with what happened at My Lai, which, after all, had taken place on LBJ's watch. That same day the *New York Times* published Laird's responses to seven hours of questions about My Lai posed a week earlier by the chair of the Senate Foreign Relations Committee, Democrat J. William Fulbright, which hardly seems like a coincidence. Asked about the delay, the defense secretary explained that he had preferred to send Fulbright a written reply for the historical record and that he had just approved it for public release. Laird declared that he was "shocked and sick" to learn of the alleged massacre. No one in the White House had heard about these events until Ridenhour's letter reached the president's desk the previous April, more than a full year after it had taken place. The administration, he assured the committee, was "determined to insure absolute compliance with our orders and with the laws of war."[61]

The army also denied any responsibility for the alleged massacre. In a statement given to the Foreign Relations Committee, it declared that the issue "was not brought to the attention of the Department of the Army, there being no apparent requirement for doing so." Colonel Oran Henderson had concluded in his report to the division commander that no massacre had occurred and no war crimes had been committed. Thus he had complied with MACV Directive 20-4, which declared it "the responsibility of all military personnel having knowledge or receiving a report of an incident or of an act thought to be a war crime to make such incident known to his commanding officer as soon as practicable." The divisional commander was not required to take further action, meaning that Henderson's report never went above division level and hence never came before the Department of the Army in Washington.[62]

The key question remained: How could there have been no war crime when photographs of the victims and a steady stream of public statements by American witnesses and Vietnamese survivors strongly suggested otherwise? The army could not deny what Meadlo had asserted on nationwide television—that a massacre had occurred and that he and Calley were two of its chief perpetrators. But the army had to show that the responsibility went no higher than the division level and that what Meadlo and others had done was an isolated incident, an aberration that resulted from rogue soldiers acting on their own and not on the basis of orders from above.

IV

In the midst of the nationwide clamor over Meadlo's interview, Hersh published his third article, "Ex-GI Tells of Killing Civilians at Pinkville," which highlighted another interview with Meadlo that included an allegation not mentioned on television that night—that Captain Ernest Medina also bore responsibility for the massacre. "I don't know if the C.O. [Commanding Officer] gave the order to kill or not," Hersh quoted Meadlo as saying in the article, "but he was right there when it happened. Why didn't he stop it? He and Calley passed each other quite a few times that morning, but didn't say anything. Medina just kept marching around. He could've put a stop to it anytime he wanted." Medina and Calley had prepared for civilian casualties by having a plan of deception in place. They warned their soldiers before the operation that if they "ever shoot any civilians," they had to make sure they were identifiable as Viet Cong. To do that, "we should go ahead and plant a hand grenade on them."[63]

With timing that seemed almost surreal to many, on the same day the *New York Times* published the story of the Meadlo TV interview and the transcript, it ran a front-page story on the U.S. Army's decision to court-martial Calley on charges of premeditated murder. According to the findings of the Article 32 investigation, Calley came under indictment for violating Article 118 of the Uniform Code of Military Justice, which defined the crimes for which a person could stand trial for "unlawfully" and "without justification or excuse" killing a human being.[64]

The murder charges fell into six specifications totaling at least 109 victims: the first for killing four persons; the second for "not less than 30" civilians; the third for three persons; the fourth for "an unknown number of Oriental human beings, not less than 70, males and females of various ages, whose names are unknown, occupants of the village of My Lai 4 by means of shooting them with a rifle"; the fifth for one male; and the sixth for a two-year-old child "whose name and sex is unknown."[65]

Major General Orwin Talbott at Fort Benning had made the decision that Calley must stand trial for murder. After heading the Article 32 investigation, Lieutenant Colonel Duane Cameron, who had commanded infantry forces during two tours in Vietnam, concluded that the evidence warranted a court martial. He had reviewed the testimonies of several former soldiers, including Meadlo, SP4 Charles Sledge, and SP4 Greg Olsen from Calley's 1st Platoon, and he had held a three-day hearing in late October in which PFC Michael Bernhardt from the 2nd Platoon and 1st Platoon sergeant Isaiah Cowan provided valuable information on the case. Cameron had also summoned 2nd Platoon sergeant Lawrence LaCroix and Sergeant David Mitchell of Calley's platoon, but they refused to testify for fear of saying something detrimental to their own cases if brought to court. Medina had testified for the defense, but other than talking about the operation, he chose not to answer the question of whether he had ordered Calley to kill civilians.[66]

Cameron had sent his report to the commanding general on November 6, recommending that Calley stand trial by "General Court Martial." Major General Talbott discussed the matter extensively with the staff judge advocate and realized that the case "was so serious that it could only be determined by a court of law."[67]

Talbott doubtless came under great pressure—from both the army and the public—in making a decision that he insisted was his own. He staunchly denied that anyone had tried to influence his decision and maintained that he had acted "solely on the Article 32 investigation."[68]

Lieutenant Colonel Tucker read the court-martial decision at a news conference at Fort Benning on November 24. The trial would take place on the base, the date depending on the time needed by the defense and the prosecution to make preparations. "It is anticipated that this will require at least a month." The trial would be open to the public, except during discussions of "classified security information." In the meantime, Calley would remain in his position at the post, free to leave for visits to nearby Columbus or, if elsewhere, after receiving permission. Was this unusual in a case involving a capital offense? Tucker emphasized that "incarceration is only used to protect a man or to make sure he's available for trial."[69]

The army's charges against Calley meant that he faced life imprisonment or death if found guilty. According to the army, he had been a chief architect of a war crime that it had initially concluded had not taken place. Not by co-incidence did the army announce on that same day, November 24, that it had appointed a three-star general, Lieutenant General William R. Peers, to lead an investigation into the Henderson report.[70]

Peers was a veteran of three wars, having served in World War II as a com-mander of the Office of Strategic Services in China, in the Korean War in army intelligence in China after a two-year stint in the CIA, and, after serving in the Pentagon, in the Vietnam War as a field commander. At the time of the Pinkville operation, he was acting commander of I Field Force and had no connection with the Americal Division in I Corps. In a memo he wrote to Westmoreland, he admitted that all his wartime experience could not have prepared him for what lay ahead—an outcome that, regardless of which way things went, meant victory for no one.[71]

Further complicating the Peers Inquiry's work was the competition be-tween the Senate and House over who would launch a separate congressional investigation—a contest won by the hawkish chair of the House Armed Services Committee, Democrat L. Mendel Rivers of South Carolina. On the same day General Westmoreland and Secretary of the Army Stanley Resor revealed the Peers appointment, Rivers announced that his investigative sub-committee would examine the charges of massacre and cover-up. Two days later, the entire Armed Services Committee opened a series of hearings.[72]

Other heavyweights were chiming in. Pulitzer Prize–winning columnist James Reston of the *New York Times* challenged Nixon and Vice President Spiro Agnew—a notable hawk and detractor of those who criticized American foreign policy—to deal with the question of culpability raised by Meadlo and others. "The main facts of this tragedy are not in dispute." The central issue now was who was at fault—the soldiers who killed the villagers, the officers who ordered the killing, or the "system" of war that prescribed the roles for both? The army had long treated My Lai 4 as a "free-fire zone," which meant the enemy controlled the village, making it open to B-52 bombing and artil-lery fire. The critical difference in the assault by Charlie Company was that its soldiers "saw the human beings in the village and killed them with their M-16s anyway, and then told their story on TV."[73]

Who was responsible? asked Reston. Meadlo, a "tragic and limited human being?" Calley, "the hard-faced lieutenant, who gave the orders?" The higher-ranking officers "who watched the carnage and let it go on?" Or "the system" for the deaths caused from afar by the B-52 bombardier and the artillery officer, who never see the faces of the men, women, and children they kill? The "big difference" in this case, Reston maintained, was that the soldier behind the M-16 "sees the human agony before he fires and the other doesn't." And yet "the end for the villagers is the same."[74]

Hersh's detailed articles based on eyewitness accounts and a confession to murder; Haeberle's graphic photos in the press and on TV; Meadlo's haunting appearance on *60 Minutes*; the news of Calley's court martial; the imminent Peers investigation—all these combined to divide Americans over what their soldiers had allegedly done at My Lai 4 and whether the U.S. Army had tried to cover it up. Meadlo's confirmation of a massacre received further support on the day after his TV interview when ex-serviceman Varnado Simpson admitted on NBC-TV that he was "personally responsible" for killing ten Vietnamese civilians at My Lai 4. The *New York Times* showed that U.S. Army publications shortly after the March 1968 assault had fabricated accounts of a great victory by American forces that resulted in 128 Viet Cong killed in action. The Americal Division's weekly newsletter, the *Southern Cross*, and the Pacific edition of *Stars and Stripes* had praised the GIs' performance in this Viet Cong stronghold without mentioning either Calley or any civilian casualties. The *New York Times* repeated these battle accounts in a front-page story, not knowing that the army reporter, Sergeant Jay Roberts, had come under great pressure from the task force commander, Lieutenant Colonel Barker, to carefully construct these highly favorable accounts.[75]

The Nixon administration nonetheless continually denounced the news coverage of the war, insisting that the antiwar demonstrations did not express the will of most Americans and encouraged the enemy by undermining the war effort. The U.S. Information Agency sent a film called *The Silent Majority* to more than one hundred countries, urging foreign observers to recognize that "the loudest sound is not the only one that should be listened to." Agnew attacked the American press for its alleged leftist leanings, which, he asserted, stemmed from the *Boston Globe*, *New York Times*, *Washington Post*, and other eastern establishment news outlets, including all three national television networks—ABC, CBS, and NBC. Postmaster General Winton Blount had just returned from Vietnam to proclaim that the antiwar protests had encouraged the enemy and were therefore "killing American boys."[76]

The controversy over the alleged massacre brought a mixed reaction in Vietnam. The North Vietnamese Foreign Ministry accused the United States of genocide, claiming that the mass murder was part of its policy toward all Southeast Asia and not the actions of a single military unit. To end this "war of aggression," the United States must totally withdraw its forces. South

Vietnam, like the American public, was divided in its reactions. The Saigon government under President Nguyen Van Thieu declared the massacre charges "totally false" and attributed the civilian deaths to "a normal and unavoidable act of war during a battle with the enemy." The leader of the opposition, Senator Tran Van Don, was a retired general and former chief of staff and defense minister who had been involved with Thieu and others in toppling Premier Ngo Dinh Diem in the early 1960s. But Don now blasted his former co-conspirator as "the valet of the Americans, who are his sole support." As chair of South Vietnam's Senate Defense Committee, he intended to ask his colleagues to appoint a panel to investigate the incident and expressed his willingness to serve on it. According to many South Vietnamese political leaders, Thieu had acted too hastily in denying there had been a massacre. How could he insist that no murder had occurred at the same time the country's ally was prosecuting one of its own army officers for murder?[77]

Two days later, the South Vietnamese Senate in Saigon approved two three-member committees to jointly inquire into the massacre, with Don heading the investigation. A great issue was at stake, he declared—the relationship between South Vietnam and the United States. Deputy Tran Ngoc Chau, a retired ARVN officer and staunch critic of Thieu, remarked that his denial of the massacre proved himself to be America's puppet. Three Vietnamese newspapers that day praised the United States for taking these deaths seriously, with one of them castigating the Thieu government's refusal to act as "cowardice and worthy of contempt."[78]

Time magazine also confirmed "the My Lai massacre"—which appears to be the earliest known use of the phrase—in its own story, based on Haeberle's grisly photos and quotes from witnesses, including Vietnamese survivors. Haeberle again described what he witnessed, as did Michael Terry and other GIs. Especially moving was the personal experience of a father, Do Chuc, whose son and daughter were killed. "My family was eating breakfast when the Americans came....Nothing was said to us. No explanation was given."[79]

Hersh meanwhile came under fire from across the political spectrum. Critics warned that his news stories had hurt the war effort and damaged the nation's influence throughout the world. Hadn't Hersh worked for Senator Eugene McCarthy's antiwar campaign for the presidency in 1968?

Hersh maintained that he was unconcerned about the charges. Years afterward he declared, "If I'm publishing something in the belief that what I'm doing is helping my country, it's going to be hard to convict me of treason." And to those military figures who urged him not to publish the story, he asserted, "It's your job to keep it secret and my job to find it out....If it's a just war and it makes sense, it's going to be reflected in the coverage." He then added, "There was something wrong with that war."[80]

By late November 1969, the U.S. Army itself appeared to be on public trial. It had aroused widespread suspicions of concealing the truth by refusing to make Henderson's April 1968 report available to the public, defending its stand by arguing that it might "be introduced into evidence in the Calley case and other proceedings." Republican senator Charles Percy of Illinois called for investigations by both the Pentagon and the Senate and accused the Defense Department of undermining the public's confidence in the Pentagon by attempting to hide a massacre that took place almost two years earlier.[81]

The Pentagon prepared for lengthy sessions, defending itself before congressional committees as increasing numbers of Americans demanded the full story about their military's actions. On November 24, Mendel Rivers of the House of Representatives took the lead in announcing that the Armed Services Investigative Subcommittee would examine the allegations of a massacre. A strong supporter of the war, Rivers knew the nation's prestige was on the line, as was the Nixon administration's peace efforts with North Vietnam. And the antiwar movement posed a major challenge. The most recent Gallup poll in late September 1969 showed that the majority of Americans thought the troop involvement was a mistake by 58 percent to 32 percent—a jump from a ratio of 54 percent to 37 percent a year earlier.[82]

Resor found it nearly impossible to ease the growing public suspicion that Washington's leaders were covering up mass murders, especially when he had himself recently seen a secret staff memorandum of November 24 that raised some highly embarrassing questions. According to its findings, numerous witnesses attested that Charlie Company had met no ground resistance and yet continued firing on defenseless noncombatants, leaving about 350 victims who were primarily women and children gathered into groups. He also learned that "responsible individuals" were aware of these actions and made every effort "to conceal that information."[83]

On November 26, the army's defense strategy became clear when Resor, accompanied by army counsel Robert Jordan and General Richard Stillwell, deputy chief of staff for military operations, answered the summons of the Armed Services Committees in both the Senate and House to testify in separate and closed hearings about the alleged massacre. The secretary of the army first read a lengthy statement detailing what his department knew about the operation in Pinkville, including a helicopter pilot's claim—Thompson's, of course—that American soldiers were mercilessly killing Vietnamese civilians.[84]

The result, Resor continued, was an investigation by the brigade commander into the accusation, an investigation that concluded that no massacre
or war crimes had occurred. Artillery preparation or cross fires during the
battle had accidentally killed about twenty noncombatants, meaning that
Viet Cong propaganda was responsible for the charge of mass murder and no
war crime had occurred. The report of that investigation therefore stayed on
the divisional level without reaching either MACV or the USARV (United
States Army Republic of Vietnam).

The Department of the Army had moved quickly on first hearing of the
incident through Ridenhour's letter of late March 1969. After a preliminary
inquiry justified decisive action, the chief of staff directed the inspector general to launch a full-scale investigation of Ridenhour's allegations. A number
of American soldiers remained under investigation for their roles in the alleged massacre, Resor noted, but the army had already filed murder charges
against two of them, Calley and Mitchell. Article 32 proceedings had uncovered sufficient evidence to order Calley to face a court martial, while Mitchell
still awaited the outcome of the investigation that would determine whether
he too would stand trial in a military court.

Resor declared that he had discussed this incident with several officers
who had served in Vietnam. "It is their judgment—a judgment which I personally endorse and share—that what apparently occurred at My Lai is wholly
unrepresentative of the manner in which our forces conduct military operations in Vietnam."[85]

For the first time, the army had admitted to mass murder being perpetrated by its soldiers at My Lai 4.

In both the Senate and House meetings, Resor assured legislators that he
had provided everything the army knew "about the tragic events that took
place in the hamlet." In covering many details, however, he did not mention
the estimated 350 Vietnamese civilians who had died in the assault. But he then
had both committee rooms darkened to facilitate showing slides of Haeberle's
photographs in color. A number of congressional members had seen the black-
and-white pictures on television or perhaps in the *Cleveland Plain Dealer*, but
the impact of the color images was much stronger. The piles of bodies torn to
pieces by M-16s and machine guns left a gory picture of blood and body matter
that sickened even the hardest of viewers—including those who had refused to
believe what Hersh had written or what Meadlo had claimed.[86]

Resor did not soften the impact of the hard truths told by these photographs by calling the incident at My Lai 4 an aberration. Democratic senator
Daniel Inouye of Hawaii walked out of the committee meeting. He had seen

tragedy in World War II, but even his loss of an arm in that conflict could not prepare him for what he saw that day. "Having been in combat myself, I thought I would be hardened, but I must say I am a bit sickened." In the House committee meeting, Republican Leslie Arends of Illinois likewise left the room. "The pictures were pretty gruesome," he explained to newsmen. "That's why I walked out. I have one of those queasy stomachs." The chair of the Senate's Armed Services Committee, Democrat John Stennis of Mississippi, emphasized that what happened "was contrary to every rule and instruction the Army has issued in connection with the conduct of the South Vietnamese operation."[87]

Democratic senator Stephen Young of Ohio was the only member of the Armed Services Committee to express concern for those who had died at My Lai 4. "It's really terrifying and horrible, looking at a Vietnam woman—a young woman—standing up and begging, with young people all about her, and knowing that she would be killed an instant later by American bullets. No one can question there was an atrocious slaughter of from 200 to 300 civilians."[88]

NO LONGER COULD one ask *whether* a massacre had occurred; the questions now were how it could have happened, who was responsible, and why it had taken so long to become public knowledge. The answers to these three queries together raised this further question: Had there been a cover-up?

Ten

THE PEERS INQUIRY HAD A SPECIFIC MANDATE: not to establish guilt and innocence in the alleged massacre at My Lai on March 16, 1968, but to determine whether a cover-up had occurred following it. Lieutenant General Peers's instructions were explicit: "The scope of your investigation does not include…ongoing criminal investigations in progress."[1] To do this, Peers headed a large investigating team, consisting of personnel from the army joined by two attorneys from law firms in New York: Robert MacCrate, a senior partner in Sullivan and Cromwell, and Jerome Walsh, associate special counsel for the commission and a partner in his own firm.

The army's Criminal Investigation Division, or CID, would continue the work it had begun the previous August, meaning that together the two inquiries would attempt to answer parallel questions. CID would investigate whether a massacre had occurred, and the Peers commission whether it was followed by a conspiracy of silence. Peers intended to present the inquiry's findings in March 1970; CID aimed for a few months after that.

I

Despite its instructions, the Peers panel soon realized the impossibility of assessing the reports and investigations with any eye toward a cover-up without examining all parts of the Task Force Barker operation in Son My Village. Testimonies began in the Pentagon on December 2, 1969, but soon expanded to include almost two weeks of on-site investigations and interrogations in Son My of Vietnamese civilians and military officials as well as U.S. military and civilian personnel, followed by another round of questioning in Washington that resulted in the interrogation of more than four hundred witnesses (some appearing more than once). The targeted completion date was March 7, 1970—about a week before the expiration of the two-year statute of limitations on military crimes on March 15. The investigative team also explored possible atrocities in three other subhamlets of Tu Cung—Binh Tay, Binh Dong, and Trung Hoa—and in three other hamlets of Son My Village: Co Luy, My Lai, and My Khe.[2]

Even if the Peers commission had had authorization to gather information aimed at criminal prosecutions, its discoveries would not have guaranteed court-martial proceedings for everyone accused. The Pentagon insisted that former servicemen were not subject to military tribunals for alleged crimes committed while in uniform. But this claim was not entirely accurate, according to an argument made on the same day the panel began work. The army's lead counsel, Robert Jordan, sent a memo to the U.S. attorney general's office, asserting that former soldiers were in fact subject to courts martial for alleged crimes committed while in the service. The problem, Jordan explained years afterward to Deborah Nelson, quoted in Nick Turse's book, was that such action could come only from a White House directive. "We would have needed the president's support to proceed, and the president of [the] United States didn't support prosecution of Vietnam War crimes."[3]

The reasons behind Nixon's stance on this issue became evident from his reaction to My Lai over the Thanksgiving holidays. On November 27, he invited Alexander Butterfield, a White House assistant who was also the architect of the taping system that would later play a large part in Nixon's resignation, to accompany him to his Key Biscayne retreat in Florida to discuss strategy. Nixon had a yellow legal pad with three pages of notes outlining his plan to minimize the impact of My Lai on his Vietnam policy.

Essentially, the president sought to undermine the credibility of those who had called it a massacre. "Check out the Claremont man," he declared, referring to Ronald Ridenhour, now a student at Claremont Men's College in California. Wasn't he Jewish and a liberal? In fact, Nixon added, according to quotations in Bob Woodward's book on Butterfield, who supplied them, "Check out talkers"—those publicly criticizing what happened at My Lai. What about Mike Wallace of *60 Minutes*? "He's far left." "The Army photographer" (Haeberle) who had sold his pictures to *Life* magazine and the *Cleveland Plain Dealer*? "How much?" His parents, thought Nixon, were "Cleveland peaceniks." Meadlo was "too smooth for a farmer." The Pentagon was "too scared" to investigate this matter, which left it to the White House. Nixon wanted his domestic adviser, John Ehrlichman, to head this effort.[4]

Nixon then called for congressional support, according to Woodward's book. "We need some ammo in the hands of some Senators.... We need a big senator—a gut fighter—a stand up senator." Perhaps drawing from his own experience uncovering communists while on the House Un-American Activities

Committee, the president wanted "some congressman who could dig into this one on a personal basis. We can feed info to them." Expose the backgrounds of everyone involved. "Discredit witnesses, discredit *Time* and *Life* for using this. Get right-wingers with us."[5]

Butterfield took careful notes on this session and marked them "Top Secret."[6]

On the plane back to Washington on November 30, Nixon revealed himself, as Butterfield told Woodward, as "a Calley advocate." "I think this fellow Calley," the president asserted, according to Butterfield, is "probably a good soldier" who might be "getting a bum rap." This "Goddamn what's his name"— Ridenhour—had told his story to Seymour Hersh. "We ought to get someone on that guy. What is that guy? Learn more about him." The president added that Ehrlichman would handle this situation. "John's got people that can get on this guy's tail. Tell Ehrlichman, I want the guy tailed. I want to know everything about him, tail him, put a tail on him."[7]

Butterfield told Ehrlichman what the president wanted, and he agreed to "take care of it."[8]

A week or so before Christmas, Butterfield informed the president that Ehrlichman had sent someone posing as a journalist to interview Ridenhour and show that he and Hersh were "the apparent driving force behind the non-government release of alleged massacre information." Ridenhour considered Hersh, Butterfield told the president, a "no-good son of a bitch" who had left the mistaken impression that he was a "government official" and then inflated Ridenhour's conversations with My Lai participants into exhaustive interviews and made a financial profit. Butterfield recommended connecting a "good lawyer" with him to exploit his "bitter feeling" toward Hersh.[9]

Butterfield further told the president that Hersh was a leftist, antiwar reporter who had worked as press secretary for Eugene McCarthy's presidential antiwar campaign in 1968 and had later secured a thousand-dollar grant to write the "My Lai story." The money came from the Edgar B. Stern Family Fund, which was "clearly left-wing and anti-Administration."[10]

On the day before the Peers commission began work, Nixon ignored the information he had on My Lai and instructed Haldeman to set up a secret "Task Force–My Lai" to undermine the efforts by the press to show that a massacre had taken place. At one point he groused about the negative publicity and declared, according to Robert Dallek and other writers, "It's those dirty rotten Jews from New York who are behind it." The makeup of the task force demonstrated its importance to the White House: Vice President Spiro Agnew, National Security Adviser Henry Kissinger, White House Press

Secretary Herb Klein, speechwriter Patrick Buchanan, and Franklyn Nofziger, a congressional liaison and chief propagandist for the administration. Their responsibility, the president made clear to Haldeman, was "to control the whole problem" by "dirty tricks" at "not too high a level." Among those measures he suggested were to "discredit one witness" (Thompson) and highlight the atrocities committed by the Viet Cong at Hué. The administration's friends in Congress might help—perhaps "a Sen[ator] or two."[11]

Rather than a senator, the president turned to the chair of the House Armed Service Committee, Mendel Rivers, who as noted earlier was a hawkish supporter of the war and an outspoken skeptic of the massacre charges. Just days earlier, Rivers had launched a full committee investigation into the My Lai case. Nofziger met with Rivers soon after the White House meeting to urge him to "vocally" support the president in all policies and "attack those who attacked him."[12]

Nixon's chief concern, of course, was that the news stories about a mass killing would further increase the opposition to America's involvement in Vietnam and undermine his program of phased withdrawal. In early September 1969, Laird had sent the president a plan to "Vietnamize the war" by withdrawing half of the American troops over the next forty-two months while leaving the remaining 267,500 forces there as long as the enemy threat persisted. The press, he complained, virtually ignored the Viet Cong's terrorist methods in focusing on such alleged events as My Lai.[13]

The president opposed the recommendation offered by Daniel Patrick Moynihan, his domestic affairs adviser, to appoint a special commission to investigate the My Lai incident. But in early December, the pressure to do something grew when Senators John Stennis of Mississippi and Margaret Chase Smith of Maine informed the White House of their joint recommendation to the president to appoint a special commission on the My Lai atrocities. They feared that congressional involvement in the affair, as they wrote in a memo to Nixon, was "rapidly leading toward a number of garish and overlapping investigations" that would interfere with the soldiers' right to a fair trial. Furthermore, they believed that the news media was "turning the entire affair into a Roman circus."[14]

Nixon nonetheless agreed with Kissinger: no commission was necessary if the issue remained only My Lai. It would be another matter if news of another incident arose. Indeed, Kissinger had recently received a report of another atrocity and referred to it in a memo to the president. A former infantryman (not identified) claimed he "witnessed many civilians shot down like clay pigeons" in the Chu Lai area—at least "sixty dead bodies—women, children and maybe a few old and decrepit men." He and others in his platoon had seen at least one hundred villagers shot in the rice paddies, including "women taken for intercourse and then shot." The Defense Department could not substantiate this report, but Laird expected more allegations "by individuals of various motives."[15]

At a televised news conference on December 8, Nixon announced that he would not consider a civilian commission to investigate My Lai unless the military's judicial process did not "prove to be adequate in bringing this incident completely before the public."[16]

"What appears was certainly a massacre," he assured the press in the same news conference, "and under no circumstances was it justified.... We cannot ever condone or use atrocities against civilians." However, he also called the My Lai massacre an "isolated incident" that did not reflect national policy and could obscure the good achieved by Americans in the war. "That is why I am going to do everything I possibly can to see that all of the facts in this incident are brought to light and that those who are charged, if they are found guilty, are punished."[17]

In the meantime, the president's secret My Lai task force would seek to sabotage that judicial process by undermining the credibility of all those making the massacre charges. With Rivers's help, Nixon hoped to cover up or at least minimize the impact of My Lai.[18]

The administration nonetheless found it impossible to quiet the media flurry over Hersh's revelations. The day before the Peers commission began its proceedings on December 2, an army major had told the *New York Times*, "We are at war with the ten-year-old children. It may not be humanitarian, but that's what it's like." *Newsweek* magazine asserted that the Viet Cong's barbarities during the Tet offensive had fueled what it called a "dink syndrome" among U.S. soldiers. About a third of the Americal Division's casualties that year had come from exploding booby traps "probably made by meek-looking farmers and grandmothers." Some soldiers held the Vietnamese in contempt and had become "casual" about killing. An American civilian official summed up the feeling: "Psychologically and morally, it's much easier to kill a 'dink' than it is to shoot a 'Vietnamese.'"[19]

Life magazine intensified the growing national debate in early December by publishing Haeberle's photos in color. Some of the photos had already appeared in the newspapers and on television, but none of these had the impact of color photographs.[20]

The popular reaction to the story and illustrations was emotional on both sides, further charging the atmosphere in which the Peers commission conducted its work. A college professor in Alabama wrote the magazine that "the whole thing has been blown up out of all proportions" in an effort "to show the United States as immoral." A veteran of World War II and Vietnam declared, "Even if this incident happened as alleged, it is an isolated incident and not American policy." But a California correspondent wrote in, "Those pictures will haunt me the rest of my life. I weep for the children murdered, and I weep for the men that murdered them." There was now a "shadow cast" on every American soldier, nationally acclaimed journalist Hugh Sidey wrote.[21]

II

On December 4, two days into its hearings, the Peers commission called Captain Medina to the stand. He denied ordering the killings and said he was not aware of a massacre, did not shoot a child, and shot a woman only in self-defense. The next morning, on Mike Wallace's CBS morning news radio program, Medina remarked that he had had problems with Paul Meadlo, who accused him of not being in the village and doing nothing to stop the alleged massacre. Medina admitted that he did not go "all through My Lai 4" and did not investigate the number of bodies because he received no reports of an "atrocity" from his men. "I was not there," he said, but "if I had been there and had known that any such thing was taking place, I would have stopped it."[22]

Meanwhile, in the early afternoon of December 5, Lieutenant Calley flew from Fort Benning with his military counsel, Major Kenneth Raby, to appear before the Peers panel. After he arrived in Washington, he tried to enter the Pentagon from the side entry, where he confronted about a hundred reporters, photographers, and spectators. As his plane's pilot and an army officer cleared the way through the crowd, Calley said nothing and stared straight ahead as he climbed the steps, only to hear a TV reporter calling out, "Lieutenant Calley! Are you sorry you couldn't have killed more women and children?" Calley said nothing as he hurried through the corridor of the Pentagon and down three flights of stairs to the Army Operations Center, where the Peers commission was holding its hearings.[23]

The highly anticipated session ended quickly: in view of the charges against him, Calley chose to remain silent on My Lai. When the commission emphasized that its major task was to decide whether the investigatory process after My Lai had been thorough, Calley agreed to make one statement only: that neither Colonel Henderson nor Lieutenant Colonel Barker had questioned him about the My Lai operation.[24]

Calley's silence meant that the Peers commission was unable to ask whether he talked with Warrant Officer Hugh Thompson. Nor could it determine the number of casualties reported to Medina by his three platoon leaders. Lieutenant Stephen Brooks had died in battle, and Lieutenant Jeffrey LaCross had guessed that his men had killed "about fifty." How did Medina justify his reported figure of ninety Vietnamese casualties?[25]

But Calley's statement raised an important question: If Henderson and Barker actually investigated what happened at My Lai, why hadn't they talked with Calley?[26]

The Peers commission was less than a week into the testimonies when it learned of Mendel Rivers's plan to have an investigating subcommittee of the House Armed Services Committee look into the alleged massacre and cover-up. Within a month, the fourteen-member subcommittee had collected enough testimony to convince Rivers to hold closed hearings.

At the subcommittee's first session on December 9, Peers and Robert MacCrate appeared at Rivers's invitation to explain their responsibilities—and perhaps ease the concern of those legislators who questioned the reliability of the army investigating itself. As Peers left the room, Rivers invited him to his office two days later for a private meeting early in the morning.[27]

Rivers's objective became evident after the first day's hearings, when he told reporters he was not yet prepared to agree with the president's assertion the night before that a massacre had taken place in My Lai. "If he knows that," Rivers remarked in a quote reported in the *New York Times*, "he knows more than I do....I've seen some pictures of dead bodies, but I haven't seen any pictures of anybody shooting anybody."[28]

Hugh Thompson testified on the second day and initially repeated what he told Colonel Wilson in his inquiry for the inspector general's office—that he had ordered his two crewmen to fire upon the American soldiers if they attempted to shoot the Vietnamese civilians he was trying to evacuate. But under the pressure of an openly skeptical congressional panel, Thompson tried to protect himself against charges of unlawfully threatening fellow soldiers by adding that he had also told his men to have their machine guns ready in the event of a Viet Cong attack. The result was that his story leaked out in two versions, opening the way for Rivers (one of the few congressional leaders briefed about Colonel Wilson's findings and thus aware of Thompson's original testimony) to tell the press that Thompson was concerned about the enemy and "didn't give us any information that would lead us to believe anybody ever committed a massacre."[29]

Other subcommittee members, stifled by Rivers's order not to talk with reporters, were shocked by his assertion that no massacre had occurred. "I don't know how he could say that," said one unidentified by Hersh.[30]

The next morning, December 11, Rivers surprised Peers at their meeting by remarking about My Lai 4, "You know our boys would never do anything like that." Peers respected Rivers's longtime support for the war in Vietnam but assured him that the investigation would be objective and thorough, warning the congressman that numerous signs pointed to an ugly incident in which U.S. soldiers murdered a large number of civilians and suggested that something went awry within the command structure in reporting these killings. Rivers's attitude made it clear that the Peers commission would face a difficult task.[31]

Later that same day, Medina appeared before the Rivers subcommittee and received a warm reception. He dismissed the talk of massacre, expressing confidence that Lieutenant Colonel Barker "believed that there was no incident of war crimes or atrocities committed at My Lai 4." Medina drew a standing ovation from the subcommittee when he asserted that he spoke "on behalf of Mrs. Barker" in calling her deceased husband "an outstanding task force commander, an outstanding soldier." Medina returned the compliment, praising the work of Rivers and his "outstanding committee."[32]

Afterward, Rivers refused to reveal what went on in the subcommittee meeting to a gathering of about fifty reporters in the corridor. But as he turned toward the elevator, someone referred to an article in the previous day's *Washington Star* that quoted an unidentified subcommittee member who claimed former Warrant Officer Hugh Thompson had testified to ordering his two crew mates to train their guns on American soldiers during the evacuation of a small group of Vietnamese civilians. Didn't that contradict your statement to the press yesterday? Rivers, now in the elevator, called the anonymous source a "damn liar" just as the doors closed.[33]

Later that afternoon, the Pentagon left the impression that no massacre had occurred by releasing a copy of the citation written in support of the Distinguished Flying Cross awarded to Thompson in July 1968. Its wording made it appear that the enemy was there and that there had been no confrontation with American soldiers. Instead, according to the citation, Thompson's heroics had saved fifteen Vietnamese children hiding in a bunker between "Viet Cong positions and advancing friendly forces" and a few moments later evacuated an injured Vietnamese child from a ditch in the midst of "intense crossfire."[34]

This award had of course come a year and a half before the army realized that a massacre had taken place and that no Viet Cong had been in My Lai 4 on March 16.

After this third day of testimony, according to Hersh, Secretary of Defense Melvin Laird (clearly not privy to the president's secret task force on My Lai) convinced Rivers to conclude the hearings in light of the furor among high department officials over his unwarranted claim to the press that there was no evidence suggesting a massacre. Secretary of the Army Stanley Resor had already admitted to a mass killing by American troops, and Rivers's public statement left the impression that a congressional whitewash was underway. "If he'd read those papers on his desk," one Pentagon official bitterly remarked sometime afterward, "he'd know what went on."[35]

At any rate, Rivers had heard enough testimony by then to appoint Democrat F. Edward Hébert of Louisiana to investigate My Lai.[36]

Rivers directed Hébert to head a special four-member "Subcommittee on the My Lai Incident," which would operate in closed executive session and independently of the Peers Inquiry. The other members of the bipartisan subcommittee were Democrat Samuel Stratton of New York and two Republicans, Charles Gubser of California and William Dickinson of Alabama. Like Rivers, Hébert was an outspoken hawk on the war in Vietnam and at one point called for a nuclear solution.[37]

Rivers told the press that his committee had gathered enough evidence to make it necessary for the subcommittee to "go into this matter in depth." When a reporter asked about the "whitewash" rumors, he indignantly denied any effort to squelch the My Lai allegations. "I ought to count to ten before I answer this," he declared. "I'm not in that business, but neither am I in the business of catering to some people who want to gut the military and destroy it at a time we should be backing them up."[38]

Hébert promised in a television interview that he would uncover the facts, "no matter where the chips fall." More than once he had privately warned Westmoreland, according to Mark Carson, against interfering with the subcommittee's work, whether holding back documents or preventing witnesses from testifying. "If this ever breaks out in the newspapers it will be a horrible mess.... If I don't get these answers, I can't stop it."[39]

Less than a week before the hearings began, in mid-April, Rivers set the tone for the subcommittee's work by lashing out at the army in a speech before six hundred people in Altus, Oklahoma. His intention, he declared, was to put a halt to the string of courts martial looming ahead. If any crimes occurred, it was the army and not the soldier who was responsible. The Pentagon was "not going to get by with this."[40]

The veneer of congressional cooperation with the Peers commission was no more than that. The two investigative teams quickly came into conflict over several procedural matters. Peers asked Hébert not to question witnesses until after the panel had taken their testimony. To placate the subcommittee members, Army Secretary Resor offered to provide the information and recommendations compiled by the Peers commission, along with the transcript of the interviews. But nearly every military and civilian figure Hébert's subcommittee wanted to question was involved in one way or another with the impending trials, and Resor requested that the subcommittee delay interrogating these potential defendants to protect their rights in the judicial process. Hébert denied the request. Almost two weeks into the subcommittee's work, Resor asked for copies of its hearings, but Hébert refused this request as well, declaring that "frank and complete statements from some of our witnesses could not be obtained without first assuring them that their testimony would not be disclosed voluntarily to anyone outside the subcommittee."[41]

It appeared that Hébert had violated the Jencks Act of 1957, which required a government agency questioning principals in a criminal investigation to make their testimonies available to the federal courts on request. Hébert had a different slant on that act. Knowing that without the transcript the army could not bring in those witnesses, he arranged to have it classified and closed for national security reasons. He then issued subpoenas to every person he and his subcommittee wanted to question. Eighteen congressional members protested Hébert's actions as an attempt to "whitewash an alleged horrible violation" of law, and Democrat Abner Mikva of Illinois wrote a lengthy legal letter chastising "the foremost lawmaking body in the land" for "obstructing administration of the very laws it writes." Hébert ignored the criticisms, determined to let nothing stand in the way of his and Rivers's plan to undermine the government's case for the massacre charges.[42]

Meanwhile, of course, the president was publicly admitting that a massacre had occurred while privately attempting to discredit this claim by means of a clandestine task force.

III

In the course of its proceedings, the Peers commission had discovered that another massacre may have taken place on March 16, 1968—at neighboring My Hoi (or Khe Hoi), which appeared on American maps as My Khe 4. Bravo Company, under the command of Captain Earl Michles, had killed about ninety civilians in this small coastal settlement in Co Luy Hamlet.[43]

Michles had died in a helicopter crash, and there was no record of his version of what happened. Of the twenty-two platoon members who either witnessed or took part in the operation, two had died in battle, eight refused to answer questions, and most of the others claimed not to remember the event. Furthermore, U.S. forces had destroyed the abandoned settlement soon afterward, leaving no traces of homes, trails, and vegetation. Finally, the few survivors of the assault had moved elsewhere, making it impossible to flesh out the story.[44]

The destruction in My Khe 4 suggests that the allegations were likely true. The day after the assault, Bravo Company burned down three of Co Luy's subhamlets, but on the next day it dropped the search-and-destroy policy to engage in a pacification effort based on the establishment of a Medical Civic Action Program supported by the task force. Concern about an investigation or perhaps a sense of remorse led to these unusual changes.[45]

In any case, due to a lack of any evidence that the victims had been enemy forces, the Peers commission put no faith in Michles's report from Lieutenant Thomas Willingham, who claimed his platoon had killed twelve armed Viet Cong.[46]

Peers later noted that Colonel Henderson did not mention My Khe 4 in his report of April 24, 1968—probably because he was not aware of what happened. And yet someone in the army at the company level or higher (or both) had "more deeply suppressed"—in Peers's words—information about these killings than those in My Lai 4. One could sense his frustration when he called My Khe 4 "an almost total cover-up."[47]

One possibility is that Resor had conceded that U.S. forces committed war crimes in My Lai 4, making it necessary for the army to keep the My Khe 4 story quiet to uphold its claim that My Lai 4 was an isolated occurrence. My Khe 4's exposure could suggest a connection to My Lai 4 as part of the combat plan and point to a higher command culpability. "When they get finished shaking this hen house, there will be a lot of big roosters falling out of the rafters," Ridenhour had told Newsweek magazine.[48]

In the course of its investigation, the Peers commission suggested a wider responsibility when it cited "many indicators of unusual events" that leaders and staff officers in the divisional chain of command should have recognized and then followed up with formal investigations and reports of possible war crimes. But no officer at any level took proper action, which left the appearance of widespread wrongdoing.[49]

Major General Koster and Colonel Henderson had insisted that artillery fired onto villages was a violation of their policy and yet did nothing to enforce that policy at My Lai 4. Captain Medina and his men had thought the artillery plan called for hitting its outer edge as a means for rooting out enemy emplacements in the tree lines. The Peers commission conceded that this action was technically in accord with the rules of engagement, but it showed no concern for civilians and "was clearly in violation of the spirit of the policy."[50]

According to the Peers panel, Lieutenant Colonel Barker bore the chief responsibility for turning My Lai 4 into a free-fire zone. Most important, he had "intentionally or negligently" furnished "false intelligence" to company commanders that all civilians would have left the village prior to the assault. The army had attempted to minimize civilian casualties by MACV Directive 525-3, which asserted that where a noncombatant lived "depends to a large extent upon factors and forces beyond his control." In the words of the Peers commission, this meant that Vietnamese "personnel living in VC-controlled areas [would] not be considered VC solely on the basis of their presence in these areas." Barker violated this directive by failing to provide for the evacuation and safety of civilians living in a combat zone and by planning and executing an "unlawful operation" that led to massive destruction of private property. He did not specifically order the killing of civilians, but "he may have created a belief" by some commanders that "they were authorized to kill any persons found there."[51]

Furthermore, the Peers commission concluded, Barker had failed to perform his duties after the operation. Despite knowing early in the morning that nearly thirty civilians had died, he "probably conspired" with Major Charles Calhoun and others to hide these casualties by submitting a "false report" that artillery fire had killed sixty-nine Viet Cong, by helping to "suppress information" regarding war crimes, and by not reporting "suspected war crimes" in accordance with MACV Directive 20-4. Finally, Barker did not report the burning of dwellings, the civilian casualties he knew about, or the allegations of war crimes sent him by Major Frederic Watke. Instead, Barker submitted "a deliberately false and misleading combat after action report" that did not mention civilian casualties and "falsely depicted a hotly-contested combat action," all apparently in "an outright effort to suppress" the truth about a massacre.[52]

Other discrepancies became evident regarding Barker's 8:40 a.m. report that Charlie Company had "counted 69 VC KIA" by small-arms fire near the center of My Lai 4. Even though his journal indicated that he had informed the 11th Brigade of this figure, the brigade's journal did not record any information pertaining to this matter until nearly an hour later, when, in two surprising changes, the cause of the deaths was switched to "artillery fire" and the location of the kills shifted to a spot nearly two thousand feet northwest of the village center and hence outside the settlement.[53]

The Peers commission noted that no one had explained the reasons for these two alterations in the brigade's journal, which division commanders should have noted as critical to establishing an enemy threat and the absence of a massacre. By nine o'clock a journal entry showed that "30–40 VC had departed the area at 0700 hours"—a half hour *before* the first American soldiers arrived at My Lai 4. The result was that after 9:40 a.m., every officer in the chain of command had been given a doubly fabricated figure: that artillery fire had killed sixty-nine Viet Cong outside My Lai 4.[54]

Thus the only Viet Cong forces in the targeted area had left before the assault began, a number far fewer than the sixty-nine enemy forces allegedly killed in action less than an hour later. Lieutenant Dennis Johnson, the Military Intelligence officer with Charlie Company, insisted that "the VC had departed the village prior to the combat assault." Lieutenant John Alaux was the company's forward artillery observer and concurred with Johnson's statement. According to the Peers commission, "the most probable source" of the inaccurate report was Captain Medina, who knew by 9:15 a.m. that no enemy forces were in the village and yet did not forward this information to division headquarters. Even though the Americal Division Operations Journal for March 16 made no reference to the Viet Cong leaving the village, it did receive one obviously "erroneous and/or altered" report referring to "lots of VC" at the same locations where Charlie Company interrogated its Vietnamese detainees.[55]

Barker, of course, had died in a helicopter crash in June 1968 and could not present his case. Nonetheless, the commission declared, Task Force Barker purposely distorted the truth by calling the civilian casualties Viet Cong, and this should have been clear to all the officers—Barker, Henderson, Watke, and Koster—who were flying over the site and saw the large number of women and children along with elderly men evacuating the area. All "references to enemy action" on that day were "entirely inconsistent with the evidence before this Inquiry, including the testimony given by these individuals."[56]

More signs of a cover-up appeared in a file containing recommendations that led to the awarding of medals for heroism to Thompson's crew member Glenn Andreotta (Bronze Star with "V" Device, posthumously), Lawrence Colburn (Bronze Star with "V" Device), and Hugh Thompson (Distinguished Flying Cross). The records indicated that Thompson had written "Eyewitness Statements" on behalf of his two crew members, and Colburn had written one supporting Thompson. The higher command, including Major Frederic Watke and Lieutenant Colonel John Holladay, had endorsed the awards as recognition of bravery in risking death in a crossfire to save fifteen Vietnamese children and for rescuing a child discovered in an area between Viet Cong and U.S. forces.

The Peers commission had no doubts about the three pilots' valor, but it did question the descriptions of their actions, along with the motives and the procedures behind the awards. On the basis of erroneous accounts of what happened that day in My Lai 4, Koster's chief of staff, Colonel Nels Parson, wrote the orders awarding the medals to the three men for courage in saving sixteen children (some were adults) while in the face of enemy fire. But the preponderance of evidence showed no enemy presence, making it appear that the officers dispensing the awards had resorted to flattery in an effort to silence those pilots making the massacre charges.[57]

IV

The Peers commission found that between March 16 and 19, American troops "massacred" a minimum of 175 but perhaps more than four hundred civilians in the two subhamlets of My Lai 4 and My Khe 4. The mass killings stemmed from "the nature of the orders" from Lieutenant Colonel Frank Barker, who presented his officers and their men with "a false and misleading picture of the Son My area as an armed enemy camp, largely devoid of civilian inhabitants." A "permissive attitude" toward the treatment of civilians had developed from the top down within the 11th Brigade, which led to "an almost total disregard" for "lives and property."[58]

According to the Peers panel, the blame started at divisional command headquarters, where Major General Samuel Koster failed to ensure the proper treatment of noncombatants and was ultimately responsible for what happened that day. When he learned of nearly thirty civilian deaths, he did not inform other command and staff members. At noontime of the following day, he still took no formal action after Brigadier General George Young told him of Warrant Officer Hugh Thompson's charges made to Major Frederic Watke and Lieutenant Colonel John Holladay. Three days later, Koster received an oral report of Colonel Oran Henderson's investigation alleging that Thompson's claims had no basis in truth, but he failed to assure its thoroughness. About mid-April, Koster again failed to act after learning from two Vietnamese sources—a report from the Son Tinh district chief based on information from the Son My Village chief, along with Viet Cong propaganda broadcasts—that U.S. forces had killed about five hundred civilians in two subhamlets. Koster thought Henderson's "so-called report of investigation" of April 24, 1968, was incomplete and yet did not reject it and demand more information. Koster claimed he ordered a formal inquiry, but the Peers commission found no record either of his appointing an officer to handle this responsibility or of a report prepared or submitted. No testimony suggests that he tried to determine what happened that day.[59]

The Peers commission therefore concluded that Major General Koster had "suppressed information" and "may have falsely testified" on several issues before the Inquiry. By confining knowledge of the incident, the investigations, the reports, and reviews to Brigadier General Young and Colonel Parson, he "may have initiated a conspiracy to withhold the facts."[60]

The Peers panel held Young accountable for failing to provide Koster with all available information. On the morning of March 18, when Young met with Henderson and three other officers in Barker's van, he did not provide "appropriate instructions" to Henderson to guarantee a full investigation. Furthermore, Young did not keep Koster apprised of its progress and "may have contributed to the impression" that Henderson was carrying out an exhaustive investigation, thus encouraging Koster to accept its findings. Young, along with Koster, failed to keep the division staff informed of these developments and "may have contributed to a conspiracy to suppress information." These divisional and task force failures led to "ambiguous, illegal, and potentially explosive orders" by Lieutenant Colonel Barker, Captain Medina, and perhaps Captain Michles, who all failed, "either deliberately or unintentionally," to prepare for the possible presence of civilians in the target area. Finally, the implementation of these orders "ultimately became the task of generally weak and ineffective leaders at the platoon level and below."[61]

The Peers commission also concluded that Henderson and at least one major staff officer (unnamed but probably Parson) "may have conspired to suppress information in an effort to deceive the division commander." Henderson had possessed "substantial knowledge" about the mass killing of noncombatants but never sent this information to Koster. Henderson's "most significant action" in hiding the truth was his "Report of Investigation" of April 24, 1968, which was "false and misleading" and continued the "original deception" played on Koster that no war crimes had occurred. Henderson "concealed the existence of war crimes" and convinced Koster there was no reason to file a report beyond the division level.[62]

One of the most critical pieces of evidence enclosed in Henderson's report was, of course, the unsigned "Statement" of April 14 that was apparently Vietnamese in origin. It asserted that Lieutenant Tran Ngoc Tan had withdrawn his atrocity charges against Americans made in his April 11 letter—a claim supporting Henderson's conclusion that no war crimes had occurred.

Tan's insistence that he had not changed his stance convinced the commission that Henderson had concocted this supposed reversal of position with the help of one or more members of his command and perhaps the Province Advisory Team. If so, this action further demonstrated that Henderson "conspired to withhold and suppress facts" relating to My Lai 4.[63]

When the Peers commission brought Henderson back for further questioning less than three months later, he claimed to have forgotten where he got the "Statement."[64]

The Peers commission switched its focus from Henderson to Koster, its members mystified over his failure to question the validity of a report based on an unsigned statement referring to two documents accusing the Americans of atrocities but not included in the package of materials supporting his conclusions. Koster understood their skepticism but maintained his position that he did not know where the statement had come from.[65]

In short, both Henderson and Koster claimed to have forgotten the source of a vital piece of evidence—the unsigned statement—contained in the April 1968 Report of Investigation that gave them what they wanted: the exoneration of American soldiers of all atrocity charges.

Then came Lieutenant Colonel Barker's turn, posthumously. His decision not to have a written plan of action contributed to what the Peers panel called "widespread confusion" among both officers and men about the "purpose and limitations" of a search-and-destroy mission. As the battle orders made their way down to the company level, they were "embellished and, either intentionally or unintentionally, were misdirected toward end results presumably not foreseen during the formative stage of the orders." Nothing indicated that the plan contained either "explicit or implicit provisions" for deliberately killing civilians. Rather, it rested on "faulty assumptions" regarding a large enemy presence and the "absence of noncombatants."[66]

The Peers commission held Captain Medina responsible for numerous war crimes. Like Barker, Medina helped plan and execute an "unlawful operation" against the hamlets that included the destruction of private property. He also contributed to the mass killing of civilians by adding a "revenge element" to the operation that made it a "grudge match" between Charlie Company and the enemy. Medina had assured his men that on their arrival in the village the only Vietnamese there would be Viet Cong or their sympathizers. He never changed his position, even though he learned before nine o'clock that morning that about forty Viet Cong had left My Lai 4 before the assault began. Furthermore, Medina mistreated a Vietnamese prisoner under interrogation and might have killed as many as three civilians. He admitted shooting a woman, but the Peers commission could not make a judgment regarding his plea of self-defense, because the act lay "outside the scope of this Inquiry."[67]

Medina, furthermore, "probably conspired" with Barker and others to "suppress information." He told his men not to discuss what happened that day and specifically advised one member of his company (PFC Michael Bernhardt) not to write his congressman. Medina's "permissive and calloused attitude" put noncombatants in danger and may have come from his attempt to run "a one-man show" in which he proved "incapable of exercising single-handed control of 100-plus soldiers."[68]

Medina's three platoon commanders—Lieutenant Calley, Lieutenant Brooks (deceased), and Lieutenant LaCross—were responsible for a large number of war crimes that included murder. Calley's 1st Platoon shot more than a hundred civilians—mainly women and children on the trail along the southern side of My Lai 4 and in a ditch on its eastern edge. Calley "directed and supervised" and "personally participated" in the "systematic killing" of these noncombatants. Brooks "expressly or impliedly" ordered his 2nd Platoon to shoot villagers as they evacuated their bunkers or in small groups of up to ten. At his direction and supervision, his platoon engaged in the "systematic killing" of perhaps one hundred elderly men, women, children, and babies in My Lai 4 and Binh Tay. He also "observed, did not prevent, and failed to report several rapes" by his men—including sodomy, rape/killings, and gang rapes. LaCross also "expressly or impliedly" ordered his 3rd Platoon to kill civilians. In the initial stages of the operation, he and his men were approaching Highway 521 when they fired on a group of Vietnamese moving southwest, killing three to fifteen. He then "directed and supervised" the "systematic killing" of many civilians in and around My Lai 4.[69]

The Peers commission also determined that the 1st Platoon leader from Bravo Company, Lieutenant Thomas Willingham, had committed war crimes in My Khe 4. By ordering "indiscriminate fire" and the use of explosives in the living areas, he opened the way for his men to kill more than ninety women and children. Although knowing that most of the victims were civilians, he submitted three phony reports to his company commander stating that his platoon had killed a total of thirty-eight Viet Cong.[70]

The result was that American soldiers at the platoon level "murdered noncombatants while under the supervision and control of their immediate superiors." The commission found no evidence of marijuana or other narcotics affecting their behavior. Their crimes were a matter of choice and "included individual and group acts of murder, rape, sodomy, maiming, and assault on noncombatants and the mistreatment and killing of detainees."[71]

And responsibility went up the chain of command. "At every command level within the Americal Division," concluded the Peers Report, "actions were taken, both wittingly and unwittingly, which effectively suppressed information concerning the war crimes committed at Son My Village."[72] A vast number of rules, regulations, and policies were in place to reduce the chances of war crimes, but the officers in charge did not enforce them and were therefore culpable for charges of dereliction of duty.

As correctives, the Peers commission recommended that the army modify its directives and training programs. Admittedly, its policies "expressed a clear intent" to assure the humane treatment of civilians, prisoners of war, and private property, but its directives were ambiguous about what a subordinate should do when his commander took part in or approved a war crime. Furthermore, the directives stated that the soldier was to report war crimes to his superior, and yet he had not received adequate training on whether to obey an order he thought "palpably illegal." America's soldiers needed more training in the procedures for reporting atrocities, as well as knowledge of the Geneva Conventions' statements on the treatment of prisoners of war and civilians.[73]

V

In mid-February 1970, Peers sent a preliminary summary of the panel's findings to Secretary Resor and General Westmoreland. He had hoped to lighten the shock of the revelations, but in explaining what happened at My Lai 4 and My Khe 4, he admitted to using "abrupt and brutal terms" that hit Resor "like a bolt out of the blue." The Secretary of the Army did not want to either diminish the tragedy or manipulate the final report released to the public, but he hoped to soften its language. Instead of referring to the victims as elderly men, women, children, and babies, could he say "noncombatant casualties"? Might he also be less graphic in describing the rapes?[74]

After making numerous revisions, the Peers commission beat the March 15 expiration of the statute of limitations by one day when it submitted *The Report of the Investigation* (known as the Peers Report) as the first of four volumes of its work to the army. The last three volumes of the collection, titled *The Report of the Department of the Army Review of the Preliminary Investigations into the My Lai Incident*, were not yet available for public perusal, but CID could use them in its ongoing investigation.[75]

On the eve of the press conference set for the morning of March 17 to announce the conclusions of the Peers Inquiry, the Pentagon raised an objection to the use of the term "massacre" in Peers's prepared statement. Peers resisted. As he explained in his own account years afterward, "I was not about to present a watered-down version and in effect said that if that was what they wanted, please leave me out." Less than a half hour prior to the conference, however, he reluctantly agreed to replace "massacre" with "a tragedy of major proportions."[76]

The Pentagon press conference began with Peers, Robert MacCrate, and Jerome Walsh seated behind a table while Resor opened the proceedings, with Westmoreland standing beside him, all of them facing a sea of cameras and newspeople jammed into the room. The army had distributed copies of the 225-page final report, extensively censored to protect the legal rights of the defendants.[77]

After Resor furnished background on the formation of the commission, he noted that *The Report of the Investigation* contained some "minor deletions." Everything was there except the footnotes referring primarily to the contents of volumes 2 and 4, which were not yet released.[78]

Resor then introduced Peers, who briefly summed up the inquiry's work before taking questions.

One of the first questions, of course, involved the central task of the commission from the beginning. Was there a cover-up at higher levels? "No," Peers replied. He explained that the panel had collected sufficient "testimony and evidence to indicate that certain individuals, either wittingly or unwittingly, by their actions, suppressed information from the incident" and kept it from passing up the chain of command. Ordinary daily reports went all the way up the command ladder—even to the National Military Command Center in the Pentagon—but "as for the knowledge of what might have transpired at Son My itself, we have no indication that this got beyond the Americal Division itself."

Peers was then asked whether evidence had been destroyed. The lieutenant general preferred not to answer that question for fear of jeopardizing the legal rights of individuals possibly going to trial. "Information was available," he explained, but "there were failures to report, there were failures in the investigations, there were failures in reviewing investigations, and these are all part of the charges."[79]

How many officers were charged? Peers referred the press members to the copy of the report in their hands and declined to go into detail about anyone named, as that might threaten that officer's legal rights. The panel did not file any charges but referred them to a group of officers, headed by Colonel Hubert Miller, the staff judge advocate of the Army Air Defense Command. They reviewed the testimony and drafted the charges before submitting them to the judge advocate general. Peers added that he was deeply concerned about what had happened and emphasized that all officers "must have extremely high standards." But this did not condemn every officer; it was "quite an isolated incident."[80] He added, using the Pentagon-approved nomenclature, "Our inquiry clearly established that a tragedy of major proportions occurred there on that date."[81]

Peers notably did not mention the massacre at My Khe 4. He had originally been willing to discuss that matter at the press conference, but high-ranking military officials thought it advisable not to do so. A senior Pentagon official involved with the report later told Hersh, "We were very much afraid of scaring off some of the B[ravo] Company witnesses." The Peers commission agreed that "the full story must await the completion of ongoing criminal investigations and any resulting prosecutions." Doubtless the Pentagon was more concerned that a second massacre would suggest that My Lai 4 was not an isolated incident and that commanders in places higher than the Americal Division were responsible for what happened.[82]

Whatever the Pentagon's wishes, however, there was no chance for keeping the story of My Khe 4 quiet. Two weeks earlier, on March 2, 1970, *Newsweek* published a story exposing the massacre and tying it to the charges recently made by the army against Thomas Willingham, who in March 1968 was a lieutenant in Bravo Company. NBC-TV followed with a report that Willingham's company had operated more than a mile to the east of My Lai 4 and that evidence suggested another mass killing. In a story confirmed by other Vietnamese, Ngo Thi De told NBC reporters that she had survived an American assault in which the soldiers had slaughtered nearly everyone in the small village. Two massacres at the same time and in the same area: Had orders come from farther up the chain of command?[83]

The issue of additional massacres came up in the Peers question-and-answer period on March 17. Asked whether similar killings had occurred on "other days" or in "other places," Peers was less than forthright in his response: "If there is, I have no knowledge of it." Based on the evidence brought before him in the investigations and his own two and a half years of experience in South Vietnam, he said, "I had no knowledge of anything that would approximate this."[84]

Another reporter pushed the issue, asking specifically about the charges made against Company B (Bravo), which did not operate in My Lai 4. Peers recognized the implications of the question and attempted to conflate the two massacres into one. Company B, he asserted, was just a short distance away to the east from the targeted village. All events of that day were "encompassed within the greater area of Son My village" rather than in My Lai 4 itself.[85]

No one followed up on the question.

The next day, an array of newspapers, including the *Baltimore Sun*, *Chicago Tribune*, *New York Times*, and *Washington Post*, published the names of the fourteen officers charged with dereliction of duty, false swearing and false testimony, failure to follow regulations, and failure to report suspected violations to higher authorities. If the officers were convicted, the penalties were up to three years of hard labor and dismissal from the army.[86]

The highest ranking officer was Major General Koster, who in June 1968 had left his command of the American Division to follow Westmoreland's footsteps in becoming superintendent of the U.S. Military Academy. He immediately assembled the 3,700 cadets (his son Samuel among them) in the mess hall to announce from its stone balcony that "action has been initiated against me" and he was resigning his position in an effort, he said, "to separate the Military Academy and you of the corps from the continuing flow" of bad publicity. "I wish to say that throughout my military career, the cherished principles of our motto—Duty, Honor, Country—have served as a constant guide to me. I shall continue to follow these principles as long as I live."

Koster received a standing ovation that lasted almost two minutes. The next day all the cadets paid tribute to him by marching before his home overlooking the Hudson River.[87]

The other thirteen officers charged were 1st Lieutenant Kenneth W. Boatman, Major Charles C. Calhoun, Major David C. Gavin, Lieutenant Colonel William A. Guinn, Colonel Oran K. Henderson, 1st Lieutenant Dennis H. Johnson, Lieutenant Colonel Robert B. Luper, Major Robert W. McKnight, Captain Ernest L. Medina, Colonel Nels A. Parson, Major Frederic W. Watke, 1st Lieutenant Thomas K. Willingham, and Brigadier General George H. Young. The press had left out Captain Eugene M. Kotouc. Second Lieutenant William L. Calley and Captain Medina already faced court-martial proceedings.[88]

The panel also listed thirty officers believed to have deliberately suppressed information about that day. No one brought charges against Chaplain Francis R. Lewis because, Secretary Resor argued, to do so would hurt the chaplain corps and its pledge of confidentiality. The secretary also considered the charges debatable. Peers disagreed but accepted the decision.[89]

The press had named the numerous officers and enlisted men involved in the alleged massacre and cover-up, and it had included murder, massacre, and assault with a deadly weapon among its list of crimes; but only *Time* and the *New York Times* specifically referred to rape, torture, and maiming. Resor called the deletions in the report "minor," but the *New York Times* insisted the released volume contained nothing new and that the censors had removed entire chapters along with scattered pieces of classified information. The only parts remaining were histories of the Americal Division and the region in Vietnam in which the events took place.[90]

Thus the testimonies containing the details of these events along with the accusations and evidence crucial to court decisions had to remain sealed until the judicial process had run its course. In the spring of 1970, the commission had released enough information to support the arguments on both sides of the issues of massacre and cover-up.

The press stories and the skeletal version of the Peers Report heightened popular suspicions of an army cover-up. The lack of access to the testimonies and specific details confirmed the skepticism of many Americans that their soldiers and officers could commit war crimes. Two earlier Lou Harris polls, one taken in early December 1969 and the other in mid-January 1970, suggested the nation's attitude toward charging its soldiers with war crimes: 67 percent of respondents thought the GIs deserved no punishment for killing civilians if acting under orders, and only 22 percent felt "moral repugnance" toward the deliberate killing of unarmed women and children.[91]

The military's reactions to the report ranged from "shock" to "pride." A Pentagon officer was not surprised by the charges, "But my God," he added, "I didn't think they would involve General Koster and General Young." Most officials at the Pentagon felt confident that nearly all the accused would go to trial and that most of those tried would be convicted. Most soldiers thought the accused were "probably guilty."[92]

Field officers were likewise split in their assessments. Battalion commanders in Vietnam praised the army for charging high-ranking officers, but one officer expressed concern that the revelations might produce a new kind of soldier who asked "Why?" in combat. A captain about to return to Vietnam worried about the next time he led his infantrymen into battle. "Do I think about tactics or do I start thinking about laying a court-martial defense?" A major with more than thirty years of experience regretted the collateral deaths but admitted to their unavoidability in war where "it's kill or be killed."[93]

The press generally praised the army for the Peers investigation. A *New York Times* editorial lauded its decision to face the atrocities at My Lai and make sure soldiers knew it would not tolerate such behavior. The *Washington Post* was even more outspoken in its support. "Those who feared a 'whitewash' by any investigating group other than a non-military one" should realize that the army had acted with "dignity and sobriety" in pursuing the facts "behind this hideous affair." The *Baltimore Sun* was more guarded in its praise. It likewise commended the army for taking action but considered what happened in My Lai predictable in a war without clear rules of conduct and purpose. "The shocking thing is that it does not come as a shock."[94]

The president, however, was not pleased with either the army or with Peers. In a phone conversation with Kissinger, Nixon accused the army of "a pretty cheap shot" in permitting its generals "to be put on the rack for the delay business." Reports of the mass killings were "covered up because it was in the interest of the country." Kissinger agreed, although inadvertently exposing his lack of knowledge of the affair by remarking that "nearly 400 people were killed there and it [went] on for days." Peers, the president remarked, was "trying to make himself look good while he kick[ed] his colleagues around." As for the massacre, Nixon added, "We know why it was done. These boys being killed by women carrying that stuff in their satchels." The best response to the Peers Report was silence. "Tell [White House Press Secretary Ron] Ziegler not to comment on it."[95]

But ignoring the Peers Report could not, in the president's words, "get it out of the way."[96]

NOT TO BE outdone by the Peers Inquiry, the Hébert subcommittee rushed into print a preliminary report on its findings that attempted to dispel the allegations of massacre and turn the critical focus onto Hugh Thompson and Lawrence Colburn, who had first reported them.

The Peers panel members could not have known it at the time, but their suspicions of the subcommittee's intentions were substantiated by its treatment of Thompson and Colburn when they testified in mid-April 1970. The transcript of the hearings did not become public for another six years, but at a press conference in Washington on July 15, the Hébert subcommittee released a report of its findings, which contained excerpts aimed at undermining the credibility of both Thompson and Colburn by showing that the army had awarded them and Glenn Andreotta (posthumously) medals for bravery in combat when no enemy was present. The army was handing out medals "like it got them out of a cracker jack box," Congressman Hébert remarked. The Distinguished Flying Cross was "sacred," and Thompson was "wearing it on his chest" for an act of valor he did not perform. The report was fifty-three pages long, more than a third of it devoted to the testimonies of Thompson and Colburn from a pool of 152 interviewed. Nixon had used his influence and his reliance on congressional friends to "discredit one witness"; Hébert and his subcommittee had decided on discrediting two.[97]

A bitter confrontation ensued in the legislative chamber, characterized by personal attacks on Thompson and Colburn by Hébert as well as other committee members. The hearings led to the revelations that someone in the Americal Division had forged the eyewitness statements allegedly written by Thompson and Colburn on behalf of each other and Andreotta for saving Vietnamese civilians during a firefight between U.S. soldiers and the enemy. If a firefight took place, no massacre had occurred, making it appear that the medals given by the army were an effort to silence Thompson and Colburn. Thompson realized during the hearings that someone had forged his signature on an eyewitness statement, which he did not write; Colburn confirmed a second forgery more than four decades later when he was sent a copy of the statement, which he had never seen before, let alone signed.[98]

In the meantime, national and international reaction to the Peers Report created a strongly charged atmosphere around the approaching courts martial of Lieutenant Calley and Captain Medina. All the while, CID quietly continued its investigation with all the Peers materials at its disposal, building a case for bringing criminal charges against a yet undetermined number of officers and enlisted men in a judicial process that soon threatened to involve the White House.

Eleven

THE PEERS INQUIRY HAD NOT ESTABLISHED either premeditated murder or a conspiracy to suppress evidence. Yet it had compiled massive amounts of circumstantial evidence, strongly suggesting that several officers and enlisted men were responsible for hundreds of murders and that others in the command chain up to and including the division level had hidden or destroyed evidence of reports and meetings discussed by many contemporaries but not found in the files. Perpetrators of the murders and cover-ups doubtless counted on others involved in either crime or both to realize that participants as well as witnesses had everything to lose by speaking out and remained silent for their own good.

It was now the army's duty to determine whether these criminal charges applied to its own people.

I

The army decided early on to hold individual trials of officers and soldiers. Both the Pentagon and the Nixon administration strongly opposed a mass trial, in part because of their claim that My Lai was an aberration. But there was another reason. Images of the Nuremberg and Tokyo war crimes trials must have flashed through their minds as they worried about the indelible stain it would leave on the army and the country.[1]

To avert such a spectacle, each indicted officer or enlisted man would undergo a separate court martial in military bases spread across the country. Major General Orwin Talbott at Fort Benning would make the final decision as to whether the inquiry justified a court martial of Lieutenant William Calley; Sergeant David Mitchell would undergo the same scrutiny at Fort Hood, Texas, as would Captain Ernest Medina, Captain Eugene Kotouc, and the bulk of the enlisted men at Fort McPherson, Georgia. All higher officers fell under the authority of Lieutenant General Jonathan Seaman at Fort Meade, Maryland.[2]

The army soon realized it lacked sufficient evidence to convict all principals involved and dropped charges against most of them. Thomas Willingham, now a captain, was the first to receive the news in early June 1970 and, in a step that further diminished the chances of exposing the murders at My Khe 4, he promptly resigned from the service. The major problem, asserted William Eckhardt, the lead prosecutor in the My Lai legal proceedings, was the virtual impossibility of presenting a convincing argument—a prima facie case—because of unavailable or non-cooperative witnesses. In August, the army dismissed charges against Sergeant Kenneth Hodges and over the next few months did the same with PFC William Doherty, Private Max Hutson, Corporal Kenneth Schiel, Private Gerald A. Smith, SP4 Robert W. T'Souvas, and Sergeant Esequiel Torres. In the words of Lieutenant Albert O. Connor, the Third Army commander, the army had "acted 'in the interests of justice.'[3]

The initial court-martial proceeding began in Fort Hood on October 6, 1970—that of David Mitchell, the sergeant from Louisiana accused of assault with intent to murder. His exoneration became certain in the opening moments when the judge, Colonel George Robinson, expressed displeasure with the government's efforts to deny defense attorneys all documents needed to cross-examine witnesses. In an allusion to the Jencks Act—which required a government agency questioning principals in a criminal investigation to make their testimonies available to the federal courts on request—he ruled that since the Hébert subcommittee had refused to provide a transcript of its hearings, no one who had appeared before that body could testify before this court. Robinson's action disallowed the testimonies of Hugh Thompson and many others who were critical to the government's case. Consequently, the army's prosecutor, Captain Michael Swann, questioned only three soldiers—PFC Dennis Conti, who saw Mitchell at the ditch; SP4 Greg Olsen, who saw Mitchell fire into the ditch; and SP4 Charles Sledge, the only one who claimed he had seen Mitchell shoot a number of Vietnamese civilians. Mitchell's civilian attorney, Ossie Brown, undercut Sledge's testimony by revealing that he had previously told CID investigators, "I believe" it was Mitchell.[4]

The jury deliberated for less than seven hours and on November 20, 1970, found Mitchell not guilty. Mitchell intended to stay in the army but soon discovered it had "flagged" his file, effectively locking him in his present position while the My Lai investigations went on, forcing him to recognize his best course was to leave the service.[5]

National interest, however, remained riveted on the imminent Calley trial. Partly this was attributable to the journalist John Sack, whose writings helped to develop the young lieutenant into a cult figure among his supporters at a time when many Americans appeared to be looking for one. What was the mood of the country, and how would the media treat Calley?

In the spring of 1970, Sack accepted an invitation from Harold Hayes, the editor of *Esquire*, to write a story on Calley. Hayes had offered the job to better-known writers, such as John Hersey, William Styron, and Garry Wills, and they had turned him down. Rejecting the advice of *New York Times* journalist and bestselling author David Halberstam, Sack agreed to take on the Calley story and in November, on the eve of Calley's trial, published the first segment of Calley's "confessions" in *Esquire*, which that year had a circulation of 1.2 million. Sack's final two pieces—in February and September 1971—joined the initial article in becoming the bulk of the book published by Viking Press in 1971 and titled *Lieutenant Calley: His Own Story*.[6]

On the cover of the November issue of *Esquire* was a picture of Calley, in uniform and broadly smiling while surrounded by four Vietnamese children. Renowned designer George Lois had convinced Hayes to approve the idea. "We'll show him with a bunch of Vietnamese kids," Lois said. "Those who think he's innocent will say that proves it. Those who think he's guilty will say that proves it." To Calley, however, Lois told a different story. "What you're saying is that you love these kids," he assured Calley. After a few photographs, he declared, "Lieutenant, this is terrific. Give me a grin." Lois admitted years later that he "bullshitted" Calley. "I showed him like a jackal…a monster." According to Frank DiGiacomo, a contributing editor for *Vanity Fair*, the cover was a "Molotov cocktail" and a "masterpiece." Calley was "the nation's Frankenstein monster…smiling."[7]

The cover caused such a national and international sensation that its publisher, Arnold Gingrich, responded to irate readers whom he thought had prematurely judged Calley guilty. "People wrote in likening the portrayal of Lieutenant Calley, surrounded by Vietnamese children, to a depiction of [Adolf] Hitler, kissing Jewish babies on their way to the gas chambers, and to [Heinrich] Himmler, fondling little Poles and Czechs, before handing them over to waiting S.S. officers." Yet readers, Gingrich declared, should ask themselves "what you would have done, if you had been there, and in this man's shoes."[8]

Thus it was in a highly charged atmosphere that the Calley trial began, on November 17, 1970, in a Fort Benning courtroom that seated only fifty-nine people. Half were reporters, the rest either military figures on the base or residents of Columbus or nearby Phenix City, Alabama. Sack occupied one of the five first-row seats allotted to Calley, who allowed him to dispense the other four seats to people of his choosing each day—including favored reporters; one girlfriend, then another, of Calley's; a TV artist; editors from

Esquire and Viking, the latter ready to release Calley's autobiography after the trial; and Hollywood director and producer Stanley Kramer. All the while, Sack kept a protective shield around Calley to fend off reporters seeking interviews—including Richard Hammer of the *New York Times*, who personally covered the trial. Sack had in effect become Calley's defender and protector. "If you knew Rusty," Sack told Hammer, "you'd know he just isn't like that at all. He's a bright, sensitive guy."[9]

The lead army prosecutor on a team of four was twenty-eight-year-old Captain Aubrey Daniel, senior trial counsel from JAG at Fort Benning and about to complete a four-year stint. Born in South Carolina but raised in the Upper South, Daniel was from a wealthy agricultural family who graduated from the University of Virginia and studied law at the University of Richmond, graduating in 1966. On his wall were his diplomas, along with a framed badge indicating his Eagle Scout certification. Drafted soon after graduation, he chose to enlist and applied for JAG. Eckhardt had been impressed by Daniel's work ethic and supported him for this assignment. Daniel appeared younger than his years and was largely inexperienced in the courtroom, but he was an unbending advocate of law and order who had voted for Nixon in 1968 and now, just months away from returning to civilian life, was keen to battle Calley's defense team, which consisted of Major Kenneth Raby, a career officer in JAG who had represented Calley during the Peers proceedings, and the well-known veteran civilian lawyer George Latimer.[10]

The chief antagonists in the court martial were, as it turned out, Daniel and Calley. According to Hammer, Daniel personified the Old South, with its strong sense of moral obligation, hard work, and right and wrong. Judge Reid Kennedy presided over the proceedings and exclaimed afterward of Daniel, "My God, he really is a Puritan, isn't he?" Calley, again according to Hammer, was the mirror opposite of Daniel. Raised in Miami, Calley reflected the moral laxness of the New South, pursuing ends regardless of means and seeming, at least according to Daniel, unable to discern "that some things could be inherently evil and wrong and others inherently good and right." Calley had at best a weak scholastic record. He admitted to failing seventh grade for cheating but insisted that all he had done was write out the answers for the final exam and share them with someone else. (When he related this story in court, someone quipped, "Can you image the guy who had to get his answers from Calley?")[11]

Latimer was the senior statesman, a sixty-nine-year-old attorney from Salt Lake City who had achieved national notoriety by successfully defending one of the eight Green Berets accused of murdering a Viet Cong spy. Hearing of the Calley case, Latimer had sent a supportive letter to the young lieutenant, expressing sympathy for what he was going through. Calley was already acquainted with Latimer's reputation, having heard friends on the base extol his ability in the courtroom. When he received this letter, he called Latimer to thank him and ask if he would defend him in court. Latimer asked only one question: "Do you believe your own self that what you did was right?" "Yes," Calley firmly responded, and Latimer agreed to represent him—pro bono.[12]

By this point, Latimer was nearing the end of a distinguished career. He had already served five years on the Utah Supreme Court when President Harry Truman appointed him to the Court of Military Appeals, where he made his mark in military law as protector of the soldier. Latimer had earlier fought with the infantry in World War II, taking part in four invasion operations in the South Pacific and amassing a number of medals for bravery. He identified with Calley, a fellow infantryman in combat who needed his help. It was clear to all that Latimer was not at his sharpest, repeatedly mispronouncing his client's name as "Collie," saying "heel-i-o-copter" throughout the trial, and continually fumbling through his papers in court. Nattily dressed, gentle and homespun in manner, sensitive about his age, and wearing a small hearing aid he tried to hide in his ear, he confidently remarked to a friend that he had "one more good case left in him."[13]

Judge Kennedy was a fifty-eight-year-old lieutenant colonel who had been promoted to full colonel at the beginning of the trial so he would outrank everyone involved in the judicial proceedings. Hammer called him "the most human figure" in the courtroom. Kennedy had enlisted in 1943 and saw military service in Europe during the Second World War. When war broke out in Korea, he joined the army again and decided to make the military his career. From 1954 to 1958, he served in the 101st Airborne Division as staff judge advocate, which was the highest legal position in a military unit, and then became part of the First Cavalry Division in Korea. When that tour came to a close, he joined the Command and General Staff College at Fort Leavenworth and sometime later moved to the Armed Forces Staff College. He had been at Fort Benning since July 1967, holding the coveted position of military judge of the army's Fifth Judicial District. Hammer wrote that Kennedy had long admired Latimer and looked forward to dealing with him in court, but that he would equally refuse to allow personal considerations to interfere with the proceedings.[14]

It became clear from the beginning that the Calley case would shape the course of other My Lai trials. If he went free, the army would recognize the futility of going forward with further prosecutions, given that the evidence against him was stronger than that against the others accused, and My Lai would go down in history as an aberration. If he were found guilty, however, a much bigger issue could emerge—that the army might have to prosecute those who had put other soldiers in the position that they had. In some ways, the future of the entire war in Vietnam was at stake.[15]

Latimer experienced an early setback in the trial when he tried to follow the pattern of the Mitchell trial by blocking the testimonies of those numerous servicemen who had appeared before the Hébert subcommittee. Kennedy, however, ruled that the Jencks Act did not apply to "statements or testimony given to a congressional subcommittee in executive session," as the *New York Times* reported. Besides, the defense had access to the information provided by most of the witnesses Daniel intended to call; they had already told their stories to the inspector general, CID, and the Peers Inquiry.[16]

Daniel knew that if he sought to prosecute anyone above Calley's rank, he would probably fail to win a guilty verdict. The jurors were six in number, five of them Vietnam veterans: Colonel Clifford Ford (a recipient of three Bronze Stars in World War II and Korea), Major Charles McIntosh, Major Carl Bierbaum, Major Walter Kinard, Major Gene Brown, and Captain Ronald Salem. Daniel realized that it was Calley on trial, not the army or the nation's political leaders. Daniel would let defense decide whether to save its client by spreading culpability to those above him.[17]

Judge Kennedy opened the proceedings by addressing Calley, who had risen from his seat at the defense table. "Lieutenant Calley, you are charged with violations of Article 118 of the Uniform Code of Military Justice. How do you plead?"

"I plead not guilty, sir."[18]

After Calley had sat down, Daniel turned to the jurors and summarized the four specifications of premeditated murder making up the army's case: at least thirty civilians on the trail just below My Lai 4; at least seventy civilians at an irrigation ditch on the eastern edge of the village; and two others at that ditch, a man wearing white apparel and possibly a monk, and a child about two years old. "He murdered them," Daniel declared, "with premeditation and with intent to kill."[19]

Daniel knew he faced a difficult task. On several occasions, a prosecution witness stopped by Calley's table on leaving the stand to pat him on the shoulder or arm and wish him good luck. Haeberle had taken pictures of the dead but did not implicate Calley and appeared to sympathize with him. Gene Oliver was another—a rifleman who drew unwanted attention as the only one of the more than one hundred GIs in Charlie Company to claim he heard enemy fire from Russian-made AK-47 assault rifles while in My Lai 4.

But Daniel faced a much bigger problem than the witnesses who openly commiserated with Calley. He had to win conviction from a jury of career officers—all highly devoted to the army and doubtless believing (or wanting to believe) Calley innocent. Daniel devoted more than a week to meticulously building his case in the packed and hushed courtroom.[20]

A pivotal moment came early in the process. After the initial assault on the morning of March 16, 1968, Daniel explained, Calley was with his radio operator, Charles Sledge, when he ordered his men to round up the villagers and take them to the intersection of the two trails along the southern perimeter of the village. Once there, Calley placed them under the guard of two privates, Paul Meadlo and Dennis Conti, accompanied by a few other soldiers. Calley and Sledge left with Meadlo standing guard while Conti also walked away and soon returned with several more civilians. As he gave his testimony Daniel gazed at Calley, whose eyes were fixed on his notepad on the table, and asserted that he had ordered Meadlo to join him in killing these "unarmed and unresisting old men, women, and children." When some of them tried to run, Calley and Meadlo shot them in "cold blood" on the trail. "Meadlo was crying," Daniel declared. "It was so repulsive...what he had to do at the direction of Lieutenant Calley."[21]

Calley suddenly looked up and, according to Hammer, "smiled broadly" at Daniel before looking back down.[22]

At the beginning of the second week, Hugh Thompson and the helicopter pilots who had hovered over the ditch gave testimonies that bolstered Daniel's descriptions of the dead. "There were a lot of bodies in there," according to Thompson. "Women, kids, babies, old men. Some were dead, some were alive," he asserted in a voice Hammer described as "muffled and choked with emotion as though he were seeing it all again." Confirmation of Thompson's story came from co-pilot Jerry Culverhouse, who was flying so low over the scene that he saw more than a hundred bodies in the ditch, many of them babies, and heard gunfire coming from alongside the culvert where there stood a black sergeant shooting survivors with his M-16. Gunship pilot Dan Millians also saw a black sergeant firing into the ditch and could hear the shots.[23]

The witnesses not allowed to testify at Mitchell's trial gave their testimony. By Thanksgiving recess, Daniel had established that U.S. forces had encountered no resistance at My Lai 4 and yet had killed two large groups of civilians on the trail and in the ditch. But on the second day back in court, he took his first major step toward clinching a conviction when he called Robert Maples to the stand. A machine gunner in Calley's platoon, Maples had been with

James Bergthold when they approached Calley and other soldiers standing at a ditch. "They were firing into the hole," Maples repeatedly declared. "I saw Lieutenant Calley and Meadlo shooting into the hole. The muzzles were down and I heard the firing." Calley ordered Maples to machine-gun the Vietnamese, but he refused. As Maples admitted to the court, he had disobeyed a direct order and nothing came of it—which raised questions about Calley's defense claim that he had no choice but to follow orders. "I saw people go into that hole and no one come out," Maples asserted. "That's all I know."[24]

In testimony confirmed by Greg Olsen, Charles Hall claimed he saw Calley talking to Mitchell at the edge of the ditch before hearing "slow, semiautomatic fire from the ditch." Olsen attested that Mitchell "raised his weapon to firing position and fired into the ditch. I heard the shots." But as he had said in his testimony at Mitchell's trial, Olsen did not *see* Calley shoot anyone. Hall declared that while crossing over the ditch with Olsen and others, "I looked back and saw people in the ditch. They were dead." "How did you know they were dead?" Daniel asked. "They weren't moving. There was a lot of blood coming from all over them. They were in piles and scattered. There were very old people, very young people and mothers. Blood was coming from everywhere. Everything was all blood."[25]

Then came a barrage of allegations against Calley that further strengthened Daniel's case. Conti provided a devastating, detailed description of Calley, Meadlo, and Mitchell killing Vietnamese in the ditch. Sledge repeated the story, asserting that Calley and Mitchell stood over the ditch less than five feet from the captives below, their rifles set on automatic as they riddled the "screaming and falling" people. When a helicopter pilot—Thompson—came and left, Calley bragged about telling him something he had said on more than one occasion: "I'm the boss here."[26]

As damning as the testimonies of Conti and Sledge were, that of another soldier in Calley's platoon, Thomas Turner, was unsettling for its content but even more so for catching the defense by surprise: Turner had never spoken to CID, any investigatory committee or journalist, or the defense.[27]

Turner not only affirmed the murder charges against Calley and Meadlo but added another brutal killing by Calley—that of a young woman. Turner had witnessed the shootings at the ditch while sitting on a nearby dike for an hour and a half, his distance from the spot ranging from seventy-five yards to less than twenty yards for a brief time. With him were Conti and Daniel Simone, but while they looked out for the enemy Turner never took his eyes off the ditch as Calley ordered the execution of about a hundred Vietnamese civilians brought there in group after group by fellow soldiers. When the shooting finally stopped, Turner explained, Calley began walking toward him and the other two soldiers still sitting on the dike just as a young Vietnamese girl approached from the side with her hands raised. "Lieutenant Calley," Turner asserted, "raised his rifle and shot her several times and she fell over into the rice paddy." While the girl lay there with several shots in her chest, Calley abruptly turned around and headed back toward the ditch while shouting at his men to line up and move out.[28]

Latimer moved to strike Turner's testimony because it introduced "into evidence a separate and distinct count of murder"; Daniel countered that the testimony was "admissible because it goes to the state of mind of the accused and to the intent to kill." Judge Kennedy later ruled that the testimony about the woman was inadmissible but that the rest of it was not. After Turner's second appearance in court in March, Kennedy explained that the new evidence would help the jury decide on Calley's guilt by ascertaining whether he had the "mental capacity to premeditate and form the specific intent to kill," "a plan or design" to kill, and "a specific intent to kill."[29]

Evidence kept mounting against Calley. James Dursi delivered a calm and exhaustive summation of the mass killings he witnessed on the trail and at the ditch. Dursi added a twist to his story that further undercut Calley's defense. He declared that the sight of the carnage had sickened him, and Calley ordered him back to the village. "He told me in a sympathetic tone," Dursi explained, "as though he actually felt what I felt." Dursi's remarks, Hammer wrote, should not be taken to suggest that Calley had redeeming qualities. They instead revealed "a killer so inured to his killing that he could stop in the middle, express concern for the stomach of one of his men, and then go back to the slaughter."[30]

Paul Meadlo surprised everyone by agreeing to testify, after earlier refusing to do so on the grounds of the Fifth Amendment. Judge Kennedy was not pleased with this refusal. "Is this the man who granted the interview on TV? I didn't notice any great reticence to tell everything he knew about My Lai in great and nauseous detail on television." Kennedy warned Meadlo that if he did not change his position, he would stand in contempt of court. "Don't look at your lawyer, Mr. Meadlo. He's not going to help you. If anyone goes to jail, Mr. Meadlo, it's going to be you and not your lawyer." Meadlo soon reconsidered. Sitting close by were an assistant U.S. attorney, a representative of the Justice Department, and two U.S. marshals, ready to place him in custody if he again refused to testify. Kennedy assured him he had a grant of immunity protecting him from prosecution for anything he said in court.[31]

Meadlo's crippling injury outside My Lai 4 became evident as he limped to the stand, watched warily—according to Hammer—by Calley. Daniel stood between his witness and Calley, blocking him from glaring at Meadlo when he first entered the courtroom. Meadlo again described the murderous scenes he recounted so graphically over television and in Hersh's newspaper articles.[32]

Meadlo added that he and his men suspected the captives of being Viet Cong and continued, "As far as I'm concerned, they're still Viet Cong." He had acted under orders, which the army had taught him to obey without question. "I was scared and really expected a big fight, really expected all hell to break out." Calley, Meadlo emphasized, "was doing his duty and doing his job." Asked if either Calley or Medina had ordered him to kill the Vietnamese, Meadlo firmly stated, "I took my orders from Lieutenant Calley."[33]

Meadlo responded to another question by explaining that he had held his M-16 on the captives because "they might attack." "Children and babies?" Daniel asked in astonishment. "They might have had a fully loaded grenade on them," Meadlo replied. "The mothers might have throwed them at us." Even though the women, children, and babies were sitting down, Meadlo said, "I thought they had some sort of chain or a little string they had to give a little pull and they blow us up, things like that....I just watched them. I was scared all the time." They never searched the Vietnamese out of fear that "they would have had a booby trap rigged up or something." When Daniel inquired whether the babies held by their mothers had ever "moved to attack," Meadlo asserted, "I expected at any moment they were about to make a counterbalance."[34]

Meadlo remarked at the end of his testimony, "Captain Medina was there before the ditch and I assumed everything was okay because if it wasn't I assumed he would put a stop to it. And he didn't so I assumed it was all right. With all the bodies lying around, why didn't he put a stop to all the killings?"[35]

On this note, Daniel concluded his case against Calley.

II

Meanwhile, outside these proceedings, The U.S. Army's Criminal Investigation Division had quietly completed its criminal investigations into what it called the "My Lai/Son My Incident" in late September 1970 and in early December terminated its inquiry into the existence of the Barker report of May 1968, the one that had found no atrocities committed in My Lai 4.[36]

CID concluded that a massacre had in fact occurred in Son My Village and that a cover-up had followed. American soldiers had "systematically killed most of the inhabitants whom they encountered. An undetermined number of Vietnamese noncombatants, 343 of whom were identified, were killed in My Lai (4) during that segment of the operation." American forces had also killed about twenty more Vietnamese civilians in the subhamlet of My Hoi (My Khe 4) on that same day.[37]

CID had investigated seventy-six complaints of criminal acts, half of them becoming the subject of twenty-five formal reports. It accused forty-six American soldiers of "murder, rape, assault with intent to commit murder, aggravated assault, maiming, and indecent assault, and wrongful disposition of an official document." Sixteen of the soldiers were still in the army; the remaining thirty had been discharged.[38]

Despite an exhaustive search of the army's files, CID, like the Peers Inquiry, had not been able to locate a copy of the Barker report. Instead, both teams of investigators discovered a trail of evasive explanations, mixed messages, lies revealed on polygraph tests, conflicting accounts of whether anyone had seen the report, and multiple lapses of memory. Based on 205 interviews, CID concluded that the Barker report "was improperly disposed of; evidence of this is the failure to locate the report of investigation at all appropriate repositories." Further inquiry failed to identify those responsible for its disappearance. CID recorded the offense in its final report on December 3, 1970: "Wrongful Disposition of an Official Document."[39]

Most likely, CID declared, Major General Koster, with or without the assistance of either Brigadier General Young or Colonel Parson (and perhaps both), had disposed of Barker's report and blamed artillery fire for the deaths of almost one hundred civilians that day. Koster at first confirmed the existence of a report but later conceded he never received a written version.[40] He had long been concerned about upholding the figure of twenty civilian casualties in the midst of reports of many more noncombatant deaths—and *not* by accident. He had also found it impossible to reconcile how American troops could kill 128 Viet Cong in battle and yet capture only three weapons. The Barker report attempted to take care of these problems by finding no war crimes.

The American public, of course, was not privy to either the CID report or the court transcript, but it was aware of Sergeant Charles Hutto's court martial, which opened in January 1971 at Fort McPherson, while Calley's trial was underway. In an earlier signed statement to CID (also unknown to the American public), Hutto admitted to machine-gunning a number of unarmed villagers. "It was murder," he now declared in court. "I didn't agree with all the killings, but we were doing it because we had been told." His defense attorney, Edward Magill, emphasized that Hutto had not considered disobeying the order "because he had never heard of an illegal order."[41]

After less than two hours of deliberation, the six army officers making up the jury acquitted Hutto on January 14, at least in part because he had been obeying illegal orders—the major argument used by the defense attorneys in the Nuremberg trials, which failed to win an acquittal of the accused Nazi war criminals. Less than a week later, Hutto resigned from the army and returned to his home in Louisiana.[42]

The decisions in the Mitchell and Hutto cases seemed to set a precedent for releasing Calley and the rest of the accused officers and enlisted men—regardless of evidence, army regulations, international law, and the Nuremberg decisions. Despite the dismissal of obedience to orders as a defense in the post–World War II trials, the military juries in the My Lai cases seemed inclined to accept it as a valid argument. The U.S. Army soon dropped all charges against the soldiers, including Private William Doherty, which happened a week after Hutto's acquittal.[43]

General Seaman recognized the message sent by these earlier trials and announced in late January that "in the interest of justice" he had dismissed all charges against Koster. He had done this on the basis of Koster's "long and honorable career," despite knowing that "some evidence" showed he had been aware of a large number of civilian casualties at My Lai 4 but failed to launch an investigation. Nonetheless, Seaman did not consider Koster guilty of "intentional abrogation of responsibilities."[44]

Seaman's decision drew a bitter reaction. Attorney Robert MacCrate from the Peers Inquiry termed it "a serious disservice to the Army" and to the American public. Several charges against Koster's men were pending, and this action "effectively cut off the orderly progress of the inquiry up the chain of command." Peers agreed and pointed out that the *Kansas City Star* had denounced the act as a "whitewash of the top man." House Democrat Samuel Stratton of the Hébert subcommittee agreed, blasting it as "a military whitewash" and "a grave miscarriage of military justice" and calling for an independent tribunal to handle the cases. The National Committee for a Citizens' Commission of Inquiry accused Seaman of commanding soldiers who committed atrocities in two major operations and now protected "a fellow general who is likewise deeply implicated."[45]

MacCrate's criticisms and the outcry in Congress prodded the Pentagon into taking punitive action against Koster and Young. In a move that Stratton cynically noted would remain unpublicized and hence would not reflect badly on the command, the army quietly gave Koster a letter of censure. But

Secretary of the Army Resor demoted him to brigadier general and Young to colonel before dropping Koster another grade and taking away both officers' Distinguished Service Medals.[46]

The two acquittals along with the dismissed charges against the remainder of the enlisted men meant that of the twenty-five officers and soldiers accused of wrongdoing, only four officers would stand trial: Calley (whose trial was already underway), Medina, and Kotouc for war crimes, and Henderson for hiding these crimes. The outcome in these cases also suggested the possibility that no one would be held responsible for what happened at My Lai.[47]

Calley's defense attorney Latimer had meanwhile assigned a young attorney on his team to read a draft of Sack's story to appear in the February issue of *Esquire* and make any necessary revisions. One passage that remained after the lawyer's review was particularly gratifying to the defense—Calley's critique of America's actions in Vietnam. "I never met a Vietnamese man, woman, or child that we really helped there. We went there to save those people, but God! We didn't give the scraps from the dinner table to them. We didn't have the common courtesy to talk their language or learn of their customs: We scorned them. And killed them. A real disgrace."[48]

Another passage, however, did not survive this revision. "I lay there and I asked myself, My god. Did you really hack up all those damned people? Did you really pull a machete out and—*kkk*! Chop into all those people and do all those horrors? Did you, and I got the answer back, Yes. I hacked up those people, I hacked up millions of people—not millions. But yes, I killed plenty of people, I killed lots of NVA, I killed lots of VC with weapons on, I killed lots of people." The magazine had intended to run this cover-line: "Did you really pull a machete out and—*kkk!* Chop into all those people and do all those horrors?"[49]

In its place were these words: "I'm sorry, I'm not myself today. I didn't think that I'd be uptight about it, talking about it. I thought, I've gone to Vietnam and I've come back. I shouldn't have any hang-up about it. But after talking about it yesterday, I don't know. I thought about it. I couldn't sleep. My country accuses me of slaughtering innocent people. Even the President calls it a massacre. I lay there and I ask myself, My god, who are they talking about?" In an effort to shift the blame to those who brought on the war, he declared, "I only know, I went to Vietnam and I did my job there the best I could. I even asked myself why did I do it? Why didn't I stand on a corner like everyone else and say, 'I won't go. It's wrong.'"[50]

Back at Calley's trial, Latimer realized the proceedings were not going well and informed the court in mid-January that he intended to call three psychiatrists to the stand in an effort to show that Calley's mental capacity had been "impaired" on the day of the assault, perhaps by "marijuana fumes." The Defense Department's *Manual for Courts-Martial* recognized mitigating circumstances that might help Calley's case: no one in the army was criminally liable for an act resulting from a "mental defect, disease, or derangement" that interfered with his capacity "to distinguish right from wrong and to adhere to the right." Calley had rejected an insanity plea, and Latimer had informed Judge Kennedy that he would not use that approach. But it now appeared—about two months into the trial—that he had changed course. Kennedy was not pleased, warning Latimer that if his questions raised issues about Calley's mental state, he would adjourn the court and have the defendant examined by the Sanity Board at Walter Reed Army Hospital. Kennedy first wanted to hear the psychiatrists without the jury in the room. He did not have to go beyond the first witness.[51]

On January 18, 1971, Dr. Albert LaVerne of the Bellevue Medical Center at New York University appeared before Kennedy and the two teams of attorneys. LaVerne had examined Calley over the Christmas holidays and concluded that he could have accidentally inhaled marijuana fumes in a closed room while checking on his men the night before the assault. "There are not many closed rooms in Vietnam," Kennedy interjected with undisguised sarcasm.[52]

Neither Latimer nor LaVerne proved convincing. Latimer declared it possible that Calley "unconsciously" inhaled second-hand marijuana smoke and had a "marijuana hangover" the following morning that, along with stress, "affected his brain." LaVerne admitted to having no evidence that Calley had inhaled marijuana smoke and insisted that on March 16, 1968, he was sane and knew the difference between right and wrong.[53]

Kennedy had heard enough to rule that Laverne and Latimer had introduced the question of insanity by expressing doubt about whether Calley could rise above his machinelike obedience to orders and, in the words of the *Manual*, "adhere to the right." If he as judge failed to instruct the jury on the insanity issue, it would constitute an error subject to reversal on appeal. He recessed the court after approving Daniel's motion to have Calley undergo psychiatric tests at Walter Reed Hospital. Latimer objected because of potential damaging revelations, but Kennedy eased his concern by ruling that the prosecution would not be privy to anything said in the examination. Within three weeks the Sanity Board found Calley "normal in every aspect" and fully capable of distinguishing between right and wrong.[54]

In mid-February 1971, Latimer tried another approach: he brought LaVerne and two other psychiatrists to the stand in an effort to show that

Calley, though sane, lacked the mental capacity to premeditate murder. No longer was the defense denying that Calley had killed civilians; Latimer and his team had recognized the futility of undermining the testimonies of numerous witnesses attesting to Calley's guilt. Latimer now argued that Calley was incapable of premeditation and thus had no specific intent to kill. He hoped to establish "reasonable doubt" about whether Calley lacked what the *Manual* called "mental responsibility" for his actions. If successful in this argument, Latimer could enter a plea for mitigation based on Calley's inability to formulate "a premeditated design to kill."[55]

Latimer first questioned Dr. David Crane from the Indiana University School of Medicine in Indianapolis, who considered Calley incapable of premeditation and of making a "complex decision." Crane seemed impressive, having served as captain in the U.S. Army Medical Corps from 1966 to 1968 before becoming division psychiatrist for the 25th Infantry Division in Cu Chi, South Vietnam. Furthermore, he had been a witness in court-martial cases involving questions of mental disease or derangement affecting combat personnel and had evaluated up to eight hundred cases of mental deterioration.[56]

But, as Daniel pointed out in a lengthy cross-examination, Crane demonstrated no expertise in psychiatry and, most important, had not interviewed Calley, despite having had the opportunity to do so. How could Calley fail to realize that deaths would result "when he gave orders for people to be killed and when he killed himself?" When Crane admitted that Calley knew that "pulling the trigger" would "bring about a loss of life," Daniel pushed harder. "He knew the people would die? He meant for the people to die?" "Yes," Crane finally replied, supporting the prosecution's claim that Calley had committed premeditated murder.[57]

The following day, February 17, LaVerne testified that his four interviews with Calley showed that he "could not plan, contrive and think on that day" because of severe "combat stress" and "psychological stress" that made him behave "in an automatic fashion as a robot." Calley was unable to question orders and "could not possibly premeditate or intend to kill on March 16, 1968."[58]

Trouble developed during Daniel's cross-examination when LaVerne requested permission to consult his notes. Both Daniel and Latimer asked to see a paper referred to by LaVerne and found it to be a copy of a lengthy preface to the question Latimer had read to him in court. More damaging, the contents of the paper came from the Sanity Board that examined Calley at Walter Reed Hospital. LaVerne maintained that he had secured this material from his interview with Calley earlier in the week but could not remember what Calley told him in their meetings. Where was the evidence gathered during the interviews? LaVerne had nothing to show and apparently could recall nothing either. He did not write the details in his notes, he explained, because he was too busy preparing for the cross-examination.[59]

Furthermore, LaVerne contended, he did not ask Calley for details. "I couldn't get him to sit down. He was jumping up and down like a jumping bean and I wasn't going to, say, pull out a pencil and paper—you don't do that with Lieutenant Calley." LaVerne explained that he had "to approach him gently and talk to him because he is under pressure, great pressure." He finally declared he could not remember what Calley said about My Lai. "I'm under stress and I am fatigued."[60]

"So am I," declared Kennedy as he abruptly ended that day's proceedings. Early the next morning, February 19, he held a conference in his chambers—without the press—where he remarked that "most of the difficulties concerned the psychiatrist." He told Calley and both legal teams that he did not want to accuse LaVerne of lying, but "if he wasn't lying, it was the next thing to it." In a face-saving effort on behalf of LaVerne, Latimer asked the court to excuse the witness on the basis of a disagreement over strategy and strike that part of his cross-examination.[61]

Kennedy agreed to do both.

The third psychiatrist, Dr. Wilbur Hamman from St. Elizabeths Hospital in Washington, D.C., testified that after five interviews he did not believe Calley mentally capable of specific intent or premeditated murder. But, Hamman emphasized, training, experience, and the stress of battle had conditioned Calley to regard all Vietnamese as possible enemies and to follow the orders he got at the briefing to "kill all the enemy, not to leave anything alive."[62]

According to Hamman, Calley admitted ordering Meadlo to "waste" the Vietnamese but argued that he did not mean to kill them. Even when telling Meadlo "I want them dead," Calley claimed this did not mean he wanted them killed.

Daniel professed to be mystified by this argument. "What's the difference between intending someone to die and intending to kill them?" Hamman told the court he had once asked Calley about this matter. "Well, you keep using the word 'waste,'" Hamman remembered saying, and "I never hear you use the word kill, why not?" "We never use kill," Calley replied. "We don't use that word. Kill refers to our teachings that we are brought up with ever since childhood—Thou shalt not kill. If you use the word kill with the troops, it causes a very negative emotional reaction, so you use the word waste, to get rid of, to destroy."[63]

Hamman explained that Calley attempted to clarify his position by denying he killed anyone in My Lai 4; his mission was "a job" in which he viewed deaths as "enemy dying" and not "humans dying." Vietnamese prisoners were not "humans" but "potential killers of himself and his men." Calley claimed he "was not killing human beings" but "destroying enemies" in accordance with "an order." In his "state of mind," Hamman asserted, Calley "did not conceive of these acts as killing but as destroying, and I am using killing in the sense of killing a human being as opposed to destroying an enemy." Calley "lacked the capacity to have will, to consciously conceive that act."[64]

III

Whether or not he had a capacity to have will, a few minutes after two in the afternoon of February 23, following nearly three months of court proceedings, Calley took the stand. He was dressed in his Class A green uniform, and he wore no decorations other than the Combat Infantryman's Badge and shoulder patches signifying the Americal Division and the Student Brigade. His feet dangled from a heavily cushioned chair too large for his small frame.[65]

To many Americans by mid-February 1971, Calley had become well-known, most notably to a sizable segment of Vietnam veterans who considered him a victim of unfair charges, but to others, according to *Time* magazine, he was "a celebrity, almost a hero." Two weeks earlier, the Vietnam Veterans Against the War had gathered in Detroit to hear more than a hundred former soldiers—including a future presidential candidate and secretary of state, John Kerry—attest to many atrocities in Vietnam. Called "The Winter Soldier Investigation: An Inquiry into American War Crimes," the gathering featured an opening speaker who insisted that My Lai was not an isolated incident and that Calley had become a scapegoat for the high-ranking civilian and military officials who drew up the policies responsible for the atrocities. Among ten thousand letters offering Calley support, twenty-five came from the highly popular conservative news commentator Paul Harvey, who declared in one of them, "I have every confidence that you are a fine military officer that we can all be proud of."[66]

Inside the courtroom, Latimer spent the first day of Calley's testimony leading him through a detailed account of his personal background before asking for a description of the battle plan for March 16, 1968. At the briefing of company commanders the day before, Calley explained, Medina emphasized that their objective in Pinkville was to destroy the enemy's headquarters at My Lai 1 near the coast and not let anyone get behind them or leave anything standing. The enemy consisted of the 48th Viet Cong Battalion and the 35th Viet Cong Heavy Weapons Battalion, which together constituted a formidable force of regulars and local cadres. Their base camp in Pinkville was a virtual fortress protected by a minefield, a ditch line, and a number of .50-caliber machine guns along the bunker line, but their main defense lay in the small surrounding villages. Once Charlie Company invaded My Lai 4, it had to destroy all opposition or else it would follow the deadly path of previous expeditions—taking fire from the rear and finding itself pinned down by mortars and heavy weapons fire as it moved toward My Lai 1. The key was to maintain rapid mobility.[67]

The subhamlets provided early warning to the Viet Cong of an assault and were ready to break it up. Once the attack force got into the targeted area, the villages would go on the offensive. "When they got you in the pocket, they would cut you to ribbons and you couldn't get back out." The 1st and 2nd Platoons would enter the village, soon followed by the 3rd Platoon, which would dust off American casualties and allow the two lead platoons to maintain the momentum of their attack.[68]

Charlie Company, Calley summarized, would begin the "high-speed combat assault" on Pinkville by quickly neutralizing My Lai 4 and then clearing My Lai 5 and My Lai 6. At that point they would band together to launch the "final assault on Pinkville" and destroy the 48th Viet Cong Battalion "once and for all."[69]

Calley explained that they were told all civilians would have left My Lai 4 a short time before the assault, meaning that the only Vietnamese there would be the enemy. When someone at the briefing asked whether the term civilians included men, women, and children, Medina declared it "meant everything." Charlie's mission was to destroy the "infrastructure," which according to "common knowledge" meant the civilian government that controlled the Viet Cong villages.[70]

The "order of the day" came from Medina, Calley testified: "Waste them." Asked when Medina had given the order, Calley replied, "The night before in the company briefing, the platoon leaders' briefing, the following morning before we lifted off, and twice there in the village, sir."[71]

Calley maintained that early in the assault Medina radioed an order to "get rid of the people" slowing his platoon's move through the village. Calley rogered him but came upon Meadlo watching over a large group of Vietnamese civilians on the southeastern trail. Calley asked if he knew what to do with these people. When told yes, Calley ordered him to get them moving to the ditch along the eastern edge of the village. At this point he saw Conti "molesting a female" off the trail and ordered him to pull up his pants and get back to his assignment. Medina called again, this time asking why Calley was disobeying his orders. Calley explained that the civilians were slowing him down, which drew Medina's hot response: "Waste the Vietnamese and get my people out in line, out in the position they were supposed to be."[72]

On returning to the trail, Calley continued, he found Meadlo still standing there with the Vietnamese and yelled at him to move those people or "get rid of them." He then left once more to check on Mitchell's position but soon heard a lot of shooting to the north—probably the 3rd Platoon entering the village. After moving up along the edge of a ditch, he came to a clearing and saw four or five soldiers firing at a group of Vietnamese in the ditch. He only knew two of the men, Dursi and Meadlo, but, he testified, "I fired into the ditch, also, sir."[73]

Calley's admission must have startled everyone in the courtroom. He had repeatedly denied involvement in the killings on the trail but now admitted to firing perhaps eight shots into the ditch without, he claimed, knowing whether he had hit anyone. In one moment, Latimer had lost his client's first line of defense. Daniel immediately tied the shootings to the charges of murder. What did you see in the ditch? "Dead people, sir."[74]

Daniel then explored the possibility of Calley's admitting to more shootings. Asked if he fired at anyone else in the area, Calley told of firing at a head moving through the rice paddy that turned out to be a small boy. The only other time he fired his weapon came near the landing zone, when a man fleeing the village jumped off the trail and into the rice paddy. Calley thought he hit him but was not certain. As for the charge that he shot a monk, he admitted that he interrogated a man but not a monk. "I butt-stroked him in the mouth, sir." The man fell to the ground, but Calley claimed he did not shoot him and that someone drop-kicked him into the ditch. Calley also denied both shooting a child running from the ditch and throwing Vietnamese into the ditch and firing at them for more than an hour.[75]

Calley explained that by the time his forces reached the eastern edge of My Lai 4, their formation had broken down and the battle plan ground to a halt. He told his squad leaders to pull the platoon together in preparation for moving out. But his troops hesitated to get back into line before hitting the next village. "I mean the fear even doubles and triples for the next one, because you know you are getting that much closer. We got through the first village all right. We are all right so far. We know sooner or later we are going to get it. That's like playing Russian roulette, but only spinning the chamber one time."[76]

Calley testified that Medina soon called him and the other two platoon leaders to meet him for lunch at the eastern terminal point of the assault—their first
time together in My Lai 4. After discussing the operation and making plans for
their next movements, Medina and his three platoon leaders walked up to My
Lai 5 and then to My Lai 6 only to find both villages deserted except for elderly
people. They then gathered their men and entered a large graveyard just west of
My Lai 1, where they met up with Bravo Company for the night.[77]

In short, Calley blamed Medina for the killings. Asked if he ever intended "to
waste any Vietnamese man, woman or child," Calley replied, "No, sir, I didn't."
His only objective was to "waste or destroy the enemy," he said. "I never sat down
to analyze if they were men, women, and children. They were enemy and just
people." Medina had declared that "everybody in that area would be the enemy
and everyone there would be destroyed, all enemies would be destroyed. We had
been taught that from the time we got there that men, women, and children were
enemy soldiers." Calley denied any responsibility for what happened. "I felt then
and I still do that I acted as I was directed, and I carried out the orders that I was
given, and I do not feel wrong in doing so, sir."[78]

Calley insisted that at their luncheon meeting he told Medina about the
shooting in the ditch and that the captain had said nothing. Asked if he told
Medina who did the shooting, Calley replied that all he told him was that
"people" had been shot in the ditch and in the village. "It wasn't any big deal,"
remarked Calley. "You didn't tell him the circumstances under which they
were shot?" "No, sir. Why should I? He knew what circumstances they were
shot under." "How did he know?" "Because he had told me to shoot them,
sir." "When?" "Both that day and the day before.[79]

Daniel now moved to counter the defense claim that Calley lacked the mental
capacity to premeditate by bringing in the three members of the Sanity Board
from Walter Reed Hospital. Major Henry Edwards had examined Calley six
times, half of them jointly with other members of the board, and concluded that
on March 16, 1968, Calley had been "free from any mental disease, defect, or derangement" and "had the capacity to form the specific intent to kill." Lieutenant
Colonel Franklin Jones likewise found no evidence of a mental illness or disorder
that would have undermined Calley's ability to distinguish right from wrong.
And Colonel Arnold Johnson, chief of the Department of Psychiatry and
Neurology, interviewed Calley for about eleven hours and found nothing suggesting a mental defect that would have prevented him from premeditating or
having a specific intent to kill.[80]

But the key question remained: Who ordered the killing? The defense had
not disproved the allegations of murder against Calley—indeed, that was

now impossible, following his admission to shooting Vietnamese in the ditch. Nor had it presented a convincing case for mental incapacity when it clumsily toyed with an insanity plea that Calley had opposed from the beginning.[81] The only avenue Latimer had left was to prove Medina was responsible for Calley's actions.

Ironically, both the prosecution and the defense wanted Medina to testify, but they first had to overcome the army's opposition. For a week, defense witnesses had asserted that Calley had acted under Medina's orders. Latimer hoped to establish this claim by questioning Medina. Daniel wanted him on the stand for the opposite reason—to show that Calley had acted on his own. The army, according to William Eckhardt, was not willing to have the government call Medina to the stand because under the rules of evidence it would have had to "vouch" for the accuracy of his testimony and thus "bless" his statement about the orders he gave. But Medina wanted to clear his name, and his attorney, the nationally known F. Lee Bailey, had filed an appeal for him to testify based on the accusation that the army had ordered Daniel *not* to call him to the stand. The matter was resolved, Eckhardt continued, when the members of the Calley jury exercised their right to call witnesses that neither party had presented. Kennedy thus summoned Medina as a witness for the court and the government did not have to vouch for his credibility.[82]

Medina took the stand the next day, on March 10, wearing a full dress uniform replete with the Silver Star and other combat decorations and at ease with himself. He first focused on the hard realities of the Vietnam War by describing in bloody detail the high number of American soldiers mangled and killed in the minefields in Vietnam. His men had not been prepared for this horror. Largely inexperienced in combat and perhaps looking for some sense of identity, they "affectionately called themselves 'Barker's Bastards.' We were illegitimate." In a comment that drew a smile from Calley, Medina declared, "Nobody wanted us."[83]

Daniel shifted the direction of the testimony, making Medina aware of the need to defend himself against claims that he had ordered his men to kill civilians. Medina faced two counts of premeditated murder—a male and a female, both unidentified. As the commanding officer of Charlie Company, he also faced charges for the deaths of at least one hundred South Vietnamese by rifles and machine guns.[84]

Turning to look directly at Calley, Medina denied ordering the killing of women and children. Nor did he make a radio call to Calley complaining about his alleged failure to follow orders. He admitted radioing Calley to speed up his progress toward the defensive position on the eastern side of the village, but he denied having any communication with him pertaining to the large number of civilians he had collected. Medina also vehemently denied telling his men to "kill everything that moves" or that any women and children there were Viet Cong. "I did not expect to find any noncombatants in the village of My Lai 4," he said. Although he was surprised to see women and children, he said nothing to either his lower or higher commanders.[85]

Medina then explained the problems he had in determining the number of Vietnamese killed in the assault. At Major Charles Calhoun's instruction that afternoon, he asked his platoon leaders for a body count. Calley said more than fifty, Brooks gave him the same number, and LaCross reported six. "Oh, my God," thought Medina. "What happened?" He knew that noncombatants had died, but not that many. He told the platoon leaders that he had seen about twenty to twenty-eight noncombatants dead and would give that body count to Calhoun.[86]

Medina insisted that it was not until the evening of March 16, at the night defensive position, that he became aware of the great number of people killed in My Lai 4. He had heard sporadic firing, but he knew that burning hooches caused the bamboo to explode with sounds like rifle shots. He denied telling anyone to get rid of the civilians, either over the radio or in person. Yet he realized that as company commander he was ultimately responsible. It might have been that night that he declared, "I will go to jail for this."[87]

In Latimer's cross-examination, Medina changed direction and surprisingly admitted to covering up the heavy number of civilian deaths. "I realized that instead of going in and doing combat with an armed enemy, the intelligence was faulty, and we found nothing but women and children in the village of My Lai 4 and seeing what had happened, I realized exactly the disgrace that was being brought upon the Army uniform that I am very proud to wear." But, he added, "I also realized the repercussions that it would have against the United States of America," as well as "my family" and "myself."[88]

Medina had perhaps also realized the statute of limitations had run out on the crime of a cover-up.[89]

"Well," Latimer indignantly asked, "what's happened now because you didn't report it? What has happened now, sir? Yes. It's worse, isn't it?" Did Calley know then, he asked, that "you were disobeying what an officer should do?" Medina insisted that he did not realize he was guilty of a felony and yet admitted, "I knew that as an officer I was responsible to report that particular action." "And you still didn't report it, knowing that you should have done it?" "Yes, sir."[90]

Medina insisted that before 10:25 a.m. he radioed his platoon leaders to stop the indiscriminate killing of civilians. Asked if his junior commanders were also surprised by the civilian presence, Medina declared that he had received no reports from them and did not become aware of the mass killings until he saw bodies on the north-south trail.[91]

Was My Lai 4 "an intermediate objective throughout this operation with the final objective somewhere else"? "No, sir," Medina declared in a response that contradicted Calley's testimony and must have surprised him and Latimer as well as others in the courtroom. The "overall mission, sir, was to close with the 48th VC Battalion which was at the village of My Lai 4, sir, and to engage it in combat and destroy it, sir." Was he planning to go to My Lai 1? Medina explained that they were supposed to join Bravo Company in a night defensive position to the west of that village. Latimer pushed for clarification. "And go to My Lai 1 the following day, is that right, or Pinkville or however you might want to classify that?" Medina replied, "No, sir, I don't recall that at all."[92]

Why would Medina assert that the combat plan did not include a final assault on the Viet Cong's headquarters at My Lai 1, as he had said at the March 15 briefing? Calley's testimony confirmed this objective, as did that of Watke, Calhoun, and Kotouc. When had anyone argued that the Viet Cong battalion was in My Lai 4 rather than in My Lai 1? My Lai 4 was the first village Charlie Company sought to neutralize before clearing others en route to My Lai 1. Had Medina attempted to declare the mission complete before news of the mass killings leaked out?[93]

Medina's story had other flaws, some of which we have seen before. He testified that he did not enter the village until somewhere between nine and ten in the morning, choosing to remain outside its southern edge but receiving no reports that the men had encountered only civilians. Latimer seemed confused. Medina said it was before 10:25 a.m. that he ordered his troops to cease fire and save ammunition. And yet he also claimed he did not realize until about 10:30 a.m. that the Viet Cong battalion was not in the village. Why, Latimer asked Medina, did you order your men to save ammunition before that time if you thought they were shooting at the enemy? Medina replied that he assumed they were shooting livestock and did not want them wasting their ammunition. "Well, how did you know they were not shooting at the enemy?" When Medina replied that he did not know this, Latimer asked, "How did you know they were shooting at livestock?" Medina replied that he had given them that instruction. "Did you see them shooting at the livestock in the village?" Told no, Latimer asked, "So, nevertheless without any information you just told them to stop shooting to save ammunition?" "I gave them instructions to conserve ammunition, yes, sir." Latimer remarked, "That's all."[94]

IV

Daniel began his closing argument on March 15, following nearly four months of court proceedings that included testimonies from about one hundred witnesses, many of whom provided either direct or circumstantial evidence of Calley's ordering and participating in the killing of a large number of defenseless Vietnamese victims, male and female, young and old. Daniel, however, realized that he only had to prove Calley guilty of one murder to win a conviction.[95]

Daniel told the court that several witnesses saw Calley order Meadlo to shoot a large number of Vietnamese in My Lai 4 and then join in the killing on the trail and at the ditch. Conti, Meadlo, and Sledge were among those who saw him order and take part in the shootings on the trail. Conti saw Calley, Meadlo, and Mitchell firing into the ditch. Maples saw Calley fire into about fifteen Vietnamese in the ditch. Turner watched Calley, Meadlo, and others fire into about a hundred people in the ditch. Sledge witnessed Calley using his rifle butt to hit an elderly Vietnamese man in the head before shooting a child attempting to escape the ditch. The defense, Daniel emphasized, had not disputed these facts.[96]

Daniel insisted he could prove his case by a combination of direct evidence stemming from eyewitness accounts and circumstantial evidence connecting Calley to the bodies in his area of operation. Calley had admitted telling Meadlo to "waste" a group of Vietnamese people, and the defense never denied that he killed people in the ditch. If Calley was responsible for killing at least one human being without justification, it followed that he had the "specific intent to kill" based on "a premeditated design." Conti, Dursi, Meadlo, and Sledge had provided direct evidence; circumstantial evidence came from Allen Boyce, Rennard Doines, Ronald Grzesik, Charles Hall, Sydney Kye, Lenny Lagunoy, Robert Maples, Greg Olsen, and Roy Wood.[97]

Daniel's summation of Dursi's testimony best exemplifies the effectiveness of this approach. Dursi testified that Meadlo was on his left when Calley ordered them to force the Vietnamese into the ditch. They began screaming as Calley said, "Start firing!" Meadlo was crying but followed Calley's order and with him began firing. Dursi refused to follow the order, and Meadlo yelled at him, "Shoot! Shoot! Why don't you shoot?" "I can't. I won't. I will not." Dursi was stunned at the sight of mothers protecting their children and people screaming and crying while being shot and falling onto each other. Calley shouted at him, "Get on the other side of the ditch before you get sick!" As Dursi made his way across the makeshift footbridge, he saw the victims below and heard the soldiers still firing as he walked away. He also glanced at a bubble helicopter flying "in the area."[98]

How many did they kill? Turning to the jury, Daniel declared that the number was not decisive for the charges. "We only have to prove that he killed at least one to satisfy that element of the offense of the fact of death, the fact of the killing just one. If you can find that he killed more than thirty, it would be satisfied, or if you can all agree that he killed twenty-five, it would be satisfied, but if you can only agree that he killed one, he can still be found guilty."[99]

Numerous witnesses saw bodies on the trail and in the ditch. Daniel briefly summarized the testimonies of each of twenty members of Charlie Company by name who saw bodies on the north-south trail pictured in Haeberle's photograph. He did the same with six defense witnesses who saw the bodies on that trail, including two pilots of Lieutenant Colonel Barker's helicopter that landed on the south side of the village, and with thirteen government witnesses who identified the victims in a photograph. Finally, Daniel slowly and methodically reviewed the testimonies of ten soldiers one by one, pointing out where they independently agreed on a string of facts. Dursi, Meadlo, Sledge, Conti, Boyce, Maples, Lagunoy, Olsen, Hall, and Grzesik—all saw the bodies in the ditch and declared that Calley had ordered and participated in the mass killings.[100]

Such a great number of witnesses, Daniel argued, could not have made up their stories. They were not questioned until after leaving the service, and they came forward years later and from different areas of the country. "Did they have an opportunity to fabricate this? There's no way, gentlemen. It has to be the truth." And, he argues, the conflicts between their accounts only made them more credible. "What would you have thought if all of these individuals came into this courtroom and told you the same story? If everybody was precise in their detail? Would that be credible to you after this length of time?"[101]

But of all those who came forth, Daniel asserted, only one told the full story and resolved the conflicts in the testimonies—Thomas Turner. Discrepancies involving the number of deaths in the ditch appeared in the witnesses' testimonies because groups of Vietnamese "were put in at a different location over a period of time, and they were seen by different people there at different times, and different people were in fact there at different times." Turner approached the ditch and remained nearby for more than an hour, watching Calley, Meadlo, and others shooting the villagers. He saw bodies in the ditch and another group kneeling along its edge as they were shot, and he saw Calley change clips while Meadlo fired into the ditch. Turner wanted nothing to do with the killings and moved a few yards north of the ditch. But when he got there, he turned around and resumed watching. More civilians continued to appear, totaling nearly one hundred people in the ditch. Turner's testimony, Daniel asserted, was consistent with all other accounts—including Calley's.[102]

Furthermore, Daniel emphasized, twelve members of the 1st Platoon placed Calley at the ditch, a fact confirmed by Calley himself when he admitted firing into those people but could give no estimates of how many men, women, and children were there. This was not important to Calley. "They were just enemy."[103]

Daniel declared that the evidence showed at least seventy people and perhaps as many as a hundred killed in the ditch. Turner and Meadlo provided this range of numbers and Thompson, Colburn, and Culverhouse confirmed them. Daniel again reminded the court that the numbers were not necessary for a conviction; he only had to prove that Calley killed at least one civilian in the ditch.[104]

Calley committed two murders witnessed by his RTO. What would Sledge have to gain by lying about the killing of an elderly man and a child?[105]

Daniel now turned to the question of premeditated murder. For this charge to apply, the shooter must intend for the person to die as a result of a decision made as little as a "split-second" before pulling the trigger. There were two ways to prove premeditated murder—by direct evidence, in which the killer tells you what he is going to do, and circumstantial evidence, which means "you just know by what he does what he intended."[106]

Both Crane and Hamman claimed that Calley lacked the mental capacity to premeditate, but under the law, Daniel pointed out, Calley could be sane and still suffer from a mental incapacity to premeditate. Without interviewing Calley or hearing his testimony, Crane offered only the opinion of a psychiatrist. And yet he admitted that Calley had the mental ability to premeditate that day even though he was incapable of making a complex decision. Hamman agreed with this assessment. "You don't have to be a genius, gentlemen, to commit the offense of premeditated murder," Daniel declared for emphasis.[107]

Daniel argued that Calley had the mental capacity to make decisions and was not delusional. He performed all the actions expected of an officer and did not seem confused. The three psychiatrists brought to the stand by the prosecution—Major Henry Edwards, Lieutenant Colonel Franklin Jones, and Colonel Arnold Johnson from Walter Reed Army Hospital—were all in the military and familiar with combat psychiatry. They unanimously agreed that Calley had the mental ability to premeditate.[108]

And yet, Daniel declared, the strongest testimony came from those who were with Calley that day, including Conti, Dursi, Meadlo, Sledge, and Turner, who all thought Calley acted in a normal fashion. Conti confirmed Meadlo's testimony that Calley ordered him to kill the Vietnamese. Dursi heard the same assertions, as did Sledge. Turner likewise showed that Calley intended to kill. The defendant, Daniel concluded, had to have known he would kill his two targets when he pulled the trigger with his rifle barrel pressed against the man's head and then shot the child at close range.[109]

The next morning, March 16, 1971, three years to the day after My Lai, Latimer tried to counter Daniel's argument by insisting that more soldiers besides Calley were involved in the killings. In the face of so much evidence, he no longer could claim his client's innocence. He also recognized the futility of establishing impaired judgment based on mitigating circumstances. Consequently, Latimer tried a new approach: he warned that convicting Calley would tarnish the army's image "beyond recognition." To widen the blame, he reminded the court that more than a hundred soldiers took part in this assault, which meant this was not "a one-man carnage." Many witnesses had testified in an effort to throw guilt elsewhere. Such "partners in crime" often try to escape punishment by accusing others of the offense, making this "a classic example" of avoiding the charge of accomplice.[110]

Latimer argued that in the midst of the chaos inside the village, it was amazing that these soldiers did not shoot each other, crowded as they were in the dense foliage and unable to see the enemy while hearing every shot fired and knowing they could die at any moment. "This is the type of warfare that fends hatred against any enemy and anyone who can aid the enemy." Latimer asserted that had he been there, "I might have suspected when I didn't find two battalions or two companies and a headquarters right in the My Lai area itself, that somewhere along the line, when I got out in the open, they might be going to mow me down."[111]

Latimer questioned the credibility of some of the key witnesses for the prosecution: Conti often strayed away from his men and "seemed to be doing something besides fighting wars"; Meadlo's "emotional state" made him "one of the most unreliable witnesses"; and Turner raised doubts about his own innocence by seeking immunity. In all the confusion of combat inside a village, an army unit cannot have some soldiers "hurting civilians, others going around looking for women."[112]

Latimer pointed out that several soldiers' testimonies supported that of Corporal Kenneth Schiel, who claimed that at the briefing "Medina stressed we were to kill everything." Schiel had no reason to lie, because he had a grant of immunity. Salvatore Lamartina remembered that Medina told them, "Go into the village and kill everything that breathed." He and others "sprayed the village." Latimer quoted from eighteen other soldiers who made the same allegation against Medina.[113]

Medina, Latimer asserted, offered "very hollow" reasons for not returning to My Lai for a body count. Going back, he knew, would expose the mass killings. Medina had to have heard every shot from the M-16s and machine guns and must have known what was going on. If he did not, "the man was not fit to be a commander." "He'd seen what happened." He "knew how his orders had been interpreted." Medina was trying to "escape responsibility." Later that evening, he expressed fear of going to prison for twenty years.[114]

Latimer declared, "For the life of me, I cannot understand why we could take a group of twenty or thirty men out of the United States Army, all good men, all good citizens, at the time they were picked up, put them over there, and have an incident like this happen unless it had been suggested, ordered, or commanded by somebody upstairs and I needn't go no further in this case than Captain Medina." Latimer could not understand why a lieutenant, "the lowest man on the totem pole, would be issuing orders like that without having some directive or orders from on high."[115]

That evening Daniel insisted in his closing argument that Calley could not avoid punishment by claiming he followed orders. His only order was to engage the enemy in My Lai 4—which meant "there was no order to round up all those men, women, and children and summarily execute them." Calley testified that they were to launch "a high-speed combat assault" aimed at clearing My Lai 4, 5, and 6 before neutralizing My Lai 1. "Does that indicate summary execution of men, women, and children?"[116]

Daniel argued that the evidence did not show that Medina ordered Calley to kill the detained Vietnamese. Medina testified that he did not give that order. Neither of the two RTOs in the command group heard such an order, nor did Calley's RTO, Charles Sledge; the 3rd Platoon's RTO, Stephen Glimpse; and its leader, Jeffrey LaCross. Only Calley claimed he received that order. "Do you think that the accused would have called Captain Medina and told him that, 'I have fifty, a hundred Vietnamese—men, women, and children—none of whom have any weapons.' And then would have received an order from his company commander to waste that many people under those circumstances? Do you believe that?" Calley never claimed to have called Medina to tell him about the people he had under control and what the circumstances were. "That was because he did not do it."[117]

Perhaps the best indication of Calley's attitude was his comment to Sledge after Thompson left: "He don't like the way I'm running the show here, but I'm the boss." Calley, Daniel asserted, "was running that show, gentlemen, on his own initiative, at his own direction."[118]

If Medina had given such an order, Daniel declared, Calley was as guilty as Medina in obeying that order. Such an order was illegal, making both men guilty of criminal intent. Any "reasonable man" would have realized the illegality of an order to gather more than thirty people on a trail, some of them children and babies, and "summarily execute" them. Any "reasonable man" would know it was unlawful to put more than seventy people in a ditch, "like a bunch of cattle—men, women, children, and babies." Any "reasonable man not only would know it, he should know it, and he could not rely upon any order to commit that, to absolve himself of criminal responsibility for that conduct."[119]

Daniel held Calley responsible for what happened at My Lai 4, regardless of an alleged order from Medina. If there was an order, Calley "joined in and he is as much to blame as anyone else who would've given that order." The law says that a reasonable man would not have obeyed that order. "What can justify, gentlemen, the shooting in cold blood of an infant or a child or any human being who's unresisting and is offering you no resistance?"[120]

Under American law, the Uniform Code of Military Justice, and the laws of warfare, Daniel declared, "all human beings are entitled to be treated humanely." And yet the defense would throw away these rules and "legalize murder." These victims were human beings, whether or not they were Viet Cong supporters or sympathizers. "They may have been Vietnamese people who just happened to have been in the wrong place at the wrong time. They may have been people who were under the control of the Viet Cong, because they had no choice, because they themselves were captives of this country's own enemy. But I ask you gentlemen, who stopped to ask them?" Did Calley ever try to determine who they were? The children? The infants? Would any court in the world have found the children or the infants guilty of an offense and sentence them to die? Yet Calley "appointed himself judge, jury, and executioner, and he convicted his prisoners without a trial." For him to assert that he fulfilled his duty and acted in the name of the United States was "to prostitute all of the humanitarian principles for which this nation stands."[121]

Daniel had concluded his remarks, and Kennedy instructed the jury that it must decide whether Calley had acted under orders. Medina denied ordering his men to kill everyone; Calley insisted that Medina ordered them to destroy anything helpful to the enemy. Twice Calley claimed that Medina ordered him to "hurry and get rid of the people and get into position" and to stop searching the bunkers and "waste the people." If the jury found that Medina had issued such an order and that Calley knew the order was illegal, "the fact that the order was given operates as no defense." The question becomes: Would a person of "ordinary sense and understanding" have realized the order was unlawful?[122]

Calley, meanwhile, waited in his apartment for the verdict, often in the company of friends while watching his large color TV. On the wall was a poster saying "No More War," and in the room was a U.S. flag flown over the Battle of the Bulge in World War II. In whiling away the time, he and his buddies kept a "body count" of roaches killed in the kitchen. Did he shoot the reindeer whose pelt was on the wall? "God no," exclaimed Calley, according to journalist Warren Rogers for the *Los Angeles Times*. "I couldn't kill a reindeer."[123]

In the late afternoon of March 29, more than four months after the opening session and thirteen days after receiving instructions from the judge, the jury had deliberated nearly eighty hours and was now ready to present its verdict in the longest war-crimes trial in American military history. Latimer complained during the wait about the money he lost every day in attorney's fees for cases back home. "Finally they're ready," Calley remarked when summoned back to court.[124]

Kennedy asked Calley and his attorneys to approach the president of the jury, Colonel Ford. After an exchange of salutes, Ford began reading the decision in a soft voice. The court by a secret written ballot and by a two-thirds vote of the members present at the time found him guilty of the premeditated murders of at least twenty-two Vietnamese civilians: Specification 1—"an unknown number, not less than 1" on the trail; Specification 2—"an unknown number, not less than twenty" at the ditch; Specification 2 of the Additional Charge—"with intent to commit murder, commit an assault upon" the child.

Calley's face flushed, his eyes widening as he stared at Ford. Calley awkwardly saluted him again before returning to the table with his defense team.

Kennedy announced that the court would hear the jury's sentence the following morning. Daniel had not called for the death penalty but for whatever punishment the jury thought "appropriate." Its choices in cases of premeditated murder were execution or life imprisonment.[125]

Calley rose to speak and, after moving from behind a high lectern to a lowered microphone, he spoke to the jury in a taut yet trembling voice. "I'm not going to stand here and plead for my life or my freedom." Short of breath, his eyes moist and his body shaking, he declared:

> I've never known a soldier, nor did I ever myself ever wantonly kill a human being in my entire life. If I have committed a crime, the only crime that I've committed is in judgment of my values. Apparently I valued my troops' lives more than I did that of the enemy. When my troops were getting massacred and mauled by an enemy I couldn't see, I couldn't feel, that I couldn't touch—that nobody in the military system ever described them as anything other than Communism. They [the army] didn't give it a race, they didn't give it a sex, they didn't give it an age. They never let me believe it was just a philosophy in a man's mind. That was my enemy out there. And when it became between me and that enemy, I had to value the lives of my troops—and I feel that was the only crime I have committed.

Drawing a deep breath, Calley concluded in barely a whisper. "Yesterday, you stripped me of all my honor. Please, by your actions that you take here today don't strip future soldiers of their honor. I beg of you."[126]

For almost two and a half minutes, Warren Rogers recalled, the only sounds in the room had been Calley's quavering voice and the drone of the air conditioner.[127]

As soon as Calley had finished his statement, Daniel rose to defend the jury's verdict. "You did not strip him of his honor," he told them. "What he did stripped him of his honor."[128]

Latimer's multifaceted strategy had failed. His gentle approach and demeanor had not swayed the jury, nor had his various tactics. Daniel and his team of prosecutors had been better prepared and proved more effective in the courtroom. In one of the most telling examples, Major Raby had spent more than a hundred hours reading and summarizing the testimonies that potential witnesses gave to CID, the Peers commission, and the Hébert subcommittee, only to have Latimer and his other associate, Richard Kay, choose not to read them. Instead, they had summaries made of the summaries. One journalist compared Latimer's defense to the bumbling performance of attorney William Jennings Bryan in the Scopes trial of 1925 in Tennessee.[129]

Latimer could never prove that Medina ordered Calley to kill; but this did not matter. As Daniel made clear, Calley as a "reasonable man" should not have obeyed such an illegal order, and Calley, of course, would have been guilty if he had acted on his own. In the end, Latimer could not overcome the massive collection of both direct and circumstantial evidence that Daniel wove together to prove his case. According to Warren Rogers, Latimer could not counter Daniel's hammering away in a "moralistic, puritanical tone" repeating the list of victims—"women, children, old men…and babies." The common belief was that Calley might get involuntary manslaughter and five years in prison. Instead, multiple eyewitness accounts of events meshed with the large number of supportive testimonies to win a murder conviction from at least four of six career army officers and veterans of war.[130]

That evening on *ABC Evening News*, however, news anchor Harry Reasoner told a nationwide TV audience that the decision was wrong. It was "ludicrous" to refer to the "laws of warfare" in the "heat of battle." He found it "too hard" to "come down to one simple and unprepared man out of the morass of all the confused and casual killing." His conclusion: "I could not have voted guilty in this trial."[131]

The strongly negative reaction to the verdict in the United States appalled Major General Kenneth Hodson, the judge advocate general of the U.S. Army. A massacre had occurred, he insisted. "It was a violation of all the rules of land warfare that I've ever known in my life. Because it was just cold-blooded killing of people who appeared to be defenseless civilians."[132]

The outspoken opposition to the conviction by uniformed Americans in Saigon must have been especially disconcerting to Hodson. Several remarks rested on the bits and pieces of news they had heard. Calley was a scapegoat—"just another victim of a war nobody wanted to fight." "I didn't want to come over here either—you don't really know who you are fighting. Women and children can shoot or frag you as easily as a man can." Calley's "platoon was being hit daily. It impaired his judgment." "I think it's wrong what he did, but they're not punishing anyone else—that's not right." From an officer: "They're getting Calley because the newspapers got hold of it and outraged so many people. The Army has to do something."[133]

Perhaps Hodson was equally puzzled by the mixed reaction in Saigon. Few Vietnamese were fully aware of My Lai, because President Nguyen Van Thieu had denied the massacre charges and barred any discussion of them on radio or television. In the meantime, those political and intellectual leaders who had learned of the killings privately criticized him for keeping the massacre and the trials from his people. One Buddhist leader spoke for many of his people in declaring that if Calley received a death sentence, he would send a cable to the military court pleading for leniency. "What is the use of another dead?"[134]

THE LIEUTENANT GOVERNOR of Georgia, Lester Maddox, responded to Calley's conviction in a manner that threatened to become a consistent theme of nationwide protest. In a letter to President Nixon, Maddox admitted to not knowing "all that transpired" in My Lai but nonetheless urged him to use the power of his executive office to free Calley from "one of the most outrageous miscarriages of justice in the history of our nation." It was wrong to make Calley the "sacrificial lamb" for the poor decisions made by our leaders in helping a government in Vietnam, which lacked the support of its own people. If the U.S. government executed Calley, Maddox wrote, "it will also be killing thousands upon thousands of other American soldiers, who, at a critical moment, will pause to wonder, '*Is this person I am about to shoot absolutely and without a doubt an enemy, or will I suffer Calley's fate if I pulled the trigger?*' "[135]

Nixon needed no persuasion: at the "Western White House" in San Clemente, California, in a mid-afternoon meeting on March 30, he told John Ehrlichman and H. R. Haldeman reassuringly, "I'll commute Calley."[136]

Twelve

AT 2:29 P.M. ON MARCH 31, 1971, Judge Reid Kennedy called the court martial of Lieutenant William Calley into session for the last time and asked Colonel Clifford Ford to read the sentence to the defendant. By secret written ballot, and with three-fourths of the members present at the time of the vote, Ford informed Calley, the jury had sentenced him to life in prison at hard labor, along with dismissal from the service and forfeiture of all pay and allowances. He would be eligible for parole in ten years.[1]

Calley weakly saluted and replied in what a reporter on the scene called "a barely audible voice," "I'll do my best, sir." Calley did an about-face, his body visibly sagging as he headed toward the military police waiting for him at the courtroom exit.[2]

"This court is closed," Kennedy declared, six minutes after it opened that afternoon and four and a half months after the court-martial proceedings had begun on November 17, 1970.[3]

Outside the building, more than a hundred people had gathered across the street, hoping to catch a glimpse of Calley. When learning the sentence, a woman in a red dress loudly denounced the court martial. "He's been crucified!" she shouted with her fist clenched. "Lieutenant Calley killed 100 Communists singlehanded. He should get a medal. He should be promoted to general." Identifying herself as Mrs. Hildegard Crochet of New Orleans, she announced that "eight concerned citizens" had accompanied her to demand Calley's freedom. She and her cohort left when ordered to do so by CID officials.[4]

Calley soon appeared, a cordon of MPs around him, his boyish face locked in a stiff smile. He acknowledged the cheering, saluting the crowd across the street as he and his escorts made their way to a waiting car. Calley had been dealt "an awful rap," George Latimer told reporters in a remark pointing to an appeal.[5]

I

Calley's sentence had been delivered at 11:35 a.m. Pacific time, and in less than two hours the chief strategists of the Nixon administration gathered in the Western White House to discuss presidential intervention in the case. Two hours after that, John Ehrlichman met again with the president, soon joined by Henry Kissinger and others. Legal counsel John Dean had reported from Washington that the president could act "now or later." Haldeman recalled that in the hours of meetings that day on various subjects, the "bigger thing" was the Calley decision.[6] No one debated whether the president should intervene; the chief question was what kind of action to take. And no one talked about the legal and moral dimensions; the major focus was the political fallout. The assumption was that intervention would boost popular support for the administration's "Vietnamization" program of gradual troop withdrawal.

At a second meeting in the afternoon of March 31, Ehrlichman passed on Melvin Laird's assertion from Washington that the president could "move in any time." According to Ehrlichman's papers, Nixon announced that he had a "strong feeling" he should act immediately. Spiro Agnew told the president that he had just learned from Governor John Bell Williams of Mississippi that his state was preparing to secede from the union unless the White House acted on behalf of Calley. The president emphasized to his advisers that he would not "delegate" this task to Laird. "It's my responsibility."[7]

In another late-afternoon meeting, the president called for a "civilian review" of the case from those of his cabinet members with legal experience and told them he would discuss the matter over the phone with Attorney General John Mitchell and Secretary of State William Rogers in Washington. At the meeting in San Clemente, Counselor Robert Finch, Secretary of the Treasury John Connolly, and Secretary of Health, Education, and Welfare Elliott Richardson agreed that the president should take "immediate action" but urged him to be "deliberate." Mitchell would chair a committee dealing with the question, Nixon explained; he wanted no one outside the White House involved.[8]

Nixon remained publicly silent that day but worked behind the scenes to cultivate support for presidential intervention. He made at least two phone calls that night to prominent political figures in Washington—House Minority Leader Gerald Ford of Michigan, a Republican, and House Representative Olin Teague of Texas, chair of the Veterans Committee and soon to head the Democratic Caucus—asking them to gauge the opinions of congressional members and, whether intentional or not, leaving the impression that a pardon was imminent.[9]

Nixon had been following the public response to the Calley case for several days and decided to tap into a potential source of support from what he had called in an early November 1969 speech the "silent majority"—his primarily white and working-class constituency from the South and the West, most of whom were hawkish on the war. Numerous Americans supported Calley as an American soldier who had simply done his job. Many of his supporters were Republican, of course, but a good number were traditional Democrats who had switched their allegiance to Nixon because of his stand on the war.[10]

A telephone survey authorized by the president involving over a thousand respondents showed that 78 percent disapproved of the Calley verdict. Within twenty-four hours, a flood of petitions, letters, and telegrams to the president and other government officials denounced the conviction. The White House announced that it had already received 5,510 telegrams, only five of them supporting the verdict. Of more than three thousand phone calls to the White House, those opposing the verdict ran about one hundred to one.[11]

Although the outcry against the verdict was bipartisan and national, the administration looked carefully at the South's reaction because of its strong support for the war and its integral role in the Republican Party's election strategy. In a letter to the president, Alabama Democratic congressman Walter Flowers declared that he was "deeply shocked" by the Calley verdict and agreed with the "nearly unanimous" sentiment of Alabamians and Americans: Calley was a "scapegoat"—a victim "held responsible for almost a decade of mistakes in Vietnam" who deserved a presidential pardon. Similar complaints came from numerous legislative leaders on both sides of the aisle, including Democratic senator Abraham Ribicoff of Connecticut, Democratic representative Joe Waggonner of Louisiana, and Republican representative Ben Blackburn of Georgia. House Republican William Dickinson of Alabama asked Nixon to pardon Calley; Ribicoff wanted him to grant clemency. But both legislators wanted the president to free Calley. Frank Moss, Democratic senator from Utah, declared his intention to prepare a resolution calling on the president to reduce Calley's sentence. Democratic senator Herman Talmadge of Georgia, a combat veteran of World War II, was "saddened to think that one could fight for his flag and then be court-martialed and convicted for apparently carrying out his orders."[12]

Protests also came from Selective Service offices across the country. Board members resigned in at least ten states, while in Georgia one draft board notified the White House that it would no longer induct anyone into the army.

A member of another board volunteered to serve a day of Calley's time in prison and called on others to do the same. A board in Kentucky unanimously agreed that Calley had been "unjustly persecuted" and subjected to "mental cruelty" resulting from the antiwar groups wanting "someone to crucify." Board members sought assurances from the administration against future draftees undergoing the same treatment, particularly when, as one put it, "men like Cassius Clay flaunt their total disregard of laws governing selective service and get away with it."[13]

Not all opposition to the verdict meant support for Calley; more than a few demanded that the government prosecute all military and political leaders responsible for the war and hence for My Lai. On the cover of *Time* magazine was the question "Who Shares the Guilt?" *Newsweek*'s coverline similarly asked, "Who Else Is Guilty?" Democratic senator George McGovern from South Dakota—also a veteran of World War II—strongly opposed the war in Vietnam and challenged Americans to focus on changing the government's policies rather than calling for more war-crimes trials. A college student in Texas declared that Calley "represents the guilt of all Americans in Vietnam" and had become the nation's "scapegoat" for all the Vietnamese deaths in the war. A Florida family who had lost a son in Vietnam in 1968 sent the president a petition calling on the court to punish everyone sharing in the guilt. The bestselling writer and renowned pediatrician Dr. Benjamin Spock, an antiwar activist, called Calley's conviction "ultimately hypocritical," declaring it "too bad that one man is being made to pay for the brutality of the whole war."[14]

Military figures had a mixed reaction to the verdict, but many wanted the prosecution to go after everyone involved in My Lai, including those who put Calley into a position of responsibility. "We can get more Calleys any time," remarked one career officer. "They're the ones we don't want." Yet much of the blame belonged to those high officials who, as one officer put it, "let this get so far out of shape." Medina called the verdict "very harsh and very severe." With his own trial approaching, he told the press that the guilt goes "all the way up" and that "all Americans must share in Calley's guilt."[15]

According to Adrian Fisher, dean of Georgetown's Law School, Calley's guilty verdict should have led to further indictments. Fisher had advised the American judges at the Nuremberg trials after World War II and asserted on NBC-TV's *Today* show that the U.S. military command must now "taste the cup" of guilt it had forced on the Japanese after the war. In 1945 the American military tribunal in Tokyo had ordered the hanging of General Tomoyuki Yamashita, the Japanese commander in the Philippines, for atrocities committed by his soldiers, though he had not been there at the time and had poor communications with his men in Manila. The U.S. Supreme Court upheld the death sentence on the basis that it was the commander's responsibility to prevent his troops from committing atrocities. The investigation into the Calley case, Fisher contended, should go up the command chain to find every person responsible for the killings.[16]

If Fisher was correct in his claims, the *New York Times* asserted, the army's decision to drop the charges against Major General Koster and other high officers suggested that the Pentagon did not want an examination into whether the so-called Yamashita principle applied to My Lai. In an effort to persuade Congress to investigate all war crimes, a group of Vietnam veterans (soon supported by the "Winter Soldiers," with future secretary of state John Kerry as a member) had organized the Citizens Commission of Inquiry into U.S. War Crimes in Vietnam (CCI) in February 1970 and held a hearing in a Washington hotel the following December. The next month its members asked the military to launch a formal investigation. "My Lai is only the tip of the iceberg," they declared, insisting that Calley served as a scapegoat "to deflect attention from the generals and the politicians." From January 31 through February 2, 1971, more than a hundred veterans from the "Winter Soldiers" testified to atrocities in a series of hearings in a motel in Detroit. Hébert instantly opposed the veterans' call for a congressional investigation, declaring that House rules barred public hearings if the testimony could defame anyone.[17]

The army realized that failure to protect its officers would hurt the corps in several ways. Not only would such an investigation further damage the army's reputation, it would put strategists in the difficult position of having to plan military operations with an eye on avoiding another My Lai. Furthermore, any soldier could face a court martial—whether he disobeyed or followed orders. As Latimer told the press, Calley was the victim of a system that "dragged him out of his home, taught him to kill, sent him automatic weapons to kill...then comes back and appoints the judge, the prosecutors, the jury and tries him."[18]

On the morning of April 1, the president met with his top two advisers, Haldeman and Ehrlichman, to discuss how to handle matters. "Calley dominated the day today," Haldeman confided to his diary. The president accused military leaders of caring less about the army's honor than "the system of which they're a part." Their chief concern was to show that they could "move expeditiously." According to Ehrlichman, Nixon believed that there was "not enough in it for us to fight for the military." The attorneys saw "no political gain for us in their argument." But, he thought, "an act of compassion" might not be "a bad thing to do at this point," though political considerations "may override" other factors. There must be "a way this time to be on the side of the people."[19]

Nixon had something specific in mind that, at least for the moment, he kept to himself. Unbeknown to Haldeman and Ehrlichman, he had that morning received notification from the Pentagon that, rather than sending Calley to the federal prison at Fort Leavenworth, it had decided to move him from the stockade at Fort Benning to his apartment just off the base entrance but still under military jurisdiction. There is no record that the president revealed this notice when he awakened his advisers in the middle of the night with his solution: he would allow Calley to stay in his apartment instead of going to prison at Fort Leavenworth. "I had that idea at 3 A.M. this morning. That's the best we can do."[20]

Actually, shortly after the sentencing, Latimer had submitted a written request for Calley to remain in his quarters, and Major General Orwin Talbott, the commanding general at Fort Benning and convening authority for Calley's trial, had promised to consider the proposal. Talbott forwarded it to Washington, where approval came from Secretary of the Army Resor, General Westmoreland, and other military figures. They had been concerned for months about containing the inevitable public outcry in the event of Calley's conviction, and this step might stem the anger.[21]

From the president's perspective, the army's decision about where to put Calley offered him the opportunity to curry popular favor. But he wanted the support of Ehrlichman and Haldeman. He admitted to them that they could not deal with the Calley case on "merits." There was "no reasonable doubt of his technical guilt, but," he added, "there is doubt regarding the motive." The question was "whether this man is a criminal who should be treated like [Charles] Manson." From Nixon's perspective, the answer was no.[22]

It is not clear what exactly Nixon meant about Calley's "motive." He had not yet seen the court-martial transcript (which was still in preparation) and could not have known that Calley had asserted that most of all he had wanted to follow what he interpreted as Medina's orders to kill the Vietnamese. No records indicate that either the president or his advisers had discussed whether such orders existed and therefore whether Calley had been under any obligation to adhere to them.

At a noon meeting with all his advisers that same day, Nixon emphasized that failure to take action would diminish public support for his gradual-withdrawal policy in Vietnam. "We've got to keep our eye on the main ball, which is to maintain our public support." A Lou Harris poll had showed that

36 percent of respondents opposed the Calley verdict, 35 percent were in favor, and 29 percent remained undecided. It also revealed that 76 percent thought Calley had followed orders in killing civilians but that 69 percent believed he was "not justified" in the killings and had become a scapegoat for others equally guilty. Perhaps most striking to Nixon and his advisers, 90 percent of Americans followed the case. It was imperative to win over the undecided voters to the notion of a pardon. After a discussion of these and other numbers, the president declared that he wanted an immediate press release announcing "his" order to relocate Calley. But first he had to make a phone call.[23]

As his advisers listened, Nixon phoned Admiral Thomas Moorer, the chair of the Joint Chiefs of Staff at the Pentagon, and ordered him to release Calley from the stockade and confine him to his apartment near Fort Benning. Putting down the phone, Nixon remarked with satisfaction, "That's the only place in the government where they say, 'Yes, sir,' instead of, 'Yes, but.'" Moorer would talk with the secretary of the army, Nixon explained. "Resor will screw it up," warned Haldeman. "He'll refuse to do it."[24]

The president's advisers did not realize that he had pre-empted the Pentagon. They circulated the story that he had risen early that morning, determined to do what he could to restore the nation's respect for its soldiers. Yet he had already made up his mind to do something prior to calling Ford and Teague in Washington the night before.[25]

Nixon's intervention threatened the Pentagon's efforts to protect the military judicial process from outside influences. He had ignored the chain of command, which required presenting such an order to the secretary of defense and instead contacted the chair of the Joint Chiefs of Staff, who called General Westmoreland about the order. But he was unavailable, and therefore Moorer phoned Resor. Thus Laird and other civilian officials in the Defense Department learned of the decision just minutes before Ziegler's press announcement in San Clemente. The Pentagon became concerned that Nixon's interference would undermine the integrity of the trial and the army itself.[26]

Actually, Nixon's chief concern was expedience. He agreed with Haldeman that he must take some decisive action before delivering his nationally televised speech on Vietnam, which was scheduled for the night of Wednesday, April 7, less than a week away. If we do nothing about Calley, he declared, popular support for Vietnamization would "evaporate."[27]

The president's "instincts" told him—as he told his advisers—to first "go through a process" of refusing to comment on the case while Calley remained in his quarters. No one could question that Calley had "a bad record." When

Haldeman asked about guilt or innocence, Nixon insisted that they could not get into that matter and that they must "uphold the conviction." Calley was technically guilty of violating the rules of engagement, even though "in [a] larger sense, [he] doesn't deserve this sentence." Without explaining what he meant by "larger sense" or why Calley's actions did not warrant his sentence, Nixon continued to keep his options open.[28]

"I haven't decided yet what the appeal procedure will be," Nixon explained, but added that when Mitchell's committee completed its study he would "personally" review the case. Ehrlichman cautioned that federal law prohibited "command influence in courts-martial." Nixon asked for the file to study, but he showed no concern over the appearance of executive interference. He would exercise his constitutional right to intervene after the appeals process. Whatever the route might be, the endpoint was already clear: "At the end I'll pardon him."[29]

Haldeman noted a consensus among his colleagues that Calley had violated the rules of engagement and committed murder. No one mentioned the Nuremberg decision that had condemned the German commanders for war crimes despite their having argued that they were simply following orders. Instead, the president's advisers agreed that Calley had acted under orders and that the court had done its duty under the military code. Nixon shed some light on what he meant by a "larger sense" when emphasizing that his responsibility went beyond the courts in showing compassion to a man under the "stress" of a "brutal war." They had to let the conviction stand as "tech[nically] correct" even at the cost of establishing a precedent that "besmirches all soldiers."[30]

Nowhere do the records of their strategy sessions indicate any discussion of the legal or moral questions about shooting groups of defenseless noncombatants. The closest the president came was his oblique reference to that "larger sense" of the matter. But based on the context of these ongoing discussions, his use of the term "legal sense" too had political objectives, which involved finding a way, in Nixon's words, of being this time "on the side of the people." Calley's actions were excessive yet defensible in a war for liberty. He had acted under orders, according to the president and his advisers—unaware, of course, that the not-yet-released court transcript of Calley's trial would raise serious doubts about this claim.

Nixon's decision to return Calley to his apartment had immediate repercussions. When a reporter asked Ehrlichman whether the president had known beforehand that the base commander at Fort Benning had intended in any case to relocate Calley, he replied in probable good faith, "No, he did not." Numerous army officers in Washington were shocked by the president's interjecting himself into an army matter. One bitterly remarked that Nixon had known all along that Calley was being released from jail. "He just beat us to the punch."[31]

At 2:30 p.m. that same day of April 1, the president, Kissinger, Haldeman, and Ehrlichman noted with approval that the "Calley cause" was spreading throughout the news circuits. Ehrlichman reported widespread concurrence with the White House's call for an act of "expiation" but urged the president to be careful to ensure that any decision not appear politically driven. They must "expedite" that decision but at the same time be "deliberate" to avoid the impression of bending to public demands. Calley could not go free, Ehrlichman emphasized, for the world would ask what the point of a trial is "if all we do is let [a] vicious man go." For the moment, however, the president's action had "taken the steam out" of the issue.[32]

Among Nixon's closest advisers, John Dean was the only outspoken opponent of presidential intervention, though solely because of the timing. On hearing of Calley's conviction, the White House counsel had read every military document available, talked with a number of attorneys well versed in military law, and come away convinced that the president should keep his hands off the case while it was under appeal. Later that day, he wrote Haldeman and Ehrlichman from Washington that the president had the right to intervene in cases involving offenses against the United States—including a court martial—on the basis of his constitutional power to grant pardons and reprieves. But these steps were not available to the president until after the appeals process had come to a close.[33]

Dean worried that when the full story emerged, it would not support a pardon. "The facts of the case show particularly aggravated conduct on the part of the accused, even taking into account the combat environment." There was no "firefight" going on when Calley had gathered the "unarmed, unresisting civilians, placed them in convenient groups, and shot them."[34]

The most critical argument in Dean's memorandum of April 1 related to Calley's admissions to the sanity board that he had been more involved with the killing than he had revealed under oath during the court martial. Dean had doubtless read an article in that day's *Washington Post* in which the writer revealed a secret report by three military psychiatrists in Washington who the previous January had conducted twelve lengthy interviews of Calley that together contradicted many of his statements made in court. The army had passed the report to Judge Reid Kennedy at the opening of Calley's trial, and in turn he showed it to the defense but not to either the prosecution or the jury; to do so, he knew, would violate Calley's constitutional right against self-incrimination. The army released the report to the public after Calley's court martial, which did not affect the jury's decision but did support it. In an account that differed markedly from his testimony in court, Calley told the sanity board that he had killed two groups of Vietnamese noncombatants in the ditch and on the trail and had also killed an elderly man.[35]

Dean warned that to intervene now "could have an adverse effect on world opinion." In any case, an appellate review would "very likely" lead to a reduced sentence. He advised the president to wait until they added all the facts.[36]

The president ignored Dean's advice.[37]

II

Both AP and UPI news bulletins headlined the White House announcement of the president's decision to move Calley to his apartment during the appeals process. Ziegler told journalists that in taking this measure the president had not acted in his role as commander in chief. This was "not a legal step," the press secretary emphasized, but an action taken on his "own initiative." Ziegler mentioned that the White House had received "more communications regarding Calley than any other incident" and that the telegrams ran "100 to 1 in favor of clemency."[38]

In San Clemente, Haldeman later noted in his diary, April 2 was "pretty much a Calley day all day." The president appealed to history in justifying his decision to change Calley's place of confinement. During the Civil War, President Abraham Lincoln had taken unilateral actions. "Presidents have this right," Nixon had insisted, "but it must be exercised personally." In the early afternoon, according to Haldeman, he again asserted his duty as president to consider the "personal" factors. He would neither "pass the buck" to a committee nor refrain from assuming the "larger view." Following a recommendation made by Richard Moore, his aide on public relations, Nixon decided that he would avoid interfering with "a fair process" by waiting to intervene until after the appeals court finished its review and before it imposed the final sentence.[39]

Nixon instructed Ehrlichman to announce this decision not to intervene yet in the Calley affair to the press the following day and to emphasize that it came after consulting a host of advisers, including the attorney general and the secretaries of treasury, defense, state, and health, education, and welfare. He would resist the popular call to free Calley or to reduce the sentence, because either step would violate the review process. In a statement that showed no awareness of the certain judicial delays noted in the documents earlier provided to Ehrlichman, the president left the impression that he could act in about two months.[40]

That same day, April 2, Laird forwarded Ehrlichman a memo setting out the president's options and warning of the consequences of an intervention. He could change Calley's place of confinement (which he had already done) by using his power as commander in chief, which ranked him above the commanding general as the convening authority; or as president, he had the constitutional right to grant reprieves, commutations, or pardons for offenses against the United States. The president as commander in chief could also order the secretary of the army to set aside or dismiss all charges. Laird warned that such an action would damage the integrity of the court-martial review system and possibly lead to serious problems: similar pleas for intervention in other cases (there were 109,345 court-martial cases in 1969 alone); criticism of alleged mass killing, a major part of antiwar sentiment; danger to American POWs in North Vietnam; and international implications for U.S. obligations to the Geneva Convention regarding the treatment of "protected persons." Laird declared that he knew of "no case in which the President or the Secretary of a Military Department has superseded the review case, after trial."[41]

Laird's warning did little to hinder the president as the news of support for his involvement in the case continued to roll into the White House. Democratic governor Jimmy Carter of Georgia considered the act a wise attempt to ease the national furor. The Calley verdict had also lowered U.S. troop morale in Vietnam, and to show the state's support for the nation's soldiers, Carter proclaimed April 5 "American Fighting Men's Day" and asked residents to display the flag and drive with their headlights on. Republican governor Edgar Whitcomb of Indiana, a decorated veteran of World War II, ordered the state's flags flown at half-mast to honor Calley's defense of the nation. Members of an American Legion Post in Ohio accused the army of making Calley the scapegoat for "worse judgments and stupidities at high levels of government" and returned their combat ribbons and decorations to the president as commander in chief. The mayor of Casey, Texas, wrote the president that Calley should not only receive clemency and a pardon but the Congressional Medal of Honor. London journalist Brian Vine put it simply: Americans did not want Calley "crucified for the sins of the high command."[42]

Most pleasing to Calley may have been the support he received from Audie Murphy, his boyhood war hero and a popular actor who had killed more than two hundred enemy troops and received more awards than any other American soldier in World War II. Murphy found the Calley verdict difficult to believe. Given the "fever pitch" of combat indoctrination calling on the soldier to kill or be killed, "I'm not so sure," he said, that "I might not have committed the same error—and I prefer to call it an error—that Lieutenant Calley did."[43]

In the meantime, the *Chicago Tribune* urged Americans to take into account the thousands of atrocities committed by the Viet Cong. As part of the Tet offensive, its forces massacred three thousand South Vietnamese civilians in Hué and threw the bodies into mass graves. Furthermore, the Viet Cong attacked the South Vietnamese village of Hoang Dieu, slaughtering one hundred civilians and wounding ninety-six, along with destroying a thousand homes and other buildings—figures that "dwarf anything that happened at My Lai." The communists started "this war of aggression and terror in Vietnam," said the *Tribune*, and leading the paper to "emphatically disavow the view of a uniquely American guilt."[44]

In the late afternoon of April 2, Alabama governor George Wallace engaged in political theater, part of his plan to run for president again in 1972. Before his state's legislature in Montgomery the previous night, he had received a rousing reception for his promise: "If I were president, I would pardon Lieutenant Calley." He went on to name Calley an honorary lieutenant in the Alabama National Guard. Now, just outside the entrance to Fort Benning and accompanied by his wife and eight state legislators, Wallace headed a long procession of visitors in front of Calley's small hillside apartment, waiting to see him. While Wallace's entourage waited outside, he talked with Calley alone for about fifteen minutes before telling the press he was confident "President Nixon will do the right thing" and pardon Calley. "I'm sorry to see the man tried. They ought to spend the time trying folks who are trying to destroy this country instead of trying those who are serving their country."[45]

Wallace then drove to nearby Columbus, Georgia, where he spoke at a rally featuring banners that read, "Free Lieutenant Calley" and "Calley for Secretary of Defense." The 3,500 or so supporters cheered as the band blared the song "William Calley, Won't You Please Come Home." The other keynote speaker was Wallace's friend Georgia lieutenant governor Lester Maddox, who had endorsed Wallace for president in 1968. No longer was the nation divided, Maddox proclaimed to the boisterous crowd. "Along came Lieutenant Calley" to bring Americans together. Wallace heartily agreed. "The Silent Majority is not going to be silent anymore."[46]

On April 3, Nixon's decision not to intervene until after the appeals process was finished when Ziegler, with Ehrlichman at his side, informed the press at Laguna Beach in California that the president would "personally review the case and finally decide it."[47] The last three words in that statement made clear that he intended to pronounce judgment.

Ehrlichman repeated Ziegler's assertion before justifying the president's involvement in the Calley case as "entirely discretionary." Under the Uniform Code of Military Justice, he explained, the only time the president became part of the review process was in cases involving the death sentence of a general or admiral. As commander in chief, however, he could express an opinion on guilt or innocence, as well as any sentences passed. The president "has a constitutional right to vest himself with the capacity of superior convening authority at any time through this process. He is not waiving that capacity."[48]

Ehrlichman emphasized that the president wanted to protect Calley's rights by familiarizing himself with "the procedure that had been followed up to now" along with his "present status." He wanted to add "that extralegal ingredient to the review process prior to the time that the sentence goes into effect, and it is qualitatively the kind of a weighing or a review that a chief executive gives a case in the pardon process." Asked what the president meant by that "extralegal ingredient," Ehrlichman replied, "I can't specify those for you. That is sort of in the heart of a man."[49]

Ehrlichman's assurances did little to ease growing concern that the president wanted to exercise "command influence." Latimer joined the *Washington Post* and the *New York Times* in criticizing Nixon for wanting to make the "final judgment" on guilt and innocence. In a blistering critique, columnists Rowland Evans and Robert Novak insisted that the president's intention as commander in chief "raises the question of objectivity at each step of this review-and-appeal process." His involvement was "strictly political," as evidenced by his putting his chief domestic adviser in charge of the effort. *Life* magazine agreed, calling the intervention "a presidential play to the political constituency Nixon so often cultivates." Wallace had portrayed Calley as a hero, thereby threatening to siphon off voters critical to the success of the Republican Party's "southern strategy" in the presidential election of 1972. The *Baltimore Sun* thought the Calley conviction appeared to be "knocking the Dixie prop" from under the president's Vietnam policy.[50]

Nixon's intervention, whatever it was to be, was not without precedent— one ironically set by himself less than a year earlier when he almost caused a mistrial in the Charles Manson mass murder trial by publicly prejudging him guilty. Joseph Califano, the head counsel of the Democratic National Committee, thought Nixon's "interference" in the Calley case, along with his public remarks during the Manson trial, left the impression of "un-Presidential behavior." One reader in *Commonweal* magazine found it difficult to believe that Nixon, a lawyer since 1937, could demonstrate such "Foot-in-Mouthism."[51]

Yet praise for the president's decision to intervene in the Calley case was widespread. A Gallup poll found that 83 percent of respondents supported Nixon's order to move Calley to his apartment. West Virginia Democratic senator Robert Byrd lauded Calley's removal from the stockade and expressed hope for clemency. Republican senator Margaret Chase Smith of Maine argued that the powers vested in the presidency allowed Nixon to review the case following the appeals process—*not* to decide guilt or innocence but to calm the public reaction to the conviction. When news of the president's action reached the House of Representatives, its members halted their debate over extending the draft to applaud what a construction worker in Kansas City called "a wonderful thing."[52]

Unknown to the public was the special status the president was according Calley. By the spring of 1971, almost eighty American soldiers charged with murder in Vietnam were in Fort Leavenworth prison. Other soldiers were there for lesser offenses—one for five years for pushing an officer and another for three years for smoking marijuana. Calley had visits from his girlfriend and other acquaintances, along with a secretary to help him handle the heavy volume of mail.[53]

Those defending the verdict were barely heard above the more vocal and much larger numbers of critics—79 percent of telephoned respondents disapproved of the court-martial decision, according to a Gallup poll in early April. The same poll found that more than 70 percent thought others shared the responsibility for My Lai, that 69 percent believed Calley a scapegoat for officers up the chain of command, and that 81 percent considered the sentence unfair. A good number of the major print media defended the decision, including the *Baltimore Sun, Charleston Gazette, New York Times, Newsweek, Time, New Orleans Times-Picayune, Wall Street Journal, Washington Star*, and *Washington Post*. The *Wall Street Journal* was particularly outspoken, registering its surprise that anyone could support exonerating Calley. Is this what this "strange coalition of super-patriots and peace marchers" wants? The *Washington Star* warned that when the United States condones such an act of "wanton murder," it "forfeits all claims to any moral leadership of this world."[54]

Yet because of the media scrutiny and coverage of My Lai, growing numbers of Americans had shifted from refusing to believe that their soldiers could commit such a horrendous crime and that the stories of atrocities were a monstrous lie perpetrated on the country by the liberal media to realizing that Calley and his men had killed a large number of defenseless civilians. It was becoming a question not of whether Calley deserved punishment but of what kind. Why should he be a scapegoat for other soldiers who participated in the killings, or for Medina and other superiors responsible for the orders that led to these killings? Did culpability go all the way to the top? Should Westmoreland share the guilt, as the Japanese general Yamashita had after World War II? "No," Westmoreland adamantly declared, according to Kenneth Auchincloss of *Newsweek*. "I feel no guilt, not in the least." The notion of comparing him to Yamashita, who had received reports of atrocities by his men and done nothing, was "absurd."[55]

And a few critics of Calley were managing to be heard. A marine lieutenant in Virginia acknowledged that his own training taught him to kill. But, he added, "we didn't kill babies." Another wondered if anyone had considered the damage this "one-man genocide squad" had inflicted on American prisoners of war. "Such men NO Army needs for they make enemies where there were none before." Former attorney general Ramsey Clark saw no basis for granting clemency to a soldier who "kills unarmed citizens that do not pose a threat to him." At Fort Benning, a captain told a reporter that Calley's conviction would convince Americans "that what Calley did isn't the way we fight wars." On the cover of a satirical magazine in London was a photograph of convicted murderer Charles Manson with the caption: "I should have joined the Army." And in a Chicago suburb, forty-one students wrote the president: "We are ten and eleven years old and afraid to grow up in America if a murderer is considered a hero."[56]

The *Washington Post* and the *New York Times* joined Evans and Novak in accusing the president of intervening for political purposes. Haldeman (or an aide) must have read the editorials; his files contain copies of each article with key points underlined. The *Post* asserted that "fanfare from the White House" indicated that the president "must have *wanted* his hand to show" because "it made political good sense." The intervention was "a calculated public intrusion at the highest level" in the judicial process. In the *Times* editorial, the writer argued that the president's intention to get involved had prejudiced the appeals process. He had given in to public pressure, something he had repeatedly emphasized a leader must not do.[57]

That same day the *Post* published selected portions of a leaked four-page Pentagon "white paper" that defended the decision to bring Calley to trial. The army insisted that the statement was not a public defense of its policies but argued that it had an obligation to file charges. According to the army's "Fact Sheet" on Son My, the Geneva Convention of 1949 required the United States as a signatory power to search for any persons accused of committing "grave breaches" in war, whatever their nationality, and to bring them to court. What happened at Son My "fits clearly under the provision."[58]

But Nixon refused to retreat from his determination to intercede and perhaps had found another reason for doing so. In a recently uncovered memorandum, speechwriter Patrick Buchanan urged him to act now, because the country was "beginning to turn on the Calley issue" and he would not go down in history as a hero. The president had to get in front of this changing public opinion—not by attacking Calley but by "defending the Army, the process of law in this country, our belief that excesses in combat will not be tolerated." This would have the added benefit of giving a "good scourging to the guilt-ridden, war-crime crowd that is on the other side of our fence, and of the national fence."[59]

"This is our position," Nixon scribbled at the end of the memo. His actions, however, suggested that his focus remained on public opinion and not the army, law, or combat excess.[60]

That same day in San Clemente, Nixon agreed with Ehrlichman to delay a decision until they had a full review and a complete record. "We'll control timing."[61]

III

A week after the verdict was announced, other reports indicated that Buchanan's worry was unfounded: opposition to Calley's sentence showed no signs of abating, which further convinced the White House that it was on the right side of the issue. Americans seemed to support the president's decision to release Calley from Fort Benning. "Citizens of Georgia for Lt. Calley" in Atlanta sent the president a billy goat wearing an Eisenhower jacket trimmed with red, white, and blue colorings and with the word "SCAPEGOAT" attached. An Oregon woman wrote the president of her intention to establish a nationwide "Ransom for Calley Fund" of one million dollars based on one-dollar contributions, and a former small-town mayor in Georgia sent a telegram asking that he pardon Calley. "That boy has gone through hell for no cause of his own." If Calley was "going to be punished," wrote a man from Texas, "why not arrest former President Truman who ordered the atom bombs dropped on Hiroshima and Nagasaki? They too, killed millions of innocent children, babies, women, old men, old women, young innocent boys and girls." A large sign displayed by a Houston gun dealer made the same point: "FREE CALLEY OR TRY TRUMAN."[62]

War correspondents in Vietnam saw numerous indications of troop support for Calley, including an artillery piece painted with the words "Calley's Revenge" and a sign declaring, "Kill a gook for Calley."[63]

ABC Evening News reported that a new song titled "The Battle Hymn of Lt. Calley" had already sold a million copies, making it an instant hit, primarily in the South. After a voice-over told the story of a young boy who wanted to be a soldier, Nashville singer Tony Nelson, to the tune of "The Battle Hymn of the Republic," honored the soldier-patriot who had led his men into enemy "rifle fire with everything we had":

> My name is William Calley. I'm a soldier of this land.
> I've tried to do my duty and to gain the upper hand.
> But they've made me out a villain, they have stamped me with a
>   brand,
> As we go marching on."[64]

The army's information office soon banned disc jockeys from playing the song over the American Armed Forces Radio Network in Saigon. It might interfere with Calley's appeals process and alienate the Vietnamese people.[65]

Members of the military jury publicly defended the verdict. Four votes were necessary for a conviction of premeditated murder. Captain Ronald Salem and Major Carl Bierbaum had voted to acquit Calley. Major Walter Kinard insisted that he did not simply say, as some had charged, "The hell with it, he's guilty." He told a *Newsweek* reporter that he had "spent thirteen days and thirteen nights trying to find something in my own mind that revealed something else."[66]

Major Harvey Brown agreed with Kinard. "We gave Lieutenant Calley every benefit of the doubt. But all those people, all those babies." What hurt the most, he said, was that "he was one of us." Brown expressed concern that the president would give in to popular pressure and pardon Calley. Asked during a radio interview whether the verdict was "a little harsh" given that the enemy used women and children in its war, Brown agreed but turned the interviewer's attention to what Calley had done to defenseless villagers in the ditch. "That was a rather harsh treatment for them…and a rather final treatment."[67]

Kinard explained that they had a "real knock-down, drag-out" battle over whether Medina had given the order to kill and, if so, whether Calley should have considered the order illegal. Unable to prove this one way or the other, they finally dropped it to say that even if Medina had issued such an order, Calley should have refused to obey. "There are some things a man of common understanding and common sense would know are wrong."[68]

The "biggest mistake" the defense had made, Kinard insisted, was putting Calley on the stand. Incredibly, he admitted to firing into the ditch from five feet away. "Why didn't he deny the whole thing? His stillness would have spoken more for him."[69]

"It had to be done," said Major Charles McIntosh.[70]

Brown soon received a death threat along with prank phone calls and joined Kinard and the other jurors in changing their home numbers. Colonel Ford removed the nameplate from his front door on the base.[71]

The White House would soon face a critical problem affecting its policy toward Calley and My Lai: a growing disenchantment with the war that could threaten Vietnamization by pushing the administration's supporters into the same camp as the antiwar groups. A Gallup poll in early January 1971 showed that dissatisfaction with the American troop involvement in Vietnam had jumped to 59 percent, three points higher than the previous poll in late May 1970, while those favorable to the involvement had dropped five points to 31 percent. Shortly after Calley's conviction, the regional head of the American Civil Liberties Union in the South, Charles Morgan, sensed a change in attitude toward the war. In Atlanta, he said in an interview quoted in the *Christian Science Monitor*, the verdict could "result in the merging of liberals and conservatives, Democrats and Republicans, and those who are pro or con the war, into a unified assault against the draft." Also quoted in newspaper articles was a Miami woman who insisted that the United States had lost the war with Calley's conviction. "How can we ask our men to fight any longer?" The American Legion commander in Philadelphia wondered, "Will servicemen have to go into battle with a battery of lawyers to find out whom they can kill?" One respondent from Washington said that the Calley affair had changed his views toward the war. "I was pro-Vietnam. My opinion of the whole war now is to get out." As the administration had worried would be the case, the Calley verdict had driven a number of doves and hawks together in calling for a withdrawal of America's forces—the former even more determined after the mass killing of noncombatants at My Lai, the latter outraged by the practical restraints placed on American soldiers. We are not a "redeemer nation," insisted theologian Reinhold Niebuhr, a staunch critic of the war. "This is a moment of truth when we realize that we are not a virtuous nation."[72]

Nixon was far from immune from criticism for his meddling, and some of it came from within the military. A U.S. Army judge advocate criticized the president for what he called an "unwarranted interference in the military judicial process." Calley was a convicted murderer whose special treatment was "plainly incomprehensible." An army captain in Vietnam declared that his men's actions stood "in stark contrast" to someone who simply gunned down women and children. A lieutenant from the Americal Division—Calley's division—angrily told a journalist, "I was sent here to fight Communist soldiers, not kill women and children." Colonel Robert Rheault, a former Special Forces commander accused of murder in the Green Beret case but never tried, denounced Calley as a murderer "for mowing down women and children." "Scapegoat, hell," declared an army major. "Calley had a gun in his hand, didn't he? A thousand, ten thousand other guys must have been in the same spot. They didn't go ape."[73]

Opposition to the president's involvement also came from outside the country. It was a "monstrous rebuke to the military courts," according to a West German columnist. The intervention was "without precedent," said a French writer in Paris; the "triumph of mob rule," declared the *London Sunday Telegraph*. The *Japan Times* reported that many Japanese felt "bewildered" by the large number of Americans who did not seem to consider Calley's actions a crime. Any defense arguments based on citing the atrocities committed by the communists did not justify what happened at My Lai. The war crimes trials after World War II had set a precedent for rejecting Calley's appeal that he had merely been carrying out orders. The Nazis, after all, had used precisely the same defense. The United States must not support one standard for its people and another for non-Americans.[74]

Despite the criticisms, the president appeared to feel that he was on solid legal ground in intervening in the case. Based on discussions with Major General Kenneth Hodson, the judge advocate general, and Assistant Attorney General William Rehnquist (the future Supreme Court chief justice), White House legal counsel Eric Fygi argued that the president's constitutional power allowed him to act. In releasing him from the stockade, the president had operated within the legal boundaries of a reprieve, and his pardoning power allowed him to approve clemency or a full pardon "at any time during the case or after execution of the sentence."[75]

Nonetheless, this legal argument did not sit well with the Pentagon. On the morning of Nixon's highly anticipated speech on Vietnam on April 7, Ehrlichman received a memo from Laird stating that the Pentagon supported Calley's conviction for a "calculated brutality of shocking proportions." Every person killed was a prisoner "under the total control of Calley's men, in a stable situation." He was not only responsible for his soldiers' acts, but he had ordered and participated in them. It rejected the notion that Calley was a scapegoat. "His act stands alone in infamy among known atrocities by U.S. forces in the war." Indeed, the Pentagon emphatically concluded, no crime "can *even remotely* be said to equal that of Calley in terms of the number of human lives involved." Setting him free would send a message to every soldier that "anything goes."[76]

The accusations against the administration sharply intensified that same morning when the *New York Times* published a scathing four-page, single-spaced letter to the president from the chief prosecutor in the Calley case. Less than a week earlier, Aubrey Daniel had sent the letter to the White House and copies to six senators: five Democrats—Harry Byrd and William Spong from Virginia, Harold Hughes from Iowa, George McGovern from South Dakota, and Edmund Muskie from Maine—and Republican Robert Taft of Ohio. The White House received the letter on the night of April 6.[77]

Daniel wrote that he was shocked by the American public's reaction to the outcome of the trial, but particularly to see the president of the United States "compromise" on the "moral issue" in the case. It was, however, even more shocking that a great number of the nation's political leaders had either failed to grasp this moral issue or simply ignored it for political gain. Daniel reminded the president of his public denunciation of what he himself called a "massacre." By intervening in the case, he had opened himself to the charge of command influence, helped turn a murderer into a hero, and left the impression that the military's judicial system was susceptible to political interference. In Daniel's mind, according to his letter, the "greatest tragedy" was the president's resort to "political expediency" in dismissing the murders of innocent people. To condone Calley's actions made Americans "no better than our enemies."

Before the president could decide how to respond to Daniel's letter, another letter of protest arrived—this one from Daniel's assistant counsel in the case, Captain John Partin. "1 April 1971 was the most discouraging night of my life," Partin wrote in condemning the intervention. The court had given Calley "every imaginable legal and discretionary advantage by every arm of the Army." It placed no restrictions on his travel and acceptance of defense funds contributed by his supporters throughout the country, and it allowed his attorneys access to all files and "unlimited funds" for travel in building their case. The jurors, Partin wrote, had wanted to acquit Calley, or at least to find him guilty of a lesser offense. The evidence, however, had made such a finding impossible. Partin asserted that the president was singling Calley out for special treatment because of the "public outcry" over his conviction and sentence. The president's actions had "defiled"—Partin's word—the prosecution's efforts, the jurors' attempts to be fair, and the military justice system itself.[78]

Nixon was furious with the two young military attorneys—especially with Daniel. He wanted to lash out but instead instructed Ron Ziegler to go before the press the following day and simply confirm receipt of Daniel's letter. To say more would be wrong, Ziegler emphasized to the news corps. "The judicial process has not ended yet."[79]

Daniel surely expected to become the target of anger, but nothing could have prepared him for the verbal abuse that forced him, like at least two of the jurors, to unlist his phone number and take the nameplate off the front of his home at Fort Benning.[80]

Daniel's letter drew a mixed reaction in the Senate, although most of the members who spoke out bitterly attacked the president. Indiana Democrat Birch Bayh had just read the letter in the *New York Times* and told the press that Nixon's involvement was an obstacle to a "truly impartial, equitable review" of the case. The president had failed to provide moral leadership and had undermined the military's judicial system. He was "playing political football with a very sensitive issue" and should "keep his mouth shut until the final reviews" were completed. Massachusetts Democrat Edward Kennedy accused the president of appealing to "the worst emotions loosed by the verdict when he should have been appealing to the best in us." Democrat Adlai Stevenson from Illinois wondered if the president understood what he was doing. Two Republicans, Robert Taft from Ohio and Hugh Scott of Pennsylvania, praised the president for attempting to restore military morale and assure the public of a fair review of the case, but another Republican, Jacob Javits of New York, declared in a speech before his peers that if Americans considered Calley a hero, "then we have changed as a people during the course of this tragic war even more disastrously than I had imagined."[81]

In the second week after the conviction, the Calley case had again captured the full attention of the president, but with a new tone. This time the reaction came with heavy criticism rather than the accustomed praise—all of which weighed upon his mind while he was gathered with his chief advisers in the Old Executive Office Building to put the final touches on his highly anticipated speech on Vietnam that evening. Daniel's letter had caused "a substantial flap," Haldeman observed. To write his letter, Daniel had gotten clearance from someone higher in the command chain. Ehrlichman recommended saying nothing in response, arguing that the controversy would go away if left alone.[82]

But Nixon would not let it pass. Already disgruntled over the Pentagon's charges, he was now livid over having to deal with what he now called this "Calley thing." In a phone conversation with Kissinger, Nixon angrily asserted that they should be discussing the real heroes in the war and not "this goddamn Calley." That the president devoted so much time to Calley on that day attests to his awareness of the political importance of the intervention, but there is also a suggestion of personal animus in his response. Nixon appeared unnerved by what he regarded as an attack on his presidency. Wasn't he the highest protector of the law? Daniel was "out of line" in accusing him of executive interference in the case. "I did not say we were going to overrule him." Nixon insisted that his decision to review the case was "completely consistent" with the judicial process. "I upheld the system."[83]

The president's argument may have fallen within the confines of the law, but it did not fit with what he earlier told his advisers. He emphasized that his administration would not interfere in the judicial process by making a judgment on guilt and innocence, and yet he insisted that as commander in chief he could review the facts in the case. What would be the purpose of a review that led to no judgment? Within two days of the verdict, he had implied he would consider judging guilt and innocence *after* the review when he asserted, "I will review it, but I am not prejudging the case." For emphasis, he repeated, "I am not prejudging it."[84]

One wonders if anyone at the April 7 meeting squirmed at the president's assurances, particularly those advisers who might have wondered how his statements correlated with what he had said at the press conference of December 8, 1969: "What appears was certainly a massacre, and under no circumstances was it justified."[85] He had also told his advisers at the first meeting in San Clemente that he would commute Calley's sentence and in a follow-up meeting that he would pardon him. Furthermore, he had appeared to favor Calley when placing him under house arrest, announcing that he would "personally review" the case and authorizing Ziegler and Ehrlichman to say he would "finally decide" the outcome.

Nixon returned to his initial suspicion that Daniel could not have written his letter on his own and blamed the army secretary for instigating it. "This must be Resor that's doing this," the president said to Haldeman. "I have learned from a source that I cannot disclose [never identified] that Resor stirred that up." Appalled by the "gross inaccuracy" of Daniel's letter, Nixon assured Ehrlichman that as for Resor, Haldeman would "have his head." The president was "hopping mad," according to Haldeman, and wanted Resor's immediate resignation. "I don't want to see him around," Nixon insisted.[86]

The president dismissed any counterargument. Alexander Haig, the deputy national security adviser, told Ehrlichman the army was "extremely embarrassed" by the letter and assured him that Daniel had written it on his own. Haig was probably correct. While it seems unlikely that Daniel would have taken such a bold action without clearing it with his superiors, no evidence has arisen that Resor or anyone else was behind the move. It may simply have been that Daniel had considered his letter the final parting shot at the president before leaving the army. But Nixon held Resor responsible for the letter. He must have gotten reinforcement for his hardline position from Haldeman's earlier warning against relying on the army secretary to handle the Calley question.[87]

Nixon hotly asserted to Haldeman that Daniel had falsely accused him of questioning the sentence. "I did not criticize the court." To comment on the verdict would have made them look like "a bunch of goddamn professors."[88]

In his anger, Nixon contradicted himself again—this time on the possibility of a pardon. Less than a week earlier he had clearly stated his intention to pardon Calley. Now, however, he insisted he had no interest in following "all the hotheads" who wanted a pardon. "We're not doing what the extremists want us to do." Without explaining what he would do, he declared that once the judicial process came to a close, he would review the case "because of the great national interest in it."[89]

THAT SAME DAY Democratic senator Harold Hughes wrote the president a letter that arrived shortly after the April 7 meeting. Hughes had received his copy of Daniel's letter the same day it appeared in the *New York Times* and thought the young attorney was sincerely concerned that the president's intervention had weakened the military's judicial system. Furthermore, his actions had raised questions about what Daniel called the "fundamental moral principle" of "the inherent unlawfulness of the murder of innocent persons." To Hughes the issue went "to the very heart of the moral purpose of the American people," which was the question of whether war—even one against "a barbaric enemy"—justified the murder of civilian men, women, and children. Hughes saw only two outcomes of this countrywide turmoil: "the reawakening of a great nation's moral purpose" or "the requiem for the American conscience."[90]

Thirteen

IN HIS NATIONALLY TELEVISED SPEECH on the night of April 7, 1971, President Nixon was upbeat about ending America's involvement in Vietnam. His plan for gradually increasing troop withdrawals over the remainder of the year would continue in sync with South Vietnam's growing capacity to take over the war without endangering, Nixon declared, either the soldiers still there or the chances for peace. "Vietnamization has succeeded." By December 1, another hundred thousand American soldiers would be home. Of the 540,000 forces serving in Vietnam when he came into office, roughly half would be out by the end of the year. "I can assure you tonight with confidence that American involvement in this war is coming to an end."[1]

I

The following day, Nixon was jubilant as he spoke with Henry Kissinger on the phone, turning to the Calley policy only after they both exulted over the speech.

Laird should "pipe down on the Calley thing," the president asserted. "We've got that in the right position. We're not defending Calley and we're gonna let it run its course."

According to the transcript, Kissinger replied, "I think that's right. And I think the judicial process should now take its normal course." He told the president that the "public furor" would have "quieted down" by the time he stepped in. Nixon agreed about the furor, which he described as a "little spasm." Americans had "a chance to pop off steam and then we came on and cooled it off a little." In the meantime, he added, "We gained a little initiative, I think, as a result of it, don't you think?"

Kissinger agreed. And "no matter what they say now, no one can construe that outburst as a dove outburst, even if it took the form, perhaps, of wanting to get out of the war. It was the frustration of the people who are not committed to win the war."

Nixon concurred, remarking, "I think the liberals really know this." He argued that they were "in shock by it, because, they were sort of hoping that the whole nation would, you know, sort of say, 'Well, now, we'll punish these...'"

Kissinger cut in. "What they wanted was a feeling of revulsion against the deed. In fact, the deed itself didn't bother anybody."

"No," Nixon declared. As a "matter of fact, the people said, 'Sure, he was guilty, but by God, why not?'" Both laughed.

"Well, Mr. President," Kissinger remarked, "I think you've done it again."[2]

It certainly appeared so to Nixon. The presiding judge in the Calley trial, Colonel Reid Kennedy, had just told the Hearst Headline Service that he supported the president's right to make the final decision and considered Captain Aubrey Daniel a young "purist" who saw only "good and evil" when "most people are in between the two extremes." But perhaps most satisfying to the president were the assurances that he was following the path Lincoln had taken during the Civil War when he intervened on a number of occasions in the judicial process. That same day, Nixon received a letter citing a scholarly article showing that in 1862 a military court in Minnesota sentenced 303 Indians to death for allegedly killing a large number of women and children. Despite public approval of the sentences, Lincoln reviewed each case and approved only thirty-nine for execution. A few days later, Nixon learned of an editorial in the *San Francisco Chronicle* claiming that on numerous occasions Lincoln commuted the death sentences of soldiers who deserted or fell asleep on sentry duty.[3]

The White House must have thought the My Lai issue was coming to a close when, later that day, the Defense and Justice Departments announced that they had insufficient evidence to prosecute the fifteen former servicemen under investigation. The draft system had led to a great turnover of personnel as service terms ended, meaning the army had lost jurisdiction over 90 percent of Charlie Company, including the fifteen suspects in the My Lai killings.[4]

Toth v. Quarles made it clear that soldiers discharged by the army were civilians and not subject to courts martial. Both departments dismissed a proposal to create a joint civil-military tribunal to try the accused soldiers. Nor could they pursue a recommendation made by the presiding justice in the *Toth* case, Hugo Black—that Congress grant the federal courts jurisdiction over this kind of case. Such a law, he warned, would save the military from "a lot of unmerited grief." Congress did not heed Black's advice in 1955 and could not pass such legislation now and apply it retroactively to those fifteen soldiers. And with civil courts having no jurisdiction over crimes committed outside the United States, the accused former soldiers were immune from prosecution.[5]

Thus by early April 1971 Calley remained the only soldier convicted from the original thirty-one enlisted men and officers suspected of involvement in the My Lai killings. Half of the remaining thirty suspects were now civilians and would not face court-martial proceedings. Of the fifteen still in the service, the courts had charged thirteen with war crimes. Eight of these soldiers had gone free after charges were dropped for lack of evidence, leaving only five to stand trial. The courts had already acquitted two (Sergeant David Mitchell and Sergeant Charles Hutto), and would soon try the last three—Captain Eugene Kotouc, Captain Ernest Medina, and Colonel Oran Henderson.

Nixon wanted to stay in front of these events and took the offensive in defending his policies. A mid-April Harris poll proved especially promising: 55 percent of Americans approved his handling of the Calley case. After instructing Ehrlichman to organize a "small working group" to explore all options regarding the other My Lai cases, the president went before a panel of six newsmen at the Annual Convention of the American Society of Newspaper Editors in Washington on April 16 and explained his reasons for intervening in the Calley affair. When an issue stirred up so many Americans, he told the panel and the large group in attendance, his responsibility as president was to address their concerns by ensuring a fair review of the decision. The secretary of defense had offered assurances that the military system of justice allowed the president to review or intercede in any case where "he believes that the national interest or the interests of the accused require it."[6]

The president also defended his decision in letters to the two lead prosecutors in the case, Aubrey Daniel and John Partin. Still stinging from Daniel's public rebuke, Nixon nonetheless reacted with restraint. In his letter to Daniel, he repeated what he told the newspaper editors at the convention—that his involvement in the Calley case was "consistent with upholding the judicial process of the Armed Forces." To Partin, he insisted that he had taken action because the case had "a significance going far beyond one man's innocence or guilt of the specific charges involved." But the president skirted the truth by declaring that he had relocated Calley only after the commanding general at Fort Benning had "independently concluded" that the stockade lacked adequate facilities.[7]

If a Gallup survey of early April was accurate, the president's position about potentially intervening in the case was popular: 79 percent of Americans polled from across the country disapproved of the jury's findings; 20 percent did not consider Calley's acts a crime because of his orders to kill; and 69 percent thought he had committed a crime but was a scapegoat. These figures virtually silenced the small number of Americans who supported the verdict and opposed the intervention.[8]

The president continued to see political gains in taking the public's side on the sentence. The army knew that to salvage credibility it had to try the three remaining My Lai cases.

The legal process resumed in late April when Captain Kotouc's trial for aggravated assault and maiming a prisoner during an interrogation began at Fort McPherson. Late in the afternoon of March 16, 1968, with several American soldiers and a few South Vietnamese National Police watching, Kotouc ordered the prisoner to lay his hand on a board with fingers spread wide and repeatedly jabbed his seven-inch-long knife between them. On the last jab, Kotouc's knife caught the suspect's finger and slit off the end. There was no question he committed the act, but he insisted the knife "slipped."[9]

The judge, Colonel Madison Wright, instructed the seven-man jury that to find Kotouc guilty of maiming under U.S. military law, they had to believe he had intentionally maimed the prisoner. But Wright added possible extenuating circumstances. Current army "regulations and directives" relating to prisoner interrogations could have led Kotouc to believe it was lawful to use "harsh and abusive language" and to "threaten violence" in order to extract information. If the jury were to determine that he was "merely offering [threatening] to do violence to the alleged victim, such an act…would be legally justified."[10]

Guided by Wright's instructions, the jury could not be certain that Kotouc had intentionally maimed the victim and, after a three-day trial and in less than an hour of deliberation, acquitted him on April 29.[11]

Attorney F. Lee Bailey had meanwhile tried various tactics to avert Medina's trial. He first attempted to raise doubt about the accusations made by soldiers to CID about the order to kill the Vietnamese villagers. His own team of investigators had interviewed a number of soldiers from Charlie Company and reported that 80 percent of them had recanted their accusatory statements to CID. But Bailey's major effort began during Calley's court-martial proceedings, when he appealed to Judge Kennedy to permit the introduction of polygraph results Bailey knew would suggest that his client was not a murderer. Robert Brisentine from CID, one of the most respected polygraph experts, had administered the test to Medina in November 1970 and testified at his

Article 32 investigation that Medina had told the truth in denying the charges of murder. Brisentine had been ready to declare at the Calley trial that he had conducted fifty thousand examinations for the army and that not one of those who passed the test had ever gone to trial. Kennedy, however, told Medina when he entered the courtroom not to mention a polygraph test.[12]

On the day of Calley's sentencing, March 31, 1971, Bailey tried again, this time sending the president a certified letter requesting his intervention in the Medina case and warning that a trial would be a "waiting trap" for the government. The army, he explained, had decided to change its criminal charges against Medina from the "specific misconduct" of "ordering a massacre" to "general responsibility" for "failing to learn of and stop a massacre." Should this notion of imputed responsibility gain credence in Medina's trial, legal scholars everywhere would think the United States had set a precedent for holding commanders responsible for all the actions of their men by invoking the "Nuremberg principle."[13]

According to Bailey, the most disturbing thing was that the army was attempting to denigrate polygraph tests. A number of experts, including those in the military, had attested to the reliability of these tests. Bailey reminded the president of his support for the polygraph during the Alger Hiss affair. A refusal to take the same position in Medina's trial would raise questions about whether he had any connection with the army's attempt to disregard the test results in Medina's case."[14]

Bailey's pressure tactics failed. Within two weeks, White House Counsel John Dean responded to his letter, saying there would be "no official Presidential involvement" in the Calley case while it was under review, making it "inappropriate" to respond to any issues relating to Medina.[15]

The public outcry against the Calley verdict had meanwhile guaranteed that Medina would stand trial. The protests against Calley's conviction had spread, and a majority of Americans continued to accuse the army of making him a scapegoat and insisted he had merely followed orders in killing the enemy. Yet the guilty verdict meant that the jury believed Medina had told the truth and that Calley had not. If the army had ever considered dismissing the charges against Medina, it could not do so now without confirming the public's charge that Calley was a scapegoat. The army, Bailey thought, felt compelled to prosecute Medina.[16]

II

A few days before Medina's trial began in mid-August, the prosecution team, headed by Major William Eckhardt, did what Bailey had warned the president they would: it dropped the charge against Medina of killing the 102 Vietnamese civilians and accused him instead of being "responsible" for their deaths.

Eckhardt was at the beginning of a long and illustrious career in the military after graduating from the University of Virginia School of Law in 1966. He had gone to Vietnam within six weeks of graduation and, as noted earlier, had defended the soldiers accused of rape and murder in the story told by reporter Daniel Lang. But he had never seen anything like My Lai. After his selection as chief prosecutor, he read the files in Atlanta and threw them against the wall; he was so sickened that he went for a long run. He found it difficult to believe that Medina had issued an order to kill, especially when the only soldiers who claimed to have heard that order were those accused of the killing. Yet Eckhardt recognized the unlikelihood of presenting enough credible witnesses to win a mass murder conviction based on an alleged order to kill everyone in My Lai 4; there were too many conflicting testimonies about what he had said or meant. Instead, Eckhardt intended to argue that when Medina realized his men were killing civilians, he did nothing to stop them. Medina's *in*action was therefore a "calculated act of murder" that resulted in at least one hundred more deaths before he finally ordered a ceasefire. Bailey was blunt about this tactic: the prosecution wanted to make his client into a "principal" who was "as guilty of the crime as if he had committed it."[17]

Medina's trial began on the morning of August 16 at Fort McPherson, with Colonel Kenneth Howard presiding, just as he had over Hutto's trial. Eckhardt had prosecuted Hutto, only to see his arguments fail to sway the jury. This time he faced one of the top criminal attorneys in the country while trying to win over a jury of five Vietnam veterans: Colonel William D. Proctor (foreman) of Georgia; Lieutenant Colonel Bobby G. Berryhill, Jr., of Georgia; Major Dudley J. Budrich of Chicago; Lieutenant Colonel Clarence Cooke of Alabama; and Colonel Robert E. Nelson, Jr., of Georgia. Eckhardt realized that the case had ramifications that went beyond this courtroom. A guilty finding against Medina would raise questions about the Calley verdict as well as the actions of other officers in the command chain.[18]

Howard made plain at the outset that the prosecution must answer the following questions: What did Medina know about the killings, and when did he know it? Just as important, what did he do after knowing it?

The prognosis for the prosecution was not good from the beginning. In the first two days of the trial, not one of Eckhardt's nine witnesses could put Medina in the village at the time of the mass killings, nor did they hear him order his men to shoot women and children, and they could not say when he called a ceasefire. The timing of the ceasefire was crucial: Medina could not be responsible for killings before he was aware of their existence. When did he learn of the killings? Without an answer to this, Eckhardt faced an uphill battle in proving that a commanding officer had failed to perform his duty.[19]

On the second day of the trial, Bailey again asked Colonel Howard to admit the results of a polygraph test previously given to Medina, a test that had supported his client's innocence of ordering the killings. Bailey knew there was little chance the court would comply with his request, and yet he also knew that in openly seeking their admission, he had indirectly introduced the findings to the jury. To decide whether or not to admit the results as evidence, Howard removed the jury from the courtroom and heard Brisentine and six other experts attest to the reliability of lie detectors. Howard nonetheless adhered to the army's court-martial manual and ruled the test conclusions inadmissible.[20]

The jury was not present at one point during the first week of the proceedings when Howard shocked Bailey by pondering the application of the Yamashita case to the Medina trial. The Yamashita verdict had set a high standard for command responsibility and, Bailey feared, posed a lethal threat to his client. Bailey also knew that Frank Murphy, the former governor general of the Philippines who had been one of the Supreme Court justices to hear the Yamashita case on appeal in 1946, had strongly dissented, warning that imposition of the death sentence meant that no officer could escape its "boundless and dangerous implications." The Yamashita decision "scared the living hell out of Medina," Bailey later wrote.[21]

When Bailey reacted strongly to the reference to the case, Howard assured him that he had not decided to invoke the Yamashita principle. Instead, according to Bailey, he intended to instruct the jurors that the court could not hold Medina "criminally responsible" for the mass murders unless they believed he was aware of the killing of civilians *and* did nothing to stop it.[22]

Bailey's understanding of the Yamashita decision was not correct, because, as Marine Corps lawyer William Hays Parks has shown, it did not establish strict liability. Admittedly, a commander with knowledge of offenses committed by his subordinates can be responsible if he does nothing to stop them. Examples of this might be a principal who commits the crime or of an officer who fails to correct the situation and is guilty of dereliction of duty. But if that officer's action—or inaction—showed "acquiescence" to his men's crime, that constituted intent to aid the offense and therefore made him culpable. "The difficulty," Parks has asserted, "lies in establishing a causal connection where acquiescence is due to dereliction of duty rather than a manifestation of specific intent." The army's field manual stated that a commander shows acquiescence in the wrongdoing "if he fails to take the necessary and reasonable steps to ensure compliance with the law of war or to punish violators thereof."[23]

Bailey shared the popular view of the Yamashita verdict—that a commander may be responsible for war crimes committed by his men without having knowledge of those actions. Months earlier, the army's general counsel, Robert Jordan, rejected the so-called Yamashita precedent. "A commander," Jordan declared, "cannot be held to be a murderer merely because one of his men commits murder." Bailey showed no awareness of the two key facets of the case: that circumstantial evidence had established Yamashita's awareness of his troops' illegal actions and that he ordered and participated in them, and that the prosecution charged at the Tokyo War Crimes Trials of 1946 that Yamashita "violated the laws of war" when he "unlawfully disregarded and failed to discharge his duty to control the operation of the members of his command, permitting them to commit brutal atrocities and other high crimes." The key word was "permitting," because it implied knowledge and acquiescence. The U.S. Supreme Court held a commander responsible for the actions of his men if he had the power to control them and did nothing to correct their behavior. Contrary to popular understanding, it did not assert "command responsibility for crimes of which a commander has *no* knowledge."[24]

Bailey's concerns for Medina were nonetheless justified. Even if he was no longer facing charges of murder, as Yamashita had been, Medina nonetheless had to show that upon learning of the killings he immediately ordered a cease-fire. And even if he escaped criminal responsibility by demonstrating he never acquiesced or intended to allow the killings, he could still be found culpably negligent for failure to act quickly—hence the importance of establishing a direct link between learning of the killings and bringing them to an end.

Bailey faced a challenge that was integral to the Yamashita issue when, in the second week of the trial, Louis Martin, a radio operator from the 3rd Platoon, took the stand as the only witness for the prosecution to place Medina inside My Lai 4 in the early stages of the massacre. Martin, as we have seen, claimed to have been with a small band of GIs from his platoon following the command group in single file through the village that morning when he saw some of the men shoot at least ten Vietnamese women and children. If so, Medina must also have seen the killings. To undermine the testimony, Bailey focused on Martin's assertion that he was sixth in line among about a dozen soldiers maintaining a distance between them of ten to fifteen feet. Not only did Martin say he was sixty to ninety feet behind Medina, he admitted that the troops often lost sight of each other because of the huts and thick vegetation. When pressed on whether he actually saw Medina in the village that day, Martin could not be certain about his presence and "assumed every-one in the line" saw the killings. He also damaged his own testimony, as Bailey remembered, by conceding that he was "not very well oriented" and "needed psychiatric treatment." Confident that the jury was aware of Martin's prob-lems and the holes in his testimony, Bailey did not push him any farther at this point in the trial.[25]

That same week, Eckhardt introduced depositions from both ARVN in-terpreters with Charlie Company, Sergeants Nguyen Dinh Phu and Duong Minh: Their written statements alleged that they were with Medina at the southern end of the village and knew what had happened. Phu saw about thirty-five bodies, mostly women and children killed by small-arms fire; Minh asserted that Medina saw about thirty bodies at the same time he did. When they asked Medina the reason for the killings, he replied, "That is the order. You don't ask questions." Eckhardt had asked the State Department to per-suade the Saigon government to allow the two interpreters to appear in court. But the ARVN command had adamantly rejected the idea, probably because it was still irate and embarrassed about having learned of the massacre and the names of the victims from the Viet Cong. It nonetheless appeared that Medina knew of the murders and had failed to take corrective action.[26]

Bailey immediately objected, wanting the depositions disallowed because he would not be able to cross-examine the two Vietnamese interpreters. When he asserted that the defense would call the White House and ask it to intervene, Judge Howard looked at him with a smile and remarked, "I don't know the number of the White House. Do you?" It so happened that Bailey did. He made the call, but the White House maintained its hands-off policy toward Medina's trial.[27]

Bailey wrote that he was livid. He had read the depositions and did not be-lieve they posed a problem, but what if another witness corroborated the charges? He proceeded to raise doubts about the depositions. Minh did not know the name of "a captain who looked Spanish" when asking him, "Why are you killing people?" Minh could not remember the name of the village and the date of the operation. Not only did he provide ambiguous and conflicting information, he had only a passing familiarity with the English language. Bailey insisted that the only chance he had to establish the "ambiguities" in the depositions would be through a cross-examination that carried the threat of perjury charges if the two interpreters were not telling the truth.[28]

Howard agreed with Bailey but had the depositions read into the record. Bailey noted with pleasure that the jury did not appear convinced by the charges.[29]

Colburn, for one, had suggested that there might have been jury tampering in the trial. On August 24, 1971, before being called to the stand to testify, he was waiting in the hallway when a two- or three-star general (Colburn could not say precisely which) and his entourage passed by and entered the jury room, near to where he was standing. The door was ajar, and Colburn remembered that he heard the general say, "Hi, John" (referring to Major Dudley J. Budrich) and exchange pleasantries with the four other jurors, expressing his hope that they would find "some nice way to get Ernie out of this mess." In an interview with journalist Nancy Montgomery, Colburn told the story, which she related in her *Stars and Stripes* article, published shortly after his death in December 2016. The Uniform Code of Military Justice declares that anyone "subject to this Code" who tries to influence the outcome of any military court proceeding would be subject to court martial and, if found guilty, would face whatever punishment that court directed.[30]

Eckhardt told me that he had been "alarmed" by Montgomery's article and asked whether Colburn had told me the same story. When I replied that he had, Eckhardt reflected for a moment, then remarked that he had heard vague rumors to that effect but discounted them. He suggested checking the trial record to see if any two- or three-star general's name appeared on the witness list, or indeed had any business in the courthouse on the day of Colburn's testimony. I did, and there was nothing in the record. Nor did the daily newspaper accounts of the trial mention the presence of either a major general or a lieutenant general at any point in the proceedings.[31]

This brief account poses yet another unanswered question about My Lai and the trials that followed.

On September 9, after other inconclusive testimonies followed by a court recess, Eckhardt persuaded Howard to allow Brisentine to appear as the prosecution's thirty-first and final witness. Eckhardt knew that the polygraph expert could not say anything about the results of the test, but he could discuss his fourteen-hour pre-test interview of Medina the previous November. He hoped that Medina had said something establishing that he had been aware of the killings earlier than the alleged ceasefire of 10:25 a.m. and yet had done nothing to stop them.[32]

Eckhardt's tactic worked. According to Brisentine, Medina had admitted in the interview that when he first saw the bodies, he should have known they had resulted from mass killings and stopped them. He did not do so because he wanted "with all his heart" to believe they had been killed by rocket and artillery fire. Brisentine's testimony indicated that Medina had not ordered the killings (as Eckhardt had already concluded), but in an important admission, he had become aware of them about ninety minutes into the operation. Thus Medina had lied during Calley's court martial when he denied knowledge of the killings before nine o'clock and was therefore indirectly responsible for a criminal act. He also admitted to Brisentine that he felt he had "lost control of his troops" two to three hours after the assault began and thought it "too late" to do anything. Medina, Brisentine declared, "did not take any steps to regain control." Not surprisingly, Medina opposed a recount because he "didn't want to go back and see the destruction. He'd seen the bodies and didn't want to see them again."[33]

Bailey realized the precarious position his client was in and tried one last time to introduce the polygraph results. On September 10, he wrote President Nixon again, expressing hope that his past public endorsement of the polygraph examination would lead him to instruct Judge Howard to admit such evidence "within the dictates of his own discretion." A few weeks later—too late to have any effect—a letter arrived, again from Dean. The White House did not fully trust a polygraph test and would not recommend a change in the court-martial manual, which, Bailey certainly knew, declared that any conclusions drawn from a polygraph test were "inadmissible in evidence" in a court-martial trial.[34]

Bailey tried another tactic. Earlier in September, he had gotten the army's permission to put Calley on the stand for the defense, claiming he had "changed his story." Bailey never explained what change he was referring to in his request, but, since Eckhardt no longer argued that Medina had ordered the killings, the only information worth securing from Calley had to relate to the new charge that Medina had been aware of the killings and had done nothing to stop them. Bailey knew that Calley's appeals process was ongoing, meaning that if he now contradicted his earlier claim to have been acting under Medina's orders, "he could be tried for perjury in his own case."[35]

Calley arrived on September 13, wearing dark glasses and a dress uniform with brass shining and the U.S. Army Infantry School patch on his sleeve with the insignia "Follow Me." Despite the anticipation generated by his appearance, it quickly became clear that Calley would not testify. He waited in a witness room while George Latimer told Judge Howard that if called to the stand, his client would plead the Fifth Amendment, choosing not to testify on the grounds of self-incrimination.[36]

It later became clear why he chose not to testify. At any rate, Calley's refusal did not surprise Bailey. "There's no need to parade him here."[37]

But Bailey later admitted that he had had another strategy in mind: using Calley's appearance as legal groundwork for bringing another army officer to the stand, Captain Robert Hicks. Shortly after Calley's conviction, Hicks had contacted Bailey, saying he had information "that could help Captain Medina." Why hadn't he spoken out during the Calley trial? "I thought Calley was in enough trouble already," Hicks replied, according to Bailey. In interviewing him, Bailey learned of a conversation Hicks had with Calley shortly after the My Lai assault that supported Medina's defense.

Eckhardt immediately objected to such testimony as hearsay, but Howard agreed to listen to what Hicks had to say without the jury present. Hicks's remarks did not impress Howard as reliable, and he ruled that they were hearsay and not admissible in court.

Bailey and Howard had disagreed on several questions during the trial, but this decision led to a bitter exchange that the *Washington Post* covered in detail.

"Your ruling was erroneous," charged Bailey. "That's not the function of the judge to rule on the credibility of a witness."

"Don't chastise the judge," Howard retorted. "Don't repeat back to the judge that he is an idiot."

"I don't recall using that term, your honor," Bailey responded. "I merely said your ruling was erroneous and I have the right to voice my objections."

"I am not ruling on credibility. The testimony was hearsay," Howard declared.

Bailey requested a conference with the judge. Howard agreed but first removed everyone from the courtroom and for two hours debated the issue with Bailey. Afterward, Howard announced that he had reversed his decision and the jury could hear the testimony.

What had caused Howard to change his mind? Bailey himself argued that it had all been part of his strategy. He had not shown any concern about Calley's decision not to testify. But his potential appearance had permitted Bailey to argue that since Calley had refused to testify, Hicks's testimony became legally permissible because he was "the next best witness" to gathering evidence about his alleged conversation with Calley. Had Calley taken the stand and pleaded the Fifth Amendment, Hicks could not have testified. Howard accepted Bailey's argument.[38]

Two days later, Hicks appeared in court, testifying that in his quarters in Chu Lai one morning in July 1968, Calley was "bragging" while telling "war stories" that eventually got around to My Lai 4. Calley declared that he and his men "didn't expect to find any civilians in the place" and were surprised when "all the people came out and started to cheer. But they shut up real fast when someone shot a water buffalo and the rest of the men opened up." Hicks testified that he had found this story difficult to believe. He knew Medina and considered him "an extremely professional commander." He said he had asked Calley whether Medina was there.

"No," Calley replied. "Captain Medina was with the 3rd Platoon."

"Did he know about this?"

"No," Calley again replied, adding that Medina was "certainly surprised."[39]

If Calley had told the truth about Medina's reaction—that he was "surprised" about the massacre—his statement posed serious consequences for both men. Had Medina been outside the village with the 3rd Platoon, he could not have been aware of the killings until later. It then followed that Calley had lied in his own trial when claiming he had obeyed Medina's orders to kill the villagers. Were Calley now to renege on his story to Hicks, Medina's jury would not be likely to believe him. In Calley's own court martial, the jury had rejected his defense based on the claim that he was following Medina's orders. Rather than risk perjuring himself in Medina's trial, Calley decided not to testify, and an hour after his arrival at Fort McPherson was on the plane back to Fort Benning.[40]

The story Calley told Hicks had not convinced anyone, but Bailey took no chances and acted quickly to squelch Martin's claim that Medina had been in My Lai 4 early in the assault. Bailey used the precedent set by Brisentine's testimony to persuade the judge to allow another polygraph expert, Leonard Harrelson, to testify about Martin's allegation. At Bailey's behest, Harrelson had interviewed Martin and now could relate what he said during their pre-test discussion. It was during that interview that Martin admitted to having "a problem with illusions and delusions" throughout his life, making it possible that his memory of Vietnamese being "mowed down by three or four GIs" was a product of his imagination.[41]

For the time being, Martin's testimony carried no weight, and Medina's claim of not being in My Lai 4 stood unchallenged.

The forecast for Medina continued to improve when it became doubtful that he had killed the young boy as charged. Michael Terry from the 3rd Platoon testified that he had seen Gene Oliver shoot the boy, leading Bailey to put him on the stand. Oliver admitted to the act, saying he felt it necessary to testify after learning from the press that the prosecution had charged Medina with the premeditated murder of the child. On that day in My Lai 4, he saw "a movement, a human form," and fired his weapon, dropping the figure "very close" to a pile of bodies near the trail. "It's only a kid," someone yelled, and the next thing Oliver heard was Medina shouting, "God damn it, cease-fire!" Medina had nothing to do with this killing, Oliver asserted. "It was what I saw." Why didn't he come forward earlier? "Because it was something I'd rather bury."[42]

Harrelson also discussed his pre-test interview of Oliver, again at Bailey's request. "In my opinion," Harrelson declared, Oliver "was telling the truth when he said he shot this little child."[43]

But the question remained as to whether Medina had lied about not being in the village until almost three hours after the assault began. Eckhardt thought so: Medina, he later told an audience at Tulane University, "calculatingly remained out once he knew what was going on, so he didn't have to see."[44]

III

Medina took the stand on September 16 and spent more than three hours refuting all the charges. He had never received any reports of civilians in the village; he did not order any killings of civilians; and he did not become aware of the huge number of slain noncombatants until he was questioned by the inspector general's officer long afterward. He had seen twenty to twenty-eight bodies but attributed them to artillery and gunship fire. He had never seen the bodies in the ditch but in the late morning had ordered a cease-fire immediately after seeing the bodies on a trail and witnessing the shooting of a boy. He shot the woman in self-defense and never intended to physically harm the prisoner under interrogation. And he castigated Calley as incompetent. In the evening of the operation, Medina said that he had questioned Calley about the charge made by Hugh Thompson that U.S. troops had slaughtered civilians in the village. Calley, according to Medina, "hemmed and hawed and wouldn't give me a direct answer." Calley, he said, ultimately guessed that they killed more than fifty civilians.[45]

At one point in the testimony, Judge Howard excused the jury from the courtroom to hear Medina discuss a conversation with Calley that without witnesses was inadmissible as evidence. Two days after the operation, Medina explained, he and Calley were alone in a field talking about the civilians killed in the ditch when Calley suddenly blurted out, "My God, I can still hear them screaming!" Medina turned to look directly at him and declared, "Look, if something happened I want to know about it. If you killed a bunch of noncombatants, you're in trouble." Calley showed no concern. "If there's an investigation, you don't have to worry about it. You had nothing to do with it. I'll take the blame. You're a family man." Medina nonetheless admitted he never investigated Calley's claim.[46]

Medina explained that he and Calley did not talk again until September 1969, when he received a phone call from Calley. Identifying himself as "Rusty," Calley declared he was "somewhere near Hawaii" and had undergone questioning by the inspector general about My Lai. "Is there anything I should do?" "Yes," Medina replied. "You'd better get you a couple of good lawyers and you'd better tell the truth." Calley reminded him of what Medina called the "promise" made to him in Vietnam—which Calley broke in his own trial a year later. "Well, I just want you to know that our deal still stands."[47]

There was no deal, Medina emphasized.[48]

Bailey's last question to Medina with the jury back in the room was, "Did you have any awareness that your men were killing innocent civilians?"

"No, sir," he replied.[49]

In his cross-examination, Eckhardt bluntly asked Medina, "Did you lose control of your company?" For the first time in his testimony, according to Bailey, Medina lost his composure when responding, "I believe I did, sir."[50]

The following day, Colonel Howard dismissed the charge against Medina for murdering the boy and, declaring that the prosecution had failed to prove Medina guilty of the premeditated murder of at least one hundred Vietnamese, reduced that charge to involuntary manslaughter. Howard added that he had dismissed the first murder charge not because of Oliver's testimony but to save the jury from having to sort through the "confusion" of determining whether the boy shot by Oliver was the correct one of five children reportedly killed and then having to deal with Medina's own uncertainty about what he might have shouted on seeing the movement, "Stop him, get him, shoot, or don't shoot…but I'm not certain." The only murder charge left was that of the woman.[51]

None of this meant that Medina's situation was less serious. In his closing argument on September 22, Eckhardt accused him of "criminal, culpable negligence" for keeping quiet about the killings because he feared they would wreck his career. Medina reported sixty-nine Viet Cong killed in action and made no personal investigation. He ordered his men to conserve their ammunition, a move that showed he realized they were not in danger and, Eckhardt emphasized, "certainly knew what they were doing in that particular village." A helicopter landed, and the pilot complained about the bodies. As Medina told Brisentine, he knew early in the morning of the operation that the 1st Platoon had collected groups of noncombatants and shot them. Yet he never examined or looked at the bodies, nor did he order an immediate cease-fire. He realized he no longer had control over his troops but waited to stop the killings and thereby condemned additional Vietnamese civilians to die. Medina "knew exactly what was going on" and chose not to act. This was "criminal negligence."[52]

At that Tulane conference years later, Eckhardt admitted that by then he had known the polygraph results, which were not admissible in court, and stated that the needle "went off the chart" when the examiner asked Medina if he had been aware of the mass killings that took place between 7:30 and

9:00 a.m. Medina had lied when he said he had not realized what happened until three hours into the operation. In Eckhardt's view, he had violated his responsibilities not only as a commander but as a soldier.[53]

After the prosecution rested its case, Bailey emphasized in his closing remarks that for the jury to convict Medina, it must believe "beyond a reasonable doubt" that he was guilty of premeditated murder in shooting the woman; that he intentionally planned to harm his prisoner; that he knew his men were "deliberately killing" noncombatants; and that he did nothing in response to this knowledge. There could be no "imputed responsibility" based on "actual awareness" of the killings that led his client to be "so negligent as to be willful and wanton and reckless" in these chaotic surroundings.[54]

Bailey also reminded the court of Medina's former commanders who had praised his conscientious behavior and sense of duty in combat. The prosecution had focused on the charge of criminal negligence, calling it an act "incompatible" with "dedication and conscientious service." To lead a "green" company into battle would admittedly tax the "most seasoned officer," especially after losing nearly thirty men to mines, booby traps, and snipers. Artillery fire on the village, an enemy force expected to be superior in numbers and experience, a "sweep" described as a search-and-destroy mission—all made it difficult to realize that the enemy was not there. This, however, should not "condemn what was and is a good officer."[55]

Bailey also issued final statements on the two other charges against Medina. If you find him guilty of murdering the woman, he told the jury, "I suggest to you that you equip every soldier with an attorney to stand with him and help him decide whether or not he's got the legal right to shoot; and our machinery of warfare will grind to a halt." And on the assault charges, Bailey argued that the army's field manual on land warfare permitted an interrogator to "threaten violence" against a prisoner who refused to talk about the enemy's location and plans—which included firing two bullets over his head. Medina never intended to hurt the prisoner; he held an "Expert's Badge" and, he testified, he tried to prevent an accidental shot by setting the safety on his rifle before placing it on the ground with its barrel facing the prisoner.[56]

After the two sides rested their cases, Colonel Howard read the jury two hours of instructions on the law. The army, he declared, had not proved Medina guilty of two of the specifications of premeditated murder—the young boy and at least one hundred Vietnamese noncombatants—which meant that Medina faced the reduced charge of involuntary manslaughter and, if found guilty, a maximum penalty of three years in prison. The jury would therefore make its decision on one specification of premeditated murder of a Vietnamese woman, in violation of Article 118 of the Uniform Code of Military Justice; one charge and two specifications of aggravated assault for using a dangerous weapon, in violation of Article 128; and one additional charge and one specification of involuntary manslaughter of not fewer than one hundred Vietnamese noncombatants, in violation of Article 119.[57]

To convict Medina of involuntary manslaughter, Howard emphasized, the jurors had to find that he had "actual knowledge" of his soldiers killing noncombatants, "plus a wrongful failure to act."[58]

Thus Howard did not in fact evoke the "Yamashita principle." Critics then and afterward complained that Howard had violated both army law and the principles that governed the war crimes trials after World War II. Had the Tokyo tribunal not sentenced Yamashita to death even though it had failed to prove he was aware of all of his men's violations?[59]

But William Hays Parks, for one, has argued that this is a mistaken assertion. Many U.S. representatives at the Nuremberg trials insisted that the "should have known test" was so broad that it "would subject the commander to arbitrary after-the-fact judgments." Eckhardt agreed with that view, later remarking that he had less chance of a conviction based on what Medina actually knew because of the difficulty in obtaining witnesses who could put him at the scene. Yet he realized that numerous observers would accuse Howard of giving "flawed" instructions and suspect the army of protecting its commanders by using standards different than those applied by the United States after World War II. Howard nonetheless told the jury that "the commander-subordinate relationship" would not by itself permit what he called "an inference of knowledge."[60]

Had Medina done nothing to stop the killing of noncombatants, he would not be guilty of murder but of involuntary manslaughter.[61]

Had Howard not removed "should have knowledge" from consideration, the prosecution would have faced the difficult task of arguing for what Parks called "an imputation of constructive knowledge" on the basis of reports and other information. It was clear that Medina did not make every effort to check on the bodies, either during the operation or afterward, when Henderson's call for a recount was rejected because Medina warned Koster of the danger in sending U.S. troops back to My Lai 4. But would this have been sufficient to win a conviction?[62]

Bailey remembered that after the jury had received its instructions on September 22, he told Medina that the army's field manual had a different wording for each verdict. If delivering a guilty verdict, the president of the jury would tell the defendant, "It is my duty as president of this court to inform you that the court, in closed session and upon secret written ballot, has found you guilty of all specifications and charges." If not guilty, he would say, "It is my duty as president of this court to *advise* you..."[63]

Just fifty-seven minutes after giving his instructions to the jury, Howard returned to the bench and announced that the jury had reached a verdict. After the five jurors re-entered the room, Colonel William Proctor as foreman turned to Medina, who stood up from the defense table and amid total silence moved to the front of the courtroom and saluted the presiding officer. "Captain Ernest L. Medina, it is my duty as president of this court to advise you..."[64]

Medina did not have to hear the rest of the words to realize that the jury had acquitted him of all charges.

Howard suppressed the spectators' cheers and applause as Medina managed to salute Proctor again before returning to his seat. Trying to hide his tears, he reached for a glass of water as his wife broke down a few feet away. The decision, he told the press outside, justified his "complete faith in military justice," even though he still intended to follow his previously announced decision to leave the service.[65]

One of the jurors, Colonel Robert Nelson, later remarked that he was "personally delighted" with the outcome. "This jury began with the assumption that Captain Medina was innocent and we waited for the government to change our minds. It's apparent from the verdict that they didn't."[66]

Howard's instructions were crucial to this decision and drew—then as now—considerable criticism, including that from Telford Taylor, the chief American prosecutor of Nazi Germany's war criminals at the Nuremberg trials after World War II. Taylor insisted that Medina had not adhered to the army's field manual of 1956, *The Law of Land Warfare*, which required the commanding officer "to take the necessary and reasonable steps to insure" that his men complied with the laws of war.[67]

Taylor's outspoken criticism of the Vietnam War made his opposition to the Medina verdict no surprise. Taylor had appeared on the highly popular *Dick Cavett Show* on TV the previous January, declaring that if the courts applied the Yamashita standard to General Westmoreland, Secretary of State Dean Rusk, Secretary of Defense Robert McNamara, and senior advisers McGeorge Bundy and Walt Rostow, "there would be a strong possibility that they would come to the same end as he [General Yamashita] did." Asked later if former president Lyndon Johnson should be on that list, Taylor replied, "I don't think I want to answer that directly at this time."[68]

In any case, Eckhardt had grappled with a host of problems in seeking a conviction of Medina as well as others on trial. His chief obstacle was

Lieutenant Colonel Barker's orders to Medina, which were vague, making it difficult to determine whether Medina had told his men to kill civilians or left the implication by issuing ambiguous directives. Numerous soldiers had a wide range of recollections of the order: that he said to kill everything that moved, that he excluded women and children, that he never gave such an order. As we have seen, Calley testified in his own trial that Medina had ordered him to "waste" the Vietnamese civilians; and yet, even if Medina used that word, he could have meant something other than kill—despite Calley's claim that Medina meant kill.

There were other issues, including the destruction of property—of homes, livestock, wells, and food stocks—anything of value to the enemy, which could mean everything. Regarding the alleged cease-fire order, some men heard it; others did not. Some thought it came at 9:15 a.m. and related only to Binh Tay; others remembered it coming after 10:30 and referring to My Lai 4. Still others claimed that being in combat obliterated all sense of time. Why would anyone check his watch? On whether Medina killed anyone, some GIs said yes; others said no. But no one testified to *seeing* him commit murder. Did Medina see bodies? Those with him in the village saw numerous bodies and asserted that he must have seen them too—just to his right on the trail, scattered throughout the village, when he had to step over a body on the pathway, in the ditch as they crossed over the bridge. But no one could—or would—testify that Medina *saw* bodies. Many Vietnamese had witnessed the killings, but Eckhardt could not call them to the stand. The South Vietnamese government would not permit the two Vietnamese interpreters to appear, and the peasants were not reliable witnesses because they could not be specific about either the time or the place of the massacre or which soldiers did what.[69]

Eckhardt knew that the key to conviction would have meant calling credible witnesses who offered testimonies that left no reasonable doubt by the jury. He had access to previous testimonies gathered by the inspector general's office, the CID investigators, and the Peers Inquiry, but most of the material was of little use in court because the interrogators did not follow up on many issues and thereby collected largely vague statements rather than specific information. Although many witnesses were willing to make allegations in private hearings, most of them were reluctant to do so in open court, perhaps knowing that their words put Captain Medina's life in the balance. They may have refused to testify, knowing they were not in the service and could ignore a request to appear. Others perhaps questioned their memories after so many months had passed—whether they saw what they thought they saw soon after the event. Some claimed not to remember—or did they choose to forget? A grant of immunity to witnesses was not an attractive inducement, because it suggested their own culpability and subjected them to possible public retribution. A few simply disappeared, either inside the United States or outside.[70]

The Calley case had proven considerably different than the trial of Medina. Six witnesses had sworn that they saw Calley order and participate in mass murders, and he himself confessed to firing into the ditch from close range. Furthermore, numerous witnesses placed him on the scenes of two hundred or more murders. Captain Daniel had had both direct and circumstantial evidence on his side. He needed only one conviction to win the case; he got twenty-two.

None of this happened in the Medina case. The CID investigator took ninety pages of testimony and concluded that Medina was guilty of the premeditated murder of at least 343 Vietnamese men, women, and children by his troops' "shooting, grenading, and stabbing." Bailey, however, claimed that his team of investigators discovered that the great majority of Charlie Company's soldiers had withdrawn their accusations made to CID. Whether or not that was accurate, most of the potential witnesses either did not show up in court, did not repeat claims made in earlier testimonies when they did appear, or, in some cases, repeated their allegations but either wilted during Bailey's cross-examinations or could not swear to have seen Medina either shoot civilians or visibly react to the large number of bodies they saw.[71]

Bailey explained the acquittal in its simplest terms: the evidence was not there to convict Medina. "In the Calley case, you couldn't escape the evidence that he had murdered children and, in my opinion, that's why they got him."[72]

After Medina's discharge from the army, the judge advocate general, Major General George Prugh, declared that the "available evidence" indicated that U.S. ground forces killed "a significant number" of Vietnamese civilians at My Lai 4. That same evidence also showed that Medina did not report these casualties to higher authorities and then lied to his brigade commander when questioned about the issue before lying two more times to army investigators. Medina's performance did not fit the professional standards of his position. Prugh recommended prohibiting Medina from re-entering the army without the specific approval of the secretary of the army and that a memorandum to this effect go into his official file.[73] It was not likely, of course, that Medina would ever re-enlist.

Not having access to court records, the public perceived a pattern in the My Lai trials that suggested an army cover-up, one intended to hide other officers' involvement in the massacre. Admittedly, the army could not have wanted an investigation to go beyond the division level, but there is no proof that it attempted to conceal culpability farther up the chain of command. The army had another great concern—that a continuing inquiry could interfere with the war effort. In 1971, of course, the war was still going on. To block the remaining judicial proceedings now would not only enhance the popular belief that its sole objective was to protect its officers, but it would further fuel the antiwar movement.

But with hindsight it seems clear that the army had not been in total control of the situation. It lacked jurisdiction over ex-servicemen and was unable to bring charges against them. David Mitchell went free by insisting that he had followed orders, and the judge barred the testimony of those former soldiers who had appeared before the Hébert subcommittee. Charles Hutto won acquittal when his defense attorney argued that his client had followed an illegal order. Lieutenant General Seaman dismissed all charges of cover-up against most of the officers—including forty-three alleged criminal acts by Brigadier General Young and Major General Koster (though Seaman sent Koster a devastating letter of reprimand, one that held him "personally responsible" for My Lai and brought his once promising career to a standstill).[74] Captain Kotouc went free on the basis of the judge's instructions, which arguably violated both American and international law. And now Medina—seemingly acquitted because Judge Howard unilaterally omitted the crucial words from the army's *Law of Land Warfare*—"should have knowledge"—in his instructions to the jury. On the basis of these impressions, the public relentlessly attacked the army for castigating Calley as a bad soldier and making him a scapegoat.

Eckhardt came to the army's defense. He admitted that its basic stance was to protect the chain of command—or "responsible command," as he termed it. But this did not translate into a conspiracy aimed at exonerating officers of responsibility for the atrocities. The army could maintain discipline, order, and control of its men only if the commanders and their troops could handle all the military contingencies of combat—including ferreting out and punishing violators of the law of war.[75]

In the end, the army had gotten what it wanted: The prosecution's inability to prove its case against Medina made it more difficult to convict anyone else in the chain of command.

Colonel Henderson alone remained to stand trial—the only one of twelve officers whose charges the army had not already dismissed.[76]

IV

In early April 1971, Colonel Oran Henderson appeared at a series of pre-trial hearings at Fort Meade that continued throughout the spring and into the summer. If nothing else, they showed that the army's chain of command was on trial. His civilian defense attorney, Henry Rothblatt, had already won a highly publicized court battle with the army, convincing it to drop murder charges against the eight Green Berets accused of killing an alleged Vietcong spy. To help undermine the charge of dereliction of duty, Rothblatt warned that if the army continued "persecuting" his client, he would call officials of higher rank, including General Westmoreland, to the stand. At a news conference held outside the courtroom on April 2, Henderson repeated his claim of innocence of any cover-up, insisting that throughout the investigation "people told me that it didn't happen and I accepted their word...especially the word of my senior commanders."[77]

However, the presiding judge, Colonel Peter Wondolowski, rejected Rothblatt's plea to disallow Henderson's testimonies to both the inspector general's investigator and the Peers commission.[78]

The Henderson trial overlapped with Medina's when it began in early August. The packed courtroom included, in addition to Judge Wondolowski, a jury of two generals and five colonels. The army's prosecuting attorney, Major Carroll Tichenor, accused Henderson of "neglect and willful deceit" in attempting to hide the My Lai killings via a sham investigation based on neither oaths nor signed statements.[79]

The prosecution seemed to strengthen its argument for a cover-up when Tichenor called Frederic Watke to the stand. Watke was now a lieutenant colonel, though in March 1968 he had been a major and commander of the 123rd Aviation Battalion, which included Hugh Thompson and the other helicopter pilots.

On the first day of his testimony, September 15, Watke explained that Thompson and at least five other pilots reported the "unnecessary killing" of Vietnamese civilians at My Lai 4. Watke said that at first he had been skeptical; he had seen no heavy combat or bodies from his own gunship, which flew overhead during the assault. But he reported these allegations that same day to Lieutenant Colonel Barker, Colonel Henderson, and Lieutenant Colonel John Holladay, and Barker had told Major Charles Calhoun to order a cease-fire. The next day, March 17, Watke and Holladay informed Brigadier General Young of the charges, who in turn informed Major General Koster. Later that same afternoon, Watke and Holladay flew to brigade headquarters to speak with Henderson about another issue, and he said nothing to them about a massacre of civilians. When a reporter asked Henderson during a court recess whether he knew at that time about My Lai, Henderson snapped, "Hell, no."

Watke also told the court of the meeting he had attended on March 18 in Barker's command van, along with Barker, Holladay, Young, and Henderson. At its end, Young instructed Henderson to investigate and submit a report to Koster within seventy-two hours. Afterward, Watke testified that Henderson had asked him to have his pilots available for questioning. Watke saw Thompson and two other pilots (Jerry Culverhouse and Lawrence Colburn) heading toward the van to talk with Henderson.[80]

On the second day of his testimony, Rothblatt's defense team raised questions about Watke's credibility. In his cross-examination, Rothblatt asserted that on April 10, 1968, Watke had falsified a statement in support of SP4 Glenn Andreotta's receiving a posthumous Bronze Star for valor at My Lai 4. According to Watke's statement, Andreotta had helped rescue Vietnamese civilians in the midst of a firefight between U.S. troops and the enemy. And yet, Rothblatt pointed out, Watke had testified to seeing no enemy in the village and claimed he had informed Henderson of the pilots' allegations of unnecessary killing. Which story was true?[81]

Watke replied that he had been mistaken in December 1969, over a year and a half after the events in question, when he told the Peers Inquiry that artillery fire had been responsible for the Vietnamese casualties. Members of the panel, he said, had asked him to "reconsider the events" given the effect they could have on his career. He realized his error upon listening to tapes of radio exchanges made during the assault on My Lai 4. To further defend his client, Tichenor had excerpts read into the record that came from a letter Watke wrote his wife two days after the operation in which he strongly suggested his awareness of the mass killings before he heard the tapes: "My people observed an unfortunate act the other day and I reported it.... I didn't make any friends but my conscience is clear."[82]

Why, then, had he falsified this statement? "I made the false statement to get Andreotta the award," Watke replied. Although Andreotta had died in action shortly after My Lai, he had performed courageously there and on other missions and deserved the Bronze Star. "The operation of March 16 was a major one in the eyes of the Division," Watke declared. Written in that vein, the statement would put the division into the position of either giving Andreotta the award or admitting that no fighting had occurred and having to explain the heavy civilian casualties. Division headquarters approved the award, thereby upholding the story of a major battle—and hence no massacre—in My Lai 4.[83]

However well-intentioned, Watke's deception had inadvertently promoted the cover-up. Still, Watke was in no judicial danger: he was among the officers whose charges of cover-up the army had earlier dismissed. Lieutenant

General Seaman nonetheless issued a letter criticizing his administrative actions.[84]

The prosecution soon suffered another setback. Among more than a hundred witnesses called during the trial were Thompson, Culverhouse, and Colburn, who all testified that they had reported the mass killings to a colonel. Though Thompson had identified Henderson before both the Peers Inquiry and the Hébert subcommittee as being that colonel, he now could not recall meeting Henderson and instead described a "heavy-set and balding" colonel; Henderson was thin and had a medium army cut of dark hair. Culverhouse likewise felt uncertain about his identification of Henderson before the Peers Inquiry and could remember only a "somewhat stocky" lieutenant colonel or colonel, and Judge Wondolowski in early October barred Colburn from attempting an identification, because his testimony would be "tainted." Colburn had by this point seen Henderson both in photographs and in person.[85]

The prosecution continued to struggle. Henderson admitted he had failed to recognize the importance of Thompson's allegations but insisted that in 1968 he did not believe that "excessive killings" had occurred and referred to the written version of his March 20 oral report (never found, as shown earlier) showing that his investigation had uncovered no war crimes. Koster had accepted Henderson's report without question, which perhaps demonstrated the major general's negligence but, more likely, simply signified his support for a finding he wanted to hear. Rothblatt had tried earlier to inform the jury that Henderson had passed a polygraph examination suggesting that he had been telling the truth when denying knowledge of the massacre and insisting he wrote a report on his investigation. But Wondolowski turned down this request, reminding the attorney that the results of lie detector tests were not admissible in court.

Rothblatt tried to circumvent that ruling by explaining that in the interests of showing the steps taken to prove his client's innocence, he would seek the court's permission to tell the jury that Henderson had voluntarily taken the examination. That transparent piece of chicanery drew a derisive remark from Tichenor. "If the government offered such testimony, the only conclusion the jury could reach is that he [Henderson] failed. If the defense offers it, the only conclusion would be that he passed." Wondolowski rejected this request as well.[86]

The pivotal moment in the trial came in mid-November when Medina appeared for the defense. He made a startling admission: he had lied to Henderson about the hundreds of Vietnamese civilians killed by U.S. forces.

Medina had made this confession earlier in the Calley trial, but the court-martial transcript was not yet open to public perusal.[87]

Two days after the assault, Medina explained, Henderson met with him in a rice field, asking about the possibility of atrocities. After telling him that U.S. artillery, gunship, and small-arms fire had accidentally killed twenty to twenty-eight villagers, Medina admitted that he had "kept from him that there were bodies on the north-south trail" and "in a group." Nor had he shared information from his platoon leaders that at least 106 civilians lay dead. "I didn't tell him that I had a feeling these people had been shot by members of my command," Medina told the hushed courtroom. "Colonel Henderson asked me whether I saw any indiscriminate wild shooting and I told him I did not." He "put his arm around my shoulder and said, 'Ernie, is there anything else I should know?'" "No," he said he had responded. "I am the father of three children, and I would not let anything like that happen." Medina told the court, "Not wanting to believe my people would do this, I tried to give the impression they wouldn't do this." Asked why he opposed returning to My Lai 4 for a recount of the bodies, he declared, "I was afraid of what I would find."[88]

Medina further explained why he had kept information from Henderson—reasons consistent with his first admission months earlier. The exposure would "disgrace" the army, have "repercussions" for America's relations with other governments, and hurt his family and his role as a father, and, he testified, "I was concerned about myself."[89]

Tichenor was appalled. "Do you realize you have completely disgraced and dishonored the uniform you wore?"

"Yes, sir," Medina replied. Less than a month earlier, he had resigned from the army with an honorable discharge. Yet he insisted he had not resigned to escape prosecution. "I just feel within myself that I cannot wear the uniform with the same pride I had before."[90]

Closing arguments in the Henderson trial came on December 16. Tichenor emphasized that the colonel was in charge of the My Lai campaign and yet never checked into the deaths of those twenty civilians he acknowledged to have occurred and then brought "dishonor, disgrace and humiliation" to his uniform by concealing the mass killings. He had, said Tichenor, "willfully failed" to conduct a thorough investigation and submitted a "hopelessly inadequate" report. Within two days of the massacre, Henderson was "beyond question" aware of what had happened and covered it up to save his career. How could he not have known of the many bodies seen by others with him on his command helicopter as it flew over My Lai 4?

In his closing remarks, Rothblatt called Henderson a "great officer" with a "reputation for veracity." Tragically, some of his men had purposely misled him on the number of civilian casualties at My Lai.[91]

Wondolowski wrapped up the day's proceedings by issuing his instructions to the jury. On Henderson's alleged failure to report a war crime, he told the jurors they "must find beyond a reasonable doubt" that he "personally and consciously thought that a war crime had occurred." To acquit him of dereliction of duty, they had to believe that he "made an honest and reasonably diligent effort to perform his duties." Finally, he told them that unless the evidence established guilt, they could place great importance on Henderson's "good character" in making their decision.[92]

The next day, December 17, the jury announced its verdict. Sixty-two days after Henderson's trial had begun, the seven jurors had heard 106 witnesses give six thousand pages of testimony and in less than four hours acquitted Henderson of all charges.[93]

Lieutenant General Peers, for one, was embittered by the outcome. Medina's revelations made his defense before the inquiry "an out-and-out lie." And, perhaps speaking for many disgruntled service members, Peers remarked that if Henderson's "actions are judged as acceptable standards for an officer in his position, the Army is indeed in deep trouble."[94]

Medina's about-face first in the Calley trial and then in the Henderson trial benefited the army. Medina's admission strongly suggested that orders to kill the Vietnamese noncombatants had not come from higher quarters and that Henderson's acquittal kept the cover-up charges at the field command level and thereby diminished the public's suspicions that they went beyond the Americal Division. Henderson was cleared of charges—as were all other officers and enlisted men, both in the division and above.

Though Medina had admitted to lying, he was a civilian and not subject to the charge of either perjury or withholding information. By the time he took the stand in the Henderson trial, he had resigned from the army and become assistant to the chairman of the board of the R. J. Enstrom Company, which manufactured the F-28A helicopter for the use of law enforcement agencies. The chair of the board and part owner of the company was F. Lee Bailey.[95]

Thus, except for Calley's appeals process, the My Lai trials came to a close. His review had already gone to the next level. On August 18, 1971, at Fort McPherson, Lieutenant General Connor had approved Calley's sentence of dismissal and forfeiture of all pay and allowances, but in a move he called "appropriate" for his offenses, he reduced Calley's lifetime confinement at hard labor to twenty years. Major Kinard, one of the jurors at Calley's trial, did not object to the reduction, noting that the sentence might have been lighter had they had more options than either execution or a life sentence. Another juror, Major Brown, was also not surprised by the reduction. The nationwide "uproar" made this decision no shock to "any reasonable man." Calley could now apply for parole after serving a third of his sentence. The fifteen thousand pages making up the trial records then went forward to the judge advocate general of the army for a decision by the Court of Military Review.[96]

In mid-February 1973 the Court of Military Review affirmed Calley's conviction and twenty-year sentence and forwarded the case to the third and final appellate stage, the Court of Military Appeals. The following December, that court affirmed the decisions of the Army Court of Military Review. Secretary of the Army Howard Callaway, who had replaced Stanley Resor shortly after Nixon's expression of displeasure, reviewed the case and in April 1974 approved the court's decision. However, in a separate action not welcomed by the Pentagon, he exercised his power of clemency to cut Calley's sentence from twenty years to ten—which, with time already served, made him eligible for parole within six months. It was a "whitewash" of the "original whitewash," the *New York Times* proclaimed. In a statement showing no familiarity with what had taken place in the appeals court, Callaway explained that "mitigating circumstances" indicated that Calley "may have sincerely believed that he was acting in accordance with the orders he had received, and that he was not aware of his responsibility to refuse such an illegal order." The judge in the Court of Military Appeals had declared that Calley was guilty whether or not he knew the alleged order was illegal.[97]

The president, given the choice of approving the army secretary's action, reducing Calley's sentence, or granting him a full pardon, approved the secretary's decision and terminated the White House involvement in the case.[98]

Nixon's tumultuous intervention in the Calley case thus came to a quiet end on May 3, 1974, when he wrote the secretary of the army, "I have reviewed the record of the case of *United States* vs. *Calley* and have decided that no further action by me in this matter is necessary or appropriate."[99] Three months later, he resigned from the presidency.

ON NOVEMBER 8, 1974, Secretary of the Army Howard Callaway announced Calley's parole, almost six months before the fall of Saigon on April 30, 1975. Within a year, on April 5, 1976, the U.S. Supreme Court rejected Calley's appeal to have his conviction reviewed, bringing this phase of the My Lai story to a close.[100]

Epilogue

THE MY LAI STORY CONTINUES

HOW SHOULD WE LOOK AT MY LAI NOW, nearly fifty years after the events? For most Americans, it was a rude awakening to learn that "one of our own" could commit the kind of atrocities mostly associated with the nation's enemies in war. Even to those who defended the American soldier, his image changed from citizen-soldier to baby killer—from poster boy hero and virtuous protector of the defenseless to cowardly murderer and rapist. It seemed impossible to reconcile My Lai with the concept of the United States as a chosen nation—an exceptional nation—built on republican principles and predestined by God to spread freedom throughout the world. In his memoirs after he had left the presidency, Nixon expressed the opinion of many Americans when he called it an aberration, unrepresentative of our country.[1]

I

From one perspective, the story of My Lai came full circle on March 10, 2008, when Pham Thanh Cong, director of the Son My War Remnant Site and a survivor of the massacre, met at My Lai with former corporal Kenneth Schiel, a participant in the killings and the first member of Charlie Company to return to the scene. Cong had lost his mother and four siblings that day in My Lai 4 and was surprised at Schiel's appearance. Less than a week before the proceedings commemorating the fortieth anniversary of the massacre, they spent three hours discussing the events of March 16, 1968. Cong described the meeting as tense, though he appreciated Schiel's effort to atone for what had happened. At first he did not admit to killing Vietnamese civilians. In the end, however, Schiel apologized even though continuing to maintain that he had been following orders.

In August 2009, Cong would learn that in the United States William Calley had spoken publicly for the first time about his role in the killings. Unlike Schiel, Calley refused to return to My Lai. Like Schiel, he claimed to have been following orders and felt no personal responsibility. To his friend Al Fleming, Calley still maintained, "I did what I had to do."[2] The news media nonetheless regarded Calley's public remarks as an apology; Cong and another survivor of that day, Tran Van Duc, were dubious. Cong wanted more than a so-called apology from Calley. "I want him to come back...and see things here." If Calley "sincerely" apologized, said Cong, "we of course would forgive him." Duc and his two sisters had escaped the massacre but did not know their mother's fate until 1975 when, in a photo displayed at the Son My War Remnant Site, he saw her lying on the ground, dead from a gunshot in the head. "A terse 'apology,'" Duc asserted, "is simply a disappointment!"[3]

Schiel and Calley substantiated an observation made by William Eckhardt, the chief prosecutor in the My Lai cases: those soldiers who killed noncombatants were the same ones to claim they were innocent because they had been following orders.

How exceptional was My Lai? In *The Guns at Last Light*, Rick Atkinson shows that in the closing months of World War II American troops committed a number of horrific crimes against the French populace after landing in Normandy in 1944. Mary Louise Roberts supports that analysis, using newly opened French documents to argue in *What Soldiers Do* that many American soldiers raped French women after landing on the continent.[4] Atrocities also took place in America's other wars, including the Mexican War, the Civil War, the Spanish-American War, World War I, the Korean War, and, most recently, in Iraq and Afghanistan.[5]

To many Americans, however, Vietnam seemed to offer more examples, perhaps in part due to the war's longevity. In *Tiger Force*, Michael Sellah and Mitch Weiss uncovered a series of atrocities and mass killings of Vietnamese civilians just below Da Nang, committed by an elite army contingent over the course of seven months beginning in May 1967. Nick Turse, in *Kill Anything That Moves*, argues that U.S. soldiers killed civilians throughout the Vietnam War as a result of government policies that made atrocities acceptable. My Lai was thus one of many.[6]

The mass killings of civilians, Turse argues, were "the inevitable outcome of deliberate policies, dictated at the highest levels of the military," and resulting in a "veritable system of suffering." These policies established the conditions conducive to atrocities—a war of attrition based on body counts, search-and-destroy missions, free-fire zones, and soldiers trained to see the enemy as subhuman.[7]

Turse draws heavily on thousands of pages of documents collected by the Vietnam War Crimes Working Group, a secret task force working out of the army chief of staff's office created by the Pentagon in 1970. The documents gathered by this wartime investigation, declassified in 1994, recorded hundreds of atrocities committed by U.S. forces in Vietnam. Eight boxes of these materials, all extracts from the now-open CID and Peers Inquiry files, focused on My Lai, however, making it stand out from the others. General Westmoreland emphasized this point in his report. "The Army investigated every case, no matter who made the allegation," but "none of the crimes even remotely approached the magnitude and horror of My Lai." Whereas many of these atrocities in other parts of Vietnam came by air and at night, every victim at My Lai was killed during the day, many of them less than five feet away while facing their killers.[8]

My Lai simply stands out, in part because of the numbers. As noted in this book's prologue, 504 victims are listed on the marble plaque located near the entrance to the museum at the Son My War Remnant Site in My Lai. The victims broke down into 231 males and 273 females—seventeen of them pregnant. More than half of those killed—259—were under twenty years of age: forty-nine teenagers, 160 aged four to twelve years, and fifty who were three years old or younger. Of the remainder, eighty-four were in their twenties and thirties, and the rest ranged from their forties to the oldest at eighty.[9]

The numbers do not tell the whole story, but they say a great deal. Calley and his platoon had executed at least two hundred Vietnamese elderly men, women, and children, seventy-seven at the trail and 123 in the ditch. Seventy-nine children were among the victims, who ranged in age from infancy to their teens and included forty-two boys and thirty-nine girls. Also slain were 120 adults, eighty-one females, and thirty-nine males.

Investigators from the Peers Inquiry and CID agreed that Lieutenant Calley and the 1st Platoon were responsible for the greatest number of deaths in My Lai 4. The Peers commission accused Lieutenant Stephen Brooks of the 2nd Platoon of numerous crimes, including ordering and participating in killing noncombatants, but by that point he had already died. The commission did not bring charges against Lieutenant Jeffrey LaCross of the 3rd Platoon. He testified that he was shocked at the number of deaths and fired his rifle only one time that day—into the air—at which point it jammed.[10]

More than forty soldiers apparently took part in killing civilians. Of all the facts that emerged from the many investigations and reports, perhaps the most chilling is that not a single soldier on the ground tried to stop the killing.

Nor did anyone try to stop the rapes. CID accused thirteen soldiers of rape, and yet no one was convicted. Witnesses could not swear to seeing penetration; others refused to come forward, some fearing retaliation. Both the victims and alleged perpetrators had scattered afterward, making it virtually impossible to find the victims and have them identify the accused. Moreover, many officers and enlisted men dismissed rape as an unavoidable aspect of war and did little or nothing to prevent it.[11]

Equally troubling is that none of the soldiers reported any of these crimes. But in fairness, to whom would they have reported them? In nearly every case, their superiors either ordered, participated in, or ignored what was going on around them. If they waited until they returned to the base, who would believe them?

Why the mass killings? The sexual assaults? The violence? Writer Tim O'Brien served with the army in Vietnam and blamed war itself, declaring that in the confusion of combat, nothing seemed real. "For the common soldier, at least, war has the feel—the spiritual texture—of a great ghostly fog, thick and permanent. There is no clarity. Everything swirls. The old rules are no longer binding, the old truths no longer true." The troops "did not know even the simple things...how to feel when seeing a dead Vietnamese, to be happy or sad or relieved....They did not know good from evil."[12]

Another Vietnam veteran, Philip Caputo, argues in *Rumor of War* that the only safeguard of decency was "the net of a man's inner moral values, the attribute that is called character." Not everyone had character. "There were a few—and I suspect Lieutenant Calley was one—who had no net and plunged all the way down, discovering in their bottommost depths a capacity for malice they probably never suspected was there." As Harry Stanley, a soldier in Charlie Company, put it two decades after My Lai, "It's just what's in the person, I think: the person himself."[13]

II

Of the figures who seemed to have "character," Hugh Thompson and Lawrence Colburn come first to mind. March 16, 1968, was "one of the saddest days of my life," remarked Thompson at a conference on My Lai at Tulane University in 1994. "I just could not believe that people could totally lose control like the way it happened." Other units had suffered losses, "but they didn't go out the next day and wipe out a village."[14]

Thompson said he learned morality in a close-knit family while growing up in Georgia. By present-day standards, he once jokingly explained, his mother and father were "abusive" and did not know what "double jeopardy" was. "If I did something wrong, my mother would get me. When my father got home from work, she would tell him, and I'd get it again. But they always taught me to help the underdog. Don't be a bully and live by the Golden Rule." His parents, he said, "taught me right from wrong."[15]

Thompson's father had served in both the army and the navy in World War II, followed by the navy reserve for more than three decades. The younger Thompson took a similar path. After graduating from high school, he joined the navy in 1961 and, after a brief time out of the service, enlisted in the army in 1966. A year later he completed flight school and departed for Vietnam, where as a helicopter pilot he crashed five times, the last time resulting in a broken back in August 1968 that took him out of the war. Lawrence Colburn later remarked that he suspected that after Thompson had exposed the massacre, someone in command placed him in a "very precarious position" by sending him to the most dangerous areas without adequate gunship protection. Whether this is true or not, Thompson stayed in the service until retiring in 1983 and was inducted into the Army Aviation Hall of Fame in 2004.[16]

Colburn likewise learned right from wrong at home. Raised in the state of Washington, he had been an altar boy for four years and, like Thompson, was humble about his actions at My Lai 4. He only did what was right, he later asserted, though he admitted that what he saw that day made it difficult to adjust to life afterward. His father had likewise provided a model, having joined the army and landed at Normandy Beach. When he died in 1964, his widow faced the challenge of raising four children, three girls and a boy. To ease the family's financial burden, Colburn dropped out of high school to join the army at seventeen but had to wait until he was eighteen before deploying to Vietnam in December 1967 as a helicopter gunner.[17]

Thompson and Colburn had not seen each other for more than two decades after My Lai when British journalist Michael Bilton brought them together in 1989. Bilton wanted to make a documentary film on My Lai, and Colburn, who lived outside Atlanta, expressed interest. After locating Thompson in Lafayette, Louisiana, Bilton convinced him to join Colburn in granting the interviews that became the basis of "Remember My Lai," the award-winning video directed by British film-maker Kevin Sim broadcasted on BBC-TV and then in the United States on *Frontline* on PBS-TV. Bilton and Sim then collaborated in writing the internationally acclaimed book that appeared in 1992, *Four Hours in My Lai*. In the meantime, Thompson and Colburn became close friends.[18]

Thompson never thought of himself as a hero, despite the accolades from Peers and many others. Peers asserted that Thompson "maintained his basic integrity in spite of everything that surrounded him. If there was a hero of My Lai, he was it." Eckhardt similarly praised Thompson's heroism.

"When you have evil, sometimes, in the midst of it, you will have incredible, selfless good. And that's Hugh Thompson." Eckhardt acknowledged that some soldiers refused to obey Calley's orders, but, he added, they did nothing to stop the killings. Colburn, however, came to their defense, maintaining that those soldiers did all they could under the circumstances. "We could just fly away at the end of the day," but they had to face each other for months.[19]

Thompson came under bitter criticism for his actions that abated only after the courts martial came to an end. When he walked into the officers' club, it was often to calls of "traitor," "communist," and "sympathizer." He received hate mail at his home in Louisiana, along with death threats over the phone at three in the morning and mutilated animals dumped on his doorstep. He said he was galled by the TV coverage of "rallies for Calley" that took place all over the country after the sentencing. How could I be "the bad guy," he once asked a reporter. "Has everyone gone mad?"[20]

Thompson thought My Lai was an aberration. "It can't happen all the time," he told Mike Wallace on *60 Minutes*. "I don't think that I could live with myself if I thought that was an everyday thing and I was part of it."[21]

David Egan, a veteran army officer and later professor of architecture at Clemson University, had been so moved by Bilton and Sim's documentary film that he began a letter-writing campaign that, with the aid of journalists, aimed at winning national recognition of the bravery of Thompson, Colburn, and the late Glenn Andreotta. The Pentagon had at first been reluctant to give awards to Thompson's two crew members, particularly in a public ceremony, but he insisted on both conditions and with public pressure got what he wanted.[22]

On March 6, 1998, the Pentagon awarded each of the three men (posthumously in Andreotta's case) the Soldier's Medal, the highest honor for valor bestowed on a soldier in a noncombat situation. The army had finally acknowledged that the awards it gave the three men in 1968 for heroism under enemy fire were erroneous, because no Viet Cong forces had been in My Lai on March 16, 1968. As the *Washington Post* put it, "The enemy was us."[23]

"We stand in honor of their heroism, and we have taken too long to recognize them," said the army chaplain, Major General Donald Shea, standing near the Vietnam Veterans Memorial in Washington. My Lai was "one of the most shameful chapters in the Army's history," declared the keynote speaker, Major General Michael Ackerman. "It was the ability to do the right thing even at the risk of their personal safety that guided these soldiers to do what they did." They "set the standard for all soldiers to follow."[24]

After accepting his medal, Thompson spoke. He thanked the army for the honor before saying, his voice trembling, "I would like to recognize all Vietnam veterans who are alive today—all across America and especially those who are on the wall right out to the left. I would like to thank all of them, who served their country with honor. In a very real sense this medal is for you." To his fellow veterans, he said, "Welcome home."

Colburn, for his part, declared it his "solemn wish that we all never forget the tragedy and brutality of war." He then quoted General Douglas MacArthur: "The soldier, be he friend or foe, is charged with the protection of the weak and the unarmed. It is the very essence and reason for his being."[25]

Following the ceremony, Thompson and Colburn walked to the black granite wall and, surrounded by the press, found Andreotta's name and used a pencil to trace the engraving onto a piece of paper to give to his mother.[26]

Over the years Thompson and Colburn participated in a number of My Lai events (including at the service academies) and gave talks, seminars, and presentations—all focusing on the importance of moral and ethical leadership in combat. Perhaps most rewarding, however, were their returns to My Lai. They received invitations to attend the commemoration of the thirtieth anniversary of the massacre in March 1998, where Vietnam veteran Michael Boehm played the mournful elegy "Ashokan Farewell" on his violin (as he had done every year since 1994) as "an offering to the spirits of dead at My Lai and for those still living at My Lai." Three years later they came back to dedicate a school and were reunited with Do Hoa, the young boy they rescued from the ditch in 1968. Colburn noted that Do Hoa "had to steal to feed himself" and spent four years in prison for petty crimes. But Boehm had helped the young man secure enough financial support to begin a new life and to become, by 2001, husband and father of a five-year-old son.[27]

For their efforts, Thompson was nominated for the Nobel Peace Prize in 2000, and a year later both he and Colburn were nominated for that award.[28]

Thompson did not accompany Colburn to the fortieth-anniversary proceedings at My Lai in 2008; he had died two years earlier—"morally wounded and despondent," according to Colburn, who was at his bedside. Soon after Thompson's death, Colburn received an increasing number of death threats, and more patrons than usual refused to do business with him in Atlanta.[29]

III

My Lai made it imperative that the army institute major changes in training aimed at developing what Eckhardt called "professional battlefield behavior."

Soldiers are trained to kill in defense of their country and must know when to use force and how much. "Ill discipline loses wars."[30]

To understand the importance of restraint in combat, soldiers and officers must learn to disobey illegal orders. The only way to bring this about, Eckhardt insisted, was "to plainly state that the intentional killing without justification of noncombatants—old men, women, children, and babies—is murder and is illegal." No one prior to My Lai had considered it necessary to teach U.S. soldiers something so "obvious"; My Lai had made the obvious necessary. Judge Reid Kennedy made clear in Lieutenant Calley's trial that no soldier could escape responsibility for following an order that a person of "ordinary sense and understanding" should know was illegal. In the U.S. Court of Military Appeals, Associate Judge Robert E. Quinn affirmed that argument, adding that it did not matter whether Calley knew the order was illegal; he had no defense for his actions.[31]

After My Lai the army felt compelled to implement reforms aimed at building a more professional military service. It produced television ads exalting work training and educational programs that better prepared soldiers for their post-army life. It improved the screening of incoming soldiers in an effort to develop an "Army of character" rather than one of castoffs or misfits. It raised the training level of both officers and enlisted personnel by emphasizing moral and ethical behavior in all situations. And it demanded strict enforcement of rules and regulations embodying what William Hays Parks called the "principle of restraint" embodied in the law of war.[32]

To its credit, the army immediately addressed the problems My Lai had exposed. It revised and expanded policy directives regarding several key issues: the reporting of war crimes; the proper treatment of civilians, noncombatants, and prisoners of war; the protection of property; the adherence to the rules of engagement; and the enforcement of the Geneva and Hague Conventions as integral parts of the law of war. It also improved the management and maintenance of file records, ensured that all photos taken by the army's photographers became its property (which, if in effect in 1968, would have kept Haeberle's photos from becoming public in 1969), called for clarification of colors in using smoke canisters to mark locations, and placed first sergeants in the field to be closer to the men and raise morale.[33]

The army also stopped using "search and destroy" in describing military operations and employed the more innocuous term "search and clear." Lieutenant General Peers thought the move wise, noting that both commanders and soldiers had sometimes misunderstood search and destroy to mean more than "seeking out and destroying enemy forces, installations, resources, and base areas"; the loosely defined term led to the killing of civilians and the destruction of their settlements and basic foodstuffs. Search and clear imposed restrictions on U.S. forces by specifically authorizing them "to clear an area permanently of organized VC/NVA main forces, including the provincial battalions, in order to eliminate the immediate enemy threat."[34]

By the mid-1970s the army had come closer to becoming a professional organization. The draft had ended in 1973, although those eligible to serve still had to register with the Selective Service System in the event of a need to revive conscription. The following year, the Department of Defense instituted the Law of War Program, which held the commander responsible for enforcing its principles, and it established training standards and educational requirements commensurate with the soldier's responsibility and position. In 1976, the army revised its field manual *Law of Land Warfare* to better protect civilians in an embattled area by specifically prohibiting the bombardment of undefended towns, villages, dwellings, or buildings; attacks on civilians, whether individual or in groups; and unnecessary killing and damage to property.[35]

The army appeared to have put My Lai in the past by the time of its first real post-Vietnam test in January 1991. Before launching Operation Desert Storm in the Gulf War, the First Armored Division commander, Major General Ronald Griffith, warned his brigade commanders: "No My Lais in this division—Do you hear me?"[36]

Two years later, in 1993, the army incorporated almost verbatim the "Nine Marine Corps Principles" into *The Soldier's Rules by the Army*. These principles held, among other things, that soldiers are not to engage noncombatants or harm those who surrender and become prisoners. They must care for all wounded, and they cannot interfere with medical workers or damage their equipment, nor can they steal or needlessly destroy property. They must treat civilians in a humanitarian way, and they must report violations.[37]

These principles were already set out in the Geneva Convention, Parks asserted, but the army wanted to make them more specific and then teach, follow, and enforce them. To prevent more My Lais, commanders must repeatedly emphasize to their military forces why they are in combat and the importance of distinguishing between "unarmed civilians, noncombatants, and those people who were, in fact, shooting at us." If the army intended to take the "moral high ground," it must develop officers and enlisted personnel with character, discipline, and an understanding of combat ethics.[38]

Lieutenant Calley, Parks declared, personified the two major problems in the army at that time: he was a poor soldier and a poor leader. He "didn't deserve to be in the United States military, much less to be an officer."[39]

To emphasize the importance of doing what was right, the army has inserted a copy of Hugh Thompson's Soldier's Award into its field manual, highlighted in a boxed quote under the heading "W01 Thompson at My Lai."[40]

Despite the army's efforts, atrocities have not become a thing of the past. Of those committed after My Lai, perhaps the best-known took place at Abu Ghraib, the American prison located twenty miles west of Baghdad, during the Iraq War. Abu Ghraib was the scene of torture, beatings, rape, degradation and humiliation, and murder—all of which happened over the course of three years, confirmed by photographs. It has been estimated but not confirmed that more than five hundred detainees (most of them civilians) died in American hands. Seymour Hersh, still tireless in his efforts to expose wrongdoing, wrote that few of the perpetrators—military police and intelligence agents—had been in combat; one could not attribute their behavior to battlefield stress.[41]

In the years since Abu Ghraib, which was perhaps the worst public relations scandal the American military had endured since My Lai, it has tried to institute further reforms.

In June 2015, after nearly two decades of work, the Department of Defense completed the updating and expansion of the U.S. Army's Field Manual 27-10 and released it as the *Department of Defense Law of War Manual*. More than 1,200 pages in length, the volume covers a multitude of issues, including attempts to correct the flaws that helped lead to the events of March 16, 1968.[42]

The echoes of My Lai (and Abu Ghraib) are unmistakable. All members of the armed services must "refuse to comply with clearly illegal orders" that violate the law of war—particularly those "orders to kill defenseless persons" who are "under effective physical control." Commands, orders, and speeches should never be "understood" as implicit authorization to violate the law of war. The commander's responsibility is to prevent his subordinates from violating the law of war. The new field manual reiterated the "grave breaches" enumerated in the Geneva Convention of 1949, the war crimes defined in MACV Directive 20-4, and the penalties set out in the Uniform Code of Military Justice. It emphasized the importance of reporting "possible, suspected, or alleged violations of the law of war," followed by a thorough investigation. And it repeated the central thrust of the War Powers Act of 1996 by declaring war crimes committed outside the United States triable and punishable under federal statutes.[43]

After Abu Ghraib, the army continued its efforts to protect noncombatants in wartime. In 2016 Congress passed the Law of Armed Conflict, which specifically confined combat engagements to military targets. Yet the continuation of atrocities in the post–My Lai era strongly suggests that the central problem in improving the army's treatment of civilians lies less in writing new laws and regulations than in having officers who enforce those already in effect.[44]

IV

Can we, fifty years later, prevent future atrocities by reaching a better understanding of what caused the massacre at My Lai? Were there any warning signs?

Just five years before My Lai, Hannah Arendt famously reflected upon the seemingly law-abiding and morally sound German citizens who followed Nazi leader Adolf Eichmann's bidding to execute millions of Jewish people. As a top officer in the SS (*Schutzstaffel*, the paramilitary security service), Eichmann was a major architect of the Holocaust, in charge of deporting Jews to ghettos and extermination camps in Eastern Europe. He had fled Germany after the war, settling in Argentina and living there under an assumed name until he was found in 1960 by Mossad, the Israeli intelligence organization, and taken to Jerusalem for trial in the civil courts. "The trouble with Eichmann," Arendt wrote after covering his 1961 trial for the *New Yorker*, "was precisely that so many were like him, and that the many were neither perverted nor sadistic, that they were, and still are, terribly and terrifyingly normal." And deeply chilling was her implication that it could happen again. "The sad truth of the matter is that most evil is done by people who never made up their minds to be or do either evil or good."[45]

This "normality," Arendt noted, "was much more terrifying than all the atrocities put together."[46]

German philosopher Bettina Stangneth has recently questioned Arendt's argument about Eichmann's "banality" by insisting it was a ruse aimed at preventing his execution. According to Stangneth, he pretended to be an innocent bureaucrat who had followed orders and yet felt "indispensable" because of his "exclusive" knowledge of the murderous program. In his private notes and taped interviews after 1945, he proved himself to be a fanatically driven National Socialist, proud of his role in the Holocaust.[47] Yet Stangneth's revelations, even if accurate, do not refute Arendt's point that banal behavior is not a guarantee against the commission of atrocities.

Historian Christopher Browning agrees with Arendt and argues that German perpetrators of the Holocaust went beyond those in the Eichmann circle: They were primarily "ordinary men," which makes it difficult to detect reliable early warning signs of genocidal behavior. His examination of a reserve police battalion in Poland involved in the Holocaust shows it was composed of normal human beings thrown into a situation conducive to committing atrocities. In an assessment that reminds one of My Lai, he found varying types of participants: those who willingly killed; those who followed orders out of a sense of duty or to protect their careers; and those who refused to kill. Yet from his study of these "ordinary men" came the realization that a person could not escape responsibility by claiming that others would have acted the same under similar conditions. They had choices. In a statement similar to that made by Harry Stanley of Charlie Company, Browning argues, "Human responsibility is ultimately an individual matter." Under intense peer pressure, who can say what any person will or will not do?[48]

Like Arendt and Browning, human rights specialist James Dawes asserts that so-called monsters are mainly "ordinary people" who do not suddenly become killers. Remorseless killing by "evil men" requires transforming them into automatons who do not realize what they are doing. Drill sergeants must teach impressionable young soldiers the skills for eliminating all threats in a binary world of good and evil. To do this, they blind the new soldiers to the world's ambiguities, erase their identity by keeping them within their own special group to promote similarity of purpose, demand unquestioned obedience to authority, stereotype the enemy as subhuman, and rely on violence as an energizing force in an escalatory process in which killing becomes less difficult with repetition.[49]

A number of people have drawn comparisons between Americans killing Vietnamese civilians and Nazis executing Jewish civilians. The Nazi firing squads avoided eye contact and blood spattering on them by shooting their victims in the back of their heads so they would fall forward into the freshly dug graves; Thompson asserted that GIs wielding M-16s and M-60 machine guns could not look into their captives' eyes and told them to turn around toward the ditch before shooting them. One young Nazi soldier noted that he and the others shot women and children to prevent them from seeking revenge later; Calley ordered the killing of women and children for the same reason. A young SS officer explained that any words suggesting execution were "completely banal and devoid of meaning once one has gotten used to them"; Varnado Simpson, a teenager in 1968, recalled that after he had shot his first victim at My Lai, the killings became easier.[50]

My Lai demonstrated with graphic clarity that U.S. soldiers are as capable of war crimes as anyone under the right circumstances. The improvements made by the army in the years since are an important step in the right direction, but they have not eliminated the problem. Ultimately, there has been no accountability and no real means to achieve it.

Historian Roger Spiller once declared that "the most frightening lesson" he learned from military history is that it is not only psychopaths who commit heinous crimes; even "ordinary" people can do the same in the right situation. "We are all," he said, "one step away from My Lai."[51]

V

My Lai was a turning point for so many reasons, not least for the ways in which it tarnished the image many Americans had of their soldiers, and that the soldiers had of themselves. Veterans came home expecting to receive a warm welcome but instead encountered widespread and vicious criticism of their actions in Vietnam.

More than a few veterans felt that Calley had cast a dark shadow over the military. Perhaps the most outspoken critic was Harry G. Summers, a retired colonel in the U.S. Army, veteran of the Korean and Vietnam Wars, and bestselling author of books on military strategy. At a 1994 conference on My Lai at Tulane University, he told the audience, "Calley and Medina ought to have been hung and then drawn and quartered and the remains put at the gates at Fort Benning to remind all who enter of the consequences. The bastard fell through the cracks." In a television interview, David Hackworth agreed with this position. Calley "should have been lined up against the wall and shot.... The guy's a murderer."[52]

"Only crime and the criminal," remarked Arendt, "confront us with the perplexity of radical evil; but only the hypocrite is really rotten to the core."[53] Both Schiel and Simpson came to realize what they had done, felt intense guilt, expressed remorse, and, in their way, atoned. Calley has provided no indication of any of these changes in attitude and will likely take his reasons and his feelings to his grave.

In the mid-1990s Tim O'Brien publicly declared at that same Tulane conference attended by Summers that military authorities today should prosecute both the perpetrators of the war crimes at My Lai and those who covered them up. Calley should have remained in jail all his life. He was no scapegoat; he committed the crimes—as did the others in Charlie Company who followed his orders and, like him, publicly admitted to the killings. O'Brien's comment echoed what Lieutenant General Peers had said fifteen years earlier: "There is no statute of limitations for war crimes."[54]

Nothing today could ease the pain of what happened at My Lai, but it is crucial that we do not allow this tragedy to slip from memory. Two instances out of many remind us of the importance of remembering how the events of that day had a lasting, deeply personal impact on both Americans and Vietnamese.

Varnado Simpson was one of numerous veterans who remained haunted by what he did at My Lai. "I just lost all sense of direction, of purpose. I just started killing in any kind of way I could kill. It just came, I didn't know I had it in me, but like I say after I killed the child my whole mind just went, it just went."[55]

Two decades after My Lai, in his hometown of Jackson, Mississippi, Simpson sat before a table covered with pill bottles as he told the story of his ten-year-old son, his photo in a frame nearby. The boy was playing in his grandmother's front yard when two boys about fourteen years old got into an argument across the street. One ran home to get a gun; the other one ran for safety—near the spot where Simpson's son was playing. The first teenager returned with the gun and fired at the other teenager but accidentally shot the child in the head. "I was in the house and I came out and picked him up," Simpson remembered, "but he died in my arms. And when I looked at him, his face looked like the same face of a child that I had killed and I said, 'This is the punishment for me killing the people that I killed.' "[56]

When asked if this self-torture would ever end, Simpson replied, "Yeah, when I kill myself, yeah, it'll come to an end. Like I said, I tried suicide three times."[57]

Simpson succeeded on his fourth attempt—this one in May 1997, at the age of forty-eight.

Truong Thi Le's life likewise changed that day in My Lai. She was having breakfast with her young son, daughter, and eight other family members, when they were ordered outside by American soldiers and taken to a group of other villagers squatting or sitting on the main trail into the village. Suddenly two soldiers raised their rifles and fired into the throng of men, women, and children. Le dropped to the ground to cover her six-year-old son. "Don't cry," she whispered as two bodies fell on them, shielding them from the gunfire. "The Americans have shot everyone. Don't cry—and see if we can survive." Le cupped her hand over the boy's mouth and lifted her head to see soldiers pointing here and there while shooting those still alive. In the silence that followed the last shot, she could hear the clicks of a camera as someone took pictures of the scene.

After the soldiers left, Le broke down in tears as she scratched and clawed among the bodies, finally finding one of her infant nephews unhurt and, with her son, took them off the trail and fled through the rice paddies to a secure area west of the village. The next day she returned to My Lai 4, where she found her home burned to the ground and all her other relatives dead—nine family members, including her father, mother, and daughter. She never saw her husband again after he left for work in the rice fields the previous morning.

More than two decades later, Le was living alone, unable to erase that day from her mind. "I think of it all the time, and that is why I am old before my time. I remember it all the time. I think about it and I can't sleep.... I hate [the Americans] very much. I won't forgive them as long as I live."[58]

We are left with the question: Why the massacre at My Lai?

In truth, there is no definitive answer because no one can reliably predict human behavior in any situation, and particularly in the stress of war.

Tim O'Brien's unit operated in the same area as Charlie Company and experienced the same trials and fears but acted differently. Each village in Pinkville was a source of terror to young American soldiers. They all individually felt rage and frustration and abject fear because of land mines and booby traps against which they could not fight, yet knowing that their next step, their next breath, could be their last. Despite all this, why didn't his unit take revenge against defenseless civilians? O'Brien's reply: *He did not know.*[59]

Despite all the reforms by the army, there are no assurances against the commission of atrocities in either combat or non-combat situations—the latter demonstrated by Abu Ghraib. What is perhaps most disturbing about My Lai is not that it stands out in the annals of wartime atrocities in the American experience, but that the factors and elements that converged there in March 1968 have converged in all wars: debilitating panic, dehumanizing rage, dissociative confusion, the heady sense of power over life and death. Other soldiers in wars before and since have experienced the cauldron of primal yet complex emotions produced by combat. They have also sometimes been badly trained and poorly led, and therefore unprepared to channel those emotions. The GIs in Charlie Company were not much different from the young men who have fought in every war. Indeed, the line between My Lai and the thousands of other operations in Vietnam in which what happened at My Lai did *not* happen seems nearly arbitrary.

But My Lai forces us to see that the line cannot be arbitrary. We have to accept that there remains a crucial difference between William Calley and Hugh Thompson. Perhaps this difference involves "character"—however we define it. I would suggest it embodies a notion of decency that was most noticeably missing at My Lai. Thompson, Lawrence Colburn, and Glenn Andreotta leave us room for hope because, unlike Calley (and others), they did not lose sight of ordinary human decency. And that, in the end, is a form of heroism.

Notes

Front Matter

1. See "Nation Remembers My Lai Massacre," *Viet Nam News*, March 17, 2008, http://vietnamnews.vn/society/174741/nation-remembers-my-lai-massacre.html.
2. For the song, see: https://www.youtube.com/watch?v=z08YYG6WJI0&index=3&list=PL7B34E3CEDEE1D4F2.

Prologue

1. See the reference to "My Lai massacre" in a Vietnamese newspaper: "Nation Remembers My Lai Massacre," *Viet Nam News*, March 17, 2008.
2. See Peers Report, 2–3, 2–4, 2–7, 2–8, 12–1. Vietnamese testimonies from My Lai 4, Binh Tay, and Binh Dong to the U.S. Army's Criminal Investigation Division (CID) investigating team provide an estimate of 163 dead in My Lai 4, including sixty-eight children. But other deaths went unaccounted for in these testimonies, driving the figures much higher than those cited above. CID Reports, Sept. 10, 25, 1970. These reports also show that in My Lai's aftermath, many of the orphaned children either struggled on their own in the countryside, moved into the homes of friends or relatives, or found shelter in barbed wire refugee camps located outside My Lai 4 and close to the mounds marking the graves of their families and friends.
3. For the discovery of the My Lai Tapes, see Celina Dunlop, "My Lai: Legacy of a Massacre," *BBC News*, March 15, 2008, http://news.bbc.co.uk/go/pr/fr/-/2/hi/asia-pacific/7298533.stm. She is the picture editor of the *Economist*.

One

1. Remarks by Zais, May 13, 1970, Hébert Hearings, 780.
2. Michal R. Belknap, *The Vietnam War on Trial: The My Lai Massacre and the Court-Martial of Lieutenant Calley* (Lawrence: University Press of Kansas, 2002), 60.
3. Ibid., 34–35, 37–38, 54, 60; Bilton and Sim, *Four Hours in My Lai*, 52, 56; James S. Olson and Randy Roberts, eds., *My Lai: A Brief History with Documents* (Boston: Bedford, 1998), 13; author's interview of Earl Tilford, historian and former Air Force Intelligence

officer in Vietnam, April 5, 2015. The estimated number of residents in My Lai 4 comes from Calley testimony to Colonel Norman Stanfield, Office of Inspector General, June 9, 1969, p. 579, My Lai Collection (VATTU).

4. Bilton and Sim, *Four Hours in My Lai*, 52; Belknap, *Vietnam War on Trial*, 38; Medina testimony, March 10, 1971, Calley court-martial transcript, 4597–98, 4601–2 (NA).

5. Bilton and Sim, *Four Hours in My Lai*, 49–50; Richard Hammer, *The Court-Martial of Lieutenant Calley* (New York: Coward, McCann and Geoghegan, 1971), 55; Calley testimony, Feb. 22, 1971, Calley court-martial transcript, 3762 (NA); Jules Loh, "Average Guy Calley Found Niche in Army," *Pacific Stars and Stripes*, Dec. 1, 1969, My Lai Collection (VATTU). For more details on Calley, see two articles by Philip Beidler: "Calley's Ghost," *Virginia Quarterly Review* 79 (Winter 2003): 30–50, and "Fort Morality," *Military History*, 23 (Dec. 2006): 56–61, as well as Arthur Everett, Kathryn Johnson, and Harry F. Rosenthal, *Calley* (New York: Dell, 1971), and Tom Tiede, *Calley: Soldier or Killer?* (New York: Pinnacle, 1971).

6. Calley's testimony, Feb. 22, 1971, Calley court-martial transcript, 3764 (NA); Belknap, *Vietnam War on Trial*, 30–31; Sack, *Calley*, 24; Bilton and Sim, *Four Hours in My Lai*, 50; Hammer, *Court-Martial of Lt. Calley*, 58–59. Calley's fear of the draft is explained in Douglas Robinson, "Murder Trial Set for Army Officer in Village Deaths," *New York Times*, Nov. 25, 1969. Calley was tone-deaf.

7. Sack, *Calley*, 25; Bilton and Sim, *Four Hours in My Lai*, 50; Belknap, *Vietnam War on Trial*, 33–34; Hammer, *Court-Martial of Lt. Calley*, 59 (commanding officer's quote); author's interview of Tilford, April 5, 2015.

8. Sack, *Calley*, 27.

9. Ibid.

10. Ibid., 27–28.

11. Ibid., 28.

12. Testimony of David Crane, Feb. 17, 1971, Calley court-martial transcript, 3462, 3769–70 (NA); Bilton and Sim, *Four Hours in My Lai*, 37, 50, 53–54; Belknap, *Vietnam War on Trial*, 42. Calley lied to the court during his trial in February 1971 when he claimed to have graduated from OCS near the top of his class. Calley testimony, Feb. 22, 1971, Calley court-martial transcript, 3768 (NA).

13. Sack, *Calley*, 29.

14. Peers Report, 4–8; Bacon testimony, Dec. 16, 1969, Peers Inquiry, 2: Testimony, book 24, pp. 56, 58 (LC).

15. Medina testimony to Col. William V. Wilson (IG), May 13, 1969, Box 1, Folder 6, pp. 255–56, My Lai Collection (VATTU); Medina testimony, Dec. 4, 1969, Peers Inquiry, 2: Testimony, book 23, pp. 73–77 (LC).

16. Leon Friedman, ed., *The Law of War: A Documentary History*, 2 vols. (New York: Random House, 1972), 1:314, 318–19; Hague Convention of 1907: Laws of War: Laws and Customs of War on Land, Hague 4 (Oct. 18, 1907), Annex to the Convention: Regulations Respecting the Laws and Customs of War on Land, in *The Avalon Project: Documents in Law, History and Diplomacy, Yale Law School*, http://avalon.law.yale.edu/20th_century/hague04.asp#art4.

17. "Principles of International Law Recognized in the Charter of the Nuremberg Tribunal and in the Judgment of the Tribunal" (1950), available online at http://deoxy.org/wc-nurem.htm. The Nuremberg Tribunal tried twenty-three military and political leaders

of the Third Reich of Germany for war crimes in the Second World War. Article 8 of the charter declared: "The fact that the defendant acted pursuant to order of his Government or of a superior shall not free him from responsibility, but may be considered in mitigating of punishment." Thus, as the tribunal indicated, "The true test, which is found in varying degrees in the criminal law of most nations, is not the existence of the order, but whether moral choice was in fact possible." Friedman, *Law of War*, 2:940.

18. Friedman, *Law of War*, 1:526.
19. U.S. Army Field Manual (FM27-10), *The Law of Land Warfare* (Washington, DC: Dept. of the Army, 1956), 3–4, 178. In the United States, the codified international rules governing a soldier's conduct in the field derived from the War Department's "General Orders No. 100," prepared at President Abraham Lincoln's direction during the Civil War by Francis Lieber of Columbia College in New York in April 1863. The War Department released a revised version in pamphlet form in April 1914, which became the basis for the 1940 edition mentioned in the text. See William F. Fratcher, "The Law of Land Warfare," *Missouri Law Review* 22 (April 1957): 143–61.
20. Michael L. Schmidt, "Yamashita, Medina, and Beyond: Command Responsibility in Contemporary Military Operations," *Military Law Review* 164 (2000): 180–81, 186. See *In re Yamashita*, 327 U.S. 1 (1946).
21. Schmidt, "Yamashita, Medina, and Beyond," 168–69; William H. Parks, "Command Responsibility for War Crimes," *Military Law Review* 62 (1973): 35–37, 81, 87–90, 97–98.
22. Schmidt, "Yamashita, Medina, and Beyond," 178–79, 182.
23. Ibid., 182–83.
24. Peers Inquiry, 3: book 2, Directives, Exhibit M-8, Force Order 5820.1 from Commanding General to Distribution List, June 3, 1967, War Crimes Investigation (LC).
25. Sack, *Calley*, 28; testimony of Wilbur Hamman (psychiatrist), Feb. 17, 1971, Calley court-martial transcript, 3675–76, 3678–79 (NA); Calley testimony, Feb. 22, 1971, Calley court-martial transcript, 3771 (NA).
26. Sack, *Calley*, 28.
27. Philip Caputo, *A Rumor of War* (New York: Holt, Rinehart and Winston, 1977), xviii.
28. Ibid., xvi.
29. Belknap, *Vietnam War on Trial*, 44; Sack, *Calley*, 55.
30. Caputo, *Rumor of War*, xviii, 57, 60, 147; Bilton and Sim, *Four Hours in My Lai*, 39; Belknap, *Vietnam War on Trial*, 43–44, 46; author's interview of Fleming, Aug. 12, 2011; Fleming quoted in Unger, "Calley," 1.
31. Bilton and Sim, *Four Hours in My Lai*, 50; Belknap, *Vietnam War on Trial*, 35–36.
32. Bilton and Sim, *Four Hours in My Lai*, 53; Sack, *Calley*, 27. Charlie Company had the distinction of being part of the historic 1st Battalion, 20th Infantry, which traced its origins to the American Civil War and had just been reactivated at Schofield Barracks in Hawaii because of the escalating war in Vietnam. Bilton and Sim, *Four Hours in My Lai*, 51.
33. Bilton and Sim, *Four Hours in My Lai*, 50–51; Peers Report, 4–9; William R. Peers, *The My Lai Inquiry* (New York: W. W. Norton, 1979), 287–89; Kimberley L. Phillips, *War! What Is It Good For? Black Freedom Struggles and the U.S. Military from World War II to Iraq* (Chapel Hill: University of North Carolina Press, 2012), 202–5, 220–21; Widmer quoted in Barak Goodman, dir., "My Lai," *American Experience*, PBS-TV, April 26, 2010, transcript, http://www.pbs.org/wgbh/americanexperience/features/transcript/mylai-transcript/; Belknap, *Vietnam War on Trial*, 40; Seymour

M. Hersh, *My Lai 4: A Report on the Massacre and Its Aftermath* (New York: Random House, 1970), 21.

34. Peers, *My Lai Inquiry*, 34.

35. Belknap, *Vietnam War on Trial*, 49; Sack, *Calley*, 30; Medina's characterization of Calley in Bilton and Sim, *Four Hours in My Lai*, 74.

36. Stories told by Calley in Sack, *Calley*, 40, 42, 44–45.

37. Ibid., 29–30.

38. Maples and Wood quoted in Hersh, *My Lai 4*, 21; Hall quoted ibid., 20; "nice guy" quote in Peers Report, 8–10. SP4 is an abbreviation for specialist fourth class and equivalent to a corporal. Linda Reinberg, *In the Field: The Language of the Vietnam War* (New York: Facts on File, 1991), 205.

39. Bernhardt interview in Christian G. Appy, *Patriots: The Vietnam War Remembered from All Sides* (New York: Penguin, 2003), 350; Shelby L. Stanton, *The Rise and Fall of an American Army: U.S. Ground Forces in Vietnam, 1965–1973* (Novato, CA: Presidio, 1985), 272.

40. Bernhardt interview in Appy, *Patriots*, 351.

41. Peers Report, 4–1; Thomas E. Ricks, *The Generals: American Military Command from World War II to Today* (New York: Penguin, 2012), 295; Stanton, *Rise and Fall of American Army*, 191, 195; Harry G. Summers, Jr., *Vietnam War Almanac* (New York: Facts on File, 1985), 77. New Caledonia served as a base for the Americal Division in the Guadalcanal campaign. Writer Tim O'Brien was a veteran of the Americal Division who explained its organization. See his account in *Going After Cacciato* (New York: Delacorte, 1978), 58–59.

42. Bernhardt interview in Appy, *Patriots*, 350; Hersh, *Cover-Up*, 29; Bilton and Sim, *Four Hours in My Lai*, 63; Ricks, *Generals*, 331; Stanton, *Rise and Fall of American Army*, 271–72, 359–60; Summers, *Vietnam War Almanac*, 78.

43. Loren Baritz, *Backfire: A History of How American Culture Led Us into Vietnam and Made Us Fight the Way We Did* (New York: Ballantine, 1985), 288–89; author's interview of Tilford, April 5, 2015.

44. Ricks, *Generals*, 295; Palmer quoted ibid., 296.

45. Bilton and Sim, *Four Hours in My Lai*, 58; Olson and Roberts, eds., *My Lai*, 9.

46. For the destruction at Quang Ngai, see Jonathan Schell, *The Military Half: An Account of Destruction in Quang Ngai and Quang Tin* (New York: Alfred A. Knopf, 1968).

47. For the Viet Cong's fear of the jungle, see Evan V. Symon and Nguyen Hoa Giai, "8 Things Vietnam War Movies Leave Out (By an Enemy Soldier)," *Cracked*, March 27, 2015, http://www.cracked.com/personal-experiences-1562-8-facts-about-vietnam-war-i-learned-as-viet-cong.html. See no. 7: "We Were Just as Scared of the Jungle as the Americans Were." For Tran Hung Dao, see Ellen Hammer, *Vietnam: Yesterday and Today* (New York: Holt, Rinehart and Winston, 1966), 43, 72–73, and Stanley Karnow, *Vietnam: A History* (New York: Penguin 2nd ed., 1997), 113, 115.

48. Bilton and Sim, *Four Hours in My Lai*, 59–60; Texas soldier's quote ibid., 60; Olson and Roberts, eds., *My Lai*, 8–9. One of the early references to collateral damage came in May 1961, when T. C. Schelling used the term in a general discussion of whether the United States should store its strategic weapons in cities and risk a Russian assault that would unintentionally kill a large number of noncombatants. The entire matter hinged on where the U.S. military dispersed its Strategic Air Command bombers. Would the Russians bear moral responsibility for collateral damage during a military operation against what they considered to be a legitimate target? See Schelling, "Dispersal, Deterrence, and Damage," *Operations Research* 9, no. 3 (May–June 1961): 363–70.

49. Medina quoted in Bilton and Sim, *Four Hours in My Lai*, 61; Sack, *Calley*, 73.

50. Sack, *Calley*, 31–32.

51. Ibid., 32; Bilton and Sim, *Four Hours in My Lai*, 62.

52. Sack, *Calley*, 33–34.

53. Ibid., 39–40.

54. Belknap, *Vietnam War on Trial*, 51–52; Bilton and Sim, *Four Hours in My Lai*, 65; Oral Deposition by Nguyen Duc Te, Dec. 8, 1970, Box 1, Folder 43, pp. 1–7, My Lai Collection (VATTU). Te claimed to have eighteen agents working in his office and another three hundred in the village. They lived in government-controlled areas, although he insisted that he had secret agents in the Viet Cong–controlled sectors as well.

55. Transcript, William E. Colby (former head of Phoenix Program and CIA), Oral History Interview 2 by Ted Gettinger, June 2, 1982, p. 6 (LBJL); John Prados, *Vietnam: The History of an Unwinnable War, 1945–1975* (Lawrence: University Press of Kansas, 2009), 327–28; Bilton and Sim, *Four Hours in My Lai*, 88. The interrogators wanted to see the blacklist, but there was no record of what happened. Te Deposition, Dec. 8, 1970, Box 1, Folder 43, pp. 10–13, My Lai Collection (VATTU).

56. Deposition by Ta Linh Vien, Dec. 8, 1970, Box 1, Folder 45, pp. 1–4, My Lai Collection (VATTU).

57. Ibid., 5–6, 8, 11, 14.

58. Ibid., 6–7, 14.

59. Kotouc testimony, Dec. 6, 1969, Peers Inquiry, 2: Testimony, book 16, p. 9 (LC); Testimony of Fred Widmer to Wilson (IG), July 15, 1969, Box 1, Folder 20, p. 997, My Lai Collection (VATTU); Testimony of William F. Doherty to Wilson (IG), May 5, 1969, Box 1, Folder 3, p. 149, My Lai Collection (VATTU).

60. Peers Report, 4–6, 4–7; Belknap, *Vietnam War on Trial*, 51; Testimony of Major Charles C. Calhoun to Wilson (IG), May 19, 1969, Box 1, Folder 8, pp. 308–9, My Lai Collection (VATTU); Bilton and Sim, *Four Hours in My Lai*, 65; Olson and Roberts, *My Lai*, 14; Sack, *Calley*, 50–51.

61. Wayne Greenhaw, *The Making of a Hero: The Story of Lt. William Calley Jr.* (Louisville, KY: Touchstone, 1971), 19–20.

62. Ibid., 20; Sack, *Calley*, 126.

63. Sack, *Calley*, 126; Greenhaw, *Making of Hero*, 20.

64. Greenhaw, *Making of Hero*, 20–21. Santellana never had the chance for revenge. Before the assault on My Lai 4, he went back to his home in Texas after the death of a family member and did not return to Vietnam. Ibid., 21.

65. For Tet and its aftermath, see William T. Allison, *The Tet Offensive: A Brief History with Documents* (New York: Routledge, 2008); Don Oberdorfer, *Tet* (New York: Doubleday, 1971); David F. Schmitz, *The Tet Offensive: Politics, War, and Public Opinion* (Lanham, MD: Rowman and Littlefield, 2005); and Ronald H. Spector, *After Tet: The Bloodiest Year in Vietnam* (New York: Free Press, 1993).

Two

1. Sack, *Calley*, 52, 54; Calley testimony, Feb. 22, 1971, Calley court-martial transcript, 3781 (NA); William T. Allison, *My Lai: An American Atrocity in the Vietnam War* (Baltimore: Johns Hopkins University Press, 2012), 25; Belknap, *Vietnam War on Trial*, 54; Bilton and Sim, *Four Hours in My Lai*, 71–72.

2. Calhoun testimony to Wilson (IG), May 19, 1969, Box 1, Folder 8, p. 311, My Lai Collection (VATTU).

3. Peers Report, 4–11, 4–12; testimony of Cecil Hall, chief of brigade radio and wire communications, April 15, 1970, Hébert Hearings, 22–25; testimony of Captain Patrick Trinkle of Alpha Company, April 15, 1970, Hébert Hearings,, 4–8; Sack, *Calley*, 80; Calhoun testimony to Wilson (IG), May 19, 1969, Box 1, Folder 8, pp. 310–11, My Lai Collection (VATTU); Bilton and Sim, *Four Hours in My Lai*, 72–73.

4. Testimony of Sergeant Lawrence LaCroix to Wilson (IG), May 2, 1969, Box 1, Folder 2, pp. 72–73, My Lai Collection (VATTU).

5. Trinkle testimony, April 15, 1970, Hébert Hearings, 8–10, 14, 18.

6. Calhoun testimony to Wilson (IG), May 19, 1969, Box 1, Folder 8, p. 312, My Lai Collection (VATTU).

7. Bilton and Sim, *Four Hours in My Lai*, 73–74; Belknap, *Vietnam War on Trial*, 88; Smail testimony, Jan. 6, 1970, Peers Inquiry, 2: Testimony, book 27, p. 42 (LC).

8. Ron Milam, *Not a Gentleman's War: An Inside View of Junior Officers in the Vietnam War* (Chapel Hill: University of North Carolina Press, 2009), 157–61; Guenter Lewy, *America in Vietnam* (New York: Oxford University Press, 1978), 155; Bilton and Sim, *Four Hours in My Lai*, 73; Belknap, *Vietnam War on Trial*, 88; George C. Herring, *America's Longest War: The United States and Vietnam, 1950–1975*, 4th ed. (New York: McGraw-Hill, 2002), 301; Robert D. Schulzinger, *A Time for War: The United States and Vietnam, 1941–1975* (New York: Oxford University Press, 1997), 279; Smail testimony, Jan. 6, 1970, Peers Inquiry, 2: Testimony, book 27, p. 13 (LC).

9. Peers, *My Lai Inquiry*, 39; PFC Louis Martin (artillery RTO) testimony, Dec. 27, 1969, Peers Inquiry, 2: Testimony, book 23, pp. 3–4 (LC); Bilton and Sim, *Four Hours in My Lai*, 74.

10. Peers Report, 4–12.

11. Medina testimony, March 10, 1971, Calley court-martial transcript, 4612–13 (NA).

12. Bilton and Sim, *Four Hours in My Lai*, 85; Bernhardt quoted in interview with Bilton, Nov. 7, 1988, Papers of *Four Hours in My Lai*, LHCMA (KCL).

13. Calhoun testimony to Wilson (IG), May 19, 1969, Box 1, Folder 8, p. 312, My Lai Collection (VATTU); Calley testimony, Feb. 22, 1971, Calley court-martial transcript, 3785 (NA); Sack, *Calley*, 64–66, 69–70; "Who Is Responsible for My Lai?," *Time*, March 8, 1971, p. 18.

14. Sack, *Calley*, 70.

15. Bilton and Sim, *Four Hours in My Lai*, 85.

16. Belknap, *Vietnam War on Trial*, 55; Sack, *Calley*, 72–73.

17. Sack, *Calley*, 57.

18. Ibid., 46, 61.

19. Ibid., 79–80.

20. Ibid., 84.

21. Medina testimony to Wilson (IG), May 13, 1969, Box 1, Folder 6, p. 249, My Lai Collection (VATTU).

22. Ibid.; Calhoun testimony to Wilson (IG), May 19, 1969, Box 1, Folder 8, p. 312, My Lai Collection (VATTU); Peers Report, 3–1, 3–2, 3–4, 5–1; Bilton and Sim, *Four Hours in My Lai*, 65.

23. Calley quoted in Sack, *Calley*, 87; Bilton and Sim, *Four Hours in My Lai*, 92.

24. Medina testimony, March 10, 1971, Calley court-martial transcript, 4613 (NA); Bilton and Sim, *Four Hours in My Lai*, 92–93; Medina quote on the number of casualties in *American Experience*, "My Lai."

25. Henderson testimony to Wilson (IG), May 26, 1969, Box 1, Folder 11, p. 450, My Lai Collection (VATTU); Henderson testimony. Dec. 2, 1969, Peers Inquiry, 2: Testimony, book 12, p. 4 (LC); Bilton and Sim, *Four Hours in My Lai*, 93–94. Henderson replaced Brigadier General Andrew Lipscomb after his one-year tour of duty.

26. Kotouc testimony, Dec. 6, 1969, Peers Inquiry, 2: Testimony, book 16, p. 2 (LC); Henderson testimony, Dec. 2, 1969, Peers Inquiry, 2: Testimony, book 12, p. 107; Henderson testimony, March 11, 1971, Calley court-martial transcript, 4706–7, 4711, 4713, 4718 (NA); Henderson testimony to Wilson (IG), May 26, 1969, Box 1, Folder 11, pp. 450–51, My Lai Collection (VATTU); Bilton and Sim, *Four Hours in My Lai*, 93–94.

27. Henderson testimony to Wilson (IG), May 26, 1969, Box 1, Folder 11, pp. 451, My Lai Collection (VATTU); Gamble testimony to Wilson (IG), June 23, 1969, Box 1, Folder 18, pp. 818–19, My Lai Collection (VATTU); Peers, *My Lai Inquiry*, 165.

28. Henderson testimony to Wilson (IG), May 26, 1969, Box 1, Folder 11, pp. 452, 476, My Lai Collection (VATTU); Henderson testimony, CID Report, Sept. 10, 1970, p. 59.

29. Henderson testimony to Wilson (IG), May 26, 1969, Box 1, Folder 11, pp. 461–64, My Lai Collection (VATTU); Peers Report, 2–2.

30. Henderson testimony to Wilson (IG), May 26, 1969, Box 1, Folder 11, pp. 481–82, 486, 488, My Lai Collection (VATTU).

31. Bilton and Sim, *Four Hours in My Lai*, 95.

32. Ibid., 88–89; Hersh, *Cover-Up*, 85–88; Peers, *My Lai Inquiry*, 157.

33. Peers, *My Lai Inquiry*, 157; Hersh, *Cover-Up*, 92–95, 97; Bilton and Sim, *Four Hours in My Lai*, 89–91. Ramsdell testified before the Peers panel on January 13, 1970.

34. The Peers commission took testimony from Ramsdell, but it remains confidential and on blank paper. Colonel Randolph Lane, an S-2 intelligence officer in Quang Ngai Province, testified that he "came in contact" with Ramsdell, but any further explanation also remains confidential. For Ramsdell's testimony on blank paper, see Ramsdell testimony (no date), Peers Inquiry, 2: Testimony, book 29, after p. 87 (LC); Lane testimony, Feb. 20, 1970, Peers Inquiry, 2: Testimony, book 29, pp. 4–5 (also blank), 22.

35. Kotouc testimony, Dec. 6, 1969, Peers Inquiry, 2: Testimony, book 16, pp. 2, 10; LaCroix testimony to Wilson (IG), May 2, 1969), Box 1, Folder 2, pp. 53–54, My Lai Collection (VATTU); LaCroix testimony, CID Report, Sept. 10, 1970, p. 26; Medina testimony, March 10, 1971, Calley court-martial transcript, 4615 (NA). Other attendees included Major Frederic Watke, commanding officer of the 123rd Aviation Battalion; Major Calhoun; and Captains Kotouc, Gamble, and Vasquez. Peers Report, 5–3.

36. Peers Report, 5–9.

37. Stephens testimony, Jan. 7, 1970, Peers Inquiry, 2: Testimony, book 16, pp. 45–48 (LC).

38. Peers Report, 2–2; Medina testimony to Wilson (IG), May 13, 1969, Box 1, Folder 6, pp. 249, 259, My Lai Collection (VATTU); Medina testimony, Dec. 4, 1969, Peers Inquiry, 2: Testimony, book 23, pp. 18–20, 78 (LC); Medina testimony, April 15, 1970, Hébert Hearings, 55–58, 84; Medina testimony, March 10, 1971, Calley court-martial transcript, 4614–15 (NA).

39. West quoted in "The Massacre at Mylai," *Life*, Dec. 5, 1969, p. 39.

40. Peers Report, 5–11, 5–12; Hein testimony, Jan. 10, 1970, Peers Inquiry, 2: Testimony, book 28, pp. 3–4 (LC).

41. Peers Report, 5–12; Medina testimony, Dec. 4, 1969, Peers Inquiry, 2: book 23, pp. 7–8 (LC); Medina quoted in Sack, *Calley*, 88; Bilton and Sim, *Four Hours in My Lai*, 97.

42. Belknap, *Vietnam War on Trial*, 40; Sack, *Calley*, 89; Kotouc testimony, Dec. 6, 1969, Peers Inquiry, 2: Testimony, book 16, pp. 49–50 (LC); Bernhardt testimony to Wilson (IG), May 8, 1969, Box 1, Folder 4, p. 189, My Lai Collection (VATTU).

43. Medina testimony to Wilson (IG), May 13, 1969, Box 1, Folder 6, pp. 248, 254, 259, My Lai Collection (VATTU); Medina testimony, Dec. 4, 1969, Peers Inquiry, 2: Testimony, book 23, pp. 7–8 (LC); Medina testimony, April 15, 1970, Hébert Hearings, 81.

44. Peers Report, 5–12; Medina testimony to Wilson (IG), May 13, 1969, Box 1, Folder 6, p. 259, My Lai Collection (VATTU); Medina testimony, Dec. 4, 1969, Peers Inquiry, 2: Testimony, book 23, pp. 7–8 (LC); Medina testimony, April 15, 1970, Hébert Hearings, 61; Kotouc testimony, April 24, 1970, Hébert Hearings, 348; Sack, *Calley*, 89.

45. Kotouc testimony, Dec. 6, 1969, Peers Inquiry, 2: Testimony, book 16, p. 50 (LC); Medina testimony, Dec. 4, 1969, ibid., book 23, pp. 18–19; Medina testimony, April 15, 1970, Hébert Hearings, 61, 82; Schiel testimony, CID Report, Sept. 10, 1970, p. 23; Testimony of SP4 James H. Flynn, Mortar Forward Observer, CID Report, Sept. 10, 1970, p. 48; Medina testimony, CID Report, Sept. 10, 1970, p. 42; Medina press interview with Peter Braestrup of *Washington Post*, Dec. 6, 1969, CID Report, Sept. 10, 1970; Medina testimony to Wilson (IG), May 13, 1969, Box 1, Folder 6, pp. 260, 279–80, My Lai Collection (VATTU).

46. Sack, *Calley*, 89–90. Calley listed twenty-one soldiers who understood their orders were to kill every living thing in My Lai 4. For their testimonies, see CID Report, Sept. 10, 1970, pp. 11, 15, 17, 20, 22, 23, 24, 25, 27, 28, 30, 31, 36, 38, 39, 48, 50. For eighteen soldiers who did not hear instructions to kill noncombatants, see ibid., 12, 14, 16, 18, 19, 21, 25, 27, 30, 31, 33, 35, 36, 47.

47. Paul testimony to Wilson (IG), June 16, 1969, Box 1, Folder 15, pp. 697–98, My Lai Collection (VATTU); Mitchell testimony to Wilson (IG), May 26, 1969, Box 1, Folder 12, p. 498, My Lai Collection (VATTU); Bacon testimony to Wilson (IG), May 22, 1969, Box 1, Folder 9, pp. 387–88, My Lai Collection (VATTU); Lagunoy testimony, May 9, 1970, Hébert Hearings, 667–68; Paul testimony, CID Report, Sept. 10, 1970, p. 46; Lagunoy testimony, CID Report, Sept. 10, 1970, p. 15–16; Bacon testimony, CID Report, Sept. 10, 1970, p. 17; Bilton interview of Bernhardt, Nov. 7, 1988, Papers of *Four Hours in My Lai*, LHCMA (KCL). Mitchell later claimed he did not interpret Medina's briefing to mean they were to kill everyone in the village, but he admitted that some of the men, particularly Calley, might have read it that way. This is a dubious argument, in that Mitchell asserted in his earlier testimony cited above that Medina told the group to "wipe them out." Mitchell testimony, CID Report, Sept. 10, 1970, p. 12. SP5 is the abbreviation for specialist fifth class, equivalent to a sergeant. Reinberg, *In the Field*, 209.

48. Gruver quoted in Jack Taylor, "Witness Says He's Haunted by Memories of My Lai," *Sunday Oklahoman*, July 9, 1972, in Tufts Collection on My Lai (U. of Mich.). See also Gruver testimony, CID Report, Sept. 10, 1970, p. 32.

49. Schiel testimony, CID Report, Sept. 10, 1970, p. 23; Martin testimony, CID Report, Sept. 10, 1970, p. 50; Flynn testimony, CID Report, Sept. 10, 1970, p. 48; Schiel Witness

Statement, Feb. 25, 1970, p. 1, My Lai Collection (VATTU); Martin testimony, Dec. 27, 1969, Peers Inquiry, 2: Testimony, book 23, pp. 5–6 (LC); Flynn testimony, Feb.11, 1970, Peers Inquiry, 2: Testimony, book 28, pp. 2–3.

50. Conti testimony, Jan. 2, 1970, Peers Inquiry, 2: Testimony, book 24, p. 28 (LC).

51. Peers Report, 2–2, 5–10, 5–11; Dahner testimony, Fact Sheet on Son My, enclosed in Maj. Gen. Karl W. Gustafson to Chief of Staff, U.S. Army, June 4, 1970, p.4, Tufts Collection on My Lai (U. of Mich.); Rushin testimony, Tufts Collection on My Lai (U. of Mich.). The Peers Inquiry uncovered no evidence suggesting any involvement by Alpha Company in war crimes and did not include its briefing in the commission's report. Peers Report, 5–9.

52. Kotouc testimony, Dec. 6, 1969, Peers Inquiry, 2: Testimony, book 16, p. 52 (LC); Kotouc testimony, April 24, 1970, Hébert Hearings, 346, 349.

53. Medina quote in Testimony of SP4 Roger D. Murray, RTO of Charlie Company, to Wilson (IG), June 14, 1969, Box 1, Folder 14, p. 672, My Lai Collection (VATTU); Medina testimony to Wilson (IG), May 13, 1969, Box 1, Folder 6, p. 261, My Lai Collection (VATTU); Bilton and Sim, *Four Hours in My Lai*, 98.

54. Bacon testimony, Dec. 16, 1969, Peers Inquiry, 2: Testimony, book 24, p. 7 (LC); Hein testimony, Jan. 10, 1970, Peers Inquiry, 2: Testimony, book 28, p. 4; Delgado testimony to Wilson (IG), July 10, 1969, Box 1, Folder 19, p. 974, My Lai Collection (VATTU); Delgado testimony, CID Report, Sept. 10, 1970, p. 27.

55. Kotouc testimony, Dec. 6, 1969, Peers Inquiry, 2: Testimony, book 16, pp. 3, 51, 53 (LC). For three examples of testimonies claiming no use of marijuana, drugs, or alcohol on the mission, see Martin testimony, Dec. 27, 1969, Peers Inquiry, 2: Testimony, book 23, p. 40; Bunning testimony, Jan. 16, 1970, Peers Inquiry, 2: Testimony, book 26, p. 49; LaCroix testimony, Jan. 22, 1970, Peers Inquiry, 2: Testimony, book 26, pp. 42–44. LaCroix thought "quite a few" in Charlie Company used marijuana, but not on the day of the assault. Ibid., 41–42. See also CID Report, July 20, 1970, p. 20; CID "Investigator's Statement," Sept. 18, 1970, p. 8, Tufts Collection on My Lai (U. of Mich.). A recent study shows that marijuana use was a symptom of something wrong within the armed forces and not a cause of My Lai's atrocities, as so much of the media at the time sensationalized it. See Jeremy Kuzmakov, *The Myth of the Addicted Army: Vietnam and the Modern War on Drugs* (Amherst: University of Massachusetts Press, 2009), 42–45, 73–74, 170.

56. See Peers, *My Lai Inquiry*, 170. For testimonies of the ten soldiers, see Alaux testimony, CID Report, Sept. 10, 1970, p. 50; Bergthold testimony, ibid., 19; Peter Delpome testimony, ibid., 34; Dursi testimony, ibid., 14; Glimpse testimony, ibid., 30; Hutto testimony, ibid., 25; Meadlo testimony, ibid., 15; Mitchell testimony, ibid., 12; Oliver testimony, ibid., 36; and Stanley testimony, ibid., 15. See also Peers Report, 12–2.

57. Peers Report, 5–13; Medina testimony, April 15, 1970, Hébert Hearings, 61; Bilton and Sim, *Four Hours in My Lai*, 93.

58. Bacon testimony to Wilson (IG), May 22, 1969, Box 1, Folder 9, pp. 391–92, My Lai Collection (VATTU).

59. Carter's Witness Statement, Nov. 6, 1969, p. 1, ibid.; Martin testimony, Dec. 27, 1969, Peers Inquiry, 2: Testimony, book 23, p. 8 (LC); Carter testimony, CID Report, Sept. 10, 1970, p. 16; Stanley testimony, ibid., 15; Bergthold testimony, ibid., 19; Widmer testimony, ibid., 45; Widmer quoted in *Frontline*, "Remember My Lai"; Garfolo quoted in Hersh, *My Lai 4*, pp. 35–36; Olsen quoted ibid., 38; Bergthold, Crossley, and Garfolo in Joseph

Strick, dir. *Interviews with My Lai Veterans*, Laser Film Corp, 1970, available on YouTube at https://www.youtube.com/watch?v=Klx4TB33BRU and https://www.youtube.com/watch?v=LDAd8i7dAWs; Peers Report, 2–2. For more than thirty soldiers highlighting Medina's focus on revenge, see two sources: CID Report, Sept. 10, 1970, pp. 14, 15–16, 17, 18–19, 20, 22, 24, 25, 26, 27, 28, 29, 32, 34, 35, 36, 40, 48, 50, and testimonies to Wilson (IG), My Lai Collection (VATTU).

60. Hodges quoted in Bilton and Sim, *Four Hours in My Lai*, 98 (interviewed by Bilton and Sim in 1989); Hodges interview in *Frontline*, "Remember My Lai." Hodges told CID in 1970 that the only villagers expected to be there were VC, but he did not recall any references at the briefing to revenge or to destroying the village or its people. Hodges testimony, CID Report, Sept. 10, 1970, p. 21.

61. Soldier's quote in Caputo, *Rumor of War*, 137.

62. Martin testimony, Dec. 27, 1969, Peers Inquiry, 2: Testimony, book 23, p. 48 (LC).

63. Bacon testimony to Wilson (IG), May 22, 1969, Box 1, Folder 9, p. 388, My Lai Collection (VATTU); Bacon testimony, Dec. 16, 1969, Peers Inquiry, 2: Testimony, book 24, pp. 6, 8 (LC). Mitchell admitted to the Peers commission that he attended Medina's briefing but refused to answer questions about its content on the grounds that it might incriminate him. Mitchell was under suspicion of assault with intent to commit murder at My Lai. Mitchell testimony, Dec. 27, 1969, Peers Inquiry, 2: Testimony, book 25, pp. 5–8. See also Peers, *My Lai Inquiry*, 173; Bilton and Sim, *Four Hours in My Lai*, 329.

64. Sack, *Calley*, 94; Meadlo testimony to Wilson (IG), July 16, 1969, Box 1, Folder 21, pp. 1011–12, My Lai Collection (VATTU).

65. Medina testimony, CID Report, Sept. 10, 1970, p. 42. Lagunoy noted that on earlier missions the soldiers received warnings not to harm civilians, but that Medina issued no such warning in this case. Lagunoy testimony, ibid., 15–16. Sergeant John Smail, squad leader of the 3rd Platoon, could not remember hearing any specific instructions about what to do with villagers found in the combat area. Smail testimony, ibid., 31. Corporal Joe Grimes, a squad leader of the 3rd Platoon, asserted that no one said anything about how to handle or process noncombatants. Grimes testimony, ibid., 33. SP4 Roy Wood of the 1st Platoon testified that they were to send detainees to platoon headquarters. Wood testimony, ibid., 19.

66. Peers Report, 5–13, 5–14, 5–15; Robert Mauro testimony, CID Report, Sept. 10, 1970, pp. 14, 15; Stanley testimony, Jan. 24, 1970, Peers Inquiry, 2: Testimony, book 25, p. 40 (LC). For the sixty-nine soldiers of the three platoons interviewed by CID in the fall of 1970, see CID Report, Sept. 10, 1970, pp. 11–37.

67. Sack, *Calley*, 88, 98; Carter's Witness Statement, Nov. 6, 1969, p. 1, My Lai Collection (VATTU).

Three

1. Peers Report, 5–6, 5–15, 5–16; Henderson testimony to Wilson (IG), May 26, 1969, Box 1, Folder 11, pp. 452, 470, My Lai Collection (VATTU); Riggs testimony, April 24, 1970, Hébert Hearings, 394–95; Peers, *My Lai Inquiry*, 167; Belknap, *Vietnam War on Trial*, 60; Bilton and Sim, *Four Hours in My Lai*, 96, 106; Hersh, *My Lai 4*, p. 46.

2. Henderson testimony, CID Report, Sept. 10, 1970, pp. 3, 59; Peers Report, 5–6, 5–17, 5–18, 6–5, 6–6, 6–9. "Web gear" refers to a belt and suspenders apparatus. Reinberg, *In the Field*, 239.

3. Peers Report, 6–5; Bilton and Sim, *Four Hours in My Lai*, 109.

4. Henderson testimony to Wilson (IG), May 26, 1969, Box 1, Folder 11, p. 453, My Lai Collection (VATTU); CID Report, Sept. 10, 1970, p. 59; Peers Report, 2–2, 5–6.

5. Testimony of Mason Young, division artillery commander at Chu Lai, April 28, 1970, Hébert Hearings, 548, 551; Lind testimony, April 30, 1970, Hébert Hearings, 607–8; Vasquez testimony, April 15, 1970, Hébert Hearings, 86–90; Peers Report, 5–7, 5–8.

6. Peers Report, 5–8, 5–16, 10–17, 10–18, 10–20.

7. Kotouc testimony, Dec. 6, 1969, Peers Inquiry, 2: Testimony, book 16, pp. 11–12, 17 (LC); Kotouc testimony, April 24, 1970, Hébert Hearings, 345–46; Peers Report, 5–8, 5–16.

8. Kotouc testimony, Dec. 6, 1969, Peers Inquiry, 2: Testimony, book 16, p. 3 (LC); Bilton and Sim, *Four Hours in My Lai*, 105.

9. Bilton and Sim, *Four Hours in My Lai*, 91; Belknap, *Vietnam War on Trial*, 61; Mary McCarthy, *Medina* (New York: Harcourt Brace Jovanovich, 1972), 15–16; Kotouc testimony, Dec. 6, 1969, Peers Inquiry, 2: Testimony, book 16, p. 9 (LC); Peers Report, 5–4.

10. Peers Report, 4–7, 5–15, 5–16; Peers, *My Lai Inquiry*, 173. Charlie Company had a field operating strength of nearly 120 men, but the number of those in the three platoons was considerably lower because of casualties and the need to assign others to administrative and logistical responsibilities. Peers Report, 4–7.

11. Sack, *Calley*, 99.

12. Peers Report, 5–6, 5–15, 5–16; Peers, *My Lai Inquiry*, 172; Allison, *My Lai*, 28, 32; Bilton and Sim, *Four Hours in My Lai*, 103–4; Hersh, *My Lai 4*, p. 47; "Massacre at Mylai," *Life*, 39 (Roberts and Haeberle), in Peers Inquiry, 3: Exhibits, book 4, Misc. Docs., Exhibit No. M-1 (LC); Henderson testimony to Wilson (IG), May 26, 1969, Box 1, Folder 11, p. 466, My Lai Collection, (VATTU); Haeberle testimony, April 23, 1970, Hébert Hearings, 250–56, 260, 277. The Peers Report of 1970 claimed that the 1st Platoon had about twenty-eight men; Calley in 1971 claimed twenty-seven. In 1979, Lieutenant General William R. Peers reduced the estimate to twenty-five. I have used his original figure of twenty-eight cited in his official report. See Peers Report, 5–15; Calley testimony, Feb. 22, 23, 1971, Calley court-martial transcript, 3787, 3845 (NA); and Peers, *My Lai Inquiry*, 173.

13. Haeberle testimony, April 23, 1970, Hébert Hearings, 250–53, 277.

14. Medina testimony, Dec. 4, 1969, Peers Inquiry, 2: Testimony, book 23, pp. 11–12 (LC); Bilton and Sim, *Four Hours in My Lai*, 106–8.

15. Bilton and Sim, *Four Hours in My Lai*, 104; Peers Report, 5–16; author's interview of Colburn, June 20, 2013. The navy used the Swift Boat, an aluminum craft, to patrol offshore and inland waters. Reinberg, *In the Field*, 212.

16. Hugh Thompson, "Moral Courage in Combat: The My Lai Story," question-and-answer session at a lecture at the Stockdale Center for Ethical Leadership, U.S. Naval Academy, Annapolis, MD, Fall 2003, available online at http://www.usna.edu/ThompsonPg1–28_Final.pdf, 21; five-part video on YouTube at https://www.youtube.com/watch?v=B6bovqjiZQ4; Peers, *My Lai Inquiry*, 66, 167, 172–73; Bilton and Sim, *Four Hours in My Lai*, 96, 102–4, 146; McCarthy, *Medina*, 14; Hersh, *My Lai 4*, p. 47; Kotouc testimony, Dec. 6, 1969, Peers Inquiry, 2: Testimony, book 16, pp. 22, 26 (LC); Colburn

interview in Appy, *Patriots*, 346; author's interviews of Colburn, June 20, Oct. 10, 2013. Andreotta was born in New Jersey and raised in Missouri.

17. Thompson in CID Report, Sept. 10, 1970, p. 8; Thompson, "The Massacre at My Lai," *Newsweek*, March 8, 1999, 64; Colburn interview, *Vietnam Magazine*, Feb. 7, 2011; Thompson quoted in David L. Anderson, ed., *Facing My Lai: Moving Beyond the Massacre* (Lawrence: University Press of Kansas, 1998), 28; Colburn interview in Appy, *Patriots*, 346–47; Colburn testimony, April 17, 1970, Hébert Hearings, 63; author's interview of Colburn, July 6, 2015.

18. Medina testimony, Dec. 4, 1969, Peers Inquiry, 2: Testimony, book 23, p. 11 (LC); Medina testimony, April 15, 1970, Hébert Hearings, 62–63; Sack, *Calley*, 100; author's interview of Tilford, April 5, 2015.

19. Calley testimony, Feb. 23, 1971, Calley court-martial transcript, 3804 (NA); Sack, *Calley*, 99–100. "Unassing" was slang for getting out of your seat quickly. Reinberg, *In the Field*, 228.

20. Sack, *Calley*, 100.

21. Ibid., 101.

22. Henderson testimony to Wilson (IG), May 26, 1969, Box 1, Folder 11, pp. 466–67, My Lai Collection (VATTU).

23. Ibid.; author's interview of Colburn, Oct. 10, 2013; Peers, *My Lai Inquiry*, 172.

24. Peers Report, 6–4; Medina testimony, April 15, 1970, Hébert Hearings, 63.

25. Peers Report, 6–4; Medina testimony, Dec. 4, 1969, Peers Inquiry, 2: Testimony, book 23, pp. 12–13 (LC); Medina testimony, April 15, 1970, Hébert Hearings, 63–64; CID Report, Sept. 10, 1970, pp. 42–43.

26. Kotouc testimony, Dec. 6, 1969, Peers Inquiry, 2: Testimony, book 16, pp. 3–4 (LC); pilot (unidentified, but Thompson) quoted ibid. 25–26; CID Report, Sept. 10, 1970, p. 47; Peers Report, 6–5.

27. Peers Report, 6–2, 6–4.

28. Calhoun quoted in Kotouc testimony, Dec. 6, 1969, Peers Inquiry, 2: Testimony, book 16, p. 26 (LC); Kotouc testimony, April 24, 1970, Hébert Hearings, 351; CID Report, Sept. 10, 1970, p. 43.

29. CID Report, Sept. 10, 1970, pp. 12, 17, 22–23.

30. Stanley testimony, ibid., 15.

31. Bunning testimony, Jan. 16, 1970, Peers Inquiry, 2: Testimony, book 26, pp. 13, 59 (LC); Mosley-Bunning telephone conversation, May 13, 1970, p. 2, My Lai Collection (VATTU).

32. Bunning testimony, Jan. 16, 1970, Peers Inquiry, 2: Testimony, book 26, p. 12 (LC); Peers Inquiry, 2: Testimony; Bunning Witness Statement, Feb. 23, 1970, p. 1, My Lai Collection (VATTU).

33. Ingle-Bunning telephone conversation, May 28, 1970, Tape 4, pp. 2–4, My Lai Collection (VATTU).

34. CID Report, Sept. 10, 1970, pp. 30–32, 55; Gibson testimony, April 16, 1970, Hébert Hearings, 130.

35. Paul Alexander, "Thirty Years Later, Memories of My Lai Massacre Remain Fresh," *South Coast Today*, March 15, 1998, available online at http://www.southcoasttoday.com/article/19980315/news/303159996.

36. Meadlo interview on *60 Minutes*, CBS-TV, Nov. 24, 1969; "Transcript of Interview of Vietnam War Veteran on His Role in Alleged Massacre of Civilians at Songmy," *New York Times*, Nov. 25, 1969; Bilton and Sim, *Four Hours in My Lai*, 111; CID Report, Sept. 10, 1970, pp. 12, 19; Calley testimony, Feb. 23, 1971, Calley court-martial transcript, 3857 (NA).

37. On mines and booby traps, see Bernhardt testimony to Wilson (IG), Army, May 8, 1969, Box 1, Folder 4, p. 216, My Lai Collection (VATTU).

38. CID Report, Sept. 10, 1970, p. 6; Don testimony (seventy-one), ibid., 25. For males working in the fields, see three of numerous examples: Nguyen Than (fifty-seven) testimony, ibid., 33; Nguyen To aka Chat (fifty-five) testimony, ibid., 35; and Do Cam (forty-two) testimony, ibid., 23. For those at market, see three examples of many: Phung Thi Chanh (seventy-three-year-old female) testimony, ibid., 23; Ngo Thi Vang (sixteen-year-old female) testimony, 36; and Nguyen Thi Hong (sixteen-year-old female) testimony, ibid., 27.

39. Keshel testimony, ibid., 58; Medina testimony to Wilson (IG), May 13, 1969, p. 262, My Lai Collection (VATTU); Peers Report, 4–13, 5–4, 5–5. The Peers commission examined the period March 1–20, 1968, and found no warning of any kind in the files of TF Barker, the 11th Brigade, or the American Division. For three of many villagers surprised by the artillery and gunfire, see Than testimony, CID Report, Sept. 10, 1970, p. 33; Don testimony, ibid., 25; and Do Thi Huu (thirteen-year-old female) testimony, ibid., 28. See also Peers, *My Lai Inquiry*, 167, 169.

40. Kotouc testimony, Dec. 6, 1969, Peers Inquiry, 2: Testimony, book 16, pp. 7–9 (LC).

41. Ibid., 55.

42. Ibid., 19; Peers Report, 2–2, 5–1, 5–2, 5–8, 5–9; Peers, *My Lai Inquiry*, 48, 167, 169; Bilton and Sim, *Four Hours in My Lai*, 206; Belknap, *Vietnam War on Trial*, 90.

43. CID Report, Sept. 10, 1970, pp. 21, 23, 26–27. I found no reports substantiating LaCroix's story.

44. CID Report, Sept. 10, 1970, p. 3; Peers, *My Lai Inquiry*, 173.

45. Bunning testimony, Jan. 16, 1970, Peers Inquiry, 2: Testimony, book 26, p. 58 (LC); weather described in author's interview of Colburn, Oct. 10, 2013; Peers, *My Lai Inquiry*, 173, 175; Belknap, *Vietnam War on Trial*, 57.

46. Medina testimony, April 15, 1970, Hébert Hearings, 65; Peers Report, 5–15, 5–16; Bilton and Sim, *Four Hours in My Lai*, 118; Peers, *My Lai Inquiry*, 170.

47. Kotouc testimony, Dec. 6, 1969, Peers Inquiry, 2: Testimony, book 16, p. 19 (LC).

48. Sack, *Calley*, 101–2.

49. Peers, *My Lai Inquiry*, 173; CID Report, Sept. 10, 1970, pp. 12, 15, 17; Cowan testimony, Oct. 30, 1969, ibid., 12, and ibid., Robert N. Zaza, "Investigator's Statement," Sept. 18, 1970, p. 4; Belknap, *Vietnam War on Trial*, 64.

50. CID Report, Sept. 10, 1970, p. 20; Delgado testimony, ibid., 27; LaMartina testimony, ibid., 28; Rodriguez testimony, ibid., 24; Hutto testimony, ibid., 25; Hutson testimony, ibid., 28; Partsch testimony, ibid., 24; Fields testimony, ibid., 20–21; Garza testimony, ibid., 21; Moss testimony, ibid., 27; Bernhardt testimony to Wilson (IG), May 8, 1969, Box 1, Folder 4, p. 204, My Lai Collection (VATTU); Widmer quoted in *American Experience*, "My Lai," transcript, 14.

51. *American Experience*, "My Lai," transcript, 13–14.

52. CID Report, Sept. 10, 1970, p. 27; Peers Report, 6–7, 6–8.

53. Bilton and Sim, *Four Hours in My Lai*, 111–12; Bergthold testimony, CID Report, Sept. 10, 1970, p. 19; Wood testimony, ibid.

54. Stanley testimony, Jan. 24, 1970, Peers Inquiry, 2: Testimony, book 25, pp. 16–18, 48 (LC); Stanley's "Witness Statement" to CID, Oct. 14, 1969, p. 3 (Bilton, My Lai Collection); Stanley testimony, CID Report, Sept. 10, 1970, pp. 12–15. SP4 Ronald Grzesik confirmed that Boyce threw a man into a well. Ibid., 16. Stanley also quoted in VWCWG, My Lai Massacre, 1969–74, Box 5, pp. 12–14 (NA).

55. VWCWG, My Lai Massacre, 1969–74, Box 5, p. 13 (NA).

56. Hersh, *My Lai 4*, 17.

57. Sack, *Calley*, 107.

58. Ibid., 107–8. Calley testified later that Medina "told me to hurry up and get my people moving and get rid of the people I had there that were detaining me." Calley testimony, Feb. 23, 1971, Calley court-martial transcript, 3812, 3889 (NA).

59. Bilton and Sim, *Four Hours in My Lai*, 118.

60. Transcript of Meadlo interview in *60 Minutes*, Nov. 24, 1989; Sack, *Calley*, 108.

61. Calley testimony, Feb. 23, 1971, Calley court-martial transcript, 3890 (NA); Sack *Calley*, 108.

62. Bernhardt interview in Appy, *Patriots*, 351; Sack, *Calley*, 108; Truong Quy in Fact Sheet, enclosed in Gustafson to Chief of Staff, U.S. Army, Jan. 21, 1970, p. 2, Tufts Collection on My Lai (U. of Mich.); Fields in Memo for Tufts by Lt. Col. Patrick D. Chisholm, Jr., Jan. 29, 1970, enclosed in Weekly My Lai Talking Paper, Jan. 29, 1970, Tufts Collection on My Lai (U. of Mich.).

63. Sack, *Calley*, 108–10, 113; Bilton and Sim, *Four Hours in My Lai*, 77, 79.

64. CID Report, Sept. 10, 1970, p. 12.

65. Sack, *Calley*, 110; Calley testimony, Feb. 24, 1971, Calley court-martial transcript, 3984 (NA).

66. Sack, *Calley*, 89, 110–11.

67. Transcript of Meadlo interview in *60 Minutes*, Nov. 24, 1989; Conti testimony, Jan. 2, 1970, Peers Inquiry, 2: Testimony, book 24, p. 32 (LC); Stanley testimony, Jan. 24, 1970, Peers Inquiry, 2: Testimony, book 25, pp. 18–19; Bilton and Sim, *Four Hours in My Lai*, 107, 120–21.

68. Conti testimony, Jan. 2, 1970, Peers Inquiry, 2: Testimony, book 24, p. 32 (LC); Bilton and Sim, *Four Hours in My Lai*, 120.

69. Conti testimony, Jan. 2, 1970, Peers Inquiry, 2: Testimony, book 24, p. 32 (LC); Bilton and Sim, *Four Hours in My Lai*, 120–21.

70. CID Report, Sept. 25, 1970, pp. 11–12; Conti testimony, Jan. 2, 1970, Peers Inquiry, 2: Testimony, book 24, p. 33 (LC); Bilton and Sim, *Four Hours in My Lai*, 121.

71. VC casualty figures in Sgt. Clement Stephens testimony (S-2 officer assigned to Task Force Barker), March 4, 1971, Calley court-martial transcript, 4306 (NA); Sack, *Calley*, 102–3, 106.

72. Sack, *Calley*, 101; CID Report, Sept. 10, 1970, p. 5.

73. Bunning testimony, Jan. 16, 1970, Peers Inquiry, 2: Testimony, book 26, pp. 57–59 (LC); Mosley-Bunning telephone conversation, May 13, 1970, p. 2, My Lai Collection (VATTU); Bilton and Sim, *Four Hours in My Lai*, 114.

74. Bunning testimony, Jan. 16, 1970, Peers Inquiry, 2: Testimony, book 26, pp. 34, 46–48 (LC); Ingle-Bunning telephone conversation, May 28, 1970, Tape 5, pp. 6–7, My Lai Collection (VATTU).

75. CID Report, June 19, 1970, p. 5; Bunning testimony, Jan. 16, 1970, Peers Inquiry, 2: Testimony, book 26, p. 48 (LC); Ingle-Bunning telephone conversation, May 28, 1970, Tape 4, p. 4, My Lai Collection (VATTU).

76. Bunning testimony, Jan. 16, 1970, Peers Inquiry, 2: Testimony, book 26, p. 58 (LC); Ingle-Bunning telephone conversation, May 28, 1970, Tape 3, pp. 9–10, My Lai Collection (VATTU).

77. Bunning testimony, Jan. 16, 1970, Peers Inquiry, 2: Testimony, book 26, p. 15 (LC); Ingle-Bunning telephone conversation, May 28, 1970, Tape 2, p. 5, Tape 4, p. 4, My Lai Collection (VATTU).

78. Bunning Witness Statement, Feb. 23, 1970, p. 2, My Lai Collection (VATTU); Mosley-Bunning telephone conversation, May 13, 1970, pp. 2–3, My Lai Collection (VATTU).

79. CID Report, June 19, 1970, p. 6; Schiel testimony, CID Report, Sept. 10, 1970, p. 23.

80. Bunning testimony, Jan. 16, 1970, Peers Inquiry, 2: Testimony, book 26, p. 16 (LC).

81. Ingle-Bunning telephone conversation, May 28, 1970, Tape 3, p. 1, My Lai Collection (VATTU).

82. Ingle-Bunning telephone conversation, May 28, 1970, Tape 3, p. 2, Tape 4, pp. 8–9, Tape 5, pp. 2, 4, 6, 7–8, My Lai Collection (VATTU); Bunning Witness Statement, Feb. 23, 1970, p. 1, ibid.

83. Bunning testimony, Jan. 16, 1970, Peers Inquiry, 2: Testimony, book 26, p. 17 (LC); Mosley-Bunning telephone conversation, May 13, 1970, p. 2, My Lai Collection (VATTU).

84. CID Report, June 19, 1970, p. 6; Schiel testimony, CID Report, Sept. 10, 1970, p. 23.

85. Bunning testimony, Jan. 16, 1970, Peers Inquiry, 2: Testimony, book 26, p. 17 (LC); Ingle-Bunning telephone conversation, May 28, 1970, Tape 3, p. 6, My Lai Collection (VATTU).

86. Bilton and Sim, *Four Hours in My Lai,* 73, 113; CID Report, June 26, 1970, p. 1; CID Report, June 19, 1970, p. 5. Others listed by Hutson as participants were Charles Hutto, Floyd Wright, Maclin Brown, Esequiel Torres, Varnado Simpson, Gary Crossley, Tom Makey, Andress Delgado, Salvadore LaMartina, and Diego Rodriguez. Ibid., 6. Zaza, Investigator, CID Report, July 20, 1970, p. 14; CID Report, June 26, 1970, pp. 1, 3–4; Bunning testimony, Jan. 16, 1970, Peers Inquiry, 2: Testimony, book 26, p. 22 (LC).

87. First Roschevitz quote in CID Report, June 26, 1970, p. 3; second Roschevitz quote in Hersh, *My Lai 4,* 52; Wood quoted ibid.; Simpson interview in Strick, *Interviews with My Lai Veterans.* See also Bilton and Sim, *Four Hours in My Lai,* 113–14.

88. CID Report, June 26, 1970, p. 3.

89. Bilton and Sim, *Four Hours in My Lai,* 115–16.

90. Ibid., 116.

91. Hersh, *My Lai 4,* 52.

92. Buchanon testimony, Jan. 8, 1970, Peers Inquiry, 2: Testimony, book 25, pp. 52–53 (LC); Bilton and Sim, *Four Hours in My Lai,* 115.

93. Bunning testimony, Jan. 16, 1970, Peers Inquiry, 2: Testimony, book 26, pp. 17–18, 60 (LC); Mosley-Bunning telephone conversation, May 13, 1970, pp. 2–3, My Lai Collection (VATTU); Peers, *My Lai Inquiry,* 175; Peers Report, 6–8.

Four

1. CID Report, Sept. 10, 1970, pp. 23, 24, 28. Wright admitted to shooting several Vietnamese males. Ibid., 29. Torres initially denied machine-gunning villagers and said it was possible that they had died in a crossfire between Charlie Company and the Viet Cong. But he later reversed his view in an interview with CID. Ibid., Jan. 9, 1970, 24.

2. Hutto testimony, CID Report., Sept. 10, 1970, p. 25.

3. Simpson testimony, ibid., 27; Hutson testimony, ibid., 28; Garza testimony, ibid., 21; McBreen testimony, ibid., 22; Simpson quote on dogs and cats in *Frontline*, "Remember My Lai"; Simpson quoted in Strick, *Interviews with My Lai Veterans*. Leon Stevenson from the machine-gun crew saw the bodies of up to twenty-five villagers, most of them women and children. CID Report, Sept. 10, 1970, p. 25. Fernando Trevino saw about fifteen bodies, some of them children, scattered along the northern side of the village. Ibid., 26. LaMartina saw up to twenty-five bodies and thought about 360 villagers had died. About halfway in the sweep, orders came to cease fire. Ibid., 28. Moss recalled three piles of about twenty dead men, women, and children in each—all shot at close range. Ibid., 27.

4. Simpson quoted in Strick, *Interviews with My Lai Veterans*; Bilton interview of Simpson in 1989, Papers of *Four Hours in My Lai*, LHCMA (KCL). See also CID Report, April 27, 1970, pp. 2–3; CID Report, May 5, 1970, pp. 1–4, and CID Report, Sept. 10, 1970, p. 27; Bilton and Sim, *Four Hours in My Lai*, 6–8, 130.

5. Bunning testimony, Jan. 16, 1970, Peers Inquiry, 2: Testimony, book 26, pp. 45–46, 49 (LC).

6. Ibid., 20–22, 60–61 (LC); Mosley-Bunning telephone conversation, May 13, 1970, p. 3, My Lai Collection (VATTU).

7. Peers Report, 6–10.

8. Garfolo testimony, Strick, *Interviews with My Lai Veterans*; Bunning testimony, Jan. 16, 1970, Peers Inquiry, 2: Testimony, book 26, pp. 22, 24 (LC); Bilton and Sim, *Four Hours in My Lai*, 117.

9. Bunning testimony, Jan. 16, 1970, Peers Inquiry, 2: Testimony, book 26, pp. 23, 61 (LC).

10. Bilton and Sim, *Four Hours in My Lai*, 132. The term "boom-boom" was slang for sex. Reinberg, *In the Field*, 26.

11. Bilton and Sim, *Four Hours in My Lai*, 131–32; CID Report, June 26, 1970, pp. 1, 4; Gonzalez on the seven women, CID Report, Sept. 10, 1970, p. 22.

12. Thomas Partsch testimony, Jan. 30, 1970, Peers Inquiry, 2: Testimony, book 26, pp. 5, 36–38, 47–48 (LC); Peers Report, 2–3; Pham Day in Memo for Tufts by Chisholm, Jan. 29, 1970, enclosed in Weekly My Lai Talking Paper, Jan. 29, 1970, Tufts Collection on My Lai (U. of Mich.); Belknap, *Vietnam War on Trial*, 68; Bilton and Sim, *Four Hours in My Lai*, 129–30.

13. Bilton and Sim, *Four Hours in My Lai*, 81–82, 117, 131.

14. Peers Report, 6–10. For the rapes and shootings of the victims (either injured or killed), see Statement by CID Investigator Roland W. Thompson, CID Report, April 28, 1970, p. 4. CID reported that 104 statements by survivors of the attack supported the charges of rape. See Thompson Witness Statement to CID, CID Report, May 25, 1970, p. 2.

15. Bunning testimony, Jan. 16, 1970, Peers Inquiry, 2: Testimony, book 26, pp. 26–27, 31 (LC); Mosley-Bunning telephone conversation, May 13, 1970, pp. 3, 7–8, My Lai

Collection (VATTU); Lt. Col. Hugh H. Riddle to Tufts, enclosed in Weekly My Lai Fact Sheet, U.S. Army, Dec. 16, 1969, p. 2, Tufts Collection on My Lai (U. of Mich.).

16. Bunning testimony, Jan. 16, 1970, Peers Inquiry, 2: Testimony, book 26, p. 27 (LC); Mosley-Bunning telephone conversation, May 13, 1970, p. 8, My Lai Collection (VATTU); Hutson testimony, CID Report, May 28, 1970, p. 4; Fields testimony, ibid.

17. Bunning Witness Statement to CID, May 6, 1970, Box 1, Folder 40, p. 1, My Lai Collection (VATTU); Mosley-Bunning telephone conversation, May 13, 1970, p. 7, ibid.

18. Bunning testimony, Jan. 16, 1970, Peers Inquiry, 2: Testimony, book 26, pp. 26, 31–32 (LC); Mosley-Bunning telephone conversation, May 13, 1970, pp. 10–12, My Lai Collection (VATTU); McBreen testimony, CID Report, May 28, 1970, p. 4. According to Bilton and Sim, Hodges was in the hooch for fifteen minutes, and the three unidentified soldiers sexually assaulted and raped her afterward. *Four Hours in My Lai*, 131.

19. Mosley-Bunning telephone conversation, May 13, 1970, pp. 8, 11, My Lai Collection (VATTU).

20. Cuong in CID Report, Sept. 10, 1970, p. 85; CID Report, May 28, 1970, pp. 1–2.

21. Bunning testimony, Jan. 16, 1970, Peers Inquiry, 2: Testimony, book 26, pp. 28, 31–33 (LC); Peers, *My Lai Inquiry*, 159.

22. Bunning testimony, Jan. 16, 1970, Box 1, Folder 34, pp. 28, 31–33, 35, My Lai Collection (VATTU); Peers, *My Lai Inquiry*, 158–59. Peers and his panel were so impressed by Bunning that, in an allusion to his plans to raise thousands of chickens on his return home from Vietnam, they remarked, "What we need around here are a few more chicken farmers." Ibid., 159.

23. Bunning testimony, Jan. 16, 1970, Peers Inquiry, 2: Testimony, book 26, p. 32, (LC); Smail quoted in Hersh, *My Lai 4*, p. 185. Later, before the Peers commission, Smail testified that he never heard of any rapes by Charlie Company in My Lai or any other operation. Smail testimony, Jan. 6, 1970, Peers Inquiry, 2: Testimony, book 25, p. 22. See also Karen Stuhldreher, "State Rape: Representations of Rape in Viet Nam," in "Nobody Gets Off the Bus: The Viet Nam Generation Big Book," special issue, *Vietnam Generation* 5 (March 1994): 3, available online at http://www2.iath.virginia.edu/sixties/HTML_docs/ Texts/Scholarly/Stuldreher_Rape.html. The Peers commission concluded that Brooks knew that several of his men "habitually raped" Vietnamese women but on March 16, 1968, "did not present, and failed to report several rapes" by his platoon in My Lai 4 and Binh Tay, nor did he report the killings of civilians as a war crime. Brooks died in battle on July 7, 1969. Peers Report, 12–33. See also Bilton and Sim, *Four Hours in My Lai*, 129–30. The Peers commission did not mention Partsch's allegation regarding Brooks in its final report.

24. Peers Report, 2–3, 6–11, 6–12; Peers, *My Lai Inquiry*, 176; Bunning testimony, Jan. 16, 1970, Peers Inquiry, 2: Testimony, book 26, pp. 28, 35–36 (LC); Mosley-Bunning telephone conversation, May 13, 1970, p. 3, My Lai Collection (VATTU).

25. Bunning testimony, Jan. 16, 1970, Peers Inquiry, 2: Testimony, book 26, pp. 28–30 (LC).

26. Peers, *My Lai Inquiry*, 175; Peers Report, 6–9.

27. Peers, *My Lai Inquiry*, 70–71; Transcript of Meadlo interview on *60 Minutes*, Nov. 24, 1989; Bilton and Sim, *Four Hours in My Lai*, 121.

28. Sack, *Calley*, 114; Sledge testimony on killings in CID Report, Sept. 25, 1970, p. 13; Sledge testimony in Calley's court-martial, Hammer, *Court-Martial of Lt. Calley*, 132–33; Stanley

testimony, Jan. 24, 1970, Peers Inquiry, 2: Testimony, book 25, pp. 16–18, 48 (LC); Stanley Witness Statement for CID, Oct. 14, 1969, p. 5; Papers of *Four Hours in My Lai*, LHCMA (KCL); Hersh, *My Lai 4*, p. 64. See also Bilton and Sim, *Four Hours in My Lai*, 122; Belknap, *Vietnam War on Trial*, 73; Allison, *My Lai*, 42.

29. CID Report, Sept. 25, 1970, pp. 10, 12. Olsen told CID investigators that he heard someone say that Calley had ordered Meadlo to "waste" them. Ibid., 8. Article 3 of the Geneva Convention of 1949 declares that both prisoners of war and detainees "shall in all circumstances be treated humanely." It specifically prohibits "any reprisal incompatible with the 'humane treatment' demanded unconditionally" in subparagraph (1). See Geneva Convention of 1949, Article 3, pp. 38–40, 45. See also Preamble, 12 (LC).

30. Turner quoted in Hammer, *Court-Martial of Lt. Calley*, 136; Belknap, *Vietnam War on Trial*, 162–63.

31. Qui quoted in *Frontline*, "Remember My Lai."

32. CID Report, Sept. 25, 1970, pp. 10, 12; Bilton and Sim, *Four Hours in My Lai*, 122.

33. Stanley Witness Statement for CID, Oct. 14, 1969, p. 8, Papers of *Four Hours in My Lai*, LHCMA (KCL); four witnesses to Calley shooting man: Stanley, Carter, Billy Carney, and Bergthold, all in CID Report, Jan. 23, 1970, pp. 1, 3. Bergthold was about six feet away when he heard a splash and saw Calley peer into the well and shoot the man. Martin claimed he heard Calley make the radio call to Medina. Bergthold testimony, March 8, 1971, Calley court-martial transcript, 4477–79 (NA); Martin testimony, March 8, 1971, Calley court-martial transcript, 4484–85. See Bilton and Sim, *Four Hours in My Lai*, 79, 122–23.

34. Grzesik's account in CID Report, Sept. 10, 1970, p. 16, and Sept. 25, 1970, pp. 9–10; Stanley testimony, Jan. 24, 1970, Peers Inquiry, 2: Testimony, book 25, pp. 34, 37–38 (LC); Bilton interview of Stanley in 1989, Papers of *Four Hours in My Lai*, LHCMA (KCL); Stanley interview in "War Hero Relives Day He Refused to Murder," *Biloxi Sun Herald*, Nov. 19, 1989, available online at http://articles.orlandosentinel.com/1989–11 –19/news/8911193407_1_stanley-lai-4-calley. See also Bilton and Sim, *Four Hours in My Lai*, 19.

35. Bilton and Sim, *Four Hours in My Lai*, 111; Stanley testimony, Jan. 24, 1970, Peers Inquiry, 2: Testimony, book 25, p. 19 (LC).

36. Maples testimony, CID Report, Jan. 24, 1970, pp. 9, 15; CID Report, Sept. 10, 1970, pp. 15, 18; Stanley testimony, CID Report, Sept. 25, 1970, pp. 11, 13; PFC William Lloyd testimony, ibid.; Stanley testimony, Jan. 24, 1970, Peers Inquiry, 2: Testimony, book 25, pp. 19, 25 (LC); Maples testimony in court, Hammer, *Court-Martial of Lt. Calley*, 113–14; Colburn interview with *Vietnam Magazine*, Feb. 7, 2011, http://www.historynet.com/ interview-larry-colburn-why-my-lai-hugh-thompson-matter.htm; Bilton and Sim, *Four Hours in My Lai*, 123.

37. Stanley testimony, CID Report, Sept. 25, 1970, p. 11; Bilton interview of Maples in 1989, Papers of *Four Hours in My Lai*, LHCMA (KCL); Bilton and Sim, *Four Hours in My Lai*, 123. The CID lists Stanley as "Randolph E.," but this has to be an error.

38. Meadlo later declared that he joined Calley, Stanley, and Simone in killing everyone in the ditch. Meadlo testimony, CID Report, Sept. 25, 1970, p. 12. Stanley and Simone denied firing at the villagers, either in the ditch or anywhere else. Ibid., 11. Stanley on Mitchell and Meadlo on Calley, Stanley, and Simone, ibid., 12. The CID found insufficient evidence for the murder

charges against Stanley and Simone. Robert Zaza, "Investigator's Statement," Sept. 18, 1970, opposite p. 39, Tufts Collection on My Lai (U. of Mich.).

39. Tuan quoted in *Frontline*, "Remember My Lai"; Mrs. Thieu's story related by Nguyen Ngoc Luong, interpreter for ARVN, in Appy, *Patriots*, 376; Stanley testimony, CID Report, Sept. 25, 1970, p. 11.

40. Stanley testimony, Jan. 24, 1970, Peers Inquiry, 2: Testimony, book 25, p. 21 (LC).

41. *American Experience*, "My Lai," transcript, 17; Hammer, *Court-Martial of Lt. Calley*, 117–18; Belknap, *Vietnam War on Trial*, 161.

42. Hersh, *My Lai 4*, 64; CID Report, Sept. 10, 1970, p. 10, and Sept. 25, 1970, p. 22. See Col. James C. Schoultz, Jr., to Chief of Staff, U.S. Army, Dec. 10, 1969, Tufts Collection on My Lai (U. of Mich.).

43. Thompson testimony, Dec. 4, 1969, Peers Inquiry, 2: Testimony, book 8, p. 34 (LC); Colburn interview, *Vietnam Magazine*, Feb. 7, 2011; Thompson, "Moral Courage in Combat," 21–22; Colburn interview in Appy, *Patriots*, 347; Hersh, *My Lai 4*, 64.

44. Thompson, "Moral Courage in Combat," 21–22; *Frontline*, "Remember My Lai."

45. Colburn testimony, Dec. 20, 1969, Peers Inquiry, 2: Testimony, book 5, pp. 7–8, 10, 12–13, 49–50 (LC); Colburn testimony, April 17, 1970, Hébert Hearings, 203–7; Colburn interview in Appy, *Patriots*, 346.

46. Thompson quoted in *Frontline*, "Remember My Lai"; Thompson, "Moral Courage in Combat," 21–22; Colburn interview in Appy, *Patriots*, 346.

47. Medina testimony, April 15, 1970, Hébert Hearings, 64–65; Medina testimony, CID Report, Sept. 10, 1970, pp. 43, 45; CID Report, Sept. 10, 1970, pp. 8–9; author's interview of Colburn, April 8, 2014; Thompson, "Massacre at My Lai"; Thompson, "Moral Courage in Combat," 22; Thompson in Anderson, *Facing My Lai*, 29; Thompson in "Back to My Lai," *60 Minutes*, March 29, 1998; Testimony of Charles Mansell, helicopter co-pilot and roommate of Thompson, April 17, 1970, Hébert Hearings, 158–59. One of the two gunships hovering overhead flew the "high" position a few hundred feet higher and was in radio communication with Thompson and the commander on the ground. Bilton and Sim, *Four Hours in My Lai*, 136.

48. Thompson interview in "Back to My Lai"; Thompson testimony, Dec. 3, 1969, Peers Inquiry, 2: Testimony, book 8, pp. 12–14 (LC); Colburn testimony, Dec. 20, 1969, Peers Inquiry, book 5, p. 15; Henderson testimony, Dec. 2, 19, 1969, book 12, pp. 9, 246; Bilton and Sim, *Four Hours in My Lai*, 126–27, 136; author's interview of Colburn, June 20, 2013; Colburn quoted in *American Experience*, "My Lai," transcript, 16.

49. *American Experience*, "My Lai," transcript, 18; Colburn testimony, Dec. 20, 1969, Peers Inquiry, 2: Testimony, book 5, pp. 35, 47, 59 (LC); Colburn interview, *Vietnam Magazine*, Feb. 7, 2011; author's interview of Colburn, Dec. 17, 2015.

50. Thompson, "Massacre at My Lai"; author's interview of Colburn, June 20, 2013, July 6, 2015; Colburn interview, *Vietnam Magazine*, Feb. 7, 2011.

51. Lagunoy testimony, May 9, 1970, Hébert Hearings, 658–60, 665; Thompson testimony, Dec. 3, 4, 1969, Peers Inquiry, 2: Testimony, book 8, pp. 10, 34 (LC); Peers, *My Lai Inquiry*, 70; Mitchell quoted in Hersh, *My Lai 4*, p. 64; Thompson, "Massacre at My Lai"; Thompson, "Moral Courage in Combat," 22. See also Belknap, *Vietnam War on Trial*, 74.

52. A "dust-off" (or medevac) referred to a medical evacuation by helicopter. Reinberg, *In the Field*, 69.

53. Stanley testimony, Jan. 24, 1970, Peers Inquiry, 2: Testimony, book 25, pp. 21–24 (LC); Peers Report, 6–12; Thompson-Calley exchanges in Sack, *Calley*, 114–15; CID Report, Sept. 10, 1970, p. 8; CID Report, Sept. 25, 1970, p. 21; Thompson's anger noted by Olsen, CID Report, Sept. 10, 1970, p. 14; Lagunoy's account of noise, ibid., 16; Sledge remembering the helicopter landing twice at the ditch, ibid., 12; Calley to Sledge in Bilton and Sim, *Four Hours in My Lai*, 138.

54. Medina quoted in Sack, *Calley*, 115; Grzesik quoted in CID Report, Sept. 10, 1970, p. 16; Olsen's account of angry discussion between Calley and the pilot, followed by Mitchell's firing into the ditch, under Calley's orders, ibid., 14, and CID Report, Sept. 25, 1970, p. 8; Thompson, "Moral Courage in Combat," 22; Andreotta quoted in Belknap, *Vietnam War on Trial*, 74, 75–76, and in Colburn interview, *Vietnam Magazine*, Feb. 7, 2011; author's interview of Colburn, June 20, 2013.

55. Olsen testimony, CID Report, Sept. 10, 1970, p. 14; Colburn interview, *Vietnam Magazine*, Feb. 7, 2011.

56. Thompson, "Massacre at My Lai"; Thompson testimony, April 17, 1970, Hébert Hearings, 225–27.

57. Peers Report, 6–11, 6–12; Colburn interview, *Vietnam Magazine*, Feb. 7, 2011; Thompson, "Moral Courage in Combat," 22.

58. Moe interviewed by CID, Jan. 12, 1970, in Zaza, "Investigator's Statement," Sept. 18, 1970, p. 6.

59. Peers Report, 5–6, 7–3; Hersh *Cover-Up*, 12; Peers, *My Lai Inquiry*, 186.

60. Peers, *My Lai Inquiry*, 186, 188; Peers Report, 7–3, 7–4. One later account claimed this was a cement bridge, but one of the survivors of the My Khe 4 massacre, Vo Cao Tai, referred to it as an "old and weak" bamboo bridge. See Peers, *My Lai Inquiry*, 188; author's interview of Vo Cao Tai, July 18, 2012. Tai was forty-one years old in March 1968. His nephew, Vo Cao Loi, referred to him as "Uncle Bay." Loi also survived the onslaught. For Loi, see Seymour M. Hersh, "The Scene of the Crime: A Reporter's Journey to My Lai and the Secrets of the Past," *New Yorker*, March 30, 2015, available online at http://newyorker.com/magazine/2015/03/30/the-scene-of-the-crime, and Michael Sullivan, "In Danang, Where U.S. Troops First Landed, Memories of War Have Faded," *Parallels*, National Public Radio, May 2, 2015, http://www.npr.org/sections/parallels/2015/05/02/403597845/in-danang-where-u-s-troops-first-landed-memories-of-war-have-faded.

61. Peers Report, 2–3, 7–4, 7–5; Hersh, *Cover-Up*, 13; Peers, *My Lai Inquiry*, 186. Another helicopter would transport the wounded soldiers to Chu Lai for medical assistance.

62. Peers Report, 7–5, 7–6; Peers, *My Lai Inquiry*, 190; author's interview of Loi, July 14, 2014.

63. Peers Report, 7–7, 7–8; Peers, *My Lai Inquiry*, 190; author's interview of Tai, July 18, 2012; author's interview of Loi, July 14, 2014; Hersh, *Cover-Up*, 14.

64. Author's interviews of Loi, July 18, 2012, July 14, 2014.

65. Author's interview of Loi, July 15, 2012; William J. Duiker, *The Communist Road to Power in Vietnam* (Boulder, CO: Westview, 1981), 196, 213.

66. Author's interviews of Loi, July 15, 18, 2012, July 14, 2014; Nhung Walsh's interview of Loi, Aug. 9, 2010; author's interview of Tai, July 18, 2012. Both of Loi's brothers died in the war in 1968, one about a week before March 16, the other months afterward. Tai was eighty-four at the time of the interview and forty-one at the time of the invasion. Loi sat

in on my interview of his uncle, many times contributing to the conversation. I want to thank Nhung Walsh, a former student of mine from Hanoi, for arranging my interviews of Loi and Tai, translating and transcribing the conversations, and sharing her interview of Loi and an article he wrote.

67. Author's interviews of Tai, July 18, 2012, and of Loi, July 15, 18, 2012; July 14, 2014; Walsh's translated summary of Vo Cao Loi, "Thảm sát Sơn Mỹ—30 năm sau" [Sơn Mỹ massacre—a recall after 30 years], *Military History Journal* 1 (1998): 68–74.

68. Author's interviews of Loi, July 15, 18, 2012; author's interview of Tai, July 18, 2012; Walsh's interview of Loi, Aug. 9, 2010.

69. Walsh's interview of Loi, Aug. 9, 2010; author's interview of Loi, July 15, 2012; author's interview of Tai, July 18, 2012; Walsh's summary of article by Loi (1998).

70. Author's interviews of Loi, July 15, 18, 2012, July 14, 2014; author's interview of Tai, July 18, 2012.

71. Author's interview of Loi, July 14, 2014; Peers Report, 2–3, 7–8; Hersh, *Cover-Up*, 17; Peers, *My Lai Inquiry*, 190; deposition by Nguyen Thi Bay (female survivor of My Khe 4), Dec. 17, 1969, CID, cited in Bernd Greiner, *War Without Fronts: The USA in Vietnam*, trans. Anne Wyburd and Victoria Fern (New Haven, CT: Yale University Press, 2009), 215.

72. Peers Report, 3–3*, 7–9; Peers, *My Lai Inquiry*, 190; author's interview of Loi, July 15, 2012; Hersh, *Cover-Up*, 15–16. There are conflicting arguments regarding why Willingham called a cease-fire before entering the village. The decision may have grown out of Michles's directive against killing women and children, or it may have come from Barker, who had issued the same instruction to Charlie Company at this time, or Michles may have given the order in response to the extraordinary amount of gunfire coming from that direction. Considerable testimony indicates that he had long stressed the importance of avoiding unnecessary killing and therefore issued this order before Bravo's 1st Platoon crossed the bridge into My Khe 4. Peers Report, 7–8, 7–9.

73. Peers, *My Lai Inquiry*, 190; Peers Report, 7–8, 7–9; Hersh, *Cover-Up*, 16–17; Homer Hall testimony, Jan. 26, 1970, Peers Inquiry, 2: Testimony, book 19, p. 31 (LC). For about a month after the massacre, Lien and another female survivor, Le Thi Tuyet, delivered motivational speeches to Viet Cong soldiers in the Quang Ngai Province People's Army. They stirred up hatred among the soldiers, particularly among the newly enlisted, by telling their story at troop deployment and at what Loi called "vowing ceremonies," where soldiers wore funeral headbands and swore to avenge the dead. Lien worked at the Son My War Remnant Site until 1995, when she died after giving birth to a son. Walsh's interview of Loi, Aug. 9, 2010; author's interview of Loi, July 15, 2012.

74. Peers Report, 2–4, 7–8, 7–9, 7–10; Hersh, *Cover-Up*, 19; Peers, *My Lai Inquiry*, 190, 192; Bilton and Sim, *Four Hours in My Lai*, 297.

75. Peers Report, 7–10.

76. Author's interview of Loi, July 15, 2012.

77. Walsh's summary of article by Loi (1998); Walsh's interview of Loi, Aug. 9, 2010; author's interviews of Loi, July 15, 18, 2012; author's interview of Tai, July 18, 2012.

78. Author's interviews of Loi, July 15, 18, 2012; Walsh's interview of Loi, Aug. 9, 2010; author's interview of Tai, July 18, 2012. Loi worked with the Political Unit until South Vietnam's "liberation" in 1975. Only then did he see his father again. Loi entered Da

Nang University four years later, but had to withdraw and stay with the military because of the war with Cambodia. In 1990, he studied at the Academy of Military Technology in Hanoi for about a year when he shifted his interests. Despite his training in engineering, he collaborated with others in writing two books, both on the military history of his home district of Tinh Khe. Author's interview of Loi, July 15, 2012.

79. Peers Report, 7–1, 7–2, 7–10, 7–11. These Vietnamese reports came in late March and early April 1968. The district chief forwarded the village chief's report to the province chief on April 11, 1968. The hamlet chief left the area before the assault and had not returned. In a highly dubious breakdown of the casualties, he alleged that the dead included fourteen civilians, but all the rest were Viet Cong: fifteen soldiers, twenty male and thirteen female cadres (including mothers of VC soldiers), and twenty-five guerrilla and supply personnel.

80. Bay deposition to CID, Dec. 17, 1969, in Greiner, *War Without Fronts*, 215–16; Peers Report, 7–2, 7–10; Peers, *My Lai Inquiry*, 192, 194; Hersh, *Cover-Up*, 18.

81. Peers Report, 7–9; Peers, *My Lai Inquiry*, 190–92. For the testimonies of the soldiers from Bravo Company, see Peers Inquiry, 2: Testimony, books 19–22 and the first testimony in book 23 (LC).

82. Author's interviews of Loi, July 18, 2012, July 14, 2014.

83. For Viet Cong nightly presence in My Lai 4, see Pham Thi Don (fifty-one-year-old female) testimony, CID Report, Sept. 10, 1970, pp. 26, 6. Loi made the same observations about My Khe 4. Author's interviews of Loi, July 15, 18, 2012.

84. Truong Quy, aka Qui (Viet Cong cadre) testimony, CID Report, Sept. 10, 1970, p. 33; Vien testimony, ibid., 36, and in "Fact Sheet: My Lai," enclosed in in Gustafson to Chief of Staff, U.S. Army, Jan. 21, 1970, Tufts Collection on My Lai (U. of Mich.); Thi testimony, CID Report, Sept. 25, 1970, p. 37, and "Fact Sheet: My Lai," enclosed in Gustafson to Chief of Staff, U.S. Army, Jan. 21, 1970; Co testimony in "Fact Sheet: My Lai," enclosed in Gustafson to Chief of Staff, U.S. Army, Jan. 27, 1970, ibid. Do Vien was later captured and imprisoned at Chu Lai. Bilton and Sim, *Four Hours in My Lai*, 281.

Five

1. Hersh, *My Lai 4*, p. 52.

2. Peers Report, 6–11; Medina testimony, Dec. 4, 1969, Peers Inquiry, 2: Testimony, book 23, p. 17 (LC); Roger Alaux testimony, Jan. 6, 1970, ibid., 22, 35; Hersh, *My Lai 4*, pp. 52–53. A *papa-san* was the GIs' term for an older East Asian male respected by youth as wise. A *mama-san* was the female counterpart. Reinberg, *In the Field*, 135, 161.

3. Hersh, *My Lai 4*, 57.

4. Bilton and Sim 1989 interview of Haeberle, Papers of *Four Hours in My Lai*, LHCMA (KCL); Bilton and Sim, *Four Hours in My Lai*, 123–24, 129.

5. CID Report, Sept. 10, 1970, pp. 30, 32, 35.

6. Ibid., 34; Polston quoted ibid., 33. Sergeant First Class Lewis H. Geis and Criminal Investigator and Chief Warrant Officer André Feher thought T'Souvas was under the influence of marijuana or drugs when interviewed. Ibid., 34. At the time of the CID investigation, T'Souvas wore an armband on his uniform saying, "ASHAMED OF

AMERICAL MURDERERS," and he admitted to using marijuana and drugs for nearly five years. Bilton and Sim, *Four Hours in My Lai*, 277–78.

7. Lopez testimony, CID Report, Sept. 10, 1970, p. 30; Flores testimony, ibid., 31; Oliver testimony, ibid., 36.

8. T'Souvas testimony, ibid., 34; Pendleton testimony, ibid., 35, and Sept. 25, 1970, p. 19; Doherty testimony, ibid., 20; Terry quoted in Hersh, *My Lai 4*, pp. 72–73. T'Souvas claimed he had put the "living dead" out of their misery. The army charged him with murder but dropped the case and gave him an honorable discharge. Two decades after My Lai, he was homeless in Pittsburgh when his common-law wife Kathleen shot him in the back of the head during a drunken struggle under a bridge over a bottle of vodka. Marylynne Pitz, "T'Souvas Convicted in Boyfriend's Death," *Pittsburgh Post-Gazette*, April 22, 1989; "My Lai Figure Dies a Drifter in a Shooting," *New York Times*, Sept. 14, 1988; Bilton and Sim, *Four Hours in My Lai*, 358–60.

9. Hersh, *My Lai 4*, pp. 53, 56; Medina testimony, April 15, 1970, Hébert Hearings, 65; Medina testimony, CID Report, Sept. 10, 1970, pp. 43–44, and Sept. 25, 1970, p. 17; Roberts testimony, CID Report, Sept. 10, 1970, p. 51; West testimony, ibid., 32.

10. Flores testimony, CID Report, Sept. 10, 1970, p. 31; Widmer testimony, ibid., 45–46; Kinch testimony, ibid., 39–40; Heming testimony, ibid., 47–48; Flynn testimony, ibid., 49; Fagan testimony, ibid., 39; Martin testimony, ibid., 50–51; Alaux testimony, ibid., 50; SP4 Floyd Wright testimony, ibid., 29.

11. Pendleton testimony, ibid., 35; Flynn testimony, ibid., 48–49; Paul testimony, ibid., 46–47; Bernhardt testimony, ibid., 25; Bernhardt testimony, Dec. 29, 1969, Peers Inquiry, 2: Testimony, book 25, pp. 13–14, 95–96 (LC); Hersh, *My Lai 4*, pp. 53–54, 59 (Bernhardt quote).

12. Carter Witness Statement, Nov. 6, 1969, pp. 1–2, My Lai Collection (VATTU); CID Report, Sept. 10, 1970, pp. 16–17.

13. First quote by Carter in his Witness Statement, Nov. 6, 1969, p. 4, My Lai Collection (VATTU); other Carter quotes in Hersh, *My Lai 4*, pp. 54, 56.

14. Bernhardt testimony to Wilson (IG), May 8, 1969, Box 1, Folder 4, pp. 184–87, 203, My Lai Collection (VATTU); Bernhardt testimony, CID Report, Sept. 10, 1970, p. 25; Bernhardt interview in Strick, *Interviews with My Lai Veterans*; Garfolo ibid.

15. Haeberle testimony, CID Report, Sept. 10, p. 51.

16. First Haeberle quote in "Massacre at My Lai," *Life*, 41; second Haeberle quote in Hersh, *My Lai 4*, pp. 54–55; Haeberle testimony, April 23, 1970, Hébert Hearings, 283, and April 28, 1970, 495–501.

17. Roberts testimony, Dec. 17, 1969, Peers Inquiry, 2: Testimony, book 14, pp. 27–30 (LC); Roberts testimony, CID Report, Sept. 10, 1970, p. 52; "Massacre at Mylai," *Life*, 44.

18. Peers Report, 6–14, 6–15; Haeberle testimony, Jan. 17, 1970, Peers Inquiry, 2: Testimony, book 11, pp. 24–25 (LC); Medina testimony, Dec. 4, 1969, Peers Inquiry, 2: Testimony, book 23, pp. 35–36, 42, 79–80; Medina testimony, April 15, 1970, Hébert Hearings, 65–67, 71.

19. Minh quote in CID Report, Sept. 10, 1970, p. 53. See also Bilton and Sim, *Four Hours in My Lai*, 125–26.

20. Kinch testimony, Jan. 21, 1970, Peers Inquiry, 2: Testimony, book 28, pp. 9, 12, 16, 28–30, 51 (LC); *American Experience*, "My Lai," transcript, 10.

21. Medina testimony, Dec. 4, 1969, Peers Inquiry, 2: Testimony, book 23, pp. 79–81, 83–84 (LC).

22. Peers, *My Lai Inquiry*, 180. Within the context of Peers's discussion, the three weapons appear to have been rifles, although he does not specifically say so.

23. Colburn testimony, Dec. 20, 1969, Peers Inquiry, 2: Testimony, book 5, p. 11 (LC); Culverhouse testimony, April 17, 1970, Hébert Hearings, 187.

24. Culverhouse testimony, April 17, 1970, Hébert Hearings, 187; Peers Report, 6–13, 6–15; Thompson testimony, Dec. 3, 1969, Peers Inquiry, 2: Testimony, book 8, pp. 10–11 (LC); Thompson, "Massacre at My Lai," *Newsweek*, March 3, 1999, 64; Colburn interview, Appy, *Patriots* 347; Angers, *Forgotten Hero of My Lai*, 79ff.

25. Colburn interview, *Vietnam Magazine*, Feb. 7, 2011.

26. *American Experience*, "My Lai," transcript, 19.

27. Thompson testimony, Dec. 3, 5, 1969, Peers Inquiry, 2: Testimony, book 8, pp. 11, 51 (LC); Henderson testimony, Dec. 19, 1969, Peers Inquiry, 2: Testimony, book 12, pp. 245–46; Thompson interviewed in Tim Sebastian, "HARDtalk: The Lessons of Vietnam," *BBC News*, May 26, 2004; question-and-answer session with Thompson and Colburn, U.S. Naval Academy, Fall 2003.

28. Peers, *My Lai Inquiry*, 71; Culverhouse testimony, April 17, 1970, Hébert Hearings, 188; Colburn testimony, April 17, 1970, Hébert Hearings, 208; Colburn interview, *Vietnam Magazine*, Feb. 7, 2011.

29. Thompson quoted in Anderson, *Facing My Lai*, 29.

30. Ibid.; Thompson testimony, Dec. 3, 1969, Peers Inquiry, 2: Testimony, book 8, p. 19 (LC).

31. Author's interview of Colburn, June 20, 2013.

32. Ibid.; Bilton and Sim, *Four Hours in My Lai*, 139; Hersh, *My Lai 4*, p. 65; Henderson testimony, Dec. 12, 1969, Peers Inquiry, 2: Testimony, book 12, pp. 132–33 (LC).

33. Question-and-answer session, U.S. Naval Academy, Fall 2003.

34. Colburn interview, *Vietnam Magazine*, Feb. 7, 2011; author's interview of Colburn, June 20, 2013; Colburn testimony, Dec. 20, 1969, Peers Inquiry, 2: Testimony, book 5, pp. 17–18 (LC); Colburn testimony, April 17, 1970, Hébert Hearings, 208–9; *Frontline*, "Remember My Lai."

35. Colburn interview, *Vietnam Magazine*, Feb. 7, 2011; author's interview of Colburn, June 20, 2013; Colburn testimony, April 17, 1970, Hébert Hearings, 210–11.

36. *American Experience*, "My Lai," transcript, 19.

37. Colburn testimony, Dec. 20, 1969, Peers Inquiry, 2: Testimony, book 5, p. 20 (LC); Angers, *Forgotten Hero of My Lai*, 81.

38. Thompson, "Moral Courage in Combat," 23.

39. Thompson's account in Anderson, *Facing My Lai*, 29–30; author's interviews of Colburn, June 20, Sept. 4, 2013.

40. First Thompson quote in *American Experience*, "My Lai," transcript, 19; second Thompson quote in Anderson, *Facing My Lai*, 30; Thompson testimony, Dec. 3, 1969, Peers Inquiry, 2: Testimony, book 8, p. 11 (LC); author's interview of Colburn, Oct. 10, 2013; Colburn interview, *Vietnam Magazine*, Feb. 7, 2011; Culverhouse testimony, April 17, 1970, Hébert Hearings, 189, 192.

41. Colburn interview, Appy, *Patriots*, 348; author's interview of Tilford, April 4, 2015.

42. Hersh, *My Lai 4*, p. 65.

43. Ibid.; author's interview of Colburn, June 20, 2013.

44. Author's interview of Colburn, June 20, 2013; Millians quoted in *American Experience*, "My Lai," transcript, 19.

45. Culverhouse testimony, April 17, 1970, Hébert Hearings, 189–90, 198; Henderson testimony, Dec. 12, 1969, Peers Inquiry, 2: Testimony, book 12, pp. 132–33 (LC); Colburn testimony, Dec. 20, 1969, Peers Inquiry, 2: Testimony, book 5, p. 20; author's interview of Colburn, Oct. 10, 2013. For Nhanh's quote, see Amy Goodman and Juan González, "Hugh Thompson's Crewmember Remembers Helping to Stop the My Lai Massacre," *Democracy Now!* Jan. 18, 2006, http://www.democracynow.org/2006/1/18/hugh_thompsons_crewmember_remembers_helping_to Stop the My Lai Massacre. See also Angers, *Forgotten Hero of My Lai*, 83–84. One of the youths died before reaching the hospital. Hersh, *My Lai 4*, p. 65.

46. Culverhouse testimony, April 17, 1970, Hébert Hearings, 189–91, 196–97, 199. That soldier was Sergeant Mitchell, ordered by Calley to finish off those Vietnamese not yet dead.

47. Medina testimony, April 15, 1970, Hébert Hearings, 69.

48. Ibid.; Culverhouse testimony, April 17, 1970, Hébert Hearings, 190.

49. Thompson quoted in Anderson, *Facing My Lai*, 28–29; Colburn interview, Appy, *Patriots*, 347; Thompson, "Massacre at My Lai," 64; Dan Kaufman, "Reconciliation at My Lai," *New Yorker*, March 24, 2013, available online at http://www.newyorker.com/news/news-desk/reconciliation-at-my-lai. Haeberle's photographs include this scene.

50. Thompson in Anderson, *Facing My Lai*, 30–31.

51. Thompson's thoughts are derived from his interview in Sebastian, "HARDtalk"; his report of these events cited ibid.; and his comments in question-and-answer session, U.S. Naval Academy; Thompson, "Massacre at My Lai," 64.

52. Angers, *Forgotten Hero of My Lai*, 87–88.

53. Peers Report, 2–3.

54. The other four soldiers, according to West, were Robert Smith, James Emerson, Ricky Neria, and Larry Polston. West testimony, CID Report, May 25, 1970, p. 6; Hersh, *My Lai 4*, p. 67; Roberts testimony, Dec. 17, 1969, Peers Inquiry, 2: Testimony, book 14, p. 55 (LC). Stanley from the 1st Platoon was an eyewitness. See his testimony in CID Report, May 25, 1970, p. 5. The CID investigation listed the eight guests as Ba Phu, Do Thi Can, Ba So, Ba Moi, Do Thi Be, Do Hoi, Do Thi Nhut, and Do Hat. Ibid. Do Vien was later captured. Vien testimony, Jan. 4, 1970, Peers Inquiry, 2: Testimony, book 32, p. 7 (LC); Bilton and Sim, *Four Hours in My Lai*, 152, 281, 283.

55. First quote in CID Report, May 25, 1970, p. 5; second and fourth quotes in Hersh, *My Lai 4*, p. 67; third quote in Belknap, *Vietnam War on Trial*, 68; Haeberle testimony, Jan. 17, 1970, Peers Inquiry, 2: Testimony, book 11, p. 17 (LC).

56. Roberts testimony, Dec. 17, 1969, Peers Inquiry, 2: Testimony, book 32, p. 22 (LC); Haeberle testimony, Jan. 17, 1970, Peers Inquiry, 2: Testimony, book 11, p. 18; Hersh, *My Lai 4*, p. 67. Stanley claimed that all six soldiers accosted both Can and Moi. See his testimony in CID Report, May 25, 1970, p. 5. One of the six soldiers, twenty-two-year-old Robert Smith from Texas, did not agree with Stanley's assertion. He told CID that he saw Gerald Smith try to "feel up" Ba So and Do Thi Can. Robert Smith testimony, CID Report, Oct. 1, 1970, pp. 1, 4. For noting the sexual assaults as a critical part of this

episode, see Valerie Wieskamp, "Sexual Assault and the My Lai Massacre: The Erasure of Sexual Violence from Public Memory of the Vietnam War," in *Mythologizing the Vietnam War: Visual Culture and Mediated Memory*, ed. Jennifer Good, Val Williams, Paul Lowe, and Brigitte Lardinois (Newcastle upon Tyne, UK: Cambridge Scholars, 2014).

57. Grzesik testimony, CID Report, May 25, 1970, pp. 5–6; Hersh, *My Lai 4*, p. 67.

58. Haeberle quoted in *Frontline*, "Remember My Lai"; Roberts testimony, Dec. 17, 1969, Peers Inquiry, 2: Testimony, book 32, pp. 6, 22 (LC); *American Experience*, "My Lai," transcript, 15; Hersh, *My Lai 4*, pp. 66–67; CID Report, May 25, 1970, pp. 5–6.

59. Haeberle testimony, Jan. 17, 1970, Peers Inquiry, 2: Testimony, book 11, p. 2 (LC). Roberts asserted, "I didn't get the impression there was any collecting area." Roberts testimony, Dec. 17, 1969, Peers Inquiry, 2: Testimony, book 32, p. 55.

60. Roberts testimony, Dec. 17, 1969, Peers Inquiry, 2: Testimony, book 32, p. 6.

61. CID Report, May 25, 1970, p. 5.

62. Ibid.; Hersh, *My Lai 4*, p. 67.

63. Haeberle testimony, Jan. 17, 1970, Peers Inquiry, 2: Testimony, book 11, pp. 2, 17–18 (LC); Roberts testimony, Dec. 17, 1969, Peers Inquiry, 2: Testimony, book 32, pp. 6, 22; Hersh, *My Lai 4*, pp. 66–68. Conflicting testimonies abound. Three witnesses to the shootings claimed that all six soldiers shot the Vietnamese. West denied the indecent assault charges but told CID that he and all five other soldiers killed the seven Vietnamese civilians. CID Report, May 25, 1970, p. 6. Stanley attested that he saw West, PFC Gerald Smith, and several other soldiers "molest and then kill about nine women and children" while Haeberle took pictures. CID Report, Sept. 10, 1970, p. 15. PFC Richard Wyatt from the 3rd Platoon saw up to nine unidentified soldiers molest and then kill seven women and children that Haeberle photographed just before their deaths. CID Report, May 25, 1970, p. 6, and Sept. 10, 1970, pp. 32–33. Three other soldiers claimed that West and Gerald Smith killed the seven Vietnamese: Grzesik, Fred Dustin, and Robert Smith, one of the six soldiers involved in the episode. Grzesik, CID Report, May 25, 1970, p. 6; Dustin, ibid., 5; Smith, CID Report, Oct. 1, 1970, pp. 1, 4. West's story lacks credibility: Emerson was in a hospital ship at the time of the incident. CID Report, May 25, 1970, p. 1. Haeberle, Grzesik, Dustin, and Robert Smith all saw either smoke coming from the muzzles of the two M-16s or West and Gerald Smith actually firing their assault rifles or pointing them at the victims lying on the ground. Roberts heard automatic fire but thought it could have come from the M-60 machine gun. Roberts testimony, Dec. 17, 1969, Peers Inquiry, 2: Testimony, book 32, p. 6 (LC).

64. *American Experience*, "My Lai," transcript, 15.

65. Hersh, *My Lai 4*, p. 68.

66. Roberts testimony, Dec. 17, 1969, Peers Inquiry, 2: Testimony, book 32, pp. 22–23, 56–57 (LC).

67. Olsen quote in Bilton and Sim, *Four Hours in My Lai*, 368.

68. John Roberts (Jay's father) testimony, April 29, 1970, Hébert Hearings, 558–59.

69. Vien testimony, Jan. 4, 1970, Peers Inquiry, 2: Testimony, book 32, p. 7 (LC); Ba So, Do Thi Can, and Do Hat identified by Do Chuc of My Lai 4 in his testimony in CID Report, May 25, 1970, p. 6, and CID Report, Sept. 10, 1970, p. 65. Truong Quy, another resident of the hamlet and a Viet Cong cadre, identified several dead in the village,

including Do Thi Be, Ba Phu, Do Thi Can, Ba So, and her daughter Ba Moi. CID Report, May 25, 1970, p. 6. The CID investigation claimed that Ba Phu and Do Hoi were among those in the house when the soldiers arrived, but Do Hoi escaped with Le Thi Huynh.

70. Huynh in CID Report, May 25, 1970, pp. 5–7; Vien testimony, Jan. 4, 1970, Peers Inquiry, 2: Testimony, book 32, pp. 2–3, 5–7 (LC). Vien presumably buried his sister Do Thi Can either before or after his son and the little girl.

71. Vien testimony, Jan. 4, 1970, Peers Inquiry, 2: Testimony, book 32, pp. 5, 7 (LC); Vien testimony, CID Report, Sept. 25, 1970, p. 36; Vien's death count, CID Report, Sept. 4, 1970, p. 8; Fact Sheet, enclosed in Gustafson to Chief of Staff, U.S. Army, Jan. 21, 1970, p. 3, Tufts Collection on My Lai (U. of Mich.); Bilton and Sim, *Four Hours in My Lai*, 152–53 (death of Do Thi Nguyen), 281 (Vien capture).

72. Hersh, *My Lai 4*, p. 68; CID Report, Sept. 10, 1970, p. 17; Bilton and Sim, *Four Hours in My Lai*, 47.

73. Hersh, *My Lai 4*, pp. 68–69; Bilton and Sim, *Four Hours in My Lai*, 133–34.

74. For this account, see Stanley testimony, Jan. 24, 1970, Peers Inquiry, 2: Testimony, book 25, p. 14 (LC).

75. Ibid., 15–16; Stanley testimony, CID Report, Sept. 10, 1970, p. 15; Hersh, *My Lai 4*, p. 69.

76. Task Force casualty report, April 6, 1968, Exhibit M-109, HQ 11th Infantry Brigade, Peers Inquiry, 3: Exhibits, book 4, p. 380 (LC); CID Report, Sept. 10, 1970, p. 4; Bernhardt testimony to Wilson (IG), May 8, 1969, Box 1, Folder 4, p. 188, My Lai Collection (VATTU). Carter insisted that his wound came from "the accidental discharge of his .45 caliber pistol." CID Report, Sept. 10, 1970, p. 17. Among the writers who consider the wound accidental, see Bilton and Sim, *Four Hours in My Lai*, 76–77, 80, 133–34; Allison, *My Lai*, 46; and Belknap, *Vietnam War on Trial*, 67. The Peers commission remained noncommittal on whether the injury was an accident. See Peers Report, 6–16, and Peers, *My Lai Inquiry*, 178.

77. Bilton and Sim, *Four Hours in My Lai*, 134.

78. Peers, *My Lai Inquiry*, 178.

79. Ibid., 180.

80. Ibid.; CID Report, Sept. 10, 1970, p. 17. Those from the 1st Platoon included Meadlo, Stanley, Lagunoy, Carter, Conti, SP4 Bruce Cox, PFC Rennard Doines, SP4 Roy Wood, Bergthold, PFC William Lloyd, and Olsen. See CID Report, Sept. 25, 1970, pp. 15–16, 18–20. Those from the 2nd Platoon included Buchanon, Fields, Bunning, Gonzalez, Diego Rodriguez, SP4 John Mower, Partsch, PFC Tommy Moss, LaMartina, and Hutson. See CID Report, Sept. 10, 1970, pp. 20–22, 24, 27–28. Those in the 3rd Platoon included Lieutenant Jeffrey LaCross and SP4 Everette Cayot. See ibid., 29–30, 32. Those from the command group included: Paul, ibid., 46, and CID Report, Sept. 25, 1970, p. 16; Haeberle, and Roberts, CID Report, Sept. 10, 1970, pp. 51–52.

81. Henderson testimony to Wilson (IG), May 26, 1969, Box 1, Folder 11, pp. 454, 459, 475–77, 480–81, My Lai Collection (VATTU); Henderson testimony, Dec. 19, 1969, Peers Inquiry, 2: Testimony, book 12, p. 234 (LC).

82. Henderson testimony, Dec. 19, 1969, Peers Inquiry, 2: Testimony, book 12, p. 234 (LC).

83. Hersh, *My Lai 4*, p. 66; Colburn testimony, Dec. 20, 1969, Peers Inquiry, 2: Testimony, book 5, p. 22 (LC); Colburn interview, *Vietnam Magazine*, Feb. 7, 2011; Kaufman, "Reconciliation at My Lai"; *American Experience*, "My Lai," transcript, 17.

84. Thompson testimony, Dec. 3, 1969, Peers Inquiry, 2: Testimony, book 8, p. 15 (LC); author's interview with Colburn, June 20, 2013; Colburn interview, Appy, *Patriots*, 348; Thompson, "Moral Courage in Combat," 23–24; *Frontline*, "Remember My Lai"; Thompson, "Massacre at My Lai," 64. Thompson made this assertion to the inspector general (quoted in Hersh, *My Lai 4*, p. 66).

85. Colburn quoted in *American Experience*, "My Lai," transcript, 20; Colburn interview, *Vietnam Magazine*, Feb. 7, 2011; Colburn testimony, Dec. 20, 1969, Peers Inquiry, 2: Testimony, book 5, p. 22 (LC); Thompson on his son on "Back to My Lai," *60 Minutes*, March 29, 1998, shown before Thompson lecture, "Moral Courage in Combat."

86. Do Hoa quoted in *American Experience*, "My Lai," transcript, 20; author's interview of Colburn, June 20, 2013. This show refers to the boy as Do Ba, but Colburn more convincingly calls him Do Hoa. Colburn saw him more than once on visits to My Lai years afterward, the last time in 2008, when Colburn had his picture taken with Do Hoa and his family. "Being reunited with the boy was just…I can't even describe it," said Colburn, who was standing with Thompson, choked up with emotion. Colburn interview, *Vietnam Magazine*, Feb. 7, 2011; Nell Boyce, "Heroes: Hugh Thompson: Reviled, Then Honored, for His Role at My Lai," *U.S. News and World Report*, Aug. 20, 2001, available online at http://www.aaezine.org/articles/vol13/13N1HughThompsonMyLaiHero1968.shtml.

87. Mansell testimony, April 17, 1970, Hébert Hearings, 152–54, 164, 158–60, 171–72; Mansell in CID Report, Sept. 10, 1970, p. 9; CID Report, Sept. 25, 1970, p. 21; Colburn testimony to Wilson (IG), June 19, 1969, Box 1, Folder 17, pp. 765, 771–72, My Lai Collection (VATTU); Colburn testimony, Dec. 20, 1969, Peers Inquiry, 2: Testimony, book 5, p. 22 (LC); Do Hoa quoted in *American Experience*, "My Lai," transcript, 20; *Frontline*, "Remember My Lai"; Angers, *Forgotten Hero of My Lai*, 87; Bilton and Sim, *Four Hours in My Lai*, 139–40; Hersh, *My Lai 4*, p. 66. See Thompson in Anderson, *Facing My Lai*, 30. Thompson remarked that in Vietnam there was always an orphanage next door to the hospital. Thompson, "Moral Courage in Combat," 24.

88. Hersh, *My Lai 4*, pp. 54–56.

89. Ibid., 72; Bunning testimony, Jan. 16, 1970, Peers Inquiry, 2: Testimony, book 26, pp. 36–37 (LC).

90. CID Report, Sept. 10, 1970, p. 5; Bernhardt testimony to Wilson (IG), May 8, 1969, Box 1, Folder 4, p. 210, My Lai Collection (VATTU); Partsch quoted in *American Experience*, "My Lai," transcript, 20. For a host of views on whether there had been a cease-fire order, see CID Report, Sept. 10, 1970, pp. 21–22, 25, 28–29, 32–33, 35–36, 38, 40.

91. Haeberle testimony, Jan. 17, 1970, Peers Inquiry, 2: Testimony, book 11, p. 53 (LC); Haeberle testimony, April 28, 1970, Hébert Hearings, 503–4; Hersh, *My Lai 4*, p. 69.

92. Peers Report, 2–3, 6–19; CID Report, Sept. 10, 1970, p. 43; Hersh, *My Lai 4*, pp. 74, 84; Bunning testimony, Jan. 16, 1970, Peers Inquiry, 2: Testimony, book 26, p. 39 (LC); Mosley-Bunning telephone conversation, May 13, 1970, pp. 3, 5, My Lai Collection (VATTU).

93. "Massacre at Mylai," *Life*, 44.

94. Peers Report, 10–2.

95. Hersh, *My Lai 4*, p. 82.

96. Kinch testimony, Jan. 21, 1970, Peers Inquiry, 2: Testimony, book 28, pp. 29–30. Kinch was an assistant gunner in the weapons platoon.

97. Hersh, *My Lai 4*, pp. 82–83.

98. Ibid., 77; MACV Communiqué, March 16, 1968, Peers Inquiry, 3: Exhibits, book 4, Misc. Docs., M-61, p. 255 (LC).

99. CID Report, Sept. 10, 1970, pp. 51–52; Bilton and Sim, *Four Hours in My Lai*, 182–83.

100. Bilton interview of Haeberle in 1989, Papers of *Four Hours in My Lai*, LHCMA (KCL); Bilton and Sim, *Four Hours in My Lai*, 183. The Peers Inquiry concluded that Roberts and Haeberle "failed to report what they had seen." Roberts wrote a "false and misleading account," and Haeberle "withheld and suppressed" his "photographic evidence of atrocities." Peers Report, 2–10.

Six

1. Jay A. Roberts, Information Office of the Americal Division's 11th Infantry Brigade, "Running Battle," [April?] 1968, Peers Inquiry, 3: Exhibits, book 4, Misc. Docs., M-58 (LC); "TF Barker Crushes Enemy Stronghold," March 22, 1968 Peers Inquiry, ibid., M-17; Hersh, *My Lai 4*, pp. 77–79. The news stories referred to Pinkville or My Lai, not yet called My Lai 4.

2. Roberts, "Running Battle"; "TF Barker Crushes Enemy Stronghold."

3. Roberts, "Running Battle"; "TF Barker Crushes Enemy Stronghold"; "U.S. Troops Surround Reds, Kill 128," *Pacific Stars and Stripes*, March 18, 1968, Peers Inquiry, 3: Exhibits, book 4, Misc. Docs., M-88 (LC).

4. "TF Barker Crushes Enemy Stronghold;" "U.S. Troops Surround Reds"; Barker quoted in Roberts, "Running Battle"; largest number killed in *Southern Cross*, Americal News Sheet of Information Office in Marine Corps base of Chu Lai, March 17, 1968, Peers Inquiry, 3: Exhibits, book 4, Misc. Docs., M-23 (LC); Americal News Sheet, March 18, 19, 1968, ibid.; San Francisco clipping of story, March 17, 1968, ibid.; *New York Times*, March 17, 1968, pp. 1, 5; Bilton and Sim, *Four Hours in My Lai*, 70.

5. Bilton and Sim, *Four Hours in My Lai*, 69–70; "TF Barker Crushes Enemy Stronghold."

6. News Release 76–68, Office of Information, U.S. MACV, March 16, 1968, Peers Inquiry, 3: Exhibits, book 4, Misc. Docs., M-61 (LC); "TF Barker Crushes Enemy Stronghold"; Roberts, "Running Battle"; *Southern Cross*, March 17, 1968, Peers Inquiry, 3: Exhibits, book 4, Misc. Docs., M-23.

7. "TF Barker Crushes Enemy Stronghold"; Hersh, *My Lai 4*, 78–79; Roberts, "Running Battle"; Westmoreland's congratulations in *Southern Cross*, March 20, 1968, Peers Inquiry, 3: Exhibits, book 4, Misc. Docs., M-65 (LC). In congressional hearings two years later, Westmoreland explained his reasoning behind the high recognition. "It appeared that the operation—with 128 Viet Cong killed and three weapons captured at the cost of only two U.S. soldiers killed—was a tactical success. In fact, from the operational reports we received, it appeared so successful that I responded with a congratulatory message." He noted that it was one of forty-seven others he sent out in his name during the first three months of 1968. Westmoreland testimony, June 10, 1970, Hébert Hearings, 837. See also William C. Westmoreland, *A Soldier Reports* (1976; New York: Dell, 1980.), 500.

8. Roberts testimony in CID Report, Sept. 10, 1970, p. 52.

9. Peers Report, 10–11; Colburn testimony to Wilson (IG), June 19, 1969, Box 1, Folder 17, pp. 765, 771–72, My Lai Collection (VATTU); Angers, *Forgotten Hero of My Lai*,

87–88; Bilton and Sim, *Four Hours in My Lai*, 139–40; Thompson quoted in Anderson, *Facing My Lai*, 31; Barry C. Lloyd, Witness Statement, Jan. 27, 1970, p. 2, Tufts Collection on My Lai (U. of Mich.).

10. Peers Report, 2–4, 10–11; Bilton and Sim, *Four Hours in My Lai*, 140.

11. CID Report, July 20, 1970, p. 8; Watke testimony, Dec. 8, 11, 19, 1969, Peers Inquiry, 2: Testimony, book 8, pp. 17, 74, 84–85, 150 (LC); Thompson quoted in Anderson, *Facing My Lai*, 31; Peers, *My Lai Inquiry*, 96–97; Belknap, *Vietnam War on Trial*, 79, 81; Angers, *Forgotten Hero at My Lai*, 88.

12. Peers Report, 10–12; Watke testimony, Dec. 8, 11 12, 19, 1969, Peers Inquiry, 2: Testimony, book 8, pp. 20, 22, 31, 72, 76–78, 85, 148, 150 (LC); Kubert testimony, Jan. 15, 1970, Peers Inquiry, 2: Testimony, book 6, p. 22; Bilton and Sim, *Four Hours in My Lai*, 140; Belknap, *Vietnam War on Trial*, 81–82.

13. Watke testimony, Dec. 11, 1969, Peers Inquiry, 2: Testimony, book 8, pp. 148–49 (LC).

14. Thompson testimony, Feb. 10, 1970, ibid., 114 (LC).

15. Watke testimony, Dec. 8, 11, 1969, ibid., 31, 85–86.

16. Peers Report, 9–10, 9–11, 9–12, 10–12; Belknap, *Vietnam War on Trial*, 81; Peers, *My Lai Inquiry*, 97; MACV Directive 20-4, April 27, 1967, ibid., 31, 262; MACV Message, "Mistreatment of Detainees and PW Prisoner of War," Feb. 12, 1968, ibid., 31, 263. See also ibid., 32, 264–67.

17. Peers Report, 9–11; Peers, *My Lai Inquiry*, 262.

18. Peers Report, 2–5, 10–12, 10–13; Watke testimony, Dec. 8, 11, 1969, Peers Inquiry, 2: Testimony, book 8, pp. 21–23, 30, 90, 102 (LC); Peers, *My Lai Inquiry*, 97; Bilton and Sim, *Four Hours in My Lai*, 140.

19. Stephens testimony, April 15, 1970, Hébert Hearings, 35, 37–39 (first quote); Stephens testimony, Jan. 7, 1970, Peers Inquiry, 2: Testimony, book 16, pp. 16 (second quote), 30 (LC); Bilton and Sim, *Four Hours in My Lai*, 107.

20. Stephens testimony, April 15, 1970, Hébert Hearings, 40–41 (quote on 40); Stephens testimony, Jan. 7, 1970, Peers Inquiry, 2: Testimony, book 16, p. 52 (LC).

21. Change of mission noted by panel member in Stephens testimony, Jan. 7, 1970, Peers Inquiry, 2: Testimony, book 16, p. 18 (LC); Calhoun testimony in CID Report, Sept. 10, 1970, pp. 55–56; Bilton and Sim, *Four Hours in My Lai*, 128, 141.

22. Ronald Ridenhour testimony, Jan. 29, 1970, Peers Inquiry, 2: Testimony, book 14, pp. 25, 42, 43; Bilton and Sim, *Four Hours in My Lai*, 140–41. Ridenhour was not at My Lai 4 on March 16 but interviewed some of the soldiers who were there.

23. Author's interviews with Colburn, April 8, 2014, Dec. 17, 2015; Anderson, *Facing My Lai*, 31; Angers, *Forgotten Hero at My Lai*, 89.

24. Medina testimony, Dec. 4, 1969, Peers Inquiry, 2: Testimony, book 23, pp. 37–38 (LC).

25. Creswell testimony, April 23, 1970, Hébert Hearings, 327–31, 333, 336–37 (quote); Lewis testimony, April 27, 1970, Hébert Hearings, 402, 405–406; Creswell in Riddle to Tufts, enclosed in Weekly My Lai Fact Sheet, U.S. Army, Dec. 16, 1969, pp. 2–3, Tufts Collection on My Lai (U. of Mich.); CID Report, Sept. 10, 1970, pp. 58, 61; Peers Report, 10–38, 10–39; Bilton and Sim, *Four Hours in My Lai*, 175; Angers, *Forgotten Hero of My Lai*, 89.

26. Peers Report, 10–38, 10–39; Lewis testimony, April 27, 1970, Hébert Hearings, 404–10 (first quote on 407; second quote on 408); Peers, *My Lai Inquiry*, 130; Bilton and Sim, *Four Hours in My Lai*, 176.

27. Creswell thought Thompson came to him as more of a friend than a chaplain, even though he was preparing Thompson for confirmation. Creswell testimony, April 23, 1970, Hébert Hearings, 331, 333. The Peers commission concluded that neither Lewis nor Creswell "took adequate or timely steps" to bring Thompson's charges to Koster, failing to realize that an investigation of war crimes through chaplain channels was "preposterous." Peers Report, 10–39, 10–40.

28. Fact Sheet, enclosed in Gustafson to Chief of Staff, U.S. Army, after Dec. 16, 1969, p. 2, Tufts Collection on My Lai (U. of Mich.); Lloyd Witness Statement, Jan. 27, 1970, p. 1, ibid.

29. Lloyd Witness Statement, Jan. 27, 1970, pp. 2–3, Tufts Collection on My Lai (U. of Mich.). Lloyd also gave sworn testimony before the Peers panel. See Lloyd testimony, Jan. 12, 1970, Peers Inquiry, 2: Testimony, book 6, pp. 8–10, 12, 15–21, 25–26. See also Major Clyde Wilson testimony, Jan. 28, 1970, Peers Inquiry, 2: Testimony, book 8, p. 31. Wilson was Watke's executive officer. Randolph Sabre of the 123rd Aviation Battalion thought the unit commander took Thompson to the command post of Task Force Barker to make a report. Fact Sheet, enclosed in Gustafson to Chief of Staff, U.S. Army, Jan. 27, 1970, ibid., p. 4.; CID Report, July 20, 1970, p. 8; other aviators' complaints, ibid., 5–7; Peers, *My Lai Inquiry*, 205; Belknap, *Vietnam War on Trial*, 82.

30. Henderson testimony to Wilson (IG), May 26, 1969, Box 1, Folder 11, pp. 456, 458–59, My Lai Collection (VATTU); Henderson testimony, Dec. 12, 19, 1969, Peers Inquiry, 2: Testimony, book 12, pp. 126, 160–61, 251 (LC); Medina testimony, Dec. 4, 1969, Peers Inquiry, 2: Testimony, book 23, p. 43; CID Report, Sept. 10, 1970, p. 5. Medina asserted that Calhoun directed him back for a recount and made no reference to either Barker or Henderson issuing this instruction. Medina testimony, April 15, 1970, Hébert Hearings, 69–70. The Peers commission declared that Henderson initiated the recount through Barker. Peers Report, 2–5, 10–4.

31. CID Report, Sept. 10, 1970, p. 5; Medina testimony, Dec. 4, 1969, Peers Inquiry, 2: Testimony, book 23, pp. 55–56; Kotouc testimony, Dec. 6, 1969, Peers Inquiry, 2: Testimony, book 16, p. 34.

32. Peers Report, 2–5, 10–4; Medina testimony, Dec. 4, 1969, Peers Inquiry, 2: Testimony, book 23, pp. 43–44 (LC); Henderson testimony, Dec. 2, 12, 1969, Peers Inquiry, 2: Testimony, book 12, pp. 42, 45, 127, 161; Koster testimony, Dec. 15, 1969, Feb. 18, 1970, Peers Inquiry, 2: Testimony, book 3, pp. 25, 28, 35, 175–77, 219; Medina testimony, April 15, 1970, Hébert Hearings, 70; Koster testimony, April 24, 1970, Hébert Hearings, 350–51; Henderson testimony, Dec. 2, 1969, Peers Inquiry, 2: Testimony, book 12, pp, 42, 45, Dec. 12, 1969, pp., 127, 161 (LC); Kotouc testimony, Dec. 6, 1969, Peers Inquiry, 2: Testimony, book 16, p. 28. Koster told the Peers commission that such a return to My Lai was not for a body count but to determine the causes of the deaths—which he did not realize was virtually impossible because the artillery had torn the bodies apart. He also asserted that the soldiers could have returned the following day or that an aero-scout team could have gathered the information wanted. See his testimony cited above, pp. 35, 219.

33. Walsh's interview of Tan, July 16, 2015.

34. Author's interviews of Vo Cao Loi, July 15, 18, 2012; Walsh's interview of Loi, Aug. 9, 2010; author's interview of Vo Cao Tai, July 18, 2012; Walsh's interview of Tan, Dec. 22, 2014.

I thank Nhung Walsh for locating now retired Colonel Tan and sharing the notes of her interview with me. I also thank Loi for facilitating Walsh's interview of the colonel. Both Loi and Tan assured me (through Walsh) that Tan was in charge of the 48th Battalion in 1968. Walsh located four articles (which she translated from the Vietnamese) that together provide circumstantial evidence for their claim. According to one, Tan was the first commander in chief of Regiment 94, Division 307, which consisted of three infantry battalions. One of these battalions was the 48th (dBB 83), which Tan commanded with its three companies. According to another article, Tan commanded that battalion of three companies at Son Tinh in Quang Ngai in 1972 through 1973. "Một thời hoa lửa" [Memories from the war], *Tin Tức Quảng Ngãi*, April 30, 2014; "Ký ức chiến tranh qua từng kỷ vật" [Memories of war through objects], *Tin Tức Quảng Ngãi*, June 23, 2016, http://quangngainews.com/news/Van-hoa/Ky-uc-chien-tranh-qua-tung-ky-vat-10291/; "Trung đoàn 94 Niềm tự hào về LLVT tỉnh Quảng Ngãi" [Regiment 94—pride of Quang Ngai's Military Force], *Báo Quảng Ngãi*, March 19, 2010, http://baoquangngai.vn/channel/2026/201003/trung doan-94-niem -tu-hao-ve-llvt-tinh-quang-ngai-1933535/; "Mũi dao nhọn" Ngô Đức Tấn ["Fierce dagger" Ngo Duc Tan], *Quân Đội Nhân Dân* [People's Army newspaper], April 10, 2015, http://www.qdnd.vn/phong-su-dieu-tra/ky-su-nhan-vat/mui-dao-nhon-ngo-duc-tan-258889. Ngo Duc Tan was born in 1936 to a poor farming family in Pho Thanh, Duc Pho, Quang Ngai province. In 1960, he joined the secret guerrilla force of Duc Pho, working as liaison officer. Two years later, he joined the army.

35. Walsh's interview of Tan, Dec. 22, 2014.
36. Ibid.
37. Ibid.
38. Peter Maslowski and Don Winslow, *Looking for a Hero: Staff Sergeant Joe Ronnie Hooper and the Vietnam War* (Lincoln: University of Nebraska Press, 2004), 46, 157–59; Military History Institute of Vietnam, *Victory in Vietnam: The Official History of the People's Army of Vietnam, 1954–1975*, trans. Merle L. Pribbenow (Lawrence: University Press of Kansas, 2002), 68, 86; Sam Adams, *War of Numbers: An Intelligence Memoir* (South Royalton, VT: Steerforth, 1994), 54–55, 79.
39. Tim O'Brien, *If I Die in a Combat Zone, Box Me Up and Ship Me Home* (New York: Dell, 1969), 125–30.
40. About 11 percent of Americans killed in Vietnam died as a result of mines and booby traps, about three times as many in either World War II or the Korean War. About 15 percent of Americans wounded in Vietnam were injured by these devices, nearly four times as many in each of those two wars. Summers, *Vietnam War Almanac*, 112.
41. Anistranski testimony, April 27, 1970, Hébert Hearings, 443–45; Lewis testimony, April 27, 1970, ibid., 412; Anistranski quoted in Peers, *My Lai Inquiry*, 129; Bilton and Sim, *Four Hours in My Lai*, 176; Hersh, *Cover-Up*, 128. Anistranski denied saying this to Lewis and denied hearing it said. Anistranski testimony, Jan. 12, 1970, Peers Inquiry, 2: Testimony, book 1, p. 6 (LC). Lewis never claimed Anistranski made the statement to him but rather that he made it to no one in particular.
42. Lewis testimony, April 27, 1970, Hébert Hearings, 417–18.
43. Anistranski testimony, April 27, 1970, Hébert Hearings, 444–45.
44. Ibid., 440, 442, 443, 448, 450; Wilson testimony, Jan. 28, 1970, Peers Inquiry, 2: Testimony, book 8, p. 17 (LC).

45. Peers Report, 2–5, 10–13, 10–14; Bilton and Sim, *Four Hours in My Lai*, 177; Belknap, *Vietnam War on Trial*, 82.

46. Holladay testimony, April 23, 1970, Hébert Hearings, 292–93; Holladay testimony, Dec. 9, 1969, Peers Inquiry, 2: Testimony, book 6, pp. 5–7, 10 (LC); Watke testimony, Dec. 8, 11, 1969, Peers Inquiry, 2: Testimony, book 8, pp. 23, 90, 101–2.

47. Holladay testimony, April 23, 1970, Hébert Hearings, 293–94; Young testimony, June 9, 1970, Hébert Hearings, 796, 806; Peers Report, 2–5, 10–13; Bilton and Sim, *Four Hours in My Lai*, 177; Belknap, *Vietnam War on Trial*, 82.

48. Peers Report, 10–14; Holladay testimony, April 23, 1970, Hébert Hearings, 296.

49. Holladay testimony, April 23, 1970, Hébert Hearings, 296; Holladay testimony, Dec. 9, 22, 1969, Peers Inquiry, 2: Testimony, book 6, pp. 10–11, 44–45, 50 (LC); Watke testimony, Dec. 8, 11, 1969, Peers Inquiry, 2: Testimony, book 8, pp. 24–25, 107.

50. Peers Report, 2–5, 10–14, 10–15; Henderson testimony, Dec. 12, 1969, Peers Inquiry, 2: Testimony, book 12, p. 182 (LC); Young testimony, June 9, 1970, Hébert Hearings, 794, 798–99, 811; Koster testimony, April 24, 1970, Hébert Hearings, 366; Belknap, *Vietnam War on Trial*, 83; Bilton and Sim, *Four Hours in My Lai*, 177.

51. Koster testimony, April 24, 1970, Hébert Hearings, 364–65; Koster testimony, Dec. 15, 1969, Peers Inquiry, 2: Testimony, book 3, pp. 30, 35, 55, 65 (LC); Henderson testimony, Dec. 2, 1969, Peers Inquiry, 2: Testimony, book 12, pp. 24–25; Koster Witness Statement to CID, Nov. 24, 1969, p. 4, Tufts Collection on My Lai (U. of Mich.); Peers Report, 2–4, 10–3; Bilton and Sim, *Four Hours in My Lai*, 177.

52. Peers Report, 2–5, 2–6, 10–15; CID Report, Sept. 10, 1970, pp. 57–58 (Young); Young testimony, Dec. 13, 1969, Peers Inquiry, 2: Testimony, book 5, pp. 10, 13–15, 18–19, 29, 39–40, 103–4 (LC); Koster testimony, Dec. 15, 1969, Feb. 18, 1970, Peers Inquiry, 2: Testimony, book 3, pp. 4, 33, 42, 49, 181–83, 191; Koster testimony, April 24, 1970, Hébert Hearings, 366–69; Fact Sheet, enclosed in Gustafson to Chief of Staff, U.S. Army, Jan. 18, 1970, p. 3, Tufts Collection on My Lai (U. of Mich.).

53. Holladay testimony, April 23, 1970, Hébert Hearings, 298–99; Holladay testimony, Dec. 22, 1969, Peers Inquiry, 2: Testimony, book 6, p. 64 (LC).

54. Koster testimony, April 24, 1970, Hébert Hearings, 366, 368; Peers Report, 2–6, 10–15, 10–16.

55. Peers Report, 2–6; Young testimony, Dec. 13, 1969, Peers Inquiry, 2: Testimony, book 5, pp. 10, 31, 39–40 (LC); Koster testimony, Dec. 15, 1969, Peers Inquiry, 2: Testimony, book 3, pp. 44–45; Koster testimony, Hébert Hearings, April 24, 1970, 369–71; Peers, *My Lai Inquiry*, 10–11, 62, 114; Fact Sheet, enclosed in Gustafson to Chief of Staff, U.S. Army, Jan. 18, 1970, p. 3, Tufts Collection on My Lai (U. of Mich.); Koster Witness Statement, Nov. 24, 1969, p.1, CID Report.

56. Peers Report, 2–6, 10–31; Young quoted by Holladay in Deposition by Holladay, Dec. 7, 1971, VWCWG, My Lai Massacre, 1969–74, Box 3, p. 42 (NARA); ibid., 43, 45, 67; Holladay testimony, April 23, 1970, Hébert Hearings, 300, 302; Holladay testimony, Dec. 9, 22, 1969, Peers Inquiry, 2: Testimony, book 6, pp. 13–14, 30, 55–57, 59 (LC); Watke testimony, Dec. 11, 1969, Peers Inquiry, 2: Testimony, book 8, pp. 112, 115; Peers, *My Lai Inquiry*, 98–99. See also Bilton and Sim, *Four Hours in My Lai*, 177; Belknap, *Vietnam War on Trial*, 83; Koster testimony, Hébert Hearings, April 24, 1970, pp. 366, 370.

57. Henderson testimony, Dec. 12, 19, 1969, Peers Inquiry, 2: Testimony, book 12, pp. 134–35A, 136, 243 (LC).

58. MACV Directive 20-4, Peers Report, 9–11, 9–12; Belknap, *Vietnam War on Trial*, 83; Peers, *My Lai Inquiry*, 100; Watke testimony, Dec. 8, 11, 1969, Peers Inquiry, 2: Testimony, book 8, pp. 25, 112 (LC); Young testimony, Dec. 13, 1969, Peers Inquiry, 2: Testimony, book 5, pp. 11–12, 23, 27, 47, 119; Holladay testimony, Dec. 9, 1969, Peers Inquiry, 2: Testimony, book 6, pp. 15–17; Koster testimony, Dec. 15, 1969, Feb. 18, 1970, Peers Inquiry, 2: Testimony, book 3, pp. 67, 100, 127–28, 186–87; Henderson testimony, Dec. 19, 1969, Peers Inquiry, 2: Testimony, book 12, p. 242; Henderson testimony to Wilson (IG), May 26, 1969, Box 1, Folder 11, pp. 454–66, My Lai Collection (VATTU); Young quoted in CID Investigator's Statement, Dec. 13, 1969, Record Group 319, p. 3 (NA), as cited by Greiner, *War Without Fronts*, 283; Riddle to Tufts, enclosed in Weekly My Lai Fact Sheet, U.S. Army, Dec. 16, 1969, p. 4 (seventy-two-hour deadline), Tufts Collection on My Lai (U. of Mich.).

59. Bilton and Sim, *Four Hours in My Lai*, 178, 179, 184, 191.

60. Peers Report, 10–33; Henderson testimony, Dec. 19, 1969, Peers Inquiry, 2: Testimony, book 12, pp. 242–43 (LC); Wilson testimony, Jan. 28, 1990, Peers Inquiry, 2: Testimony, book 8, pp. 13–15; Peers, *My Lai Inquiry*, 108.

61. Peers Report, 10–32; Henderson testimony, Dec. 2, 12, 19, 1969, Peers Inquiry, 2: Testimony, book 12, pp. 7–8, 142–43, 245 (LC); Thompson testimony, Dec. 3, 1969, Peers Inquiry, 2: Testimony, book 8, pp. 16–17.

62. Henderson testimony, Dec. 2, 12, 19, 1969, Peers Inquiry, 2: Testimony, book 12, pp. 9, 132–33, 142–43, 245–48 (LC); Thompson testimony, Dec. 3, 4, 5, 1969, Feb. 10, 1970, Peers Inquiry, 2: Testimony, book 8, pp. 17–18, 34, 45, 51, 121; Peers, *My Lai Inquiry*, 55, 70; Angers, *Forgotten Hero of My Lai*, 127.

63. Henderson testimony, Dec. 12, 1969, Peers Inquiry, 2: Testimony, book 12, pp. 130, 132–33, 134–35A, 144 (LC).

64. Peers Report, 2–6, 2–7, 10–32.

65. Author's interview of Colburn, April 8, 2014; Colburn testimony, April 17, 1970, Hébert Hearings, 220–21; Colburn testimony, Dec. 20, 1969, Peers Inquiry, 2: Testimony, book 5, pp. 24–25, 29–32, 34, 42, 47 (LC).

66. Author's interview of Colburn, April 8, 2014.

67. Peers Report, 2–6, 10–32; Peers, *My Lai Inquiry*, 74, 74n3, 99, 108; Colburn testimony, April 17, 1970, Hébert Hearings, 220–21; Culverhouse testimony, April 17, 1970, Hébert Hearings, 186, 193–95, 198, 201; Culverhouse in Riddle to Tufts, enclosed in Weekly My Lai Fact Sheet, U.S. Army, Dec, 16, 1969, p. 3, Tufts Collection on My Lai (U. of Mich.); Culverhouse testimony, Jan. 10, 1970, Peers Inquiry, 2: Testimony, book 6, p. 28 (LC); Bilton and Sim, *Four Hours in My Lai*, 178–79; Allison, *My Lai*, 62; Belknap, *Vietnam War on Trial*, 159.

68. Peers Report, 2–6; Henderson testimony, Dec. 19, 1969, Peers Inquiry, 2: Testimony, book 12, p. 249 (LC).

69. Peers Report, 6–20; Bilton and Sim, *Four Hours in My Lai*, 164–65; Belknap, *Vietnam War on Trial*, 39, 99; Allison, *My Lai*, 54–55, 100.

70. Peers Report, 6–20; Allison, *My Lai*, 55; Bilton and Sim, *Four Hours in My Lai*, 165 (Meadlo's quote); Calley's quote in Belknap, *Vietnam War on Trial*, 88; Meadlo in

transcript of interview, *60 Minutes*, Nov. 24, 1969, in *New York Times*, Nov. 25, 1969. Squad leader L. G. Bacon remembered Meadlo proclaiming, "I'll get even with you, sir. I'll get even with you if it's the last thing I do." Bacon testimony, Dec. 16, 1969, Peers Inquiry, 2: Testimony, book 24, pp. 41–42 (LC).

71. Hersh, *Cover-Up*, 141–42; Medina testimony, Dec. 4, 1969, Peers Inquiry, 2: Testimony, book 23, pp. 56–57 (LC); Bacon testimony, Dec. 16, 1969, Peers Inquiry, 2: Testimony, book 24, pp. 4, 38–40; Bunning testimony, Jan. 16, 1970, Peers Inquiry, 2: Testimony, book 26, p. 41 (on mass burnings); Peers Report, 6–20. That same day of March 17, Bravo Company burned the coastal villages of Co Lay 1, 2, and 3. Peers Report, 7–12. See also Bilton and Sim, *Four Hours in My Lai*, 167–68, and Allison, *My Lai*, 56–57. See chapter 2 of this work for a discussion of the "bouncing Betty" mine.

72. Sack, *Calley*, 76.

73. Hersh, *Cover-Up*, 143–44; Kinch quoted in "Massacre at My Lai," *Life*, 44; Peers Report, 6–20; CID Report, Sept. 10, 1970, pp. 5, 41, 45, 49, 50 (testimonies of witnesses); Hein testimony, Jan. 10, 1970, Peers Inquiry, 2: Testimony, book 28, p. 17 (LC); Medina testimony, Dec. 4, 1969, Peers Inquiry, 2: Testimony, book 23, pp. 57–58; Richard Hammer, *One Morning in the War: The Tragedy at Son My* (New York: Coward-McCann, 1970), 160–61.

74. Peers, *My Lai Inquiry*, 82; Medina testimony, Dec. 4, 1969, Peers Inquiry, 2: Testimony, book 23, pp. 58–60; Walsh's interview of Tan, Dec. 22, 2014; Bilton and Sim, *Four Hours in My Lai*, 169–70.

75. Henderson testimony, Dec. 12, 1969, Peers Inquiry, 2: Testimony, book 12, p. 126 (LC); Medina testimony, Dec. 4, 1969, Peers Inquiry, 2: Testimony, book 23, pp. 61–62; Medina testimony to Wilson (IG), May 13, 1969, Box 1, Folder 6, p. 272, My Lai Collection (VATTU); Bilton and Sim, *Four Hours in My Lai*, 172–73, 228.

76. Blackledge testimony, May 9, 1970, Hébert Hearings, 695, 698; Luper testimony, April 27, Hébert Hearings, 458; Peers, *My Lai Inquiry*, 56; Medina testimony to Wilson (IG), May 13, 1969, Box 1, Folder 6, p. 272, My Lai Collection (VATTU); Henderson testimony to Wilson (IG), May 26, 1969, Box 1, Folder 11, p. 478, My Lai Collection (VATTU); Henderson testimony, Dec. 2, 1969, Peers Inquiry, 2: Testimony, book 12, p. 83 (LC).

77. Peers, *My Lai Inquiry*, 56; Henderson testimony, Dec. 12, 1969, Peers Inquiry, 2: Testimony, book 12, pp. 144, 159 (LC); Bilton and Sim, *Four Hours in My Lai*, 172.

78. Henderson and Medina quoted in Blackledge testimony, May 9, 1970, Hébert Hearings, 694; Peers Report, 10–33, 10–34.

79. Medina testimony to Wilson (IG), May 13, 1969, Box 1, Folder 6, pp. 258, 271, My Lai Collection (VATTU); Henderson testimony, Dec. 12, 1969, Peers Inquiry, 2: Testimony, book 12, p. 158 (LC).

80. Medina testimony, April 15, 1970, Hébert Hearings, 73–74.

81. Henderson testimony, Dec. 12, 1969, Peers Inquiry, 2: Testimony, book 12, p. 158 (LC).

82. Henderson testimony, Dec. 2, 1969, Peers Inquiry, 2: Testimony, book 12, p. 10; Medina testimony, Dec. 4, 1969, Peers Inquiry, 2: Testimony, book 23, p. 24; Henderson testimony to Wilson (IG), May 26, 1969, Box 1, Folder 11, pp. 455–56, 459–60, 478, My Lai Collection (VATTU); Peers Report, 6–11, 10–9.

83. Medina testimony, Dec. 4, 1969, Peers Inquiry, 2: Testimony, book 23, p. 24 (LC); Medina testimony, April 15, 1970, Hébert Hearings, 64; Kotouc testimony, April 24,

1970, Hébert Hearings, 353–54; Riggs testimony, April 24, 1970, Hébert Hearings, 397–98; Peers, *My Lai Inquiry*, 95; author's interview of Colburn, April 8, 2014.

84. Medina testimony to Wilson (IG), May 13, 1969, Box 1, Folder 6, pp. 266–67, My Lai Collection (VATTU); Peers Report, 6–14.

85. Medina testimony to Wilson (IG), May 13, 1969, Box 1, Folder 6, p. 266, My Lai Collection (VATTU); Henderson testimony to Wilson (IG), May 26, 1969, Box 1, Folder 11, pp. 454–56, My Lai Collection (VATTU); Colburn testimony to Wilson (IG), June 19, 1969, Box 1, Folder 17, p. 775, My Lai Collection (VATTU); Henderson testimony, Dec. 2, 1969, Peers Inquiry, 2: Testimony, book 12, pp. 8–9 (LC); CID Report, Sept. 10, 1970, pp. 43–45.

86. Henderson testimony, Dec. 12, 1969, Peers Inquiry, 2: Testimony, book 12, p. 158 (LC).

87. Ibid.

88. Henderson testimony to Wilson (IG), May 26, 1969, Box 1, Folder 11, pp. 455–56, My Lai Collection (VATTU); Henderson testimony, Dec. 2, 12, 1969, Peers Inquiry, 2: Testimony, book 12, pp. 37, 82, 105 160 (LC); CID Report, Sept. 10, 1970, p. 59.

89. Medina testimony to Wilson (IG), May 13, 1969, Box 1, Folder 6, p. 271 (Medina quoting Henderson), My Lai Collection (VATTU); Medina testimony, April 15, 1970, Hébert Hearings, 74. Luper overheard Medina's defense of his action and found it "quite valid." Luper testimony, April 27, 1970, Hébert Hearings, 458.

90. Medina testimony, Dec. 4, 1969, Peers Inquiry, 2: Testimony, book 23, p. 70 (LC).

91. Henderson testimony, Dec. 19, 1969, Peers Inquiry, 2: Testimony, book 12, pp. 252–54.

92. Henderson testimony, Dec. 2, 12, 1969, ibid., pp. 108–9, 179; Henderson testimony to Wilson (IG), May 26, 1969, Box 1, Folder 11, p. 490, My Lai Collection (VATTU); Peers Report, 2–7. One hundred meters is equivalent to 328 feet.

93. U.S. Army, Field Manual 27-10, *Law of Land Warfare*, 178–79; quote from Roger S. Clark of the Rutgers School of Law, "Medina: An Essay on the Principles of Criminal Liability for Homicide," *Rutgers-Camden Law Journal* 5 (Fall 1973): 78. See also Kenneth A. Howard, "Command Responsibility for War Crimes," *Journal of Public Law* 31 (1972): 7–22.

Seven

1. Henderson testimony, Dec. 2, 1969, Peers Inquiry, 2: Testimony, book 12, pp. 9–10 (LC); Henderson testimony to Wilson (IG), May 26, 1969, Box 1, Folder 11, p. 478, My Lai Collection (VATTU).

2. Henderson testimony, Dec. 2, 12, 1969, Peers Inquiry, 2: Testimony, book 12, pp. 7, 42, 99, 171 (LC), Dec. 12, 1969, ibid., 171; Ronald Ridenhour testimony, Jan. 29, 1970, Peers Inquiry, 2: Testimony, book 14, p. 27. Ridenhour was a Vietnam veteran who exposed the My Lai 4 massacre to governmental leaders in Washington. See chapter 8 of this work.

3. Henderson testimony, Dec. 2, 1969, Peers Inquiry, 2: Testimony, book 12, pp. 42–43; Belknap, *Vietnam War on Trial*, 93; Allison, *My Lai*, 63.

4. These exchanges in Henderson testimony to Wilson (IG), May 26, 1969, Box 1, Folder 11, p. 458, My Lai Collection (VATTU).

5. Bilton and Sim, *Four Hours in My Lai*, 174.

6. Ibid.

7. Henderson testimony, Dec. 2, 12, 1969, Peers Inquiry, 2: Testimony, book 12, pp. 42–43. 171 (LC); Peers, *My Lai Inquiry*, 57.

8. Henderson testimony, Dec. 12, 1969, Peers Inquiry, 2: Testimony, book 12, pp. 171, 174 (LC).

9. Henderson testimony, Dec. 2, 1969, ibid., 27, 35; Henderson testimony to Wilson (IG), May 26, 1969, Box 1, Folder 11, p. 480, My Lai Collection (VATTU).

10. Medina testimony, April 15, 1970, Hébert Hearings, 75; Stephens testimony, April 15, 1970, Hébert Hearings, 41–43; Medina testimony, Dec. 4, 1969, Peers Inquiry, 2: Testimony, book 23, pp. 64–65 (LC); Stephens testimony, Jan. 7, 1970, Peers Inquiry, 2: Testimony, book 16, pp. 32–33.

11. Stephens testimony, Jan. 7, 1970, Peers Inquiry, 2: Testimony, book 16, pp. 19, 33 (LC); Stephens testimony, April 15, 1970, Hébert Hearings, 51–52.

12. Gibson testimony, April 16, 1970, Hébert Hearings, 121; Henderson testimony, Dec. 2, 12, 19, 1969, Peers Inquiry, 2: Testimony, book 12, pp. 39–40, 178, 256 (LC).

13. Gibson testimony, April 16, 1970, Hébert Hearings, 123–24; Peers, *My Lai Inquiry*, 57–59; Hersh, *Cover-Up*, 161; Allison, *My Lai*, 64–65; Henderson testimony, Dec. 2, 1969, Peers Inquiry, 2: Testimony, book 12, p. 47 (LC); Belknap, *Vietnam War on Trial*, 93, 108.

14. Medina testimony, Dec. 4, 1969, Peers Inquiry, 2: Testimony, book 23, p. 65 (LC); Bacon testimony, Dec. 16, 1969, Peers Inquiry, 2: Testimony, book 24, pp. 4, 37 (Bacon quoting Medina), 54; CID Report, Sept. 10, 1970, pp. 5, 49.

15. CID Report, Sept. 10, 1970, pp. 5, 55; Gustafson to Chief of Staff, U.S. Army, Jan. 24, 1970, enclosed in Talking Paper, Jan. 24, 1970, Tufts Collection on My Lai (U. of Mich.); Rickey Neria testimony in Riddle to Tufts, enclosed in Weekly My Lai Fact Sheet, U.S. Army, Dec. 16, 1969, pp. 4–5, Tufts Collection on My Lai; Kinch testimony, Jan. 21, 1970, Peers Inquiry, 2: Testimony, book 28, p. 40 (LC).

16. Medina testimony, Dec. 4, 1969, Peers Inquiry, 2: Testimony, book 23, p. 66 (LC); Medina to Bernhardt in Ridenhour testimony, Jan. 29, 1970, Peers Inquiry, 2: Testimony, book 14, pp. 26, 28, 29; Bernhardt testimony, Dec. 29, 1969, Peers Inquiry, 2: Testimony, book 25, pp. 24–25, 113, 114; Ridenhour letter to various U.S. government officials, March 29, 1969, Peers Inquiry, 3: Exhibits, book 4, Misc. Docs., M-83, p. 5; Bernhardt testimony to Wilson (IG), May 8, 1969, Box 1, Folder 4, p. 197, My Lai Collection (VATTU); CID Report, Sept. 10, 1970, pp. 14, 35, 43, 44; last Bernhardt quote from his interview by Bilton and Sim and in their *Four Hours in My Lai*, 180. Medina later asserted to the Peers commission that he told Bernhardt that in lieu of an investigation it would not be wise to write his congressman. Medina testimony, Dec. 4, 1969, Peers Inquiry, 2: Testimony, book 23, p. 66.

17. Ridenhour testimony, Jan. 29, 1970, Peers Inquiry, 2: Testimony, book 14, p. 27 (LC).

18. Guinn testimony, April 29, 1970, Hébert Hearings, 565–66; Bilton and Sim, *Four Hours in My Lai*, 186; Allison, *My Lai*, 67; Letter from Census Grievance Cadreman, March 18, 1968, in Peers, *My Lai Inquiry*, 276–77; Belknap, *Vietnam War on Trial*, 80; Douglas Valentine, *The Phoenix Program* (New York: William Morrow, 1990), 345.

19. Allison, *My Lai*, 67; Koster testimony, April 24, 1970, Hébert Hearings, 373; Koster testimony, Dec. 15, 1969, Feb. 8, 1970, Peers Inquiry, 2: Testimony, book 3, pp. 39, 54–56, 66, 74, 188, 193, 195–96 (LC); Henderson testimony, Dec. 12, 1969, Peers Inquiry,

2: Testimony, book 12, p. 182; Peers, *My Lai Inquiry*, 58. The Peers commission concluded that Henderson "deliberately misrepresented both the scope of this investigation and the information he had obtained." Peers Report, 2–7.

20. Henderson testimony, Dec. 2, 12, 1969, Peers Inquiry, 2: Testimony, book 12, pp. 51, 181 (LC); Peers, *My Lai Inquiry*, 58–59.

21. Henderson testimony, Dec. 2, 12, 1969, Peers Inquiry, 2: Testimony, book 12, pp. 95–97, 110, 126, 182 (LC).

22. Peers Report, 5–7, 5–8, 5–17. See also chapter 3 of this work.

23. Henderson testimony, Dec. 2, 1969, Peers Inquiry, 2: Testimony, book 12, p. 106 (LC).

24. Ibid., 107.

25. Henderson testimony, Dec. 12, 1969, Peers Inquiry, 2: Testimony, book 12, p. 183 (LC).

26. Henderson testimony, Dec. 19, 1969, ibid., 250.

27. Ibid., 249–50; Henderson testimony to Wilson (IG), May 26, 1969, Box 1, Folder 11, p. 459, My Lai Collection (VATTU).

28. Henderson testimony, Dec. 19, 1969, Peers Inquiry, 2: Testimony, book 12, pp. 246–47 (LC).

29. Adcock testimony, April 17, 1970, Hébert Hearings, 134–37, 143, 148. Adcock remembered that Lieutenant James Cooney was the pilot and that the brigade operations officer, Major Robert McKnight, might have been with them. The latter seems unlikely, since Adcock recalled seven on board and accounted for a pilot, a co-pilot, and two gunners, along with himself, Henderson, and Luper. Ibid., 148.

30. Ibid., 141–43, 148–49.

31. Bilton and Sim, *Four Hours in My Lai*, 144; Luper testimony, April 27, 1969, Hébert Hearings, 456–59, 461; Henderson testimony, Dec. 2, 1969, Peers Inquiry, 2: Testimony, book 12, p. 19 (LC).

32. The Peers commission called Henderson's questioning of Charlie Company a "totally meaningless action." Peers Report, 10–34; see also 2–6, 2–7; Hersh, *Cover-up*, 135–36, 138.

33. "Congratulatory Message from General Westmoreland," Americal News Sheet, March 20, 1968, Peers Inquiry, 3: Exhibits, book 4, Misc. Docs., M-65, p. 267 (LC).

34. Holladay testimony, April 23, 1970, Hébert Hearings, 307–8 (quote on 307); Holladay testimony, Dec. 9, 22, Peers Inquiry, 2: Testimony, book 6, pp. 21, 61, 70 (LC); Koster and Henderson comments, March 27, 1968, Peers Inquiry, 3: Exhibits, book 4, Misc. Docs., M-90; Keshel testimony, Jan 19, 1969, Peers Inquiry, 2: Testimony, book 31, pp. 42–43 (Confidential Extracts).

35. Holladay testimony, April 23, 1970, Hébert Hearings, 307–8.

36. Ibid., 309–10.

37. Ibid., 310, 320; Bilton and Sim, *Four Hours in My Lai*, 182–83, 195.

38. Guinn testimony, April 29, 1970, Hébert Hearings, 567, 572; Peers Report, 10–48.

39. Guinn testimony, April 29, 1970, Hébert Hearings, 566, 576, 580, 581, 586–87; Henderson testimony, Dec. 2, 1969, Peers Inquiry, 2: Testimony, book 12, pp. 100–101 (LC); Peers, *My Lai Inquiry*, 64; Allison, *My Lai*, 67–68.

40. Guinn testimony, April 29, 1970, Hébert Hearings, 566–67; Peers Report, 10–49; Peers, *My Lai Inquiry*, 64, 152; Peter Braestrup, "Vietnam Probe Widens," *Washington Post*, Nov. 22, 1969; Bilton and Sim, *Four Hours in My Lai*, 186–88. Guinn later admitted that it might have been sometime after he had originally thought, but he insisted that he gave

Henderson the report. Yet he did not know where he got his handwritten memorandum. Henderson testimony, Dec. 2, 1969, Peers Inquiry, 2: Testimony, book 12, pp. 101–3 (LC).

41. Bilton and Sim, *Four Hours in My Lai*, 186, 297, 309; Peers, *My Lai Inquiry*, 185–86, 188, 190, 192; Allison, *My Lai*, 48–49.

42. Henderson testimony, Dec. 2, 1969, Peers Inquiry, 2: Testimony, book 12, pp. 52–52A (LC); Peers, *My Lai Inquiry*, 60; Fact Sheet on My Lai Investigation, in Gustafson to Chief of Staff, U.S. Army, Nov. 18, 1969, pp. 1–2, Tufts Collection on My Lai (U. of Mich.); Chronology of Action Taken Since March 16, 1968, enclosed ibid., 1; Talking Paper, Gustafson to Chief of Staff, U.S., Nov. 17, 1969, Tufts Collection on My Lai. Tan submitted his findings on March 28. Bilton and Sim, *Four Hours in My Lai*, 186–87.

43. Koster Witness Statement, Nov. 24, 1969, pp. 3, 6, CID, Tufts Collection on My Lai (U. of Mich.); Koster testimony, Dec. 15, 1969, Peers Inquiry, 2: Testimony, book 3, pp. 15–16, 97, 113, 115 (LC).

44. Riggs testimony, April 24, 1970, Hébert Hearings, 394–96; Balmer testimony, April 27, 1970, Hébert Hearings, 463, 467–68.

45. Hersh, *Cover-Up*, 75; Koster Witness Statement, Nov. 24, 1969, pp. 6–7, CID, Tufts Collection on My Lai (U. of Mich.). Peers termed Koster's timing in publishing the rules of engagement "ironic." Peers, *My Lai Inquiry*, 118.

46. Koster Witness Statement, Nov. 24, 1969, p. 7, CID, Tufts Collection on My Lai (U. of Mich.).

47. Ibid., 6; Koster to all commanders, "The Safeguarding of Noncombatants," March 24, 1968, Peers Inquiry, 3: Exhibits, book 2, pp. 615–16, Directives, M-9 (LC); Koster testimony, Dec. 5, 1969, Peers Inquiry, 2: Testimony, book 3, pp. 96, 98.

48. Koster testimony, April 24, 1970, Hébert Hearings, 362.

49. Addendum enclosed in Koster to CID, Dec. 2, 1969, p. 2, Tufts Collection on My Lai (U. of Mich.); Henderson testimony to Wilson (IG), May 26, 1969, Box 1, Folder 11, pp. 489–90, My Lai Collection (VATTU).

50. Chronology of Action Taken Since March 16, 1968, in Gustafson to Chief of Staff, U.S. Army, Nov. 18, 1969, p.1, Tufts Collection on My Lai (U. of Mich.); extract of Barker's Combat Action Report, in Peers Report, 11–7. For a full copy, see "Lieutenant Colonel Barker's Combat Action Report" in Peers, *My Lai Inquiry*, 268–71.

51. Barker's Combat Action Report, March 28, 1968, Peers Inquiry, 3: Exhibits, book 3: Reports, 2, Exhibit R-2, p. 405 (LC); Stephens testimony, Jan. 7, 1970, Peers Inquiry, 2: Testimony, book 16, p. 47.

52. Chronology of Action Taken Since March 16, 1968, in Gustafson to Chief of Staff, U.S. Army, Nov. 18, 1969, p. 1, Tufts Collection on My Lai (U. of Mich.). The Peers commission called Barker's combat action report "misleading and deceptive," a "pure fabrication" of "a hotly-contested combat action." It "can only be considered an effort by LTC Barker deliberately to suppress the true facts and to mislead higher headquarters into believing that there had been a combat operation in Son My Village on 16 March involving a hotly contested action with a sizable enemy force." Peers Report, 2–10, 11-7. In mentioning no civilian casualties, Peers stated, Barker's last two paragraphs on the evacuation of the wounded and control over the population become "nothing short of ludicrous" when taking into account the hundreds of dead noncombatants at My Lai 4. Peers, *My Lai Inquiry*, 59.

53. Henderson testimony, Dec. 2, 1969, Peers Inquiry, 2: Testimony, book 12, pp. 66–67 (LC); Peers, *My Lai Inquiry*, 59; Frosch discussed in Guinn testimony, April 29, 1970, Hébert Hearings, 569–71; Bilton and Sim, *Four Hours in My Lai*, 189.

54. See chapter 4 of this work.

55. Peers, *My Lai Inquiry*, 114, 118, 119–20.

56. Peers Report, 10–30. The Peers commission concluded that Koster's "decision contributed, either wittingly or unwittingly, to the suppression of information about the My Lai incident." Peers, *My Lai Inquiry*, 120.

57. Milloy testimony, May 13, 1970, Hébert Hearings, 769; Koster testimony, April 24, 1970, Hébert Hearings, 364; Peers, *My Lai Inquiry*, 120. Peers alleged that Koster's countermanding order prevented the possible exposure of hundreds of civilian deaths and "seemed to have set the stage for the cover-up." Henderson's "lack of action was still another facet of the cover-up." Ibid., 204, 205.

58. MACV Directive 20–4 in Peers Report, 9–11; Peers, *My Lai Inquiry*, 119–20. Henderson's oral report eventually became the basis of a written version known as the "Report of Investigation." Ibid., 119.

59. Koster Witness Statement, Nov. 24, 1969, p. 5, CID, Tufts Collection on My Lai (U. of Mich.).

60. Keshel testimony, April 27, 1970, Hébert Hearings, 422; Bilton and Sim, *Four Hours in My Lai*, 188; Hersh, *Cover-Up*, 194–95. Anistranski's job was to provide monetary compensation to civilian families with injuries, but he never went to My Lai 4. Anistranski testimony, Jan. 12, 1970, Peers Inquiry, 2: Testimony, book 1, p. 7 (LC); Anistranski testimony, April 27, 1970, Hébert Hearings, 438; Peers, *My Lai Inquiry*, 126–27, 155.

61. The Peers commission was never able to determine what was in that folder. Peers, *My Lai Inquiry*, 155.

62. Keshel testimony, April 27, 1970, Hébert Hearings, 423.

63. Addendum enclosed in Koster to CID, Dec. 2, 1969, p. 1; Koster testimony, Feb. 8, 1970, Peers Inquiry, 2: Testimony, book 3, pp. 141, 166 (LC).

64. Peers Report, 10–37, 10–55, 10–56; Young testimony, June 9, 1970, Hébert Hearings, 801; Peers, *My Lai Inquiry*, 108; Henderson testimony, Dec. 2, 1969, Peers Inquiry, 2: Testimony, book 12, pp. 56–57, 61–62 (LC). Koster later confirmed that the helicopter pilot's allegations, combined with those made by villagers, had necessitated a written report and an immediate investigation. CID Report, Sept. 10, 1970, p. 56.

65. Henderson testimony, Dec. 2, 12, 19, 1969, Peers Inquiry, 2: Testimony, book 12, pp. 69, 184, 261, 264–65 (LC); Parson in Fact Sheet, enclosed in Gustafson to Chief of Staff, U.S. Army, Jan. 27, 1970, p. 4, Tufts Collection on My Lai (U. of Mich.); Peers, *My Lai Inquiry*, 108. The Peers commission concluded that the report was either "a figment of Henderson's imagination" or "he kept it to himself." Ibid., 109.

66. Gustafson to Chief of Staff, U.S. Army, Jan. 24, 1970, enclosed in Talking Paper, Jan. 24, 1970, Tufts Collection on My Lai (U. of Mich.); Bilton and Sim, *Four Hours in My Lai*, 186–87; Peers, *My Lai Inquiry*, 137–38; Hersh, *Cover-Up*, 190–91. The village chief's name was Dinh Luyen Do.

67. Tan's Letter to Province Chief, April 11, 1968, in Peers, *My Lai Inquiry*, 279; ibid., 137–38; Henderson testimony, Dec. 2, 1969, Peers Inquiry, 2: Testimony, book 12, pp. 52–52A

(LC); Bilton and Sim, *Four Hours in My Lai*, 186–87. Luyen's report also emphasized that during the Viet Cong's withdrawal, American helicopter gunships wounded another forty-eight Viet Cong and more than fifty-two guerrillas and self-defense forces.

68. Henderson testimony, Dec. 2, 1969, Peers Inquiry, 2: Testimony, book 12, pp. 52–52A, 54–55 (LC); Talking Paper, Nov. 17, 1969, Tufts Collection on My Lai (U. of Mich.); Fact Sheet on My Lai Investigation, in Gustafson to Chief of Staff, U.S. Army, Nov. 18, 1969, p. 2, Tufts Collection on My Lai; Chronology of Action Taken Since 16 March 1968, enclosed in Gustafson to Kanamine, U.S. Army, Nov. 23, 1969, p. 1, Tufts Collection on My Lai; Peers, *My Lai Inquiry*, 60. Peers declared that Khien and other senior commanders "probably" were "apprehensive about what they might find, and, above all, they had not wanted to report upon the actions of an American unit." Ibid., 140. The copy of Tan's April 11 letter held by the Peers commission contained a slightly different wording of the subject line: "Allied Operation at Son My assembled and killed civilians." Ibid., 279.

69. Henderson testimony, Dec. 2, 1969, Peers Inquiry, 2: Testimony, book 12, pp. 263–64 (LC); Peers, *My Lai Inquiry*, 59–61, 121, 150.

70. Peers Report, 10–56, 10–59, 10–89, 10–90; Henderson testimony, Dec. 2, 12, 1969, Peers Inquiry, 2: Testimony, book 12, pp. 57, 69, 95, 186–87, 189 (LC); Robert Gerberding testimony, Jan. 27, 1970, Peers Inquiry, 2: Testimony, book 11, pp. 41, 57; Henderson testimony to Wilson (IG), May 26, 1969, Box 1, Folder 11, p. 455, My Lai Collection (VATTU); Peers, *My Lai Inquiry*, 53, 59, 61, 108, 121. Another English translation calls the title of the broadcast, "The American Devils Divulge Their True Form." Ibid., 273.

71. Henderson testimony, Dec. 2, 1969, Peers Inquiry, 2: Testimony, book 12, p. 57 (LC); Tan's letter of April 11 in Peers, *My Lai Inquiry*, 279. For Henderson's full report, see ibid., 272–76. See also Peers Inquiry, 3: Exhibits, book 3, Reports, R-1 (LC).

72. Koster testimony, April 24, 1970, Hébert Hearings, 374–755; Holladay testimony, April 23, 1970, Hébert Hearings, 302–4, 306; Holladay testimony, Dec. 9, 22, 1969, Peers Inquiry, 2: Testimony, book 6, pp. 19, 66 (LC); Peers Report, 10–58, 10–59. The Peers commission declared that Henderson's report "strongly suggests a conscious effort to deceive." Peers Report, 10–60.

73. Henderson testimony to Wilson (IG), May 26, 1969, Box 1, Folder 11, p. 479, My Lai Collection (VATTU); Henderson testimony, Dec. 2, 12, 1969, Peers Inquiry, 2: Testimony, book 12, pp. 69, 194, 263 (LC); Peers, *My Lai Inquiry*, 108. S-2 of the 11th Brigade got a copy. Chronology of Action Taken Since March 16, 1968, enclosed in Gustafson to Kanamine, Nov. 23, 1969, p. 1, CID, Tufts Collection on My Lai (U. of Mich.); Fact Sheet on My Lai Investigation, in Gustafson to Chief of Staff, U.S. Army, Nov. 18, 1969, p. 3, CID, Tufts Collection on My Lai.

74. Peers Report, 10–50; Hersh, *Cover-Up*, 192.

75. Peers Report, 10–60; "Statement" signed by Rodriguez, April 14, 1968, Peers Inquiry, 3: Exhibits, book 4, p. 129, M-30 (LC); Hersh, *Cover-up*, 180, 184, 193; Peers, *My Lai Inquiry*, 140; Rodriguez testimony, April 24, 1970, Hébert Hearings, 388–92.

76. Rodriguez testimony, April 24, 1970, Hébert Hearings, 389; Dawkins testimony, April 30, 1970, Hébert Hearings, 619; Hersh, *Cover-Up*, 191–93; Rodriguez testimony, Jan. 24, 1970, Peers Inquiry, 2: Testimony, book 30, pp. 7–8 (LC); Peers, *My Lai Inquiry*, 151–53; Bilton and Sim, *Four Hours in My Lai*, 187. Gavin denied hearing of any massacre report.

Guinn denied talking with Rodriguez about the charges relating to civilian casualties and could not remember seeing the April 11 letter. Guinn testimony, April 29, 1970, Hébert Hearings, 584–85.

77. Peers Report, 10–51; Allison, *My Lai*, 70; Tan quoted in Hersh, *Cover-Up*, 193–94; Peers, *My Lai Inquiry*, 193–94. Bilton and Sim conclude that Rodriguez's statement "falsely claimed that Tan wasn't really sure whether the allegation was true." Bilton and Sim, *Four Hours in My Lai*, 187.

78. Peers Report, 10–60.

79. Peers, *My Lai Inquiry*, 150. Peers quote ibid., 140.

80. Hersh, *Cover-Up*, 202–3; Peers Report, 10–52.

81. Peers Report, 10–65; CID Report, Sept. 10, 1970, pp. 56, 59; Koster Witness Statement, Nov. 24, 1969, pp. 1–2, CID, Tufts Collection on My Lai (U. Of Mich.); Koster testimony, Dec. 15, 1969, Feb. 8, 1970, Peers Inquiry, 2: Testimony, book 3, pp. 82, 158–59, 161 (LC); Henderson testimony, Dec. 2, 1969, Peers Inquiry, 2: Testimony, book 12, p. 71; Peers, *My Lai Inquiry*, 61–62, 115–16, 121.

82. Henderson testimony, Dec. 2, 1969, Peers Inquiry, 2: Testimony, book 12, pp. 54, 71–72 (LC).

83. Ibid., 73–75; Koster testimony, Dec. 15, 1969, Peers Inquiry, 2: Testimony, book 3, pp. 87–88, 91; Peers Report, 10–66; Peers, *My Lai Inquiry*, 121, 203; Koster Witness Statement, Nov. 24, 1969, p. 4, CID, Tufts Collection on My Lai (U. of Mich.); CID Report, Dec. 3, 1970, p. 1.

84. Henderson interview with Tufts, July 29, 1970, in Memo by Tufts for Sec. of General Staff, July 31, 1970, Dept. of the Army, Tufts Collection on My Lai (U. of Mich.); Maj. Leon A. Young to Tufts, July 30, 1970, enclosed in Weekly Son My Talking Paper, July 30, 1970, Tufts Collection on My Lai; Lt. Col. Sinclair L. Melner, Infantry Chief, U.S. Army, to Commanding Officer, U.S. Army CID Agency, April 9, 1970, Lessons Learned, After Action Report, The CID Investigation of the My Lai/Son My Incident, Dec. 10, 1970, p. 2 plus Tabs, U.S. Army, Tufts Collection on My Lai; Koster Witness Statement, Nov. 24, 1969, pp. 2–3, CID, Tufts Collection on My Lai. Koster remembered the delivery date because Henderson's leg was in a cast from a wound from a grenade tossed by a VC suspect. Ibid., 4; Peers, *My Lai Inquiry*, 61. Koster thought he discussed the allegations with General Cushman, his immediate superior and commanding general of the 3rd Marine Amphibious Force. Koster declared that his talking with General Lam made it appropriate to inform Cushman. He never considered it necessary to bring the matter before either MACV or the ARVN. Koster testimony, Dec. 15, 1969, Peers Inquiry, 2: Testimony, book 3, pp. 38, 50, 93 (LC).

85. Chronology of Action Taken Since March 16, 1968, enclosed in Gustafson to Kanamine, Nov. 23, 1969, p. 1, Tufts Collection on My Lai (U. of Mich.); Henderson testimony, Dec. 19, 1969, Peers Inquiry, 2: Testimony, book 12, pp. 263–64 (LC); Medina testimony quoted ibid., 270; ibid., 271; Peers, *My Lai Inquiry*, 121–22, 203. The Peers commission's "inescapable conclusion" was that "no such formal report of investigation ever existed." Peers Report, 10–66. Koster later admitted he never knew who authored the so-called Rodriguez Statement. Ibid.

86. Henderson testimony, Dec. 19, 1969, Peers Inquiry, 2: Testimony, book 12, p. 271 (LC).

87. Ibid., 272.

88. Ibid., 56–57, 61–62. Henderson offered a weak defense in citing his unfamiliarity with the reporting procedures on atrocities. He did not believe a copy of this document was on file in brigade headquarters. The 11th Infantry Brigade was in a state of flux, and it was some time before the documents were once again in one place under division control. There was no "brigade set of documents." Ibid. See MACV Directive 20–4, April 27, 1967: "Inspections and Investigations, War Crimes," in Peers Inquiry, 3: Exhibits, Bk 1 (Directives), D-1 (LC); Peers, *My Lai Inquiry*, 31; MACV Directive 20-4, ibid., 261–62; MACV message of Feb. 12, 1968, ibid., 263.

Eight

1. Ridenhour testimony, Jan. 29, 1970, Peers Inquiry, 2: Testimony, book 14, pp. 3, 9, 17 (LC); Ron Ridenhour, "Jesus Was a Gook," in "Nobody Gets Off the Bus: The Viet Nam Generation Big Book," special issue, *Viet Nam Generation* 5 (1994): 1.7, available online at the Sixties Project website, http://www2.iath.virginia.edu/sixties/HTML_docs/Texts/Narrative/Ridenhour_Jesus_01.html, http://www2.iath.virginia.edu/sixties/HTML_docs/Texts/Narrative/Ridenhour_Jesus_02.html; CID Report, Sept. 10, 1970, pp. 61–62; CID Report, Sept. 25, 1970, p. 20; LaCroix testimony to Wilson, May 2, 1969, p. 68, My Lai Collection (VATTU); Bilton and Sim, *Four Hours in My Lai*, 215.

2. Ridenhour letter, 2; Ridenhour testimony, Jan. 29, 1970, Peers Inquiry, 2: Testimony, book 14, pp. 17–18 (LC). In his letter, Ridenhour misspelled Calley's name as Kally.

3. Ridenhour testimony, Jan. 29, 1970, Peers Inquiry, 2: Testimony, book 14, pp. 52–53 (LC).

4. Ridenhour-Gruver story in Bilton and Sim, *Four Hours in My Lai*, 214–16; Belknap, *Vietnam War on Trial*, 101–2; Allison, *My Lai*, 76–77; *Frontline*, "Remember My Lai"; George Esper, " 'It's Something You've Got to Live With': My Lai Memories Haunt Soldiers," *Los Angeles Times*, March 13, 1988; "Four Hours in My Lai."

5. Ridenhour testimony, Jan. 29, 1970, Peers Inquiry, 2: Testimony, book 14, p. 34 (LC). Ridenhour did not learn that My Lai 4 was the name of the village until about sixteen months after talking with Gruver. Ridenhour, "Jesus Was a Gook," 1.5.

6. Ridenhour testimony, Jan. 29, 1970, Peers Inquiry, 2: Testimony, book 14, pp. 18, 21, 22 (LC).

7. Ibid., 18–19, 21; Ridenhour, "Jesus Was a Gook," 1.6–7.

8. Ridenhour testimony, Jan. 29, 1970, Peers Inquiry, 2: Testimony, book 14, pp. 19–20 (LC); Ridenhour, "Jesus Was a Gook," 1.8, 2.1–2, 6; Ridenhour letter, 3; *Frontline*, "Remember My Lai"; Bilton and Sim, *Four Hours in My Lai*, 216.

9. Ridenhour testimony, Jan. 29, 1970, Peers Inquiry, 2: Testimony, book 14, pp. 18–22 (LC); Ridenhour, "Jesus Was a Gook," 1.4.

10. Ridenhour testimony, Jan. 29, 1970, Peers Inquiry, 2: Testimony, book 14, pp. 21–22 (LC); Ridenhour letter, 4; Bilton and Sim, *Four Hours in My Lai*, 216. Torres was in the 2nd Platoon and not under Calley's command. In mid-October 1968, Ridenhour came across Torres, who giggled when referring to "all them people we killed at Pinkville." LaCroix had misled Ridenhour into thinking that Torres was talking about acts committed under Calley's direction. Torres later stood accused of war crimes of his own. Ibid., 78–79, 115, 130, 181; CID Report, Sept. 4, 1970, p. 9. SP4 John Mower testified that he saw Torres

machine-gun six men and women. He was a machine-gun crew member with Torres in the 2nd Platoon. Mower testimony, CID Report, Sept. 10, 1970, p. 24.

11. Ridenhour testimony, Jan. 29, 1970, Peers Inquiry, 2: Testimony, book 14, pp. 23, 69 (LC); Ridenhour letter, 3–4; Bilton and Sim, *Four Hours in My Lai*, 218.

12. Ridenhour testimony, Jan. 29, 1970, Peers Inquiry, 2: Testimony, book 14, pp. 23, 26, 29, 43 (LC); Ridenhour letter, 3–5.

13. Ridenhour testimony, January 29, 1970, Peers Inquiry, 2: Testimony, book 14, pp. 24–25 (LC).

14. *Frontline*, "Remember My Lai"; Bilton and Sim, *Four Hours in My Lai*, 371.

15. Ridenhour testimony, Jan. 29, 1970, Peers Inquiry, 2: Testimony, book 14, p. 61 (LC); Allison, *My Lai*, 77–78; Ridenhour letter, 1, 2, 4; *Frontline*, "Remember My Lai"; "My Lai Massacre"; CID Report, Sept. 10, 1970, p. 62; CID Report, Sept. 25, 1970, p. 20; Belknap, *Vietnam War on Trial*, 103–4.

16. Ridenhour letter, 4–5.

17. Churchill quoted ibid.; Ridenhour testimony, Jan. 29, 1970, Peers Inquiry, 2: Testimony, book 14, pp. 61–62 (LC); Bilton and Sim, *Four Hours in My Lai*, 220–21; Belknap, *Vietnam War on Trial*, 103–4; Allison, *My Lai*, 78.

18. Bilton and Sim, *Four Hours in My Lai*, 208–13; Glen to Abrams, Nov. 27, 1968 (NARA), cited ibid., 210–12. For widespread atrocities in Vietnam, see Nick Turse, *Kill Anything That Moves: The Real American War in Vietnam* (New York: Henry Holt, 2013).

19. Bilton and Sim, *Four Hours in My Lai*, 213. The military intelligence officer was Kenneth Osburn, who served in Vietnam from September 1967 to December 1968. Osburn statement to Dellums Committee, April 27, 1971, in Citizens Commission of Inquiry, ed., *The Dellums Committee Hearings on War Crimes in Vietnam: An Inquiry into Command Responsibility in Southeast Asia* (New York: Random House, 1972), 106, 108, 117, 125, 127. Democratic congressman Ronald Dellums of California chaired this ad hoc committee in response to the My Lai massacre. Charles Lane suggests that Powell contributed to the My Lai cover-up through his shallow investigation. See Lane's article "The Legend of Colin Powell," *New Republic*, April 17, 1995, 20–32. Richard Harwood sharply disagrees in his article "Damned If You Don't: Colin Powell's Supposed Sins of Omission," *Washington Post*, April 10, 1995. Powell insists in his autobiography that he knew nothing about the My Lai massacre at the time he wrote his memo. See Colin Powell, *My American Journey* (New York: Random House, 1995), 143–44. For questions about what Powell knew and when he knew it, see John Barry, "The Very Model of a Political General," *Newsweek*, Sept. 11, 1995, 31. For additional questions about Powell's behavior, see David Corn, "Questions for Powell," *The Nation*, Jan. 8, 2001, 5. Robert Parry and Norman Solomon claim that the army whitewashed My Lai. See their article "Powell Media Mania," *Extra!*, Jan. 1, 1996, http://fair.org/extra-online-articles/powell-media-mania/.

20. Belknap, *Vietnam War on Trial*, 104–5; Ridenhour testimony, Jan. 29, 1970, Peers Inquiry, 2: Testimony, book 14, p. 64 (LC); Westmoreland, *Soldier Reports*, 494–95; Bilton and Sim, *Four Hours in My Lai*, 220–21; Allison, *My Lai*, 78. Westmoreland had become chief of staff on July 3, 1968, after serving as the commander of MACV since June 1964.

21. Westmoreland testimony, June 10, 1970, Hébert Hearings, 832, 838; Bilton and Sim, *Four Hours in My Lai*, 220–21; William Wilson, "I Had Prayed to God That This Thing Was Fiction," *American Heritage* 41 (Feb. 1990): 44–53; Belknap, *Vietnam War on Trial*, 105; Peers, *My Lai Inquiry*, 8.

22. Bilton and Sim, *Four Hours in My Lai*, 220–21. According to a Gallup Poll of late January 1969, 52 percent of Americans thought involvement in the war a mistake and 39 percent did not. These figures were comparable to polls taken in early August and late September 1968, which for the first time since early April 1968 showed a majority against the war. See Mark Gillespie, "Americans Look Back at Vietnam War," Gallup News Service, Nov. 17, 2000, http://www.gallup.com/poll/2299/americans-look-back-vietnam-war.aspx.

23. Westmoreland testimony, June 10, 1970, Hébert Hearings, 832; Whitaker Memorandum for Record, "Preliminary Inquiry Concerning Alleged Massacre of All Vietnamese Residents of My Lai by U.S. Soldiers," April 17, 1969, Peers Inquiry, 3: Exhibits, book 4, Misc. Docs., M-98, pp. 359–62 (LC); Bilton and Sim, *Four Hours in My Lai*, 221–22; Allison, *My Lai*, 78–79.

24. Westmoreland testimony, June 10, 1970, Hébert Hearings, 837–38.

25. Wilson, "I Had Prayed to God," 44, 46; Belknap, *Vietnam War on Trial*, 105; Bilton and Sim, *Four Hours in My Lai*, 222–23.

26. Wilson, "I Had Prayed to God," 46–47; Belknap, *Vietnam War on Trial*, 105–6; Allison, *My Lai*, 79.

27. Wilson, "I Had Prayed to God," 48; Belknap, *Vietnam War on Trial*, 106.

28. Wilson, "I Had Prayed to God," 47–48; Allison, *My Lai*, 79; Bilton and Sim, *Four Hours in My Lai*, 223.

29. Wilson, "I Had Prayed to God," 48.

30. Ibid.

31. LaCroix testimony to Wilson, May 2, 1969, p. 71, My Lai Collection (VATTU). Calley's name remained misspelled, this time in the written transcript of LaCroix's testimony.

32. This exchange ibid., 69, 71.

33. Ibid., 56, 62–64, 78–79.

34. Ibid., 84–85; Bilton and Sim, *Four Hours in My Lai*, 224–25.

35. LaCroix testimony to Wilson, May 2, 1969, pp. 56, 60, 62, My Lai Collection (VATTU). On the ARVN issue, see Bernhardt testimony to Wilson, May 8, 1969, My Lai Collection, 188; Medina testimony to Wilson, May 13, 1969, My Lai Collection, 248, 269; Cowan testimony to Wilson, May 23, 1969, My Lai Collection, 444. On medical aid, see Bernhardt testimony to Wilson, May 8, 1969, My Lai Collection, 208, and Medina testimony to Wilson, May 13, 1969, My Lai Collection, 264. Bilton and Sim, *Four Hours in My Lai*, 224–25.

36. Wilson, "I Had Prayed to God," 49; Doherty testimony to Wilson, May 5, 1969, pp. 134–35, My Lai Collection (VATTU).

37. Doherty testimony to Wilson, May 5, 1969, pp. 136–37, 139, 144–46, My Lai Collection (VATTU).

38. Wilson, "I Had Prayed to God," 49; Bernhardt testimony to Wilson, May 8, 1969, pp. 184–85, My Lai Collection (VATTU).

39. Bernhardt testimony to Wilson, May 8, 1969, pp. 187, 196, 202, My Lai Collection (VATTU).

40. Medina testimony to Wilson, May 13, 1969, pp. 239, 254, My Lai Collection (VATTU).

41. Ibid., 254, 256–57, 260, 266, 283.

42. Ibid., 272; Bilton and Sim, *Four Hours in My Lai*, 227–29; Belknap, *Vietnam War on Trial*, 107.

43. Medina testimony to Wilson, May 13, 1969, pp. 245, 258–59, 274, My Lai Collection (VATTU); Widmer testimony to Wilson, July 15, 1969, My Lai Collection, 982–83, 987.

44. Wilson, "I Had Prayed to God," 49.

45. Belknap, *Vietnam War on Trial*, 107–8.

46. Ibid.; Calhoun testimony to Wilson, May 19, 1969, pp. 318, 320–21, 326–29, My Lai Collection (VATTU); Wilson, "I Had Prayed to God," 50.

47. Henderson testimony to Wilson, May 26, 1969, pp. 454–55, My Lai Collection (VATTU); Wilson, "I Had Prayed to God," 50; Bilton and Sim, *Four Hours in My Lai*, 229–31; Allison, *My Lai*, 80.

48. Wilson, "I Had Prayed to God," 50–51.

49. *United States ex rel. Toth v. Quarles*, 350 U.S. 11 (1955); Alfred H. Kelly and Winfred A. Harbison, *The American Constitution: Its Origins and Development*, 4th ed. (New York: W. W. Norton, 1970), 871–72; Belknap, *Vietnam War on Trial*, 112. See also Joseph W. Bishop, "Court-Martial Jurisdiction over Military-Civilian Hybrids: Retired Regulars, Reservists, and Discharged Prisoners," *University of Pennsylvania Law Review* 112 (Jan. 1964): 317–77.

50. Belknap, *Vietnam War on Trial*, 98–99.

51. Ibid., 99–100; Sack, *Calley*, 134–37, 146–47.

52. Sack, *Calley*, 147; Calley testimony to Stanfield, June 9, 1969, p. 576, My Lai Collection (VATTU).

53. This exchange in Calley testimony to Stanfield, June 9, 1969, p. 577, My Lai Collection (VATTU); Sack, *Calley*, 147; Belknap, *Vietnam War on Trial*, 98; UCMJ, art. 109, pp. 137–38; art. 118, pp. 143–44 (LC).

54. Calley testimony to Stanfield, June 9, 1969, pp. 577, 581–83, My Lai Collection (VATTU); Belknap, *Vietnam War on Trial*, 109; Allison, *My Lai*, 80–81.

55. Wilson, "I Had Prayed to God," 50–51; Belknap, *Vietnam War on Trial*, 108–9; Allison, *My Lai*, 80.

56. Wilson, "I Had Prayed to God," 51.

57. Ibid.; Belknap, *Vietnam War on Trial*, 108.

58. Wilson, "I Had Prayed to God," 51.

59. Millians testimony to Wilson, June 18, 1969, pp. 734–35, 739, 752, 754, My Lai Collection (VATTU); Colburn testimony to Wilson, June 19, 1969, p. 765, My Lai Collection.

60. Widmer testimony to Wilson, July 15, 1969, pp. 990, 992, 994, 997, 1002, 1005, My Lai Collection (VATTU); Bilton and Sim, *Four Hours in My Lai*, 127–28.

61. Widmer testimony to Wilson, July 15, 1969, pp. 1005–6, My Lai Collection (VATTU).

62. Wilson, "I Had Prayed to God," 52.

63. Meadlo testimony to Wilson, July 16, 1969, pp. 1010–12, My Lai Collection (VATTU).

64. Ibid., 1011–12; Wilson, "I Had Prayed to God," 52; Belknap, *Vietnam War on Trial*, 109–10. The standard clip for an M-16 assault rifle before 1970 was twenty rounds but afterward became thirty. Experience, however, showed that a fully loaded clip often jammed the rifle and led soldiers to load seventeen to nineteen rounds. Author's interview of Tilford, June 27, 2015.

65. Meadlo testimony to Wilson, July 16, 1969, pp. 1012–13, My Lai Collection (VATTU); Wilson, "I Had Prayed to God," 52. Wilson alluded to the *United States ex rel. Toth v. Quarles* case of 1955.

66. Meadlo testimony to Wilson, July 16, 1969, p. 1013, My Lai Collection (VATTU).

67. Ibid.

68. Ibid.

69. Ibid.

70. In his article of 1990, Wilson asserted that Meadlo knew he was liable for everything he said but nonetheless declared, "I don't care," and told the story again. Wilson, "I Had Prayed to God," 52–53. The transcript of the interview does not verify this claim.

71. Meadlo testimony to Wilson, July 16, 1969, p. 1014, My Lai Collection (VATTU).

72. Ibid., 1014–15, 1017–19, 1021.

73. Wilson, "I Had Prayed to God," 52.

74. Ibid., 6–7; Belknap, *Vietnam War on Trial*, 109–10.

75. Wilson, "I Had Prayed to God," 53.

76. Ibid., 46, 53; Belknap, *Vietnam War on Trial*, 110; CID Talking Paper, Aug. 7, 1969, Tufts Collection on My Lai (U. of Mich.).

77. CID Investigation of My Lai/Son My Incident, Dec. 10, 1970, pp. 2–3, Tufts Collection on My Lai (U. of Mich.); Westmoreland, *Soldier Reports*, 495; Bilton and Sim, *Four Hours in My Lai*, 237, 239–40; Feher quoted ibid., 239; Belknap, *Vietnam War on Trial*, 110; Allison, *My Lai*, 81.

78. Haeberle testimony, April 23, 1970, Hébert Hearings, 261, 267. Less than a week later, Haeberle raised the number to more than one hundred black-and-white pictures. Haeberle testimony, April 28, 1970, Hébert Hearings, 524; Bilton and Sim, *Four Hours in My Lai*, 240–41; Haeberle, CID statement, Aug. 25, 1969, pp. 4–5, quoted ibid., 241.

79. Haeberle testimony, April 23, 28, 1970, Hébert Hearings, 261, 264, 266, 525, 530, 543–44; Biographical sketch of Haeberle in Gustafson to Chief of Staff, U.S. Army, Dec. 6, 1969, p. 2, Tufts Collection on My Lai (U. of Mich.); Haeberle testimony, Jan. 17, 1970, Peers Inquiry, 2: Testimony, book 11, p. 5 (LC); Bilton and Sim interview of Haeberle in 1989, Papers of *Four Hours in My Lai*, LHCMA (KCL); Haeberle statement to CID, Aug. 25, 1969, pp. 4–5, quoted in Bilton and Sim, *Four Hours in My Lai*, 240–42; Bilton and Sim interview of Haeberle quoted ibid., 242.

80. Bilton and Sim, *Four Hours in My Lai*, 242.

81. Simone quoted ibid., 243.

82. Ibid., 243–44; Boyce statement to CID, Aug. 28, 1969, pp. 2–7, quoted in ibid., 244.

83. Olsen statement to CID, Aug. 28, 1969, p. 8, quoted ibid., 245.

84. Bilton and Sim, *Four Hours in My Lai*, 245–46.

85. CID Talking Paper on My Lai, Sept. 10, 1969; Bilton and Sim, *Four Hours in My Lai*, 246.

86. Belknap, *Vietnam War on Trial*, 114.

87. The source was Montgomery reporter Wayne Greenhaw. See his work *Making of a Hero*, 175–76. Greenhaw did not identify the two colonels by name. See also Robert Miraldi, *Seymour Hersh: Scoop Artist* (Lincoln: University of Nebraska Press, 2013), 9.

88. UCMJ, art. 32, pp. 47–49 (LC); CID Talking Paper on My Lai, Sept. 10, 1969; CID After Action Report, Dec. 10, 1970, p. 3; Belknap, *Vietnam War on Trial*, 114–15; Bilton and Sim, *Four Hours in My Lai*, 248–49.

89. Bilton and Sim, *Four Hours in My Lai*, 248–50.

90. Ibid., 235–36, 250; "Army Accuses Lieutenant in Vietnam Deaths in 1968," *New York Times*, Sept. 7, 1969. For the Green Berets case, see Jeff Stein, *A Murder in Wartime: The Untold Spy Story That Changed the Course of the Vietnam War* (New York: St. Martin's, 1992).
91. Bilton, *Four Hours in My Lai*, 250–51.

Nine

1. Miraldi, *Hersh*, 1–3; Bilton and Sim, *Four Hours in My Lai*, 251–52. My account of Hersh's investigation rests primarily on his own statements both in print and in public talks. In a telephone conversation with him, I noted the inconsistencies in detail and wondered which accounts were accurate. Hersh dismissed the discrepancies as unimportant and attributed them to his attempt to recall the facts after so many years had passed. Author's telephone conversation with Hersh, Jan. 23, 2015.
2. Miraldi, *Hersh*, 3, 5; Bilton and Sim, *Four Hours in My Lai*, 251.
3. Miraldi, *Hersh*, 7; Bilton and Sim, *Four Hours in My Lai*, 251–53.
4. Seymour Hersh, "Vietnam War: My Lai Massacre," keynote address at Tulane University, New Orleans, Dec. 2, 1994, http://www.c-span.org/video/?62006-1/vietnam-war-lai-massacre%20December; Philip J. Stern, "Seymour Hersh and the Hunt for Lt. William Calley," Fund for Investigative Journalism, 2009, available on YouTube at https://www.youtube.com/watch?v=sR3-tc54VPU; Hersh interview in "Seymour Hersh, My Lai Massacre," *Investigating Power*, 2012, http://www.InvestigatingPower.org (no longer online).
5. Miraldi, *Hersh*, 7–8; Hersh, "Vietnam War."
6. Miraldi, *Hersh*, 9–12; Hersh, "Vietnam War"; "Seymour Hersh and the Hunt for Lt. William Calley," Hersh interview in "My Lai Massacre"; Hersh radio interview by Brooke Gladstone, "40 Years Later: Hersh on My Lai," *On the Media*, Aug. 15, 2008, http://www.onthemedia.org/story/131080-40-years-later-hersh-on-my-lai/transcript/.
7. Miraldi, *Hersh*, 12; Hersh, "Vietnam War"; Hersh interview by Gladstone. Calley had had an ulcer since he was nineteen years old.
8. Hersh, "Vietnam War."
9. Ibid.; Peter Braestrup, "U.S. Officer Is Accused of Mass Viet 'Murders': Army Probing Charge GI Killed Viet Civilians," *Washington Post*, Nov. 13, 1969; Robert M. Smith, "Officer Kept in Army in Inquiry into Killing of Vietnam Civilians," *New York Times*, Nov. 13, 1969; Bilton and Sim, *Four Hours in My Lai*, 253–54; Miraldi, *Hersh*, 17–19; Obst quoted ibid., 18; Bradlee quoted ibid., 20. *Newsweek* magazine called the Dispatch News Service "an antiwar offshoot of Washington's radical Institute for Policy Studies." See "The Calley Case," *Newsweek*, Nov. 24, 1969, 45. According to British historian Kendrick Oliver, most "American journalists chose not to disturb the silence over the darkest aspects of the national war effort." See his *The My Lai Massacre in American History and Memory* (Manchester, UK: Manchester University Press, 2006), 24. Hersh won the George Polk Memorial Award in February 1970 for his early reporting of the My Lai 4 massacre and the Pulitzer Prize for International Reporting in that same year for his book *My Lai 4*.
10. See Greenhaw's account in his *Making of a Hero*, 28–42.
11. Ken Roberts to author, July 18, 2013, enclosed in email from Jenkins to Roberts; Greenhaw, *Making of a Hero*, 28–42.

12. Greenhaw, "Ft. Benning Probes Vietnam Slayings," *Alabama Journal*, Nov. 12, 1969. The *Alabama Journal* was an afternoon newspaper that became part of the *Montgomery Advertiser* in the mid-1990s.

13. Hersh, "Lieutenant Accused of Murdering 109 Civilians," *St. Louis Post-Dispatch*, Nov. 13, 1969, reprinted in *Reporting Vietnam: American Journalism, 1959–1975* (New York: Library of America, 1998), 413–17. Hersh referred to the Pinkville massacre, but that name soon became interchangeable with Son My or My Lai and ultimately My Lai 4 when focusing on that particular subhamlet.

14. Ibid.

15. Ibid.

16. Ibid.

17. CID Talking Paper on My Lai to Army Chief of Staff, Nov. 13, 1969, Tufts Collection on My Lai (U. of Mich.).

18. Ibid.

19. Bilton and Sim, *Four Hours in My Lai*, 255; Miraldi, *Hersh*, 21.

20. Jon Nordheimer, " 'I'm Beginning to Feel the Pressure,' Says Officer Linked to the Murder of Vietnamese Civilians," *New York Times*, Nov. 14, 1969.

21. Miraldi, *Hersh*, 18–19; David E. Rosenbaum, " 'March Against Death' Begun by Thousands in Washington," *New York Times*, Nov. 14, 1969.

22. Peter Braestrup, "U.S. Officer Is Accused of Mass Viet 'Murders,' " *Washington Post*, Nov. 13, 1969; Robert M. Smith, "Army Names 2d Soldier in Mass Murder of Vietnamese," *New York Times*, Nov. 15, 1969; "Ex-G.I. Says He Stirred Army into Action on Alleged Slayings," *New York Times*, Nov. 16, 1969.

23. Henry Kamm, "Vietnamese Say G.I.'s Slew 567 in Town: Vietnamese Assert G.I.'s Killed 567 Unarmed Civilians in Village," *New York Times*, Nov. 17, 1969. The article reported that the killings took place in the village of "Songmy."

24. Miraldi, *Hersh*, 20–21, 26; Ridenhour quoted ibid., 21; Seymour Hersh, "Hamlet Attack Called 'Point-Blank Murder,' " *St. Louis Post-Dispatch*, Nov. 20, 1969, reprinted in *Reporting Vietnam*, 417–22. Doherty was the unidentified soldier.

25. Hersh, "Hamlet Attack"; Belknap, *Vietnam War on Trial*, 114–15.

26. Hersh, "Hamlet Attack."

27. Ibid.

28. Ibid.

29. Ibid. Terry had earlier testified that he and Doherty engaged in mercy killings at the ditch.

30. Joseph Eszeterhas, "1st Photos of Viet Mass Slaying: Cameraman Saw GIs Slay 100 Villagers," *Cleveland Plain Dealer*, Nov. 20, 1969, pp. 1, 5b; Gayle Powell, "Eyewitness accounts of the My Lai massacre; story by Seymour Hersh," ibid., 5b; Hersh, "GIs Call Viet Killings 'Point-Blank Murder,' " ibid.; Haeberle testimony, April 23, 1970, Hébert Hearings, 268; Haeberle testimony, April 28, 1970, Hébert Hearings, 536; Miraldi, *Hersh*, 21; Eszterhas interview by Ellen Hetzel, "From News Hound to Hollywood Animal," Feb. 20, 2004, for the Poynter Institute for Media Studies in Saint Petersburg, Florida, available online at http://www.poynter.org/2004/from-news-hound-to-hollywood-animal/21132/. The Poynter Institute is a non-profit school for journalism that owns the *Tampa Bay Times*.

31. Evelyn Theiss, "Images of My Lai Atrocities Shook Nation, Even in War: The *Plain Dealer* Was the First to Publish Images of Massacre," *Cleveland Plain Dealer*, Nov. 20, 2009.

32. Evelyn Theiss, "Photographer Destroyed Photos of Soldiers in the Act of Killing," *Cleveland Plain Dealer*, Nov. 20, 2009; Bilton and Sim, *Four Hours in My Lai*, 259–60. Apollo 12 marked the second mission to the moon; the first, Apollo 11, landed there in July. Ibid., 234, 261.

33. Theiss, "Photographer Destroyed Photos."

34. David D. Van Tassel and John J. Grabowski, eds., *The Encyclopedia of Cleveland History*, 2nd ed. (Bloomington: Indiana University Press, 1997). A joint effort of Case Western University and the Western Reserve Historical Society of Cleveland, Ohio, available online at https://ech.cwru.edu.

35. Haeberle interview in Eszterhas, "Cameraman Saw GIs Slay 100 Villagers," reprinted in Jo Ellen Corrigan, "Plain Dealer Exclusive in 1969: My Lai Massacre Photos by Ronald Haeberle," *Cleveland Plain Dealer*, Nov. 20, 2009.

36. Haeberle interview, *Cleveland Plain Dealer*, Nov. 20, 1969.

37. Haeberle testimony, April 23, 1970, Hébert Hearings, 281; Theiss, "Photographer Destroyed Photos."

38. Haeberle's photos in *Cleveland Plain Dealer*, Nov. 20, 1969; Bilton and Sim, *Four Hours in My Lai*, 260. CBS paid the *Plain Dealer* five hundred dollars for permission to show its front page and the photos. Ibid.

39. Miraldi, *Hersh*, 24.

40. "The Calley Case," *Newsweek*, Nov. 24, 1969, 45; "An American Nightmare," editorial, *New York Times*, Nov. 22, 1969; Stein, *Murder in Wartime* (Green Berets case); Daniel Lang, "Casualties of War," *New Yorker*, Oct. 18, 1969, reprinted in *Reporting Vietnam*, vol. 1, *American Journalism, 1959–1969* (New York: The Library of America, 1998), 709–67. William G. Eckhardt defended the accused soldiers in court. Eckhardt later became the chief prosecutor in all the ground action My Lai cases in federal court and is now on the faculty of the University of Missouri-Kansas City School of Law. Author's interview of Eckhardt, Jan. 19, 2017. Lang's story also detailed the death threats made to the soldier (unidentified) who witnessed the incident after he turned in fellow squad members and testified at numerous courts martial as they attempted to cover up what happened. This story became the basis of a Hollywood movie with the same title. See Turse, *Kill Anything That Moves*, 223–24.

41. Fred Emery, "US Authorities Disturbed over Massacre Allegations," *London Times*, Nov. 20, 1969; "A Case for Inquiry," editorial, n.d., ibid.; *Daily Sketch*, editorial, n.d., quoted in Miraldi, *Hersh*, 22.

42. Laird memo (prepared by his deputy, David Packard) to the president, "My Lai Atrocity," with attachment, "Statement of Facts and Circumstances," Sept. 3, 1969, enclosed in Kissinger to H. R. Haldeman (chief of staff), "Lieutenant Calley Case," Nov. 21, 1969, NSC Files, Vietnam Subject Files, Box 118 (RNL); Kissinger memos to the president, "My Lai Atrocities," "The Incident at Mylai," Dec. 6, 8, 1969, ibid.

43. Kissinger-Laird telephone conversation, Nov. 21, 1969, Thomas Blanton and Dr. William Burr, eds., "The Kissinger Telcons," National Security Archive Electronic Briefing book no. 123, May 26, 2004, National Security Archive (George Washington University), http://nsarchive.gwu.edu/NSAEBB/NSAEBB123/. Klein quoted in William M.

Hammond, *Public Affairs: The Military and the Media, 1968–1973* (Washington, DC: Department of the Army, 1996), 231.

44. Kissinger-Laird telephone conversation, Nov. 21, 1969, "Kissinger Telcons" (NSA).

45. Robert M. Smith, "26 Are Investigated in Vietnam Deaths," *New York Times*, Nov. 22, 1969.

46. Ibid. Jordan alluded to the *United States ex rel. Toth v. Quarles* case of 1955.

47. Haeberle testimony, April 23, 1970, Hébert Hearings, 269–71, 273. Eszterhas later regretted his role in this story. In the *Evergreen Review*, he published an article entitled "The Selling of the My Lai Massacre," in which he criticized the *Plain Dealer* for "the way the photographs were published." The paper fired him in September 1971. Eszterhas shifted career directions, first taking a position with *Rolling Stone* magazine before becoming a highly successful screenplay writer and producer in Hollywood by the early 1990s. Among his movie credits are *Basic Instinct* and *Basic Instinct 2*, *Showgirls*, and *Flashdance*. Eszterhas interview; *New York Times*, May 28, 1972; Bilton and Sim, *Four Hours in My Lai*, 260, 264n.

48. Miraldi, *Hersh*, 24–25.

49. Ibid., 25.

50. Ibid.

51. Ibid., 25–26.

52. Hersh interview by Gladstone; Bilton and Sim, *Four Hours in My Lai*, 260–62.

53. Miraldi, *Hersh*, 23; Bilton and Sim, *Four Hours in My Lai*, 260–61; UCMJ, Art. 32, pp. 47–49 (LC).

54. Hersh quoted in Miraldi, *Hersh*, 26; Bilton and Sim, *Four Hours in My Lai*, 260–61; Belknap, *Vietnam War on Trial*, 120–21; Hersh, "The Scene of the Crime."

55. Wallace's interview of Meadlo, Nov. 24, 1969, in "Transcript of Interview of Vietnam War Veteran on His Role in Alleged Massacre of Civilians at Songmy," *New York Times*, Nov. 25, 1969. See also Bilton and Sim, *Four Hours in My Lai*, 262.

56. Bilton and Sim, *Four Hours in My Lai*, 261; brief video clip of interview in "Back to My Lai." See David K. Shipler, "Mike Wallace: The Question That Changed America," *The Shipler Report: A Journal of Fact and Opinion*, April 10, 2012, http://shiplerreport .blogspot.com/2012/04/mike-wallace-question-that-changed.html. Shipler declared that the question "And babies?" was "like a punch in the stomach" and became the basis of one of the most powerful antiwar posters of the time. Shipler wrote for the *New York Times* for more than two decades and received the Pulitzer Prize for General Non-Fiction.

57. For Meadlo's parents, see mother's interview on *CBS Evening News*, Nov. 25, 1969, quoted in Bilton and Sim, *Four Hours in My Lai*, 263, and father's quote in J. Anthony Lukas, "Meadlo's Home Town Regards Him as Blameless," *New York Times*, Nov. 26, 1969. Meadlo's parents also quoted in "My Lai: An American Tragedy," *Time*, Dec. 5, 1969, 32.

58. "War Veteran Says He Killed 35 to 40 in Songmy Sweep: Veteran Says His Unit Killed Villagers," *New York Times*, Nov. 25, 1969.

59. Ridenhour quoted in Anderson, *Facing My Lai*, 55; "War Veteran Says He Killed 35 to 40 in Songmy Sweep."

60. E. W. Kenworthy, "Resor Called to Testify about Alleged Massacre," *New York Times*, Nov. 26, 1969, 10.

61. Ibid.

62. Ibid.; MACV Directive 20-4, April 27, 1967, in Peers Report, 9–11, 9–12; extracts of directive in Peers, *My Lai Inquiry*, 261–62.

63. Seymour Hersh, "Ex-GI Tells of Killing Civilians at Pinkville," *St. Louis Post-Dispatch*, Nov. 25, 1969, reprinted in *Reporting Vietnam*, 422–27.

64. Ibid.; UCMJ, Art. 118, pp. 143–44 (LC).

65. Douglas Robinson, "Murder Trial Set for Army Officer in Village Deaths," *New York Times*, Nov. 25, 1969; Belknap, *Vietnam War on Trial*, 114; Bilton and Sim, *Four Hours in My Lai*, 254–55.

66. Belknap, *Vietnam War on Trial*, 114–16.

67. Ibid., 115.

68. Ibid., 115–16.

69. Robinson, "Murder Trial Set." Calley visited his family in Miami on one of the occasions that he left the post since he was charged with murder in early September. Ibid.

70. Ibid.

71. Memo for Peers from Westmoreland and Resor, Nov. 26, 1969, Peers Report, 1–6; Westmoreland, *Soldier Reports*, 495; Robert M. Smith, "Army Will Review Study of '68 on Alleged Killings," *New York Times*, Nov. 25, 1969; Bilton and Sim, *Four Hours in My Lai*, 293–95.

72. Belknap, *Vietnam War on Trial*, 137.

73. James Reston, "Washington: The Massacre of Songmy: Who Is to Blame?" *New York Times*, Nov. 26, 1969.

74. Ibid.

75. Simpson in Kenworthy, "Resor Called to Testify"; "Army Reported Killing 128 of Enemy at Songmy," *New York Times*, Nov. 26, 1969. See chapter 6 of this work for a discussion of these stories.

76. Agnew and Blount in "The Administration v. The Critics," *Time*, Nov. 28, 1969, 19. On another occasion, Simpson admitted to killing up to twenty-five Vietnamese civilians that day in Son My. See Bilton and Sim, *Four Hours in My Lai*, 7.

77. "Massacre Report Denied by Saigon," *New York Times*, Nov. 22, 1969; Charles Mohr, "Hanoi Charges Genocide by the U.S.," *New York Times*, Nov. 26, 1969; Henry Kamm, "Foe of Thieu Sets Massacre Inquiry," *New York Times*, Nov. 26, 1969.

78. Henry Kamm, "Saigon Senate Will Investigate Alleged Atrocity," *New York Times*, Nov. 28, 1969. The quote came from the newspaper *Chinh Lun*. Ibid.

79. "The My Lai Massacre," *Time*, Nov. 28, 1969, 17–19. Like Seymour Hersh, *Newsweek* referred to the location as Pinkville at this time, although by early December 1969 it used Song My. For Pinkville, see "The Calley Case," *Newsweek*, Nov. 24, 1969, 40–41. For Song My, see "Song My: A U.S. Atrocity," *Newsweek*, Dec. 1, 1969, 35–37, and "The Killings at Song My," *Newsweek*, Dec. 8, 1969, 33–36, 41. The *New York Times* also referred to Songmy. See "Massacre Report Denied by Saigon," Nov. 22, 1969; Robert M. Smith, "Army Will Review Study of '68 on Alleged Killings," *New York Times*, Nov. 25, 1969; and Henry Kamm, "Foe of Thieu Sets Massacre Inquiry," *New York Times*, Nov. 26, 1969.

80. Hersh quoted in Anderson, *Facing My Lai*, 75–76; Miraldi, *Hersh*, 19, 30–32. Hersh had a falling-out with McCarthy and left the campaign after three months. Ibid., 2.

81. Smith, "Army Will Review Study of '68."

82. Mark D. Carson, "F. Edward Hébert and the Congressional Investigation of the My Lai Massacre," *Louisiana History* 37 (Winter 1996): 61–79; Gillespie, "Americans Look Back

at Vietnam War," Gallup News Service, Nov. 17, 2000, http://www.gallup.com/
poll/2299/americans-look-back-vietnam-war.aspx.

83. Bilton and Sim, *Four Hours in My Lai*, 264–66.

84. Kenworthy, "Resor Called to Testify"; Resor's testimony in "Statements by Ziegler, Resor
and Stennis," *New York Times*, Nov. 27, 1969. Ron Ziegler was Nixon's press secretary.
John Stennis was a Democrat from Mississippi and chair of the Senate Armed Services
Committee.

85. Bilton and Sim, *Four Hours in My Lai*, 266.

86. Ibid., 266–67.

87. Resor, Inouye, Arends, and Stennis quoted in Hersh, *My Lai 4*, p. 159. See also
"Statements by Ziegler, Resor and Stennis."

88. Young quoted in Hersh, *My Lai 4*, p. 160.

Ten

1. Peers Report, 1–1, 1–2, 1–3, 1–6; E. W. Kenworthy, "Panel on Songmy Questions Calley,"
New York Times, Dec. 6, 1969; Peers at Pentagon press conference, March 17, 1970,
available on YouTube as "Peers-MacCrate Press Conference," https://www.youtube.com/
watch?v=021eVBvEXhI; Peers, *My Lai Inquiry*, 15; Belknap, *Vietnam War on Trial*,
122–23. See also Joseph Goldstein, Burke Marshall, and Jack Schwartz, *The My Lai
Massacre and Its Cover-Up: Beyond the Reach of Law? The Peers Commission Report with a
Supplement and Introductory Essay on the Limits of Law* (New York: Free Press, 1976), 33.

2. Peers Report, 1–2, 1–3, 1–4, 1–16; Peers, *My Lai Inquiry*, 245. The panel learned that the
Vietnamese did not use the name My Lai 4 in referring to the subhamlet but called it
Thuan Yen, part of Tu Cung Hamlet.

3. Citation and quote in Turse, *Kill Anything That Moves*, 242. Turse shows that Jordan sent
his memo to the assistant attorney general bearing the subject line "Trial of Discharged
Servicemen for Violation of the Law of War" (Dec. 2, 1969). He also cites Jordan's email
to Deborah Nelson, as well as her interview of Jordan in 2006. Ibid., 343nn68–69.

4. Bob Woodward, *The Last of the President's Men* (New York: Simon and Schuster, 2015),
53–54. Butterfield is the subject of this work.

5. Ibid.

6. Ibid., 54.

7. Ibid.

8. Ibid.

9. Ibid., 54–55.

10. Ibid., 54.

11. The "Task Force–My Lai" document is dated December 1, 1969, and comes from the
Haldeman diaries housed in the Nixon Library in Yorba Linda, California. Michael
Bilton and Kevin Sim first uncovered this story over two decades ago in their book
published in 1992, *Four Hours in My Lai*, 321. Ken Hughes from the Miller Center
Presidential Recording Program at the University of Virginia called Haldeman's note
"an important piece of evidence that Nixon interfered with a war-crime prosecution."
Hughes quoted in Evie Salomon, "Document Points to Nixon in My Lai Cover-up
Attempt," *60 Minutes, Overtime*, CBS-TV, March 23, 2014, http://www.cbsnews.com/

news/document-points-to-nixon-in-my-lai-cover-up-attempt/. See Robert Dallek, *Nixon and Kissinger: Partners in Power* (New York: HarperCollins, 2007), 185–86; Anthony Summers, *The Arrogance of Power: The Secret World of Richard Nixon* (New York: Viking Penguin, 2000), 333–34; and two publications by Trent Angers: *Forgotten Hero of My Lai* and "Nixon and the My Lai Massacre Coverup," *New York Post*, March 15, 2014, available online at http://nypost.com/2014/03/15/richard-nixon-and-the-my-lai-massacre-coverup/.

12. Bilton and Sim, *Four Hours in My Lai*, 321; Lyn Nofziger, *Nofziger* (Washington, DC: Regnery Gateway, 1992), 98–100; Angers, "Nixon and My Lai Massacre Coverup."

13. Laird memo to president, Sept. 4, 1969, "Vietnamizing the War," U.S. Department of State, *Foreign Relations of the United States, 1969–1976*, vol. 6, *Vietnam, January 1969–July 1970* (Washington, DC: U.S. GPO, 2006), 358–67 (hereafter *FRUS*). For Nixon and Vietnamization, see George C. Herring, *America's Longest War: The United States and Vietnam, 1950–1975*, 4th ed. (New York: McGraw-Hill, 2002), 281–82; Jeffrey Kimball, *Nixon's Vietnam War* (Lawrence: University Press of Kansas, 1998), 72–73, 137–39; Dallek, *Nixon and Kissinger*, 125–27.

14. Moynihan memo to president, Nov. 25, 1969, NSC Files, Vietnam Subject Files, Box 118 (RNL); Action Memorandum for Kissinger from Staff Secretary in White House, Dec. 2, 1969, ibid.; Memorandum for the president and Kissinger from Bryce Harlow, Nixon's senior political adviser, Dec. 3, 1969, ibid.; Kissinger to Nixon, Dec. 6, 1969, ibid.; Kissinger memos to the president, Dec. 6, 8, 1969, "My Lai Atrocities" and "The Incident at Mylai," ibid.; Nixon's agreement with Kissinger on no commission, *FRUS*, vol. 6, *Vietnam, January 1969–July 1970*, 508n4; Belknap, *Vietnam War on Trial*, 134–37.

15. Memorandum from John R. Brown III to Kissinger (contains Chu Lai atrocity report), Dec. 2, 1969, NSC Files, Vietnam Subject Files, Box 118 (RNL); memorandum from Laird for Kissinger, Dec. 11, 1969, ibid; memorandum from Kissinger for Nixon, Dec. 12, 1969, ibid.

16. David Rosenbaum, "President Pledges Penalty for Any Guilty at Songmy," *New York Times*, Dec. 9, 1969.

17. President's News Conference of Dec. 8, 1969, *Public Papers of the Presidents of the United States: Richard Nixon, Containing the Public Messages, Speeches, and Statements of the President, 1969* (Washington, DC: U.S. GPO, 1971), 1003–4; Richard Nixon, *The Memoirs of Richard Nixon*, 2 vols. (New York: Warner, 1978), 1:619–20.

18. Angers, "Nixon and My Lai Massacre Coverup"; Evie Salomon, "Document Points to Nixon in My Lai Cover-up Attempt," *60 Minutes Overtime*, CBS-TV, March 23, 2014, http://www.cbsnews.com/news/document-points-to-nixon-in-my-lai-cover-up-attempt/; Jonathan Block, "Nixon May Have Tried to Discredit Witnesses in My Lai Massacre to Quell Growing Public Relations Fiasco," *Daily Mail* [UK], March 24, 2014; Lauren McCauley, "Does New Look at Documents Reveal Nixon's Hand in My Lai Cover-Up?" *MintPress News*, March 25, 2014, http://www.mintpressnews.com/new-look-documents-reveal-nixons-hand-lai-cover/187470/.

19. Army major quoted in Henry Kamm, "GI's Near Songmy Doubt Any Massacre," *New York Times*, Dec. 1, 1969; "GI's in Battle: The 'Dink' Complex," *Newsweek*, Dec. 1, 1969, 37.

20. "Massacre at Mylai," *Life*, 36–44.

21. Harry Fletcher of Montgomery, AL; Col. Ray Smith of Fort Sill, OK; Stella Swain Rico of Los Angeles, CA; and Katherine Farris of Pullman, WA, all quoted in *Life*, Dec. 19, 1969, 46–47; Peers, *My Lai Inquiry*, 18; Hugh Sidey, "In the Shadow of Mylai," *Life*, Dec. 12, 1969, 4.

22. Medina testimony, Dec. 4, 1969, Peers Inquiry, 2: Testimony, book 23, pp. 38–39, 43–44, 46, 48, 61, 79–80 (LC); Kenworthy, "Panel on Songmy Questions Calley"; Richard Homan, "Army Panel Hears Calley Testimony," *Washington Post*, Dec. 6, 1969. To reporters on the day following the hearings, Medina declared, "I did not shoot any child in My Lai. I did not order any massacre in My Lai. I did not see any massacre at My Lai." Quoted in "And Then There Were Ten," *Newsweek*, March 23, 1970, 37.

23. Calley testimony, Dec. 5, 1969, Peers Inquiry, 2: Testimony, book 24, p. 6 (LC); Homan, "Army Panel Hears Calley Testimony"; John Sack, "Confessions of Lt. Calley," *Esquire* (Nov. 1970), 115; Sack, *Calley*, 14; Kenworthy, "Panel on Songmy Questions Calley."

24. Calley testimony, Dec. 5, 1969, Peers Inquiry, 2: Testimony, book 24, pp. 5–6.

25. Peers, *My Lai Inquiry*, 70, 179–80.

26. Bilton and Sim, *Four Hours in My Lai*, 300–301.

27. "Background on the My Lai Hearings and Report," https://www.loc.gov/rr/frd/Military_Law/pdf/MyLai_bckgr.pdf; Peers, *My Lai Inquiry*, 19–20; Belknap, *Vietnam War on Trial*, 137–38.

28. Belknap, *Vietnam War on Trial*, 137–38; "Rivers Differs with Nixon on Songmy," *New York Times*, Dec. 10, 1969.

29. Hersh, *My Lai 4*, pp. 167–68; Bilton and Sim, *Four Hours in My Lai*, 233–34; "Pilot's Testimony Is Cited by Rivers," *New York Times*, Dec. 11, 1969.

30. Hersh, *My Lai 4*, p. 168.

31. Peers, *My Lai Inquiry*, 20–21; Belknap, *Vietnam War on Trial*, 138; Bilton and Sim, *Four Hours in My Lai*, 285.

32. Hersh, *My Lai 4*, p. 168; Allison, *My Lai*, 89.

33. Robert M. Smith, "A.C.L.U. Asks Laird to Drop Case against Calley," *New York Times*, Dec. 12, 1969; *Washington Star*, Dec. 10, 1969, cited in "Rivers Picks Four to Study Son My: He Orders Inquiry 'in Depth' as He Ends Hearings," *New York Times*, Dec. 13, 1969; William Kling, "Rivers Orders Special Probe of My Lai Massacre Reports," *Chicago Tribune*, Dec. 13, 1969.

34. Smith, "A.C.L.U. Asks Laird to Drop Case against Calley."

35. Hersh, *My Lai 4*, pp. 168–69.

36. Michael J. Davidson, "Congressional Investigations and Their Effect on Subsequent Military Prosecutions," *Journal of Law and Policy* 14 (April 18, 2006): 300–301.

37. "Background on My Lai 4 Hearings and Report"; "Rivers Picks Four to Study Son My"; Carson, "Hébert and Congressional Investigation," 64; Charles DeBenedetti, *An American Ordeal: The Antiwar Movement of the Vietnam War* (New York: Syracuse University Press, 1990), 210 (Rivers's support for nuclear weapons); Belknap, *Vietnam War on Trial*, 138. The Hébert subcommittee also included former congressmen Porter Hardy, a Democrat from Virginia, and Indiana Republican Charles Halleck as special consultants. Hébert Report, 2.

38. "Rivers Picks Four to Study Son My"; Robert M. Smith, "Search for the Truth of Songmy," *New York Times*, Dec.14, 1969.

39. Carson, "Hébert and Congressional Investigation," 68 (first quote); Bilton and Sim, *Four Hours in My Lai*, 291 (second quote).

40. Rivers quoted in Associated Press, "Seeks My Lai Trial Halt," *New Orleans States-Item*, April 11, 1970. See also Carson, "Hébert and Congressional Investigation," 68.

41. Belknap, *Vietnam War on Trial*, 138–39; Hébert to Resor, April 27, 1970, in Carson, "Hébert and Congressional Investigation of My Lai Massacre," 68.

42. Author's interview of William Eckhardt, lead prosecutor in the Medina case, July 2, 2015; William G. Eckhardt, "My Lai: An American Tragedy," *UMKC Law Review* 68 (Summer 2000): 684–85; congressional opposition and Mikva's letter cited ibid., 684–85n50.

43. Peers Report, 7–1; Peers, *My Lai Inquiry*, 184–85, 197–98.

44. Peers Report, 7–2; Hersh, *Cover-Up*, 22–23; Peers, *My Lai Inquiry*, 185.

45. Peers Report, 7–2; Hersh, *Cover-Up*, 23–24; Peers, *My Lai Inquiry*, 185–86, 194.

46. Peers Report, 7–8.

47. Peers, *My Lai Inquiry*, 198.

48. "Song My: A U.S. Atrocity?," *Newsweek*, Dec. 1, 1969, 35; Bilton and Sim, *Four Hours in My Lai*, 309; Hersh, *Cover-Up*, 25.

49. Peers Report, 10–16, 10–17.

50. Peers Report, 10–18, 10–21, 12–20.

51. Peers Report, 9–8, 10–18, 10–22, 12–20; MACV Directive 525-3, "Combat Operations: Minimizing Noncombatant Battle Casualties," Oct. 14, 1966, Peers Inquiry, 3: Exhibits, book 1, Directives, D-6, p. 1 (LC).

52. Peers Report, 2–10, 2–12, 10–5, 12–20, 12–21, 12–23, 12–24, 12–25. Barker died in a helicopter crash in June 1968, along with Captain Michles of Bravo Company.

53. Peers Report, 10–23.

54. Peers Report, 10–24, 10–27.

55. Peers Report, 10–27, 10–28.

56. Peers Report, 10–24, 10–25, 10–26.

57. The documents relating to the award nominations are in the Peers Inquiry, 3: Exhibits, book 4, Misc. Docs., M-42, M-43, and M-44 (LC). The "V" Device was a small bronze letter V with decorative serifs at the top and worn on the medal to signify valor in combat. In late April 1968, Barker recommended an award based on Medina's "tactical planning" and "coolness under fire," which saved many troops' lives and led to his company's killing close to 150 Viet Cong "while sustaining minor casualties." Major General Koster and his Awards Board, however, turned down the recommendation, although they approved Henderson's later request to award a Silver Star to Medina for bravery in saving the lives of his men during the February 23, 1968, minefield explosions. After Barker's death in June of that year, he posthumously received the Purple Heart and, for his performance in heading Task Force Barker, the Legion of Merit and the Bronze Star with Oak Leaf Cluster, the citation for the latter noting his "outstanding leadership and guidance." Bilton and Sim, *Four Hours in My Lai*, 205–6.

58. Peers Report, 8–11, 12–1.

59. Peers Report, 12–9, 12–10, 12–11, 12–12.

60. Peers Report, 12–12.

61. Peers Report, 5–5, 8–10, 8–11, 12–12, 12–13, 12–14.

62. Peers Report, 2–10, 10–31, 12–2, 12–3, 12–16, 12–17.

63. Peers Report, 12–17; Peers, *My Lai Inquiry*, 202–3. For a discussion of this controversy, see chapter 7 of this work.

64. Henderson testimony, Feb. 16, 1970, Peers, *My Lai Inquiry*, 295.

65. Koster testimony, Feb. 18, 1970, ibid., 220–21.

66. Peers Report, 8–2.

67. Peers Report, 2–2, 5–13, 6–11, 6–14, 8–2, 8–14, 10–33, 12–29, 12–30.

68. Peers Report, 8–11, 8–12, 8–14, 10–7, 12–30.

69. Peers Report, 2–3, 6–6, 6–8, 6–9, 6–10, 6–12, 12–2, 12–32, 12–33, 12–34. On Brooks's commission of rape, see chapter 3 of this work as well as Bilton and Sim, *Four Hours in My Lai*, 129–30.

70. Peers Report, 12–32; Peers, *My Lai Inquiry*, 185, 192, 197.

71. Peers Report, 12–1, 12–2. Three officers stood accused of maiming and torture: Kotouc, Medina, and Michles. Peers Report, 12–29, 12–30, 12–31. Eleven officers came under suspicion of conspiracy: Barker, Calhoun, Gavin, Guinn, Henderson, Koster, Kotouc, McKnight, Medina, Parson, and Young. Peers Report, 12–12, 12–14, 12–17, 12–19, 12–20, 12–21, 12–22, 12–24, 12–26, 12–28, 12–29, 12–30. Eight officers allegedly provided false or distorted battle reports: Barker, Henderson, Kotouc, McKnight, Medina, Michles, Roberts, and Willingham. Peers Report, 12–15, 12–21, 12–25, 12–28, 12–29, 12–30, 12–31, 12–32, 12–35. Thirteen officers allegedly gave false or misleading testimony: Calhoun, Gavin, Guinn, Henderson, Hutter, Johnson, Koster, Kotouc, McKnight, Medina, Vasquez, Watke, and Willingham. Peers Report, 12–12, 12–17, 12–18, 12–22, 12–24, 12–26, 12–28, 12–29, 12–30, 12–31, 12–32. And twenty-eight officers allegedly failed to report war crimes: Alaux, Barker, Boatman, Brooks, Calhoun, Calley, Creswell, Gavin, Guinn, Haeberle, Henderson, Holladay, Colonel Dean Hutter, Johnson, Koster, Kotouc, LaCross, Chaplain Lewis, 2nd Lieutenant Michael Lewis, Luper, McKnight, Medina, Michles, 1st Lieutenant John Mundy, Parson, Roberts, Watke, and Young. Peers Report, 12–10, 12–12, 12–13, 12–15, 12–18, 12–19, 12–20, 12–21, 12–22, 12–23, 12–24, 12–25, 12–27, 12–29, 12–30, 12–31, 12–33, 12–34, 12–35.

72. Peers Report, 2–9, 2–11, 2–12, 2–13, 12–3.

73. Peers Report, 12–7, 12–8.

74. Peers, *My Lai Inquiry*, 210–11, 214; Belknap, *Vietnam War on Trial*, 127.

75. Peers, *My Lai Inquiry*, 211, 213–14. The full report remained closed to the public until November 13, 1974, when Secretary of the Army Howard Callaway authorized the publication of volumes 1 (The Report of the Investigation) and 3 (Exhibits). The entire report is at the National Archives and Records Administration in College Park, Maryland, and at government depository libraries. Volumes 1, 2, and 3 are available online through the Library of Congress: http://www.loc.gov/rr/frd/Military_Law/Peers_inquiry.html. All four volumes are on microfilm. For a guide to the microfilm collection, see Robert E. Lester, ed. and comp., *The Peers Inquiry of the Massacre at My Lai* (Bethesda, MD: University Publications of America, 1997). The names of witnesses in the fourth volume on CID Statements remain coded with no key available. Volume 1, the Peers Report, summarized the findings and recommendations of the inquiry, which, Callaway remarked in a news release of that day, "concludes a dark chapter in the Army's

history." Goldstein, Marshall, and Schwartz, *My Lai Massacre and Its Cover-Up*, 1–3; News Release, Nov. 13, 1974, Office of Assistant Secretary of Defense (Washington, DC).

76. Peers, *My Lai Inquiry*, 211, 214, 216–17 (Peers quote on 217); Bilton and Sim, *Four Hours in My Lai*, 308–9; Belknap, *Vietnam War on Trial*, 127; Turse, *Kill Anything That Moves*, 229.

77. "Peers-MacCrate Press Conference"; William Beecher, "Army Inquiry Charges 14 Officers in Suppression of Songmy Facts; West Point's Head, Accused, Quits," *New York Times*, March 18, 1970; Bilton and Sim, *Four Hours in My Lai*, 309.

78. Peers Report, ii.

79. "Peers-MacCrate Press Conference"; Beecher, "Army Inquiry"; Fred Farrar, "Generals Face My Lai Charge," *Chicago Tribune*, March 18, 1970; Peter Braestrup, "2 Generals, 12 Others Charged in My Lai Case," *Washington Post*, March 18, 1970; "Songmy: The Army Brings Charges," *Washington Post*, March 19, 1970.

80. Colonel Hubert Miller, staff judge advocate of JAG, drafted and submitted the charges against eleven officers; Col. Robert Miller did the same with two other officers; and Lieutenant Colonel Charles Bauer assumed the responsibilities for one. The latter two JAG attorneys were members of the Peers Inquiry. Peers, *My Lai Inquiry*, 214–16; Belknap, *Vietnam War on Trial*, 128–29; "Peers-MacCrate Press Conference."

81. Beecher, "Army Inquiry"; Muriel Dobbin, "West Point Commander, 13 Other Army Officers Charged in My Lai Case," *Baltimore Sun*, March 18, 1970; Hersh, *Cover-Up*, 248–49; Belknap, *Vietnam War on Trial*, 128; "Peers-MacCrate Press Conference."

82. William Beecher, "Songmy Data Lag Laid to 2 Groups," *New York Times*, March 19, 1970; Hersh, *Cover-Up*, 250; Peers Report, 7–2.

83. "Another Song My?," *Newsweek*, March 2, 1970, 4.

84. Hersh, *Cover-Up*, 250–51.

85. "Peers-MacCrate Press Conference"; Hersh, *Cover-Up*, 250–51; Bilton and Sim, *Four Hours in My Lai*, 309–310.

86. Lawrence Van Gelder, "Shock and Pride Are Voiced about Son My Study," *New York Times*, March 19, 1970.

87. Dobbin, "West Point Commander"; Braestrup, "2 Generals, 12 Others Charged in Mylai Case"; Beecher, "Army Inquiry"; Farrar, "Generals Face My Lai Charge"; "Miasma of My Lai," *Time*, March 30, 1970, 16–17; "The Generals Accused," *Newsweek*, March 30, 1971, 18–19; David Stout, "Gen. S. W. Koster, 86, Who Was Demoted After My Lai, Dies," *New York Times*, Feb. 11, 2006. The army reassigned Koster to Fort Meade, where he became deputy to Lieutenant General Jonathan Seaman, commander of the First Army.

88. "Miasma of My Lai," 16; Farrar, "Generals Face My Lai Charge"; Dobbin, "West Point Commander"; Van Gelder, "Shock and Pride Are Voiced about Son My Study". Peers included Kotouc on his list of officers. Medina, like Calley, was already slated for court-martial proceedings. Peers, *My Lai Inquiry*, 214–15.

89. Peers, *My Lai Inquiry*, 212–13, 215. For the entire list of thirty officers, see ibid., 212–13, and Peers Report, 12–9 through 12–35.

90. "Miasma of My Lai," 16; "Judgment on My Lai," *New York Times*, March 19, 1970; Beecher, "Songmy Data Lag Laid to 2 Groups".

91. Peter Steinfels, "Some Facts for the State of the Union," *Commonweal*, Jan. 23, 1970, 446.

92. Van Gelder, "Shock and Pride Are Voiced about Songmy Study."

93. Braestrup, "2 Generals, 12 Others Charged in My Lai Case"; Van Gelder, "Shock and Pride Are Voiced about Songmy Study."

94. "Judgment on My Lai"; "Songmy: The Army Brings Charges," *Washington Post*, March 19, 1970; "14 Officers," *Baltimore Sun*, March 19, 1970.

95. Nixon-Kissinger telephone conversation, March 17, 1970, Kissinger Telcons (NSA). Despite Kissinger's claim, the killings at My Lai occurred on a single day.

96. Ibid.

97. Hébert quoted in Mike Miller, "My Lai Report Attacks Army: The 'Cracker Jack' Medals," *Washington Daily News*, July 16, 1970, Papers of William Westmoreland, Box 25, Folder on Mylai War Crimes, Lyndon B. Johnson Library (Austin, TX); Hébert Report, 4; "Background on My Lai Hearings and Report."

98. Hébert Report, 4, 7, 14–20, 22, 37, 40–41; Distinguished Flying Cross awarded to Thompson, July 1, 1968, General Order 3601, Col. Parson, Chief of Staff, office, Americal Division, Peers Inquiry, 3: Exhibits, book 4, Misc. Docs., M-44 (LC); Bronze Star with "V" Device awarded to Andreotta (posthumously), April 23, 1968, General Order 2137, Col. Parson, Chief of Staff Office, Americal Division, ibid., M-42; Bronze Star with "V" Device awarded to Colburn, May 14, 1968, General Order 2585, Col. Parson, Chief of Staff Office, Americal Division, ibid., M-43; author's interviews of Colburn, July 1, 6, 2015; Allison, *My Lai*, 73–74; Peers, *My Lai Inquiry*, 243. For an opposing view of Thompson's "Eyewitness Statement" on behalf of both Andreotta and Colburn, see Peers, *My Lai Inquiry*, 243, and Bilton and Sim, *Four Hours in My Lai*, 204–5. Thompson later threw away his award because he did not want to be part of a cover-up. Angers, *Forgotten Hero*, 160. The forged eyewitness statements are in the files of the Peers Inquiry at the Library of Congress.

Eleven

1. Hammer, *Court-Martial of Lt. Calley*, 36–37.

2. Ibid., 38–39.

3. Ibid., 39; CID Investigation of My Lai/Son My Incident, Dec. 10, 1970, pp. 5–6; CID Report, Feb. 22, 1971, p. 1; CID Report, Feb. 23, 1971, pp. 1, 4; CID Report, March 2, 1971, pp. 1–2; CID Report, Jan. 21, 1972, p. 1; Summary court martial of Willingham, June 9, 1970, in Administrative Review of Son My Cases, n.d., VWCWG (NARA); author's interview of Eckhardt, Jan. 19, 2017; Peers, *My Lai Inquiry*, 227; Allison, *My Lai*, 91, 93; Belknap, *Vietnam War on Trial*, 226–27; Bilton and Sim, *Four Hours in My Lai*, 330.

4. William T. Allison, *Military Justice in Vietnam: The Rule of Law in an American War* (Lawrence: University Press of Kansas), 97; Allison, *My Lai*, 90, 92; Belknap, *Vietnam War on Trial*, 142, 224–25; Bilton and Sim, *Four Hours in My Lai*, 329; "Trials: A Second Soldier Charged," *Time*, Jan. 12, 1970, 11; "One Not Guilty for My Lai," *Time*, Nov. 30, 1970, 10.

5. Hammer, *Court-Martial of Lt. Calley*, 41; Belknap, *Vietnam War on Trial*, 225, Allison, *My Lai*, 92.

6. Carol Polsgrove, "Joy Boys," Part 1, in *It Wasn't Pretty, Folks, but Didn't We Have Fun? Esquire in the Sixties* (New York: Norton, 1995), 219–20; Edd Applegate, *Literary Journalism: A Biographical Dictionary of Writers and Editors* (Westport, CT: Greenwood,

1996), 117. For the first essay, see John Sack, "The Confessions of Lt. Calley," *Esquire*, Nov. 1970, 113–19, 227, 229. For the second and third parts, see the issues of February 1971, 55–59, 114, and September 1971, 85–89, 224, 226, 228. Calley and Sack accepted a hundred-thousand-dollar advance from Viking Press for the scheduled publication of Calley's memoirs in mid-September 1971, an expanded version of the three articles that appeared in *Esquire* magazine. "Calley and Writer Get $100,000 Book Advance," *New York Times*, April 9, 1971. William Styron, who had turned down *Esquire*'s invitation to write a story on Calley, four years earlier published a book titled *The Confessions of Nat Turner* (New York: Random House, 1966).

7. See Frank DiGiacomo, "The Sixties: The Esquire Decade," *Vanity Fair*, Dec. 20, 2006, available online at http://www.vanityfair.com/culture/2007/01/esquire200701. For the background of the November cover, see Alex Hoyt, "The Story Behind the Iconic Andy Warhol 'Esquire' Cover," *Atlantic*, June 7, 2012, available online at http://www.theatlantic.com/entertainment/archive/2012/06/the-story-behind-the-iconic-andy-warhol-esquire-cover/258196/.

8. Letters in "The Sound and the Fury," *Esquire*, Feb. 1971, 30; Sack's response, ibid.; "Editor's Note," ibid. Heinrich Himmler was a military commander and major architect of the Nazi extermination camps.

9. Warren Rogers, "Calley Convicted of Murder in My Lai Deaths," *Los Angeles Times*, March 30, 1971; Hammer, *Court-Martial of Lt. Calley*, 73–74, 171–73; Allison, *My Lai*, 100; Belknap, *Vietnam War on Trial*, 145–46; Bilton and Sim, *Four Hours in My Lai*, 264. Hammer received the *New York Times*'s Publishers Award in 1971 for covering the trial. See also Hammer, *One Morning in the War*, 100–101, 133–35, 194–95.

10. Hammer, *Court-Martial of Lt. Calley*, 50–51, 53; "Capt. Aubrey Daniel: Able Trial Lawyer," *Washington Post*, April 7, 1971; "The Captain Who Told the President Off," *Newsweek*, April 19, 1971, 30 (Daniel's background); author's interview of Eckhardt, July 9, 2015; Belknap, *Vietnam War on Trial*, 146–48; Bilton and Sim, *Four Hours in My Lai*, 264; Allison, *My Lai*, 96.

11. Hammer, *Court-Martial of Lt. Calley*, 54–55; Belknap, *Vietnam War on Trial*, 146–47.

12. Hammer, *Court-Martial of Lt. Calley*, 60–61; Belknap, *Vietnam War on Trial*, 148.

13. Hammer, *Court-Martial of Lt. Calley*, 60–62, 90, 107; Belknap, *Vietnam War on Trial*, 147–48.

14. Hammer, *Court-Martial of Lt. Calley*, 67; Belknap, *Vietnam War on Trial*, 149; Allison, *My Lai*, 96.

15. Hammer, *Court-Martial of Lt. Calley*, 71.

16. Homer Bigart, "Calley Jury to Hear Witnesses Barred in First My Lai Trial," *New York Times*, Nov. 11, 1970; Belknap, *Vietnam War on Trial*, 152.

17. Belknap, *Vietnam War on Trial*, 154–55; Hammer, *Court-Martial of Lt. Calley*, 72; Stephen Lesher, "Inside the Jury Room," *Newsweek*, April 12, 1971, 33; Arthur Everett, "Calley Draws Life Term for 22 Deaths at My Lai," *New Orleans Times-Picayune*, April 1, 1971.

18. Hammer, *Court-Martial of Lt. Calley*, 74–75.

19. Ibid., 75.

20. Ibid., 81–82, 84–85, 102–3; Joseph Dimona, *Great Court-Martial Cases* (New York: Grosset and Dunlap, 1972), 253; Allison, *My Lai*, 97.

21. Hammer, *Court-Martial of Lt. Calley*, 77–78.

22. Ibid., 78.

23. Ibid., 105–8.

24. Ibid., 108, 113–15; Allison, *My Lai*, 98; Belknap, *Vietnam War on Trial*, 161.

25. Hammer, *Court-Martial of Lt. Calley*, 116–18; Allison, *My Lai*, 98.

26. Hammer, *Court-Martial of Lt. Calley*, 121–34; Belknap, *Vietnam War on Trial*, 162; Allison, *My Lai*, 98–99.

27. Hammer, *Court-Martial of Lt. Calley*, 134.

28. Turner's first appearance in court, Dec. 8, 1970, recounted ibid., 134–42; Turner's second appearance, March 5, 1971, Calley court-martial transcript, 4371–76 (NARA); "Lieut. Calley at Bay," *Time*, Dec. 21, 1970, 14; Belknap, *Vietnam War on Trial*, 162–63; Allison, *My Lai*, 99. Calley later denied shooting the girl, declaring that the only other time he fired his gun in this area was when he saw a head move through the rice, only to find out he had killed a young boy. Wilbur Hamman (psychiatrist) testimony, Feb. 22, 1971, Calley court-martial transcript, 3722, 3724 (NARA); Belknap, *Vietnam War on Trial*, 72–73.

29. Latimer-Daniel exchange and Kennedy's ruling on Turner, Dec. 8, 1970, in Hammer, *Court-Martial of Lt. Calley*, 137–39; Kennedy's final ruling on Turner, March 5, 1971, Calley court-martial transcript, 4376 (NARA); Belknap, *Vietnam War on Trial*, 163.

30. Dursi's first court appearance on Dec. 8, 1970, recounted in Hammer, *Court-Martial of Lt. Calley*, 142–47; Dursi's second appearance, March 5, 1971, Calley court-martial transcript, 4376–86 (NARA); Belknap, *Vietnam War on Trial*, 163; Allison, *My Lai*, 99.

31. Hammer, *Court-Martial of Lt. Calley*, 118–21, 152–53; Dimona, *Great Court-Martial Cases*, 255; Belknap, *Vietnam War on Trial*, 164–65; Allison, *My Lai*, 98–99.

32. Hammer, *Court-Martial of Lt. Calley*, 153; Belknap, *Vietnam War on Trial*, 165.

33. Hammer, *Court-Martial of Lt. Calley*, 154, 158–59; Belknap, *Vietnam War on Trial*, 165–66.

34. Hammer, *Court-Martial of Lt. Calley*, 161–63.

35. Ibid., 163; Allison, *My Lai*, 101; Belknap, *Vietnam War on Trial*, 166.

36. CID Investigation of My Lai/Son My Incident, Dec. 10, 1970, p. 8.

37. Ibid., 6.

38. Ibid.

39. Ibid., tab G.

40. Fact Sheet on Son My, enclosed in Gustafson to Chief of Staff, U.S. Army, June 4, 1970, p. 3, Tufts Collection on My Lai (U. of Mich.); Koster written statement, Nov. 24, 1969, in CID Investigation of My Lai/Son My Incident, tab G.

41. Hammer, *Court-Martial of Lt. Calley*, 41–42; Allison, *My Lai*, 92–93; Belknap, *Vietnam War on Trial*, 225–26; Bilton and Sim, *Four Hours in My Lai*, 329–30; "My Lai: A Question of Orders," *Time*, Jan. 25, 1970, 24; Daniel St. Albin Greene, "When Can a Soldier Say No?," *National Observer*, Jan. 18, 1971, Westmoreland Papers, Box 25, Folder on My Lai War Crimes (LBJL).

42. Hammer, *Court-Martial of Lt. Calley*, 41–42; Allison, *Military Justice in Vietnam*, 98; Belknap, *Vietnam War on Trial*, 225–26; Eckhardt, "My Lai," 692n72.

43. Hammer, *Court-Martial of Lt. Calley*, 42; Belknap, *Vietnam War on Trial*, 226; Allison, *My Lai*, 92–93; Bilton and Sim, *Four Hours in My Lai*, 330.

44. Hammer, *Court-Martial of Lt. Calley*, 42–43; Fred P. Graham, "General Cleared of Mylai Charges," *New York Times*, Jan. 30, 1971.

45. Peers, *My Lai Inquiry*, 224, 254; Hersh, *Cover-Up*, 266–67; Graham, "General Cleared of Mylai Charges"; Samuel Stratton, "The Army and General Koster," *New York Times*, March 8, 1971; "Justice for the General," *Newsweek*, Feb. 8, 1971, 21.

46. Peers, *My Lai Inquiry*, 221, 223–25; Belknap, *Vietnam War on Trial*, 233–34; Bilton and Sim, *Four Hours in My Lai*, 325–28; Hammer, *Court-Martial of Lt. Calley*, 42–43. Young retired in June 1971 and Koster in January 1973. Koster later sued in the Court of Claims for restoration of his medal. The court denied the request in what Eckhardt called "an extremely scathing opinion—far worse than his official censure." Author's interview of Eckhardt, Jan. 19, 2017.

47. Hammer, *Court-Martial of Lt. Calley*, 43–44.

48. For the essay, see Sack, "Continuing Confessions of Lieutenant Calley," *Esquire*, Feb. 1971, 55–59, 114 (quote).

49. Polsgrove, *It Wasn't Pretty, Folks*, 224–25.

50. Ibid., 225; Sack, "Continuing Confessions of Lieutenant Calley," 114. The February essay is almost identical to a section in Sack's book appearing later that year, *Calley*, 51–85. In the book, Calley concluded that all Vietnamese were Viet Cong and then put a different slant on some of the same words he had used in the segment deleted from the magazine article. "I thought, *Damn it, what do I do? Hack up all these damned people? Pull a machete out and kkk? Chop up all of these people?* That's what the VC themselves will do." Sack, *Calley*, 84.

51. Allison, *My Lai*, 102; U.S. Department of Defense, *Manual For Courts-Martial United States 1969*, rev. ed. (Washington, DC: GPO, 1969), ch. 24, p. 1, available online at https://www.loc.gov/rr/frd/Military_Law/pdf/manual-1969.pdf. See also Belknap, *Vietnam War on Trial*, 172.

52. Kennedy quoted in Homer Bigart, "Sanity Unit Finds Calley 'Normal': Army Panel Rules on Officer Charged in Mylai Deaths," *New York Times*, Feb. 17, 1971.

53. Allison, *My Lai*, 101–3; Belknap, *Vietnam War on Trial*, 172.

54. Allison, *My Lai*, 102–3: Belknap, *Vietnam War on Trial*, 172–73; Bigart, "Sanity Unit Finds Calley 'Normal.' "

55. Hammer, *Court-Martial of Lt. Calley*, 226; Belknap, *Vietnam War on Trial*, 174; Bigart, "Sanity Unit Finds Calley 'Normal' " ; *Manual for Courts-Martial*, ch. 24, p. 2.

56. Crane testimony, Feb. 16, 1971, Calley court-martial transcript, 3455–59, 3461, 3466–67 (NARA).

57. Allison, *My Lai*, 103; Hammer, *Court-Martial of Lt. Calley*, 227–29; Homer Bigart, "Two Doctors Say Calley Lacked Ability to Premeditate Slayings," *New York Times*, Feb. 17, 1971.

58. Laverne testimony, Feb. 17, 1971, Calley court-martial transcript, 3574, 3583, 3585–86 (NARA). See Belknap, *Vietnam War on Trial*, 172–76, 244, 282; Allison, *My Lai*, 102–4.

59. LaVerne testimony, Feb. 18, 1971, Calley court-martial transcript, 3596 (NARA).

60. Calley court-martial transcript, 3596 (NARA), 3597; Bigart, "Two Doctors Say Calley Lacked Ability to Premeditate Slayings."

61. LaVerne testimony, Feb. 18, 1971, Calley court-martial transcript, 3598–99 (NARA). Daniel thought that at the end of the doctor's testimony there was enough evidence to justify an examination into whether he had perjured himself. But he decided not to push the issue. Ibid., 3599.

62. Hamman testimony, Feb. 19, 1971, Calley court-martial transcript, 3596 (NARA), 3614, 3624–26, 3628, 3655, 3667, 3735, 3737, 3755–56; Belknap, *Vietnam War on Trial*, 175–77.

63. Hamman testimony, Feb. 22, 1971, Calley court-martial transcript, 3717, 3734–35 (NARA). Hamman's testimony belies Calley's boot camp experiences with the sergeant who graphically demonstrated to his men how to kill the enemy before the enemy killed them. See chapter 2 of this work.

64. Ibid., 3716, 3720, 3741, 3743–44; "Calley's 'Confession,'" *Newsweek*, March 1, 1971, 21–22.

65. Belknap, *Vietnam War on Trial*, 145; Dimona, *Great Court-Martial Cases*, 266; Hammer, *Court-Martial of Lt. Calley*, 74.

66. Richard Stacewicz, *Winter Soldiers: An Oral History of the Vietnam Veterans Against the War* (Chicago: Haymarket, 1997), ix, 232, 235, 240 283, 316–17, 433; Christian G. Appy, *The Vietnam War and Our National Identity* (New York: Viking, 2015), 265–66; Turse, *Kill Anything That Moves*, 238–39; Allison, *My Lai*, 114; Belknap, *Vietnam War on Trial*, 210; Anderson, *Facing My Lai*, 114; "The Hero Calley," *Time*, Feb. 15, 1971, 14. The term "Winter Soldier" comes from *The Crisis*, Thomas Paine's pamphlet written during the Revolutionary War, when he tried to lift the spirits of the Continental Army at Valley Forge in the winter of 1776 with the words "These are the times that try men's souls. The summer soldier and the sunshine patriot will, in this crisis, shrink from the service of their country; but he that stands it *now*, deserves the love and thanks of man and woman." See *The Crisis* in William M. Van der Wyde, ed., *The Life and Works of Thomas Paine*, 10 vols. (New Rochelle, NY: Thomas Paine National Historical Association, 1925), 2:263. For the antiwar documentary film *Winter Soldier* of 1972 by Stoney Road Films, Winterfilm, Inc., see https://www.youtube.com/watch?v=CvNDkzi_HEE.

67. Calley testimony, Feb. 23, 1971, Calley court-martial transcript, 3791, 3794, 3797–98 (NARA); Belknap, *Vietnam War on Trial*, 54, 60; Allison, *My Lai*, 23.

68. Calley testimony, Feb. 23, 1971, Calley court-martial transcript, 3799–3800.

69. Ibid., 3792–93.

70. Ibid., 3793, 3796–97.

71. Ibid., 3821.

72. Ibid., 3809, 3812–15.

73. Ibid., 3815–16.

74. Ibid., 3816–17; Belknap, *Vietnam War on Trial*, 179; Dimona, *Great Court-Martial Cases*, 270.

75. Calley testimony, Feb. 23, 1971, Calley court-martial transcript, 3818–21 (NARA); Sack, *Calley*, 115.

76. Calley testimony, Feb. 23, 1971, Calley court-martial transcript, 3809, 3826 (NARA).

77. Ibid., 3828–31.

78. Ibid., 3832–34.

79. Ibid., 3874–76, 3950–52.

80. Psychiatrists' testimony, Feb. 25, 26, 1971, ibid., 4003–4, 4009–10, 4012, 4057, 4065–66, 4103, 4113–15. Edwards and Jones testified the first day, Johnson the second.

81. Dimona, *Great Court-Martial Cases*, 265.

82. Author's interviews of Eckhardt, July 9, 2015, Jan. 19, 20, 2017; Dimona, *Great Court-Martial Cases*, 274. Bailey had recently won a highly publicized acquittal in a retrial of Dr. Sam Sheppard for the murder of his wife. The story inspired a popular TV series of the early 1960s and a Hollywood movie three decades later, both titled *The Fugitive*.

83. Dimona, *Great Court-Martial Cases*, 274–75.

84. Medina testimony, March 10, 1971, Calley court-martial transcript, 4597 (NARA).

85. Dimona, *Great Court-Martial Cases*, 276; Medina testimony, March 10, 1971, Calley court-martial transcript, 4635, 4646, 4649–50, 4658, 4669, 4671, 4682 (NARA).

86. Medina testimony, March 10, 1971, Calley court-martial transcript, 4632 (NARA).

87. Ibid., 4640–42.
88. Ibid., 4682–83; Homer Bigart, "Medina Rejects Calley Account," *New York Times*, March 11, 1971.
89. Belknap, *Vietnam War on Trial*, 183; Allison, *Military Justice in Vietnam*, 99.
90. Medina testimony, March 10, 1971, Calley court-martial transcript, 4683 (NARA).
91. Ibid., 4683–84.
92. Ibid., 4695.
93. Ibid., 4696. See Watke testimony, March 3, 1971, Calley court-martial transcript, 4220–22 (NARA); Calhoun testimony, March 4, 1971, Calley court-martial transcript, 4263, 4268; and Kotouc testimony, March 5, 1971, Calley court-martial transcript, 4359–61.
94. Kotouc testimony, March 5, 1971, Calley court-martial transcript, 4696–98 (NARA).
95. Daniel's closing argument, March 15, 1971, Calley court-martial transcript, 4773, 4777–78, 4783 (NARA).
96. Ibid., 4781, 4783.
97. Ibid., 4783–90, 4592–93.
98. Ibid., 4797–98.
99. Ibid., 4795.
100. The twenty witnesses from Charlie Company were Roger Alaux, Frank Beardslee, Dennis Conti, Jerry Culverhouse, James Dursi, Fred Dustin, Gary Garfolo, Joe Grimes, Ronald Grzesik, Ronald Haeberle, Calvin Hawkins, David Hein, Jerry Heming, Calvin Hodde, Leo Maroney, Paul Meadlo, Gene Oliver, John Paul, Richard Pendleton, and Charles Sledge. The six defense witnesses were Michael Bernhardt, Martin Fagan, Stephen Glimpse, Thomas Kinch, and the two pilots of Barker's helicopter, Christopher Garbow and Dean Lind. The thirteen government witnesses were Beardslee, Culverhouse, Dustin, Garfolo, Grimes, Haeberle, Hawkins, Hein, Heming, Hodde, Maroney, Paul, and Pendleton. Ibid., 4790–4803.
101. Ibid., 4803.
102. Ibid., 4803–5.
103. Ibid., 4804–5.
104. Ibid., 4807.
105. Ibid., 4808–9.
106. Ibid., 4810.
107. Ibid., 4810–13; Hamman testimony, Feb. 22, 1971, Calley court-martial transcript, 3739 (NARA).
108. Daniel's closing argument, March 15, 1971, Calley court-martial transcript, 4813–15 (NARA).
109. Ibid., 4815–18.
110. Latimer defense, March 16, 1971, Calley court-martial transcript, 4843, 4845 (NARA).
111. Ibid., 4847–48.
112. Ibid., 4850–52.
113. Ibid., 4854–55. The eighteen other soldiers were Alaux, L. G. Bacon, Bernhardt, Jay Buchanon, Fagan, James Flynn, Glimpse, Leonard Gonzalez, Elmer Haywood, Kinch, Barry Lloyd, James McBreen, Maroney, Louis Martin, Meadlo, Oliver, Thomas Partsch, and Charles West. Ibid., 4855–56.
114. Ibid., 4860–62.
115. Ibid., 4863.

116. Daniel's closing argument, March 16, 1971, Calley court-martial transcript, 4836 (NARA).

117. Ibid., 4837.

118. Ibid.

119. Ibid., 4838–39.

120. Daniel's response, March 16, 1971, Calley court-martial transcript, 4881 (NARA).

121. Daniel's closing remarks, March 16, 1971, Calley court-martial transcript, 4882–83 (NARA).

122. Kennedy's instructions, March 16, 1971, Calley court-martial transcript, 4906–908, 4911 (NARA).

123. "'I Couldn't Kill…,'" *Newsweek*, March 29, 1971, 26; Warren Rogers, "The Trial of Lt. Calley—A Study in Contrasts," *Los Angeles Times*, April 4, 1971.

124. Rogers, "Trial of Calley"; Rogers, "Calley Convicted in My Lai Deaths."

125. Jury verdict, March 29, 1971, Calley court-martial transcript, 5043–44 (NARA); vote count regulation in UCMJ, art. 52, pp. 75–76 (LC); Homer Bigart, "Calley Guilty of Murder of 22 Civilians at Mylai; Sentence Expected Today," *New York Times*, March 30, 1971; Belknap, *Vietnam War on Trial*, 189; Allison, *My Lai*, 111.

126. Warren Rogers, "Calley Pleads for Honor of All GIs; Seeks No Mercy," *Los Angeles Times*, March 31, 1971; "Text of Calley Statement," *New York Times*, March 31, 1971; Calley's statement, March 30, 1971, Calley court-martial transcript, 5071–72 (NARA).

127. Rogers, "Calley Pleads for Honor of All GIs."

128. Daniel's final statement, March 30, 1971, Calley court-martial transcript, 5072 (NARA).

129. Rogers, "Trial of Calley." Biology teacher John Scopes violated Tennessee law by teaching the theory of evolution in his classroom. Bryan led the prosecution and was no match for the defense attorney, Clarence Darrow.

130. Rogers, "Trial of Calley."

131. Harry Reasoner, *ABC Evening News*, March 30, 1971, in Westmoreland Papers, Box 25, Folder on My Lai War Crimes (LBJL).

132. "Remember My Lai"; Bilton and Sim, *Four Hours in My Lai*, 324.

133. Gloria Emerson, "Saigon G.I.'s Indignant over Calley Ruling," *New York Times*, March 31, 1971.

134. Ibid. For the Thieu government's reaction to the massacre, see chapter 9 of this work.

135. Maddox to Nixon, March 30, 1971, White House Central Files, Subject Files, 1969–74, National Security—Defense (ND), Box 10 (RNL).

136. Notes on Ehrlichman and Haldeman meeting with Nixon, March 30, 1971, White House Special Files, Staff Member and Office Files, John Ehrlichman Papers, Box 5: JDE meeting with President (3) 1/5/71–4/21/71 (RNL). The San Clemente meetings are not on tape.

Twelve

1. Jury sentence, March 31, 1971, Calley court-martial transcript, 5077, 5079 (NARA); Arthur Everett, "Calley Draws Life Term for 22 Deaths at My Lai," *New Orleans Times-Picayune*, April 1, 1971; vote tally requirement in UCMJ, Sect. 852, Art. 52 (2), p. 75 (LC); Warren Rogers, "Calley Sentence: Life at Hard Labor," *Los Angeles Times*, April 1, 1971, 27.

2. "Judgment at Fort Benning," *Newsweek*, April 12, 1971, 27; Homer Bigart, "Calley Sentenced to Life for Murders at My Lai 4; Lengthy Review to Begin," *New York Times*, April 1, 1971; "Clamor over Calley"; Everett, "Calley Draws Life Term."

3. Calley's sentence, March 31, 1971, Calley court-martial transcript, 5079 (NARA).

4. Bigart, "Calley Sentenced to Life"; Holger Jensen, " 'Bum Rap,' Enlisted Men Say of Calley," *Charleston Gazette*, April 1, 1971; Joseph Kraft, "Lt. Calley No Media Hero," *Washington Post*, April 4, 1971.

5. Bigart, "Calley Sentenced to Life"; Rogers, "Calley Sentence," 1.

6. H. R. Haldeman, *The Haldeman Diaries: Inside the Nixon White House* (New York: G. P. Putnam's Sons, 1994), 264; Ehrlichman and Kissinger meeting with Nixon, March 31, 1971, Ehrlichman Papers, Box 5: JDE meeting with President (folder 3) 1/5/71–4/21/71 (RNL).

7. Ehrlichman and Kissinger meeting with Nixon, March 31, 1971, Ehrlichman Papers, Box 5: JDE meeting with President (folder 3) 1/5/71–4/21/71 (RNL). Williams publicly declared that his state was "about ready to secede from the union." Williams quoted in Belknap, *Vietnam War on Trial*, 192. Spiro Agnew was vice president. In the Nixon Library, the Tape Subject Logs from the Oval Office meetings in April 1971 show the administration's concern over the polls, not only in matters relating directly to the Vietnam War but also regarding the president's policy toward Calley. See Nixon White House Tapes, Tape Subject Log, available online at https://www.nixonlibrary.gov/virtuallibrary/tapeexcerpts/ (RNL).

8. President's meeting with advisers, March 31, 1971, Ehrlichman Papers, Box 5: JDE meeting with President (folder 3) 1/5/71–4/21/71 (RNL).

9. Rowland Evans, Jr., and Robert D. Novak, *Nixon in the White House: The Frustration of Power* (New York: Random House, 1971), 396.

10. Rick Perlstein, *Nixonland: The Rise of a President and the Fracturing of America* (New York: Scribner, 2008), 444, 446–47; Richard Reeves, *President Nixon: Alone in the White House* (New York: Simon and Schuster, 2001), 14, 104, 307; Kimball, *Nixon's Vietnam War*, 175, 249–50; author's interview of Tilford, June 27, 2015.

11. Telephone survey, April 1, 1971, University of Missouri-Kansas City, http://law2.umkc.edu/faculty/projects/ftrials/mylai/SurveyResults.html; Robert Barkdoll, "Drive Under Way for Nixon to Pardon As Protests Grow," *Los Angeles Times*, March 31, 1971; "Wires to Nixon Rap Conviction by 100–1 Ratio," *Los Angeles Times*, April 1, 1971; Belknap, *Vietnam War on Trial*, 192–94; Memo from Alexander Butterfield, White House counsel, to Haldeman, March 31, 1971, H. R. Haldeman Papers, Box 115 (RNL); Evans and Novak, *Nixon in the White House*, 395; Perlstein, *Nixonland*, 556.

12. Evans and Novak, *Nixon in White House*, 398; Linda Charlton, "Many in U.S. Perturbed by Conviction of Calley," *New York Times*, March 31, 1971; Congressman Walter Flowers of Alabama to Nixon, April 1, 1971, NSD Papers, Box 10 (RNL); "Calley Conviction," *Congressional Quarterly Almanac 1971*, 853.

13. "Draft Board in Georgia Resigns Over Verdict," *Los Angeles Times*, March 31, 1971; Local Board of Selective Service System in Pittsfield, Illinois, to Nixon, April 1, 1971, NSD Papers, Box 10 (RNL); Charlton, "Many in U.S. Perturbed by Conviction of Calley," 18; Evans and Novak, *Nixon in the White House*, 395; "Opposition to Calley's Conviction and Sentence Grows in Nation," *New York Times*, April 2, 1971; John Darnton, "Decision by Nixon on Calley Hailed," *New York Times*, April 3, 1971; "Protests at Verdict Continue

to Grow," *Washington Post*, April 4, 1971; H. G. Salisbury, chair of Selective Service System Board, to Nixon, April 21, 1971, NSD Papers, Box 10. In Georgia, the Quitman board ended inductions, and a member of the Houston County board offered to serve Calley's time. The local board in Kentucky was in Prestonsburg. Clay was a heavyweight boxing champion later known as Muhammad Ali, who was a conscientious objector to serving in the Vietnam War on the basis of his religious beliefs. Charged with draft evasion, he was convicted and stripped of his first title, won in 1964, but he appealed all the way to the Supreme Court, which in 1971 overturned his conviction. The ten states were Arkansas, Florida, Georgia, Illinois, Kansas, Michigan, Montana, Tennessee, Virginia, and Wyoming.

14. *Time*, April 12, 1971. See "Clamor over Calley." See also *Newsweek*, April 12, 1971. The full title on its cover was "The Calley Verdict: Who Else Is Guilty?" See two articles in that issue, "Judgment at Fort Benning," 27–29, and Kenneth Auchincloss, "Who Else Is Guilty?," 30–32. Charlton, "Many in U.S. Perturbed by Conviction of Calley," 18; Denise Maddox (student at Eastfield College in Texas) to Nixon, April 1, 1971, Letters in NSD Papers, Gen ND 8/Calley, Box 10 (RNL); Darnton, "Decision by Nixon on Calley Hailed." Mr. and Mrs. Arthur Hunt and family in Florida sent the petition in April 1971.

15. "Clamor over Calley"; Charlton, "Many in U.S. Perturbed by Conviction of Calley"; "My Lai Verdict Draws Nation's Fire," *Charleston Gazette*, April 1, 1971.

16. Fred P. Graham, "Impact of Calley Trial," *New York Times*, March 31, 1971.

17. John W. Finney, "Liberals Seek 'War Crimes' Inquiry," *New York Times*, April 1, 1971; Stacewicz, *Winter Soldiers*, 235–36; DeBenedetti, *An American Ordeal*, 307; Allison, *My Lai*, 114. The veterans' organization that had founded the CCI talked with liberal Democrats, headed by Representative Bob Eckhardt of Texas, who with three colleagues announced in a TV news conference their intention to hold public committee hearings. Ibid. *Pravda*, the Communist Party's newspaper in Moscow, likewise called Calley a "scapegoat" and denounced the trial as part of "a whole series of machinations by the Pentagon to save from justice most of those involved in the crime." The Soviet news agency *Tass* asserted that "the main initiators of this bloodbath escaped punishment." See "Pravda Scores Pentagon," April 1, 1971, *New York Times*.

18. Graham, "Impact of Calley Trial."

19. Haldeman Notes, April 1, 1971, Haldeman Papers, Box 43 (RNL); *Haldeman Diaries*, 265.

20. Notes on meeting of April 1, 1971, Erlichman Papers, Box 5 (RNL); Haldeman Notes, April 1, 1971, Haldeman Papers, Box 43 (RNL); *Haldeman Diaries*, 265.

21. "Clamor over Calley"; Everett, "Calley Draws Life Term"; Evans and Novak, *Nixon in White House*, 395–97; *Haldeman Diaries*, 265–66. As secretary of the army, Resor could put Calley in "any place of confinement under the control of any of the armed forces or in any penal or correctional institution under the control of the United States, or which the United States may be allowed to use." UCMJ, art. 58 (a), p. 81 (LC). See Rowland Evans and Robert Novak, "Chain of Command Jolted," *Washington Post*, April 8, 1971. This article appeared in the *Pittsburgh Post-Gazette* a day later under the title "Nixon's Interference: 'Strictly Political.'"

22. Haldeman Notes, April 1, 1971, Haldeman Papers, Box 43 (RNL); *Haldeman Diaries*, 265; President's meeting with advisers, April 1, 1971, Ehrlichman Papers, Box 5: JDE

422 Notes to Pages 295–298

meeting with President (folder 3) (RNL). Nixon referred to Charles Manson, found guilty of murder on numerous counts, along with three accomplices, just two days earlier by the court in Los Angeles in a case then making nationwide headlines.

23. Evans and Novak, *Nixon in White House*, 395–97; *Haldeman Diaries*, 265–66.

24. Ehrlichman notes on April 1, 1971, meeting, Ehrlichman Papers, Box 5 (RNL); *Haldeman Diaries*, 265–66.

25. President's meeting with advisers, April 1, 1971, Ehrlichman Papers, Box 5: JDE meeting with President (folder 3) (RNL); Evans and Novak, *Nixon in White House*, 396–97; *Haldeman Diaries*, 265–66.

26. Evans and Novak, "Chain of Command Jolted."

27. *Haldeman Diaries*, 265, 266; Kimball, *Nixon's Vietnam War*, 250–51.

28. President's meeting with advisers, April 1, 1971, Ehrlichman Papers, Box 5: JDE meeting with President (folder 3) (RNL).

29. For the law referred to by Ehrlichman, see U.S. Code, chap. 47—UCMJ, subchap. 7—Trial Procedure, Sect. 837, Art. 37, pp. 53–54—unlawfully influencing action of court. The law forbids any court authority or "commanding officer" from influencing "the action of a court-martial or any other military tribunal…in reaching the findings or sentence in any case." See the text of the law online at http://www.gpo.gov/fdsys/pkg/USCODE-2011-title10/html/USCODE-2011-title10-subtitleA-partII-chap47-subchapVII-sec837.htm. See also president's meeting with advisers, April 1, 1971, Ehrlichman Papers, Box 5: JDE meeting with President (folder 3) (RNL).

30. President's meeting with advisers, April 1, 1971, Ehrlichman Papers, Box 5: JDE meeting with President (folder 3) (RNL).

31. White House Press Conference of Ziegler and Ehrlichman, April 3, 1971, Dean Papers, Box, 14 (RNL); "Clamor over Calley."

32. President's meeting with advisers, April 1, 1971, Ehrlichman Papers, Box 5: JDE meeting with President (folder 3) (RNL).

33. Memo from Dean to Ehrlichman and Haldeman, April 1, 1971, Dean Papers, Box 14 (RNL); John Dean, *Blind Ambition: The White House Years* (New York: Simon and Schuster, 1976), 34–35.

34. Memo from Dean to Ehrlichman and Haldeman, April 1, 1971, Dean Papers, Box 14 (RNL). Neither the court-martial transcript nor the Peers Report was available to the administration at this time.

35. See William Greider, "Calley's Sanity Data Reveals Conflicts," *Washington Post*, April 1, 1971. A shorter version of Greider's story appeared that same day in the *Los Angeles Times* and yet either no one in the San Clemente White House read it or none of them considered it important enough to share with the president. See Greider, "Calley Told Different Stories, Report Says," *Los Angeles Times*, April 1, 1971.

36. Memo from Dean to Ehrlichman and Haldeman, April 1, 1971, Dean Papers, Box 14 (RNL).

37. Dean, *Blind Ambition*, 35.

38. AP and UPI news bulletins, April 1, 1971, Dean Papers, Box 14 (RNL). UPI declared that "the only incident rivaling the Calley sentencing in prompting an outpouring of public sentiment was Nixon's decision last May to send U.S. forces into Cambodia." See also Linda Charlton, "President Orders Calley Released from Stockade," *New York Times*, April 2, 1971.

39. *Haldeman Diaries*, 266; Dean, *Blind Ambition*, 166–67, 194*; President's meeting with advisers, April 2, 1971, Ehrlichman Papers, Box 5: JDE meeting with President (folder 3) (RNL).

40. *Haldeman Diaries*, 266; Haldeman Notes, April 2, 1971, Haldeman Papers, Box 43 (RNL).

41. Belknap, *Vietnam War on Trial*, 199; Memo from Daniel J. Murphy, U.S. Navy Military Assistant, to Ehrlichman, April 2, 1971, enclosed in Memo on Calley Case, April 2, 1971, NSC Files, Vietnam Subject Files, Box 118 (RNL).

42. "Opposition to Calley's Conviction and Sentence Grows in Nation," *New York Times*, April 2, 1971; "Clamor over Calley"; Commander Ernest Bader, Kettering Post of American Legion in Ohio, to Nixon, April 2, 1971, NSD Papers, Box 10 (RNL); Mary Beene, mayor of Casey, Texas, to Nixon, April 2, 1971, NSD Papers, Box 12; Brian Vine, "U.S. Rejects Calley Verdict," *London Express* (n.d.), enclosed in Bob O'Connell of Denver, Colorado, to Ziegler, April 18, 1971, ibid.

43. "Opposition to Calley's Conviction and Sentence Grows in Nation"; "Nixon Decision Draws Praise in House," *Los Angeles Times*, April 2, 1971.

44. "The Opposite Side of the Coin," *Chicago Tribune*, April 2, 1971. Copy in Charles Colson Papers (RNL).

45. Wallace quote in Perlstein, *Nixonland*, 467.

46. Linda Charlton, "Verdict Protested Anew; 3 Try to Jail Themselves," *New York Times*, April 1, 1971; "Lieutenant Calley and the President," editorial, *Life*, April 16, 1971, 40; James T. Wooten, "Gov. Wallace Sees Calley," *New York Times*, April 3, 1971; Kenneth Reich, "Wallace Visits Calley, Backs Him at Rally," *Los Angeles Times*, April 3, 1971; R. W. Apple, Jr., "Nixon Planning to Clarify Calley Case Intervention," *New York Times*, April 9, 1971; Evans and Novak, *Nixon in White House*, 395; James S. Baugess and Abbe A. DeBolt, eds, *Encyclopedia of the Sixties: A Decade of Culture and Counterculture*, 2 vols. (Santa Barbara, CA: ABC-CLIO/Greenwood, 2012), 1:99.

47. Murray Seeger, "Nixon to Decide Calley Punishment," *Los Angeles Times*, April 4, 1971.

48. White House Press Conference of Ziegler and Ehrlichman, April 3, 1971, Dean Papers, Box, 14 (RNL); Seeger, "Nixon to Review Calley Case." On the question of findings and sentence, see UCMJ, art. 64, p. 89 (LC). See also ibid. art. 71 (d), p. 103: "The convening authority may suspend the execution of any sentence, except a death sentence." White House Press Conference of Ziegler and Ehrlichman, April 3, 1971, Dean Papers, Box, 14 (RNL); Robert B. Semple, Jr., "Nixon Declares He Will Review the Calley Case," *New York Times*, April 4, 1971.

49. White House Press Conference of Ziegler and Ehrlichman, April 3, 1971, Dean Papers, Box, 14 (RNL); Semple, "Nixon Declares He Will Review the Calley Case."

50. Latimer in Robert B. Semple, Jr., "Calley Lawyer Wants Fast Action by Nixon," *New York Times*, April 5, 1971; Robert D. McFadden, "Calley Verdict Brings Home the Anguish of War to Public," *New York Times*, April 4, 1971; Carroll Kilpatrick, "Nixon Will Make Final Decision in Lt. Calley's Case," *Washington Post*, April 4, 1971; Evans and Novak, "Chain of Command Jolted." On this point, see Rowland Evans and Robert Novak, "Bad Politics in Calley Case," *Washington Post*, April 9, 1971; "Lieutenant Calley and the President," 40; Philip Potter, "Analysis—Calley's Conviction Appears to Be Hurting President Nixon in the South," *Baltimore Sun*, April 2, 1971, in Westmoreland Papers, Box 25, Folder on My Lai War Crimes (LBJL).

51. "Remarks on Manson and Statement in Washington," *New York Times*, Aug. 4, 1970; "Manson Trial Proceeds Despite Nixon Comments," *New York Times*, Aug. 4, 1970; Robert B. Semple, Jr., "Nixon Calls Manson Guilty, Later Withdraws Remark," *New York Times*, Aug. 4, 1970. Calafano quoted in R. W. Apple, Jr., "Nixon Planning to Clarify Calley Case Intervention," *New York Times*, April 9, 1971; John Deedy, "News and Views," *Commonweal*, April 23, 1971, 154.

52. "Gallup Finds 79% Disapprove of Verdict," *New York Times*, April 4, 1971; West Virginia Democratic Senator Robert Byrd to Nixon, April 3, 1971, NSD Papers, Box 10 (RNL); UPI news bulletin, April 3, 1971, ibid.; Associated Press, "House and Nation Applaud, Cheer 'a Wonderful Thing'" (n.d.), ibid., Box 12 (RNL); "Nixon Action Draws Praise from House," 10; Charlton, "President Orders Calley Released from Stockade."

53. Bilton and Sim, *Four Hours in My Lai*, 341–42; "Second Thoughts about Calley," *Newsweek*, April 19, 1971, 30.

54. "Gallup Finds 79% Disapprove of Verdict"; "A *Newsweek* Poll on Calley's Fate," *Newsweek*, April 12, 1971, 28; "Second Thoughts on Lt. Calley," *Wall Street Journal*, April 7, 1971; "A Nation Troubled by the Specter of My Lai," *Washington Sunday Star*, April 4, 1971, in Papers of Westmoreland, Box 25, Folder on Mylai War Crimes (LBJL).

55. Auchincloss, "Who Else Is Guilty?," 31.

56. Darnton, "Decision by Nixon on Calley Hailed"; "Letters to the Editor: More Reaction to the Conviction of Lieutenant Calley," *Washington Post*, April 4, 1971; "Clamor over Calley." The jury in January 1971 found Manson and four accomplices guilty of murdering seven people in California, including Hollywood actress Sharon Tate, and in March sentenced them to death. In 1972, however, California abolished the death penalty, and all five received life sentences.

57. "The Calley Case and the President," *Washington Post*, April 4, 1971, and "The President and Mylai," *New York Times*, April 4, 1971. Copies of both articles in Haldeman Papers, Box 115 (RNL).

58. "Incident at Son My," U.S. Army Command Information Fact Sheet, April 2, 1971, NSC Files, Vietnam Subject Files, Box 118 (RNL); "Partial Text of Army's Fact Sheet on Mylai," *Washington Post*, April 4, 1971; James M. Naughton, "Trial Is Defended by Army," *New York Times*, April 3, 1971.

59. Memo from Buchanan to President, "The Calley situation," April 5, 1971, POF Files, Box 10 (RNL).

60. Ibid.

61. President's meeting with advisers, April 5, 1971, Ehrlichman Papers, Box 5: JDE meeting with President (folder 3) (RNL).

62. Memo from Dick Cook (White House aide) to Ehrlichman, April 7, 1971, Dean Papers, Box 14 (RNL); McFadden, "Calley Verdict Brings Home Anguish of War to Public"; "Clamor over Calley"; Memo from Daniel Carr, White House Reception and Security Unit, to Noble Melancamp, Staff Assistant to President, April 5, 1971, NSD Papers, Box 10 (RNL); Judy Wheeler of Coos Bay, Oregon, to Nixon, April 7, 1971, enclosed in Undated and unidentified newspaper article, "CB Woman Seeks Calley 'Ransom,'" ibid.; front-page story and pictures of the former Georgia mayor, Mrs. B. B. Cook, in the *Anderson (SC) Independent*, April 9, 1971, ibid., Gen ND 8/Calley (RNL); Texas letter unidentified but dated April 12, 1971, and quoted in Jonathan Lurie, *Pursuing Military*

Justice: The History of the United States Court of Appeals for the Armed Forces, 1951–1980 (Princeton, NJ: Princeton University Press, 1998), 218n53; Houston sign in "Judgment at Fort Benning," 27. The Republican states were Arizona, California, Georgia, Iowa, Kansas, New Jersey, New York, North Carolina, Pennsylvania, Tennessee, and Vermont. The Democratic states were Connecticut and Indiana.

63. "Clamor over Calley"; A. J. Langguth, "Death, Taxes and Bob Kerrey," *Los Angeles Times*, May 6, 2001; A. J. Langguth, *Our Vietnam: The War 1954–1975* (New York: Simon and Schuster, 2000), 581.

64. *ABC Evening News*, April 6, 1971, available online by subscription at the Vanderbilt Television News Archive, http://tvnews.vanderbilt.edu/program.pl?ID=15323; "Judgment at Fort Benning," 28; C Company featuring Tony Nelson, "Battle Hymn of Lt. Calley," Plantation Records, PL-73, available on YouTube at https://www.youtube.com/watch?v=4JoacW7w0BY.

65. *ABC Evening News*, April 6, 1971; Langguth, "Death, Taxes and Bob Kerrey"; Alvin Shuster, "U.S. Command in Vietnam Bars 'Battle Hymn of Calley' from Radio Network, Citing Pending Appeal," *New York Times*, May 1, 1971; "Calley 'Hymn' Is Barred in Vietnam," *San Bernardino (CA) County Sun*, May 2, 1971; Allison, *My Lai*, 112; Belknap, *Vietnam War on Trial*, 191; Langguth, *Our Vietnam*, 581.

66. Stephan Lesher, "Inside the Jury Room," *Newsweek*, April 12, 1971, 33.

67. Lesher, "Inside the Jury Room," 33–34; Warren Rogers, "The Trial of Lt. Calley—a Study in Contrasts," *Los Angeles Times*, April 4, 1971; William Greider, "Mass Murderer Becomes a U.S. Hero," *Chicago Sun-Times*, April 6, 1971; Associated Press, "Lawmakers Hail Action by Nixon" (no date or newspaper source), newspaper clipping in NSD Papers, Box 12 (RNL); "Clamor over Calley."

68. Lesher, "Inside the Jury Room," 33.

69. Ibid., 34; "Calley Juror: 'We're Not Ogres,'" *Washington Post*, April 1, 1971.

70. Lesher, "Inside the Jury Room," 34.

71. "Lawmakers Hail Action by Nixon"; Greider, "Mass Murderer Becomes U.S. Hero"; Charlton, "President Orders Calley Released from Stockade." A copy of Greider's article is in the NSD Papers, Box 12 (RNL). Greider's article appeared one day earlier in the *Washington Post* under a different title, "Calley's Trial: The Moral Question and Battlefield Laws," April 5, 1971.

72. Gillespie, "Americans Look Back at Vietnam War" (Gallup poll); Charlton, "Many in U.S. Perturbed by Conviction of Calley," 18; George W. Ashworth, "Calley Case Prods New Look At War," *Christian Science Monitor*, April 2, 1971, in Westmoreland Papers, Box 25, Folder on My Lai War Crimes (LBJL); Henry Brandon, "Calley: Where Can the American Conscience Rest?," *Sunday Times* (London), April 4, 1971, ibid.; "Nation Troubled by Specter of My Lai"; Richard Hammer, "Symbol of a Divided and Embittered Nation," *New York Times*, April 4, 1971; McFadden, "Calley Verdict Brings Home Anguish of War to Public."

73. Lyman Hozove (U.S. Army Judge Advocate) to Nixon, April 8, 1971, NSD Papers, Box 10 (RNL); Cpt. William Francisco to Nixon, April 10, 1971, NSD Papers, Box 15; "Clamor over Calley," (Rheault), 20 (Lieutenant Tom Schmitz from Americal Division); Drew Middleton, "Army Officers Disturbed by Calley Case Outcome," *New York Times*, April 10, 1971.

74. West German, French, and British reaction cited in "Second Thoughts about Calley," *Newsweek*, April 19, 1971, 29; "The American Conscience," *Japan Times*, April 8, 1971, enclosed in Fred and Carol Peng to Nixon, April 10, 1971, NSD Papers, Box 15 (RNL).

75. Memo from Fygi to Dean, April 6, 1971, Dean Papers, Box 14 (RNL). The president's power to grant reprieves and pardons comes from Article II, Section 2, of the Constitution.

76. Memo from Haig to Ehrlichman, April 7, 1971, enclosed in information sheet from Laird, Dean Papers, Box 14 (RNL).

77. "Text of Calley Prosecutor's Letter to the President," *New York Times*, April 7, 1971. See analysis of the letter in "Calley Prosecutor Asserts Nixon Undermines Justice," *New York Times*, April 7, 1971, and Daniel to Nixon, April 3, 1971, Ziegler Papers, Box 18 (RNL). A copy of Daniel's letter, though misdated April 1970, is on the website created by Daniel Linder of the University of Missouri–Kansas City School of Law, "Famous American Trials: The My Lai Courts-Martial 1970," at http://law2.umkc.edu/faculty/projects/ftrials/mylai/daniels_ltr.html. Daniel was close to leaving the army at the time of this letter. Belknap, *Vietnam War on Trial*, 203–4; Allison, *My Lai*, 113.

78. Partin to Nixon, April 4, 1971, Ehrlichman Papers, Box 5: JDE meeting with President (folder 3) (RNL). On Daniel, see "The Captain Who Told the President Off," *Newsweek*, April 19, 1971, 30.

79. Louis Harris, "Public Opposes Calley Sentence," *Washington Post*, April 5, 1971; AP news wire bulletin, April 7, 1971, in Ziegler Papers, Box 18 (RNL); John W. Finney, "President's Calley Move Arouses Political Debate," *New York Times*, April 8, 1971; "Captain Who Told President Off," 30.

80. "Capt. Aubrey Daniel: Able Trial Lawyer," *Washington Post*, April 7, 1971. A copy of this article is in the NSC Files, Vietnam Subject Files, Box 118 (RNL).

81. Finney, President's Calley Move Arouses Political Debate"; "Calley Conviction," 853–54.

82. *Haldeman Diaries*, 269.

83. Nixon-Kissinger telephone conversation, April 7, 1971, Nixon Tape 001–021, Miller Center of Public Affairs (UVA); Nixon meeting with advisers in Old Executive Office Building, April 7, 1971, Nixon Tape 246, Part I (246a), Miller Center of Public Affairs. These recordings are available online at http://millercenter.org/presidentialrecordings/nixon. On the possible adverse effect of the Calley affair on the president's withdrawal policy in Vietnam, see "Judgment at Fort Benning," 29.

84. Nixon meeting with advisers in Old Executive Office Building, April 7, 1971, Nixon Tape 246, Part I (246a), Miller Center of Public Affairs (UVA).

85. "The President's News Conference of December 8, 1969," *Public Papers of Presidents, Nixon, 1969*, 1003.

86. Nixon meeting with advisers in Old Executive Office Building, April 7, 1971, Nixon Tape 246, Part I (246a), PRC, Miller Center of Public Affairs (UVA); Haldeman Notes, April 7, 1971, Haldeman Papers, Box 43 (RNL).

87. Memo from Haig to Ehrlichman, April 7, 1971, NSC Files, Vietnam Subject Files, Box 118 (RNL); President's meeting with advisers, April 1, 1971, Ehrlichman Papers, Box 5: JDE meeting with President (folder 3) (RNL).

88. Nixon meeting with advisers in Old Executive Office Building, April 7, 1971, Nixon Tape 246, Part I (246a), PRC, Miller Center of Public Affairs (UVA); Haldeman Notes, April 7, 1971, Haldeman Papers, Box 43 (RNL).

89. Nixon meeting with advisers in Old Executive Office Building, April 7, 1971, Nixon Tape 246, Part I (246a), PRC, Miller Center of Public Affairs (UVA).

90. Hughes to Nixon, April 7, 1971, Ziegler Papers, Box 18 (RNL); "President's Calley Move Arouses Political Debate."

Thirteen

1. Richard Nixon, "Address to the Nation on the Situation in Southeast Asia," April 7, 1971, *Public Papers of the Presidents of the United States: Richard Nixon, Containing the Messages, Speeches, and Statements of the President, 1971* (Washington, DC: GPO, 1972), 522–27.

2. "Kissinger Telcons," April 8, 1971, Nixon Tape 001–053, PRC, Miller Center of Public Affairs (UVA).

3. "Calley Judge Backs Nixon on Review of the Trial," *New York Times*, April 10, 1971; T. W. Evans to President, April 8, 1971, NSD Papers, Box 10 (RNL). Evans cited a scholarly article by Emanuel Hertz titled "Abraham Lincoln—The Jurist of the Civil War," *New York University Law Quarterly Review* 14 (May 1937): 473–501. Royce Brier, ed., "The Captain and The President" (no date), clipping enclosed in Bill Lane, President and Publisher of *Sunset Magazine*—Sunset Books, Menlo Park, CA, to Haldeman, April 12, 1971, NSD Papers, Box 10 (RNL); Haldeman to Lane, April 16, 1971, ibid. Brier noted that Lincoln had commuted the sentences "for the duration."

4. Eckhardt, "My Lai," 680.

5. "U.S. Drops Efforts to Try Ex-G.I.'s Over Mylai," *New York Times*, April 9, 1971; *United States ex rel. Toth Quarles, Secretary of the Air Force*, 350 U.S. 11 (1955); Kelly and Harbison, *American Constitution*, 871–72; Belknap, *Vietnam War on Trial*, 112. Not until 1996 did Congress rectify this problem with the War Crimes Act. "Whoever, whether inside or outside the United States, commits a war crime," the act declared, was subject to prosecution whether "a member of the Armed Forces of the United States or a national of the United States." The federal district courts would handle violations of the Law of War. War Crimes Act of 1996, Title 18, United States Code, Section 2441, pp. 562–63, available online at http://www.gpo.gov/fdsys/pkg/USCODE-2011-title18/html/USCODE-2011-title18-partI-chap118-sec2441.htm; Eckhardt, "My Lai," 682; Gary D. Solis and Fred L. Borch, *Geneva Conventions* (New York: Kaplan, 2010), 248. In mid-May 1971, Dean called for a law authorizing the military to try former soldiers for a war crime committed while in uniform, but he did not succeed. Memo from Dean to Ehrlichman, Haig, and Bud Krogh, May 14, 1971, NSC Files, Vietnam Subject Files, Box 118 (RNL).

6. Bilton and Sim, *Four Hours in My Lai*, 346; Memo from Ehrlichman to Kissinger, April 15, 1971, NSC Files, Vietnam Subject Files, Box 118 (RNL); Memo from Dean to Haig, April 15, 1971, ibid.; "Panel Interview at the Annual Convention of the American Society of Newspaper Editors," April 16, 1971, *Public Papers of Presidents, Nixon, 1971*, pp. 538–39; "Excerpts From an Interview in Washington with the President by Six Newsmen," *New York Times*, April 17, 1971.

7. Nixon to Partin, April 19, 1971, Ehrlichman Papers, Box 5: JDE meeting with President (folder 3) (RNL); Nixon to Daniel, April 21, 1971, ibid.; Belknap, *Vietnam War on Trial*, 205–6.

8. "A *Newsweek* Poll on Calley's Fate," Gallup survey commissioned by *Newsweek* of early April 1971 in "Judgment at Fort Benning," 28; Gallup survey also referred to in Stephan Lesher, "The Calley Case Re-examined," *New York Times*, July 11, 1971.

9. Bilton and Sim, *Four Hours in My Lai*, 147–48; Hammer, *Court-Martial of Lt. Calley*, 44–45; Belknap, *Vietnam War on Trial*, 227; Allison, *My Lai*, 121.

10. Lt. Col. Matthew O'Donnell, JAG, Special Assistant to the Assistant Judge Advocate General for Military Law, "Memorandum of Law," n.d., 1, 4, 6, 8, VWCWG, RG 319, My Lai, 1969–74, Box 4 (NARA); "Administrative Review of Son My Cases," May 17, 1971, ibid.; Allison, *My Lai*, 121; Belknap, *Vietnam War on Trial*, 227; Bilton and Sim, *Four Hours in My Lai*, 346–47; Wright's instructions, ibid., 347.

11. Hammer, *Court-Martial of Lt. Calley*, 44–45; Allison, *My Lai*, 121; Belknap, *Vietnam War on Trial*, 227; "Courts-Martial: Finger Exercise," *Newsweek*, May 10, 1971, p. 37. *Newsweek* commented that "after the blood-chilling tale of wholesome murder" that came from Calley's trial, the chopped-off finger of a Viet Cong suspect was "an uncommon amount of military to-do about very little. The Vietnamese National Police took the prisoner away and shot him.

12. F. Lee Bailey, *For the Defense* (New York: Atheneum, 1975), 63–67. Bailey also filed a motion charging the army with exercising command influence in the case, but this effort likewise failed. Ibid., 68–69, 71; Belknap, *Vietnam War on Trial*, 228.

13. Bailey to Nixon, March 31, 1971, Dean Papers, Box 14 (RNL); Dean to Bailey, April 13, 1971, ibid.; Belknap, *Vietnam War on Trial*, 218–19.

14. Bailey to Nixon, March 31, 1971, Dean Papers, Box 14 (RNL). Hiss was a member of the State Department whose loyalty to the country became suspect after Whittaker Chambers, a senior editor for *Time* magazine and former member of the Communist Party, accused him of being a communist. Nixon was a member of the House Un-American Activities Committee as a California congressman and became nationally known after the investigation. Hiss was found guilty of perjury but not of treason.

15. Dean to Bailey, April 15, 1971, Dean Papers, Boxes 14 and 15 (RNL). Dean told Ehrlichman that the president was following a "course of non-involvement" in the Medina case based on his Calley policy. Memo from Dean to Ehrlichman, April 13, 1971, ibid.

16. Bailey, *For the Defense*, 59–60.

17. William G. Eckhardt, "Command Criminal Responsibility: A Plan for a Workable Standard," *Military Law Review* 97 (1982): 1–34; Bailey, *For the Defense*, 79; Anderson, *Facing My Lai*, 41–42; Allison, *My Lai*, 117; Belknap, *Vietnam War on Trial*, 229–30; Bilton and Sim, *Four Hours in My Lai*, 348.

18. McCarthy, *Medina*, 5–6.

19. Homer Bigart, "Prosecution Says That Medina 'Chose Not to Intervene' at Mylai," *New York Times*, Aug. 16, 1971; Homer Bigart, "Nine Witnesses Unable to Place Medina at Site of Mylai Slayings," *New York Times*, Aug. 18, 1971. For the Medina trial, see Bailey, *For the Defense*, 25–128; Eckhardt, "My Lai," 678–80; Belknap, *Vietnam War on Trial*, 228–33; Allison, *My Lai*, 116–21; Bilton and Sim, *Four Hours in My Lai*, 347–49; and McCarthy, *Medina*. McCarthy covered the trial for the *New Yorker*. Bailey had represented Medina in Calley's trial. Hammer, *Court-Martial of Lt. Calley*, 45.

20. Bailey, *For the Defense*, 83, 85, 87; Allison, *My Lai*, 118; *Manual for Courts-Martial*, ch. 27, "Rules of Evidence," para. 142e, p. 27–25 (LC). For the discussion of the reliability of the

polygraph involving the experts, prosecution, defense, and the judge, see an extract of that meeting on August 19, 1971, in Calvin B. Anderson, U.S. Army Court Reporter, to White House, Aug. 27, 1971, Dean Papers, Box 15 (RNL).

21. Bailey, *For the Defense*, 87–88; Parks, "Command Responsibility for War Crimes," 35.

22. Bailey, *For the Defense*, 88.

23. Parks, "Command Responsibility for War Crimes," 37, 80–81; U.S. Army Field Manual 27-10, *Law of Land Warfare*, ch. 8, sect. 2, para. 501, pp. 178–79; Schmidt, "Yamashita, Medina, and Beyond," 179–80, 186–87, 193–97.

24. Jordan quoted in "Whose War Crimes?," *Newsweek*, Feb. 22, 1971, 29; Parks, "Command Responsibility for War Crimes," 87–88.

25. Bailey, *For the Defense*, 92–94, 112; Homer Bigart, "Witness Places Medina in Mylai," *New York Times*, Aug. 25, 1971; Allison, *My Lai*, 118, 120.

26. For their depositions, see Phu's testimony, CID Report, Sept. 10, 1970, p. 53, and Minh's testimony, ibid.; Phil Gailey, "Viets Tell What They Saw at My Lai," *Washington Post*, Sept. 9, 1971; author's interview of Eckhardt, Sept. 3, 2015.

27. Bailey, *For the Defense*, 96.

28. Ibid., 96–97; Bigart, "Medina Said to Have Felt He Lost Control of Troops"; author's interview of Eckhardt, Aug. 3, 2015; Eckhardt closing argument, Sept. 22, 1971, My Lai Incident—March 16, 1968: The Trial of Captain Ernest Medina (court-martial transcript), MS74-27, Box 4, vol. 1, p. 3447 (WSU).

29. Bailey, *For the Defense*, 102.

30. Author's interview with Colburn, April 8, 2014; Nancy Montgomery, "Larry Colburn: The Last 'Hero' of My Lai," *Stars and Stripes*, Dec. 21, 2016; Montgomery email to author, Jan. 25, 2017; UCMJ, Art. 37, pp. 53–54; Art. 98, pp. 128–29.

31. Author's interview of Eckhardt, Jan. 24, 2017. Brigadier General (one-star) Andrew Lipscomb testified as a defense witness, but he did not take the stand until September 15, and after speaking on behalf of Medina, returned home to Florida. Lipscomb was commanding general of the 11th Brigade while training in Hawaii and led Medina and the others to Vietnam in December 1967. Colonel Oran Henderson replaced him on March 15, 1968—the day before My Lai—and Lipscomb left the army later that year. Lipscomb testimony, Sept. 15, 1971, Medina court-martial transcript, MS74-27, Box 3, vol. 2, pp. 2992-2994 (WSU). For Colburn's presence at the trial on August 24, see Bigart, "Witness Places Medina in Mylai." The "witness" referred to in the title of the article was Louis Martin.

32. "Bailey", *For the Defense*, 98, 103; Eckhardt, "My Lai," 680; "Polygraph Expert to Testify for Army in Medina Trial," *Baltimore Sun*, Aug. 28, 1971; "Judge's Ruling Enjoined, So Medina Trial Is Recessed," *Washington Post*, Aug. 28, 1971; "Army Rests Case Against Medina," *New York Times*, Sept. 10, 1971; "The Army Calls Its Final Witness at Medina Trial," *Baltimore Sun*, Sept. 10, 1971; "Witness Testifies Medina Told Him of Losing Control," *Washington Post*, Sept. 10, 1971.

33. Bailey, *For the Defense*, 99, 103–4; Eckhardt, "My Lai," 679–80; Homer Bigart, "Medina Said to Have Felt He Lost Control of Troops," *New York Times*, Aug. 28, 1971; "Army Rests Case Against Medina," *New York Times*, Sept. 10, 1971; "Army Calls Its Final Witness at Medina Trial"; "Witness Testifies Medina Told Him of Losing Control"; Allison, *My Lai*, 118.

34. Bailey, *For the Defense*, 105–6. Two years later, Bailey noted, he was watching the Watergate Committee hearings on television when Dean offered to take a polygraph test

to support his claims of corruption in the White House. His words were almost the same as those in Bailey's letter to the president. Ibid., 106–7. For the prohibition against polygraph tests in court-martial trials, see *Manual For Courts-Martial*, ch. 27, para. 142e, pp. 27–25 (LC).

35. Bailey, *For the Defense*, 103; Homer Bigart, "Calley to Appear at Medina's Trial," *New York Times*, Sept. 9, 1971.

36. Bailey, *For the Defense*, 107; Peter Braestrup, "Ex-Rifleman Says He, Not Medina, Killed Mylai Boy," *Washington Post*, Sept. 14, 1971; "Calley Excused from Testimony at Medina Trial," *Baltimore Sun*, Sept. 14, 1971; "Judge Concedes to Bailey on Medina Witness," *Washington Post*, Sept. 16, 1971 (reporter not identified); Homer Bigart, "Medina Defense Gains Two Points," *New York Times*, Sept. 16, 1971. "Follow Me" became the battle cry of the U.S. Infantry after its return to the Philippines during World War II in October 1944. A statue of a charging soldier serves as a memorial honoring the U.S. Infantry School at Fort Benning.

37. Bailey, *For the Defense*, 107; Homer Bigart, "Medina Witness Admits Shooting Boy," *New York Times*, Sept. 14, 1971; McCarthy, *Medina*, 53.

38. Bailey, *For the Defense*, 107, 111, 113, 116; Bigart, "Medina Defense Gains Two Points"; "Judge Concedes to Bailey on Medina Witness"; McCarthy, *Medina*, 53–54.

39. Bailey, *For the Defense*, 111; Homer Bigart, "Medina Trial Told That Calley Said Killings Surprised Captain," *New York Times*, Sept. 15, 1971; "Lt. Calley Quoted at Mylai Trial," *Washington Post*, Sept. 15, 1971; Bigart, "Medina Defense Gains Two Points"; "Judge Concedes to Bailey on Medina Witness."

40. Bailey, *For the Defense*, 111; Homer Bigart, "Calley Sentence Is Cut to 20 Years from Life Term," *New York Times*, Aug. 21, 1971; Braestrup, "Ex-Rifleman Says He, Not Medina, Killed Mylai Boy."

41. Bigart, "Medina Defense Gains Two Points"; "Judge Concedes to Bailey on Medina Witness."

42. Bailey, *For the Defense*, 108–9, 112; Allison, *My Lai*, 119; Bigart, "Medina Witness Admits Shooting Boy"; Braestrup, "Ex-Rifleman Says He, Not Medina, Killed Mylai Boy."

43. Bailey, *For the Defense*, 112.

44. Eckhardt, "Command Criminal Responsibility," 13; Anderson, *Facing My Lai*, 47.

45. Belknap, *Vietnam War on Trial*, 181–83; Allison, *My Lai*, 118–19; "Uninformed, Medina Says," *Baltimore Sun*, Sept. 17, 1971; Homer Bigart, "Medina Defends Actions at Mylai," *New York Times*, Sept. 17, 1971; "Medina Takes the Stand, Puts Blame on Lt. Calley," *Washington Post*, Sept. 17, 1971.

46. Bigart, "Medina Defends Actions at Mylai"; "Medina Takes the Stand"; Bailey, *For the Defense*, 119–20.

47. Bailey, *For the Defense*, 120.

48. Bigart, "Medina Defends Actions at Mylai."

49. Bailey, *For the Defense*, 120.

50. Ibid.; Eckhardt, "Command Criminal Responsibility," 14.

51. Bigart, "Medina Witness Admits Shooting Boy"; Homer Bigart, "A Medina Charge Reduced by Judge," *New York Times*, Sept. 18, 1971; Phil Gailey, "101 of 102 Medina Murder Counts Cut: Judge Reduces, Dismisses 101 Medina Murder Counts," *Washington Post*, Sept. 18, 1971; "Medina Charges Eased By Judge," *Baltimore Sun*, Sept. 18, 1971.

52. Eckhardt closing argument, Sept. 22, 1971, Medina court-martial transcript, MS74-27, Box 4, vol. 1, pp. 3440–42, 3446–47 (WSU); Eckhardt, "Command Criminal Responsibility," 13, 22. Brisentine also emphasized Medina's concern about the impact of the deaths on his career. "Polygraph Expert to Testify for Army in Medina Trial," *Baltimore Sun*, Aug. 28, 1971.

53. Anderson, *Facing My Lai*, 43.

54. Bailey closing argument, Sept. 22, 1971, Medina court-martial transcript, MS74-27, Box 4, vol. 1, pp. 3459, 3461, 3469, 3472 (WSU).

55. Ibid., 3466–69.

56. Ibid., 3475–77, 3480–81; Bailey, *For the Defense,* 123–24; Phil Gailey, "Medina Is Found Innocent: Commander at Mylai Free on All Counts," *Washington Post*, Sept. 23, 1971. See U.S. Army Field Manual, 27-10, *Law of Land Warfare*, Provisions 89 and 93, pp. 36, 37.

57. Howard's instructions to jury, Sept. 22, 1971, Medina court-martial transcript, MS74-27, Box 4, vol. 1, pp. 3498–3501 (WSU); Homer Bigart, "Medina May Get A Lesser Charge," *New York Times*, Sept. 22, 1971.

58. Howard's instructions to jury, Sept. 22, 1971, Medina court-martial transcript, MS74-27, Box 4, vol. 1, p. 3521 (WSU); Fred P. Graham, "Impact of Calley Trial," *New York Times*, March 31, 1971.

59. U.S. Army Field Manual, 27-10, *Law of Land Warfare*, 178–79.

60. Author's interviews of Eckhardt, Aug. 9, Sept. 10, 2015; Jan. 19, 2017; Eckhardt, "My Lai," 688–89n63; Eckhardt, "Command Criminal Responsibility," 18–20: Howard's instructions to jury, Sept. 22, 1971, Medina court-martial transcript, MS74-27, Box 4, vol. 1, p. 3521 (WSU).

61. Howard's instructions to jury, Sept. 22, 1971, Medina court-martial transcript, MS74-27, Box 4, vol. 1, pp. 3521, 3523–24, 3528 (WSU); UCMJ, Art. 119, p. 144; Parks, "Command Responsibility for War Crimes," 12.

62. Parks, "Command Responsibility for War Crimes," 89–90.

63. Bailey, *For the Defense*, 124.

64. Ibid., 124–25.

65. Jury's deliberation, Sept. 22, 1971, Medina court-martial transcript, MS74-27, Box 4, vol. 1, pp. 3552, 3557 (WSU); jury's decision, ibid., 3556–57, 3559; Bailey, *For the Defense*, 124–25; Homer Bigart, "Medina Found Not Guilty of All Charges on Mylai," *New York Times*, Sept. 23, 1971; "Medina Is Acquitted of All My Lai Charges," *Baltimore Sun*, Sept. 23, 1971; Gailey, "Medina Is Found Innocent"; "Medina Intends to Quit Army When Trial Ends," *Los Angeles Times*, March 31, 1971. Medina left the army on October 15, 1971. Memorandum of Law, n.d., VWCWG, RG 319, My Lai, 1969–74, Box 4 (NARA). See also Kathryn Johnson, "Acquitted Medina—Not Bitter but Leaving," *Washington Evening Star*, Sept. 22, 1971.

66. Bailey, *For the Defense*, 125.

67. Telford Taylor, "The Course of Military Justice," *New York Times*, Feb. 2, 1972; U.S. Army Field Manual, 27-10, *Law of Land Warfare*, 178–79; Telford Taylor, *Nuremberg and Vietnam: An American Tragedy* (Chicago: Quadrangle, 1970), 53. Guenter Lewy argues that "there is general agreement" that Howard's instructions were "wrong." See his study, *America in Vietnam* (New York: Oxford University Press, 1978), 360.

68. Neil Sheehan, "Taylor Says by Yamashita Ruling Westmoreland May Be Guilty," *New York Times*, Jan. 9, 1971; Parks, "Command Responsibility for War Crimes," 2n2.

69. Author's interview of Eckhardt, Sept. 3, 2015.

70. Ibid.

71. CID Report, Sept. 10, 1970, p. 92; Bailey, *For the Defense*, 63.

72. Johnson, "Acquitted Medina."

73. Prugh, JAG, Summary Sheet, Personnel Action Concerning Former Cpt. Ernest Medina, April 10, 1972, VWCWG, RG 319, My Lai, 1969–74, Box 4 (NARA).

74. R. W. Apple, Jr., "Parole of Calley Granted by Army Effective Nov. 19," *New York Times*, Nov. 9, 1974; Belknap, *Vietnam War on Trial*, 234. Koster remained in the army until 1973 as deputy commander of the Test and Evaluation Command at the Aberdeen Proving Grounds in Maryland. He died in January 2006. Stout, "Gen. S. W. Koster, 86, Dies."

75. Author's interview of Eckhardt, July 28, 2015.

76. Peers, *My Lai Inquiry*, 221–22; Bilton and Sim, *Four Hours in My Lai*, 325.

77. Douglas Robinson, "Henderson Trial: More Is Involved Than a Colonel," *New York Times*, Nov. 29, 1971; Hammer, *Court-Martial of Lt. Calley*, 45; Douglas Robinson, "Hearings Start on a Mylai Case," *New York Times*, April 3, 1971.

78. Bilton and Sim, *Four Hours in My Lai*, 349.

79. Allison, *My Lai*, 122–23.

80. For the September 15 testimony, see Douglas Robinson, "Helicopter Chief Says He Told Henderson of Killings at Mylai," *New York Times*, Sept. 16, 1971; Peter Braestrup, "Henderson Notified of Mylai, Jury Told," *Washington Post*, Sept. 16, 1971; Charles Whiteford, "Witness Says My Lai Study Was Ordered," Sept. 16, 1971, *Baltimore Sun*.

81. Allison, *My Lai*, 123. For the September 16 testimony, see Douglas Robinson, "Officer Testifies on False Report of Mylai," *New York Times*, Sept. 17, 1971; Peter Braestrup, "Phony Citation Described," *Washington Post*, Sept. 17, 1971; Charles Whiteford, "False My Lai Report Admitted," *Baltimore Sun*, Sept. 17, 1971.

82. Watke testimony, Dec. 8, 10, 11, 12, 19, 1969, Peers Inquiry, 2: Testimony, book 8, pp. 17, 69, 79–80, 83, 101, 104, 112–14, 142–43, 148–52 (LC); Watke to wife, March 18, 1968, Peers Inquiry, 3: Exhibits, book 4, Misc. Docs., M-12; Peers, *My Lai Inquiry*, 100–101.

83. Robinson, "Officer Testifies on False Report of Mylai"; Braestrup, "Phony Citation Described"; Whiteford, "False My Lai Report Admitted." For Watke and Holladay's experiences in reporting Thompson's accusations, see chapter 6 of this work.

84. Peers, *My Lai Inquiry*, 222.

85. Hersh, *Cover-Up*, 267–68: Douglas Robinson, "Pilot Tells Trial of Mylai Report," *New York Times*, Sept. 21, 1971; Peter Braestrup, "Ex-Pilot Fuzzy on His Report of Mylai Affair," *Washington Post*, Sept. 21, 1971; Charles Whiteford, "Henderson Trial Hits 2 Snags," *Baltimore Sun*, Sept. 21, 1971; "Henderson Trial Witness Is Barred," *Washington Post*, Oct. 7, 1971; Douglas Robinson, "Henderson Gains a Point at Trial," *New York Times*, Oct. 7, 1971; Charles Whiteford, "Judge Rules for Henderson," *Baltimore Sun*, Oct. 7, 1971; Hébert subcommittee *Report*, July 1970, p. 28; Peers Report, 10–32.

86. "Judge Postpones Decision on Henderson's Lie Test," *Washington Post*, Oct. 6, 1971; Douglas Robinson, "Colonel's Defense Seeks to Tell Jury of Lie Test," *New York Times*, Oct. 6, 1971; Charles Whiteford, "Henderson Lawyers Battle to Conceal, Reveal Data,"

Baltimore Sun, Oct. 6, 1971. Medina left the army with an honorable discharge on October 15, 1971. CID Report, Jan. 21, 1972.

87. Medina testimony, March 10, 1971, Calley court-martial transcript, 4682–83 (NARA); Homer Bigart, "Medina Rejects Calley Account," *New York Times*, March 11, 1971.

88. "Medina Admits Withholding Facts, Lying about My Lai Massacre," *Baltimore Sun*, Nov. 16, 1971; "Medina Testimony Backs Henderson," *Washington Post*, Nov. 16, 1971. Douglas Robinson, "Medina Says He Lied to Colonel about Mylai Toll," *New York Times*, Nov. 16, 1971; "Medina Testimony Backs Henderson," *Washington Post*, Nov. 16, 1971; "Lies about My Lai," *Time*, Nov. 29, 1971, p. 39; Bilton and Sim, *Four Hours in My Lai*, 349; Belknap, *Vietnam War on Trial*, 183; Allison, *My Lai*, 123–24.

89. Robinson, "Medina Says He Lied"; "Lies about My Lai," 39.

90. Robinson, "Medina Says He Lied"; "Lies about My Lai," 39.

91. Douglas Robinson, "Colonel Called a 'Disgrace' and 'Great' in Trial Debate," *New York Times*, Dec. 16, 1971; Allison, *My Lai*, 122–24; Bilton and Sim, *Four Hours in My Lai*, 350; Belknap, *Vietnam War on Trial*, 233. The brigade's artillery commander, Lieutenant Colonel Robert Luper, testified to seeing at least fifteen bodies on a trail south of the village and hearing no radio reports of enemy resistance while on the command helicopter with Henderson. It was "another routine operation," Luper declared. Douglas Robinson, "Officer at Colonel's Trial Tells of Bodies at Mylai," *New York Times*, Sept. 10, 1971; Peter Braestrup, "Henderson Aide Thought Mylai Was 'Routine,'" *Washington Post*, Sept. 10, 1971.

92. Douglas Robinson, "Army Jury Gets Henderson Case," *New York Times*, Dec. 17, 1971. Henderson had also distinguished himself with a host of medals from thirty years of service that included World War II, Korea, and Vietnam. Before the Vietnam War, he had earned four Purple Hearts, an Air Medal, five Silver Stars, and five Bronze Stars—two of the last ones for valor. In Vietnam, he received the Legion of Merit, the Vietnamese Cross of Gallantry, and the Vietnamese Medal of Merit. Bilton and Sim, *Four Hours in My Lai*, 207.

93. Douglas Robinson, "Col. Henderson Acquitted in Last of the Mylai Cases," *New York Times*, Dec. 18, 1971; David Goeller, "Col. Henderson Is Acquitted of Mylai Coverup Charges," *Washington Post*, Dec. 18, 1971; Belknap, *Vietnam War on Trial*, 233.

94. Peers, *My Lai Inquiry*, 83, 226. Henderson stayed in the army, becoming commandant of the Indiantown Gap Military Reservation in Pennsylvania. He came under mandatory retirement in 1974 after holding the rank of colonel for the maximum of five years. Michael T. Kaufman, "Oran Henderson, 77, Dies; Acquitted in My Lai Case," *New York Times*, June 5, 1998.

95. "Medina Intends to Quit Army"; Robinson, "Medina Says He Lied."

96. Bigart, "Calley Sentence Is Cut to 20 Years"; James T. Wooten, "Calley Juror Says Verdict Offered Few Options," *New York Times*, Aug. 21, 1971. The document immediately follows the Calley court-martial transcript (NARA).

97. Memo from Dean to President, Feb. 16, 1973, Dean Papers, Box 15 (RNL); "No-Fault Command," editorial, *New York Times*, April 19, 1974; R. W. Apple, Jr., "Parole of Calley Granted by Army Effective Nov. 19," *New York Times*, Nov. 9, 1974; Memo from J. Fred Buzhardt to President, "Review of United States vs. Calley," May 3, 1974, POF, Box 50 (RNL); "Calley Sentence Upheld by Nixon," May 5, 1974, *New York Times*. *U.S. v. Calley*, No. 26,875, U.S. Court of Military Appeals, 22 USCMA 534, Dec. 21, 1973; Herman L.

Goldberg and Frederick A. C. Hoefer, "Army Parole System," *Journal of Criminal Law and Criminology* 40 (1949–50): 158–69 (see 160); Allison, *Military Justice in Vietnam*, 102; Allison, *My Lai*, 115; Belknap, *Vietnam War on Trial*, 245; Bilton and Sim, *Four Hours in My Lai*, 355.

98. Memo from Buzhardt to President, "Review of United States vs. Calley," May 3, 1974, POF, Box 50 (RNL); "Calley Sentence Upheld by Nixon."

99. Memo from Nixon to Secretary of Army, May 3, 1974, Buzhardt Files, Legal Papers and Transcript, *Calley v. Nixon*, Box 50 (RNL). Three years earlier, Nixon had predicted such an ending when he told Kissinger after the speech on Vietnamization on April 7, 1971, that he would let the Calley matter "run its course." Nixon-Kissinger telephone conversation, April 8, 1971, Nixon Tape 001–053, PRC, Miller Center of Public Affairs (UVA).

100. Calley's parole came ten days short of the required one-third of his term. His early parole resulted from a temporary release on bail ten days before his term was over, when a federal district judge in Georgia, J. Robert Elliott, overturned his conviction based on alleged legal violations in his court-martial. The U.S. Court of Appeals by an eight-to-five vote reversed Elliott's decision and reinstated Calley's conviction. Circuit Judge Griffin Bell wrote the dissent, arguing that congressional refusal to release transcripts of testimonies (see chapter 10 of this work) provided grounds for a reversal of Calley's conviction and an examination of this evidence to determine whether it warranted a retrial. Rather than send Calley back to jail for the final ten days of his sentence, the army waived that last segment as serving no purpose. Wayne King, "Court Orders Calley Freed but the Army Will Appeal," *New York Times*, Sept. 26, 1974; Wayne King, "Calley Released; No Condition Set," *New York Times*, Nov. 10, 1974; Lesley Oelsner, "High Court Denies Appeal by Calley," *New York Times*, April 6, 1976. For the dissent, see Eckhardt, "My Lai," 885–86, 686 n. 54; author's interview of Eckhardt, Jan. 19, 2017; Belknap, *Vietnam War on Trial*, 252–53.

Epilogue

1. Michael Novak, "The Battle Hymn of Lt. Calley…and the Republic," *Commonweal*, April 30, 1971, 183–84; Nixon, *Memoirs*, 1:620; Richard Nixon, *No More Vietnams* (New York: Arbor House, 1985), 37.

2. Author's interview of Cong, July 14, 2012; Nhung Walsh's interview of Cong, Jan. 2008; Cong quoted in "My Lai Massacre: Lt William Calley Apologises More Than 40 Years After Vietnam," *Telegraph* (London), Aug. 27, 2009. Before the Kiwanis Club in Columbus, Georgia, on August 19, 2009, Calley declared, "There is not a day that goes by that I do not feel remorse for what happened that day in My Lai. I feel remorse for the Vietnamese who were killed, for their families, for the American soldiers involved and their families. I am very sorry." Calley quoted in Dick McMichael, "William Calley Apologizes for My Lai Massacre," *Columbus (GA) Ledger-Inquirer*, Aug. 21, 2009; author's interview of Fleming, Aug. 27, 2011.

3. For press coverage, see Associated Press, "Ex-Army Lieutenant Involved in Vietnam Massacre Apologizes," Aug. 22, 2009; "Calley Apologizes for My Lai Massacre," *Atlanta Journal-Constitution*, Aug. 19, 2009; "My Lai Massacre: Lt William Calley Apologises More Than 40 Years after Vietnam," *Telegraph* (London), Aug. 27, 2009; Frank James, "William Calley Makes

First Public Apology for Vietnam War's My Lai Massacre," *The Two-Way* (National Public Radio blog), Aug. 21, 2009, http://www.npr.org/sections/thetwo-way/2009/08/william_calley_makes_first_pub.html; "My Lai Officer Apologizes for Massacre," NPR Transcript, Aug. 21, 2009; "Calley Apologizes for Role in My Lai Massacre," *Los Angeles Times*, Aug. 22, 2009; "Ex-Officer Apologizes for Killings at My Lai," *New York Times*, Aug. 23, 2009. William Eckhardt did not acknowledge an apology. See "Calley Apologizes for Role in My Lai Massacre," MSNBC, Aug. 22, 2009. Cong quoted in "My Lai Massacre: Lt William Calley Apologises More Than 40 Years after Vietnam"; Duc's story in a comment he wrote (Feb. 9, 2010) on "Why William Calley Chose to Speak at the Kiwanis Club," *Dick's World* (blog), Aug. 21, 2009, https://dicksworld.wordpress.com/2009/08/21/why-william-calley-chose-to-speak-at-the-kiwanis-club/#comment-1469, and Tim King, "Reunion at Site of My Lai Massacre: Survivor Duc Tran Van and Photographer Ron Haeberle," *Salem-News.com*, July 14, 2012, http://www.salem-news.com/articles/july142012/my-lay-duc-haeberle-tk.php. Duc's response to Calley's public remarks also appeared in a comment to David Calleja, "The My Lai Massacre—Vietnam's Holocaust," *Foreign Policy Journal*, Feb. 24, 2010, http://www.foreignpolicyjournal.com/2010/02/24/the-my-lai-massacre-vietnams-holocaust/#comment-937293489.

4. Rick Atkinson, *The Guns at Last Light: The War in Western Europe, 1944–1945* (New York: Henry Holt, 2013); Mary Louise Roberts, *What Soldiers Do: Sex and the American GI in World War II France* (Chicago: University of Chicago Press, 2013).

5. For atrocities in other American wars, see Paul A. Kramer, *The Blood of Government: Race, Empire, the United States and the Philippines* (Chapel Hill: University of North Carolina Press, 2006), and Charles J. Hanley, *The Bridge at No Gun Ri: A Hidden Nightmare from the Korean War* (New York: Henry Holt, 2001). For Iraq and Afghanistan, see Allan R. Millett, Peter Maslowski, and William B. Feis, *For the Common Defense: A Military History of the United States from 1607 to 2012*, 3rd ed., (New York: Free Press, 2012), 646–47, 665. The most infamous abuse involved waterboarding, which simulated drowning in an effort to extract information and was employed in interrogation centers in Abu Ghraib Prison during the Iraqi War, Guantanamo Bay Naval Base in Cuba during the war in Afghanistan, and in Europe.

6. Michael Sellah and Mitch Weiss, *Tiger Force: A True Story of Men and War* (New York: Little, Brown, 2006); Turse, *Kill Anything That Moves*.

7. Turse, *Kill Anything That Moves*, 6, 22, 23; Bill Moyers, "Nick Turse Describes the Real Vietnam War," *Moyers and Company*, Feb. 8, 2013, http://billmoyers.com/segment/nick-turse-describes-the-real-vietnam-war/; Robin Lindley, "The Brutal War on Vietnamese Civilians: Interview with Nick Turse," *History News Network*, May 27, 2013, http://historynewsnetwork.org/article/152039. See also Deborah Nelson, *The War Behind Me: Vietnam Veterans Confront the Truth about U.S. War Crimes* (New York: Basic Books, 2008). Nelson collaborated with Turse in writing a series of articles for the *Los Angeles Times* that dealt with American war crimes in Vietnam. See, for example, "A Tortured Past," *Los Angeles Times*, Aug. 20, 2006.

8. Westmoreland, *Soldier Reports*, 501; Nick Turse, "A My Lai a Month," *The Nation*, Dec. 1, 2008, https://www.thenation.com/article/my-lai-month/; Nelson, *War Behind Me*, 1–2. Bernd Greiner claims to be the first writer to publish a book using these army documents. See his study, *War Without Fronts*, 10–11.

9. The figure on the number of pregnant women comes from Hersh, "Scene of the Crime." The rest of the information comes from the plaque itself. See list of victims in Angers, *Forgotten Hero*, 223–26.

10. LaCross testimony, Jan. 10, 1970, Peers Inquiry, 2: Testimony, book 27, p. 26 (LC); Belknap, *Vietnam War on Trial*, 220–21; Bilton and Sim, *Four Hours in My Lai*, 125. LaCross, according to his medic's testimony, looked for Medina to explain the killings. Peers Report, 6–14. According to the Peers Inquiry, Charlie Company's three platoons had killed "at least 175–200" Vietnamese civilians, including men, women, children, and babies in My Lai 4. But its figures rested on the testimony and claims only of American personnel. CID estimated that the number "may have exceeded 400." Peers Report, 2–3, 3*.

11. CID Investigation of My Lai/Son My Incident, Dec. 10, 1970, p. 8, Tufts Collection on My Lai (U. of Mich.); Witness Statement, May 25, 1970, pp. 1–2, Tufts Collection on My Lai; Fact Sheet on Son My, enclosed in Gustafson to Chief of Staff, April 28, 1970, p. 3, Tufts Collection on My Lai.; CID Report, May 28, 1970, pp. 1–2, 4–5; CID Report, Sept. 10, 1970, p. 85; Bunning Witness Statement to CID, May 6, 1970, p. 1, My Lai Collection, Box 1, Folder 40 (VTTU); Peers Report, 12–33; Belknap, *Vietnam War on Trial*, 55; Susan Brownmiller, *Against Our Will: Men, Women and Rape* (New York: Simon and Schuster, 1975), 32, 99–101, 103–5. The Uniform Code of Military Justice defined rape as a soldier's forceful "act of sexual intercourse with a female not his wife" and declared that guilt necessitated "penetration, however slight." A guilty verdict could lead to death or whatever other punishment the court martial imposed. UCMJ, art. 120, p. 145 (LC).

12. Tim O'Brien, *The Things They Carried* (Boston: Houghton Mifflin, 1990), 88. See also O'Brien, *Going After Cacciato*, 320–21.

13. Caputo, *Rumor of War*, xviii; *Frontline*, "Remember My Lai"; "My Lai Massacre," part 2; Stanley testimony, Jan. 24, 1970, Peers Inquiry, 2: Testimony, book 25, p. 38 (LC). See also "War Hero Relives Day He Refused to Murder," *Biloxi Sun Herald*, Nov. 19, 1989, available online at http://articles.orlandosentinel.com/1989-11-19/news/8911193407_1 _stanley-lai-4-calley.

14. Anderson, *Facing My Lai*, 32.

15. Question-and-answer period following Thompson's lecture, U.S. Naval Academy, 1, 26.

16. Rebecca Leung, "An American Hero: Vietnam Veteran Speaks Out about My Lai," *60 Minutes*, CBS-TV, May 6, 2004, http://www.cbsnews.com/news/an-american-hero/.

17. Author's interview of Colburn, July 18, 2015.

18. Angers, *Forgotten Hero of My Lai*, 152–55. "Remember My Lai" received the British Academy Award and an International Emmy. The third member of the helicopter team, Glenn Andreotta, perished in combat less than a month after My Lai. Andreotta came from an Italian American family in New Jersey, headed by a father who had joined the Air Force during World War II. The young boy developed a love for flying when his father bought a Piper Cub airplane and took him and his cousin Jim into the air. Colburn described his crewmate as "quiet, modest, and unassuming" but possessing "raw courage and selflessness." Andreotta was in his second tour in Vietnam by March 16, 1968, when he rescued the little boy from the ditch. Author's interviews of Jim Andreotta, Nov. 11, 2015, and of Colburn, Nov. 24, 2015.

19. Peers, *My Lai Inquiry*, 158, 242–43; Nell Boyce, "Heroes: Hugh Thompson: Reviled, Then Honored, for His Role at My Lai," *U.S. News and World Report*, Aug. 20, 2001.

20. Boyce, "Heroes"; Thompson lecture, U.S. Naval Academy, 27.

21. Thompson lecture, U.S. Naval Academy, 27; Thompson quoted in "Return to My Lai," *60 Minutes*, Dec. 13, 1999 and Anderson, *Facing My Lai*, 33.

22. Angers, *Forgotten Hero of My Lai*, 168–69, 173.

23. David Montgomery, "30 Years Later, Heroes Emerge from Shame of My Lai Massacre," *Washington Post*, March 7, 1998; Boyce, "Heroes."

24. "3 Honored for Saving Lives at My Lai," *New York Times*, March 7, 1998; Montgomery, "30 Years Later"; "Official Citations for Saving Lives at My Lai: Chief Warrant Officer Hugh C. Thompson Jr.," *Washington Post*, March 7, 1998; Richard Goldstein, "Hugh Thompson, 62; Saved Civilians at My Lai," *New York Times*, Jan. 7, 2006; Jessica Bujol, Associated Press, New Orleans, "My Lai Hero Hugh Thompson Jr. Dies at 62," Jan. 7, 2006; *Frontline*, "Return to My Lai"; Angers, *Forgotten Hero of My Lai*, 155–56. The army had already examined its training program to determine where it had gone wrong. Already in place was a requirement that every potential officer study My Lai and watch a videotape highlighting Thompson's comments.

25. Thompson and Colburn's remarks in "Army Honors 2 Vets Who Put Lives on Line to Stop Massacre at My Lai," *Deseret News*, reprinted in *Boston Globe,* Aug. 22, 2015.

26. "30 Years Later"; author's interview of Colburn, Oct. 12, 2015; author's interview of Jim Andreotta, Sept. 12, 2015. For the awards ceremony, see Angers, *Forgotten Hero of My Lai*, 176–80.

27. Author's interview of Colburn, July 1, 2015; " 'Blood and Fire' of My Lai Remembered 30 Years Later," CNN, March 16, 1998, http://www.cnn.com/WORLD/9803/16/my.lai/. The song, written by Jay Ungar, expresses the suffering of wives of husbands fighting in the U.S. Civil War and provides the soundtrack for Ken Burns's documentary series *The Civil War*. For the documentary film directed by Nguyen Van Thuy and produced by Boehm, see *The Sound of the Violin in My Lai* (1999), available on YouTube at http://www.youtube.com/watch?v=SKq62meVA3k. Boehm founded Madison Quaker, Inc., in Wisconsin to help the Vietnamese in numerous ways, including extending loans to women and establishing a Peace Park, a primary school, and free dental care. Kaufman, "Reconciliation at My Lai"; Ben Stocking, "U.S. Soldier Returns to My Lai on 40th Anniversary, Finds Hope at the Scene of a Massacre," Associated Press, March 15, 2008, http://legacy.utsandiego.com/news/military/20080315-1219-vietnam-mylai.html; interview of Colburn, "My Lai," *American Experience*, PBS-TV, April 26, 2010, http://www.pbs.org/wgbh/americanexperience/features/transcript/mylai-transcript/ and http://video.pbs.org/video/1475790127/; Kaufman, "Reconciliation at My Lai." Venture capitalist George Sarlo, founder of the Sarlo Foundation in California, financed the digging of a well and bathroom facilities for the school. Author's interview of Colburn, Sept. 13, 2016.

28. Author's interview of Colburn, Sept. 13, 2016; Angers, *Forgotten Hero of My Lai*, 230.

29. Author's interview of Colburn, July 1, 2015.

30. Author's interview of Eckhardt, Aug. 10, 2015.

31. Eckhardt, "My Lai," 693, 693n73; William G. Eckhardt, "Nuremberg—Fifty Years: Accountability and Responsibility," *UMKC Law Review* 65 (Fall 1996): 1–14; *U.S. v. Calley*, 22 USCMA 534, Dec. 21, 1973. For early Army reforms, see "Ounce of Prevention," *Newsweek*, April 19, 1971, 35.

32. Parks, "Command Responsibility for War Crimes," 101.

33. Peers, *My Lai Inquiry*, 238–41.

34. Ibid., 29–30; Peers Report, C 20.

35. Comments by William Hays Parks, "The Geneva Conventions at 60: Taking Stock," Law Library of Library of Congress, American Red Cross, and the Friends of the Law Library of Congress, Dec. 3, 2009, available on YouTube at https://www.youtube.com/watch?v=1py84CJGJnQ; U.S. Army Field Manual 27-10, *The Law of Land Warfare* (July 15, 1976), 19, available online at http://www.globalsecurity.org/military/library/policy/Army/fm/27-10/CHANGE1.htm.

36. Quoted in Eckhardt, "My Lai," 671.

37. Ibid., 695n76, 698; Army Regulation 350-41, Training in Units (March 19, 1993), ch. 14–3, p. 23, U.S. Army Heritage and Education Center Digital Collections, available online at http://cdm16635.contentdm.oclc.org/cdm/ref/collection/p16635coll11/id/1447.

38. Comments by Parks, "Geneva Conventions at 60"; author's interview of Parks, Nov. 14, 2015; Anderson, *Facing My Lai*, 129.

39. Anderson, *Facing My Lai*, 130–31. See also Peter Karsten, *Law, Soldiers, and Combat* (Westport, CT: Greenwood, 1978), 37–38. Vietnam veteran David Hackworth called the Calley affair "a microcosm of everything that was wrong with the Army." See his *About Face*, 772. See also Ron Milam, *Not a Gentleman's War: An Inside View of Junior Officers in the Vietnam War* (Chapel Hill: University of North Carolina Press, 2009), 2, 113.

40. Millett, Maslowski, and Feis, *For the Common Defense*, 598. See *Army Field Manual FM22-100* (Washington, DC: Department of Army, Aug. 1999), ch. 2–10: "The Leader and Leadership: What the Leader Must Be, Know, and Do," available online at https://archive.org/stream/milmanual-fm-22-100-Army-leadership---be-know-do/fm_22-100_Army_leadership_-_be_know_do#page/n47/mode/2up.

41. Seymour M. Hersh, "Torture at Abu Ghraib," *New Yorker*, May 10, 2004, available online at http://www.newyorker.com/magazine/2004/05/10/torture-at-abu-ghraib; Millett, Maslowski, and Feis, *For the Common Defense*, 647, 665.

42. Office of General Counsel of the Department of Defense, *Department of Defense Law of War Manual* (June 2015), available online at http://www.defense.gov/Portals/1/Documents/pubs/Law-of-War-Manual-June-2015.pdf.

43. Ibid., 1057–59, 1060n31, 1070–73, 1082–83, 1101–4. Parks withdrew from helping to write this massive volume about three years before its publication, complaining that it had become politicized. See W. Hays Parks, "Update on the DOD Law of War Manual," 1–6, in Robert Chesney, "Hays Parks on the Demise of the Law of War Manual," *Lawfare* (blog), Dec. 8, 2012, https://www.lawfareblog.com/hays-parks-demise-dod-law-war-manual.

44. Rod Powers, "Law of Armed Conflict (LOAC), The Rules of War," *The Balance* (podcast), Sept. 15, 2016, https://www.thebalance.com/law-of-armed-conflict-loac-3332966; John Tirman, *The Deaths of Others: The Fate of Civilians in America's Wars* (New York: Oxford University Press, 2011), 311. For a discussion of these matters, see chapter 1 of this work.

45. Hannah Arendt, *The Life of the Mind*, 2 vols. (New York: Harcourt Brace Jovanovich, 1978), 1:180.

46. Hannah Arendt, *Eichmann in Jerusalem: A Report on the Banality of Evil*, rev. ed. (New York: Viking, 1965), 276–77.

47. Bettina Stangneth, *Eichmann before Jerusalem: The Unexamined Life of a Mass Murderer* (New York: Alfred A. Knopf, 2014), 364–65, 367.

48. Christopher R. Browning, *Ordinary Men: Reserve Police Battalion 101 and the Final Solution in Poland* (1992; New York: HarperCollins, 1998), xx, 168–70, 173, 188, 189.

49. James Dawes, *Evil Men* (Cambridge, MA: Harvard University Press, 2013), 52–57, 62–63, 66–68, 79–81, 85; interviews of Dawes in Gal Beckerman, "Conversations with Evil Men," *Boston Globe*, April 28, 2013, available online at https://www.bostonglobe.com/ideas/2013/04/27/conversations-with-evil-men/xxMikxrBBRBUTWnhaTodwK/story.html, and "Any Good from Evil?" *The Brian Lehrer Show*, WNYC Radio, May 13, 2013, available online at http://www.wnyc.org/story/292646-washington-news-nj-transit-during-sandy-mammograms-evil-men/.

50. Richard Rhodes, *Masters of Death: The SS-Einsatzgruppen and the Invention of the Holocaust* (Oxford: Perseus, 2002), 114, 124–25, 146.

51. Author's interview of Spiller, Aug. 21, 2015.

52. Anderson, *Facing My Lai*, 187; interview of Hackworth by Steve Gillon, "My Lai Massacre," *As It Happened*, History Channel, 1998; Hackworth, *About Face*, 772–73.

53. Hannah Arendt, *On Revolution* (New York: Viking, 1963), 103.

54. O'Brien in Anderson, *Facing My Lai*, 175–76; Peers, *My Lai Inquiry*, 252–53, 256.

55. *Frontline*, "Remember My Lai."

56. Ibid.; Bilton and Sim, *Four Hours in My Lai*, 6–8.

57. *Frontline*, "Remember My Lai."

58. For this account, see Truong Thi Le "Witness Statement," CID, Dec. 28, 1969, Papers of *Four Hours in My Lai*, LHCMA (KCL); Bilton and Sim interview of Truong Thi Le, 1988, ibid.; Truong Thi Le testimony, CID Report, Sept. 10, 1970, pp. 73–74, and Sept. 25, 1970, p. 29; "Remember My Lai"; Bilton and Sim, *Four Hours in My Lai*, 22–23, 157–58.

59. Interview of O'Brien, "My Lai," *American Experience*; Anderson, *Facing My Lai*, 174, 177–78.

Bibliography

PRIMARY SOURCES

Unpublished Sources

Kings College, London, United Kingdom
    Papers of *Four Hours in My Lai*. Liddell Hart Centre for Military Archives.
Library of Congress, Washington, DC
    Background on the My Lai Hearings and Report. Available online at https://www.loc.gov/rr/frd/Military_Law/pdf/MyLai_bckgr.pdf.
    F. Edward Hébert Subcommittee. "Investigation of the My Lai Incident." Hearings of the Armed Services Investigating Subcommittee of the Committee on Armed Services House of Representatives, 91st Congress, 2nd Session. Washington, DC: GPO, 1976. Available online at http://www.loc.gov/rr/frd/Military_Law/ML_investigation.html.
    F. Edward Hébert Subcommittee. "Investigation of the My Lai Incident." Report of the Armed Services Investigating Subcommittee of the Committee on Armed Services, House of Representatives, 91st Congress, 2nd Session. Washington, DC: GPO, 1970. Available online at http://www.loc.gov/rr/frd/Military_Law/ML_investigation.html
    Peers Inquiry. Available online at http://www.loc.gov/rr/frd/Military_Law/Peers_inquiry.html.
Lyndon B. Johnson Library, Austin, Texas
    Colby, William E. Transcript, Oral History Interview 2, June 2, 1982, by Ted Gettinger.
    Papers of William Westmoreland, Box 25, Folder on Mylai War Crimes.
Miller Center of Public Affairs, University of Virginia (Charlottesville, Virginia)
    Richard M. Nixon Tapes. Presidential Recording Program. Available online at http://millercenter.org/presidentialrecordings/nixon.

National Archives, College Park, Maryland

    Calley, William L. Court-martial transcript. Vietnam War Crimes Working Group, Central File, RG 319, My Lai Massacre, 1969–74. Available online at https://catalog.archives.gov/id/921641?q=MY%20LAI%20MASSACRE (created in 1970 and declassified in 1994).

National Security Archive, George Washington University, Washington, DC

    Blanton, Thomas, and Dr. William Burr, eds. "The Kissinger Telcons." National Security Archive Electronic Briefing book 123, May 26, 2004, http://nsarchive.gwu.edu/NSAEBB/NSAEBB123/.

Richard M. Nixon Library, Yorba Linda, California

    H. R. Haldeman Diaries.

    Henry A. Kissinger Telephone Conversation Transcripts (Telcons), Home File.

    NSC Files, Vietnam Subject Files.

    Nixon White House Tapes, https://www.nixonlibrary.gov/virtuallibrary/tapeexcerpts/.

    Oral Interviews, H. R. Haldeman.

    President's Office Files.

    White House Central Files, Subject Files, 1969–74, National Security—Defense (ND).

    White House Special Files, Staff Member and Office Files.

University of Michigan, Ann Arbor

    Colonel Henry Tufts Collection on My Lai.

    U.S. Army, Criminal Investigation Division Reports.

U.S. Army

    Be, Know, Do. Army Field Manual FM22–100. Washington, DC: Department of the Army, Aug. 1999. Available online at https://archive.org/stream/milmanual-fm-22-100-army-leadership---be-know-do.

    The Law of Land Warfare. Field Manual 27-10. Washington, DC: Department of the Army, July 1956; rev. ed., July 15, 1976. Available online at http://www.globalsecurity.org/military/library/policy/army/fm/27-10/CHANGE1.htm.

U.S. Army Heritage and Education Center

    Digital Collections, http://cdm16635.contentdm.oclc.org/cdm/ref/collection/p16635coll11/id/1447.

U.S. Department of Defense

    Manual for Courts-Martial United States 1969. Rev. ed. Washington, DC: GPO, 1969. Available online at https://www.loc.gov/rr/frd/Military_Law/pdf/manual-1969.pdf.

Office of General Counsel of the Department of Defense. *Department of Defense Law of War Manual*, June 2015. Available online at http://www.defense.gov/Portals/1/Documents/pubs/Law-of-War-Manual-June-2015.pdf.

Uniform Code of Military Justice, 1949. Available online at https://www.loc.gov/rr/frd/Military_Law/pdf/morgan.pdf.

Vietnam Center and Archive, Texas Tech University, Lubbock, Texas

My Lai Collection, http://www.virtualarchive.vietnam.ttu.edu/starweb/virtual/vva/servlet.starweb?path=virtual/vva/virtual.web.

Wichita State University, Wichita, Kansas

My Lai Incident—March 16, 1968: The Trial of Captain Ernest Medina (court-martial transcript), MS74-27. Available online at http://special-collections.wichita.edu/collections/ms/74-27/74-27-A.HTML. University Libraries, Special Collections.

Published Sources

Documentary Collections, Congressional Documents, and Periodicals

Applegate, Edd. *Literary Journalism: A Biographical Dictionary of Writers and Editors*. Westport, CT: Greenwood, 1996.

Avalon Project: Documents in Law, History and Diplomacy, Yale Law School, http://avalon.law.yale.edu/.

Baugess, James S., and Abbe A. DeBolt, eds. *Encyclopedia of the Sixties: A Decade of Culture and Counterculture*. 2 vols. Santa Barbara, CA: ABC-CLIO/Greenwood, 2012.

Citizens Commission of Inquiry, ed. *The Dellums Committee Hearings on War Crimes in Vietnam: An Inquiry into Command Responsibility in Southeast Asia*. New York: Random House, 1972.

Friedman, Leon, ed. *The Law of War: A Documentary History*. 2 vols. New York: Random House, 1972.

Goldstein, Joseph, Burke Marshall, and Jack Schwartz. *The My Lai Massacre and Its Cover-Up: Beyond the Reach of Law? The Peers Commission Report with a Supplement and Introductory Essay on the Limits of Law*. New York: Free Press, 1976.

Lester, Robert E., ed. and comp. *The Peers Inquiry of the Massacre at My Lai*. Bethesda, MD: University Publications of America, 1997.

Olson, James S., and Randy Roberts, eds. *My Lai: A Brief History with Documents*. Boston: Bedford, 1998.

Public Papers of the Presidents of the United States: Richard Nixon, Containing the Public Messages, Speeches, and Statements of the President, 1969. Washington, DC: GPO, 1971.

Public Papers of the Presidents of the United States: Richard Nixon, Containing the Public Messages, Speeches, and Statements of the President, 1971. Washington, DC: GPO, 1972.

Reinberg, Linda. *In the Field: The Language of the Vietnam War.* New York: Facts on File, 1991.

Reporting Vietnam. Vol. 1, *American Journalism, 1959–1969.* New York: Library of America, 1998.

Reporting Vietnam: American Journalism, 1959–1975. New York: Library of America, 2000.

Van Tassel, David D., and John J. Grabowski, eds. *The Encyclopedia of Cleveland History.* 2nd ed. Bloomington: Indiana University Press, 1997. Available online at https://ech.cwru.edu.

U.S. Department of State. *Foreign Relations of the United States, 1969–1976.* Vol. 6, *January 1969–July 1970.* Washington, DC: GPO, 2006.

Memoirs, Personal Accounts, Interviews

Anderson, David L., ed. *Facing My Lai: Moving Beyond the Massacre.* Lawrence: University Press of Kansas, 1998.

Appy, Christian G. *Patriots: The Vietnam War Remembered from All Sides.* New York: Penguin Books, 2003.

Bailey, F. Lee. *For the Defense.* New York: Atheneum, 1975.

Caputo, Philip. *A Rumor of War.* New York: Holt, Rinehart and Winston, 1977.

Dean, John. *Blind Ambition: The White House Years.* New York: Simon and Schuster, 1976.

Haldeman, H. R. *The Haldeman Diaries: Inside the Nixon White House.* New York: G. P. Putnam's Sons, 1994.

Nixon, Richard. *The Memoirs of Richard Nixon.* 2 vols. New York: Warner, 1978.

Nixon, Richard. *No More Vietnams.* New York: Arbor House, 1985.

Nofziger, Lyn. *Nofziger.* Washington, DC: Regnery Gateway, 1992.

Peers, William R. *The My Lai Inquiry.* New York: W. W. Norton, 1979.

Powell, Colin. *My American Journey.* New York: Random House, 1995.

Ridenhour, Ron. "Jesus Was a Gook." In "Nobody Gets Off the Bus: The Viet Nam Generation Big Book." Special issue, *Viet Nam Generation*

5 (March 1994). Available online at the Sixties Project website, http://www2.iath.virginia.edu/sixties/HTML_docs/Texts/Narrative/Ridenhour_Jesus_01.html, http://www2.iath.virginia.edu/sixties/HTML_docs/Texts/Narrative/Ridenhour_Jesus_02.html

Sack, John. "The Confessions of Lt. Calley." *Esquire*, Nov. 1970, 113–19, 227, 229 (part 1); Feb. 1971, 55–59, 114 (part 2); and Sept. 1971, 85–89, 224, 226, 228 (part 3).

Sack, John. *Lieutenant Calley: His Own Story*. New York: Viking, 1971.

Schell, Jonathan. *The Military Half: An Account of Destruction in Quang Ngai and Quang Tin*. New York: Alfred A. Knopf, 1968.

Vo Cao Loi. "Thảm sát Sơn Mỹ—30 năm sau" [Sơn Mỹ massacre—a recall after 30 years]. *Military History Journal* 1 (1998): 68–74.

Westmoreland, William C. *A Soldier Reports*. New York: Dell, 1980. Originally published in 1976.

Author Interviews

Jim Andreotta
Lawrence Colburn
Pham Thanh Cong
William G. Eckhardt
Al Fleming
Mark Folse
Seymour Hersh
Pete Maslowski
Roger Spiller
Michael Stedman
Earl Tilford
Vo Cao Loi
Vo Cao Tai

Multimedia

Felder, Christoph. *Inside My Lai: The Power of Images*. Christoph Felder Film Production, forthcoming.

Goodman, Barak, dir. "My Lai." *American Experience*. PBS-TV, April 26, 2010, http://video.pbs.org/video/1475790127/. Transcript available at http://www.pbs.org/wgbh/americanexperience/features/transcript/mylai-transcript/.

Remember My Lai. Produced by Kevin Sim and Michael Bilton of Yorkshire Television in UK, Judy Woodruff, "Frontline," PBS-TV, May 23, 1989.

Sim, Kevin. *Four Hours in My Lai.* BBC-TV. 1989.

Tran Van Thuy, dir. *The Sound of the Violin in My Lai.* 1999. Available on YouTube at https://www.youtube.com/watch?v=SKq62meVA3k.

Vietnam Veterans against the War. Winter Soldier." Stoney Road Films, Winterfilm, Inc., 1972.

SECONDARY SOURCES

Books

Adams, Sam. *War of Numbers: An Intelligence Memoir.* South Royalton, VT: Steerforth, 1994.

Allison, William T. *Military Justice in Vietnam: The Rule of Law in an American War.* Lawrence: University Press of Kansas, 2007.

Allison, William T. *My Lai: An American Atrocity in the Vietnam War.* Baltimore: Johns Hopkins University Press, 2012.

Allison, William T. *The Tet Offensive: A Brief History with Documents.* New York: Routledge, 2008.

Angers, Trent. *The Forgotten Hero of My Lai: The Hugh Thompson Story.* Rev. ed. Lafayette, LA: Acadian House, 2014.

Appy, Christian G. *The Vietnam War and Our National Identity.* New York: Viking, 2015.

Arendt, Hannah. *Eichmann in Jerusalem: A Report on the Banality of Evil.* Rev. ed. New York: Viking, 1965.

Arendt, Hannah. *The Life of the Mind.* 2 vols. New York: Harcourt Brace Jovanovich, 1978.

Arendt, Hannah. *On Revolution.* New York: Viking, 1963.

Atkinson, Rick. *The Guns at Last Light: The War in Western Europe, 1944–1945.* New York: Henry Holt, 2013.

Baritz, Loren. *Backfire: A History of How American Culture Led Us into Vietnam and Made Us Fight the Way We Did.* New York: Ballantine, 1985.

Belknap, Michal R. *The Vietnam War on Trial: The My Lai Massacre and the Court-Martial of Lieutenant Calley.* Lawrence: University Press of Kansas, 2002.

Bilton, Michael, and Kevin Sim. *Four Hours in My Lai.* New York: Penguin, 1992.

Bourne, Peter G. *Men, Stress, and Vietnam.* Boston: Little, Brown, 1970.

Browning, Christopher R. *Ordinary Men: Reserve Police Battalion 101 and the Final Solution in Poland.* New York: HarperCollins, 1998. Originally published in 1992.

Brownmiller, Susan. *Against Our Will: Men, Women and Rape.* New York: Simon and Schuster, 1975.

Dallek, Robert. *Nixon and Kissinger: Partners in Power.* New York: HarperCollins, 2007.

Dawes, James. *Evil Men.* Cambridge, MA: Harvard University Press, 2013.

DeBenedetti, Charles. *An American Ordeal: The Antiwar Movement of the Vietnam War.* Syracuse, NY: Syracuse University Press, 1990.

Dimona, Joseph. *Great Court-Martial Cases.* New York: Grosset and Dunlap, 1972.

Dower, John W. *War Without Mercy: Race and Power in the Pacific War.* New York: Pantheon, 1986.

Duiker, William J. *The Communist Road to Power in Vietnam.* Boulder, CO: Westview, 1981.

Evans, Jr. Rowland, and Robert D. Novak. *Nixon in the White House: The Frustration of Power.* New York: Random House, 1971.

Everett, Arthur, Kathryn Johnson, and Harry F. Rosenthal. *Calley.* New York: Dell, 1971.

Gershen, Martin. *Destroy or Die: The True Story of Mylai.* New Rochelle, NY: Arlington House, 1971.

Greenhaw, Wayne. *The Making of a Hero: The Story of Lt. William Calley Jr.* Louisville, KY: Touchstone, 1971.

Greiner, Bernd. *War Without Fronts: The USA in Vietnam.* Translated by Anne Wyburd and Victoria Fern. New Haven, CT: Yale University Press, 2009.

Grossman, David. *On Killing: The Psychological Cost of Learning to Kill in War and Society.* Boston: Little, Brown, 1995.

Hackworth, David H. *About Face: The Odyssey of an American Warrior.* New York: Simon and Schuster, 1989.

Hammer, Richard. *The Court-Martial of Lieutenant Calley.* New York: Coward, McCann and Geoghegan, 1971.

Hammer, Richard. *One Morning in the War: The Tragedy at Son My.* New York: Coward-McCann, 1970.

Hammond, William M. *Public Affairs: The Military and the Media, 1968–1973.* Washington, DC: Department of the Army, 1996.

Hanley, Charles J. *The Bridge at No Gun Ri: A Hidden Nightmare from the Korean War*. New York: Henry Holt, 2001.

Herring, George C. *America's Longest War: The United States and Vietnam, 1950–1975*. 4th ed. New York: McGraw-Hill, 2002.

Hersh, Seymour. *Cover-Up: The Army's Secret Investigation of the Massacre at My Lai 4*. New York: Random House, 1972.

Hersh, Seymour. *My Lai 4: A Report on the Massacre and Its Aftermath*. New York: Random House, 1970.

Hughes, Ken. *Fatal Politics: The Nixon Tapes, the Vietnam War, and the Casualties of Reelection*. Charlottesville: University of Virginia Press, 2015.

Karsten, Peter. *Law, Soldiers, and Combat*. Westport, CT: Greenwood, 1978.

Kelly, Alfred H., and Winfred A. Harbison. *The American Constitution: Its Origins and Development*. 4th ed. New York: W. W. Norton, 1970.

Kimball, Jeffrey. *Nixon's Vietnam War*. Lawrence: University Press of Kansas, 1998.

Kramer, Paul A. *The Blood of Government: Race, Empire, the United States and the Philippines*. Chapel Hill: University of North Carolina Press, 2006.

Kuzmakov, Jeremy. *The Myth of the Addicted Army: Vietnam and the Modern War on Drugs*. Amherst: University of Massachusetts Press, 2009.

Langguth, A. J. *Our Vietnam: The War, 1954–1975*. New York: Simon and Schuster, 2000.

Lewy, Guenter, *America in Vietnam*. New York: Oxford University Press, 1978.

Lifton, Betty Jean, and Thomas C. Fox. *Children of Vietnam*. New York: Atheneum, 1972.

Lurie, Jonathan. *Pursuing Military Justice: The History of the United States Court of Appeals for the Armed Forces, 1951–1980*. 2 vols. Princeton, NJ: Princeton University Press, 1998.

Maslowski, Peter, and Don Winslow. *Looking for a Hero: Staff Sergeant Joe Ronnie Hooper and the Vietnam War*. Lincoln: University of Nebraska Press, 2004.

McCarthy, Mary. *Medina*. New York: Harcourt Brace Jovanovich, 1972.

Milam, Ron. *Not a Gentleman's War: An Inside View of Junior Officers in the Vietnam War*. Chapel Hill: University of North Carolina Press, 2009.

Military History Institute of Vietnam. *Victory in Vietnam: The Official History of the People's Army of Vietnam, 1954–1975*. Translated by Merle L. Pribbenow. Lawrence: University Press of Kansas, 2002.

Millett, Allan R., Peter Maslowski, and William B. Feis. *For the Common Defense: A Military History of the United States from 1607 to 2012*. 3rd ed. New York: Free Press, 2012.

Miraldi, Robert. *Seymour Hersh: Scoop Artist*. Lincoln: University of Nebraska Press, 2013.

Nelson, Deborah. *The War Behind Me: Vietnam Veterans Confront the Truth about U.S. War Crimes*. New York: Basic Books, 2008.

Nguyen, Lien-Hang T. *Hanoi's War: An International History of the War for Peace in Vietnam*. Chapel Hill: University of North Carolina Press, 2012.

Oberdorfer, Don. *Tet*. New York: Doubleday, 1971.

Oliver, Kendrick. *The My Lai Massacre in American History and Memory*. Manchester, U.K.: Manchester University Press, 2006.

Peck, M. Scott. *People of the Lie: The Hope for Healing Human Evil*. New York: Simon and Schuster, 1983.

Perlstein, Rick. *Nixonland: The Rise of a President and the Fracturing of America*. New York: Scribner, 2008.

Phillips, Kimberley L. *War! What Is It Good For? Black Freedom Struggles and the U.S. Military from World War II to Iraq*. Chapel Hill: University of North Carolina Press, 2012.

Polsgrove, Carol. *It Wasn't Pretty, Folks, But Didn't We Have Fun?* New York: W. W. Norton, 1995.

Prados, John. *Vietnam: The History of an Unwinnable War, 1945–1975*. Lawrence: University Press of Kansas, 2009.

Reeves, Richard. *President Nixon: Alone in the White House*. New York: Simon and Schuster, 2001.

Rhodes, Richard. *Masters of Death: The SS-Einsatzgruppen and the Invention of the Holocaust*. Oxford: Perseus, 2002.

Ricks, Thomas E. *The Generals: American Military Command from World War II to Today*. New York: Penguin, 2012.

Roberts, Mary Louise. *What Soldiers Do: Sex and the American GI in World War II France*. Chicago: University of Chicago Press, 2013.

Schmitz, David F. *The Tet Offensive: Politics, War, and Public Opinion*. Lanham, MD: Rowman and Littlefield, 2005.

Sellah, Michael, and Mitch Weiss. *Tiger Force: A True Story of Men and War*. New York: Little, Brown, 2006.

Solis, Gary D., and Fred L. Borch. *Geneva Conventions*. New York: Kaplan, 2010.

Spector, Ronald H. *After Tet: The Bloodiest Year in Vietnam*. New York: Free Press, 1993.

Stacewicz, Richard. *Winter Soldiers: An Oral History of the Vietnam Veterans against the War.* Chicago: Haymarket, 1997.

Stangneth, Bettina. *Eichmann Before Jerusalem: The Unexamined Life of a Mass Murderer.* New York: Alfred A. Knopf, 2014.

Stanton, Shelby L. *The Rise and Fall of an American Army: U.S. Ground Forces in Vietnam, 1965–1973.* Novato, CA: Presidio, 1985.

Stein, Jeff. *A Murder in Wartime: The Untold Spy Story That Changed the Course of the Vietnam War.* New York: St. Martin's, 1992.

Summers, Anthony. *The Arrogance of Power: The Secret World of Richard Nixon.* New York: Viking Penguin, 2000.

Taylor, Telford. *Nuremberg and Vietnam: An American Tragedy.* Chicago: Quadrangle, 1970.

Thayer, Thomas C. *War Without Fronts: The American Experience in Vietnam.* Boulder, CO: Westview, 1985.

Tiede, Tom. *Calley: Soldier or Killer?* New York: Pinnacle, 1971.

Tirman, John. *The Deaths of Others: The Fate of Civilians in America's Wars.* New York: Oxford University Press, 2011.

Turse, Nick. *Kill Anything That Moves: The Real American War in Vietnam.* New York: Henry Holt, 2013.

Valentine, Douglas. *The Phoenix Program.* New York: William Morrow, 1990.

Waller, James. *Becoming Evil: How Ordinary People Commit Genocide and Mass Killing.* 2nd ed. New York: Oxford University Press, 2007.

Woodward, Bob. *The Last of the President's Men.* New York: Simon and Schuster, 2015.

Articles and Essays

Beidler, Philip. "Calley's Ghost." *Virginia Quarterly Review* 79 (Winter 2003): 30–50. Available online at http://www.vqronline.org/essay/calley%E2%80%99s-ghost.

Beidler, Philip. "Fort Morality," *Military History* 23 (Dec. 2006): 56–61.

Bishop, Joseph W. "Court-Martial Jurisdiction over Military-Civilian Hybrids: Retired Regulars, Reservists, and Discharged Prisoners." *University of Pennsylvania Law Review* 112 (Jan. 1964): 317–77.

Calleja, David. "The My Lai Massacre—Vietnam's Holocaust." *Foreign Policy Journal*, Feb. 24, 2010. Available online at http://www.foreignpolicyjournal.com/2010/02/24/the-my-lai-massacre-vietnams-holocaust/.

Carson, Mark D. "F. Edward Hébert and the Congressional Investigation of the My Lai Massacre." *Louisiana History* 37 (Winter 1996): 61–79.

Clark, Roger S. "Medina: An Essay on the Principles of Criminal Liability for Homicide." *Rutgers-Camden Law Journal* 5 (Fall 1973): 59–79.

Davanzo, Jeannine. "Note: An Absence of Accountability for the My Lai Massacre." *Hofstra Law and Policy Symposium* 3 (1999): 287–312.

Davidson, Michael J. "Congressional Investigations and Their Effect on Subsequent Military Prosecutions." *Journal of Law and Policy* 14 (April 18, 2006): 281–328.

Eckhardt, William G. "Command Criminal Responsibility: A Plan for a Workable Standard." *Military Law Review* 97 (1982): 1–34.

Eckhardt, William G. "My Lai: An American Tragedy." *UMKC Law Review* 68 (Summer 2000): 671–703.

Eckhardt, William G. "Nuremberg—Fifty Years: Accountability and Responsibility." *UMKC Law Review* 65 (Fall 1996): 1–14.

Goldberg, Herman L., and Frederick A. C. Hoefer. "Army Parole System." *Journal of Criminal Law and Criminology* 40 (1949–50): 158–69.

Howard, Kenneth A. "Command Responsibility for War Crimes." *Journal of Public Law* 31 (1972): 7–22.

Kelman, Herbert C., and Lee H. Lawrence. "Assignment of Responsibility in the Case of Lt. Calley: Preliminary Report on a National Survey." *Journal of Social Issues* 28, no. 1 (March 1972): 177–212.

Lippman, Matthew. "Humanitarian Law: The Uncertain Contours of Command Responsibility." *Tulsa Journal of Comparative and International Law* 2 (Fall 2001): 1–95.

Parks, William H. "Command Responsibility for War Crimes." *Military Law Review* 62 (1973): 1–104.

Savage, Paul L., and Richard A. Gabriel. "Cohesion and Disintegration in the American Army: An Alternative Perspective." *Armed Forces and Society* 2 (Spring 1976): 340–76.

Smidt, Major Michael L. "*Yamashita, Medina*, and Beyond: Command Responsibility in Contemporary Military Operations." 164 *Military Law Review* (2000): 155–234.

Stuhldreher, Karen. "State Rape: Representations of Rape in Viet Nam." In "Nobody Gets Off the Bus: The Viet Nam Generation Big Book." Special issue, *Viet Nam Generation* 5 (March 1994). Available online at http://www2.iath.virginia.edu/sixties/HTML_docs/Texts/Scholarly/ Stuldreher_Rape.html.

Wieskamp, Valerie. "Sexual Assault and the My Lai Massacre: The Erasure of Sexual Violence from Public Memory of the Vietnam War." In

Mythologizing the Vietnam War: Visual Culture and Mediated Memory, edited by Jennifer Good, Val Williams, Paul Lowe, and Brigitte Lardinois, 127–43. Newcastle upon Tyne, U.K.: Cambridge Scholars, 2014.

Novels

O'Brien, Tim. *Going After Cacciato*. New York: Dell, 1978; Delacorte, 1978.

O'Brien, Tim. *If I Die in a Combat Zone: Box Me Up and Ship Me Home*. New York: Dell. 1969.

O'Brien, Tim. *In the Lake of the Woods*. Boston: Houghton Mifflin, 1994.

O'Brien, Tim. *The Things They Carried*. Boston: Houghton Mifflin, 1990.

Index

Being Mary Bennet

JC PETERSON

HARPER TEEN
An Imprint of HarperCollins Publishers

For Ian

You are tolerable, I suppose

Being Mary Bennet

ONE

IT IS A TRUTH UNIVERSALLY ACKNOWLEDGED that no one should spend her eighteenth birthday at the library.

That's according to Adhira Fitz, accidental roommate and apparent birthday expert. According to me, Marnie Barnes, academic extraordinaire and solitude expert, libraries make for fabulous birthdays. I would say something about being surrounded by your closest confidantes and bosom friends, but even I realize that makes me sound like your great-aunt Maude, the one with three too many cats and opinions on brocade.

The Ambrose Bierce Library on the campus of Pacific Crest Academy is cocooned in the thick hush of hundreds of books and a head librarian who only wears soft-soled shoes. Deep within the stacks, I've commandeered my favorite corner table and spread out my textbooks and notes with precision—books to the right, stacked by size, and highlighters to my left. Everything in its right place. *Me* in my right place, surrounded by my book BFFs without a soul bothering me. Nothing could make my birthday heart happier.

Bzzz. Bzzz.

Ugh. Nothing save maybe putting my phone on silent. I push aside the book I'm about to crack open and snatch my phone out of my bag, balking at Adhira's name. We don't talk on the phone. We don't *chat*. We happen to share living quarters until the PCA Housing Board realizes their mistake and puts me in a single room like I've repeatedly requested.

"Yes?" I hiss, tight-lipped.

"You're not hiding alone in a library on your birthday, Marnie. I won't allow it."

Well, that's preposterous. I'm not alone. (See: aforementioned book BFFs.)

I swivel around to check for the librarian, then hunch and cup a hand over my mouth: "I'm not *hiding*, Adhira. I'm *working*."

Talking on phones is verboten in the Bierce Library. Just last week, the librarian caught Ophelia Lawson and literally threw her brand-new iPhone—Kate Spade case and all—out the window. Though, by the triumph smeared all over her father's face when I spied him leaving the headmaster's office, PCA staff will likely refrain from any more phone defenestration.

"Unacceptable," Adhira says much too loudly.

That shakes a cough loose. "Excuse me? I have an essay to complete for British History and my presentation to write for my Hunt Prize entry."

A presentation for which I'm woefully unprepared. A twist of sourness heats my stomach. If I don't wow the Hunt Prize committee with a project idea . . . if I'm *rejected* from entering the program . . .

"Exactly. You deserve a break. I've got to finish my costuming workshop, then I'm coming to rescue you," Adhira says, like I need rescuing.

"Wait, no—"

"See you soon!" She hangs up, and I'm left with the prickling sensation that I lost an argument I didn't know I was having.

A shadow darkens my untouched notebook.

"I believe," a flat, deliberately bored voice begins, "there's a name for someone who gets me in trouble for using a phone, then turns around and uses one herself."

A groan swells in my throat and breaks against my tongue. I drop my phone like it's acid and glance at Ophelia Lawson over my glasses.

"Hello, Lia."

And, okay. Maybe I *did* tell the librarian she was being loud, which led to the whole "phone chucked out the window" incident. But a library is for studying and reading, not fraternizing with your friends. She was *giggling*. Giggling!

Lia casts a long look over my assembled books and crosses her arms. "You took every book on Queen Mary. How is anyone else supposed to do that stupid essay you got us assigned?"

First of all, the essay isn't stupid. Queen Mary is fascinating. She was called "Bloody Mary," and no one nicknamed "bloody" *anything* turns out to be a homebody who got all her daily fiber. Second of all—

"I simply asked if we had any homework, Lia. Rather we get the assignment now than just before the weekend, right?" Some people are just ungrateful. Lia's icy eyes cut to the books again. Oh so casually, I lean on them in case she tries to make off with one.

Lia grumps. "Whatever." She sweeps a sheet of long blond hair over her shoulder, pausing to give me one of her patented Lia Disapproves sneers before she spins on a heel and stalks off. She is not, it should be noted, wearing soft-soled shoes. Her stomps crack against the wood floors all the way across the library. Maybe she'll make Daddy solve this for her too. There'll be a "no homework" rule instituted. My eyes roll so hard, my head is in danger of tipping off.

Pacific Crest Academy is one of the premier boarding schools on the West Coast, an institution where senators, Silicon Valley executives, and stars send their teen daughters. (Fact: three of my fellow PCA students are the progeny of reality show stars.) Homework shouldn't simply be a requirement. It should be lauded for how it's preparing us for college and beyond. Unfortunately, some of my fame-adjacent class-mates seem to disagree.

My phone buzzes again, this time with a text: *All done. On my way over.*

Great. I've taken exactly zero notes for this essay. And I haven't even opened my Hunt Prize notebook. Can't a girl spend her birthday how she wants? Preferably in quiet reflection with a favorite book. Or at least getting ahead on an assignment or two.

A wriggle of trepidation worms down my spine. What if Adhira has planned something? What if she *invited* people? The wriggle tunnels deep and gets bitey, and I curl a hand against my stomach.

The last time someone planned a party for me without my knowledge, it was my mother. She invited all the ladies from the club and their tanned, statuesque daughters to celebrate my sixteenth. And nobody came. *Nobody.* Mother was mortified—for herself, of course—and used the Party That Wasn't as a truly delightful opportunity to enumerate all the ways I could improve myself to attract friends. It started with "Stop eating all the leftover cake, Marnie" and ended with "I can't believe you ate all that cake just to spite me. Don't come crying to me when you can't fit into your prom dress."

I didn't go to prom, so joke's on her.

But the memory of that particular humiliation is hot behind my eyes. It spurs me to stand, do something so the sting doesn't turn into something worse like—horror of horrors—tears. I scoop up my notebooks and shove them into my bag next to *Costumes of the Elizabethan Stage*, which I've already checked out, then hesitate over the rest. I snatch up one, *The Madness and Mystery of Queen Mary*, and leave the rest behind to go hide. I'll text Adhira later that something came up and—

"Oh, good, you're already packed."

The book drops and hits the table with a thump.

"Adhira. Hey. I was actually about to . . ."

The issue is, I haven't thought up an excuse yet, so the sentence puffs away to nothing. Adhira stares at me for a second, her eyebrows pulled together, then she goes about stacking my books on the nearby cart so I can retrieve them later. We're both new seniors at PCA this year—me from San Jose and her from Toronto. In these past two months, the girl has learned my ways. It's all very disconcerting.

"You and this library," she mutters to herself.

"Are in a mutually beneficial relationship," I finish for her. Then, feeling very smug, I brandish *Costumes of the Elizabethan Stage* from my bag. "*And* I grabbed this for you. It's the one you were trying to track down, right?"

Adhira's eyes light up. "Oh, it is! Thank you!"

The head librarian shushes us, and Adhira tilts her head toward mine. "But you're still not celebrating your birthday in a library," she whispers, "impossible-to-check-out book or no."

With that, I'm bundled out the door and stumble down the

library steps. Outside, low clouds scuttle across the San Francisco sky, casting the formerly bright October day in flat shadows. I shove my hands deeper into my cardigan pockets and hunch my neck. The wind off the Pacific snaps with a wet sort of cold and sends a frizz of my dirty-blond hair into my eyes. I tuck it behind my ear and push my glasses back up my nose.

PCA takes up a full city block in the hilly heart of San Francisco, but within its tall fences, our little school is a quiet green oasis, windy Pacific air notwithstanding. Across the terraced central courtyard, the PCA cafeteria nestles squat between the stately old arts and humanities building and the new glass-and-steel science building, home of the trendsetting Girls in Tech incubator. The science building isn't named yet, but the rumor is it'll soon be dedicated in honor of the incubator's founder: Thomas J. Barnes Science Hall. As in, my father. Who texted me this morning to cancel our lunch plans because he was too busy incubating, or whatever.

"I was thinking I could buy you dessert," Adhira says, smiling wide. She has a way of smiling that makes her dark eyes sparkle and her brown skin go all glowy. My rare smiles more resemble those charts doctors use so patients can point out their level of physical pain. Or so I was told by my mother when she got the proofs back from my sister's wedding.

"They've got chocolate cake at the caf today," I venture. I should know, because I definitely ate a piece by myself earlier.

Adhira tilts her pointed chin and hooks a thumb in the

opposite direction—toward the blue-and-green painted steps leading to Alcott House and the main gates that open to the bustle of San Francisco. "I had something different in mind."

As a rule, I don't go in for things that are different. There's too much variability in "different." I chew on Adhira's proposal as she drags me along the steep gravel path toward the edge of the courtyard.

"I guess we could walk over to Bardo for some tea," I say as we pass the fountain of Athena with an owl on her shoulder.

Adhira blows out a breath, ruffling her dark bangs. "You're going to like this, Marnie. Promise."

"I won't."

"You will. Come on." Adhira plants both hands on my shoulders. This is more physical contact than I strictly allow, but she is a hugger. She hugged me the first time we met— on move-in day—and I nearly recoiled in abject horror. I've gotten her down to one hug a week, but it's taken hard work and dedication. I don't know why she hasn't given up on this "friend" thing and hung out with other girls at PCA, but here we are. Her nose scrunches up. "Please? I promise it'll be fun."

"Fine." But I shift my shoulders to toss Adhira's hands off and lift my chin, like I didn't just give in to the smallest, most determined Canadian girl I know.

We stop at the top of those famous Pacific Crest Academy painted steps. At eye level, the turrets and gables of Alcott

House and the soaring arches of the Edison Auditorium at the
bottom of the hill stare back.

"I'll call a car!" She grins and yanks her phone out of her
pocket. "Dev and Tilda can't wait to meet you!"

Wait. What?

TWO

THE HIRED CAR DIVES DOWN Russian Hill and across Market, burrowing into the impossibly hip Mission. I do some burrowing of my own, but try as I might, I'm not able to disappear into the brown leather seat.

The darkening streets buzz with bicyclists on fixies swerving around cars and groups in line for the Korean taco food trucks. Mom once went on an all-fermented diet. I spent three months offended on Korean food's behalf because of the ways Julia Barnes disrespected kimchi.

"I can't stay out late," I say to Adhira. The art of the pre-excuse is one I've honed over the years. "My Hunt Prize presentation is in three days, and unlike you, I still have no idea what I'm going to pitch. Plus, I've got a volunteer shift at the library tomorrow afternoon for story time."

"I thought you settled on Once Upon a Doggie for the project?"

"First, a giant no to that name. Second, why would I want to spend the next six months covered in poodle hair?" Poodles aren't winning the Hunt Prize.

Adhira shrugs, but it's still peppy. I don't know how she does it. Even when deep in concentration at her dress form, her mouth lifts in a natural smile. Last month, my niece told me I look like Viola Swamp when I read. In my defense, I was into an intense passage in *A Great and Terrible Beauty*. But is there any defense for looking like an actual witch?

"Then pitch that lecture series on Feminism and Shake-speare," Adhira counters. She peers out the window, the streetlights slashing orange over her hair. "You'll figure it out, Marnie."

Except I quite possibly *won't* figure it out, and either way I have to present to Headmaster Finch and the Hunt Prize committee, which includes Lia's foul-faced father. Who *definitely* would rather his name be on the science building—among other reasons to hate me (*cough* Lia's phone *cough*).

It's easy for Adhira to act unconcerned. Her pitch was accepted nearly a month ago and she's already found mentors at Academy of Art University—the illustrious Dev and Tilda I'm about to meet. It is now the twenty-third of October, and if I don't have my project accepted and the mentorship paperwork filed by the first of November, I'll be a normal senior. I might as well schlep back to San Jose since the Hunt Prize is only for PCA seniors, anyway.

A wave of exhaustion hits me again, making this entire birthday journey a totally irresponsible venture. Even if my pitch is accepted, I still have so many more steps to go. I'll have to secure a mentor—usually some VIP from the community—and then, most daunting of all, I'll have to actually implement the project. Plus, there's the Hunt Prize fair in December, which weeds out the weaker projects, advancing no more than twenty finalists. Then the big final speeches are the culmination of all our projects in the spring. The winner is awarded a medal, some money, but most importantly prestige. The sort of prestige that looks really good on college applications if, for example, you want to attend Stanford and have great grades but not a ton of extracurricular padding (*ahem*). Two senators, a handful of CEOs, and at least one social media influencer have won in the past. And, oh yeah, my older sister.

She won the prize nearly a decade ago, with a project on saltwater marsh reclamation in San Francisco Bay. Not that I'm trying to live up to Perfect and Amazing Lindy Barnes™, it's just that I *need* to win the Hunt Prize. And if Mom starts gushing about me ad nauseam and Dad stops canceling lunch plans, that'll be a pleasant side effect.

The car swerves toward the curb and stops, jolting me from my thoughts.

Adhira grins out my side of the car toward a crowded restaurant called Satchel & Pine. "Dev told me this place is amaze."

"—ing," I helpfully finish for her.

Adhira leans across me to push my door open and practically shoves me out onto the sidewalk. "No lecturing tonight," she says, warning in her tone.

"I was correcting, not lecturing," I admonish, pushing my glasses back up my nose.

Adhira cuts a brown-eyed glare my way, so I turn away and peer at this apparently amaze(ing) place. Two garage doors on either side of the entrance are open, and the music wafting out sounds like a singing saw. Inside, it's all man buns and maroon lipstick, and I am hopelessly out of place.

"I promise, you'll like Dev and Tilda. You guys have a ton in common."

Doubtful. My toes curl in my clogs. "Theater people are so . . . dramatic." I get enough of that with four sisters and an excitable mother.

Adhira dramatically rolls her eyes, proving my point quite nicely. "It's only Dev and Tilda, not any of the performers. We're only dramatic about a kick-ass bustle, eh?" She holds up her hand for a triumphant high five that will never come.

"I don't know, Adhira," I hedge, already looking for the exit before we've even walked through the door.

"Marnie Elizabeth Barnes," she says, deploying my full

name so I know it's serious. Funny, but I don't know her middle name. "You are to march inside this instant and have a wonderful birthday, do you hear me? Stop judging this place and"—Adhira screws up her face for a moment—"give it a try, okay? There are places other than the library and Bardo you may like. Stop hiding."

"I'm not hiding." Why have I had to say this twice today already? "I'm just very busy."

After a second, Adhira sighs. "I'd be a terrible roommate if I ignored your birthday. Let me be your friend, okay?"

All my indignation puddles at my feet. My friend. She's under the impression that the PCA Housing Board matched us as roommates based on some compatibility in our applications. Except it was all a mistake. I never filled out a roommate application because I'd requested a single room, and I definitely gave a strangled choke instead of telling her the truth when she brought up the application on move-in day. Now, nearly two months later, it feels too late to correct her. Except . . .

Guilt bloops in my stomach at the memory of the letter I hand-delivered to the housing board a couple of weeks ago— the third such letter reminding them of my request for a single room. But truthfully, I'm much better on my own.

If I were alone, there'd be no one currently nudging me toward heavy black velvet curtains and into a restaurant. A restaurant that is, okay, not as annoying as I imagined. Between the man buns and maroon lipstick are deep leather booths and framed vintage maps on the walls. Hanging above, milky-white lamps cast everyone in a moody, glamorous light. A giant age-smoked mirror to my right shows my complexion transformed from consumptive to almost luminous.

"See?" Adhira gushes.

"I see!" I say, like someone on the receiving end of a tent-revival miracle.

Adhira grins and hauls me to a booth at the back and two people with matching swoopy half-shaved haircuts; the guy's hair is black and the woman's white-blond. Adhira introduces me, and instead of saying hello I freeze up, audibly gulp, then go for a stiff stare. Miss Personality Plus, that's me.

Dev Mehta and Tilda Williams return my stare, though I don't miss the way Tilda flicks her heavily winged eyes up and down my outfit. I tug at the edges of my sack dress pockets, then shove my hands into my cardigan pockets—that's right, I'm double-pocketed.

"Your cardigan," Tilda says. "Did you add the embellishments yourself?"

I glance down at my cardigan, and it glances back. It's covered in embroidered orange cats in various attitudes. My favorite is the snoozing tabby curled in a ball above my left pocket. "My sister got it for me last year. From some online place, I think."

Honestly, clothes aren't my forte. Or makeup. Or small talk. Or . . . you get the picture.

"It's so unique," Tilda says, in what is most certainly not a compliment. She's dressed head to toe in black, which, combined with her bright white hair, makes her look like Goth Santa.

Adhira slides into the deep olive-green booth, already talking fast with Dev. I wobble onto the edges of my clogs for a second, dithering. But then Dev frowns at me.

"Are you going to sit, or . . . ?"

Right. Standing awkwardly at the head of the table is not the best option. I bumble my way into the booth, the backs of my thighs squeaking across the leather. This is all going splendidly; is it a surprise yet that I don't seek out social moments?

Adhira's voice bubbles with excitement as she dissects the local production of *Ali Baba and the Forty Thieves* she helped costume. It was part of her Hunt Prize project to create costumes using all recycled and sustainable products, and *Time Out San Francisco* called it "a play" that "happened." There's still scavenged turquoise sateen all over our dorm room that's given me flashbacks to the two and a half weeks Mom declared she'd taken up sewing and hauled her grandmother's Singer and a collection of vintage cloth out of storage.

All my attempts to decipher the talk of bodices and darting makes desperation ping in my brain. I have nothing substantive to add. Why can't Adhira be into modern-day retellings of *Anne of Green Gables*?

Dev idly plays with a sprig of some sort of roughage sticking out of his drink, then leans forward, eyes bright. "Thank god the director didn't get his way with the flying carpet," he hisses with gossip. "It would've been wall-to-wall shag pile to get Morgiana off the ground."

Tilda cackles with laughter, but I've lit up. Finally, something I can work with!

"Actually, there aren't any flying carpets in *Ali Baba*."

All aforementioned cackles screech to a stop. Ah, yes. Here I am. Your friendly neighborhood mood killer. But honestly, it would be totally incongruous to add a flying carpet to that story. A tiny bit of research would have told anyone that.

Adhira looks at me with big eyes, which I apparently take to mean "do go on," so I say, "You're thinking of one of the other stories from *One Thousand and One Arabian Nights*. If you didn't know, that's the source material."

Silence. Though Tilda's slow blink speaks volumes.

Maybe Adhira's "do go on" eyes were actually "shut up, now!" eyes.

"Right." Dev glances at Adhira, then back to me. "You're into books, aren't you?"

Adhira nods for me, even though Dev said "into books" like I was "into murder."

"She's read, like, everything." A twinge of desperation stretches the edge of Adhira's voice. I have a sneaking suspicion she's rethinking introducing me to her mentors. "And she interns at the city's central library. That's how she came up with her best Hunt Prize idea."

I side-eye her, but Dev and Tilda are side-eyeing me. It's a side-eye circle. I sit on my hands and kick the back of one clog against the booth. I should have just stayed on campus. These two clearly don't like me. I mean, I don't care, except I sort of do.

"So it's called Once Upon a Doggie," Adhira begins, considering I've gone chatty as a clam.

"I'm not calling it that."

They blink at me, so I sigh and take over since I have no choice now. "Basically, it's using the library's bookmobile to set up at animal shelters so kids can practice their reading with adoptable dogs."

"Fiction for Fido," Dev pipes up.

Uh, no.

"Oh! Ruff Reading," Adhira says.

Also no.

"Puppy Periodicals!"

"Periodicals are magazines, not books," I say.

Tilda, who's been quiet, catches my eye. There are little muscles quivering on either side of her mouth, then she quirks a brief smile. "That's actually a rad idea."

A little squidge of pride pops in my chest to have a cool older person think the idea is good. Maybe it *is* the best idea of all my options. Maybe this'll be the thing that makes my teachers and parents and generally everybody stop saying "Oh, you're Lindy's little sister! She's so Perfect and Amazing™!" before trailing off and staring at me like they don't know what went wrong in the eight and a half years between her birth and mine.

"Do you have a shelter you're partnering with?" Dev asks.

That squidge of pride deflates with a *pffffft*. I rub at the end of my nose, then say, "Not yet."

"My little brother's friend at USF volunteers at a shelter in Outer Richmond," Dev says as he scrolls through his phone. "I'll give you his contact info."

"Oh yeah. Of course." By which I mean: nope. There's no way I'm going to cold-call some dude who's the friend of the brother of a guy I've literally just met. I have to psych myself up to call my own mother.

"What's your number?"

Dev looks up from his phone expectantly, but all I can muster is a weak, "What?"

He puffs his cheeks out in a big sigh, then grabs the coaster from under his drink and scrawls the number for someone named Whit. I nod as I look at it, like I live in a world where I will ever, in ten million years, call this guy.

"Seriously, call him," Dev presses, like he could read my thoughts. "He's really nice—and *hot*, if you're into guys."

"I'm not— I mean. Yeah, I'm into guys, but not—" *Oh god.* Dev waggles his eyebrows and my cheeks burn. *Panic!* I don't talk about boys with friends. And I *certainly* don't talk about boys with absolute strangers. The edge of the coaster is soggy under the press of my fingernail, and I start blurting words to change the subject. "I mean, I'm not even sure this is the project I'll end up pitching. No offense, but this is a big deal to me. I think I've got a chance to do something actually important, you know? I'm not going to jump at the first thing if I want to win the prize."

Beside me, Adhira stills. "What, like working on plays is unimportant?"

"No! I mean, the spirit of the project is to, you know, help people. If I want to win the Hunt Prize—"

"I'm hungry," Adhira announces quite suddenly. "Are you hungry? Let's eat. Dev, can you recommend—"

"Is that your only goal? To win some prize?" Tilda interrupts, her eyebrows winging low. "Because I hate to break this to you, honey, but that isn't helping anyone but yourself. Maybe don't be shitty about Adhira's project."

It takes a second for the words to burst past my teeth. "I wasn't! I just need something better!"

Tilda's glare could freeze a penguin. "You're being really rude." She scoots out of the booth and stands. "And for the record, the arts are just as important as whatever bullshit you're going to come up with. Adhira, you don't have to listen to this."

Dev scoots out behind Tilda, and Adhira is right behind them, wringing her hands together. She pauses, sucks in a breath like she has something to say to me. But then she clamps her mouth shut and dashes after Dev and Tilda.

I really wasn't trying to be shitty. It's just that she's working on making some pretty dresses—which is great and fine and good for her!—and I have the ability here to make people's lives better. I mean, if I can actually settle on a project.

Guilt prickles my skin, and I squirm to relieve the feeling. Dev and Tilda abandoned their cocktails when they stormed off, so I push them across the table. That's all I need right now, for someone to ID me and kick me out. I peek around the booth to see Adhira at the front of the restaurant talking with Dev and Tilda. She's using her hands a lot. Not a good sign. But then Tilda's eyes snap to mine, and I dart back with a little huff.

Heat crawls up my chest, probably making me blotchy, and my hair sits hot and itchy against the side of my neck. I grab the tail of my long blond braid and throw it over my shoulder. Okay, so I could have gone about that a different way. I peer around, careful not to be caught spying on the others.

That's when I see him.

My heart takes off like a shot, thumping so hard I can scarcely breathe. Hayworth Wellesley rests one elbow against the sleek copper bar, looking for all the world like a posh alcohol advertisement. He's fresh out of a concurrent bachelor's and master's program, the youngest venture capitalist at Bright Star Capital in Palo Alto, a former California all-state lacrosse midfielder, and newly engaged to Sara Nguyen, my sister's best friend.

And he's the love of my life.

Not that he knows that.

THREE

HAYWORTH WELLESLEY.

Giddiness is a Tilt-A-Whirl inside my chest. I don't know whether to shrink deeper into the booth and creep on him or sprint over and throw myself into his capable arms.

And they are capable. When I was thirteen and Hayes almost nineteen, I tagged along with my older sisters and their friends to Seacliff Beach. I think Mom made them take me so I'd actually get a summer tan, which was probably item #11 on the Julia Barnes List of Appropriate Beauty. Anyway, I got caught in a riptide, and it was Hayes—atop his boogie board— who saved me. Like, literally saved my life. He was so frantic to reach me, he clocked me on the head with his board. I still have a half-moon scar at my hairline, my token of his heroism.

I fell in love with him the instant he dragged me onto his boogie board and held me tight, and have never since been untrue.

He's tall and blond, like a Norse god, and the cut of his jawline makes knives jealous. His eyes—not on me at the moment, but eminently picturable—are a wind-whipped sea blue. Now, one hand is curled around the stem of a cocktail glass, and his crisp gray suit has a slight luster in the overhead lighting.

Look at me, I silently yearn. *Look at me.*

Then—oh, holy mother of god—he does, and heat blazes up my neck. The Tilt-A-Whirl in my chest throws me headlong off the ride.

A half second too late, I raise a hand at him. Hayes tilts his chin, confusion drawing his eyebrows together.

"Hi, Hayes," I burst out. "I didn't see you there!"

My lie is . . . not spectacular, seeing as I was practically swooning over him not two seconds ago.

But Hayes's expression clears, and the smile gracing his beautiful face makes my stomach explode into a million butterflies of pure flappy joy.

"Marnie," Hayes says, crossing to me. "What are you . . . ?"

"Birthday."

He frowns again. Even his frown is amazingly perfect.

"I mean, *my* birthday," I clarify.

Okay, here's how this should go. Hayes will light up and immediately buy me a celebratory dessert, one demonstrating he understands the hidden nuances of my personality. Then he'll slide into the booth beside me and we'll share a laugh. Probably some old chestnut about his now-*ex*-fiancée, Sara.

Then his hand will slide across the table to mine, our fingers touching. Then he'll—

"Hello," Hayes says, dragging out the *o* and tapping the table in front of me.

I choke on the fantasy and peer up at Hayes. He tugs at his tie and glances around. "Sara and I will have to owe you a dessert. Root beer float, right?"

He remembers. He bought me a root beer float after the doctor stitched up my forehead. I'm too flustered to do more than squeak, so Hayes taps the table with two fingers and checks his watch. "Rain check, okay? I'm meeting a client in, like, five. But will Sara and I see you at your sister's big dinner Friday?"

I'm already nodding. "Yeah, yup. See you there, Hayes."

It's the same day as my presentation to the Hunt Prize committee, and until zero-point-one seconds ago, I hadn't planned on attending.

Hayes stares at me for another second, and my heart beats wildly when he smiles again. It warms me all the way down to my toes. Then he turns away and also smiles at Adhira, who's returned to the table. He probably likes seeing me with friends. He's such a good guy.

Adhira's expression, though, is ringed in metaphorical fire. She ignores Hayes and rudely jerks her arm away when he lightly brushes past her. Her reaction to Hayes makes all those butterflies in my stomach drop dead. *Way to go, Adhira, you butterfly butcher.*

"That was Hayes," I blurt, then sigh, snuggly and sloppy with love. I'm also playing with the end of my braid like a damn schoolgirl. I mean, which I am, but I've never been described as a schoolgirl. Even in kindergarten, I was Marnie Barnes: Serious Scholar.

Adhira slices her eyes toward Hayes's retreating back and pulls a face.

As a rule, I don't share such personal details—such as my yearslong devotion to a guy almost six years older than me—but the background on my laptop is a close-up of Hayes with his arm around me taken last summer at Mom's annual Melanoma Awareness Pool Party. Adhira apparently put two and two together.

A deep sigh drops her bunched shoulders. "That is no good, Marnie."

"What does that mean?" I look up so fast, one finger catches in a tangle of my braid and yanks a chunk free.

When Adhira doesn't answer, I glance down at Tilda's nearly full cocktail on the table. This is a Hayes-Positive Zone. I don't want to hear whatever she has to say. So I won't. "You know, these are called coupe glasses, and the story goes they're modeled after Marie Antoinette's—"

"He's such a—"

"—boob," I finish.

Adhira presses her lips together. "Come on, Marnie. Guys like that . . . I don't want you to get hurt."

"It's just a dumb crush." But Adhira stares hard at me until I drop my eyes. We both know I don't think of Hayes as anything as pedestrian as *a crush*.

"I know we don't know each other super well yet, but as your roommate . . . as hopefully your friend, I don't want to see the same thing happen to you that . . ." She trails off, her gaze far away. Then she shakes herself out of it and leans onto the table, her chin jutted. "Bad things happen when you trust the wrong people, and Hayes is all sorts of wrong people."

"That's absurd," I snap back, glaring. "You saw him for, what, one second?"

"Don't give me that look," Adhira warns.

I give her an even saltier look.

She throws up her hands, sending a half-dozen gold bracelets jangling down her arm. "Besides, I should be angry at *you*."

"What? Why should you be mad at me?"

Adhira stares. Oh, right. That. Okay, so it wasn't exactly love at first sight between me and her mentors, but that's no reason to go after Hayes.

"I respect Dev and Tilda, and they're really helping me with my project. Even if *you* don't think it's going to save the world."

"I never said—"

"No, let me finish. I've had to deal with you judging me

enough about . . . everything." Adhira's knuckles press harder against the table, and she tilts closer.

"I've never—" I start again.

She silences me with a look, and my knees go all jelly.

"You don't have to say a thing for me to know you're *always* judging, Marnie. But the housing board saw something in our roommate questionnaires that said we'd be a good match, and that's got to *mean* something," she says, exasperation thinning the edges of her voice. I almost tell her the truth, but her blazing eyes meet mine, and I swallow my words. "I wanted you to meet my mentors because I like them and they've become a big part of my new life here, but you had to go all . . . all Mary Bennet on me."

Shock sucks the air right out of my lungs. So *that's* what she thinks of me. I'm the dowdy, lecture-prone sister from *Pride and Prejudice* no one likes.

"Sorry, forget it," Adhira mumbles.

Hidden under the table, I've got one hand fisted against my thigh.

"Sorry, but I won't just 'forget it.'" I lift my face to hers, defiant. "So I'm Mary? Good. She's about the only one who had any sense anyway."

My pulse throbs in my neck, heat crawling into my cheeks. I need her to leave. Now. Before she sees what her accusation is doing to me. "Did you need anything else?" I keep my voice as chilly as I can.

Adhira won't quite look at me as she says, "Dev and Tilda invited me to an underground recycled fashion show. I came back to ask if you wanted to join."

A rueful laugh crawls up my throat. "Yeah, no."

She pauses, her face contracted in a frown. "Are you sure? I don't want to leave you alone on your birthday."

I sit back hard against the booth and cross my arms. After a moment, Adhira shuffles away, and my big show of strength withers until I'm a mush of goo on the seat. They'll have to hire professional crime scene cleaners to get rid of me.

Mary Bennet.

She thinks I'm Mary Bennet. The sullen, forgotten sister. The *ugly* one who everyone wants to fade into the background entirely so they can get on with their happily ever after.

The accusation burrows, gnawing through my brain and exposing all the insecurities hiding there.

She's wrong. There's no way I'm Mary Bennet. I can't be, because there's no world in which Hayes would choose Mary, no possibility of Mary standing out in her own family, no future for Mary winning the Hunt Prize.

How could Adhira have been so mean? Okay, so I could have made a better first impression with her mentors, but was I truly so terrible as to merit the Mary bomb? Surely not. Right? Before I can stop myself, I grab Tilda's forgotten cocktail and gulp it down in one go. Would Mary Bennet do that? No, ma'am.

First lesson: an entire cocktail on an empty stomach does not a happy Marnie make.

Second lesson: there are some things even *Jane Eyre* can't fix. I know, I was just as surprised.

But after rereading the same paragraph a half-dozen times, I give up, click off my bedside lamp, and flop back into bed.

In the darkness, the brooding gray-orange of a nighttime city bleeds through my paned window and makes a patchwork of the wall beside me. Across the narrow space, the glow-in-the-dark arms of my desk clock show it's nearly weekday curfew. Great, so Adhira insulted my very being and doesn't have the decency to get back before curfew. It's highly irresponsible to stay out so late on a school night. Didn't she think of how it might disturb her roommate?

This is why I need a single room. I wouldn't be up tossing and turning, unable to even relax with one of my favorite books because my roommate may be fending off a murderer . . . or a drug fiend . . . or hippies who are into upcycled corduroy.

I said as much in my latest email to the PCA Housing Board, sent off an hour ago with our dorm RA, Ms. Johnson, copied. As I reminded them—*again*—Dad paid extra for a single. Discomfort wriggles through me. Dad didn't seem to remember he'd paid for that single when he helped me move in. I swallow the thought. The discomfort is probably the alcohol.

If I were in a single room, I'd be happily reading about a

taciturn older man who seduces the governess while his wife is locked in the attic. Or blissfully recalling my serendipitous meeting with Hayes earlier. Instead, I'm checking my phone for the millionth time. It's quarter to ten. Worry blooms in my chest, but I quash it with indignation. I'm up, and yet not reading or fantasizing about my first kiss with Hayes, because Adhira is being irresponsible. When she gets home, I'm going to—

The door handle squeaks, and I dive over onto my other side, facing the wall. The bed squeaks underneath me, long after I've frozen in place.

There's a creak and a click, and then our room goes still.

"Marnie?" Adhira hisses.

Grumble. Grumble. "What?"

"You're up?"

I sigh loudly and turn over, sitting up against my headboard. "I am now, I guess."

My bed sags at the edge, and I squint into the gloom to see her looking at me.

"I'm sorry your birthday was, you know . . ." Adhira sighs, and I nearly tell her it's okay. Anything to stop talking more about this whole *you're one of literature's famous wet rags* thing. Or from me having to acknowledge that my behavior might have earned the moniker tonight.

"I don't know why you want to be my friend," I say aloud before withering into dust. My god, I sound like a mutant. I sound like *Mary*. The truth about the roommate issue gathers behind my teeth. She deserves to know. And also, she should learn to stop putting so much stock in whatever magic she thinks the housing board used to pair us. It is seriously impractical to her future success in life.

In the shadows, the outline of Adhira's arm drifts toward mine, but she pulls back. "You want to know why? Because earlier, you checked out a book you knew I needed, even though I didn't ask you to."

"That's hardly a reason to declare someone a friend," I huff.

"No, but it's something. Look, I know we may not be what either of us . . . expected. As roommates, I mean. We both probably wanted someone, you know, *different*."

Okay, so I may have fired off a snippy email saying basically this, but I can't deny my vanity is bruised.

"But the thing is," Adhira says. "When you let your guard down, you're great. You're funny and smart and confident, if you'd get out of your own way."

That makes my mouth turn down. "Thanks, that's helpful. I need to stop trying, is what you're saying."

"No! It's just . . . you have a million excuses lined up to never go outside your very narrow comfort zone. No room for error, but no room for anything else either." Adhira's growing louder. In the orange gloom, her hands cast shadows over my face, her bracelets tinkling exclamation points. "I mean, think of the clothes thing. I'd love to design some stuff for you, but you won't even give me a chance."

I cough on a retort. She knows what I think of her little designs. The first month living together, Adhira did all these drawings of clothes she thought I'd like, but I shut that down. There's no reason to pretend I'm fashionable. I have more important things to do than worry about silly stuff like that.

"Well, maybe you should stop trying so hard," I shoot back. "You said it yourself: we don't mesh." There's a horrible note of petulance in my voice that makes me cringe.

In the shadows, Adhira pushes her hair over her shoulder and twists her hands together. "At home, I had all these friends, and then I . . . things changed. I've got to trust in something again, I've *got* to, and I'm choosing to trust in the housing board." She pauses for a second that stretches, and I wonder exactly what happened in Toronto to make her flee across the continent, but I'm pretty devoted to my anger right now, so I stay silent.

"Just because something's hard, that doesn't mean it's not worth it. I'm alone here in San Francisco, but I've got you. And I'm not going to let you talk yourself into thinking we can never be friends simply because we're different on the surface."

Adhira's words poke at the cracks in my armor. But I spackle them over and scowl at her. "You don't know anything about me."

She laughs at that, which makes me grimace. "Oh, yes, I do. I've met your family. You've got all those sisters and *that mother* and you think you've got to stand out from all that, find your . . . I don't know . . . *thing* to make yourself worthy."

"You're an only child," I say, reminding her she isn't the only one who's met the respective families. Adhira's mother is also a hugger. It was a traumatizing move-in day on the personal bubble front.

"Yeah, but I've got, like, forty-five cousins and all my aunties, and when I'd spend summers in India with my grandparents I'd feel lost and just, like, unsure of what I brought to the table."

Adhira sighs and reaches over the narrow space between our beds to flip on her desk lamp. Great, now she can see how fabulously well I'm taking all this. "When I was twelve, I decided I'd be the most Canadian girl ever and spent the entire summer trying to convince everyone I was intensely into hockey. And they all saw right through it. *That's* what I meant when I said you were like Mary Bennet. Whenever I'd watch that movie, I'd think that if Mary stopped trying so damn hard to achieve, like, this sister-obliterating greatness, she'd realize she was happier with *goodness*."

My hands are jerky when I snatch my comforter up tighter around my waist. Obviously, I should remind Adhira the *movie* was based on a masterpiece of a novel. Except . . .

What Adhira just said, about Mary trying to outshine her sisters and failing miserably . . . her words reverberate through me, echoing the thoughts that have plagued me ever since I can remember. That I'm not good enough. That my sisters are *great*, but I'm only tolerable.

No, not tolerable. Barely *tolerated*. That every time I open my mouth, others are simply waiting for me to be done. I can almost see it whenever I speak: the invisible eye roll, the droop of shoulders that *oh god, Marnie is going to lecture again.*

I wrap my arms around my chest and glare. "If you loved Toronto so much, you should have stayed there."

Adhira startles and sucks in a breath, and I'm certain for one awful second she's going to slap me. But then her shoulders sag and she shoves away from me. I don't react, not even when she punches her finger against the light switch and heaves herself into her bed. Her bed makes an L against mine, our headboards at right angles. I can't see her, but I hear every tiny movement, every muffled sniffle.

I hate Adhira in this moment. I hate that she's trying to be my friend. And I hate that she's dug down to expose my awful truth. I am Mary Bennet. The thought tears through me, wild and raw.

Everybody longs to be the Lizzy in their own life, the vivacious, witty beauty destined for greatness. No one wants to be Mary. Hell, even Mary didn't want to be Mary. The fact is: if Adhira's right, I'm not the protagonist in my own life.

If I ever want to find my rightful place in my family and stand on my own, I simply *cannot* be that person. And Hayes . . . even if he never chooses to love me, I want to be a person who *could* earn him.

I must change. I *have* to change.

FOUR

TRADITIONALLY, THERE ARE TWO TYPES of responses when one is faced with doom. One either faces and fights . . . or retreats.

I have chosen retreat. In the three days I've trudged through since the Bennet Birthday Boondoggle, I've uttered maybe ten words to Adhira—words like *are you done with that* and *no.* Even yesterday, when I scrubbed the bathroom clean even though it was Adhira's turn (it was definitely because it needed to be done and not because I was feeling bad and knew it was her least-favorite chore) and she said thank you when she returned from class, I shrugged and went back to my book. A book that was definitely *not Pride and Prejudice.* I have heroically locked away the Mary Bennet comparison into a dark, musty corner of my mind.

Adhira tentatively smiled and thanked me for cleaning the bathroom again this morning, and I grunted in reply. And now, on this smudgy, gray Friday morning, with nary a thought of Mary Bennet, I dress in my PCA uniform.

Uniforms aren't a daily requirement at Pacific Crest Academy, which disappoints me to no end. When Lindy attended PCA—back when I was an owl-eyed seven-year-old—students wore chic green plaid skirts, crisp white button-downs, and navy blazers with gold buttons. Gold buttons! I used to sneak into Lindy's room and try on her extra blazer, twisting in the mirror to admire the flash of the gold buttons.

But sometime between then and now, the required uniform has become an only-for-special-events uniform. Apparently it happened around the time Lia's father joined the board, when his older daughter, Desdemona, transferred to PCA.

That's right, the infamous Silicon Valley executive Casper Lawson named his daughters after doomed women in Shakespearean tragedies. That's got to say something about his psyche.

Also, that means I blame the demise of the uniform on Lia. Because, obviously. All roads (of blame) lead to Lia.

So back to the uniform; I'm getting a few sideways looks this Friday as I tromp to my dorm after morning block. But I'm too focused on watching where my clogs are going to pay too much attention.

This uniform makes me feel competent. Wearing it means I don't have to figure out a professional outfit for my Hunt Prize entry presentation. I'll be crisp and gold-buttoned when I meet with the committee in an hour to pitch my possible projects. We're technically allowed to prepare three separate pitches, though I know for a fact Lia only needed one, thanks to daddy. Whatever. Bully for her. I'll present all three, and the committee can choose their favorite. . . .

Or deny all three. If that happens, I'm done. Goodbye, Stanford. This is where my Mary Bennet-ness would *well, actually* me about the fact that I also haven't secured a mentor—a necessary requirement to competing for the Hunt Prize. But as I've established, Mary's been banished.

The impending meeting makes hot tar gurgle up my throat. Arms held tight around my books, I climb the stairs to the second floor and pause outside my door. Silence. Which is all fine and good, but also I was studying at Bardo last night and witnessed a spectacular breakup between our classmate Polly Osgoode and her boyfriend. There were thrown drinks and screaming; it was glorious. I kind of really want to gossip with Adhira about it, but see: awkward silence.

Moving quietly, I inch the door open and peek inside. The coast is clear . . . ish. Immediately, my eyes are drawn to a little orange-striped box on my desk. I know that box. That's a Piephoria box.

I drop my bag, because screw schoolwork when there's pie

to be had, and touch the outside corner of the box. Gently. Reverently. Maybe a bit drooly. Inside, a silky brown chocolate chess pie awaits.

A piece of torn notebook paper under the box reads:

> *Good luck with your presentation. I know you'll do great!*
> *—Adhira*
> *PS What do you think about calling it Bark Books?*

A thrill of joy arcs through me, and not because I'm about to make out with a slice of my favorite pie from my favorite pie place. Adhira didn't need to do this for me. I'm not sure I deserve a slice of gloopy, from-a-can cherry pie—the most disgusting of the pie varieties—let alone chocolate chess.

And yet . . . she did. The edge of my lips tug upward for a heartbeat, then I plop down at my desk and slice open the sticker holding the box shut. The first bite is what I imagine being seduced is like. The pie is practically complimenting the health of my hair and my straight teeth as it slides down my throat.

Side note: perhaps I should read novels written after 1940 or, you know, actually be pursued by a living human so I know what seduction entails. I doubt straightness of teeth comes up often.

I take three amazing bites of the pie, then push it back. Improvising, I cut out a little pennant using a bright yellow sticky note, attach it to an orphaned chopstick, and plunge it into the pie. Now a cheery flag proclaims, *Finish Me! (And thank you!)*

I maybe should have added an *I'm sorry about telling you to go back to Toronto*, but there isn't room.

Buoyed by kind deeds and chocolate—*piephoric*, some might say—I grab my project binder and head out to finally pitch my Hunt Prize.

"Down to the wire, Ms. Barnes," Headmaster Finch says by way of greeting. He meets me at the front steps of Alcott House and ushers me inside.

It's a stately stone Queen Anne, the original PCA building, and it smells like old books.

"I'm excited to pitch the committee," I tell him, projecting competence that I only partly feel. "I'd be honored to compete in the Hunt Prize."

Honored, and also daunted. Headmaster Finch leads the way through the hallowed halls of Alcott House, where old photographs of winners adorn the walls, looking down on me with expectation. The Hunt Prize was started a century ago by philanthropist Theodora Hunt, with the aim of connecting debutantes of PCA with causes they could champion as respectable (marriageable) society ladies. Today, it's open to any PCA senior and judged by a twenty-person panel of staff, PCA board members, and local Bay Area leaders. I'm pitching the selection committee just for entrance into the prize. No thinking what will happen if I don't even get to participate.

Headmaster Finch is known for his themed bow ties, and today's is maroon with gold lightning bolts. He glances at me. "Our fifth committee member is unfortunately out today, so Mr. Lawson will be voting for himself and the board."

Excuse me?

He pulls the conference room door open for me. "Please, take a seat."

My confidence gutters just as three heads turn to stare. Among them is Casper Lawson, who has apparently curated the same bored expression his daughter favors. He's definitely not one for themed bow ties, and instead is wearing the tech guy uniform of Patagonia vest over a checked button-down. He deigns to glance from his phone to me for only a second.

And he counts for two votes today. Great.

The room is quiet in that hazy sort of way that comes from thick wallpaper and thicker carpet. It just makes me horribly aware of how loud I'm breathing. I need an approved project and a mentor by November first, which is just six days away. Then I need to give up food and sleep to launch and make a splash at the fair in December, where only the highest-rated projects will get into the finals. Great. Perfect. Totally doable.

Seated at Headmaster Finch's right, a woman with a cotton candy fluff of orange hair leans forward. "What have you got for us, Ms. Barnes?"

What I've got is a whole lot of undigested pie about to come up.

"I have three options I'm excited about." *Lies. Dirty lies.*

Mr. Lawson, at the far end of the group, makes some sort of grunt of irritation but doesn't look up from his phone.

I fidget with the cuffs of my button-down, open my binder, and stand taller. I never actually took that offered seat. *Okay, Marnie. You can . . . possibly do this.*

"First . . ." I stop to clear the creaks from my voice. "I was thinking of a project to rehabilitate the natural shoreline of the Sacramento River just south of Vallejo."

A petite, ancient woman in enormous black-framed glasses next to Lady Orange Hair tilts her chin. "Didn't your sister do something similar?" Great, so this woman shares the memory and skin elasticity of an elephant.

Headmaster Finch's gaze is sharp as he regards me. "Yes, her work not only won her the Hunt Prize but led to the expansion of the National Estuarine Research Reserve in the bay."

She also made me wear horribly uncomfortable contacts with my bridesmaid dress so as not to ruin her wedding photos, so let's not jump straight to the deification of Lindy Barnes-Drake just yet.

"Well, my project would be significantly different," I begin, flipping to a yellow tab in the binder. They've buffed this dumb table to a mirror shine, so I can practically see the flop sweat gathering on my upper lip. Headmaster Finch shifts in his chair.

Lady Orange sits back. "She looked fantastic at the Oscars. I hosted a watch party to support her."

"I, for one," warbles the Ancient One, "think her otter

- 41 -

documentary was far and above the best of the documentaries."

"Yes," I manage, trying to insert myself back into the conversation. "We were all disappointed when she lost. But she's been down in Houston shooting a new doc."

That perks them up.

"Oh, what is it?" the old lady asks.

"Perhaps we should get back to Marnie's project," Headmaster Finch cuts in.

Lady Orange actually groans. I'm losing the room. Casper Lawson taps away at his phone, and the Ancient One slowly cleans her glasses. Make that, already lost it. My brain is in full meltdown, screeching for me to change the subject, but when I fumble for a new tab—any tab—the gold buttons on my blazer snag the binder's edge and topple it to the carpet. Gold buttons, how could you betray me like this?

"Anyway, the river rehab was just my first idea," I shout up to them from under the table. My clammy hands can't quite get a grasp on my binder, and it's taking every ounce of determination not to curl up under here and shrivel away. Finally, I toss the binder back up to the table and crash into a seat. The clock on the wall snickers at me.

"I've also done research into a homeless buddy system. You know, like kids who have accountabit—accoob"—*pause, breathe*—"accountabilli-buddies," I finally manage.

Casper smirks. "You'd have to be able to pronounce it first."

My cheeks pulse with heat. You know what I can pronounce?

That Casper Lawson is a plague on humanity.

Desperation claws at my back, so I shove my shoulder blades down and squash it. The clock behind Headmaster Finch shows that exactly five minutes have passed since I walked in here, yet already my first two ideas have been shot down. This is my last chance to show Mom and Dad I'm as good as Lindy. That I'm *better*. That I can get into Stanford just like her.

I flip to my final tab and steel my nerves. "I intern at the downtown library, where they use a bookmobile for outreach events. My intern advisor there, Daniel Wong, gave me the green light to pursue a program to bring books to animal shelters."

Lady Orange looks up at that. "And do what, exactly?"

"Do the dogs need to learn how to read?" Mr. Lawson drawls, finally joining the conversation. *Welcome, Mr. Lawson, now please leave.*

"Obviously the dogs can't read. I mean, they can learn a huge variety of commands and have a powerful ability to sense emotions in humans, which I'd argue is a sort of reading. There was this study—"

The Ancient One cuts me off. "Ms. Barnes, we know the dogs wouldn't be reading."

"Right. Of course. The project would be for children. And, um, dogs."

She nods for me to continue, but I'm too flustered to remember the next part of my pitch. The binder's protector sheets are slick under my fingers and the words are as jumbled on the page as they are in my head, but I take a deep breath and try to ignore the impatient eyes on me. I drop one hand to my side and dig nails into my palm, then look up again.

"I meant to say, the program would serve two functions and benefit both the kids and the dogs. The children would practice reading to the animals, and the shelter would run an adoption event for the dogs."

Lady Orange smiles, and Headmaster Finch nods thoughtfully. "Interesting," he begins. "Do you have any research to show reading to the dogs would be helpful for the—"

"Nope," Mr. Lawson snorts, with all the sensitivity of a ham-fisted narcissist.

"Excuse me?" Headmaster Finch says. By his clipped tone, it wasn't a question.

Mr. Lawson finally looks at me. "Sorry, Ms. Barnes, but the selection committee made an agreement not to approve any animal-related projects after a student's Corgis for the Congo project went . . . poorly."

"But I'm not sending dogs anywhere," I splutter, hysteria starting to grab hold of my heart. "I mean, unless they're adopted. Then they'll be going home."

"I don't care if every single stray in the Bay Area is adopted."

Blackness rings my vision, and I'm not sure I remember how to breathe. Why is Mr. Lawson being so awful to me? He's an über-rich Silicon Valley guy who's here because he wants his name on the science building. What does he get for being mean? Is this all because of the phone incident with Lia? This is my last viable project idea. I've *got* to make this work. I scan the bullet points on the page before me, but there's nothing about contending with an entitled monster who once posed for a *Wired* cover story titled "The Law Returns to Silicon Valley" wearing a sheriff's badge and cowboy hat.

"I've already got a shelter to partner with," I blurt out, remembering the near-forgotten coaster scrawled with a name. "I promise, there'll be no dogs harmed. This will help kids *and* dogs, and I think it could be a really great project."

Mr. Lawson is buried back in his phone, like my pitch and I are beneath him, but the other three adults are nodding, even smiling.

"What are you calling it?" the Ancient One asks.

I think of Adhira's suggestion, of her gesture of pie, and I say, "Bark Books."

Headmaster Finch sits back in his leather chair and regards me. "I like it, Ms. Barnes. It's unique and practical. Shall we vote?"

My stomach is voting to evacuate my body, and I grip the edge of the table.

"All in favor?"

My lungs shrivel to raisins, but three hands rise and air whooshes back in. Casper Lawson voted no for himself and the board. But his noes weren't enough. I'm in. I'm officially competing in the Hunt Prize. Goose bumps race down my arms and legs.

"Congratulations, Ms. Barnes. Your project is approved. Have you secured a mentor?"

"Um," I squeak.

The Ancient One pipes up. "It's a shame you can't ask your sister. I'm sure she'll be helping you behind the scenes, but she won the prize too recently to be your school-sponsored mentor."

Ha. Like Lindy would take time out of saving the world to help me with a school project.

"Are we about done here?" Mr. Lawson drawls.

The Ancient One flares her nostrils so decisively her giant glasses jostle. I don't want to jump to conclusions here, but I think I love this woman immensely.

Headmaster Finch leans back and steeples his fingers. "You're close to the deadline. Have you considered asking your father, Marnie?"

A muscle twitches in my eye. Lindy had three mentors vying for her project, and none of them were relatives. Dad has been asked a few times to be a Hunt Prize judge but has always declined. I once heard him tell Mom he "doesn't play that game anymore." Which was a real blow to Mom, who loves nothing more than a game of societal Chutes and Ladders.

I don't want to go begging my father. The thought of it makes my insides go squigglier than they already are. "I'll figure it out."

A minute later, I stumble out of Alcott House into a watery afternoon, the sky overhead dithering between rain or shine. My legs sting with pins and needles, making the ground squishy and disconnected. I walk in a daze, and when I look up, the library is before me. A sigh whispers up my throat and threads past my teeth. I can almost feel my tension start to fall away at the thought of sitting in my favorite nook with a book.

Yet just as I approach the big oak doors, Lia Lawson stalks out.

"Dogs, huh?"

I don't have any energy for Lia right now. "What?"

Lia lifts her phone and shakes it, flashing a shark smile. "Your Hunt Prize project. Is that why you're in that dumb uniform, to impress the selection committee?" Even at her meanest, she sounds perpetually bored, her words crackling away to nothing and full of wide-open, lazy vowels.

She smirks at me. "Daddy got my project approved more than a month ago. Tennis lessons for low-income kids. Daddy says it's definitely going to win."

"Okay," I say, utterly exhausted. I didn't realize how much time I'd been pouring into this pitch. And I still need to complete my English essay. I don't have it in me to defend my idea again to Lia.

Lia shrugs and flounces by me, but the sound of her heel grinding against the flagstone as she turns makes me shiver with distaste.

"You know, I'm surprised you want to work with dogs.

You've always struck me as a crazy cat lady."

Lia turns and stalks off toward Hawthorne Hall before I can say anything, not that I had much of a comeback. I mean, she's not wrong. I walk right up to the stone arch encasing the doors and press my forehead to it. It's cool against my skin, solid where I feel so very mushy. I stand like that for a long time, the sky spitting tiny, insincere droplets of rain down on my neck and shoulders. Finally, I sigh and stand tall.

I should be happy, proud. My project has been approved! (Pending mentor agreement, a Mary-sounding voice nags.) Yet the thought of metaphorically tap dancing onstage and impressing another adult right now—even if it's only Dad—scoops out any last energy and throws it in the bin.

My hand is on the door, almost into the safety of the library, when there's a terrible screech of metal on metal, a crunch of gravel, and then a car honks.

A car honks, like, *right* behind me.

FIVE

THERE IS A CAR ON the upper lawn of Pacific Crest Academy.
Four wheels straddle the gravel walkway in front of Bierce
Library, like the driver didn't notice the "road" had suddenly
narrowed. Those four tires sink into the soft grass, leaving a
trail of churned tread marks leading from the school's pedestrian Hawthorne Gate.

Words fail me. One quick blink, but the car is still there.
Still parked, right in front of me. Almost like it's there for
me. . . .

And that's when I recognize the car. And the driver. Words
aren't simply failing me. They've ceased to hold any meaning.

There's a mechanical whir as the BMW's window rolls
down. I scurry closer and somehow splutter past my incredulity,

"Lola? Aren't you supposed to be in Paris?"

And I mean the *ooh la la* Paris, not the one in Texas.

My sixteen-year-old sister ignores the question. She shoves sunglasses up into her faded pink hair, and they flash off the reflection of my gold-buttoned blazer. "I'm supposed to drag you up to Lindy's thing."

My heart tries to cliff dive out of my chest. Lindy's thing. As in, where Hayes will be. My fingertips fizz, then fizzle. *How* could I forget a potential Hayes interaction? Man, the Hunt Prize is really screwing with my priorities.

"Can I change first?" A school uniform is hardly the thing one wears if one is trying to sort-of woo an older man. Not that I'm doing that. He's engaged. I just . . . I mean, maybe he'll notice I'm a mature eighteen-year-old now and realize Sara Nguyen isn't for him. We'd wait at least six months to announce our intentions, obviously, so as not to seem improper.

"Why do you need to change?" Lola barks the question, snagging my daydream at the edges and yanking it out from under me.

"Because Hayes" is not a good answer. Neither is "because Hayes would never fall for Mary Bennet." Nor is "because I'm in love with our family friend." Instead, I settle for a shrug.

Lola rolls her eyes. "Don't be difficult, Mar. It's not like anyone is going to think *you're* going for sexy schoolgirl. Just get in."

Okay, let's weigh my options *and ignore the fact that my sister basically said I'm incapable of being alluring.* I could pretend none of this happened and walk away. Or I could get in the car with a person who ran over a goose her first time behind the wheel and failed her driver's test three times.

Lola flops her forehead against the steering wheel, a long, bleating honk like so many dying geese issuing from the car. I jerk my gaze around the courtyard. Empty, thank every god who ever existed. Maybe procrastinating until four on the very last Friday for Hunt Prize presentations was a small miracle. Most students are off campus or gone for the weekend. I scurry around the hood and yank open the passenger door, pointedly ignoring the fresh gouges in the black paint. Without a word—and before I can buckle in and cross myself for divine protection—Lola throws the car into drive and wheels around the lawn toward the gate.

"This isn't actually a—"

There's a shrill metal-on-metal screech, then she pops through the gate to the sidewalk. Lola puts on her blinker for reasons that will remain a mystery until the end of days and swerves into traffic, bumping down the curb with another ominous screech from the undercarriage.

"What?" Lola stares at me. One hand fiddles with the radio and the other untangles her sunglasses from her hair.

"Eyes on the road," I squeak.

Lola rolls her eyes again—she's a champion eye-roller—but turns back to the road, slamming on the brakes just in time to avoid a fender-bender. And I suffer the first of many heart episodes. Luckily, once she gets us onto Highway 101 in the forested Presidio, the only thing I have to worry about is running headlong into a tree.

"Where's Kat?" I venture once we're safely across the Golden Gate Bridge headed north. Lola and Kat relish the whole "twin" thing, so it sits a bit odd to be alone with Lola. Honestly, it's weird to be alone with any of my sisters, whether they're older or younger.

Lola scowls. "She had some debate club thing in Petaluma, so she's coming with Joss."

"Debate?" Kat and Lola are only eighteen months younger than me, but the list of things we have in common begins and ends with DNA. The last I knew, Kat had been asked to leave the Crenshaw Day School production of *My Fair Lady* for giggling too much. I can't imagine her interested in presenting thoughtful, logical arguments for fun.

Lola's scowl only deepens. "Yeah, Kat joined the nerd squad while I was away." She cuts a glance my way and smirks. "Looks like you're not the only Barnes desperate to prove you're the smart one."

"You're smart, Lola. If you applied yourself. I could help you come up with a study schedule." Under the ever-changing hair, flair for drama, and disaffected attitude, my little sister could probably be smart . . . ish.

Something between a snort and a groan hisses out of Lola's

mouth. "Nice try, Mar. No, I'm the screw-up and everyone knows it."

I press my lips together and stare ahead, unsure what to say. And then too long passes for anything I say to seem genuine. The traffic of San Francisco has melted away, leaving the road curving and empty.

The whole reason Lola was shipped off to France was because of boy drama (because, of course). He was a senior to her sophomore, and he was also definitely dating one of Lola's popular friends. They were caught, there were pictures, and it all led to the social media page Lola Barnes Is a Thot. That's how she and Kat—a Lola loyalist—ended up sitting with me at lunch last spring when it all went down. "It" being a tray of cafeteria chili onto Lola's head and then a screaming match between Lola, her former friends, and the dumb boy. Somehow *I* got pulled into the principal's office along with the rest of the hormonal idiots and was given a three-day suspension for fighting when all I was trying to do was eat my turkey sandwich and read *War and Peace* in, you know, peace. The Russians have nothing on high school drama.

The turmoil was partly how I convinced Mom and Dad I should transfer to PCA. As for Lola, France was supposed to be her fresh start. But if she's home seven months early . . .

I squeeze my hands between my knees and peek at Lola. She's in worn gray jeans and a slouchy black tee that looks like it lost a fight with a rabid raccoon. There are gold spikes dangling from her ears, the pointed ends painted black.

"How was France?"

Lola shrugs. "Very French. I ate a bunch of disgusting food. Like snails and shit. *Le directeur* at the awful school completely disregarded my dietary needs."

Lola's dietary needs usually consist of Taco Bell Party Packs and enough Diet Coke to quench a nation's collective thirst.

"Do you want to tell me what—?"

"No, Marnie," Lola says forcefully. The speedometer inches higher with her words. "I don't want to talk about France."

We lapse into the sort of comforting silence usually reserved for opposing political factions and don't speak another word the rest of the drive. After a few minutes, I pull out my dog-eared copy of *Jane Eyre* and ignore Lola's grumble.

At a lonesome stretch of Highway 1, we turn west toward Bolinas. The town clings to the edge of the Point Reyes shore, desolate in a way that is deliberate. A few years ago, there was a travel guide that tried to make a big splash about Bolinas, and the townspeople responded by taking down all road signs pointing their way.

The fog creeps through the dense trees hugging the road, painting the landscape in blue shadows. If I wasn't hurtling headlong toward my family with an erratic sister behind the wheel, I'd almost long to lose myself in the bleak romance of the trees. (And then very romantically be found by a strapping man riding a horse. Does Hayes ride horses? I'll have to ascertain.)

Lola cranks the wheel and veers off the main road outside of town toward a long drive. On either side, gnarled cypress trees stand sentinel. Lindy and Will live in a giant old beach house of weathered wood they call The Shack. Though perhaps they don't quite know the definition of a "shack," seeing as *Town & Country* featured their extensive renovations with six pages of glossy photos and an interview some would call self-indulgent. It's certainly the fanciest shack that ever was.

Through the trees, The Shack appears in a field of heather and thistle, the ocean in a mood behind it. Lola slows the closer we get to the house. There are three vehicles already parked in the circular drive.

Lola's knuckles where she grips the steering wheel pop white, and she sighs heavily as she turns the car off. "Ready for a wonderful evening hearing how we can never stack up to our perfect older sisters?"

We share a look—deeper than the usual careless glance or angry glare. A look of sisterly solidarity. I almost smile. Almost reach for her.

Then she slides from the car and says, "At least you're dressed like a pompous idiot, so Mom'll give me a break."

Okay then.

SIX

THE MINIVAN IN FRONT OF us has a stick-figure family on the back window—two moms and three little kids—so my oldest sister, Joss, is already here with her wife and the triplets. The Tesla in front of that is Dad's . . . but the Range Rover in front of that . . .

My stomach flops. Is Hayes already here? I smooth my hands down my pleated plaid skirt and peek in the side mirror. No weird zits, no crusts of pie on my lips. "Is that Hayes's new SUV?" I say casually to Lola as I try to rub life into my limp hair.

She grimaces. "Gross, Mar. Do you still have a crush on him?"

"What? No! I never—" My voice issues thin and high, and

my cheeks pulse with heat. I crane my neck to make sure no one can hear Lola. She stalks closer and stops in front of me.

"He moved in next door to us when you still picked your nose. Don't be weird."

"I never picked my nose, Lola." *I definitely did.* "And I'm not being weird. I simply wondered. Last I knew, he had that sports car."

Fact: it was a Porsche Boxster in the paint color Speed Yellow with an MSRP of $68,600. Not that I looked it up or anything.

Lola glares at me—there's the sisterly look I know so well—but before she can insult me further, the front door opens.

"Girls!"

Both of us go still, though my stomach is currently trying to sidestep out of my body. Sara Nguyen, Hayes's fiancée, grins wide at us and waves.

Here's the thing, the horrible thing. Sara is great. She and Lindy have been friends since elementary school, when our parents transferred Lindy and Joss to Crenshaw Day. So the fact that I've secretly been in love with Hayes for five years? Okay, yeah, they didn't start dating until Hayes's final year at Stanford, so I got my claim in first. But still. I had migraines when they got engaged in August. I'll need to retire to a dark room for a week after their wedding in February. My fingers drift up to my half-moon scar and trace the edges, finding comfort in the physical manifestation of what binds me to Hayes.

I mean, it's all innocent fantasy, right? To love him unrequited like a heroine in my favorite novels, pining for him but never winning him. There's something so romantic about it all. But that doesn't mean I actually expect to *date* Hayworth Wellesley, Flawless Specimen.

Ah, but there's a dark knot of truth hidden inside me: I don't know if I'd say no. If Hayes cornered me tonight and tried to kiss me, I don't know if I'd walk away from that.

My stomach sours in a cocktail of guilt and envy and the littlest bit of hatred every time I see Sara, and today is no exception. Lola and I schlep toward the door and give Sara hugs and cheek kisses just as the triplets—my two nephews and niece—burst past and race toward feral freedom. They bound toward Lola, howling like a pack of wild dogs and drawing a genuine smile from her. Joss and Edie favor something called free-range parenting, which I thought was reserved only for chickens.

"Hi, hi, hi!" Joss calls as I trip my way inside. She's bent over the marble countertop in The Shack's enormous kitchen and doesn't look up at us, instead waving a hand in our direction. The artisanal lightbulbs overhead turn the wispy white-blond hair escaping her bun into a halo. It's apt, seeing as Joss's main thrust in life is to be as angelic as possible. Currently, she's using tweezers to apply gold leaf to mini-tarts. See, *angelic*.

"Ooh, are those from the bakery?" I ask. Edie owns a famous bakery north of here called Sonoma Sugared. Joss stays home since the triplets were born, but she's usually around the bakery or mastering some new craft.

Joss straightens and balks as she finally looks up at me. "Marnie. We weren't expecting you."

I rub the end of my nose in answer. You know what's a spectacular feeling? Uncertainty that you're welcome at your family's get-together. Especially when it seems like Barnes (Original Recipe) sometimes forgets to make room for Barnes (New Edition).

Joss is eleven years older than me, so sometimes she feels more like an aunt than a sister. And right now, she feels a bit like a bouncer. Mom and Dad had Joss and Lindy—the inverse to sweetness-and-light Joss—when they were really young. *Young and in love and too dumb to care for success* is how Mom explains it. Then Dad's first tech company, Invigor, made a metric crap-ton of money (technical term), and Mom quit her job as a pharmacist to become the Gala Queen of Silicon Valley. Joss and Lindy were already eleven and nine, respectively, but Mom and Dad had me, then Lola and Kat in quick succession. I don't know if it's because Mom wanted more kids or because she was bored and suddenly very rich.

"Lindy and Will are out back on the deck with Dad, and Kat is here somewhere," Joss says, her hands a flurry of movement as she plates the mini-tarts. "Edie, darling, did you see Marnie's here?"

Lola charges through the door and lets her leather bag drop off her shoulder. "I'm here, too, you know."

Edie Rivera turns from where she's been arranging a

rainbow of macarons and shares a look with Joss—the sort of unspoken communique only partners seem to share—and pulls a grin a half second too late. Edie's hair is short and artfully ruffled, and she always wears black, winged eyeliner that accentuates her dark brown eyes. The one time I tried to make eyeliner wing out, I poked myself in the eye so violently I had to go to the optometrist for an eye patch. Which, let me tell you, glasses *and* an eye patch don't make a great first impression your freshman year of high school.

Lola picks at her peeling nail polish. "Don't know why you're losing your mind about Marnie."

"Because," Joss says, smiling beatifically at Lola, "it's not every day your little sister turns eighteen."

Warmth fills my chest at that. Then it warms even more to see Edie hustle over to the fridge. "We were going to send this home with your parents to drop off for you, but since you're here . . ."

Yes? I lean forward, expectant. She used to make this amazing lemon cupcake with a candied lemon rind on top that literally tasted like dreams. And I say that as someone who knows the definition of literally.

"Oh, happy birthday," Lola says with a note of distraction, bringing me down a notch. "Why didn't you come home to celebrate?"

"I was too busy with—"

"School," Lola finishes for me. "Yeah, we all know."

Edie produces the signature Sonoma Sugared matte black box from the fridge and slides it across the marble slab to me. "Happy birthday, Mar."

I trace the edge of the box and grin down at lemon perfection. "Thanks, Edie! You even took it out of retirement for me."

Joss slips her arm through Edie's elbow and smiles. "You're worth it."

Lola grumps, and Joss shushes her, but I'm lost in my lemon lust. Honestly, it's not just the cupcake. No one but Mom and Dad ever remembers my birthday, so the fact that Edie specially made my very favorite cupcake, it means a lot. Especially since Mom would take one look at this delicious present and pointedly stare at my hips, which are getting no favors from my heavily pleated skirt.

Joss keeps chatting, but I don't quite hear until she says Mom's name. My gaze lifts from the cupcake. Where *is* Mom? She's usually stationed in the living room, with a white wine spritzer in hand.

"Is she not here?" I probably sound too hopeful.

Joss and Edie share another look. "The kids were a bit spirited earlier, so Mom went to lie down."

Spirited is one way to put it. Behind Joss in the living room, Jonah, Theo, and Elle are scaling the stone fireplace like orcs attacking Minas Tirith.

"Is anyone else coming?" I ask, the picture of nonchalance. *Nice job, me.*

Out of thin air, Sara leans against the counter next to me, and I startle with guilt. She sighs, and the lights glint off her giant engagement ring and her glossy black hair in equal adoration. I feel like curdled milk in comparison. "It's only us. Poor Hayes has been chained to the office for the last week. His boss expects so much of him."

Obviously, I detest his boss for working my beloved so hard.

"He wanted to come tonight," she continues. She smiles softly at me and squeezes my hand. "He considers you family." My hand jerks. I don't want him to consider me family, unless he means "by marriage." Sara, though, doesn't seem to notice. "Honestly, I've barely seen him lately. He's working on securing financing for some new app. It's almost like . . ." She trails off and shrugs.

But I'm suddenly on high alert. Maybe Sara and Hayes are on the outs. She's three years older than him; what can they possibly have in common? I mean, that'd be awful and everything, and, okay, she's gorgeous and accomplished and shockingly young to be the director of a national youth arts nonprofit by age twenty-seven, but maybe Hayes has realized he needs someone more . . . me.

Sara waves a hand and taps the cover of my Hunt Prize binder sitting on the counter. I schlepped it in with my bag, since Lola's car is *this close* to being declared a biohazard. "Oh, Lindy said you're going for the Hunt Prize. What project are you pursuing?"

I mutter something noncommittal about reading dogs, then

make a big show of opening the box to reveal the cupcake. And honestly, that first wafting scent of lemon makes me forget everything else. The whipped frosting is featherlight and has a sheen of iridescent sugar coating the top. Two delicate curls of candied lemon rind swirl atop the frosting like a little neon welcome sign.

I've got the cupcake in my hands, nearly to my mouth . . . when someone shrieks. The cupcake shivers out of my hand and plops back to the box.

"The lights, Joss," Mom cries from down the hall. "Dim the lights."

Lola rolls her eyes, then turns down the kitchen lights, leaving us in the diffuse twilight slanting in from the peaked wall of windows facing the ocean.

Mom stumbles from the hallway holding her head. She pinches the bridge of her nose and plucks a green bottle of Perrier from the fridge. The air in the room zaps with tension, uncertainty for whatever mood Julia Barnes has brought with her.

My mother is a lottery winner cautionary tale. Today is a wonderful example: she's dressed in head-to-toe cherry red, each article of clothing emblazoned with the word *Gucci* (including her exposed bra straps). Her long hair is highlighted bleached blond to within an inch of its life, and her lips are pink, puffy slugs—too fat and shiny to do much more than lounge there.

"Sorry you're unwell, Mom," Joss says, actually sounding genuine. She's the only one of us who seems to take Mom's many lamentations seriously. "But I promise, we've got a surprise planned that'll make you really pleased."

Mom sips the sparkling water. "As long as it's not food. I'm still so nauseous." She presses long fingernails—also red—to her chest.

"Actually, you mean nauseated," I say. Which, hello there, Mary Bennet.

Mom's knife-sharp, dark brown eyes find mine. "That cupcake will go straight to your hips," she announces, letting a long, judgmental gaze linger on my wide skirt.

"Mom!" Joss protests.

"Oh, don't be like that, Joss, I'm teasing her. You have no sense of humor."

Neither does Mom.

And right now, neither do I. Maybe I should gather my cupcake and hitchhike home.

Yet before I get a chance to stash the cupcake in my bag, the glass doors slide open and Dad walks in from the back deck with Lindy and Will. My older sister married Will Drake a little over a year ago, and to Mom's eternal disappointment, they kept it simple. Probably because Will, some Silicon Valley golden boy, seems to loathe three-quarters of those he meets. I can't imagine his guest list was super deep (I say with all kindness, considering a fictional redheaded orphan is one of my best friends). Either way, Will is mostly sullen around us Barneses.

But right now, he's practically beaming. His cheeks dimple from trying to hold back a smile. Next to him, Lindy, too, is grinning. One corner quirks up higher than the other. It's Dad's smile. She's *Dad's* daughter, from her square chin to her dark hair. That has always gnawed at me, that Lindy is the most like Dad, yet I am a copy of Mom. My dark blond hair is her natural color, and my brown eyes match hers. Even my tendency to be hippy is thanks to her genes.

I've always wondered if that's why Dad is closer to Lindy than me. Maybe if I *did* ask him to mentor me for the Hunt Prize, he'd see how much we have in common. We'd develop those little in-jokes like he has with Lindy and share interesting articles. I could ask him to mentor me, I could . . . if the mere thought of asking him didn't pinch like failure, and if he wasn't currently smiling at Lindy with such soppy affection.

No, he'll always choose Lindy over me. She's excelled at everything she's ever tried—from the Hunt Prize to her documentaries to that fawning *Town & Country* piece where she casually dropped the word *solipsism* and I had to look it up.

She's perfect and I'm . . .

Gnawing jealousy snarls and sinks teeth into the back of my neck. I'm living inside a story where my sister is the protagonist, the girl who gets it all. I have to concentrate not to let this bitter taste at the back of my throat overwhelm me.

"Dad." I cross the space, trying to get his attention. He'll look up from Lindy and focus on me. I'll ask him to be my mentor right now, and he'll say yes.

Kat emerges from the den, glances up from the phone in her hands, and frowns at me. "What are you doing here?"

I ignore her. Yes, yes, no one considered Marnie would join the family dinner. "Dad," I say again, urgently now. He still doesn't look at me.

He's staring at his favored daughter, then pressing a kiss into her hair. I stop, suddenly unsure. Lindy's eyes are bright, her fingers caught up with Will's.

"We're having a baby," Lindy announces, then starts laughing and crying at the same time.

The room erupts in movement and congratulations, but I'm frozen.

"Oh, thank the Lord," Mom yells. "About time!"

Will shakes his head, but Lindy laughs. "Oh, we know, Mom. Your last birthday card to me simply said, 'Your ovaries are drying up.'"

"I would never write something like that," Mom says.

She definitely would.

Mom flaps her hand and totters over to Lindy, grabbing her around the neck in a crushing hug before hauling Will into the embrace too. He's stiff, but even I can't miss the joy in his dark eyes.

Among the hugs, Lola slips past the group—even Kat— and out onto the back deck. I shuffle back and forth on my feet. "Dad," I try one last time. His eyes take a moment to find mine. "Can I talk to you for a minute?"

Dad's got his arm around Will's shoulders, and Joss is talking about something called hypnobirth, and Mom keeps grabbing Lindy's shirt to see if her stomach is protruding yet. It is, slightly. That gives me pause. I've never considered Lindy the maternal type.

"What do you need, Marnie?" He doesn't leave the group.

I take a step away from my family. "I wanted to ask you about the Hunt Prize."

Dad looks back to Lindy, then to me. "Come celebrate with your sister first."

"Yeah." But I don't. I follow Lola out onto the deck.

She's leaning against the deck railing, looking over the cliff's edge to the tumble and churn of the tide against the rocks below. The evening gathers gray around us, but my little sister's profile cuts through the fog. Then—surprise of surprises—she sniffles and rubs roughly at her cheeks.

"Can you go back inside, please? I'm not up for one of your Marnie lectures right now." Lola's voice is thick, and she won't look at me.

I've never seen Lola like this. She screams and rages and shrieks. But this . . . this quiet sadness . . . it's something I understand too intimately. I cross the deck, then hesitate, my fingertips nearly brushing her shoulder.

I turn away and lean against the railing next to her. "We'll just brood in silence."

Lola flicks hard at another tear and faces me. "I'm embarrassed."

I don't look at her. "About what?"

"About what? Seriously? I was supposed to come swanning back home after nine months abroad all mature and amazing, and instead I hated it. Like, every second of it."

A strangled groan whines up Lola's throat. "And what do I come home to? You're, like, a genius at your new school; Kat didn't want to skip with me today because she was hanging out with her new friends; and our perfect older sister is having a perfect baby. It sucks."

She's silent for a long time, long enough that I fill the void with something very, very dumb.

"Would a genius be in love with an engaged man?" I say it toward the sea, but Lola snatches the confession off the wind.

"Holy shit, in love? With *Hayes?*" She stands taller, and I shiver with instant regret. "What are flesh-and-blood men to the perfection of books?"

I make a *pshhh* sound, but, well, I did once say that exact thing to Lola and Kat. In my defense, they were going on about some guy with a brick for a brain. Lola is still eyeing me.

"He saved my life, Lo. He threw himself into danger for *me*. That bonds two people together in a way that can never be undone."

Lola scrunches one side of her face. "Um, that is not how I remember it."

"You weren't even there."

"I definitely was. Don't you remember? Mom made Joss and Lindy take all of us. And all I remember is Hayes looking a total fool trying to impress some girls with his boogie board, but now you're saying he, like, saved your life?"

Her words butt up against my memories, but they don't match. I can picture it so clearly . . . me caught in the riptide, frantic . . . Hayes rushing to my aid, so desperate to save me he cracked my skull. . . .

Lola rolls her eyes. "Okay, believe whatever you want. He's also *Hayes*. I love him too. *Not like that*"—she adds hastily, palms toward me—"but he's, like, one hundred percent Silicon Valley schmooze."

My fingers dig into the wood railing. "No, he's not. He's thoughtful and kind. You just don't know him."

Usually, this is where Lola would get into her fighting stance. If there were a glass nearby, she'd grab it in case she needed to throw a drink in my face. Instead, she chews on her lip, then asks, "What will you do?"

"Stand up dramatically at their wedding and object?"

Lola honest-to-god gasps.

"Come on. I'd never do that. I'll probably settle with sulking in the corner and ruining all their wedding photos. Take that, perfect union."

A gust of wind tugs at Lola's powder-pink hair, and she shoves it out of her eyes. I've judged her harshly for so many years—for the tantrums and demands and brash belief that she deserves a spotlight—but maybe we can start over. She didn't get the chance in France, but *I* can give her a new chance.

Behind us, the glass door slides open, and Kat calls out to us. "What are you two hiding out here for?"

"Oh, the debate queen appears," Lola says. Kat and Lola are fraternal twins, and though they look very similar, Lola's lips are thinner, her chin sharper. And now her short pink hair is at odds with Kat's long blond waves.

"Shut up, Lo."

Lola laughs and crosses to her twin. "Did you know the capital of Massachusetts?"

Kat pokes Lola's arm. "I do know it, but that's not what debate club is about. Really, why are you out here?"

Lola shrugs, then grins at me, her eyes glinting. "Oh, Marnie just totally cheered me up! She is *way* more pathetic than I am."

The warmth in my chest is drenched in cold fog. Why did I think it could be different, that *I* could be different? The twins flounce back inside, and I'm left staring. Heat presses behind my eyes, and I duck my chin when I slip back inside. Dad is in the living room, leaning against the back of the couch and watching Lindy and Will.

"Dad, can I talk to you now?"

"Hm?" His gaze drifts to me.

"Tom!" Mom calls from the kitchen. "Tom, come help!"

"Dad, I just have a quick question." I'm desperate. I can feel it in my bones.

"Tom! The tarts!"

Dad rubs a hand down his jaw. "Sorry, Marnie. Come find me in a bit."

I don't know what else to do, so I follow him into the kitchen. Where only a smear of frosting and smattering of crumbs mark the place where my birthday cupcake sat.

"Where'd my cupcake go?" I ask aloud to no one in particular.

Mom tuts. "I gave it to the triplets. Why, did you want it?"

As she says it, the kids sprint by with the remnants of lemon cake littering their cheeks.

I hate that I'm upset by this. I hate how my throat grows tight and my eyes sting. "Mom, that was from Joss and Edie for my birthday."

Mom arches one eyebrow. "Oh, so now we're allowed to publicly celebrate your birthday? When I tried to throw you a party, you had a fit."

She pats my cheek—harder than a loving tap—and sets my blood boiling. "Be a good girl and grab the party favors, will you? Joss was a total beast and knew about the baby, so she made these adorable gender reveal poppers just for me. You know how disappointed I was that she kept the triplets' gender a secret."

"Gender is a construct. You actually want to know the sex of the baby."

Mom's shiny lips tighten at the corners. "Please don't be difficult, darling."

No words can make it past my clenched jaw, and it wouldn't

matter if they could. Mom flits away, already stream-of-consciousness talking about everything Lindy and Will need to do to prepare for the baby.

Before me, my family is all laughter and chatter. My family . . . who I'm not sure would notice if I wasn't here. If I excised myself from this story, would anyone notice? Without consulting me, my feet inch backward, bit by bit, until I'm pressed against a corner cabinet with hard marble knuckling into my spine. Discomfort shifts through me; my throat has gone tight. My eyes feel hot and too big for my head. And I feel . . . *stupid*. Stupid for feeling this way, and for caring, and for showing up when it's clear I wasn't invited, not really.

I'm Mary Bennet at the Netherfield Ball, obliviously playing piano to the derision of others. I'm Mary Bennet shrewishly pronouncing the family should devote themselves to quiet reading instead of making new acquaintances.

I'm Mary Bennet. Always.

I'm—

"Marnie."

Joss smiles at me, then nods at the counter behind me. "Will you help me pass these out?" She reaches around me to grab half of the delicate silver poppers, stuck all over with "Boy or Girl?" stickers. "Mom made such a big deal about the triplets, I thought this could be a peace offering. I was up half the night making them!"

I palm the rest of the poppers and circle the room, handing them out until there's only one left, and I'm standing before Lindy, handing it over.

There's not one for me. It's absurd how much that stings. I blink hard and stare at the end of the popper resting in Lindy's palm. A wisp of blue tissue paper leaks out.

"What do you think, Mar? I know it's silly to do this just to keep Mom from a meltdown, but I am excited to find out the sex! Between Will and me, we're kind of hoping for a boy." She leans in conspiratorially. "We've got enough women in this family, don't you think?"

"Statistically, it's about fifty-fifty."

Lindy laughs. "I hope your statistics are wrong."

"I mean, that's not how statistics work." *God, shut up, Marnie.*

"Oh, Marnie, never change." She's smiling, but all I hear is the insult.

Lindy turns back to Will, and the rest of us hover close. She's a meteor, burning brightly and fiercely and outshining all others without even trying. And me . . . where do I fit in that analogy? A lot of the time, I feel like an asteroid. Lumpy and dull and careening through my little orbit trying to force others to see me. But I've never become a meteor. I've never burned.

Mom holds up one manicured nail toward Lindy and rushes over to hand me her phone. "Since you don't have a popper. Won't a video be special? The whole family here finding out what our Lindy's having."

Sara steps away from the group. "Julia, I'll take the video."

"Don't be silly, Sara. You're as much family as anyone else."

Mom looks at me expectantly, her phone still held out between us. But the implication is there. That I'm interchangeable.

The air is stuffy, choking. Fingers reaching down my throat and stopping my breath. And there I am careening again, heading toward Dad at the far end of the assembly—I'm unable to shine, even for a moment.

"I need to go," I choke out. Dad puts his popper back down on the table and tilts his chin at me. "I'm not feeling great," I continue. "I have a ton of homework. Can you drive me?"

Dad fishes his keys out but frowns, his attention back on Lindy. Lola and Kat are chanting *boy or girl . . . boy or girl*, and Lindy is laughing about something with Joss.

"Dad, please," I say, my voice low and desperate.

"Marnie," Mom says loudly, making the whole group look at me. "Stop being ridiculous pretending you're going to storm out. Do you need me to take the video? I'm only the grandmother, after all."

My heart stumbles over itself as I stare at Dad, waiting for him to tell Lindy his other daughter needs him. I *am* being ridiculous; that's the thing making an ache bloom behind my ribs. I'm being ridiculous, but I can't stop myself now. I want Dad to choose me in this moment. I want . . .

Dad sighs and presses the keys into my hand. "Take my car. Park in my spot in the teachers' lot and call as soon as you arrive." His hand is heavy on my shoulder; he squeezes once, then looks away from me.

It all crashes down, like I'm crumbling from the inside out. Until there's a hollowness carved out inside my chest that lets the wind whistle through my cracks. She won again.

My words are hard-bitten and cold, aimed directly at Lindy. "It's a boy. Surprise."

San Francisco shimmers orange across the bay, and it's only as I cross the bridge that the haze lifts from my brain.

Crap. I *really* screwed up back there, didn't I?

Don't answer that. We all know I just won Barnes Bingo. I mean, I could hear Mom wailing before I'd even shut the door behind me. Making my mother cry is practically the free square in Barnes Bingo, then there's: ruined a surprise, made a scene, and surely disappointed my father all in one go. That sort of tantrum is usually reserved for Lola.

I've always considered my solitary existence a point of pride. I was independent, inscrutable. And—perhaps, maybe, sometimes—lonely. But it was a romantic sort of loneliness. Then why does my life suddenly feel so empty? Is it because I've put a name to it? No. If I'm Mary, it's because my family has made me this way. *They* did this to me. I point Dad's Tesla toward PCA and put my foot down.

The streets are shrouded through the Presidio, but the city throws off sleep as I navigate Cow Hollow. I should go full Lola and park in the middle of the courtyard. Maybe do a few doughnuts beforehand to really make my mark. Instead, I do one better and pull into Headmaster Finch's reserved spot in the staff lot. My act of defiance is short-lived, though, and I back up and park in Dad's spot.

I heave myself up the stone steps of Hawthorne Hall and schlep toward my dorm room. Light shines from under the door, and I can faintly hear the warbling of some indie band. I burst through the door and startle Adhira, midway through some new design sketch.

We came to a sort-of truce at Camp Pie, but the last time we were face-to-face, it was nothing but anger, accusations, and hurt. We haven't even made eye contact since that night. But right now, she takes one look at me and jumps to her feet.

"Marnie, what's wrong?"

"You're right," I announce, breathing hard.

The truth is press, press, pressing against my skin, trying to scratch free of me any way it can.

Adhira frowns and pushes hair off her face, smudging charcoal pencil along her forehead. "Right about what?"

I drop my bag, and my shoulders drop with it. "I'm Mary Bennet." My eyes flick up to hers, then away. "I'm Mary Bennet, and I don't want to be. Will you help me?"

SEVEN

HELP ME.

It's such a simple command when the task is, say, reshelving books in the children's library. You read the numbers on the spine and roll your cart to the correct shelf. But asking for help to change the very essence of who you are? Not so simple.

In the past thirty-six hours, I've missed nine calls from my mother, ignored five texts from my sisters on our group chat, and watched four Bollywood movies. That last one was Adhira's idea. It was admittedly sweet of her, but also like giving a drowning man a bathing cap. It's a nice gesture, but not exactly helping the situation.

Which leads me here. My family probably hates me, and even Adhira has apparently taken all she can since she vanished an hour ago, leaving me prone in bed wearing novelty pajamas featuring pizza slices floating in space and scouring *Pride and Prejudice* for every mention of Swamp Monster Mary.

Each new delightfully awful description pricks behind my eyes, hard enough that I sit up, shove my glasses up into my hair, and pinch at the bridge of my nose. What does one do when confronted with the truth of one's nature? Is the answer to reread a nineteenth-century burn book about one's life and copy every pertinent passage in a journal? No? Well, too bad.

The descriptions of Mary are scant in *Pride and Prejudice*, but maybe that's because she's such a turd of a person. This is my personal favorite. (And by personal favorite, I mean it makes me want to go all Mrs. Rochester and lock myself in an attic.)

Mary had neither genius nor taste; and though vanity had given her application, it had given her likewise a pedantic air and conceited manner, which would have injured a higher degree of excellence than she had reached.

I underline the words *pedantic* and *conceited* so hard, my pen rips through the page of my journal. Under my pillow, my phone rings again, but I ignore it.

If I were Lizzy Bennet—the heroine my heart longs to inhabit, but who is currently being played by Lindy—I would've laughed. A musical laugh that makes men like Mr. Darcy (*cough* Hayes *cough*) remember me far into the night. My laugh is more choking chortle, like a bullfrog suffering from postnasal drip. If I were Lizzy, I would've already put this behind me and come out the other side stronger. I . . . haven't done that. Though I guess I can mark that down to having "neither genius nor taste."

A whine starts deep in my gut and rumbles upward. I fall back against my pillow and finally pull out my phone. I don't yet know how to confront Mary, but I *can* confront the mess I made with my family.

The gist of the ignored group texts: horror (Kat); awful glee (Lola); annoyance (Lindy); rationalization (Joss); then a final one from Lindy saying it wasn't a big deal, but I'd better smooth things over with Mom.

Speaking of. A highlight from one of my mother's many voice mails: *"Why would you ruin one of the few joys in my life?"*

Wonderful. But then there's one more missed text from Lindy, sent only to me. *I understand why family stuff is awkward for you and you know I don't care about some lame sex reveal party, but the way you acted hurt me and Will. Can we talk about it?*

My fingertips hover over my phone, unsure how to respond. Regret and shame skitter down my skin, making me squirm. I press my lips together and squint at Lindy's text, but I can't figure out a way past this horrid disappointment. It drags at me, churns inside me, and I shove the phone back under my pillow without responding.

Maybe my family made me this way, but I don't *want* to be like this. I don't *want* to be awkward or a disappointment. Mary would never earn Hayes's love. She'd never win prizes or equal her sister or make her father proud. I can't allow myself to be Mary Bennet.

I slide my glasses back down onto my nose, turn to a new page in my journal, and write out in large block letters:

ON BEING MARY BENNET:
A DETERMINATION TO THWART DESTINY

Underneath, I write a contract with myself.

I, Marnie Elizabeth Barnes, hereby do swear to root out and destroy Mary Bennet. I will not allow myself to be pedantic, conceited, or insensible. I will not allow myself to die alone with fifteen cats, having never been kissed. I will change who I am, no matter the cost, to cast off Mary Bennet.

Signed,
Marnie Barnes / October 28

Writing it helps. I carefully tear the page from the journal and shuffle over to the corkboard above my desk, tacking it in place. There. It's official. Ish.

Next up: Bark Books. I can't stomach the thought of begging Dad again to mentor me, but I can set up the partner shelter. Yesterday, Adhira asked Dev to send her Whit's social media handles so I could make sure I wasn't partnering with a serial killer, but I haven't yet checked him out. I open my laptop, pull up Instagram, and type in Whit's name: @Whit_SF.

His feed is mostly landscapes, available dogs at the shelter, and food (including a mouthwatering photo with the caption: *My mom's ramen beats your mom's ramen.*). The few featuring his face show a Japanese American guy with a wide smile. There's one of him in a hat and sunglasses flashing an admittedly gorgeous smile atop a mountain peak, and another of his toes painted sparkly purple. (Caption: *Uncle on duty. I think I'm more of a pale pink, not [checks bottle] Unicorn Poop. #NiecesInCharge*

It's all so wholesome I might die. But . . . at least I'm not dying because he's got a basement full of heads. He seems like a nice guy. And, um, Dev wasn't wrong about his hotness. Not that I'm in any way interested. This is all strictly business. I shake the nerves from my fingers and cold text Whit.

Hi! My name is Marnie. Dev shared your info and said you may be interested in partnering for a dog adoption program. Can you give me a call or text so we can set up a meeting at your shelter?

Okay. Check. Next item on the Defeating Mary agenda: I better take stock not just of my insides, but my outsides. Because if we're bringing up horrid truths, the most horrid one of all is that I thought my insides were killing it, so who cared about my outsides. Turns out, I'm a dung heap through and through.

The part of my brain that longs to "say something very sensible, but knows not how" clears its throat and dutifully reminds me outward appearance doesn't matter. It's all a contrived social construct that holds women to impossible beauty standards.

But the other part of my brain wants Hayes to do a cartoon double take next time he sees me.

I toss my phone onto my bed and stand before the full-length mirror behind the door. The confidence I'd felt texting Whit whistles out of me like a deflating balloon. I ruffle fingers through my hair, scrubbing life into my follicles. Adhira has bouncy, thick hair like she walked off the set of a shampoo commercial. I pull my hands free, and my hair wilts like one of those fast-forward videos of dying flowers. I wilt with it. My shoulders cave in; my stomach puddles at my Space Pizza knees. If I were hanging in a museum, I'd be titled, *A Study in Defeat: The Girl Who Realized She Was Mary Bennet and Died from It.*

Somewhere within the heap of my comforter, my phone rings—probably Mom again—but I've already dramatically flopped to the ground. One can't simply get up once one has dramatically flopped.

Just as the phone stops ringing, the door handle behind me turns.

"Go away!" I shout.

"Marnie?" Adhira's voice is muffled at the crack in the door. "What's going on?"

"I've died. Come back later."

Adhira does nothing to honor my dying wish and shoves the door open. Her shadow darkens my thousand-yard stare.

"I'm giving up." Hayes will never see me as anything but a

little sister. Whit will never contact me. Dad basically rebuffed my mentor advances.

She plants a hand on one cocked hip. "Well, you still need to eat."

Even in death, I can't miss the fact that she's brought food that smells like a deep-fat fryer and is spreading grease stains across the bottom of the brown paper bag. My stomach rumbles.

"No, just leave me here. You'll forget about me after a while."

"You'll probably start smelling eventually."

I sigh—long and deep and death-rattling—then slump into a seated position right as my phone dings with a voice mail. Adhira disassembles the bag to reveal two veggie burgers and a mess of fries, but then she stills, her eyes on my corkboard.

"What's this about?" She jams a finger at the contract and turns to me, her lips pursed in disapproval.

I'd wager she knows exactly what this is about, which means she doesn't approve of my contract. So I decide to ignore her. One finger held up, I unearth my phone and click on the voice mail.

A pleasantly deep voice starts speaking. "*Uh, hi. This is Whit, from Paws and Claws.*"

I put the voice mail on speaker for Adhira to hear. "*Dev told me about your project last week and said you may be in touch. It sounds like a great idea. I know this is kind of last minute, but the outreach coordinator and I are around this afternoon if you want to come*

by the shelter to talk about it. Paws and Claws of Outer Richmond.
Four forty-five, okay?"

Adhira points at me with a fry. "You're going to go, right?"

My nod is slow to start. Okay, so I still don't have a mentor.
And there are only three days left to secure one. But suddenly
with this call from Whit, the Hunt Prize is possible.

The inside of my cheek is getting raw from gnawing at it,
but I flick my eyes to her and say, "Yeah, I think so. He got
back to me way faster than I expected."

Adhira claps her hands together like an excited seal. "Yay!
Bark Books is a go? You like that name too?"

We still haven't spoken about our fight or the Pie Peace
Accords. But it doesn't quite seem necessary. Something warm
and bright flares inside me. "It's the perfect name, Adhira."

She shimmies her shoulders in pride and takes a big bite of
her veggie burger.

But I can't eat. Whit's response means I now am expected
to act. Like, *right now.* I glance at my contract, then back to
Adhira—with her bouncy hair and expert mascara and clothes
with nary a Space Pizza. I pick at the hem of my tee and chew
on the words in my mouth.

"So do you have time for, uh, a makeover montage?"

A frown creases Adhira's forehead, drawing her dark eyebrows together. "No, I'm not doing that for you."

That pulls a chuff of surprise from me. "You won't?"

Adhira kneels in front of me and grabs my wrists. I don't
even wince, which is a triumph in and of itself. "No. I see

that . . . whatever it is up there on your corkboard. I won't be a part of that. Makeup and clothing and all that, for me, it's a way to boost my confidence, show off my personality, you know?" Adhira swallows and stares at me intently. "If you think it'd do the same for you, I'd love to help, but I'm only helping if it's something you want. Not something you think you should want. You may not see it, Marnie, but you're pretty great just as you are, if you'd stop second-guessing yourself."

I'm not sure I believe her. If I'm already pretty great, I'd have more friends and a family that doesn't consider me an inconvenient afterthought.

But also, there's a fizz of excitement at my feet, and it's bubbling upward. Mary would scoff at caring for clothes or hair. She'd think it beneath her. Just like I always have. Yet the way Adhira talks about confidence . . . it sounds nice. I think of Lindy, who always looks competent in her own Lindy way. I bet she never resorted to wearing her school uniform to a Hunt Prize event.

I scramble to my feet and tug Adhira up with me. The fizziness makes my chest light. "I want your help. I think it'd be"—and I'm not lying when I say this—"fun."

Adhira grins. "It *is* fun! And it's so empowering, just you wait." She's practically vibrating with anticipation. "The start of Bark Books is the perfect opportunity to embrace confident Marnie."

I suddenly feel very much in over my head, so I let out a squeak. "Makeup?"

Adhira nods like a general. "Makeup. Let's go."

She marches me into the bathroom and starts rifling through her makeup bag. I own exactly three items: mascara that's gone clumpy, an eye shadow duo gifted to me by Mom in my stocking last Christmas (used twice), and concealer for any breakouts. Adhira owns enough brushes to paint Van Gogh green with envy.

Yet she only hands over two items: a little pot of creamy blush and a deep green pencil.

"The green'll bring out the golden brown in your eyes, and you can have this blush. They were in those free gifts with purchase that only work for white girls. You've got mascara already. Let's keep this simple."

She swoops in to help when I hesitate—which is about every three seconds—and in a couple of minutes she zips up her bag. The whole process is actually a lot less painful than I've always imagined.

Adhira pulls out some dry shampoo next and rubs it into my scalp. "My bouncy secret. Well, sort of. I have great hair."

"And modesty to boot." I meet her eyes in the mirror, and one corner of my mouth quirks upward.

"Confidence, Marnie!" She holds up one finger like it's her mantra. I mean, one could do a lot worse for a mantra. "I've got great hair, and you've got great hips."

I start to groan, but she silences me.

"Confidence?" I am dubious, at best.

"Confidence!" Adhira commands, then walks me into our shared closet.

"Have you ever considered Junior ROTC?" I tease as she looks through my things. "I'm sure the armed forces would be happy to have you."

She ignores me and instead pulls out two pieces of clothing I've never paired—a green-and-white striped skirt and black tee declaring "I like big books and I cannot lie." Then she piles on a pair of my black tights, a light wash jean jacket I've never worn, and a pair of her black ankle boots.

My teeth grind together. "I don't know," I say through lockjaw.

"Give it a try." Adhira grins. "You can always change if you don't like it. It's not like I shaved your head or pierced your nipples."

"Oh my god." I hug my clothes to my piercing-free chest.

"See! That's what makes fashion so much fun!"

And, okay, I'm kind of warming to her excitement. Adhira flits into the bathroom, and I change. I've just pulled the tee down when she pops out of the bathroom like the dictionary definition of *exuberance*.

She stares at me for a moment, then, like she's in slow motion, Adhira's hands drift up to her mouth in what I can only assume is silent horror.

She absolutely screeches. I jump back a foot and basically break my ankle in the too-small boots. I tug at the shirt, trying to yank it down around my butt.

"Oh. My. *God.*" Adhira scurries closer and fusses with my shirt, tucking it in and hiking my skirt higher on my waist. "Girl, you look *amaze.*"

I start to add the "ing," but her next words stop me.

"But how do you feel?"

My heart gallops, so I can barely breathe. I stare at myself in the mirror and twist side to side. The jacket skims my hips, and with the shirt tucked in—something I've never considered—I marvel at the way my waist dips in and the skirt follows the curve of my legs.

I feel . . . capable. Like a girl who could run Bark Books with ease and win the Hunt Prize. My shoulders straighten; my chin lifts. I feel *confident.*

"I know, right?" she says, beaming. She hands over gold studs for my ears and a handful of her ever-present bangles from her aunts in India.

Adhira didn't *need* to do this for me. She didn't need to try and be my friend. But she did. Before I can stop myself, I pat her on the shoulder and nearly smile. It's a fleeting, scared thing, but it darts across my face, then ripples into a confused frown. I didn't realize until this moment that smiling feels so peculiar. Maybe I should add smiling to my anti–Mary contract.

"Thank you," I say, and I mean it.

Adhira grins. "Now go impress everyone with your genius

idea, and we'll celebrate later."

I grab my bag, my backup binder—since I forgot the original at Lindy's—and head toward the door. Nothing is going to ruin my mood right now. *Nothing*.

And that's when it starts raining.

EIGHT

TWO BUS CHANGES, ONE PHONE in a puddle, three wrong turns, and a twelve-minute walk later, I drag my waterlogged carcass toward Paws & Claws of Outer Richmond. It's not supposed to rain like this in the fall, but tell that to my dripping wet hair. My boots squeegee against the concrete, each step murdering my heels, and my jacket has become a denim sarcophagus.

Any confidence I'd scrounged up dribbled into my boots and leaked away somewhere around the Polk Street bus stop. Nerves had me pull out my book for a bit of solid familiarity, which made me miss my last bus stop. Which means I'm late, with no way to tell Whit (see: dead, waterlogged phone). My stomach writhes, a pit of snakes.

The sign on the window says Paws & Claws closed twenty minutes ago, and the waiting room beyond the glass door is dark and empty. Yet when I muster the courage to tug on the door, it opens. Beyond the blue plastic chairs lining one wall and a corkboard tacked with Polaroids of dogs, cats, various rodents, and what looks like an iguana, there's a shut door with "Staff" painted on it.

Goose bumps prickle my skin, and panic floods my brain. I missed it, didn't I? I missed my meeting, which'll mean I missed my chance, which'll mean I won't win the Hunt Prize. It's all downhill from there. I think of a lifetime of Mary-ness and force myself to say, "H-hello?"

Nothing. A muffled dog bark makes me jump.

Overhead, the fluorescent lights hum, casting everything in a bruised light. I yank my phone out of my pocket and shake it, like that will make a difference. The screen remains black and unresponsive.

With the daring of a dormouse, I inch toward the staff door. It's nearing half past five, but maybe Whit waited almost forty-five minutes for me. Totally reasonable request. My hand is on the door, but I'm frozen. I should just go. Put my phone in some rice and call with an apology. Or text. Yeah, texting is safer. I release the handle like it's fire and spin around, eyeing the door to rain-soaked freedom.

"Can I help you?"

The soles of my boots protest long and loud as I turn back

toward the voice. An Asian guy around my age has stuck his head around the staff door, and he's staring. There's no mountaintop smile or sparkly purple toes, but this is definitely Whit.

"Are you Marnie?"

I answer by rubbing dripping water off my eyelashes and palming my dead phone. "Do you happen to have any rice?"

Whit tilts his head to one side, eyes narrowed. ". . . No?"

"Oh, god, I—I didn't mean—" I stammer, realizing a second too late that I just sounded like a horrible person. I hold up my phone, flustered. "I dropped my phone in a puddle, so I got turned around getting here. I'm usually very punctual. You're Whit, right?"

Another pause. He's still staring at me like a curiosity in the zoo. He slides through the door to lean against the wall and roughs a hand through his black hair. "We thought you were a no-show, so the outreach coordinator left." His gaze flicks behind me, and I follow his eyes to a wall clock. "I'm about to leave too."

Disappointment bunches between my shoulders. "Maybe I can leave some info with you? It's all laid out in this . . ." I yank my presentation binder from my bag and thrust it toward him. "Please?"

His jaw works as he fidgets with the door handle. I'm still holding the binder out to him, expectantly, hopefully. I try for a smile that probably only bares my canines—appropriate— and notice the paper under the binder's plastic cover has gone soggy at the edges, the ink bleeding.

Whit scrubs a hand through his hair again, making it stick up on one side. "Look, I've got to meet my sister for an, uh, event in an hour, but I can give you a few minutes."

A sharp exhale whooshes out of me, and I hug the binder to my chest. I'll have to make this pitch absolutely dazzling. Really wow him with my knowledge. I'm already running through the pertinent facts in my head. Studies about dog behavior and student reading scores.

Whit opens the door wider to usher me through, but a frown pulls his eyebrows low. His eyes dart to mine, then away. "Do you, ah, want to use the bathroom first?"

Well, that's a bit odd. "No, I'm fine."

"Maybe you should use the bathroom," Whit says again, his voice strained. He waves in my general direction. "You've got . . . under your eyes."

Frowning, I swipe a finger under my eye. It comes back smudged with black. A horrified squeak jumps off my tongue.

Whit grimaces. "I'll be in the outreach office when you're done. Second door on the right."

I squelch-run my way down the hall where he pointed and shove my way into the bathroom. And swallow down a yelp. I look like something that crawls out of your vents to steal your soul. My hair is plastered to my head, hanging like viscera around my face. Black mascara makes raccoon eyes and runs down my cheeks. Panicking, I grab a handful of paper towels and scrub.

"Crap," I mutter to my reflection, dancing back and forth

in agitation. "Crappity crap." I scrub harder, making my skin red and angry, but after a harried minute my face is wiped clean. I scrape my hair into a ponytail and shake the nerves out of my hands. I don't look at myself in the mirror—because screw that girl—then head back to Whit, every step making the tsunami in my stomach roil and churn.

I allow myself a deep, shuddering breath, then step into the room Whit indicated. He sits behind a cluttered desk, posters featuring frolicking animals tacked on the wall behind him. One poster is of a horse, which I'm pretty sure aren't up for adoption here at Paws & Claws of Outer Richmond. The desk and chair are a cheap, blue-flecked laminate, and one of the posters is hanging at an odd angle.

"You're missing a . . . ," I start, pointing at the missing tack causing the poster of an orange cat to sag. Whit leans back in the chair and raises dark eyebrows. "Never mind."

Instead of insulting my possible program partner's design choices, I tug out the binder again and plop it on the desk. "Anyway, if you want to, you know, look through the proposal."

I'd practiced a speech, a presentation. I'd come up with some cute tidbits about dogs. Something about tail movements? And all of it—every last word—is gone. My brain is hopelessly blank, soaked through with rainwater and defeat. My failure quakes through me, and I collapse into the rickety chair across from Whit, toeing out of my boots in the hope that'll make them dry faster.

Whit frowns and flips through the papers, one of his hands

fidgeting against the desk. I stare at that hand, unable to look anywhere else. His fingers are long with a faint crescent of dirt under his nails, and I follow the line of his arm up to his shoulder, then his face. His eyes are still on the first page, but even with his head tilted down, I pick out the fringe of his eyelashes and the blunted point of his chin.

Whit glances at me, his eyes dark brown like mine, and I drop my gaze. Heat flares up my neck to be caught staring.

There's a rustle of movement and the creak of an old chair from Whit's side of the desk, then he says, "Can I keep this to read and share with Monica?" The dismissal at the edge of his voice makes it plain he'll never get past page one. "I'm just a volunteer, but the outreach coordinator will be in touch if she's interested."

The rejection surges through me, pushing me up and out of the chair. I thought he said Bark Books sounded like a great project? So the problem isn't *it* . . . it's— "Give me a chance," I blurt. "It," I amend, cheeks burning. "Give *it*. The program. Did you know a dog recognizes distinct human voices?"

Whit's mouth tugs at one side. "I did know that."

"And for shelter animals, who may have gone through trauma, children are more soothing. They aren't intimidating."

He sits back, arms crossed. The sleeves of his plaid shirt are rolled up to his elbows, and I watch a muscle jump in his forearm. "Kids can also be loud and startle animals, especially those that are already nervous."

A terrible sense of dread grips the back of my neck. I don't have a chance in hell at the Hunt Prize. Bile scours my throat, and I barely fight the urge to *leave*.

"I didn't mean to insinuate I knew more than you." Without looking, I grab for my bag but only snag one strap, upending the entire thing. A groan of frustration builds in my chest, and I crash to my knees to start shoving things back in. My boots are still under the desk, leaving me only in my black tights.

"I'm not . . ." I push my slipping glasses back up my nose. "I did my research. And I . . . I think this would be great for the kids and the dogs." God, how much did I have in my bag? Pens have rolled under the desk, my wallet and two small notebooks are under the chair, and a tin of mints has burst open. I hear more than see Whit get up and kneel beside me, helping to gather my things.

"In my head," I say, eyes on the ground as I pick up my things. I scan for the last thing missing—my book—and mumble past my clogged throat. "I picture kids sitting in front of each kennel, practicing their reading. It can be intimidating for them too, learning to read. But the animals won't judge. I picture dogs—even the shy ones—listening. Reading . . . I don't know if you like to read, but it can still your mind like nothing else can, and I think that's true for the dogs too."

Finally, I peek at Whit. He's crouched next to me, his mouth screwed to one side. He reaches under the leg of the desk, his arm brushing against my back—warm and shocking in a way that makes me arch away from him. He yanks the book free, and I watch in confusion as his eyebrows wing high and his mouth opens in a little "huh?" of surprise.

My worn, broken-spined copy of *Anne of Green Gables* is held up between us. Whit's eyes find mine, and he smiles. I haven't a clue why, and it only makes my shoulders inch upward in defense.

"You seem like an *Anne* girl. Is that weird to say?"

I snatch the book out of his hands, certain it's meant as an insult. Everything people say about my books is an insult.

"Sorry," Whit says quickly. "My two older sisters became obsessed with these books when we were stationed in Japan."

Oh. The hardness in my mouth softens.

Whit's smile widens, and his eyes grow warm. "I'm an air force kid. When I was little, my mom talked my dad into doing two tours in Japan, since her parents grew up there. Anyway, the books were turned into anime in Japan decades ago, and Anne was massive."

We're still crouched on the cheap carpet, but I make no move to stand.

"My sisters talked our parents into going to Prince Edward Island for summer vacation when I was ten, for this tour," Whit says, shaking his head at some memory. There's humor in his voice when he says, "They made me dress up like Gilbert Blythe."

"Gilbert Blythe was my first crush," I offer for reasons that cannot be explained other than my insatiable need to humiliate myself at every turn. I often like to picture Hayes as my own Gilbert Blythe. There's this scene in one of the later books where Gilbert kisses the nape of Anne's neck. First, I had to look up the definition of *nape*, and then I pictured Hayes kissing me there. Basically, Lucy Maud Montgomery was responsible for my sexual awakening.

Whit laughs, bringing me back to this strange moment. "Anne Shirley was my first crush. Actually, make that a tour bus full of Japanese teens *dressed* as Anne Shirley."

Unsure of what to say to that, I tuck the book into my bag and peek up at Whit. "You've really been to PE Island? You know, Lucy Maud Montgomery was said to have written the books during these lovely twilights overlooking the fields outside Cavendish. The actual Green Gables farm was just up the road from there and belonged to her cousins."

Whit cocks his head to the side, staring at me in either surprise or concern for my *Anne* obsession. "You know, I did know that. It was on the tour." Whit pauses, his palms pressed against his thighs. Then he stands and offers me his hand.

After a moment, I take it and let him pull me to my feet.

He drops my hand as suddenly as he offered it and shoves his fingers into the pocket of his dark jeans. He checks his phone. "I really do have to go; Hana will kill me if I'm late." Whit fades away and rubs at the back of his neck. Then he looks back at me, and I don't look away. "I think maybe we got off to a bad start. Monica will love this program, and since I'll be the one running point on it from our end . . ." He hesitates for a moment before he extends his hand out to me. "Partners?"

Then his fingers curl in for half a heartbeat. "Wait, what are you calling the program?"

"Bark Books."

Whit smiles wide. His mountaintop smile. The sort that makes his eyes seem to glow with warmth. "I like it. To Bark Books, then, Anne Girl."

I take his hand and shake it, my heart a puff of cloud in my chest. "To Bark Books."

NINE

TO BARK BOOKS, THEN, ANNE GIRL.

Whit's voice rustles through me all the way down Balboa toward the number 91 bus. I almost don't notice the slow destruction of my heels in these boots.

There was a timbre in his voice that warmed me from the inside. Or maybe that's just him. He smiles like he means it. For the first time, real excitement shivers down my spine at the prospect of devoting myself to this project. I'm going to figure out my phone and call Dad as soon as I get back to Hawthorne Hall.

Whit called me Anne Girl. I barely see where I'm stepping as I get on the bus and plop into a seat, my paperback clutched to my chest. A sigh escapes me, all very Anne-like. Perhaps we can be bosom friends. My sigh chokes off with a gurgle and heat floods my face so suddenly the old lady sitting next to me scoots away.

Not *bosom* friends. Purely platonic friends. No bosoms involved. I clamp the book harder against my chest, flattening said bosoms. Not that they need more of that.

Anyway.

Whit comparing me to my heroine is quite possibly the second-best compliment of my life. Of course, the best compliment I've ever received was the time I helped Dad move a box of books—Mom called them "ugly old paperbacks," which was just very rude—and Hayes playfully squeezed my bare arm and told me to put my guns away. I exclusively wore sleeveless shirts for a month after.

The bus trundles uphill, and I glance out the window. The old Queen Annes—many painted white with bright trim in this part of town—stair-step up the hills. It's still cloudy, but bright, like the sun wants to come play. I imagine the cool air on my face, maybe a peek of the sun. I imagine Anne Shirley walking across fields with a smile on her face. She wouldn't take a bus when there was a glorious day to enjoy. I yank the string to signal a stop, gather my bag, and dart outside.

It's a common misconception that winter in San Francisco is foggier than summer, but it's actually the reaction of the cold Pacific waters meeting the warmth on land that creates those famously thick fogs, meaning foggier summers. Also, the fog is called Karl, and I don't know why, but I approve.

Karl is off doing his foggy thing elsewhere today, so I peel off the jacket, slide on my sunglasses, and start climbing.

By the crest of the first hill on Hyde, my lungs sear. But it's the good sort of searing. The ficus trees lining the street twist above my head toward the clearing sky, and the scent of coffee wafts out of a shop on the corner and into my nose. Across the city toward the bay, an orange sunset gilds the bridge and water and sets something loose inside me—something that unspools and deepens my breath. Behind me, a cable car dings, rounding the corner of California on its charge uphill to disgorge tourists at the top of famously twisty Lombard Street (which, as it happens, is a block from campus). And though I'm still kind of waterlogged and my heels are surely worn to the bone, I keep walking.

By the top of the second hill, I make plans to run on the PCA gym treadmill every morning and completely cut out carbs. I will spend money on activewear instead of books and take up indoor cycling and tell everyone I meet about it. I bet there's an app to track it ("it" being how much I brag about working out, obviously). That app promises to change the world. I grew up in the South Bay, after all, so I know every app needs to promise to change the world.

By the top of the third hill, I eye two pigeons fighting over a half-eaten doughnut and seriously consider throwing down. So perhaps that's a no on deleting carbs. I'll simply run a bit longer at the gym. Or, you know, go to the gym. I'm only vaguely aware of where it is on campus. Lia probably knows. Lia can probably do all the craziest upside-down yoga poses and has an Instagram account solely dedicated to her practice. It definitely *does not* change the world.

But more than anything—more than the doughnut-envy or the gasping lungs or the hill-jellied knees or the Lia derision—there's a snap and sizzle in my nerves, my fingertips, my chest. I *proved* to Whit that Bark Books is a good idea. Me. Anne Girl. Pride breaks free of the little cage around my heart and sings down my skin. Pride that is well and truly earned. You hear that, Mary Bennet? Who's a pedantic fun-suck now?

A flash of movement from within Swensen's Ice Cream arcs across my vision. A watch—cobalt face, silver links—catches my attention. Almost like . . .

Hayes. My body turns to marshmallow and moonbeams. He's just a foot away beyond the plate glass. It must be fate, to see him here on this day. There's no other option. Mary has practically withered away to a husk.

And that's when a bright blond ponytail flicks the plate-glass window, and every gooey, shiny emotion coursing through me curdles. Because who is seated at the round table with Hayes? No one but Lia herself.

Lia swirls a little spoon through her ice cream, then licks it, attention on Hayes. My feet fuse with the sidewalk. I gape at them, trying to piece together how a girl I loathe and a man I love came to be sharing a little round table at the ice cream shop. I stare until they must feel me. They both notice me at the same time, but their reactions are opposites: Lia sneers, but Hayes startles.

"Marnie!" Hayes jogs out the door, but Lia remains where she is, glaring at me.

"Why are you—?" My fingers grasp my bag so tight, my fingernails embed in my palm. "I mean, how do you know—?"

Hayes raps on the window and holds up one finger toward Lia. She shrugs and takes another bite. He swings his attention back to me and angles away from Lia.

"You know Lia? Her dad asked my boss for a favor with some school project. The Hart Prize or something. You don't say no to Casper Lawson. Don't tell her, but it's irritating." His gaze flicks over to Lia, then back to me, and he rolls his deep blue eyes. "Like, come on, bro, I'm already crazy busy."

My emotions veer from jealousy to irritation. Poor Hayes. Always going above and beyond to help.

"Who's crazy busy?" Lia appears behind Hayes, her evil grin set to eleven. "Never mind. Look at you, Marnie! All dressed up!" She turns to Hayes. "Marnie usually wears pajama pants and fuzzy cardigans to class." She puffs her lips into an exaggerated pout like, *poor thing.*

"I—what?" I manage through a throat that is currently on fire. Lia's shirt ends at her rib cage and shows off three inches of tanned stomach. I fold my arms across my own middle.

Why am I wearing a shirt with a book pun on it? *Why?*

My hatred for Lia is a bonfire burning me up from the inside. I try to regain the advantage and jut my chin toward Hayes. "I'm competing for the prize too. Actually, I'm headed back to campus right now after a highly successful planning meeting."

Hayes cuffs me lightly on my shoulder. The moonbeams return. "Oh, good for you, Mar! Wait. I remember now—is this the thing that Lindy won?" And there they go again.

Lia scrunches up her nose in mock excitement. "Good for you! I thought she'd have to beg her *dad* to mentor her! Can you imagine? I had two local dignitaries vying to mentor me. And now, of course," she adds, smiling indulgently at Hayes, "I've got the geniuses at Bright Star Capital on my team."

Hayes's chest puffs up at being called a genius, and I'm overcome with the genius idea to shove Lia into traffic.

"I'm just happy to help," he says to Lia. "So who *did* you end up choosing as a mentor, Mar?"

Lia looks at me with big eyes, triumph oozing from her pores.

"I, uh . . . I mean—"

Lia lets me squirm for a long moment, then tugs her phone from her pocket and checks it. "Hayes, can we go over one more thing before you go? Tennis for Truants will be *so* much better with you helping me out."

Then Hayes is gone with a distracted goodbye, and I'm left behind.

I spent one wonderful afternoon under the delusion that I could be more. That I could prove my worth to Dad, to Lindy, to Hayes. But I'm incapable of that. In just a matter of minutes, Lia has cut away at the tender scaffolding of confidence and exposed the small, sorry creature underneath. Nothing but Mary, all the way down.

TEN

IT'S HALLOWEEN, WHICH MEANS TOMORROW is the official deadline to turn in my mentorship paperwork. And every time I pull out my phone to text Dad, Lia floats before me like a poltergeist.

I thought she'd have to beg her dad to mentor her! Can you imagine!

Honestly, it's just very rude of her. I can wallow in self-pity perfectly fine without Lia needing to remind me of my many failures. Of the indisputable fact that Hayes now definitely sees me as a child who still needs Daddy's help.

Maybe I can make a case for being a modern woman and write my own name on the mentorship paperwork? I'm self-mentored. That's the sort of gumption the judges would appreciate, right?

I flop back onto my bed and tug the covers overhead like a very mature woman.

Call your father, Marnie, the mature me admonishes.

Screeeeeeech, immature me tantrums.

Because here's the thing. I've hemmed and hawed about Dad mentoring me, but everyone assumed it was a given. He's my dad; what is he going to say, no? He's on campus all the time running his tech incubator, and other than sitting on the board of Sara's youth arts nonprofit and volunteering for the annual Point Reyes bird count, Dad is retired. What reason would he have to say no to me?

Except . . . except, what if he does? The possibility roars in my ears, steals my breath. I couldn't capture his attention at the fiasco at Lindy's house, and since then he hasn't reached out. My sisters have contacted me, even Mom, but Dad . . . silence. Do I rank so lowly to him that he hasn't even realized? And if that's the case—

A horrible sort of ache presses at the back of my ribs. Why doesn't Dad notice me? What about me makes him so careless with his fatherly duties?

Through the muffle of batting and cotton, I hear a distant creak and click of the door opening. My comforter is hauled off and thrown to the floor without a single bit of regard for my existential crisis. My hair snaps with static, but that's nothing to the lightning storm forking through Adhira's eyes.

"Enough," she commands, hands on hips.

"Excuse me?" I massage the crease from between my brows.

"Get your ass out of bed." When I whine, she swipes the air, silencing me. "Nope. You had a setback, eh? Get over it. You have the ability here to fix your situation, so it's on you to act. Trust me, not everyone has the opportunity you do. Have you called your dad yet?"

My answer is to roll over and plant my face into my pillow.

And Adhira's answer is to grab my ankle and pull. "Call. Your. Dad," she grinds out. She gives one more tug, and my entire body flops to the ground. Beyond the shock of how, exactly, Adhira Fitz found the strength to pull me out of bed is a little kernel of agreement. That kernel goes *pop* and releases a knot of tension that's been pounding through my brain. She's right. The Hunt Prize can be mine, if I really want it. And oh, I want it so badly my muscles quiver with it.

She hands over my new phone—the old one was well and truly dead—and, fingers trembling slightly, I call my dad. This is it. This is the solution.

Except he doesn't answer.

I peer at Adhira, and she shrugs. "Text him."

Yes, ma'am.

Hey, Dad, can you call me? I need to talk to you about the Hunt Prize.

Adhira nods, then holds a hand out to me. "Good. Now to take your mind off that, you can come to Haunt the Grounds with me tonight."

I splutter on an excuse. Haunt the Grounds is the annual PCA Halloween festival, a nighttime frolic with music, haunted surprises, and elaborate displays created by former graduating classes. It's a big alumni event that brings in lots of money from former students and their families. All current students can attend for free, but that doesn't mean I want to.

"I don't have a costume," I start, letting Adhira pull me to my feet.

"And it's not as if you live with a girl who has a key to the theater closet and a future career in costume design."

Okay, so she unfortunately has a point there.

"Come on," she says, softer now and her eyes wide with pleading. "I really want to go. It's supposed to be a ton of fun."

"So go." I don't see how I'm necessary here.

Adhira frets with her fingers. "I don't want to go alone. It's been kind of, um, hard to make new friends here." She rubs at the end of her nose and scrunches her face up.

"You? But you're so nice!"

Adhira huffs out a breath that ruffles her dark bangs. "I'm working through some trust issues." Trust . . . it's the second time she's brought it up, and I itch to know what happened in Toronto but don't want to pry.

Then Adhira brightens and shoots me with finger guns. "But I *trust* that we'll have a great time together! Come on, Marnie. Please say yes."

My attention shifts from Adhira to my Mary contract.

What would Mary do? She'd definitely be anti-fun, wouldn't she? My stomach gurgles with nerves, but I nudge Adhira's shin with my toe and say, "Okay."

She jerks her chin up, and her smile is so incandescent I nearly have to shade my eyes. "Really?"

"I can't promise I won't complain the entire time, but I'll go."

My, what a selfless saint I am. Watch out, Mother Teresa, I'm coming for you.

Adhira clutches my hands and squeals, then she darts to her desk and whips out a cloth tape measure.

My affirmation squeaks. "What is that for?"

"Measurements, silly!"

My measurements are: laughable—passable—horror show.

Adhira ignores my cringe and lifts my arms to measure my bust (the laughable part of the equation). She works quick, tongue between her teeth and fingers sure as she moves to my waist (passable) and my hips (horror show). She skips back to her desk, jots something down on a scrap of paper, and is nearly out the door before she stops. "I have to pop over to the costume closet, then I'll be back. Shower and blow-dry your hair, please."

Shower *and* blow-dry my hair. What's next; will the Halloween Drill Sergeant expect me to shave my legs? This isn't the PCA Little Miss Pageant. But I schlep myself to the bathroom and do what is required of me.

I'm yanking a brush through my dried hair a little later when Adhira knocks. I peek out the door, steam whirling around me. She thrusts a dress of maroon velvet and gold brocade at me.

"Whoa." I'm not sure I even know how to put this thing on.

"You're Ophelia!"

"Like, Lawson?"

Adhira pulls a face. "Well, actually, like the tragic love of Hamlet. Think how much it'll annoy Lia if you upstage her costume by *being* her. You know she's going to be a sexy kitty cat or something."

Upstage Lia? Now we're talking. I grab the dress and eventually figure out how to wrangle it onto my body.

The gray Halloween day fades to a gray Halloween evening as we get ready. Number of return calls or texts from my father: zilch. His silence worries through me, but I try to tamp it down for Adhira's sake.

Adhira flits around my head, putting the finishing touches to my hair and makeup. "Ophelia Drowned," she finally pronounces, unable to hide the satisfaction in her voice. And why should she? She's turned me into something both beautiful and terrifying.

I marvel at my reflection in the mirror, afraid to touch anything. I wish Hayes could see me in this costume, looking almost—I can't believe I'm about to think this—*sultry*. Heat curls in my stomach, and I clear embers from my throat. Adhira pokes a few more pins into my hair, and I focus on her work.

She's painted my skin blue and gray, like a drowned wraith. My lips are silvery, and deep gray circles haunt my eyes. She's even painted creepy midnight-blue veins spidering across my cheeks and chest. My hair flows down my back in a loose braid, tendrils tugged free like they've been caught in a current.

And the dress . . . I smooth my hands down the soft velvet swathed at my waist. Gold threading weaves vines along the bodice's neckline, and the rich velvet sweeps into a brocade train.

Adhira joins me at the mirror and turns side to side. She's an haute couture solar system, all swirling starlight and stardust spangled across her black leotard, tights, and flats. Planets sprout from her topknot and dangle around her head in a planetary halo. Her eyes are rimmed in thick false lashes, iridescent droplets at the end of each lash.

Adhira beams at me. "I'm going for the Bauhaus look," she explains, and I nod so as not to look stupid. She hands over a light-up skull—"In case you want to go for Hamlet's soliloquy," she says—and then she steps into a tutu. There are planets perched within the black netting, and I can spot Jupiter, Saturn, even a tiny Mercury hiding in there.

"Wow" is all I can say.

"Wow to you too. Ready?"

Outside our door, laughter fills the hallways. A sense of adventure and mischief takes hold of my chest and makes me fizzy.

I grab Adhira's elbow, and we charge out into the night.

Pacific Crest Academy glitters.

Adhira and I duck under an archway rippling with black streamers and follow the curve of the gravel path that tilts steadily downward toward the library. The sloped campus is laid out in blinking orange lights and shimmering white strands. The night vibrates with shrieks, laughter, and ghoulish music.

A laugh starts behind my navel and bursts up through me. I slap my hand against my mouth to stifle it, but then Adhira slips her arm through mine. The night crackles around us, phosphorescent with possibility. I let it grab me, carry me away. My laughter runs free, popping and loud and wonderful. I'm wearing the costume of a tragic dead girl, yet I feel startlingly alive.

One of Adhira's planets bumps my cheek, and her tutu rasps against my gown, but I don't pull away.

"What should we do first?" She has to shout over the excitement of our fellow students, teachers, and alumnae running riot over the grounds.

My gaze trips around the courtyard, dizzy with options. The student orchestra plays spooky music on the library steps, and the statue of Athena sports a blinking orange witch's hat and a billowing black cape. The choir roams the grounds in matching shrouds, chanting what sounds like a medieval dirge. I am drifting closer to the singing ghouls, entranced by their unearthly music, when they grind to a halt.

Whispers disturb the air, and I clutch Adhira's arm as the ghosts stand there, frozen. Like they're waiting for something. Watching us from behind their faceless shrouds.

Then they thrust their hands overhead and shriek as one, and every student within fifty feet of them jumps back and screams. My heart cracks against my ribs, but I descend into giggles again. Adhira presses a hand to her chest and mutters in what I'm fairly sure is Hindi.

"This way." I point my chin in the opposite direction of the ghost choir.

We weave and wander, past the head librarian shilling fortunes from within a Professor Trelawney costume and a troupe of light-up dancing skeletons wobbling on stilts. Most of the teachers, I recognize. The students, though . . . they're almost all a mystery. Behind the makeup, masks, and elaborate costumes, we're faceless. It's freeing, the way this costume makes my spine unfurl and shoulders straighten. For tonight—just tonight—I'm not Marnie or Mary. I'm *anything*. I'm limitless. And that is a powerful sensation.

With a little skip, I gather my gown's train and face Adhira, my glowing skull friend pressed to my cheek. "Let's do the haunted garden."

She bobs her head side to side and blinks. "I didn't think you liked scary things."

I shrug and laugh. "I don't, but Ophelia *loves* them." To

prove my point, I plant a kiss on the skull's forehead.

Adhira still doesn't move, so I grab her hand and pull her onward. It's a haunted garden; it can't be *that* scary. *Ooh, vampire roses.*

But it is that scary. Scarier.

And not because the zinnias are zombies.

Because Lia Lawson leans against the low stone wall guarding the entrance, sliding one hand over her tail. She *is* a sexy cat, because of course she is. She's flanked by two sycophants, all of them wearing matching rhinestone cat ears and black unitards. The only Halloween disturbance on Lia's flawlessly made-up face is a black triangle on her nose and painted-on whiskers. Her false eyelashes look like spiders, but I don't think that's intentional.

"Oh my god, the renaissance fair has arrived." Lia flicks her tail. Beside her, the girls chuckle, as is required. "What are you supposed to be, Marnie?"

"I'm Ophelia."

Lia goes still, and her matte red lips tug down in disgust. "Ew," she sneers. "That's, like, really weird, Marnie. Are you stalking me?"

My shoulders hunch. My spine curls. And all that power sizzling though me only minutes ago goes flat and dull. How stupid. How utterly stupid of me to think dressing as Ophelia would somehow cow Lia.

"Don't be an asshole, Lia," Adhira snaps. "What are you? A sexy kitty cat? How original."

Lia rolls her eyes. "Some of us have real parties to go to tonight. Daddy and I are invited to, like, the most exclusive event being thrown by Bright Star Capital out on Alcatraz."

A flare of jealousy arcs through my chest. Lia gets to see Hayes again, yet I don't. I wish Hayes could see me in this costume, on this night. We could lock Lia into a cell together. It'd be so romantic.

Lia pushes off from the garden wall and stalks closer, her eyes glittering with malice. "Anything you want me to tell Hayes? I mean, not that he'll think to ask about you. It's obvious *that's* all one-sided." She smirks in a way that clearly says she recognized the way I looked at him outside Swensen's.

She knows my secret. It's a punch to my gut, a kick to my ankles. Adhira grabs hold of my elbow and squeezes tight as I force out, "He's a family friend."

"Mm-hmm." Lia twirls the end of her tail. "Anyway, nice job looking so"—she drops her tail and eyes my costume—"*tragic.*"

Lia nods to her friends, and they slink past. Her threat clutches at my heart. Mary would hide; she'd play the mouse. I can't let that happen. Courage finds my tongue. "Better a tragic heroine than a pussy in a push-up bra."

Lia glares at me over her shoulder. "Bitch," she snarls.

Adhira wraps her hands around my wrists and tugs until I turn away from the bit of night into which Lia disappeared. "She won't say anything."

My mind whirs. "She might."

Would Hayes believe her? Maybe I should text him right

- 117 -

now to warn him. But then if she doesn't . . . I pull away from Adhira and press the heels of my hands against my eyes. "She ruins everything!"

"She just wanted to scare you."

I peek at Adhira from between my fingers. "Then full marks to Lia."

Adhira is quiet when she asks, "Why is she so mean to you?"

The sting of memories pricks behind my eyes. In sixth grade, she recorded me reciting my poem "Window Friend" and posted it online with a video of her laughing. In eighth grade, she taped tampons all over my locker when she heard I'd gotten my first period (thanks to Mom and one too many white wine spritzers at the club). I never once retaliated. Mom already made it plain she'd prefer if I were more like Lia. *Be more outgoing,* she'd say. *Put down those books for once and talk to a real human.*

The memories cling like slime at the back of my throat. I swallow them down and twist my fingers together. Why does Lia pick on me? "Because I'm an easy target, I guess."

"So don't be easy." Adhira's voice has gone granite. She holds out her hand to mine, and after a second, I take it. "Let's be difficult women, shall we?"

Difficult women. Adhira's words work through me. Lia got the better of me outside Swensen's the other day. All because I'm afraid people will judge Dad mentoring me? Let them judge. Then let them realize I've earned my place. Dad may mentor me, but at least I don't need him to be a judge like Casper.

I squeeze Adhira's fingers. "Hey, you're a good friend."

Then I pull out my phone and call Dad. He answers on the first ring. "Marnie! I was just about to call you back."

Air sucks into my lungs, and I say in one big whoosh: "Will you be my mentor? For the Hunt Prize, I mean. Not just generally. Though I guess I've always—"

"Of course, my dear," Dad interrupts. "I'd love to mentor you."

Relief ripples down my spine.

"Really?" I clear the shock from my voice. "I mean, perfect. Okay, talk soon." Then I hang up abruptly and bite down on a delirious laugh.

Adhira tips back her head and howls. "To difficult women!"

I cackle and spin in a circle, my costume swirling around me. I did it. I actually did it! Hunt Prize, here I come.

ELEVEN

MY HUNT PRIZE TRIUMPH SHOULD cast today in rainbows—I am officially in the contest and have a mentor!

But it doesn't. Turns out, Mary is still creeping. I sit on a cold bench in a corner of the PCA garden and blame her for how much I've cyberstalked both Lia and Hayes the last two days. There's been nothing of note, but that hasn't eased the panic. The Halloween confrontation has burrowed down deep and festered. I can't shake the feeling—an irritant scraping me raw—that I didn't properly *earn* my spot. That I'm only in the contest because I was desperate and Dad pitied me.

What if he doesn't really want to mentor me, or what if he doesn't really believe in my project? It's not as spectacular as Lindy's. Surely I'm just going to disappoint him.

A shiver works through me and I stretch my shoulders against the bench. The day is cold pea soup, so thick I can barely decipher the headmaster's cottage beyond the redwood grove. I check my phone and suppress another shiver—this one mental. There's only ten more minutes before my first official meeting with my Hunt Prize mentor, aka Dad, aka He Who Had No Choice in the Matter.

I snap my paperback closed: not even my girl Anne can distract me. I stow the book and stand. From here on out, the only Hunt Prize option is to be flawless. And/or better than Lia. It's the only way to prove I deserve this opportunity. The expectation is a weight at the bottom of my lungs, dragging down every breath.

Right now, that means arriving on time.

The gravel crunches under my clogs, only to be swallowed up by the dampening fog. The path wends through a row of rhododendrons—their long, thin leaves drooping with dormancy—and toward a side entrance to the soaring glass angles of the science building.

Dad is only on campus a couple of times a month for his Girls in Tech incubator, but the school gave him an office all the same. Everything inside the building echoes—sounds bouncing off glass walls and open-backed wood staircases. Everywhere else on PCA is nooks and crannies, dark wood and warm light, so this ultramodern building makes my senses go sideways. I'm in Dad's territory now.

Behind the frosted glass door to his office, shadows move. I rap on the door, then push it open.

"Hey, Dad! How's—"

But it's not Dad staring at me.

It's Lindy. Lindy, for whom I ruined her baby's sex reveal last time I saw her. Does she hate me? I'd hate me. Sure, she said she didn't *really* care in our group chat, but who knows if that's true.

I backpedal and ram a shoulder against the door. My sister tilts her chin and stares.

"I'msorryabouttheparty," I shout in her general direction.

She and Dad share a look. Not a casual glance—the sort that clearly says, *oh yeah, we've all gossiped about you.* Lindy recovers first. "It's really not a big deal." Her eyes slide to Dad. "I mean, Mom flipped, but nothing new there."

"Your mother was excited," Dad says, ever the apologist. He shrugs, then says, "I'll go get us some drinks, then we'll get to work on your Hunt Prize. Lindy, herbal tea for you?"

She rubs the gentle swell of her belly and nods. Dad eyes me. "What's your order, Marnie?"

He knows Lindy's order, but not mine. The realization squeezes my throat. "Coffee?"

"Black?"

I don't drink coffee, but it's what came out of my mouth, and now I've got to run with it. "With sugar, please. Raw sugar, if available." I have no idea where this order is coming from. Also, I don't know what raw sugar is, specifically.

Then Dad leaves, and I turn away from my sister and her dark, inquisitive eyes.

"You seem distracted."

"What?" I was staring at the back wall, squinting like it'd tell me what to say to Lindy if I only looked hard enough.

"Exactly."

I scrub a hand against my cheek. I can't help but wonder if she's here because she doesn't want to share Dad. Or if Dad asked her because he doesn't want to waste his time just with me.

"Sorry, it's just—" It's not like I can tell Lindy a) I'm afraid Lia will tell Hayes I love him, or b) I suspect her motives for being here. So I say the next thing that pops into my mind. "Lia Lawson called me a bitch the other night."

Oddly, Lindy grins. It's cockeyed and full of mischief. "Did you earn it?"

My mouth flops open like a dying fish. Lindy shrugs. "There's nothing quite as satisfying as earning a 'bitch.' I usually take it to mean I'm doing something right."

She says it like it's a badge of honor, and it shakes me. I've never thought of it that way.

"Anyway, get in here already!"

I'm still hovering at the doorway, and I cast about for a place to sit and stash my things. Lindy's at ease, moving in a way that shows she's been here often. I've only visited Dad here twice. Envy bubbles hot in the pit of my stomach.

"So sorry I didn't tell you I was coming." Lindy digs through her leather tote. "But you left your Hunt Prize binder at my house after the . . ." She peeks up at me and rolls her eyes. She finally tugs free the binder and hands it over. "Anyway, I read your proposal, and I love it. Dad and I were texting yesterday and he said he was mentoring you, so I piggybacked on this meeting. I'd love to help out, if I can."

"Oh." Effusive, I'm not. Dad never texts just me. But then he's back before I can offer more, and I'm suddenly facing them both sitting on a couch like a cozy little team while I'm over here by myself in a black leather club chair being grilled on the inner workings of Bark Books. Black coffee with two raw sugar packets is, by the way, disgusting.

Dad gets sidetracked comparing Bark Books to the annual Point Reyes bird count, and then Lindy shares a fun anecdote about mistaking an avocet for a cormorant at the last bird count, which *har har har* did I know Lindy and Dad have done the bird count together for the last decade? No, I did not. And I haven't said a word in ten minutes even though this is, ostensibly, about *my* Hunt Prize but instead I'm sitting here like a blue-footed booby watching the Dad and Lindy Show and feeling very, very forgotten. *Forgotten by Her Family: The Marnie Barnes Story.*

Lindy sighs and seems to remember I'm here, veering back toward the topic at hand. Maybe I'll become one of those nuns who wall themselves into the convent with just little windows for food delivery. *Maybe you'll remember me when I'm in your walls wailing for cheeseburgers, Lindy.*

She leans forward and regards me. "One thing the judges will ask you at the final presentation—at least they did the year I won—"

Thanks for the reminder, sis.

"—is *why* you chose this project."

Why? Because I want to finally be ranked with Lindy. Because I'd love for Dad to focus on my accomplishments for once and maybe invite me to the annual bird count even though birds are kind of gross. Because I want to prove to Lia I earned it. None of those answers will suffice.

I lean back in my chair and stare out the window at the Greenwich Garden Path behind campus. It's a wall of green separating us at PCA from the flat-roofed Italianate houses beyond. And it offers nothing in the way of a real answer. The silence between us cracks under the weight of my ineptitude. Leave it to me to strain for attention, then wither at the first sign of it.

"Can I offer something?" Lindy says when I remain silent. Her voice is softer now. "You wrote in your proposal about shy readers, and it made me think of you. I remember catching you reading to yourself in the mirror."

Heat crawls up my neck. It pokes behind my eyes and makes me duck my chin. How was I such a lonely child when I was surrounded by family? What was—*is*—wrong with me?

"Marnie?" Dad asks gently.

Why do I want this? I close my eyes, my chest tight and my hands clenched. And then, unbidden, I think of Whit's smile when I finally convinced him to give Bark Books a try. He believes in this project, and Lindy does too. She must, to spend her afternoon with Bark Books. Right?

"Because," I finally say, "because I wanted to share these words that were bursting inside me but I . . . I didn't have anyone to share them with. So I read to my reflection and pretended it was someone else listening. I think for young readers like that, they'll find a patient listener in these dogs, you know? And maybe the dogs will get a little hint of the worlds they may find outside the shelter."

Self-consciousness prickles when I finally peek at my dad and sister. They're both still, watching me closely in a way that makes me shift with discomfort. Dad sucks in a little breath and looks away, rubbing at the corner of one eye. It's Lindy who comes over and squats next to my chair. "Oh, Marnie," she whispers, dragging me into a hug. Her hair smells like it always has, like herbs and apples. I'm stiff for a moment, then make myself relax. "You always had us."

The stiffness is back. Did I? Because it never felt like that. Lindy was always off doing whatever Lizzy protagonists do. She had no need for a Mary. I was inconsequential to her story. But I can't tell her that.

"Yeah," I reassure her. "I know." The words are thin and hollow.

Lindy pats my back and returns to sit with Dad, who's composed himself. We pull out the binder and wade away from the murky waters of feelings and back to solid ground. By the time the steel wool clouds out the window have bruised purple and black, we've hammered out most of the program details, assigned tasks and due dates, and come up with a plan for the launch.

I leave with ideas and homework and inspiration bouncing around my skull. And under that, uncertainty. Dad and Lindy were energized and engaged—notwithstanding their little bird nerd interlude—but I'm not sure working with my family is the best idea.

If I'm honest, the sole reason I want to win the Hunt Prize is to earn my place among my older sisters. But more than that, what if it doesn't matter? What if *nothing* will give me equal footing—equal *love*—within my family? What if all they see is Mary? What if that's all there is to see?

Outside the science building, I crush the binder to my chest and suck in a misty breath. No, I won't accept defeat so easily. If I improve myself enough, I'll not only win the Hunt Prize, I'll earn my place in my family.

TWELVE

THERE ARE FEW PLACES THAT delight me as much as a quiet library, but Bardo comes close.

The coffee shop is across the street from campus and always packed with PCA students hunched over homework among the would-be novelists and trust-fund hipsters. Today, five days after my planning meeting with Dad and Lindy, I thread through the mismatched wooden tables with a backpack weighed down with homework, Hunt Prize materials, and a brick of anxiety. Tomorrow I've got another planning meeting for Bark Books before dinner with Mom and Dad. It's always a fun game to guess which Mom I'll be dining with: I Hate San Francisco Mom, I'm Definitely Dying Mom, or Weirdly Exuberant Until You Say the Wrong Thing Mom.

But pushing through the nondescript door at the back of Bardo, the weight on my shoulders lightens.

The courtyard at Bardo is a thing of beauty. It's narrow but deep, surrounded on all sides by tall brick walls crawling with ivy. Fuzzy moss is a carpet underfoot, and an enormous tree in the center spreads lantern-hung branches overhead. The wonderful weather means the tables are nearly all full, but I snag one at the back.

Back inside, I've ordered a pot of Earl Grey for myself and a large chai for Adhira when a voice makes my stomach twist. I spot him on his phone three people behind me in line.

Hayes.

Hayes at Bardo.

My hands go stiff against my embroidered wallet. Is he . . . is he here because of *me*? Maybe he knows Bardo is where PCA students like to study, so of course he'd look for me here. A mad dash of excitement sprints through my chest, until I can barely breathe.

"Miss?" The cashier eyes me. "That's eleven dollars."

Hands quaking from Hayes proximity, I struggle to open my wallet.

I sense him next to me before I turn. Also, he's worn the same Givenchy cologne for years, and the scent gives him away.

"I'll get it," Hayes says, leaning around me with a credit card held out to the cashier. His arm brushes my shoulder, sending shivers down my skin. He approached *me*. My heart is a herd of wild ponies. "And add an almond milk latte with three shots of sugar-free caramel."

Behind us, someone grumbles. Probably jealous this perfect specimen isn't buying their drink too. I flick my eyes up to Hayes, then away. "Thank you."

He scans the coffee shop. "I promised you a birthday dessert, right? The tea will have to do for now."

I don't squeal, but my stomach throws a dance party. He remembered my birthday!

We move down the counter to await our drinks. Hayes peers over the counter at the barista. "Hey, bro. Can you make mine a twenty ounce?"

The barista frowns and glances at the cashier.

"I meant to order the twenty. I'll go throw another couple bucks in the tip jar."

The barista hesitates, then switches out Hayes's to-go cup with the next larger size.

Hayes turns back to me and leans an elbow on the bar. His face is sun-kissed and his teeth blindingly white when he smiles at me. He stares intently, and I fight the urge to look away. "Little Marnie, all grown up. You're an adult now."

"Yup," I squeak. I ever so subtly push a long hank of hair behind my shoulder, exposing the nape of my neck. It's very kissable, I think. I imagine Gil kissing Anne there and experience a blooming ache deep in my body that makes said neck prickle with heat.

"I've got a table in the back," I say, after clearing the

pubescent creak out of my throat. "If you want to . . ." Would finishing that with "take my virginity" be appropriate? Probably not.

Hayes grabs his drink and even offers to hold the chai while I balance the wooden tray with my pot of Earl Grey and accoutrements. His gray-checked button-down is rolled up to the elbows, and the sight of his manly forearms handling the hot drinks is enough to make me all aflutter with longing.

We head out to the magical courtyard, like two people totally together and in love, and I kick my laptop bag off the chair to free a seat for Hayes.

"You're making a habit of running into me in San Francisco." My god, I'm flirting!

Hayes's gaze circles the courtyard, then rounds back to mine. He has a way of looking at a person like you're the only one in the world, the only one who matters. My heart swells so much it nudges my lungs out of the way. Not that I need lungs when I have Hayes's blue eyes giving me life. "Ha ha. Yeah," he says. "Need to make sure you're not getting corrupted by the city. It's a whole different beast than the South Bay."

My mind latches onto the word *corrupted*. Hayes wants to protect me. I nearly swoon into my pot of tea. Mouth clamped against another squeal, I sit on my hands to keep from pawing at this perfect man and somehow speak past my galloping heart.

"Did you hear about Lindy and Will?"

Hayes snorts out a laugh. "Oh yeah. What is it with women

and wanting babies? Sara won't stop talking about it."

"I don't want babies," I practically shout. See? Maybe being with an older woman like Sara really *isn't* the right thing for Hayes!

He stares at me for a moment, a moment sparking with the sort of unspoken longing I imagine coursed between Lancelot and Guinevere. Before I can say anything, something pithy and nonchalant like "I love you with every fiber of my being," Hayes blinks quickly, glances at his phone, and stands.

"I've gotta run. Just needed a little"—he shakes his latte at me, and I assume he means *caffeine*, not *a chance to see you*—"before this high-profile cocktail reception in Pacific Heights. The guest list is crazy tight, so I've got bring my A game. Wish me luck, Mar!" Then he's gone.

My heart belly flops and my inner Mary gives me an *I told you so* look. So he wasn't here for me. Yet he still went out of his way to chat. I feel like I went skydiving, and it was exhilarating and amazing, but then I broke both legs on impact. I'm left in a puddle on the mossy ground, blathering incoherently.

Adhira finds me there sometime later and scoops me back into my seat and pours me tea. It is an exceptionally long time before I remember the existence of homework or Bark Books.

Twenty-four hours later, I stand in front of the San Francisco Public Library's bookmobile with my volunteer advisor, librarian Daniel Wong, plus Dad and Whit. I entered this meeting with a healthy dose of optimism—Whit called me Anne Girl last time I saw him!—but that excitement has drained away.

Whit circles the bookmobile, one hand hooked behind his neck. "It'll fit out front, but that's all street parking," he says, eyeing the vehicle.

Daniel, Dad, and I follow behind. We've spent the last half hour folded into pint-sized chairs in the children's library talking through the program, but now we're in the loading bay, where Booker the Bookmobile lives. The vehicle—a converted minibus—is painted sea-foam green with a bright blue octopus on the side, a different book held in each tentacle. The octopus is also wearing glasses, which is my favorite touch. I imagine octopi being very literate and quite snobby about their reading tastes.

Daniel nods at Whit's parking concerns. Whit has had a lot of concerns. And comments. And general thoughts on Bark Books. It's turned into an irritation between my shoulder blades, something I long to scratch. I wriggle my shoulders and jump in before Daniel can answer. "In the past when I've volunteered on Booker duty, Daniel clears it with the city and they hood a couple parking meters."

"But Whit has a point," Dad adds, making disappointment pinch behind my eyes. "That's a lot of Saturdays to clear with the city. And it's taking spots for potential participants."

Daniel, bless him, steps in. "I scoped it out last Saturday; we'll be fine. I think what we need to focus on now is the book selection. Marnie, do you have a list for me to pull?" He turns to Dad and Whit. "Marnie is aces at matching kids with books."

Whit nods. "We have cats and other animals too. Quite a few rabbits at the moment, actually. Maybe I can help—"

"All the books will be dog-themed," I clarify, scowling in Whit's direction. Someone apparently needs a reminder who's heading up this project. I angle away from him and say, "Daniel, I'll get you a list by Monday."

Dad turns to Daniel. "Mr. Wong, I just need to get some insurance information for the bookmobile." With a wave and grin, Daniel leads Dad through the loading door and back into the bowels of the library.

Lindy texts as they're leaving: *Sorry I can't be there tonight. Just wanted to remind you to make sure Bark Books is on the library events calendar. Free marketing for you!*

I'm left alone with Whit and the niggling annoyance that Lindy keeps butting in. Whit shoves his hands into the pockets of his dark gray pants and tilts back onto the heels of his beaten-up leather boots. "So we're thinking the Saturday before Thanksgiving? That's less than two weeks away."

What, are he and Lindy coordinating on questioning my abilities? Outside the open bay doors, yesterday's blue sky has given way to a miserable evening of cold drizzle, and I'm cursing myself for forgoing tights. It's damp in the loading bay, and our voices echo off the concrete. I hook the toe of my white canvas sneaker around the back of my calf and rub warmth into my skin.

"It'll be a soft launch, but it'll be nice to work out the kinks. Though there shouldn't be many. I have worked hard on this program." My voice comes out harsher than I wanted, but I'm the one in charge here.

He takes a step closer, and his dark eyes slide to mine. "Sorry if I was asking too many questions. It's such a rad project and I just want it to go well." He screws his lips around, and my skin prickles. "It's obvious you've put a ton of thought into everything, but if you want to brainstorm or anything, there's a cafe—"

"*There* you are!"

Mom's voice makes me jump, and a nervous laugh rattles my chest. I step back from Whit, pushing cold space between us. When did we get so close, and why do I feel like I was just caught? I'm standing by a bookmobile, for god's sake. Nothing untoward happens in a bookmobile.

Mom and I have only exchanged terse texts since I ruined grandmotherhood for her, but in true Mom fashion, her storms blow out as fast as they blow in.

"Do they make you take out the garbage, darling? I thought you said you volunteered with the kids. I encountered three transients before I found anyone to point me in the right direction."

She shakes her umbrella, sending water droplets flying, then shivers. "It was gorgeous at home. I don't know why you made us come all the way here to meet you."

Every bit of my body sighs. So she's I Hate San Francisco Mom tonight. Yay. "Dad's here for Bark Books stuff. It was his idea to make it a birthday dinner."

"It's your birthday?" Whit asks.

"A couple weeks ago, it was."

"Who are you?" Mom asks with her usual grace. She's regarding Whit with the sort of shrewdness she usually reserves for the semiannual sale at Nordstrom.

A groan gathers behind my clenched teeth.

"Oh." Whit nearly stumbles over himself to cross the loading bay to Mom. "I'm Whit. I volunteer at the shelter where Marnie's launching Bark Books." He holds out his hand for her to shake, and she offers a floppy wrist instead, like she expects him to kiss it.

"Whit? Like, Whitney?"

Whit's back is to me, but I don't miss the way his shoulders bunch. "Um, it's Eugene Whitlock Jr. actually," he says, voice tightening. It hits me then that he's talked about his mom, sisters, and nieces on social media, but the only mention of his dad was when he explained that he was in the US Air Force. Whit clears his throat and says to Mom, "But everyone calls me Whit."

"Yes, I do see why you wouldn't want to go by Eugene. What a terrible name to saddle a handsome young man with."

"Mom!" Heat flares in my chest.

Whit stares at the ground. "Yeah, um . . ."

"Julia, there you are!" Dad is back, and he doesn't seem to recognize that Mom is, once again, bringing shame to the Barnes name.

My eyes collide with Whit's. "Okay, gotta go. I'll talk to you soon to figure out launch specifics." Then I wrap my fingers around Mom's forearm and drag her out of the loading bay.

"Marnie! Settle down! I need to open my umbrella before this awful rain ruins my hair any further. I know you don't care about such things, but I do."

Spoiler alert: her hair has been ruined since 2007 when she started bleaching it. I'm pretty sure some of that bleach leaked into her brain too, because no sane human would insult someone's name *to their face*.

Dad jogs ahead and starts the Tesla, and we both jump in. And, okay, yes, I can feel my hair frizzing already too, but that is the least of my worries. I'll have to apologize to Whit for my mom's appalling behavior.

"I meant to say earlier," Dad says from the front seat, his eyes on me in the rearview mirror. "You look nice."

I smooth my hands over my dress, and smile. "Thanks. Adhira took me shopping a couple days ago to celebrate starting the Hunt Prize, and—"

"Yes, it hides those hips," Mom adds.

"—and I loved the pattern," I finish, my voice small. I

hadn't thought anything about it hiding my body when I tried it on. I usually order clothes online, but Adhira dragged me to a local shop in Cow Hollow. This dress is navy blue with tiny white silhouettes of cats all over it, small enough they look like squiggly dots if you don't look too closely. Adhira gushed about it being a "fit-and-flare" dress to highlight my figure, but I was most excited about the cats. Though less so when she said I wasn't allowed to pair it with my cat cardigan. We'll see about that.

I tug at the cuffs of my jacket and huddle down into the leather seat. Absently, I stroke the minuscule back of one of the cats on my thigh.

"I thought we could go to that noodle place in the Ferry Building," Dad says, easing into traffic. "You always like that."

"Noodles are the last thing Marnie or I need, Thomas," Mom says.

My hips feel a mile wide and made of cottage cheese. "Yeah, Mom's right." Outside the car window, the rain is lashing, streaming down the glass. "What about that salad place on Market?"

"Salad? For dinner?" Dad only enjoys green lettuce-y things if they're atop a burger.

"You heard her, Tom. She's the birthday girl; let her pick."

Mom and Dad drop me back at school an hour later, and my stomach is already grumbling. I'm not sure if it's because dinner consisted of various kales or because I spent the last sixty minutes hearing Mom compare my Hunt Prize project to Lindy's. Did I know she won? Yes, yes I did. Did I know she also got a second award from the California Environmental Pioneer Society or her new documentary was accepted into South by Southwest?

Or that Lola lost weight in France and is now a dress size smaller? Or that Joss's Etsy shop is already selling out of her embroidered wall hangings? Or that Kat finally quit debate club to go back to choir?

Welcome back, Mary Bennet. You might be on your way to winning the Hunt Prize, but you'll never compare to your sisters.

THIRTEEN

I HAVE IN MY POSSESSION: thirty-five dog-themed books; fifteen multicolored floor cushions; seven Bark Books posters to hang; two welcome signs; and one stress headache.

After ten days of intense preparation, it's finally time to launch Bark Books. We bumble across town in Booker, drawing waves and honks in equal measure. I'm perched on a little fold-down chair—a bookmobile jump seat—across from children's librarian Beth Moreno on our way to the official launch of Bark Books.

From the driver's seat of Booker the Bookmobile, Daniel catches my eyes in the rearview mirror. "Excited?"

My phone pings with a text from Lindy: *It's going to be great! Remember to take pictures!*

"Pictures." When Daniel frowns, I clarify: "Sorry. I can't forget to take some pictures."

No pressure or anything, but today needs to go perfectly. Today sets the tone for the entire program. Possibly my entire life. Dad and I have met every afternoon this week to finalize the launch plan, and I woke up to encouraging texts from Lindy and Joss.

Beth lifts her foot—clad in a platform heel I have no idea how she manages—and nudges my shin. "Let me handle the photos. You've got enough to do."

"No, no. I can do it."

Unless no one shows up, and it's just me taking selfies with dogs. Beth included the launch on the children's library online calendar—*okay, Lindy's idea was good*—and Daniel plugged it at story time yesterday, but still. I should've gotten Joss to bring the triplets.

What if one of the kids has an allergic reaction to a dog? Or what if a parent asks for book recommendations based on Lexile measure? What if a kid bites a dog?

But there's neither time nor room for additional spiraling, because Daniel slows and pulls Booker up in front of Paws & Claws of Outer Richmond. Out the window, I spot Whit leaning against the stucco building. He lifts one hand in a wave and ambles over, and my heart races with nerves. This is *my* program. Mine. And if something goes wrong, I'm the only one to blame. I press my palm to my chest for a moment to try and tamp down this hammering against my ribs.

"Are you nervous?" Beth asks.

"No." My breath lodges in my throat. Traitor. "You know, medically, it's good to get your heart rate up every—"

"You designed a great program, Marnie," Beth interrupts. "And Daniel and I are here to help if anything goes amiss."

"Right. Yeah, of course." Mary Lesson #5,927: no one wants to hear the underlying statistics of things.

Beth grabs the camera bag and declares she'll take all the photos. I'm too close to passing out with anxiety to argue.

Booker swings open, and Whit is there. My legs are shaky when I stand, and I grip a shuttered bookcase to keep from toppling over. Whit holds out a hand, but I skirt him to clamber down from Booker on my own. Our last encounter runs circles in my head—him questioning my skills.

Whit, though, is grinning. "Excited? The dogs are all looking their best."

Excited isn't the word I'd use right now. I manage a grimace and yank the clipboard out of my tote, a pen poised over my printed list. "We should run through the checklist."

"Oh, dueling checklists." Whit's mouth quirks, and he holds his phone up. "I have one too."

I blink slowly. "Yes, well, mine is the official one."

The smile falters and a crease ghosts between his eyebrows. "I brought out a good group of dogs and set up a table with information on adoption."

"Perfect." I make a check through one bullet point, then reach back into the bookmobile and grab seven rolled-up posters explaining the rules for a successful "reading to dogs" experience. "I need your help hanging these posters. We only have a half hour before the kids arrive."

Whit clears his throat and hooks a hand behind his neck. "Well, I actually already put up a few posters."

My pen hovers over the *hang informative posters* bullet point. "Of what?" Hopefully not those ratty animal posters from the office. The overall effect we're aiming for is competence, not "poorly hung inspirational cats."

Daniel and Beth join us at the back hatch and nod hellos to Whit. Beth lifts her camera and takes a quick snapshot in which I'm no doubt looking put out and surly, my patented look. I suck in a deep breath that doesn't seem to dislodge the boulder in my throat.

"Show me," I say to Whit.

He salutes, and it only makes my scowl deepen. His shoulders are relaxed, his smile easy when he glances at Daniel. How can he be at ease when I feel like a metal wire pulled so taut I'm in danger of snapping clean in two?

Daniel anchors the doors open to Booker and hauls out a bright sandwich board. "We'll join you two inside once we get Booker opened up."

My mind careens back to my checklist. "I was thinking of rearranging the featured books by reading level."

"If we get to it." Daniel is smiling too. How am I the only one freaking out? There is only one thing marked off my checklist and—I glance at my phone—twenty-seven minutes to go. My stomach plummets toward my knees.

"Right, yeah, okay. Whit?" I jerk my head toward the animal shelter and take off at a speed about two clicks shy of "fire evacuation."

"If you don't like them, we can take them down." Whit jogs around me to open the staff door. "But I thought they made the adoption room look bright and welcoming, and I tried to match the colors from the cushions you ordered. My sister knows a bit of graphic design, and I just—" He finally pauses at the end of the hall. In front of us, double glass doors lead to a rectangular adoption room, three sides of the room spaced with kennels. He pulls the door open and works his jaw. "I really hope you like them, Marnie."

But all I see—all I can possibly see—is that Whit didn't believe I could do this on my own. He's exactly like Lindy, texting and emailing me all this week with ideas under the guise of support.

I hold out my posters to him without even glancing at what he put up. "I think we'll go with these instead."

We're nearly fifteen minutes into the official start of Bark Books before the first kid shows up. Dad paces the sidewalk, Whit has stuck his head out the front door to check on us three times, and I've recounted every misstep of my life.

Relief floods my senses so thoroughly I nearly rush around the table outside Booker to haul the kid and his mom into a hug.

It's Dexter, a bespectacled young boy who never misses Saturday read-a-thons, and his equally wire-framed mother.

"Hi! Hello! Welcome!" The grin yanking on my mouth feels downright rabid, so I clamp my hands onto the side of the table and reel it in. "We're happy you've come today." There. That's better. Staid, yet cordial. Definitely not breaking down sobbing inside that someone finally showed up.

Dexter's mom ruffles his dark hair. "It's all he's been talking about for days."

Behind me, Booker jostles and Beth peeks out of the back hatch. "Dex! I thought I'd see you here today." Beth hops down from Booker—landing flawlessly on her tall heels—and joins me behind the book table to snap a few photos. Her full skirt swishes against my sensible gray pants. "Miss Marnie has a great selection of books to choose from, and then follow the signs inside to the reading room. There are lots of dogs waiting to hear you read to them!"

"And," I add, looking at Dexter's mom, "don't forget to read the rules posted inside. They'll give you tips for reading to the dogs."

Dexter and his mom take their time choosing a book, and by the time he makes his selection, there are already two more kids with their adults walking up. For the first time all day, I take a deep breath that actually fills my lungs all the way to the bottom. Maybe this will turn out okay.

Two hours pass quickly with Daniel and me helping the kids pick books, Beth taking photos, and Dad on coffee and water duty. There's a fairly good turnout of kids I recognize from library story times. The little girl at the front of the line presses a new book to her tummy—one about the first dog to go to space—and runs back into Paws & Claws with her dad in tow. She's on her third book and was very chatty about the black-and-white spotted dog she's been reading to inside.

Dexter steps back up and tilts his pointed chin at me. "Do you have anything on iguanas?"

My mouth screws to one side. "I don't think so." I pluck up a picture book about a puppy snuffling through a garden. "You might like this one, though. No iguanas, but there are some snails and slugs in it."

Dexter's lips purse. "No, thank you. I asked the man inside, and he said there's an iguana named Ralph I could read to. I don't think Ralph wants to hear about dogs. Or snails and slugs."

Sure, but this isn't Iguana Books, is it? "Dex, we're reading to dogs today. That's the program. The man inside must have told you wrong."

The man inside is most definitely Whit, who I will most definitely murder at my earliest convenience.

Before Dexter can argue, a girl named Amelia leans out of line. "Is Dexter reading to iguanas? I want to read to the cats."

The girl behind her squeals. "I love cats! Are there any ponies here?"

"Okay, kids," I say loudly, trying to nip this mini mutiny in the bud. Their parents seem oblivious to the growing revolt. Panic thrums against my throat. This is supposed to be about kids reading dog books to dogs, not some animal free-for-all. Someone in the back of the line roars and announces he's reading to dragons. The line dissolves, a horde of kids rushing my carefully planned book table.

"That's enough!" I plant my hands over my precious, appropriately-dog-themed books and don't budge, even as my glasses slip down to the tip of my nose. The raiding party in front of me is a fuzz of movement. Someone's sticky hand tries to wrench a book out from under my palm.

"Kids," Daniel says, voice firm.

The children freeze, and I shove my glasses back up my nose. The scrum parts for Daniel and Whit, their eyes big.

"Sorry, Mr. Daniel," Dexter says, voice tremulous. Daniel is usually made of gumdrops and giggles during story time.

"What's the issue, Miss Marnie?"

My stomach gurgles. It all seems silly now. I push hair off my forehead and try to rearrange the books. "Dexter wants to read to Ricky the iguana."

"Ralph," Dexter and Whit correct me at the same time.

"Right. But I only have dog books." I glare at Whit as I say this, but he doesn't seem to notice.

Whit looks between Dexter and the books, then picks up one about a dog's adventure in the jungle. "Well, Ralph is adoptable, and I'd hate to think he'd miss out on a great story just because he wasn't born a dog."

"And I want to read to a cat," Amelia pipes up. "Mom says we can't adopt a dog anyway."

My molars grind together. This is wholly *not* in the spirit of the program.

"I think that's a great idea, Amelia." Daniel lays a hand on my forearm, but it only makes a muscle jump under my skin. "We'll be here again next week, so we'll make sure to have books on all sorts of animals. How does that sound?"

The children cheer. I feel like a warty old hag, defeated by two knights. "Okay!" I say, my voice as tight as my clenched jaw. "Sounds great! Can do!"

Daniel only sort-of-slyly pushes me from behind the table. "You've been manning the features table for a while. Why don't you take over inside Booker pulling some more titles. Beth took some great photos you can look through too."

Grumble. Grumble. "Yeah, of course, Mr. Daniel." One of the kids smirks at me. Next time I see her, I'll recommend she reads *Where the Red Fern Grows* and wipe that smile right off her face.

It's quiet inside Booker, so much so I can hear the whoosh of blood pumping in my ears. Things had been going so well. Hadn't they? Did the parents not read my very clear rules posted inside? I mean, how can I be expected to run a program if no one will follow the rules? Or maybe . . .

I sit down hard on one of the jump seats and rock my ankles side to side in my sneakers. Maybe it wasn't the adults or the kids. Maybe it was me. Why *shouldn't* Dexter be able to read to other animals? If that makes him happy and helps him be a more confident reader, it doesn't matter if he's reading to a cocker spaniel or a cod.

"Marnie?" Dad hauls himself into Booker and takes the seat across from me. He's a tall, broad-shouldered man, and the sight of him folded onto the narrow seat is somehow endearing. He hands me a bottle of water from a bag stashed under a bookshelf. "What's wrong?"

I roll the water bottle between my palms. "I screwed up out there. I'm sorry."

Dad sits back and rubs a hand down his stubbly face. When I was small, I loved nothing more than to curl in his lap and scratch my palm against his cheek. "You got a little short-sighted, that's all. This is *your* program, Marnie, and you've done an amazing job organizing it. Have you been inside yet?"

I shake my head no and stare at the ground.

Dad grabs an assortment of books off the open shelves next to his seat and hands them over. "Go take a look inside. See how your program is actually going, okay? I think it'll help."

⌿

Dog shampoo is the first thing I notice inside. The scent somewhere between sudsy and syrupy, and the room is thick with it. A dog in the kennel closest to me yips, and it echoes off the tiled walls. But the room is mostly quiet, the low murmur of nearly a dozen kids and their various adults reading to the animals. The sound soothes the whitecaps inside me. A wide smile, unfettered by my normal tics and uncertainties, crawls across my face.

One boy is stretched out on his cushion in the corner of the room, his skinny arm straining through the bars of the kennel. A shaggy mutt lies with his nose pressed to the boy's palm, and whenever the kid stops reading, the dog licks his wrist. As his pages dwindle, I kneel at the boy's shoulder and hand him a new book from the pile in my arms so he can keep reading. My heart is swoopy inside my chest and seems too big to fit properly behind my ribs.

Standing up, my heel knocks against a discarded roll of posters, and the bottom one unfurls from the rest. My eyes catch at the top, on the silhouette of a dog sitting next to an open book. A logo for Bark Books. A logo I never even considered designing. But Whit did. My chest warms; it's perfect.

I kneel before the poster and unroll it all the way. Then the next one. And the next. Whit was right; he matched the background colors of the various posters with the cushions I ordered. Each poster highlights a different aspect of Bark Books. There are facts about how the dogs and kids will benefit—all lines I recognize from my program binder that I left with Whit the first time I met him.

My swoopy, soaring heart thumps hard and my stomach twists, a mixture of joy and guilt swirling inside me. Whit wasn't trying to take over my program. He obviously loves these animals and wanted to make Bark Books a success. I scoop up the discarded posters and set about making it right, replacing my stodgy, colorless posters with Whit's. There are only two left in my hands when Whit joins me. Instead of taking down my posters, he simply adds his next to mine.

Then he sits down on an empty cushion in front of an occupied kennel at the far end of the room and scoots over to make room for me.

The dog in the kennel before us whines and nuzzles his nose against the door, and Whit absently reaches out and sticks his fingers through the bars to stroke at the dog's fur.

I stare at the dog instead of Whit, which makes it easier to say, "You read my proposal. That . . . means a lot to me."

Whit's long fingers curl gently around the dog's ear. "Of course I read it."

The dog in the kennel makes me cock my head, trying to decipher how exactly he came to be. His wiry fur is mottled gray and tan. He's got the long, stout body of a big dachshund, but the boxy head of a schnauzer. There are scraggly whiskers hanging from his mouth, but his ears are silky-looking and flop over.

I peek over at Whit. "Sorry I was short earlier. My sister won the Hunt Prize and it was this massive deal."

"This is going to be a massive deal too, I can tell." He grins at me, and warmth fills my chest. "Great cardigan, by the way. I almost wore my cat shirt too, but my boss wanted me to represent." He points at his soft gray tee, emblazoned with the Paws & Claws logo. The way it fits, the slightest bit snug across his chest and shoulders, makes my throat go oddly tight.

I long to say something witty, but *definitely* know not how at the moment. Luckily, the peculiar-looking dog presses his wet nose to the kennel door and whines loudly for attention.

"Yeah, yeah." Whit pushes his hand back through the kennel bars to continue petting him. He nods toward the dog. "Meet Sir Patrick Stewart."

A coughing laugh tumbles past my teeth. "Excuse me?"

Whit scratches the dog behind his floppy ears. "His family surrendered him before I started volunteering here. Even worse, they called him Stewie at home."

The dog tilts his whiskery chin and whines.

"I know, Sir Patrick. What you had to put up with." Whit gives the dog a nice scratch.

"He's not been adopted yet?"

Whit's smile droops. "He's not a puppy anymore, and not everyone understands Sir Patrick's got a big personality to make up for his lack of . . . *commonplace* appearance."

The mutt turns his eyes on me, his expression all, *humans, am I right?*

I wriggle my hand through the bars and stroke Sir Patrick's

back. His fur is scratchy under my palm, but his warm little body is soft. He scoots his butt so he can lean harder into my ministrations. I've only ever believed in love at first sight in my cherished novels, but I fall hard for Sir Patrick Stewart right then and there. "You'd think they could have at least called him Sir Pat for short."

Whit shrugs. "They were the sort that surrendered a seven-year-old dog because they were too busy for him, so it doesn't surprise me they'd call him Stewie."

"Sir is much better," I say.

"Or The Most Honorable Patrick."

"Or A Knight of Her Majesty's Realm."

Whit grins. "I like that one."

Sir Patrick Stewart yips and nudges Whit's hand, and he pets him again. With his arm stretched out, I notice a small tattoo hidden just inside his elbow, a thin outline of a hexagon with a beautiful brushstroke symbol inside. It looks like kanji, one of the Japanese scripts, but I'm too timid to ask the meaning. Instead, we fall into silence, but it's not the sort that makes me nervous. It's the sort where I could imagine sitting with Whit in a park, or at a coffee shop. On a date. A wash of hope ripples down my skin.

"You know, I could use help with more brainstorming. At the library, you mentioned . . ."

A little line appears between Whit's eyebrows when he looks at me. I see it, and yet I'm still babbling. The words plop out of me, uncontrollable. "Maybe we could go get a coffee after this? Or food? I'll even consult your checklist."

The line between Whit's eyebrows deepens. A horrible sense of humiliation crawls up my spine, curves long fingers around my neck, and finally shuts me up.

Whit pulls his hand from the kennel and brushes his palm down the thigh of his jeans. It takes him a long time to answer. "That'd be great. But, uh, I have a, um, date in a couple hours."

A date. Not with me.

My skin goes tight and flushed. "Oh, I didn't mean like—"

"Yeah," Whit jumps in. "Obviously. I know."

I scramble to my feet and busy my hands straightening my cardigan, cleaning my glasses, anything to avoid looking at Whit. "I'd better check on Randy the iguana."

"Ralph."

"Right," I say, already turning away. "I'm going to ralph."

FOURTEEN

I ASKED OUT A GUY.

I asked out a guy and he said no.

I asked out a guy and he said no and now I need to keep working with him and—

"Marnie."

Our Zipcar veers around a corner, jerking me back to attention. Less than twenty-four hours after Dategate, Adhira asked me if I wanted to check out the Land's End Labyrinth with her and Dev, and when Mary thought *absolutely not* I said yes.

From the front seat, Adhira looks up from her phone while Dev flicks on the blinker and glances behind, awaiting my answer.

"Sorry, what?"

Dev finds a gap in traffic and guns it onto Balboa. "I said," he repeats, "isn't Whit hot? If Ravi wouldn't murder me for making a pass at his friend . . ."

"He's not— I didn't—" My god, why is it so hot in here? Dev seems to have cranked the heater up to Satan's Beach Bungalow, and now my cheeks burn.

Adhira whips her face toward me so fast she nearly tumbles into the minuscule back seat. "Oh my god. He *is* hot. It's all over your face."

I scrub any emotion from my face, but Adhira just grins wider.

"Why didn't you say anything when you got home yesterday!"

"Because there's nothing to say!" Except at that moment we pass Paws & Claws of Outer Richmond and my eyes betray me by tracking the outside of the building as we barrel by.

Was Whit in there, all moony-eyed from his date last night? Was he giving Sir Pat a scratch and telling him about the New Love of His Life? *Shut it, brain. We don't care either way.*

In desperation, I reach for a change of subject and shove Whit from my thoughts. "So this labyrinth."

"I've wanted to walk it ever since I moved here! There's one at Trinity Park at home, and they're just very insightful, you know?"

I do not know.

"I'm just happy for the excuse to dodge the dramaturge at the playhouse," Dev says. He skids into a spot in front of the painted Lincoln Steps and cuts the engine. "He's a *nightmare* and keeps insisting we use *actual* silk from the 1880s."

"Still?" Adhira asks. "He didn't like the taffeta Tilda and I tracked down for you?" She's obviously heard about this guy before, while I try to sneakily look up the definition of *dramaturge* on my phone.

I bumble out of the car and fiddle with my bag. I was all defiant against Mary earlier when I told Adhira I'd join her, but now I'm not so sure. Adhira and Dev have so much in common—they didn't need a (nonexistent) roommate questionnaire telling them they could be friends. I work my jaw back and forth and fight the fear that I'll just be trailing behind them all afternoon.

But then Adhira pauses at the foot of the painted steps and grins at me. "Coming?"

It's a wash of relief through my system. Dev hops sideways up a few steps, making the climb a dance. The steps are painted like a botanical Art Deco wonder; the floral motif marches up the stair steps in spikes and baubles of green, yellow, and orange.

At the top, the wind picks up, and the scent of rain teases. But it's gorgeous up here near the very edge of the continent, and I breathe deeply. We follow a trail through stands of Monterey pines across the vast green park toward a jut of land.

Adhira pauses at the start of the labyrinth and squares her shoulders. "Ready?"

"Oh, come to me, insight," Dev declares, clutching his chest.

It pulls a chuckle from my throat. "Show me thy destiny!"

"*My* destiny," I say through a laugh. "Unless this labyrinth has a destiny."

Dev tilts his chin. "You don't know its life, Marnie."

"Please don't embarrass me," Adhira says, but she's smiling, and I feel a bit like I've been set up on a friend date and our matchmaker is spying on us.

"Sorry," Dev and I say at the same time.

The Land's End Labyrinth is nothing more than a series of precise stones laid out in a pattern. I expected something with more . . . I don't know, fanfare, maybe? But this is decidedly modest and doesn't seem particularly insightful. Yet with the clouds piling behind the Marin Headlands across the bay, and the fog rolling fast and thick atop the water, I feel like I'm clinging to the edge of the world. There's something about the steady thunder of the ocean against the rocks and the wind-twisted trees at our backs that pricks like electricity against my skin. Maybe I really *can* uncover some new insight about myself. Dig under my Mary-ness to the truth of who Marnie is.

A gust of wind tugs hair from under the hood of my raincoat and whips it across my face. Two paces ahead, Adhira's head tilts down, burrowed deep in her bright red raincoat. The stone-lined path curves inward, circling toward the center and, supposedly, destiny.

Or, apparently, thoughts of Whit. He invades my mind again as I follow the path.

Which of my favorite heroines asked out their intended? How many stuttered through a strange half-ask they didn't even realize they were doing until it was already too late and now they can never look that person in the face again?

None of them, that's how many. They simply remain dazzlingly beautiful and oftentimes frail and eventually consumptive, and the romantic interest comes around. Fervently. Ardently.

I stop dead. *Anne Girl.* Whit called me Anne Girl. And then he went on a date with someone else. God, I'm an idiot.

Behind me, Dev jabs me in the ribs. "You're lagging, Barnes," he scolds, but when I glance behind, a wide grin creases his cheeks. I make a show of rolling my eyes and turn back to our circular quest.

I tuck my escaped hair back under the hood of my blue raincoat and concentrate on the whole exercise. Step over step, I follow the curving path toward the center, and my mind curves with it. Thoughts swirling around themselves and inward toward a conclusion that feels just out of reach. Which of my favorite heroines asked out their intended? Well, first of all, Whit is not my "intended." That distinction belongs to Hayes. Obviously. *He* is my destiny. So, really, I'm not an idiot. I was simply lost in the moment of Bark Books going well.

The toe of my boot nearly collides with Adhira's heel, and I pull up short. We've reached the middle.

"Oh!"

Adhira spins, and her eyes are wet even though the first, fat drops of rain are just now plopping onto our hoods.

"Oh," I say again. I rub at my nose and am about to take a step back to give her some space when Dev comes charging into the center. We should have timed this all better.

"Adhira, honey, are you okay?" Dev reaches around me to squeeze Adhira's shoulder.

Adhira blubbers through a smile. "I'm fine."

I mean, she doesn't *look* fine. Her nose has gone quite red, and her eyes are threatening to spill over.

"Honestly, guys. More than fine." She's still smiling, but the tears are really flowing now. Adhira grabs hold of us both and tugs us into a three-person hug, which in my recent past would have been two too many people for my comfort. But I'm hit very suddenly—like a big slap across the cheek from insight, perhaps?—with the realization that I don't mind this. And then a slap on the other cheek . . . and my friend is crying for *reasons* and I've been so shortsighted in my own determination to thwart Mary that I haven't done anything to help.

"Do you, ah, want to talk? About it?" *Wow. Nice, Marnie. Nearly human.*

Adhira hiccups. "No, just having you two here was exactly what I needed."

Except for hearing her sniffle after our fight on my birthday, I've never actually seen Adhira cry. And while I know *something* happened in Toronto that made her come here, she's always acted like it was well behind her. But now I'm not so sure. Whatever it was, as her friend—and I've realized quite strongly that Adhira *is* my friend—I need to get out of my Mary-ness and be there for her.

Just maybe not *right* now. The rain has really picked up, the wind with it. I can be there for her from the warmth of our dorm room, okay?

"So should we . . ." I mime skipping straight over the stones out of the maze.

That makes Adhira hold me tighter. "We can't only go halfway! We'll lose all the gained insight!"

Then she's off, following the tight path as it slowly unspools toward the exit. Dev catches my eye. "You don't want to *lose* insight. Can you imagine?" He grins at me and follows Adhira. For the first time, I realize why she wanted me to get to know Dev.

"The horror." I say it just loud enough for him to hear.

We're soaked by the time we trek back across the park to the top of the Lincoln Steps. Dev announces that he has the car for another hour and he's taking us all to In-N-Out. It's by Fisherman's Wharf and overrun by tourists, yet we snag a corner table by the door and tear into greasy food and shakes.

The "insight" gained from the labyrinth isn't quite sitting right in my belly. It tussles with my burger for supremacy. If Hayes is my destiny, why do I feel so . . . let down? There should be fireworks and a song-and-dance number. Sparks shooting across my vision. Instead, I feel oddly disappointed. I want more. A big gulp of milkshake freezes a spot between my eyes, and I glance around, trying to distract myself from all this uncomfortable introspection.

There's a sign tacked to the door, the letters and words all backward.

CLOSED THANKSGIVING

Thanksgiving. "Adhira, are you flying home for Thanksgiving?"

She pauses, the grilled cheese from the secret menu halfway to her mouth. "Well." She sets the grilled cheese back down. "Canadian Thanksgiving was last month."

Unbidden, I picture Adhira at PCA all alone, heating up a single-serving turkey dinner in the cafeteria microwave. I've never once been alone on a holiday. I've fantasized plenty about spending Easter with a book and some chocolate eggs, but it's the fantasy of someone who knows they'll always be surrounded by family. The thought of Adhira alone makes my chest tighten.

"Come home with me for the weekend." I don't chew on the words. I spit them right out and then peek at Adhira for her reaction.

She's silent for a second that stretches wide with the specter of discomfort.

"Are you sure?" she finally says. "I don't mind a weekend by myself. I could use the time to finish up my booth design for the Hunt Prize fair."

Dev rolls his eyes. "You're already so prepared."

Adhira nods. "But don't you think I should add one more costume sketch? And I'm still working on the swatches."

Sure, that sounds reasonable, but something in her voice makes me insistent. "Come on. You'll be doing me a service. I mean, be prepared for Dad telling *way* too many dumb jokes, but my older sister's wife always brings an amazing dessert."

Adhira blinks fast, then she scoots her chair like she's coming in for another hug, but I hold my hands up. "You already hugged me at the labyrinth. Don't push it."

But she's laughing, and I'm smiling, and I feel in this moment like I did the right thing.

From deep within my raincoat pocket, my phone rings. I pull it out and nearly drop it into my fries. It's destiny calling.

"Hayes." I breathe out, half afraid I'm having a stroke and have lost the ability to read. He never calls.

Adhira and Dev share a look. "Yippee," she says, voice flat. "The boogie board superhero."

My shoulders hunch in defense. "I think you mean the guy who saved my life."

"Answer if you're going to answer," Dev says, but in a way making it clear answering the call is *definitely* the wrong move. But, seriously, what does he know? In all my books, the heroine is pursued. It's simply fact. And right now, Hayes is calling me.

I'm out the door and huddled under the yellow awning before the Judgment Twins can get in any more jabs.

"Hayes! Hi!"

"So, listen," he says, launching right in. "Plans changed, and I'm headed to your folks' for Thanksgiving."

My heart jumps and I choke on a giggle.

"I'm driving down from Petaluma and Sara's meeting me there, so I figured, hey, I should give my favorite Barnes sister a ride to San Jose."

Favorite. He called me his favorite. Heat rises in my chest and burns away anything I could possibly say. The air in my lungs vaporizes, which leads to some serious serial killer breathing. A ride. *Ohmygod a ride.* With Hayes. In his car. This is it, my moment. Like when Gilbert gives Anne a ride alone in his carriage, and yeah, they don't heavily make out, but that doesn't mean it won't happen for me and—

A flash of movement within the restaurant shatters my illusions.

"Um," I say, my eyes on the glass windows through which Adhira and Dev are *clearly* watching my every move. "My roommate is actually coming home with me for Thanksgiving."

There's a pause. An awful pause. "I've got the Porsche."

My fingers twist up in the cord of my hood and a vision of me sitting next to Hayes in his Porsche revs in my mind. And Adhira will . . . My twisted-up fingers yank hard.

"I . . . I don't know. How will Adhira get there?"

"She'll figure it out. Come on, don't make me drive all on my own. I was looking forward to catching up."

I picture him on the other end of the phone, his lovely lips turned down in disappointment. Because of me. Last year, Hayes helped Dad with a small project, and when he returned from a coffee run he brought me a mocha Frappuccino even though I'd not asked for one. It was so sweet it made my teeth hurt, but I drank the whole thing and used the plastic cup to hold pens on my nightstand. He noticed me when no one else did. How can I possibly say no to him now?

Through the window, Adhira and Dev are practically smashed against the pane. I flap a *stop staring already!* hand at them, then consult my shoes. They're muddy from our walk back from the labyrinth. I'd asked for insight, but all I have is indigestion. Adhira already planned on being alone for the long weekend. It's not like she was looking forward to Thanksgiving with my family. And, oh god, Mom will definitely be wearing her problematic Thanksgiving dress. It'd actually be kinder, right? To *not* bring Adhira?

Except . . . My heart twists.

"Sorry." I can't believe what I'm doing. Marnie Barnes: Enormous Dumbass. "We'll drive down with Lindy and Will like I planned. But I'll see you there!"

"Your choice." Hayes's voice is clipped, and he's fast to get off the phone. My stomach sloshes with undigested shake and uncertainty.

I don't know what that labyrinth did, but I don't think it did anything for my insight, that's for sure.

"There's something very lovely about an empty campus," I sigh, my cheek pressed to the cool glass. Below our dorm room window, PCA is deserted. I wonder, has Hayes already left for Mom and Dad's house? Is he lonely without me? I swallow down a spike of regret and pivot away from the window, where Adhira is packing her weekend bag. I'm doing the right thing bringing her to Thanksgiving. Although—

"I need to warn you about my mom."

Adhira looks from the two dresses she was considering to me. "I've met her, remember?" She rolls up one dress and carefully stashes it in her bag before tugging it out and replacing it with the other option.

"Yeah, but she's . . . a lot on holidays. It's like seeing Julia Barnes performance art and it's . . . I mean, she wears this certain dress almost every Thanksgiving she calls—"

My phone pings announcing Lindy and Will's arrival, and Adhira frets, shifting on her feet. "Do I look okay? I don't know how dressy—"

I almost say something flippant about how it doesn't matter, but I stop and smooth away that reaction. She's asked me no more than ten times how dressy everyone is at my house for Thanksgiving. Wearing the appropriate clothes is Adhira's way of showing she cares, I've learned in the past few weeks. Honestly, I usually wear jeans and a tee, but the rest of my family *does* dress up. And maybe it's Adhira's influence, or my quest to banish Mary, or the fact that Hayes will be there, but this morning I put on my navy dress with the tiny cats. I read my contract to myself and felt *very* proud.

I, Marnie Elizabeth Barnes, hereby do swear to root out and destroy Mary Bennet. Check.

I will not allow myself to die alone with fifteen cats, having never been kissed. Check . . . ish.

"Adhira," I say, putting on my best reassuring tone, "you look fantastic." She's wearing a shift dress with a graceful boatneck in an eggplant color that makes her skin glow. Also, I didn't know what half those terms meant before I moved in with her.

My phone pings again, and I dash out a quick text: *Sorry! Coming!*

We march across campus and find Will's black Audi idling in the staff lot. For a twist of a second, I picture sliding into the passenger seat of Hayes's Porsche. But then Lindy jumps out of the passenger seat, scattering the daydream. "Marnie! I love your dress!"

I return the compliment with true grace: "Look at your stomach!" I practically screech.

Lindy grins, and Will reaches over and rubs her belly, which has well and truly popped since the last time I saw her. "We got to week twenty, and this little boy was like, *hello, I'm here!*" I've never witnessed Will this smiley in the four years I've known him.

"You look beautiful," Adhira says, which is perhaps a tad more gracious than I was. She holds out her hand to Lindy, then Will. "Adhira Fitz."

"Are you of the Seattle Fitzes, by any chance?" Will asks. "They've been enthusiastic proponents of a sustainable travel app I've been beta-ing. They really understand emerging markets."

Adhira blushes and tucks hair behind her ear. "Uh, no. The Toronto Fitzes. I don't think my parents are into emerging markets. But they did use Airbnb when they came to move me into school."

Will stows our bags, and as he's helping Lindy back into the car, I lean close to Adhira. "I think the Toronto Fitzes are *miles* better than those snobby Seattle Fitzes anyway," I whisper in my snootiest accent.

An airy laugh whooshes out of her. "Don't even mention the Miami Fitzes in my presence. They are the worst."

"The *worst*." I slide into the back seat and grin at Adhira next to me.

After I invited her to join us for Thanksgiving, I spent a few days cycling through all the worst-case scenarios and second-guessing my invite. But now, as much as I'm nervous for how my family will behave, I'm excited to have a friend by my side.

Lindy swivels to look back at us as Will takes the on-ramp toward 280 South. "I wanted to check out Bark Books Saturday, but I've got an investor meeting. Can I take you out to dinner after?"

My eyebrows shoot high, but I school them. Lindy's never taken just me out for dinner. I pinch my mouth closed to stop a manic smile and say, "That sounds nice."

"Joss wants to come too," Lindy adds before turning back around.

I nod, then Will glances in the rearview mirror. "Lindy told me Casper Lawson's daughter is at your school too. How is that? In all my business dealings with Casper, he's . . ."

"A douchecanoe?" Lindy pulls a face as Will chokes on a laugh. "Dad can't stand him."

That news makes my chin tilt. I never knew that about Dad. Mom is always cozying up to Lia's stepmom at the club. She once made me and Lia be partners in a charity badminton match that was, you know, horrific.

But then Lindy moves on to chatting with Adhira about her costume and design contacts in the film industry and I forget all about it. Between the four of us, we talk about general life news, music, and—oddly—there's a tangent on our favorite seasons based on allergies. Will is blowing his old talking record out of the water.

So much so, I almost startle as he turns right onto my family's road, a winding ribbon of asphalt that snakes upward into the Los Altos Hills northwest of San Jose. Beyond enormous trees and around blind corners, mid-century-turned-mansion homes cling to the cliff edges. The entire drive seems to have taken half the time it usually does, and I haven't once taken out my book to pass the time. Weird, but this human interaction has been, dare I say, enjoyable.

Maybe this Thanksgiving will be different.

FIFTEEN

MAYBES ARE DREAMS FOR THE DELUDED.

The house is crawling with people. I mean, the triplets are *literally* crawling along the back of the enormous white sectional. Mom screeches a hello at us and an acrid scent of smoke burns my nose.

"Lindy, my darling!" Mom's so excited, she even puts down her chardonnay and two-steps over. She's wearing the aforementioned Thanksgiving outfit, a tan suede dress with turquoise cowgirl boots and a load of yellow topaz jewelry. She calls it her Pocahontas dress and I've lost hours of my life trying to educate her on why this is wrong. But here we are.

"Sorry for the awful stench. Your sister lit a tea towel on fire."

"On accident," Lola bellows from the living room.

"She says." Mom kisses Lindy on both cheeks—how continental of Julia Barnes—then tries to go in for Will, but he scoots around her. He catches my eye and smirks guiltily, then gratefully accepts a cocktail floating with pomegranate arils and a lemon twist from Sara.

There's a lemon twist in my stomach too—Hayes asked *me* to ride with him, but I wonder why he wasn't traveling with Sara. Does she know he offered me a ride? It's a strange sensation to both hope for Hayes's eternal love and dread the guilt whenever I see Sara.

Adhira's overnight bag knocks the back of my calves and drags my attention away from Sara.

"Thanks for having me, Mrs. Barnes," Adhira says.

Mom grabs her arm and pulls her deeper into the great room, though she doesn't offer to take the bag. "Oh, we always welcome guests. I do love to entertain, you know." She leans in conspiratorially, like she and Adhira are old gossips from way back. "Even though Mr. Barnes can be absolutely awful about it all. I'm happy Marnie brought home a friend who isn't imaginary."

"Mom!"

Mom ignores me—perhaps the root of my childhood imaginary friends. She gets her claws into Adhira and drags her away while complimenting her complexion and hair.

Under the burned-tea-towel smell, it's all apples and

nutmeg. It's warm and soft, seemingly at odds with the glass-and-concrete modernism of Mom's remodel. The art on the walls is "directional," as she tells anyone who lingers too long, but translates to "my designer picked it out and I have no clue what I'm looking at." Mom isn't one for art, directional or otherwise. Though she's very proud of the boudoir portraits hanging above her and Dad's headboard.

From behind the makeshift bar set up atop the breakfast bar, Sara is mixing more drinks while chatting with Lindy.

"Marnie, you want one?" she asks, shaking a new cocktail. "Virgin, obviously."

Low blow, Sara.

"Meh, I'm . . ." I don't bother to finish the sentence the second I hear the laid-back drawl that often populates my dreams.

He's here. Past Lola and Kat, who are bickering about something (I'm guessing boys), past the triplets currently disemboweling a pillow, past Joss flapping her hand at the triplets and calling for Edie to help. There. Sliding into view by Dad and Will, who're shaking hands in hello. Hayes's blond hair is lustrous under the living room lights, and his skin hints at a tan like he spent a weekend on the water.

My heart goes pitter-patter. I grab the weekend bags as an excuse and dart closer. Hayes tugs at the cuffs of his charcoal-gray suit and palms his phone, holding it up to show Will and my dad something.

Oh so casually, I sidle up next to him at the fireplace and listen in.

". . . and the designer, on my request, is even mocking up a sliding bar to choose your level of diversity, which I think will go over well with our demographic."

A rainbow of birds singsong in my chest. Of course Hayes would care about ensuring diversity in his new venture! He's so considerate like that.

The smile on Dad's face curdles, though, and he holds up a hand. "Son, we're here to celebrate Thanksgiving, not talk tech."

Well, that seems rather rich. That's all Dad and Will usually do. Will, for his part, slides a finger under his collar and searches the room for Lindy.

"Tom, come on now," Hayes presses. "This is a prime opportunity—"

"Let's go check on the turkey," Dad says, cutting him off.

What turds, to not even give Hayes the chance. He's not made a fortune in Silicon Valley yet, unlike the two of them. I gather my courage around me like barbed wire and prepare to wholeheartedly show Hayes that at least I appreciate him.

Hayes's shoulders stiffen, and the side of his neck has gone blotchy. "So sorry I bothered you with all this." He emphasizes the word *bothered* to Dad's back. "Of course, I'm already close to securing Casper Lawson's support."

Dad stills and angles back to us. "I would caution you before working with that man."

"He's the most powerful man in the South Bay."

"Power doesn't make him a smart investor." Dad's cheeks

are pricked with color, and he pulls his shoulders up and back, standing to his full height. Dad's usually bent over something— an old computer, books about birds, his grandchildren. He's rarely imposing, but right now he commands silence.

Lindy had mentioned Dad not liking Casper, but now I wish I'd asked her why that was, exactly.

"Oh, I know what you think of Casper Lawson. Who can forget what you did to him?" Hayes adds after a moment, piquing my interest even more. Then he whirls to me, acknowledging me for the first time, and I startle. "Marnie! Let me help you with that bag."

He plucks my tote off the floor and marches toward the hallway leading to the bedrooms, leaving me to scurry after him with the two weekend bags. He slows, passing three closed doors—Lola's room, Kat's room, a guest bathroom— and I clear my throat. Timidly, I bump open the last door on the right and show him into my room. Hayes tosses my tote on the bed, books and my laptop spilling out.

"I'm sorry about that, Mar." His jaw is tight and his nostrils flared. He starts pacing. "I shouldn't have lost my temper."

I drop my bags and nearly fall over myself holding out my hands to him. "No! He was being an absolute boor to you! To not even consider your project. Which sounds brilliant, by the way."

"Thank you. At least someone in this family recognizes what I can offer. We'll have to work on him, right? Make him see this is something worth his time." *We. He called us we.* Hayes catches his reflection in the mirror over my dresser and pauses to push a stray hair back into place, then resumes pacing.

In the breath of silence between us, that name—Casper Lawson—sneaks back up on me and nips at my ankles. I chew on my lip, then ask, "What did you mean, about my dad doing something to Mr. Lawson?"

"You don't know?" He stops pacing and regards me.

The shake of my head is small and jerky. I remember Adhira asking me why Lia was so mean to me, but I always assumed it was because of who *I* was, not anything to do with Dad. Have her years of torment been Dad's fault?

"That's for your father to explain, not me," he finally says. "Though he's probably too embarrassed to, with how he acted."

Hayes has been all manic energy, but now he stills and peers around my room.

"It's funny, isn't it? All my years living next door, and I've never been in your room." Stuffed animals gather dust on my white rocking chair in the corner, and the bed skirt is blue ruffles. His gaze turns back to me, and my skin prickles. I slide sweaty palms against the skirt of my navy dress and shuffle a bit on my tan wedge heels.

The air is stretched thin between us.

Hayes plucks Master Bunbun off the rocking chair and tosses the floppy stuffed rabbit between his hands. He smirks and steps closer. "Stuffed animals? You're *definitely* not a kid anymore."

The air whooshes from me. His eyes are steady on mine; he takes another step closer. It happens in an instant—I jolt away from him. The reaction is instant, undeniable, and absolutely the opposite of what I've always fantasized. I'm alone in this room with a man I've swooned over for nearly all my teen years. I'm alone in this room with a man engaged to a woman I've known all my life. And I really, really shouldn't be.

"I've got to get back," I mutter, eyes on the rug.

Hayes laughs. "Come on, Mar. I was just joking. I've known you forever; I thought I was allowed to joke around with you."

I push my glasses back up my nose and make myself look up so I don't seem like a miserable bore. "You can. I didn't mean—"

"It's just." He cuts me off and reaches out to lay a warm palm on my arm, and I fight the overwhelming urge to tug away. "Maybe you can help me get your dad on board with this project. I could come meet you in the city? We can do dinner and catch up and maybe come up with something. My treat."

I don't want to be alone with him. He's marrying Sara . . . Sara, who is currently mixing drinks just down the hall from us. There can never, *ever* be anything between us. It's always made me feel so, I don't know, *romantic,* to consider myself a tragic heroine who will die alone but true to her one love. But this? This reality?

I don't want this.

He finally lets go, and I grab hold of my wrists behind my back, squeezing tight to quiet my shaking fingers.

"Mom cornered Adhira," I manage. "I've got to go."

I bolt out of my bedroom and force myself to walk in the hallway, even though my muscles beg me to run. The great room is hot and loud, and this stupid dress is itchy and too heavy for the eighty-degree day. I peek at Sara, then away when I catch her eyes on me. The guilt on my face is probably obvious as an ax wound.

What do I do? The wrongness of it all skitters down my spine. Do I tell Sara . . . but what is there to actually say? And how do I explain to her why my encounter just now with Hayes felt off without betraying my own devotion to him? There's a sourness in my gut that won't be tempered. I owe her . . . *something*, but I don't know what that is. And I don't even know how to begin to say any of it aloud.

Instead, I veer the opposite way and head toward Mom, who *does* still have Adhira trapped between the dining room table and the big glass doors to the backyard. I join them just as Mom says, "Huh. I didn't know your people celebrated Thanksgiving. What on earth are you giving thanks for?"

Adhira blinks quickly. "Canadians? Uh, the bountiful harvest and terrible colonialism, just like Americans. Though I think my dad is most excited for the annual CFL double-header."

My mother's smile goes brittle. "Yes, of course. Canadians.

I guess you would celebrate a good harvest too. Do you like my dress? I think of it as my—"

"Want me to show you around?" I practically shout.

"That'd be great!" Adhira answers in a waterfall of words.

And we both straight-up flee.

"I saw you go down that hallway alone with Hayes."

The way Adhira says his name makes my stomach clench, but I breathe around it. "He helped me with the bags."

We've holed up in the downstairs movie room, but I glance up at the ceiling as I say it, like Sara may hear. The music and talking on the main floor have been reduced to an indistinct rumble.

Adhira's mouth tightens and the tip of her finger pauses over the spine of one of the thousands of movies Dad has collected and alphabetized. "Uh-huh."

I groan and flop into an armchair. They're made of some high-tech material that makes me sink deep into the cushion, until I'm getting an upholstered hug. Yet it doesn't hug away the hard pit of *something* in my stomach. I've longed for real attention from Hayes for years, then my body straight-up betrays me when I finally get it. Obviously, I am defective.

But that doesn't feel right. I'm a whole bunch of mixed-up feelings, but then an *awful* possibility invades. Hayes said he was joking, so I obviously misread the situation, embarrassed myself in front of him, made my unrequited love painfully obvious, and must immediately check myself into a nunnery.

Instead of telling Adhira my nun plans, I ask, "Do you happen to know anything about Casper Lawson getting . . . in trouble, maybe? Or, like, humiliated?"

Adhira glances over her shoulder. "Only in my dreams. He hosted a table read for my theater class last month then, I swear to god, he critiqued everyone's style and how it inhibited Lia's natural talent. It was . . . I mean, if he were my dad, I would have died. But I don't think Lia has enough humanity to feel embarrassed."

A shiver of disgust rolls up my spine. "He's like a Shakespearean villain."

"Except worse."

"'Thus do I ever make my fool my purse,'" I say, quoting Iago's famous soliloquy in *Othello*.

"And thus am I an absolute human boil," Adhira shoots back. She collapses back into her own armchair and goes quiet.

"Speaking of human boils . . . I'm sorry I abandoned you with my mom."

She grimaces. "I know I shouldn't say anything bad about your mom."

"Oh, yes. You should."

"She's kind of really offensive, isn't she?"

"Kind of? She's one hundred percent offensive. But if you call her on any of it, she'll tell you to calm down. Or she'll bring up her ace card." I affect her childish voice and purse my lips in the smile Mom makes when she knows she's about to win. "'Well, your father doesn't seem to have a problem with me, Marnie. So if I'm so awful, you must have an issue with him too.'"

Adhira picks at an invisible thread on the arm of the chair. "I miss home." Her words are small.

"I'm sorry." Fifteen minutes with Mom, and she's ready to drop out and fly home. "I, uh, I kind of figured something happened in Toronto to make you come all the way here for senior year. Do you, um, want to talk about it?"

Adhira leans her head back against the chair and tilts her chin to look at me. Her mouth parts, and I wait. Because the thing is, I *want* to know what happened to my friend. I want to be able to talk her through it. To help her love it here.

But then her lips press together and she sighs through her nose. After a second, she stares at the ceiling and says, "No, I don't. Sorry."

The rejection stings, even though I know Adhira enough by now to be certain she didn't mean it as a slight. Pushing my way through the awkwardness and out of the chair, I hold out a hand to her. "No problem. I want to show you something."

She follows me down the hall and into a little-used corner of the basement, where my great-grandmother's sewing machine and vintage cloth hide in archival boxes.

"My mom's grandma was a seamstress, so we've got a lot of her old stuff." I pull the lid off one box—one of dozens—and stare down at neat rows of bolts, the colors organized in a gradient. Behind me, Adhira gasps.

Her fingertips dance across the cloth. "These are phenomenal. Look at how crisp the colors in this calico are!" Her eyes are bright when she looks at me. "I scour the vintage shops in the city, but it's hard to find anything predating the fifties."

It warms my chest to see the joy radiating off Adhira's face. I bump her shoulder. "Yeah, hearing you and Dev talk about it reminded me these were even down here. They're going to waste. You want some of it?"

Adhira's hands press against her chest. "No, I couldn't possibly." But her eyes linger on the cloth bolts.

One stands out to me—it's a soft cream cloth pricked with delicate flowers in hues of muted rose and celery green. I slide it from the box and hold it out to her. "Please, take it. Take a few. You can give them a better life than moldering away in a box."

Adhira squeezes the cloth and my fingers. "Marnie, you're one of the good ones. For a while, I thought everyone was crap, but you're not." She waits a beat, then grins. "Hayes is still crap, though."

The table practically sags with the weight of food—tangy cranberry sauce and tureens of gravy, mountains of boiled potatoes and two types of stuffing. Peeking out from under the porcelain bowls and platters is a deep maroon tablecloth and a lace runner. Four separate tablescapes of creamy flowers are jammed in between, and candlelight glints off the crystal glasses. And in the middle of all this is an enormous carved turkey.

Mom holds court at one end of the fourteen-seat table, Dad at the other, with all of us in between arranged by calligraphy place cards. Hayes is smashed between Mom and my nephew Theo with Sara across from him and out of my line of vision. I've already embarrassed myself once in front of Hayes, so let's leave it there.

Hayes's eyes flick to mine, and my stomach churns so violently I burp. Charming.

"I thought," Dad begins, dragging me away from my newest humiliation, "we could each say what we're most thankful for this year. I can start. I'm thankful for the time with my wonderful, talented daughters the last few weeks." He nods at me as he says it, and a sunshine glow warms my skin. Maybe I can salvage this.

The thanks go around the table, ranging from *my health, fragile as it is* (Mom) to *the excellent boiled potatoes* (Hayes) to *new shoes* (that'd be Lola). When it's my turn, I'm still not sure what to say.

"I'm thankful for . . ."

"Books!" Kat grins at me from across the table.

"I mean, always."

Lola waggles her eyebrows dangerously. "The love of an older man!"

Heat surges up my neck and I force myself to not look to Hayes. "What? No, Lola. God."

I'm about to be thankful for this giant carving knife I'll plunge into my sister's black heart, but next to me, Adhira whispers, "Bark Books?"

"Yeah," I say, surprised by my conviction. I *am* thankful for Bark Books and everything it's brought to my life already. I look at my family—though still studiously avoiding Hayes— "I'm thankful for Bark Books."

Dinner is less stab-inducing after that low blow from Lola. For her part, she's quiet afterward and seems to at least feel an approximation of shame. Mom has also been on her best behavior, cocooned with Sara, Edie, and Hayes. She let Edie and Joss bring all the desserts, which is better than two years ago, when she ordered "pumpkin mousse and graham cracker shards served in a martini glass" from a trendy San Jose bakery (now out of business). Even despite a puking incident involving dessert and a certain young nephew named Jonah, Mom has proclaimed zero headaches. We've all slowed down, leaning back and chatting over each other. The floor-to-ceiling windows beyond the long table are fogged over, and the lights shimmer against them with a golden glow.

The room is lulled, the fourth pie half-eaten, and I'm warm and sleepy. Kat stretches her arms overhead, then leans forward to drag her fork through the bowl of whipped cream. "Dad has been talking up Bark Books." She licks the tines of her fork. "Honestly, Mar, it sounds pretty great."

Lindy speaks up. "You should come to one! Every Saturday

at Paws and Claws. I can't make it this Saturday, but you'll tell Sir Pat I miss him, Marnie?"

Lindy had texted me demanding dog pics last week, and fell hard for Sir Pat. It makes sense, since her next doc is *Not Without My Doggo*, about a man in Houston who wouldn't evacuate in a hurricane without his shelter dogs. I scroll to an adorable shot of Sir Pat with his snout rested on his crossed paws and show it around.

I'm all warm and fuzzy inside from Dad and my sisters being so supportive. It's like my Thanksgiving dinner is giving me a hug. "I'd love it if you came, you guys! Adhira, you should come too!" *Look at me, exclaiming things all over the place!*

"When is it again?" Hayes asks. Thanksgiving dinner kicks, and I clamp my mouth shut. He scoots down to nab the open seat next to Kat. "You know I'm always up for supporting you Barnes ladies."

And you know what, he is. He comes to our family meals and indulges Mom's inane themed parties. Come on, body, get with the program. I'm not a complete idiot; I know my reaction is because of the guilt I feel toward Sara, who's currently in the kitchen loading the dishwasher with Edie. But in that moment, alone and close with Hayes, it felt more immediate than that. More like . . . *revulsion.* I shake away that word just as Adhira speaks.

"I'll trade you one Bark Books for one tour of the Winchester Mystery House."

The table groans, and it's not just from the leftover food and jumble of haphazardly stacked china.

"No, no, no. That place is a tourist trap," Hayes insists.

"What?" Edie pokes her head around the kitchen wall. "That place is creepy and awesome!"

"Okay, and you also held a séance for your bachelorette party," Lindy retorts.

"And you and Joss communed with your great-grandma, so cool it," Edie teases.

"Both of you, quiet down," Mom says, one hand at her chest. "All this talk of dead people. It's too macabre."

Lindy catches my eye and snorts. Mom is obsessed with true crime shows.

"You're too right, Julia," Hayes cuts in. "There are much nicer places to go around here."

That makes me narrow my eyes. Nicer, maybe, but not what Adhira wants.

"If you want, I could meet you both for lunch and show you around," he presses, like I wasn't born and raised in the San Jose area. "There's this great spot near Santana Row. Very hard to get in, but I know a guy." Hayes leans forward, his hair less shiny than it was earlier and his voice too eager. I tilt away from him.

It's been nearly five years since I pledged my love—my *everything*—to Hayworth Wellesley. And I'm suddenly not certain I should anymore.

SIXTEEN

PUMPKIN PIE FOR BREAKFAST IS severely underrated.

This is our second morning choosing dessert over something boring like hard-boiled eggs, and I have no regrets. After breakfast, Adhira raids my closet and helps me choose an outfit for today's Bark Books: cropped jeans and a white button-down embroidered with comically long wiener dogs. I used to wear it open over a dress, but she buttons it halfway and ties the ends "to show off your waist." She suggests a stacked heel, but I suggest she stop dreaming and slip into my clogs. As a consolation, I let her do my hair in a messy topknot and pull out the earrings I bought yesterday after our Winchester Mystery House tour. The tassels are bright blue like today's morning sky and hang nearly to my shoulders.

I twist my head back and forth and let them shimmy in my earlobes. They make me feel—please never tell anyone I'm saying this—*sassy*.

Mom and Dad have some sort of charity event, Kat and Lola refused to get up, Joss is probably wrangling the triplets, and Lindy is meeting with an investor for her documentary, so it's just me and Adhira on the train north to Paws & Claws. She can't stay long because she has a progress meeting with Dev and Tilda, but the fact that she's coming to support me is sunshine on my face. We even get into the city early and grab pastries and coffees for everyone, though I have to guess Whit's order. When we walk up to Paws & Claws, Daniel and Whit are lugging crates out of Booker to set up the display table.

"Hey, guys!" I hold up the coffees like a trophy and bound toward them. There's an undeniable spring in my step. Would we call it a *sassy* step? I daresay we would. We hand out the coffees and almond croissants, then Adhira makes big eyes at me and Whit, announces she requires dog snuggles, and runs off. Daniel follows her a minute later.

Last time I saw Whit, I sort of, kind of asked him out. Does he remember? Definitely, right? But I stomp down the desire to squeak and scurry away and instead lift my chin and ask, "How was your date?" at the same moment that he says, "Thanks for the cold brew."

We stare at each other. I say, "Yeah, of course" at the exact moment he kind of . . . groans? What a totally natural conversation we're having!

Whit leans back against Booker's open rear door and takes a sip of his drink. I pick a slivered almond off the top of the croissant and sit down inside the bookmobile's door. After a second, Whit joins me, our feet dangling and our legs nearly touching. I'm aware of how close he is, how nearly hidden we are in the shadows inside Booker. My heart kicks and I swallow hard.

Whit stares out the door. "It was really, um, first date-y. Those are always kind of weird, especially when your sister sets them up."

I nod, like I've ever been on a first date.

"Anyway, how was your Thanksgiving?" Whit changes the subject with the deftness of a bulldozer.

"Well, my nephew started crying so hard about not getting second dessert he puked, and then when I tried to get everyone to play Bananagrams, my mom announced she didn't feel like spelling. So pretty standard, actually. But Adhira was there, which was nice, and Hayes too."

I mention Hayes almost out of habit. As in, it's been my habit to always mark Hayes's location in relation to me. If I were being introspective right now, I'd probably say I brought him up to prove to Whit I'm not hung up on asking him out and *also* have members of the opposite sex in my life. But I'm definitely not feeling introspective at the moment. I roll my lips together and run the pad of my finger against my scar. Yup, still there—still a memento binding me to Hayes.

"Is that your brother?"

My cheeks prickle with heat. "Oh, um, no. He's a close family friend."

Silence opens between us, and I'm not sure what to fill it with. I want to keep talking to Whit, I want to ask him how his Thanksgiving was or how many nieces he has, but he jumps down from Booker, then holds out his hand to help me down. This time, I take it, and a current races between our palms. It's a shock to my system, reverberating deep in the base of my spine, and I tug my hand away from his.

Whit works his jaw and looks away. "Want to go over the checklist before the kids arrive?"

"I'm sure everything is fine." Also, I already went through it on the train up. He follows me around to the table under Booker's retractable awning, and I lift one of the new titles: "As promised, I come bearing iguana books."

"Nice!" Whit rifles through the titles until I bat his hand away and rearrange them how I like. This is easier, with my hands busy and not aching to grab his fingers again. Whit plucks one book before I can stop him and holds the cover up. "I hate to break it to you, Marnie, but we don't have any adoptable otters."

I snatch the book back. "How was I supposed to know? I covered all my bases this time. These kids will be able to read to dogs, cats, dragons, iguanas, one otter, two rabbits, and a moose."

Whit laughs, deep and musical. "Well, thank god our

adoptable moose won't have to go another week without being read stories." He pauses, peers around, then leans close over the book table. "I also come bearing surprises."

Suspicion makes my gaze narrow. Then my eyebrows crawl high when he points at the little illustration peeking over the pocket of his black tee. It's a simple line drawing of a cat, just the head visible. "I told you I had a cat shirt. I feel like you didn't believe me last time."

"I didn't," I say, lips quirked to one side. "Still don't."

Then Whit hooks one finger into the pocket of his tee and tugs it down, revealing the illustrated kitty giving me the finger.

A gasp whisks past my teeth, but that makes Whit laugh so hard that my cheeks go spectacularly warm. "That's so inappropriate! We're working with kids!"

He leans close again, and I can smell something clean, like fresh sea air, on his skin. It only makes the flames in my cheeks stoke higher. "It'll be our secret, then. Deal?"

Someone clears his throat, and I jump back from Whit like I got caught with a severed head. Daniel stares at us with all the opacity of tissue paper.

"Sorry to interrupt." His grin is wicked, innuendo dripping from his words.

"What? You weren't! Why would you . . . ?" I shuffle through the books, totally screwing up my careful display. Cats are jumbled with dogs, iguanas with otters. "I'm all done setting up here, and we're good to go!" Why am I yelling? *Stop yelling, Marnie.* "Excited for today!" I practically scream.

Whit shoots me a look, but there's a stain of pink in his cheeks and his eyes are bright. He nods at Daniel and shoves his hands into his pockets. "Well, I've got to go groom the moose, but I'll see you guys inside."

Daniel silently mouths the words *groom the moose.* "Is that some euphemism?" He shakes his head, but laughs. "I get why you'd want to groom his moose, Marnie. But maybe don't in front of the kids?"

"I'm not— I don't—" I suck in a breath and grip the edges of a book about a lost rabbit. "He was joking about one of the books I brought."

"Uh-huh." Convinced: Daniel is not.

Neither am I, honestly. "I'm serious, Daniel. I kind of asked him out, and he said no, okay? We're just friends."

"Oh, Marnie." Pity sugars his words.

"Which is as it should be," I say over him, choking on the excuse. "We're here to work, not . . . dally. Dallying never leads to anything good. I'm strictly anti-dallying." I have no idea why I keep saying the word *dally*, but there's no stopping me now. "Dally-free, is what I say."

Daniel frowns, so I crank my head away from him as the first kids wander up with their adults. The humiliation dissipates— slowly—as I pair kids with books. Plenty of kids still choose dog books, but enough of them light with excitement at the prospect of other animals that it boosts my confidence.

An hour passes quickly, and after Adhira leaves, I dig out the library camera. "I'm going to head inside to take some photos," I tell Daniel. "I'm planning a slideshow on a monitor at my fair booth."

He nods. "How's that going?"

The fair is only a couple weeks away, and I'm woefully behind. Less than half of the Hunt Prize participants advance past the fair, so I've got to nail this. I've compiled most of the materials I'll need, but I haven't actually done anything with them yet. The year Lindy won, she re-created a healthy salt-water marsh, complete with live animals. And I'm not saying that's why I emailed Whit last week asking if he could bring some dogs to the fair, but . . .

Daniel stares.

"It's going great!" I tap the edge of the lens to my forehead in a salute and head inside.

It's slow work, getting the photos. I need waivers from the parents to use any face shots of the children, which takes more time than actually taking the photos. After a bit, I focus on the animals. That'll probably play well with voters at the fair. Though who knows if it can compete with whatever nonsense Lia is cooking up.

A text from Lindy interrupts my focus: *Puppy pics please! Sir Pat is the love of my liiiiiiife.*

My grin curls reading it. I circle over to the scruffy mutt

and do a few glamour shots—he's a willing participant—and text them to Lindy. Her response is fast.

Thanks! Sir Pat is the only thing getting me through this investor meeting. See you later for dinner!

I don't know exactly when Lindy and I started to have our own conversations—not just, like, sister-wide discussions—but it's . . . nice. Still unusual, but nice.

A few minutes later, I'm having trouble focusing the camera on one of the dogs when a shadow falls over me.

"Which dog should I buy?"

The voice skitters across my skin. I'm squatting on the concrete floor, and I have to crane my neck to look up at him.

"Hayes?" I say his name like a question. He shouldn't be here. That's the first thing I think.

Yet the innuendo that icked me out at Thanksgiving is gone. Maybe I really did overreact. He was definitely just joking, right? Right now, his smile is uncertain, and it helps to quell my reservations. I say his name again, making the exclamation point clear. That makes his smile hitch higher. He fiddles with his watch. "Hope this is okay. The program sounded dope and I wanted to come support you."

I scramble to my feet. Across the room, Whit glances our way.

"No, it's great! Thanks for coming." Almost all of me means it. The holdout, though, fights being ignored.

I don't want him here.

Hush, self.

Hayes swipes a hand through his hair and peers around. "Do I get the official tour?"

I do my best to show him around the kennels and explain the program, but I'm also trying to take photos of the kids as I go, and Hayes is kind of in the way. But it's sweet of him to come! I have to remind myself of this several times. I'm working very hard to remain charmed by his surprise visit. It doesn't help that Whit is tracking us like a damn bloodhound.

We circle the space and end up at Sir Pat's kennel at the same time as Whit. Hayes glances at him, and steps closer to me. He tugs at the wisps escaping my topknot. "Was this dog your inspiration for your hair today, Mar? That's a major dog 'fro on this ugly mutt, isn't it?"

His laugh is, like, ten percent too loud. Embarrassment spikes in my gut, but it's for *him*. When I don't laugh, he nudges my shoulder.

"I'm joking! Maybe I'll buy this one."

I roll my lips in and clamp down.

On Hayes's other side, Whit visibly stiffens. "He can be adopted, not sold."

Hayes holds up his palms. "Whoa, dude. Didn't mean to offend. Who are you?"

Whit's fingers are stiff as his shoulders, but he holds out his hand toward Hayes. "Whit," he introduces himself. "I'm helping Marnie with her Hunt Prize project."

Hayes pumps Whit's hand too forcefully. "Hayworth Wellesley, of Bright Star Capital." He nods toward Whit's arm. "Sick tattoo. I got one just like it on my shoulder when I was in Thailand. The dude said it means 'golden warrior.'"

Whit's eyebrows twitch, and my cheeks burn with second-hand embarrassment. There is no possible way Hayes's tattoo means anything other than "loud tourist."

"What's yours mean?" Hayes barrels on, oblivious.

Whit says very evenly, "My Japanese name."

"Cool." Hayes says it like punctuation and angles away from Whit toward me. "Hey, so everything seems to be under control here. Can you sneak out early? Walt's got it." He juts his chin back toward Whit, who has a small muscle jumping in his jaw. My stomach knots up tight.

"His name is Whit."

"Okay, sure," Hayes says, but I'm pretty sure he wouldn't remember Whit's name if I asked him right now. "I was hoping we could talk more about my new project and how we can get your dad on our side."

We. Our.

My throat tightens. "This is *my* project. I'm not going to leave early."

Hayes shrugs. If he can sense my discomfort, he doesn't show it. "Another time, then." He slings an arm around my shoulders in a half hug, and I freeze. How many times have I imagined melting into him, feeling his arms strong around me like they were that day in the ocean? But once again, my body physically recoils away from him. And this time, it's hard to deny: I didn't do anything wrong—he did. The way he acted, the way he almost seemed to be flirting with me.

Hayes's phone rings, and he answers immediately, absently waving at me in goodbye, and I'm left staring at Sir Pat. He whines at me.

"For what it's worth, I like your hair." Whit's voice is clipped, and he strides away.

I don't see him again until we've packed up Booker. Joss and Lindy are meeting me at the library to head to dinner, and despite the weirdness with Hayes, I'm excited to see them. I duck into the staff bathroom and check my reflection. You know what, I think my hair looks good. *So take that, Hayes.*

I haul my weekend bag over my shoulder—I haven't had a chance to drop it off at PCA yet—and push the door open. And nearly collide with Whit. He's pacing, worrying a groove in the tile floor just outside the women's bathroom.

A sigh whooshes out of him. "Marnie." His feet still, and he hooks a hand behind his neck. "I need to apologize, about earlier."

"Oh yeah," I mumble, but I feel like *I* should be the one apologizing for Hayes's behavior.

"I just . . . I really hate it when people talk about buying pets like they're a new love seat or something."

"I'm sure that's not what he—" I stop myself. No, that's

exactly what Hayes meant. His family cycled through expensive Italian greyhounds like they were last year's Mercedes. "You don't need to apologize."

My hand drifts toward his arm, but I tug it back and curl my fingers in on themselves. The only light in the hallway comes from the open door of the volunteer office, and it brews a sort of intimacy I'm not sure I want with Whit. Shadows fall over his high cheekbones, his neck.

"Besides, it's obvious Sir Pat only has eyes for you. You're the only one who should be able to adopt him." I force a shaky laugh. Despite my earlier anti-dally position, this feels very much like dallying.

The tension in Whit's face dissipates and half a smile pulls at one corner of his mouth. "I would if I could. My mom's apartment doesn't allow animals." He scrubs a hand through his hair and cringes. "And I guess I just admitted out loud I'm a nearly-twenty-year-old college student who still lives with his mom." He grimaces and darts his eyes around the hallway, then taps his fingers against the phone sticking out of his pocket. I should say goodbye; Daniel's probably waiting for me. But my feet linger. All of me wants to linger, to find excuses to talk to Whit. He swallows, and I watch the bulge of his Adam's apple bob in his throat.

"So that was Hayes . . . you said he's a family friend?"

I chew on the inside of my lip and run a finger along the half-moon scar. Whit's eyes track the movement.

"What's that about?" He shuts his mouth quickly and holds up his hands. "Sorry, that was rude."

I shrug. I hadn't consciously touched my scar. "Hayes actually saved my life when I was younger. I got caught in a riptide and he saved me. That's how I got this scar."

Whit balks. "Whoa. Really?"

Usually, retelling this story fills me with pride, but now confusion sits uneasily under my skin. It's always been such a defining moment—Before Hayes Saved Me and After. But that horrible moment in my bedroom has scooped out the foundations of my dedication to him. I feel wobbly now, unsettled.

"It was a long time ago," I finally say, swiping my hand through the air, trying to erase the talk of Hayes between us.

"Oh, okay. Yeah, so actually . . ." Whit shifts back and forth on his feet. "I have an extra ticket to a traveling exhibit at the Academy of Sciences. It's on the domestication of dogs. It might be useful to fill out your project, right? You wanna check it out?"

Is Whit asking me out on a date? That can't be right. Maybe he means I'll buy the second ticket off him and we'll go separately. Yeah, that's probably it.

"Tomorrow at noon?" he asks.

My chest squeezes, almost painfully. "That could work," I choke out. "It would be good for my project."

Don't think of it as a date.

Not a date.

Not a—

"It's a date, then," Whit says, totally throwing off my internal monologue.

"Right, yeah. Okay. See you then."

Whit grins. I grin. There's more grinning happening than is strictly natural. Then I uncover my good sense and escape back to Booker. I need to tell someone. Adhira already texted me not long after she'd left with just Whit's name and a bunch of fire emojis. It's not every day a girl who was previously destined to die alone and be devoured by her cats gets a surprise visit by last year's *Silicon Valley Gossip*'s most eligible bachelor *and* gets asked out on a date. Except if it wasn't a "date" date. Maybe he meant, like, a physical date on the calendar. I mean, the word *date* can mean any number of things, so I don't want to jump to conclusions.

I'm still so busy overthinking literally everything that we're back at the library and I'm wandering through the loading bay before I register Joss standing in front of me.

"Have you heard from Lindy? She's late." A delicate frown pulls her brows together. She pushes white-blond flyaways off her forehead and glances at her phone.

I haven't actually. That's very un-Lindy-like.

"Maybe we should head to the restaurant?" It's only a few blocks from the library in Hayes Valley. And, yeah, I have considered if I chose the restaurant based on the Hayes connection.

"Yeah . . ." Joss's voice is soft and one hundred percent unconvinced.

We've just settled in her car when her phone rings. Her eyes snap to it and she puts the call on speaker.

But it's not Lindy. My heart goes sideways. My lungs deflate.

It's Will, and he's sobbing.

SEVENTEEN

JOSS STOPS AT THE PARKING LOT entrance at the hospital in Santa Cruz. "I don't know where to go. Is she in the emergency room?" She fidgets with her hair, the steering wheel, her collar.

"Dad said she was in Labor and Delivery."

"But the baby." Joss chokes back tears.

The baby. I stare at my lap and try my hardest not to think about it. About *him*.

A car beeps behind us, and Joss lurches forward. Finally, I point her toward the valet.

"Thank you," I mutter at the weedy kid who takes Joss's keys. Joss is frozen on the sidewalk, staring at the hospital doors and breathing hard. I've never seen her this lost. It unmoors me, to see my sunshine-and-warm-cookies big sister completely undone.

I slide my arm through hers, and she grabs me tight. "Together," I say.

Then the sliding glass doors whir open, and we're propelled inside.

"I'm looking for Lindy Barnes," I tell the nurse sitting behind the desk. "Drake," I amend quickly. "I mean, Lindy Drake."

Before she can consult her computer, the scent of burned air—like frayed wires and electricity—envelops me. I sink into Dad's hug. He always smells slightly of some new invention. Mom constantly complains and buys him cologne, but his scent calms the stuttering of my heart the tiniest bit.

"Marnie," Dad whispers into my hair, my name a lament. Fear eats away at me.

Dad hugs Joss and wipes her tears with his thumbs, then leads the way into a waiting room with fluorescent lights buzzing overhead and cheap laminate furniture. There are people gathered holding pink or blue balloons; smiling older women clutching teddy bears and little girls proudly sporting Big Sister badges.

And then there's us. Lola and Kat are curled in chairs on either side of our mother, whose face is puffy from crying. Her hair, always so meticulous, is thrown into a sloppy ponytail. Dad falls backward into a chair opposite.

"What happened?" I ask him, not sitting. Now that I'm here, my nerves sizzle and snap like so much of Dad's old tech he likes to disassemble for fun.

"A car ran a red light. She got T-boned. That's how . . ." Dad's voice fades.

There's a tightness in my throat, making it hard to swallow. "But she'll be okay?"

Mom scoffs, but her hands flutter like trapped moths in her lap. "The doctors only wanted to talk to Will, like we're not even here. Like we don't care our daughter might well die. Maybe they'll talk to us then."

"Julia," Dad growls, but his voice cracks.

Lola lifts her head from Mom's shoulder and glares. "Don't make this about you, Mom. Don't you dare." She scrambles to her feet and stalks off toward the coffeemaker, Kat following. They huddle together, Lola's faded pink hair brushing up against Kat's long, dark blond waves.

"I need to see her." Joss's voice is thick.

Mom shoves her chin out. "Oh, *you* should be allowed in? I guess we know where you think Dad and I rank with Lindy."

"Mom, I don't mean it like that."

Dad's shoulders droop. "We're lucky our girls have each other, Julia. Lindy has Joss, Lola has Kat, just like it should be."

Mom shrugs and goes back to staring at the far wall, her fingers worrying together, and I wrench my mind from the glaring error my dad made. The fact that he didn't include me.

That I have no one. It hollows me out.

"She just came out of surgery," Dad explains. "The accident cracked her hip. A femoral neck fracture. That's how . . ." Dad presses the back of his hand against his mouth until his breathing smooths. "The impact caused a placental abruption. It means the placenta detached from her uterus. They got her in for an emergency C-section, but it was too late."

All I can see when I close my eyes is the way Will pressed his hand against Lindy's pregnant belly. Heat sears up my throat, and I swallow hard. I'm afraid I may be sick.

My mind whirs, looking for reason or a way out or *something*. The baby was less than twenty-three weeks along, if I remember right, so there was no chance of survival. It's not like they lost their toddler. But even as I try to convince myself this is their silver lining, it still sounds wrong in my head.

They'd decorated a nursery. Last week, Lindy texted pictures to our group chat. They painted walls and put together a crib and bought a little stuffed bunny with a knit gray body. And there will never be a baby to hug it tight.

A film of tears obscures my vision, and I collapse into the chair, unable to stand any longer. I don't know how long I sit, but the world outside the windows bruises to purple. Will stumbles out into the harsh light of the waiting room sometime later and says we can't see her tonight. Because they were trying to save the baby, she was put under general anesthesia and reacted poorly coming out of it. Then he disappears back down the hall.

It's another while still when Dad squeezes my arm and says he's booked us all a hotel next door for the night. Wordlessly, we head over—Joss, Lola, and Kat in one room, and me with Mom and Dad in the other. For the first time in my life, I am the solo child alone with my parents. How often have I craved this? Yet all I want in the world right now is for my sisters to be here.

The night passes in fits and starts, and a mushy gray dawn is cold against my face when I finally give up and pad into the bathroom to shower. When I come out, Mom and Dad are dressed and ready to head back to the hospital.

It's mid-morning and I'm using the last of my phone's battery to update Adhira when Will slumps into the chair beside me. A million ways to say *I'm sorry* lodge in the back of my throat. Mom darts over and yanks him into a hug, but he stiffens.

"Don't hold back, Will, darling. It's okay to cry." Mom pulls back to check for tears—the only proper sign of sadness to my mother—and goes in for another hug. The poor man is already miserable, and I know more than most a Julia Barnes hug isn't what he wants right now.

"Have you eaten?" I ask.

Mom pauses her hug to scowl at me. "How can you be hungry at a time like this?"

"I'm asking Will. He needs to eat."

His head falls, and after a minute, he mumbles something to his lap.

Dad lifts Mom's purse and holds out a hand to her. "Let's all take a walk, Julia. I saw a coffee shop around the corner. Everyone needs some caffeine."

Joss, Kat, and Lola all stand, but I stay seated. "I'll take Will to the cafeteria here."

I've hooked onto this idea, that making him eat is a concrete way to help.

"You don't have to—" Will begins but doesn't finish. Without a word, he stands and follows me, and for the first time in nearly a day, I feel like I'm doing something real, something helpful.

In the cafeteria, Will pushes powdered eggs around his plate. The coffee is the only thing he seems to swallow. "You and Lindy know exactly how to . . . I don't know, *deactivate* your mother." He sits back, and a smile ghosts at one corner of his mouth. "Sorry to make her sound like a bomb."

His admission pulls a rueful laugh up my throat. "I never thought of it that way, but you're right. She *is* a bomb."

"It's more than just that, though. Lindy, she always talks about how similar you two are. Not only the books, I mean. She . . . she always means to be more involved with you. It's why she wanted to help with Bark Books. But isn't that the bullshit thing about life? You only focus on what's right in front of you, what's immediate, and you don't appreciate . . ."

Will trails off and goes back to shoving eggs around. And I'm struck by a couple of things. First, I realize I've never been alone with Will. And second, Lindy thinks we're alike? I honestly assumed she never thought about me. I thought her interest in Bark Books was a territorial Dad Grab. Guilt burns in my bones at how many years I've let my jealousy chip away at our relationship. And yet . . . if she cared so much, she could have done *something* before her sudden interest in my Hunt Prize to make it known. I shake off the thoughts and try to force down the rest of my yogurt.

"Can I see her?"

Will's hand goes tight around the handle of his fork, but he nods. "She'd like that. Yesterday was . . ." He scrubs a hand down his face and tries to take a sip of coffee, but his hand shakes. "She was already under by the time I got here, the baby was already . . . Usually they do a regional anesthesia, you know, but they were trying to go fast to save him. Seeing her on the table like that . . ." His voice breaks, and I reach across the table to grab his hand.

We dump the rest of our uneaten food, and Will leads the way down a quiet, dimly lit hall. The beep of monitors echoes out of cracked-open doors, and the air is tinged with the antiseptic scent of cleaning products. He pauses outside a propped-open door at the end of the hall. There's a small green sign tacked to the outside—a leaf dripping rain. Or maybe that's a tear.

Will's mouth is tight when he looks at me, and I have to drag my attention away from that horrible little card. Is that how they signify the patient within suffered more than an accident? A clip-art crying leaf?

"She looks really beaten up," he chokes out. "Just so you're . . ."

"I want to see her." I also want to run away and pretend none of this is happening.

Will knocks softly, and I shuffle in behind him, unsure where to look, not wanting to stare.

Because she looks awful. My heart nearly stops to see my sister like this. Lindy towers in my mind, a woman of near-perfection to whom I can never compare. Witty where I'm stumbling; sharp where I'm stifled; a quick laugh where I'm locked inside my own insecurities. Part of me has hated Lindy for how easily she bests me. All of me hates *me* right now for ever wanting to see her taken down. Not like this. Never like this.

Her skin is mottled purple from her forehead to her collarbone, bruises disappearing into the neck of her hospital gown. Cuts along the left side of her face are shiny yellow with ointment, the deeper ones bisected black from stitches. Her left wrist is wrapped in bandages, and her left ankle is in a cast. Under the thin blanket, her stomach bulges, like she's still pregnant.

She cranes her neck as we enter and winces in a hello. I sit by her bed and rest my palm on the blanket by her hand. After a second, she takes it. We don't talk. I don't know what to say.

Will and I intermittently watch TV and take turns getting coffee. The rest of the family drifts in and out: Joss can't stop crying, and it puts me on edge. Lola and Kat move as a unit, and Dad keeps commenting on the weather. After a while, Mom starts painting her nails, even though the smell of the polish sears against the scent of cleaner. My weekend bag is in Dad's car, so all I have is my now-dead phone, my wallet, and my battered copy of *Jane Eyre*. But even that can't quite hold my attention. Instead, I make it my day's mission to get Will to eat and have partially succeeded.

Sometime in the late afternoon, Joss leaves and takes the twins with her. Edie is getting on an emergency flight home from Sydney, where she was judging a baking show, but she won't be home for another fifteen hours and the triplets are with a friend.

The hours are marked by nurse rotations. The worst is when they check her C-section incision. The nurse presses on Lindy's belly, and I watch my sister screw up her face in pain. Nowadays, the nurses tell us, they don't give out narcotics, but they've made an exception for my sister.

It's near nightfall when any of us stir.

"Tom," Mom says, "I can't go another day in these clothes. I smell like a morgue."

Lindy flinches, but Mom doesn't notice.

Dad takes a long time nodding, then stands and claps a hand on Will's shoulder. "Son, why don't you come with us. We'll drive you up to your house and pick up a few things. Lindy, sweetheart, is there anything you want?"

Lindy's right hand drifts toward her stomach, then she drops it at her side and shakes her head tightly.

"I can't go, Tom." Will's voice cracks from disuse.

"No, Will, go," Lindy says. "I'll be fine here tonight. What am I going to do, run away?"

"I'll stay," I say, before even considering it.

"You have school—"

"Lindy, I can stay. Let me be useful."

After a second, she nods. They leave a few minutes later, and the silence stretches between us, sticky with discomfort. It makes my shoulders hunch and my hands curl in toward my lap. I want to say I'm sorry for her loss, but I don't know how. Don't know if it'll make everything worse to even bring it up.

"I'm—"

Lindy talks over me. "I'm sorry I wasn't able to come celebrate Bark Books with you."

"Oh," I say. "I'm just happy you want to be involved."

As I say it, I realize I mean it. It's been *fun* exchanging texts with Lindy, more than I thought it could be.

Lindy tilts her chin to look at me, and I force myself not to stare at the bruises disfiguring the side of her face. "You've always loved that book, haven't you?" She flicks her eyes to

Jane Eyre, sitting abandoned in my lap.

"I'm a big fan of secret wives and house fires." I cringe at the stupidity of the statement as soon as I say it.

A laugh tightens to a cough in Lindy's throat. "I always thought it was a bit too . . . florid for me, I guess. I fancied myself a *Secret Garden* sort of girl." She adopts a posh accent. "Because I was very mature and pragmatic, of course."

"Except Mary was obviously fated to be with Dickon, and it's a tragedy it doesn't happen."

Lindy nods. "A crime, truly. Dickon was my first literary crush. Well, him and the animated fox from *Robin Hood*."

"Ooh, yes," I enthuse, leaning forward and almost forgetting Lindy's injuries. Look at me, talking sexy anthropomorphic animals with my older sister!

Lindy makes to sit up, but hisses in pain, her hand pressing low to her abdomen.

"Do I need to call someone?" I lurch to my feet, panic crackling.

"No." She winces as she concedes to her pillow. "It's the incision from the C-section. I'm supposed to roll onto my side, but that's not exactly easy with three shiny new screws holding my hip together." Lindy goes silent for a moment, then looks at me. "Can you move the head of my bed up a bit? I hate lying here all day."

I fiddle with her motorized bed, trying to get the angle perfect, then ease back into my chair, unsure what to do now. The moment we just shared seems unreachable. I grab the remote and flip through the channels, but I don't recognize anything. All these years pretending I'm too good to watch television has kind of painted me into a corner. Finally, I flip onto some movie where people are wearing pretty gowns Adhira would insist on analyzing and still my channel-flipping finger.

"Oh, this is a good one." Lindy sighs.

It takes a moment before the character names click together.

"Wait, is this *Sense and Sensibility*?"

Lindy peers at me in disbelief. "Are you telling me you've never actually watched it?"

"I mean, I've read it plenty of times."

"Right, but you weren't lying about never watching these adaptations? Marnie, girl. You're missing out."

My lip curls, but it's more from routine than anything. "That's what Adhira keeps saying."

"I guess I should have come home more, huh?"

I was ten when she left for college. I was in awe of her, but sometime along the way, it turned to jealousy. I think back to Will's words yesterday. All these weeks I've been seeking an explanation for her involvement in Bark Books that can live in tandem with the monster that is my jealousy, but maybe it was never that.

My eyes are on the screen when I say, "Yeah, I would've liked that."

"But at least you had Kat and Lola . . ."

"No. I didn't."

Lindy sucks in a breath at that, then tries to smile easily. But it's thin at the corners. "The last time we all had some sister time to ourselves was at my wedding, wasn't it?"

Memories and a horrible sense of humiliation spider up my spine. Lindy's wedding. Where I was deemed not attractive enough. I shouldn't say anything. It makes me sound sour and petulant. I really shouldn't—

"I mean, except for me having to squint the whole time because you didn't want me wearing my glasses."

Lindy's chin jerks. "What?"

Uncertainty suddenly makes my stomach twist. "My glasses. You said they ruined your wedding photos."

"I *never* said that." There's danger in her tone. "Who told you that?"

It hits me suddenly, so absolutely, air punches past my teeth. *Mom.* Mom told me Lindy made that request. I don't say a word, but the angles of Lindy's face turn to murder, and I drop my chin.

"Jesus, Marnie. Look at me."

I manage to look somewhere above her eyebrows, which are winged low and sharp as a knife.

"Whatever Mom told you . . . I would *never* say something like that."

"Oh," I say, mouse-quiet to my lap. "Maybe I misheard. . . ."

Lindy grunts a laugh. We both know Mom wouldn't think twice about lying to get what she wants.

We go back to the movie in silence, but I'm aware of how

every movement seems to catch Lindy's attention, how we're two sisters perhaps just now lamenting at the deep, wide, churning sea between us. On screen, the tragically romantic character Marianne is carried home in the rain by the dashing Colonel Brandon. Lindy reaches over and wraps her cool hand around my wrist.

"I'm sorry, Marnie. I'm sorry I left you alone with her. All I could see was my own freedom. I didn't think of my sister. I didn't consider . . ."

For once in my life, I don't try to cover my emotion with facts and figures and denial. I turn my hand over and grasp Lindy's palm and squeeze her tight, even though I can't quite make myself look away from the screen.

"I'm sorry you lost the baby," I whisper.

A hitch catches her breath. "They let us hold him."

"Oh, Lindy." I shift from the chair to her bed to curl next to her and smooth her hair away from her forehead, careful with her bruises and cuts. "I'm so, so sorry."

Tears trace down her cheeks and soak into her thin hospital gown. "They kept him warm, and when I finally became lucid enough, they wrapped him in a little blanket and let us say goodbye. I could almost see who he was going to become. My son. My beautiful son."

I let her cry against me and tuck the sheets around her when she falls asleep before letting exhaustion drag me over to the narrow cot in the corner. When we wake the next morning, Will is already there. I tug on Lindy's sweatshirt over my day-old clothes and pad out to find us some coffee.

When I return, Will and Lindy are close together, his forehead pressed to her hand. It's a tender moment that I shouldn't witness, but it shatters through me, breaking apart the hardened shell I built between me and my sisters.

I've wasted years being jealous of my sisters—for their beauty or wit or bawdiness or friends. I've spent weeks convincing myself Lindy fit neatly into the Lizzy archetype, someone for whom only good things happen, whether they were deserved or not. But that's not right. It probably never was. Lindy has hidden triumphs *and* sorrows that would never make it to the page. We all do. Something aches within me—I'm desperate to know my sisters.

A few hours later, I realize it's time to return to my life. Joss is on her way back this afternoon, and Will should have some time alone with his wife. There is loss here they shouldn't feel compelled to share with anyone else. He offers to drive me to the train station to head back to PCA, and I don't try to demur. Before I go, I pause and look at my sister.

Then before I can talk myself out of it, I lean close and kiss her forehead. "I love you, Lindy."

She grabs my fingers and squeezes. "I love you too, sis."

The sea separating our lives has calmed, and it's clear enough that I can see the bottom. I could walk across to Lindy if I tried. The realization soothes something in me I never quite knew needed balm.

EIGHTEEN

I'M DRAGGING WITH EXHAUSTION BY the time I approach the iron gates of PCA. Gray mist curls across the school grounds beyond the gate, smudging the edges of campus. The trees outside are brown and bare, their limbs as cracked as my smile.

But a sigh escapes me. I'm home.

Last night at the hospital, I'd forgotten to get my weekend bag out of Dad's car, so I only have Lindy's borrowed sweater over clothes I've worn since Saturday. Habit has made me check my dead phone a dozen times on the train north and streetcar across the city. My wallet is in one hand, my book in the other, the pages fat with the drizzle. The chilly walk from the streetcar stop to here has sunk into my skin and pricks out goose bumps all along my arms.

In the gloaming, rectangles of yellow light from the dorm windows fight a losing battle against the fog. My clogs clack dully against the steps to the upper level of the courtyard in front of Hawthorne Hall, and I rush into the warmth. Yet every step closer to my dorm room makes the reality of the upcoming Hunt Prize fair settle heavier on my shoulders. I'm behind. *Really* behind. Being in the hospital with Lindy was like being on a different planet. A planet without deadlines or a de facto popularity contest in less than a week that will determine if I move on to the final round of the Hunt Prize.

Fingers of anxiety clutch my throat and make it hard to swallow. Maybe if I drop dead they'll posthumously award me a memorial Hunt Prize. Or everyone *else* can keel over and they'll have no choice but to award me the winner. A wince bristles my skin. Well, aren't I an awful human being.

It's quiet and shadowed in our room: nearly dinnertime on a Monday. Adhira's probably at the cafeteria. I flick on the light and squint. My eyes feel as if someone poured a pound of sand into them, but I spot my weekend bag sitting atop my neatly made bed. Dad must have dropped it on his way taking Will home. I dig through the bag for my phone charger and plug it in. It's so dead it doesn't even turn on at first.

I slump backward onto my bed, throw my glasses beside me, and have just let my eyes drift shut when my phone dings approximately half a million times. Almost blindly, I reach for it and drag it up to my face. I'm nearsighted, so I don't need my glasses to read all the missed texts, but it still takes a minute for everything to sink in.

I've missed a ton of messages from Adhira and my sisters. I click onto the group chat first: there's a text from Lindy an hour ago wishing me good luck at the fair on Saturday. That started a back-and-forth from my sisters offering their help: cookies from Joss and Edie; a whisper campaign about Lia's project I'm *pretty* sure Lindy is joking about; Lola has offered her good looks; and Kat jumped in to tell Lola it wasn't that sort of event.

I'm tired and sad and in desperate need of a shower, but a smile unfurls across my face as I join the thread.

I'll def take some cookies, thanks. And Lola and Kat, you're welcome to come and vote for my project!

I hit send as Adhira opens the door. She rushes over and wraps me in a hug. "Oh, Marnie."

My phone is still in my hands, and that's when I see it. Three more missed texts.

From Whit.

Hey, I'm here.

Are you coming?

I'm going in. Hope everything is okay. I'll see you around, I guess.

"Oh, shiiiiiiiiiiiit."

Adhira pulls back, her mouth pulled down in a frown. My stomach churns. My date with Whit. I *totally* forgot my date with Whit. I shove my phone at Adhira and scramble off my bed.

"What do I do?" I fidget on the balls of my feet like I'm on coals. Adhira reads the texts, and I flap a hand. "We were supposed to meet at Academy of Sciences yesterday to go to an exhibit."

"For a *date?*"

"I don't know!" I wail. I collapse into my desk chair and hold my head in my hands. But bending over like this makes me distinctly aware I want to puke.

"Can you tell him what happened?"

A groan rumbles out of me. "I don't know." The thing is, my sister and Will are sort of famous. Not, like, nationwide famous, but they're kind of a Big Deal in the South Bay: the tech scion who's made bank and his vivacious documentarian wife. Texting their tragedy to someone doesn't feel right, even if I trust him. I tell Adhira this; she chews on her lips and hands the phone back to me.

"This has to come from you," she says.

I start and delete a half dozen different responses, but how do you say *So, there was a family emergency and I spent a few days in the hospital with my sister and it was awful but also I think I had a breakthrough with my family, or at least with my sisters* without it sounding like an excuse? Finally, I settle on a short response, then throw my phone down.

I'm so sorry! Family thing came up. I'll explain when I see you at the fair.

He'll still come to the fair, right? I mean, he has to or I'm doomed. *Dooooooomed.* I'm counting on cute dogs. I *need* some damned cute dogs. Except if he hates me now and—

My phone dings and I lunge for it. Then groan in disappointment to see *Mom.*

He hasn't read it.

Still hasn't read it.

Adhira stretches out a leg and nudges my knee. "I understand if you're exhausted or don't want to talk about Lindy, but I did something for you."

I peek up from between my fingers. She kneels on my bed and grabs something unwieldy from behind my headboard—it must have been hiding in the space between our L-shaped beds.

"I know you lost prep time for the fair and you were already behind." She lugs a giant piece of cardboard down in front of her and opens up two folds. It takes a second to realize what I'm looking at, and when I do, surprise chokes me. The cardboard is full of photos and glued printouts from Bark Books.

"I found Daniel's contact info and got him to email me some photos," she explains.

The choking surprise reaches my eyes, makes them blurry. I seize Adhira in a hug, bury my face into her shoulder, and bawl.

Holy Anne Shirley. I'm crying. Sobs roll up my chest and break free, wet and loud.

Her arms tighten around me. "I'm sorry, Marnie. Is Lindy going to be okay?"

Another sob, this one like a wounded animal. Adhira's hand is on my back, rubbing in circles.

I nod against her shoulder, smearing tears and probably more snot than is proper. I'm crying for Lindy, for what she lost and the emptiness she's going home to. But under my sadness for my sister is something deeper. Something so powerful it scares the bejesus out of me.

Adhira is here for me. I don't know what I've done to deserve her. She doesn't need to be here for me, but she is. Because . . .

Because she's a real friend. A rare, beautiful, wonderful friend who likes me for who I am.

Another wounded animal claws up my throat and groans all over Adhira's pretty blue sweater I'm definitely ruining. I pull back and swipe at my eyes and under my nose.

"Thank you," I manage through great, gulping hiccups. "You didn't need to—"

She squeezes my shoulders. "I know. I wanted to; that's what friends do."

Oh god. Here I go again. Uncontrollable emotions are pretty terrible, frankly. How do Mom and Lola cope with this every damned day of their lives? To mask my tears, I make a big show of inspecting the trifolded cardboard, which fools exactly no one, but at least she gives me some space to get ahold of myself.

Below some lovely hand lettering that mirrors the font

of the Bark Books logo, Adhira has pasted two of the posters Whit made about how the program benefits animals and
kids. In the middle panel, there's a great photo of children
lined up in front of Booker with me in the background helping them choose books. Under that are some stats on the
effectiveness of the program so far, including the number
of children who've attended and what animals have directly
been adopted because of Bark Books.

"An iguana?" I point at the bottom line. My voice is only
partly blubbering.

"I called the shelter earlier to get numbers. A little boy
came in yesterday and adopted it."

A grin tugs at my lips. Somewhere, Ralph the Iguana is
going to lead a wonderful life with Dexter.

As composed as possible, I turn to Adhira. There's still a
wet spot staining her sweater. How does one recover gracefully after sobbing all over one's roommate? "I don't know
how to thank you enough," I finally say. "What can I do for
you?"

Adhira cocks her chin, then her eyes narrow in glee. "Oh,
don't worry, I have something in mind. It's just not ready yet."

Well, that's ominous.

NINETEEN

I'M SWEATING. NEVER A GOOD sign.

For the past five days, I've survived on coffee and snacks, and all I want to do is crawl into bed and pull a Rip van Winkle. But first, I've got to survive the Hunt Prize fair, which starts in—I check my phone, the same phone Whit still hasn't texted—*eep!* A half hour.

The gilt-and-fresco lobby of the Edison Auditorium swarms with students and mentors putting the finishing touches on their project booths. One of said booths boasts an honest-to-god children's choir. Another is testing some sort of seizure-inducing strobe light.

And me? I've got dog-themed books, three dozen iced sugar cookies shaped like dogs from Edie's bakery, and an extreme lack of cute puppies.

Worry and dread skirmish in my stomach, and my breath ratchets higher. Whit should be here by now. That's what we agreed upon . . . at least before I stood him up. The last time I checked my phone (i.e., five minutes ago), I could tell he'd read my text from Monday. Over the week, there have been a few instances of the dreaded text bubbles, but nothing.

If Whit and the Puppy Posse show up, I've got a real chance. If not . . . the stomach skirmish escalates. The casualties are really starting to pile up.

Best not think about the *if nots*.

Behind my table, Kat hides monitor cords for my slideshow, and Lola, sporting furry dog ears and a collar, helps by inspecting her nails.

She swipes one of the cookies Dad is fretting over. "Should you have the cookies separated by breed?"

Dad looks to me. "Ask the boss."

The boss is busy checking the levels on the hanging, blown-up Bark Books photos. "They're fine, Lola." I don't bother to check the cookie layout, but add, "And don't eat any more unless you've got a token for me."

Those tokens used by the public to vote during the fair count toward half my score, and Lola definitely doesn't have any.

Lola recommits to her lime-green nails with a harrumph. "That's bribery."

"Duh."

Lola and Kat disappear, and I rearrange the book selection

again. We're all set: Adhira's trifold is to one side, with the slideshow running in the center, the cookies in front to bribe voters, and the displayed books on the right side. I'm pretty proud of how it all came together, save for the giant, gaping hole to the right. I've set out water bowls, a floor of towels, and some portable fencing for the dogs that are definitely coming.

I chew my lip and force down a whine. Instead, I focus on repositioning the locked metal voting box. Yesterday, I made a paper flag to stick up from the box. It declares: *Woof! That's "thanks" in dog!* At the time, I thought it was *very* cute, but it's going to look pretty dumb if there are no actual dogs present. I *need* these dogs. There are forty-two contestants in the Hunt Prize this year, and no more than twenty will advance past this fair. The judges' scores on merit, promise, and presentation count for half my final score, but the rest is up to the voting public—current and former students, families, and various locals—and their five tokens.

The public voting aspect is what's terrifying. Quantitative scoring rubrics, I can handle. Popularity contests? Not so much. There's only so much the judges' scores can do when a thousand people are swayed by a chance to win free massages for life or whatever.

I lift hair off my neck and fan myself. It's broiling in here, and I wore thick tights under my skirt-sweater combo that are basically steaming my legs to sauna sausages. My knit sweater is embroidered with a schnauzer and itches like crazy.

I really need to stop ordering clothes online. Nowhere in the description on WhimsicalAnimalWear.com did it say this sweater was made of reused cat scratching posts.

Dad interrupts my mini breakdown. "Everything looks perfect, Marnie. Why don't you go find Adhira and you two can scope out the competition?"

Sure. Yeah. But before I go, I crack and text Whit.

Fair starts in 1/2 hour. Where are you?

Okay, maybe I could have been more apologetic, but I don't have time for responsibility shirkers at the moment. If he doesn't come, fine. I'll make it wor—

My phone pings and I jump out of my skin. But it's Lindy.

Good luck tonight! Love you!

All I can muster is a thumbs-up emoji, then I take off toward Adhira.

Hers is just two booths down, but I pull up short and stare. I helped her haul the dress forms and garment bags over to the Ed this morning, but this is the first I've seen her finished booth. The centerpiece is a Frankenstein's monster of a dress form, but in a good way. The left side of the form shows the underpinnings—half a boned corset and hooped crinoline cage; while the right side shows the finished product—a maroon, raw silk ball gown with lace trimmings, a draped bell sleeve, and furbelows aplenty. And wow, I didn't realize until right this second how many costume design terms I've picked up from Adhira.

Hanging behind the dress are sketches, one that makes me gasp. It's the fabric, the cream fabric from my great-grandma, now envisioned as a gorgeous floor-length gown with a gracefully scooped neckline, cap sleeves, and a green ribbon tied around the empire waist.

I force myself to look away from the beautiful sketch, and try to find Adhira, but she's not at her booth. Instead, Dev and Tilda stand at the side, both living mannequins in Adhira designs.

"Where's Adhira?"

"Outside for some fresh air." Dev doffs a lustrous black top hat and bows. "What do you think?"

I sink my fingertips into a square of green velvet fabric on the table. "You look smashing."

"Oh, smashing! Tilda, did you hear that? I'm *smashing*."

Beside him, Tilda blinks imperiously at me from behind black netting pulled over her face. I swallow hard. So I'm still on that one's shit list.

"Seriously, Adhira is *so* winning this thing."

That makes Tilda's frown turn upside down. Or, at least, a bit more sideways. "Make sure to tell Adhira that. She's nervous."

"She shouldn't be. This is fantastic."

Dev grins at me. "And everything is reused, recycled, or ethically sourced."

I didn't know one was supposed to ethically source fabric,

but I nod thoughtfully all the same.

Out of nowhere, a hand clamps down on my elbow. "Marnie," Adhira hisses in my ear. Her eyes are wide when I turn, and her mouth is pulled down in a grimace. "Have you seen Lia's booth?"

My knees jelly. "Why?"

She lets go of my elbow, but only to grab hold of my wrist. "Come on."

She drags me away, every step making my heart thump a little faster. What does Lia have at her booth? Roger Federer?

We pass dozens of student booths, many of which have brought metaphorical jazz hands to this thing. Another brought them, literally, in the shape of a senior citizen jazz dance troupe. One contestant's project is a free traveling clown school for kids. She brought stilts, juggling balls, and even a bunch of throwing knives to try. Because what is a children's clown school without throwing knives.

I start counting as I go, which is doing jack for my nerves. Forty-two contestants, and I'm going to be beat by that one . . . maybe that one . . . *definitely* that one. If these dogs don't show, I'm a goner.

We haul ourselves up the sweeping staircase to the wide mezzanine and the rest of the booths. Over the railing, my fellow contestants buzz around down below, and if I lean just so, I can see my booth. There's Dad puttering around. But it's still dog-free. Disaster nips at my neck. Directly overhead hangs a gargantuan chandelier. Maybe it can fall on me à la *Phantom of the Opera* and put me out of my misery.

With an effort I drag my gaze from my dog-free booth and turn to find Lia's booth beside me. It basically punches me in the face.

Adhira's hand claws at mine, and we both freeze. "See? This is . . ."

"Preposterous." I breathe out the word and stare.

Her booth is stuffed with video monitors—a slideshow of her posing with kids in her branded Tennis for Truants polo, a news segment about the project hosted by a local morning anchor. There's an archway made of tennis balls and branded polos, sweaters, and caps to purchase.

But it's the thing *next* to the booth that really makes me want to puke. Lia has erected a bespoke virtual reality system that has nothing to do with her actual project, but *a lot* to do with wooing voters. If the smiling cardboard cutout is to be believed, VR Serena Williams will coach your backhand.

Lia flounces out from behind her table. She's wearing tennis whites, including about four separate articles of branded Tennis for Truants gear.

"Isn't it amazing? My mentor and I worked *extra hard* to get this system." She pouts like all that *extra hard* work has made her *extra tired*. We all know this is actually thanks to her *extra douchebag* dad. But not just her dad. Hayes helped her with this too. Just how much that guy is screwing me over drips acid into my stomach.

Lia smirks and flips her high ponytail, which is honestly

perfect for yanking out in a cat fight. Not that I plan on pushing her down the stairs. No, I'll settle with dumbfounded horror and a strong need to scream. That'll show her.

"Good luck, Lia," Adhira says, clench-jawed.

Lia blinks slowly, and a vicious smile curls. "Don't forget to enter the drawing! It's for an all-expenses-paid trip to the French Open."

And that's it. The death knell. There's no way I'm advancing. The reality of it is a dying star in the center of my chest, pulsing with heat and imminent implosion.

The room has lost focus—the Ed a swirl of rich colors and frenzied movement—as Adhira and I trudge back downstairs.

"How did she—" I'm mumbling.

"Yeah, I don't know," Adhira mumbles back. "I'm done."

That focuses me. "No, you're not." I grab her arms and give her a little shake. "That sketch you did, using my great-grandma's old fabric . . . it's so pretty I could cry."

"Well, that's a relief."

I tip my chin. "Why?"

Adhira purses her lips. "No reason."

"Really, Adhira, your booth is perfect. And it showcases *your* talent, not just who your dad knows."

"Yours is great too, Marnie."

We've reached said booth, and I sweep my hand out toward the empty kennel area. "Yeah, except the guests of honor are a no-show. How can cookies and a slideshow compete with Serena Williams and a trip to France?"

Dad must hear my lament, because his hands settle on my shoulders. It makes my sweater dig into my skin, and I work not to squirm.

"Did you see Lia Lawson's booth?"

Dad sighs. "I did." I open my mouth, but he talks over me. "You've developed a fantastic project, Marnie, and you deserve to move on to the final round." He nods at Adhira. "You too, Adhira. Don't let Lia get into either of your heads."

Nice try, Dad. He takes a phone call from Mom, who's at the hospital with Lindy, and I'm left with probably-manic eyes, a real lack of famous athletes, already-sore feet, and tights that keep sagging in the crotch. I lean against my table to give my feet some relief, but that makes my sweater scratch against my waist. Blood pulses at my neck, my wrists, behind my knees. Everything is a disaster. An absolute, terrifying, head-pounding disaster.

I clamp my bottom lip between my teeth. "I'm losing these tights," I growl at Adhira, healthily taking out my nerves on inanimate objects.

"But the doors are opening!"

Desperation has made me bold. The first voters filter in through the auditorium doors, but they're a few booths away.

"Cover me." I shimmy my navy houndstooth skirt up my thighs and rip the tights down to my knees. I peel them off and throw them under my booth, where they shall remain for the rest of time.

The air from outside is cool against my naked legs and it

helps, if only a little. Adhira crushes me in a quick hug and darts back to her booth, and I plaster on a desperate smile.

The minutes drag by, and Whit still isn't here. A few voters drift by my booth and pretend to read stats as an excuse to swipe a cookie, but I only see two tokens drop into my voting box. The children's choir apparently only knows five songs and starts cycling through them again. Somewhere behind me, a group of people collectively gasp. Maybe someone got a throwing knife through the palm?

Dad has returned to chat with voters, but I can't stop myself from checking the door for Whit again, and again, and . . .

Oh *no*.

Hayes just walked in, Casper Lawson at his side. My heart stutters.

Why the hell is he here? And why is he showing up with Casper? Did Lia's dad *actually* fund his app like he said might happen at Thanksgiving? Next to me, Dad presses his knuckles to the table. A cunning smile—so like Lia's—unfurls across Casper's face, and he nods my way. Hayes looks spooked, his smile thin and his eyes darting.

"Tom." Casper saunters toward my booth. He's got on a fleece vest and his wind-whipped blond hair is probably thanks to a team of stylists and a wind machine.

"Casper." Dad lifts his nose, his mouth tight. The blazing hot room is suddenly arctic.

"Hi, Hayes," I try. His proximity used to make me fizzy

with delight. But tonight his company leaves me slightly uncomfortable and very confused. That VR machine in Lia's booth is because of him.

"Hey, Marnie," he mutters, then lets loose with a nervous giggle and checks to see if Casper is paying attention. The sound of that sniveling laugh makes me shiver. "Mr. Lawson invited me to—"

"To see some of the worthy Hunt Prize candidates," Casper finishes for him. Hayes bobs his chin in a nod. Casper, winner of Worst Judge Ever, flaps his hand until an aide hovering nearby pushes a clipboard into it. He glances around my booth, then sighs and writes a few things on a hidden paper.

The smile he deigns to give me is thin. "Thank you for your effort, Ms. Barnes."

My stomach plummets out of my body and tunnels into the earth. "There are dogs coming." The words burst out of me, and Casper squints.

"I don't see any."

My mouth opens, closes. "They're running late."

"Did you not know what time the fair started?" He turns away from me toward Hayes. "That other judge I was telling you about, the philanthropist, is over there. Are you coming?"

Hayes palms the five tokens in his hand. "Ah, just a minute, Mr. Lawson."

"Suit yourself."

Then he's gone, and I'm face-to-face with Hayes, my

feelings slippery and hard to grasp. Where is the man who was hugging me, asking me out for lunch dates, and talking all about *we* and *us*? Or am I just now seeing the real Hayes for the first time?

"Remember what an absolute monster Lindy was the year she competed for this?" Hayes says. "It was all she talked about for months."

My defenses rear up like spikes. He knows my sister is still in the hospital, and he wants to make fun of her? I suck in a breath. "What are you doing here?"

Hayes searches the crowd before his attention drifts back to me. "I had a business meeting with Mr. Lawson, and he suggested we come to see Bright Star's contribution. I got Lia some sick VR tech. You should go see it."

"Yeah," I choke out past my dust-dry tongue. "I saw."

And then, from somewhere close, a dog woofs.

My heart kicks in my chest and I have to bite down on the inside of my cheeks to hide my smile as Whit maneuvers through the big front doors with Sir Pat prancing on his lead beside a loping cocker spaniel, and with an enormous lop-eared bunny cradled in one arm. As if he were the Pied Piper, a bunch of cooing voters follow him.

The world tilts under my feet, and I have to hold tight to the table as he walks up. He won't quite look at me, which is probably for the best since I'm fairly certain I'm the definition of flop sweat right now.

"You came," I breathe out.

Whit busies himself with securing Sir Pat's lead around the table leg. "I said I would."

My fingers knot together. Hayes steps closer, attention on Whit. Everything is off-kilter. It makes my stomach twist into more tangles than my fingers. It's almost like Hayes is . . .

No, there's no way. There's no earthly way Hayes would be *jealous* of my Bark Books partner.

But then he runs a light hand down my arm. "Have you been to see Lindy?" he asks, suddenly concerned for my sister.

I drop my chin and focus on the floor.

"Such an awful thing to happen." He's talking too loud and standing too close. "That was the same hospital I took you to, do you remember? You made me so scared that day, Mar."

He puts his hand on my shoulder again and squeezes, and I fight the urge to shrug him off. Whit isn't looking at us—willfully, it seems—but instead works on getting the bunny set up with what looks like a miniature cat cave.

I want him to look at me. I want to explain. I want to try for another date with him.

I want Hayes to leave me alone.

Whit stands suddenly and dumps the rabbit into my arms. "Hold Candace for a second, will you? I need to fill the water bowls."

Whit unearths an enormous metal water bottle from his backpack as the bunny—Candace—buries her nose into the crook of my arm, butt shivering. *Yeah, you and me both, bunny.* Voters gather around us, cooing at the animals and checking out my booth. But my attention skitters between Whit and Hayes. The air between them snaps with something dangerous, like frayed wires humming.

Hayes angles to stand between me and Whit and tilts his face closer to mine, his voice low. "We still need to discuss some things, like we said we would at Thanksgiving. Dinner soon, just you and me?"

There's a storm brewing in my chest; it's becoming hard to breathe past the piling clouds. But the way Hayes keeps pressing . . . it leaves me with an undeniable suspicion that Hayes is playing me, that he *wants* something from me. But what can he expect to get from an eighteen-year-old girl? What should he *want* when he's marrying in just two months?

Hayes's dinner invite hangs unanswered between us, and he waves a hand through the awkward silence. "Irregardless, good luck."

"Regardless," I say back automatically.

"What?"

I toe at the ground. "You mean regardless. Irregardless isn't a word. It's a double—"

"Yes, I know." The angles of his face go rigid. "I know that. You don't need to correct me. It's an awful trait."

Whit shoots to his feet, and his eyes when they land on me are hard. Then he pivots to Hayes, his mouth a slit. "That's enough."

Hayes lifts one eyebrow. My mouth drops open, and I snap it closed. Whit is defending me—at least, I think that's what he's doing—and Hayes seems deathly bored. It makes my fingers itch to slap him.

Whit's chest rises and falls fast. "We've got work to do, so stop hanging around being insulting."

Hayes's smile simmers, but I don't miss the way he searches the crowd, making sure no one heard Whit's reprimand. He fumbles over his feet as he leaves, and I can finally breathe. In my arms, Candace seems to be sleeping.

"Thank you," I say to Whit.

He's gone silent again. He turns on his heel and finishes getting the cocker spaniel comfortable in the pen while Sir Pat sits tall outside the wire boundary, obviously proud of his status.

"Can I pet the bunny?" a younger girl intrudes, oblivious to my strife. I only sort of look at her, my mind a thousand miles away. "I said, can I pet the bunny?" The girl's lips thin with impatience. I eye her, then the snoozing bunny, then the single token in her right hand.

"Of course! The dogs would love a nice pat too!"

She giggles and runs her fingers along Candace's long, floppy ear.

"He's so soft!"

"He's a she," Whit replies, his expression stony.

"Well, *she's* adorable." The girl turns to the woman next to her. "Isn't she, Mom?"

The woman eyes me. She's wearing a silk scarf knotted at her neck and enough bright gold jewelry that I'm certain her name is Mitsy. Mom would love her. "How much for the bunny?"

"Um . . ." There's another wooden token resting on the woman's palm.

"Candace is available for adoption at Paws and Claws of Outer Richmond," Whit grinds out. There are already three people lining up to give the fluffy spaniel a pet. "Pending application approval."

Despite Whit's less-than-stellar mood, both mother and daughter drop tokens into my box and move on.

In a lull a few minutes later, I turn to Whit and poke his arm with Candace's paw. "Candace is *hoppy* you're here."

My attempt at humor falls so flat, it's practically my chest situation. Whit blinks at me. He seems to chew on his words for a second before he says, "You could've said you didn't want to go to the exhibit. I was going anyway."

Whit extracts Candace from my arms and nudges her into her hutch, and I'm left with the hard-edged reality of my epic screw-up. Nothing fluffy about it. But there are more people approaching my booth, and I've got a job to do. I tack on a smile and answer questions about the program, the same few phrases tumbling out of my mouth. The dull thunk of tokens dropping into my box matches the pace of cookies disappearing from the tray.

Whit's presence next to me is angry and raw, but he's playing nice too. Chatting up voters about the available animals at Paws & Claws and dropping statistics about kids and reading. But there are shards of glass between us, a broken line we can't—or won't—cross. And I hate it, this feeling. I hate that I'm the reason he's mad.

Dad circles back at some point to man the booth—this fair lasts four hours and a girl has to pee—then leaves to get Lola and Kat dinner.

Finally, in a break in the last trickle of voters, I reach toward Whit, nearly touch him. "I owe you an explanation."

Whit crosses his arms, and I notice a small muscle pulsing in his forearm. "Yeah, you do."

I hurt him, and he deserves to know why. The truth gathers at the back of my throat. I steady myself before speaking, but even then it's hard to smooth the cracks.

"My older sister got into a car wreck. She . . . she survived, but she was pregnant, and . . ."

I blink fast and force myself to meet Whit's gaze. His eyes have softened, and he scrubs a hand through his hair. "Shit, Marnie. I'm sorry."

I have to look away to save myself from publicly crying. "And I did screw up, Whit. I totally forgot about meeting you at the museum, but I stayed in the hospital with Lindy Saturday and Sunday night."

"No, I understand." He rakes fingers through his hair again, making it stand on end in whorls. "I'm sorry I jumped to conclusions without giving you a chance to explain. Can I blame it on parent issues without sounding like a whiny asshole?"

"Um, parent issues are the reason behind *every* bit of my crap behavior." I flash a grin at him and nearly laugh with relief when he returns the smile. That wonderful smile that warms his face up from the inside.

He opens his mouth, takes the tiniest step closer. Anticipation swirls around me, until it sings under my skin. He sucks in a breath, just as Sir Pat—who's been sitting like a champ this whole time—flops to the ground and noses under the booth skirting. His tail flops against the carpet with a great thwack, butt wiggling, and he scoots deeper under the booth. A frown flits across Whit's face, and he kneels next to the dog.

"What's got you so excited?" He gently tugs Sir Pat out from under the booth. Whit cocks his chin and grabs at something slobbery and brown hanging out of Sir Pat's mouth.

Realization hits me like a bucket of cold water to the face. "Wait!" I shriek. Voters around me crane necks, but all I can see is Whit . . . and my abandoned tights. His hand is wrapped directly over the crotch, and my face erupts in heat at the same time he apparently recognizes what he's holding. I snatch them out of his hands and shove them into my bag.

"I got warm," I stutter. "I mean, it's stupid hot in here, and I'm already in a winter sweater."

"It's not a big deal." Yet his face is lit with a barely concealed laugh. It breaks free of him right as Sir Pat lunges for the pantyhose prize in my bag.

A whine escapes me, and Whit laughs harder.

"Just beware," he says. "I stashed a pair of my boxer briefs under there too."

"Shut up."

"I got warm!"

"Shut up!"

My face is so blazing hot, I'm pretty sure my skin is melting off.

I can barely look at him as he ushers Candace into a carrier and starts packing up the animal supplies. The spaniel, Edgar, leans his snout over the wire barrier and breathes on my hand with a *floof*. I interpret it as solidarity, but then he nudges my hand onto his head for some scratches.

"Hey, really." Whit clips on Edgar's lead and unhooks Sir Pat's from the table leg, then loops both in one hand. "It's not a big deal, Marnie. I live with all women. I've seen tights. I've folded enough princess underwear to last a lifetime."

"I'm not wearing princess . . ." My tongue flops fat in my mouth before I can utter the word *underwear* in front of Whit.

"Who's a princess?" Dev pops around the corner with Adhira. "Other than you, Marnie, dear." He spies Whit and claps him on the shoulder. "Whit! You didn't even come say hello to Ravi's favorite older brother?"

"Aren't you his *only* brother?"

Dev bobbles his head and picks up a cookie.

"I expect a token for that," I insert.

Adhira sidles over as Dev and Whit chat. "So. He came." She grins and waggles her eyebrows. "Did you kiss and make up?"

I hiss a bunch. It's a lot like a goose, honestly. Whit turns back to me, and Adhira flips around so he can't see her face. *He's hot*, she mouths.

A tug of muscle behind my navel makes me squirm. Whit *is* hot. His face is in profile as he laughs with Dev. The straight nose, the curve of his mouth. He's only a few inches taller than me, but lean with muscle. I can see it in the way his shoulders flex when Edgar the spaniel pulls at his lead. My heart is a bellows, pushing heat through my body as I stare.

Then he turns and I nearly yelp. "I've got to get these pups home. Let me know the results, will you?"

Then he's gone. And it hits me suddenly that if I don't advance past this fair, I mean that in the forever and ever sense.

TWENTY

IT'S BEEN FIFTEEN HOURS SINCE the fair closed, and I've
marked every single one with a minor breakdown. The inside
of my cheek is shredded, and I've plucked an entire duck out of
my down pillow. Now my hands flop to my lap, and a tempest
of tiny feathers puffs up.

"Please just get it over with, Dad."

Dad sits down at my desk and swivels the chair to face me,
the weak winter light turning my dorm room watery gray.
He flips over the sealed manila envelope and slips on reading
glasses to squint at the instructions stuck to the back.

"I don't care about the rules." It all comes out in a big
breath, and Dad raises an eyebrow. Okay, jeez, yes, I care about
the rules. But I'll care more once I know where I came in the

fair. Did I advance? Will Dad be proud of me?

"Focus on the positive, Marnie." His voice is soothing and steady. It's the same voice he used to talk Mom down when another woman wore the same Oscar de la Renta gown at a charity auction.

The positive, right. My forehead rests against my knees, and my breath shallows. I don't watch, but hear a *snick* when Dad breaks the envelope's seal, then the dry rasp of papers sliding out.

My fingers and toes prickle. Am I having a stroke? All signs point to probably. Dad's got one leg crossed over the other, the papers balanced on his crooked leg. In order, he nods, goes *hmm*, then frowns.

I follow every tiny change in expression, certain of the worst. I'm following the Julia Barnes Breakdown Template™ practically point by point. Next, I need to look off in middle distance, sigh, and press my hand to my heart.

Pull it together, Marnie. I sit up straighter on my bed and fold my legs in, elbows on my knees. If the stroke doesn't get me first, it'll be the terrible anticipation.

Dad's eyebrows twitch upward. He rustles the papers on his lap, clears his throat, and looks at me. "The prize committee decided to only advance eighteen projects this year."

Ohgodohgodohgod.

"And yours was one of them."

My heart soars, then plummets back into my chest just as

fast. If I advanced, why does Dad appear so perplexed?

"What's wrong?"

"Hmm? Nothing's wrong."

Then why isn't he cheering? Why aren't *I* cheering? I cantilever out and snatch the papers off Dad's lap. My eyes fly over the front side of the score sheet with my tally and the judges' comments, too fast to really take anything in. At the bottom, there's the number nineteen, but it's crossed out and changed to eighteen.

"The important thing to remember is that you *did* advance," Dad says.

My chest is hollowed out, my throat tight. "But then why . . . ?"

I search his face for an explanation. Dad's smile darts, then retreats. "Yours and another project had tied for the last advancement spot. Headmaster Finch had to be called in to break it." He reaches over and squeezes my knee, then gently takes the papers back before I can flip them over to see the rest of the project rankings. "I'm proud of you. This is a momentous thing you've done."

Yet I don't feel anything even in the same zip code as proud, and Dad certainly doesn't sound it. I swallow hard. I'm disappointed, and I fear he is too. Goose bumps race down my spine. "Who was the other? The project I tied with?"

Dad consults the other side of the paper, where all the projects are listed by score. "Um, a children's choir."

Great, so I'm definitely making a bunch of kids cry. Just your normal Sunday. I spread my palms against my comforter, focus on the coolness against my skin. I *did* advance. But was it earned? What if I'm meant to be number nineteen? Behind Dad, my Mary contract catches the watery light.

I, Marnie Elizabeth Barnes, hereby do swear to root out and destroy Mary Bennet.

Root out and destroy. Have I?

Mary would focus on the negative. Try to argue her way into believing she'd been wronged, that it wasn't her fault others couldn't understand her genius. I search my emotions. Okay, I do feel sorry for myself, but I'm not conceited enough to believe I presented the best project at the fair. What I do believe is that my project has the *potential* to be the best, as long as I work my hardest at it. I can still make Dad proud of me.

And more than that. I think of my friendship with Adhira. The way I smile when I'm around Whit. The bond I've started to forge with my sisters. I flick my gaze away from the contract and roll my shoulders back. So I tied for last. I still made it through to the finals, and there are twenty-four PCA girls finding out right now their Hunt Prize is over. I have a few more months to prove myself, and I intend to make good on this chance.

Dad sighs and looks up. "I'm afraid this is my fault."

That makes my chin jerk. "What?"

"I thought Casper Lawson would be able to be an adult about all this, but I think I was wrong."

My eyebrows draw together.

"Almost all of the judges were complimentary. Honestly, just glancing at the comments plus the token tally, you should have scored in the top ten." Dad pauses, and I lean forward.

"Okay . . . ?"

Dad clears his throat and looks down at the scores again. "But Casper Lawson scored you low across all three metrics."

"That's not fair!" It's hard to keep the whine out of my voice.

"You're right."

I have to know. "How did Lia score?"

Dad shifts in his seat.

"So that good, then?" When he doesn't answer, I lean forward. "Why doesn't Casper like our family?"

Dad's features tighten. He looks a lot like Lindy in this moment—the focus and intensity. "It doesn't matter. What matters is that my family did nothing wrong, and Casper should know that."

But what Dad doesn't deny is that *he* did nothing wrong, and I remember what Hayes said: there's bad blood between Casper and my father, and, perhaps, Dad doesn't talk about it because he's embarrassed.

Yet as I'm about to press him, the door swings open and Adhira bounds through. She's smiling with her entire body, and I scramble off my bed.

"You made it through?" Her wide grin is all the answer I need. "I knew it!"

She squeals and grabs me in a hug. "You too!"

Dad pats us both on our shoulders and slips out, but I watch him go. He's always been so gentle, so careful with his words. I've seen myself in his love of books, his quirkier passions, the way he remains a bit detached from the Sturm und Drang of our family.

What could he possibly have done to Casper Lawson to make him hate us so much?

Whatever it was, it didn't make the internet. Or if it did, it's tucked so far into the corners I can't find it. The only oblique mentions I uncover in my Google searches are vague lines about Casper's "return to Silicon Valley" and "moving on from a tumultuous past." But nothing mentioned in conjunction with my father.

My searching is cut off abruptly by a more pressing issue: finals week. Dad could have challenged Casper to a duel in the middle of the Golden Gate Bridge, but with exams upon me, I have neither time nor energy to track that record down. Even Bark Books is on hiatus until after break. The frantic days of studying and tests do make the time go quickly, and by the following Friday it's all over. Nearly all the students are packing up and taking off for Aspen or Tahiti or, I don't know, Disney. Parents and siblings crawl over the campus, and the dorm practically vibrates with stomping feet and rolling luggage. Adhira, too, is headed out for break.

"Anywhere exciting?"

She rolls her clothes and packs them precisely in her suitcase. "Would you call Toronto exciting?"

I shrug. "I've never been."

"Then you should know it's called the Capri of Ontario."

"Wait. Really?"

Adhira breaks. "No! Don't get me wrong, I *love* Toronto. You should come visit! But it's going to be very cold and gray this time of year."

She's inviting me to visit? Excitement rustles through me. I've never been invited to visit a friend! Possibly because Anne Shirley wasn't sending out invites to Green Gables. And she wasn't real. (*Hush, she's plenty real.*)

"I'd love—"

My phone buzzes. It's Hayes: *Congrats on advancing to the finals! We should celebrate.* :)

The rustling excitement takes a sharp left. Sure, he's congratulating me, but he had five tokens in his hand at the fair, and I'm pretty positive none of them ended up in my locked metal box. I dither over the keypad, then type out a flat *thanks.* He doesn't even get an exclamation point. I put the phone—screen side down—onto my desk.

"Anyway, I'd love that!" I continue. My fingers fiddle with the desk drawer. I have a wrapped gift for Adhira in there, but we didn't talk about presents, and I don't want her to feel weird or like she has to get me something, and oh, what the hell. I yank open the drawer and lift out the package. It's a book—because I am nothing if not on brand—a memoir by a famous costume designer.

"Here." I trip across the floor to shove the present into her hands. "It's nothing big or anything, but I wanted—"

Adhira peels back the wrapping paper (cats lounging in lemon trees on a minty green backdrop) and grins. "Oh, Marnie, thank you! This is lovely. I love Edith Head's costume design!"

"You're welcome," I manage around the relief flooding my system. I've never been great at presents.

She nudges my shoulders. "I have something for you too . . . but it's not ready yet."

It occurs to me she *doesn't* have a gift for me and I've made her feel guilty. "Oh yeah, sure. No worries."

"Promise, Mar. It's going to be great."

All too soon, her parents text that they're waiting for her in the parking lot. She's not even left yet, and I find I'm already missing her. It's a peculiar sensation.

She pauses at the door of our dorm room, her suitcase in hand. "Hey, have a great Christmas, Mar."

"You too, Adhira. I'll see you after break."

She presses her lips together for a moment, then bursts out, "Maybe sooner."

Then she sprints off and I'm confused. Merry Christmas?

TWENTY-ONE

THERE'S SOMETHING BEGUILING ABOUT a lazy Christmas. Or, day *after* Christmas.

Yesterday came with all the requisite paper ripping and squealing and triplet mayhem. But today, Dad, Kat, and I enjoy each other's quiet company on the drive to Lindy's. The promise of a languid day with my sisters kindles warmth in my bones. And then there's a jolt of shock that I would think such a thing. A few months ago, the only sisters I was keen to spend any time with were the March girls. (Except Beth, obviously. She's the worst. Oh, Lord. I'm the Beth March of *Little Women*, aren't I?)

We've spent the day playing board games and snacking, and now the last teaspoon of afternoon sunshine is diffuse

and dreamy through the enormous wall of windows pointing toward the sea. The only light comes from the glowing
Christmas tree tucked next to the fireplace.

I'm stretched out on the couch, the sleepy-warm laziness
of the holidays like a fat Christmas goose nested on my chest.
Over at the dining room table, Dad, Kat, and Will are playing
some sort of card game that keeps making Kat say "no fair."

But it's Lindy who I search for when I peek up from my
spot on the couch. It's been nearly a month since I stayed with
her at the hospital. We've texted a ton, even chatted on the
phone a couple times—which is a Big Ask for me, honestly—
but until today I hadn't seen her. She and Will requested to
spend Christmas Day alone, and even Mom obliged without
too much drama.

Today, she's been pleasant but detached. Fear pinches at the
base of my neck, and a needling voice whispers that all the
supposed bonding we did in the hospital didn't mean to Lindy
what it meant to me.

I go searching for reassurance and find it in the den. She's
perched precisely on a high-backed chair and staring out the
window. Her walker is within reach and her lips are thin.

"Lindy?" For a second, she doesn't react. Outside the big
windows, shadows creep in. It takes a moment to realize the
whoosh and crash I hear is the surf against the rocks below the
windows and not my heart. "How's it going?"

Lindy considers for a long moment, chin tilted. She stretches
out her left ankle, still cocooned in a fracture boot, and a wince

twitches the edge of her features. "Better today." She nods at the chair opposite hers, and I sit. She smiles, but her blue eyes are a flat winter sky. "Thank you again for the book."

I reach up and finger the new enamel pin on my sweater. "And thanks for the pins." She got in touch with an artist who created otter swag for her first doc and special-ordered me a set of adorable dog pins. The one I'm wearing now is a doe-eyed Lab.

A smile—a real smile—flits across Lindy's features. It masks the silvery-pink scars etched into the side of her face. "I think I'm going to use these same designs for some *Not Without My Doggo* promotion."

"You definitely should." I pause. She was supposed to premiere at South by Southwest but pulled out. "How are you feeling about South By?"

Lindy shrugs, but then she lets the facade crack. "Honestly? It's been hard. I love this film and I want to give it my all, but film festivals are *hard*. You have to be on, and I can't . . ." She stares down at her hands, her fingers twisted in her lap. "It still hurts," she says quietly, a palm going to her stomach. "If I move a certain way, it hurts and it's this visceral *memory* of him, of where he lived. I told the people at South By about the car accident, but I couldn't bring myself to tell them about the baby."

We lapse into silence, the constant surge of the ocean matching our breath.

"Hey," Lindy says quietly after a while, "I know I texted

you about it, but congratulations on advancing to the final round of the Hunt Prize. It's a big deal, and you should be proud of yourself."

I bounce my heel against the leg of my chair. "Yeah, thanks."

Does she know I tied for last? And would it matter if she did? Those old pangs of jealousy sizzle in my chest. I douse them and make myself look straight at my sister.

"I need to tell you something."

Lindy crooks one eyebrow. "Should I be nervous?"

"No. I mean, maybe?"

The other eyebrow joins its twin.

"I've spent years being jealous of you. You were this perfect older sister who did everything first, everything better than I could ever hope to. I watched everything through this . . . this prism." Lindy opens her mouth to speak, but I keep going. "I'm not trying to get sympathy or anything, I just needed to tell you. A few months ago, I realized I wanted to change, and I'm trying, but it's been difficult. It's like . . ." I roll my lips together, searching for the way to say what I want to say. "I'm not the protagonist, right? I'm the Mary Bennet in this life and you . . . you're the Lizzy. But that's not fair and I don't even know if it's right, but it's how I've seen you and I . . . I need you to know I'm trying to change."

My shoulders pull back; my neck lengthens. A weight has lifted, telling someone other than Adhira this awful little truth of mine. Lindy, though, has darkened to thunderclouds. She grabs her walker and presses upward to stand, and I am fairly certain she's about to storm out in an awkward, slow fashion, but then she stops at one of the brimming library shelves and pulls down a book. She tosses it to me, then eases back toward her seat.

The title of the book is *Wide Sargasso Sea*, and the cover features a dark-haired woman standing amid a riot of greenery. The cover is peaceful, a slight hint of a smile on the woman's muted expression. I've heard of it before, of course. *Wide Sargasso Sea* is written as a sort of prequel to *Jane Eyre*, told from the point of view of Mr. Rochester's deranged, pyromaniac wife, called Antoinette in this book. It was written by Jean Rhys, more than a hundred years after my beloved *Jane Eyre*.

"Bullshit," Lindy pronounces, settling into her chair.

"Pardon?" That's not exactly what I was expecting from her.

"Bullshit. You are not Mary Bennet, Marnie. And even if you were, that doesn't make you any less a protagonist in your own life." Lindy jabs a finger at the novel's cover. "Every person is the main character in their own story, even the women stuffed in the attics."

It hits me very suddenly that Lindy and I speak the same language: *books*. Suddenly, I recognize my sister not just as family, but as a kindred spirit.

Lindy runs a hand through her dark hair. "Did you know it

was Mom who called me a bitch for the first time? Trust me, I've heard plenty of guys in my field mutter it behind my back, but it was Mom who said it first. I was fourteen and I refused to go to some dumb event with her. It *killed* me, to think my own mother thought that about me, but I've learned something since then. I can make the life I want, but I need to be willing to not give a single shit about what others think of me. I fought like hell to be my own protagonist. And you can too."

I'm speechless. But under the shock of my sister's revelation is a stroke of boldness. Lindy made the life she wanted. I can too. Instead of competing with my sister, I should emulate her freedom.

Lindy lifts her chin. "I found this in a used bookstore when I was about your age. Read what's written on the inside cover."

The cover is stiff under my fingers, the edges brittle. Scrawled on the title page in black ink are two short lines:

To us tower-bound women. Break free.

My fingers brush over the few words, feel them sink into my skin. "Who wrote that?"

"I have no idea, but I can still remember how reading it made me feel. That's what's important, Marnie. How do those words make you feel?"

I press down, feel the give of the pages under my hand, and close my eyes. And I feel connected—to my sister, to all those fighting fear to become who they want to be. My eyes flutter open, and I sigh.

"I feel . . . limitless."

Lindy smiles. "Life is not a rose garden, Marnie. But you can make it something wild and wonderful, if you choose. I've always preferred wildflowers anyway."

Life is not a rose garden.

The conversation with Lindy still plays in my head nearly two days later. Well, that and the words of Jean Rhys. I'm curled into a corner of the couch, the book against my knees and my thoughts running roughshod.

The book is hauntingly beautiful and sad, and it works its way under my skin. The unnamed Englishman in the novel—obviously Mr. Rochester of *Jane Eyre*—pokes at a spot between my eyes. There is something too familiar about this depiction of him that makes me want to stop reading, stop thinking, but I keep turning the pages. The Mr. Rochester of *Jane Eyre* had always thrilled me with his intense taciturn drama. With the tragic romance of it all. But this Mr. Rochester is something else entirely. Erratic with his affection, making Antoinette—and by extension, me—question what's real and imagine wildly to fill in the blanks.

He almost reminds me of . . . I snap the book shut and catch my breath. Hayes. He reminds me of Hayes. Am I the Antoinette to Hayes's Mr. Rochester? Or is it Sara? The thought drips through me like acid, that he's playing both of us. As if he can sense my thoughts, my phone dings with a text from him. It's a dumb dog meme and a short note: *Saw this and thought of you!*

But is this Hayes being genuine or toying with my emotions for the hell of it?

One thing is certain: Sara deserves to know about this behavior, but I'm out of my depth here. This has gone from a fantasy to a horrible sort of reality that has left me unmoored. I don't know how to navigate my way back to solid ground, to a way to talk to Sara. But the truth is a nut in the center of my chest, hard and solid and something I can no longer deny.

I shove the book under a decorative pillow. I need to stop thinking for, like, two seconds.

Our house perches at the top of a hill, the shade trees clustered around the tiered back deck giving way to wide-open views of the forested coastal mountains. During Mom's most recent renovation, the designers turned the entire back of the house into giant sliding glass doors and created a multistoried deck with an outdoor kitchen, lap pool, and hot tub that *Luxurious Landscapes Quarterly* called "a masterpiece of woods and water."

Today, it's where I find Mom and Kat. They're at the patio table, Kat on her phone and Mom writing out Christmas thank-you cards. I'm in my Space Pizza jammies and an enormous PCA hoodie, and—Christmas miracle—Mom doesn't even say anything about what pizza grease will do to my complexion when I flop onto the chair next to her. (It doesn't matter that the pizza in question is printed on pajamas. Julia Barnes doesn't let logic stand in her way.)

"What a nice surprise, Marnie, dear," she says, patting my hand.

Kat leans back and looks at me with big eyes. *Don't mention Lola*, she mouths.

"What are you whispering about?" Mom asks. "Not your sister, I hope. I can't even say her name without my heart giving me pains."

Kat catches my attention and rolls her eyes. Mom and Lola are either plotting to get matching tattoos or trying to murder each other. There is no in between.

"Mom, I have a question." I wasn't exactly sure what my plan was as I came out here, but it's starting to solidify. "Do you know what happened with Dad and Casper Lawson?"

She flaps a manicured hand toward her chest. "Oh, that whole mess. I don't even want to talk about it."

Pause. Pause.

She takes a sip of water and dabs at the corners of her mouth with a finger. "I was completely stonewalled from any and all events in the Bay Area for *months* afterward. Months! The only thing that saved me was when Casper left his first wife and she disappeared back to whatever awful place she came from. And good riddance, I say. Now I'm invited to galas nearly every week! I can barely keep up, but keep up I must. It's good for our family name, you know."

Kat perks up. "I'm Mom's plus-one at the Chips and Cheers Latin Fiesta tonight!"

I'm losing control here. "Mom, the thing about Casper. What happened, exactly? *When* did it happen?"

Mom purses her fat, shiny lips. "You were five or six, I think? It was the year Charlotte Montclair got food poisoning at the Save the Snails Parisian Dinner event."

"Oh, Maggie's mom?" Kat leans forward and grins. "She *totally* screwed up the high note in her solo at the winter concert."

Mom titters. "Like mother, like daughter. Always trying to be in the spotlight."

"Mom. Casper."

"Oh, right. Well, it was something about work. Why don't you ask your father? Oh, Hayes!"

My heart skitters and I whip around so fast, my head nearly snaps off. But he's not here. Relief rushes into my lungs.

Mom is reading a text on her phone. "How lovely! He wants to pop over with a little Christmas gift." She sighs. "It's always been one of life's great disappointments he didn't wind up with Lindy or Joss."

"Mom, Joss is gay," Kat reminds her, like she's not familiar with her eldest daughter's wife of five years.

"Yes, well, Hayes would have made a wonderful husband." Mom taps away at her phone. "Perfect! He'll be here in an hour." Her eyes shift to me. "Marnie, darling, I know it's only Hayes and *he* doesn't care what you're wearing, but could you freshen up a bit?"

And that's my cue to nope on out of here.

"Sorry, Mom. Gotta run. I've got plans with . . ." And I flee to my room. I have no plans. I barely know anyone with whom to *make* plans. But I am not ready to face the possible Mr. Rochester in my life quite yet.

But what about the Gilbert Blythe of my life?

Whit. I could call Whit. Maybe go into the city and meet him for coffee? We've texted twice since I told him the news about the fair, and it's been nice. Friendly. But the memory of when I accidentally asked him on a date sticks in my mind. I'm standing in the middle of my bedroom, bouncing back and forth on the balls of my feet. I can't call Whit. That's ridiculous. I snatch my cell phone off my nightstand and stare at the screen. Simply out of curiosity, I check the train times to San Francisco.

A muffled screech buffets the back of my teeth. What am I thinking? I don't make rash decisions. I once made a pros and cons list for whether or not I'd name my future cats with a literary theme. (The future Chaucer, Brontë, and Tolstoy will love their names.) My reflection in the mirror catches my attention. My cheeks are pink and my hair is wound into a messy braid. But there *is* mascara on my dresser, and I've gotten pretty good at it. And the polka dot navy sweater thrown over the back of my chair—a Christmas gift from Kat and Lola—isn't unflattering.

No, Marnie. Just . . . no.

But maybe?

If I waffle any more, I'll be covered in syrup.

In a flurry of movement, I select Whit's number and squeeze my eyes shut as tight as I can.

Maybe he won't pick up. Or he's busy with the girl he'd gone on a date with and is now surely his girlfriend. Yes, that'll be it. He won't be free, then this decision will be made for me, and—

"Hello?"

TWENTY-TWO

WHIT WAITS FOR ME NEAR the junction of narrow Montgomery Street and the Filbert Steps, which carve their way up the side of Telegraph Hill. The collar of his dark jacket is pulled up against the misty day, and his hair has a dull luster in the low light. He grins when he spots me and holds up a hand in hello, and my heart kicks quite suddenly.

Maybe this wasn't a great idea. For some reason, I can't see Whit without comparing him to Hayes. Seeing them together at the fair a few weeks ago has left me decidedly discombobulated. For nearly five years now, my unrequited love for Hayes has been a constant. It wove itself into my narrative, that I was tragic and true and would someday be rewarded for my constant heart. It's been . . . *easy*. Like the decisions about who I was—who I *am*—were preordained. And I can't lie; it's also made me feel superior to Lola and even Kat and their messy, dramatic love lives.

Yet there's the way Whit makes my skin tingle, makes my heart almost ache from beating so hard. What if my feelings for Hayes aren't a tragic romance straight out of a Brontë novel? What if it was nothing more than a childhood obsession? Lord, no one tell Adhira I admitted that.

But the word still lances through me. *Obsession.* It's difficult to breathe past the gaping Hayes-shaped hole in my psyche. I paper it over as I walk toward Whit. He doesn't deserve to be compared to Hayes. He's his own man, one I like a surprising amount.

I press myself back together, force my mind away from Hayes, and smile at Whit as I climb the first few steps to where he waits, leaning against the railing with one ankle hooked over the other.

"Are we searching for parrots?" No one quite knows how, but a flock of bright-green parrots have made their home among the trees and gardens of Telegraph Hill.

"I thought we'd climb to the top," Whit says, pushing off the railing and hopping up a step.

I crane my neck, but the stairs zig and zag uphill, hemmed in close on both sides by wild greenery and stair-stepped houses. Above it all, the round Coit Tower—rising from the top of the hill—peeks through the mist. It's an art deco icon, full of murals and amazing views of the city and Bay Bridge. I've only been once, and we drove to the top of the hill.

"It's kind of late. Is it open, or are we breaking in?" I ask, like he's suddenly going to reveal his penchant for breaking and entering.

A crease works into one cheek. "Are you telling me you're *not* into some light crime?"

I cut him a look and climb a set of steps beside him. He breaks and nudges my shoulder. "I actually didn't think about going in. I thought we'd just take a walk and enjoy the views. I brought snacks."

"Fine," I say, biting back a grin and hauling up another set of stairs. "But only because you brought snacks."

Talking with Whit eases my mixed-up mind. That's the thing I've noticed that makes me believe we're truly friends: it's never all that hard to fall into conversation with Eugene Whitlock Jr. He's a lot like Adhira in that way.

The stairs are narrow and steep, so for the next few minutes it's less about the talking and more about trying not to breathe like a pug with collapsed nasal cavities. Whit pauses at a landing and tugs a water bottle out of his backpack. He takes a long drink then hands it over to me without a word, and I hesitate only a second before taking it. It's intimate, sharing the water, and though it's cool in my throat, it kindles a warmth in my belly.

"I'm surprised you called," Whit says. "But it gave me a great excuse to escape. I love my family, but all of us in that apartment on school holidays—" He breaks off and scratches idly at the hollow of his throat. "It's a bit much."

I hand back the water and we start climbing again, finally

reaching the top of the hill. The shady park is just one set of stairs away, and the mist is tinged with the scent of the ocean.

"I wanted to ask," I say as we follow the path upward. "You said your tattoo is your Japanese name?"

Whit glances at me, then grins. "Yeah. Golden Warrior."

I elbow him in the ribs. "Shut up! You know his tattoo means, like, 'Pig Parade' or something."

"Oh, definitely," he says. "Also, Thai script is way different from kanji, hiragana, or katakana."

Whit rubs at his ribs where I elbowed him then lets his hand drop. The ridge of his knuckles brushes my hand, and it's suddenly very, very warm up here. He speaks like nothing has happened. Which, I mean, it hasn't. Definitely nothing happening here.

"Mine is the kanji script for Kaito, my middle name," he says, touching the spot where his small tattoo is hidden beneath his jacket. "My dad might have made me a junior, but Mom made sure I had a Japanese name too."

We crest the hill and stop, and I suck in a breath that fills the bottom of my lungs. "That's beautiful," I say on an exhale. And I mean it all. The story behind his tattoo and the lingering heat where his hand brushed mine, and the park in front of us.

Tall trees encircle the base of the tower, and the air around us is still, waiting. A tabula rasa. I am too, I realize. A hundred different futures are just beyond my fingertips, waiting for me to choose. What comes next for me? My blood thrums at the possibilities.

The cool, damp weather has chased away the tourists, so it's nearly deserted. We follow a path toward a small break in the trees, and Whit finds a wooden bench. I join him as he digs into his bag and produces a thermos of hot chocolate and a crinkly pouch of Chocorooms, little mushroom-shaped cookies with a chocolate cap.

My smile hitches to one side. "I didn't bring anything."

"You gave me the excuse, remember? My niece Molly got this makeup kit for Christmas and keeps trying to get me to be her model. I've been poked in the eye a dozen times already."

"Please tell her to take pictures next time you've got a full face on." I accept a cookie and pour us both mugs of hot chocolate. "Christmas Day, my nephew Theo went outside to the deck and peed all over the window during dinner."

Whit chokes on a bite of cookie. "That's amazing. We all went to Honolulu last year to visit old air force friends, and my other niece Annie dug a hole in the beach, stripped down, and peed in the hole in front of everyone. I thought my mom was dying she screamed so loud."

A laugh bubbles up and spills past my teeth. "Obviously, we never were an embarrassment to our families, right?"

Whit clanks his mug of hot chocolate against mine. "Obviously."

"Where all have you lived?" There's so much about Whit I want to learn. I wonder if he thinks the same about me.

He chews another cookie and counts on his fingers before answering. "We moved every two years until I was sixteen, so South Korea, Oklahoma, Germany, Florida, Japan, North Dakota, Honolulu, then back to Japan. My dad was stationed twice at Yokota, outside Tokyo, so I guess that's where I spent the most time. The last time was right before my parents divorced and my mom moved us back here to where she grew up."

"Do you want to move back? To Japan, I mean."

Whit regards his hands. The mug of hot chocolate rotates in his palms, and a small muscle jumps on the side of his jaw. "Sometimes? But even though I'm half Japanese, living around military bases is a lot different from actually *living* overseas. I went to American schools on base and everything. Plus, all my family is here. Hana and her girls are living with us since her divorce, and my middle sister is in grad school in LA. And my mom . . ." Whit roughs a hand through his hair and hooks his palm behind his neck.

"Sorry. I don't mean to pry."

"No." The crease between his eyebrows smooths when he looks at me. The mist clings to his eyelashes, and I curl my fingers inward to keep myself from touching a droplet of water. "Since my dad left, my mom kind of relies on me to be the man of the family, you know? And now that Hana and her girls are there too . . . I'm it, I guess. I love being there for them, but I've spent the last year sleeping on a cot in the corner of the living room so my sister and the kids could have my room."

"I have four sisters," I say, nodding. Though I don't add our house also has five bedrooms and seven bathrooms.

Whit hands over another cookie. "So, do you think you'll stay in San Francisco or head elsewhere for college?" Whit asks it lightly, but his fingers worry at the button of his jacket.

"Oh, stay," I say, without an ounce of uncertainty. Out across the city, the lights atop the Bay Bridge blink in the gloom. We're surrounded on all sides by buildings and life, yet it feels like we're the only two people in the world right now. "This city has my heart. What about you?"

Whit puts his empty mug down and slings one arm behind the back of the bench. "I'm here at least through college. In fact, a few friends asked me to move in with them next year." Whit's throat bobs with a swallow. "I can't believe I'm about to admit this, but, as much as they can annoy me, moving away from my family . . ." His eyes find mine, and he quirks up one side of his mouth. "How was it for you? Moving away."

I want to say something useful, but all I know is my own small experience. How sheltered it must seem compared to his, a guy who's not yet twenty, but who has lived around the world and taken up the mantle for his family. But, he asked me. He wants my opinion. It warms me up from the inside, like a dozen mugs of hot chocolate.

"It was hard, but not." Whit tilts his chin to one side and frowns. "I mean . . . it took moving away from home to realize who I could be. Or, maybe, who I hope to be. At home, I was only ever the girl my family decided I was. And that person . . ." I shake my head, clearing the Mary Bennet-ness from the dark corners of my mind. "Before I left for PCA, I'd never taken a train by myself, or a bus, or barely even driven by myself outside San Jose. The things that used to frighten me exhilarate me now. And, I mean, you've obviously already done all those things," I continue. "You grew up around the world and I grew up literally forty miles from here. But I guess I mean the freedom to try something, completely on your own, without that immediate safety net. It's worth it."

Whit grins, and it makes heat spread up my neck. He pulls his arm from the back of the bench and laughs under his breath.

"What?" The one time someone actually asks for my opinion, and I mess it up. Classic Mary/Marnie.

Instead of rolling his eyes and proclaiming me a dolt, Whit sits back so we're side by side on the bench and nudges my shoulder with his own. "You give good advice."

Oh. *Oh.* The heat in my neck flames higher and consumes my cheeks.

Whit's smile falters. "I'd have to get a paying job and leave Paws and Claws. There's no way I can swing school, a job, *and* volunteering at the shelter as much as I do."

Not volunteer. Not see me. The thought hollows me out, letting the winter mist creep in. But Whit is my friend. And apparently I give good advice.

"You should still do it." I'm surprised at how certain I sound.

Whit blinks fast. "You think?"

"If it means going after something you want? Definitely."

But what do I want? I peer at him and feel the answer glinting inside me.

His voice is low when he says, "I'd miss Bark Books."

"Bark Books would miss you too."

He opens his mouth to say something, tilts his body to face me. His leg brushes my thigh as he does, sending sparks showering down my skin. "Marnie."

His phone buzzes, severing the connection. Whit checks his phone and swears. "I'm supposed to be at the tailor in fifteen minutes."

My eyebrows rise in question. Whit rubs a hand against his jaw. "Okay, promise you won't laugh?"

Something in the tone of his voice makes me needle. "I make no promises."

Whit groans. "So I go to these dances with my sister. Very formal things, really. But she's had a hard year, and it makes her happy. Plus, the old ladies there love me."

A flash of Whit invades my mind. Bowing to a partner, doing the two-step with little old ladies. I've got to admit, it sounds unbearably cute.

"Like, a square dance?"

Whit grimaces. "Different century."

Well, now I'm intrigued.

"But the big annual gala is in a week, and Hana talked me

into getting a whole new . . . thing for it. And she's apparently already at the tailor and threatening to murder me if I'm not there."

"Go! Go!" I'm laughing, shooing Whit off. "Don't get murdered!"

He scoops up the cookies and thermos, his phone dinging at him again. He turns away, then back. Regards me.

"This has been nice, Marnie."

A smile unfurls across my lips. "Agreed."

Whit tugs at the collar of his jacket. The lines of his face are sharp: the swoop of his cheekbones, the thick slash of his eyebrows, the blunt edge of his chin. But then he licks his lips slightly, and my knees turn to jelly.

His voice is low and full when he says, "We should do this again sometime. Soon."

My blood fizzes. "Agreed. Soon."

TWENTY-THREE

SOON DOESN'T COME SOON ENOUGH.

In the last week, we've tried twice to get together for another date-non-date, but my grandparents were visiting from Arizona until yesterday, and Whit's been watching his nieces while his sister and mom are out of town for a single parenting retreat.

Unfortunately, Whit's not the only one trying to arrange seeing me. Hayes keeps texting, like, *constantly*. It's always under the guise of "catching up." There's something too smarmy—too desperate—about his texts. I mean, if *I* kept getting one-word replies, I'd probably get the hint, right?

I've started an email to Sara probably three dozen times. But what can I say? *So, your fiancé has been texting me in an aboveboard, friendly way?* It's not like he's sent me a photo of his genitalia. My cheeks flare with heat at the thought.

And yet. *Ugh*, and yet. Every time my phone dings with a new text, my heart flips over. A smaller flip than it used to be, but a flip nonetheless. Speak of the devil. I'm stretched out on a chaise longue with a book on my chest, Lola painting her toenails next to me, when my phone pings.

My chest squeezes, I roll my eyes, but then a delighted smile curls on my face when I see Whit's name.

Sir Pat misses you. The text from Whit accompanies a close-up of my favorite scruff monster with his grizzled chin tilted.

I curve forward and hunch over my phone. *He wouldn't miss me if he knew I was Team Cat.*

Whit's reply comes fast. *Little-known fact: Sir Pat is really into cats. To a weird degree, honestly.*

I knew I liked him for some reason.

"Who're you flirting with, Marnie?" Lola eyes me, Barbie pink nail polish in one fist.

I shove my phone under my thigh. "What? I don't know— No one!"

Lola freezes, and her eyes narrow. "Who is it, Marnie?"

"No one!" I practically screech. One of the great disappointments in life is that Lola (and, oh god, Lia) know about Hayes.

My traitorous phone pings. Lola perks up. "You have another text."

Ping.

"Two texts."

I pull a face and peek at my new texts.

Hayes: *In SF today. Free for coffee?*

Whit: *When are you back at PCA? It's too quiet here w/o Bark Books kids crawling all over the place.*

Lola tracks every twitch as I read the texts and respond. Hayes gets a flat *no* and Whit gets: *Sunday. Give Sir Pat my regrets.*

"You're smiling." Lola says it like I'm disemboweling a pigeon in front of her.

My nostrils flare. "And you're prying."

"It's what I do best, dear sister." She singsongs her response and goes back to her toenails. "It's definitely a boy."

"It's not a—"

One boy texts back.

Whit: *No one is reading to the moose. He's very depressed. Send help.*

To my eternal disappointment, the other boy texts too: *Oh I get it. Have time for what's his name but not me.*

What the hell? Detective Lola is still eyeing me, and I've practically got whiplash going between the two chats. My emotions veer between giddiness and annoyance, and Hayes's latest text clubs my "single-word replies only" strategy to death.

Come on. You know I've always made time for you.

I punch send and the text whooshes straight to . . .

Shiiiiiiit. I sent it to Whit. Every particle of blood drains my face. I squeak, jump off the chaise, and bolt inside. My fingertips tremble, but I manage to type a quick response: *Sorry! That was meant for Hayes.*

Text bubbles taunt for somewhere between three seconds to three millennia before Whit responds: *Got it.*

Then silence.

I barricade myself in my room and pull out a battered copy of *Anne* to cleanse my body of the texting horrors. Sometime later, I faintly hear the doorbell ring, but I don't move. I'm to the part in *Anne of the Island* where Gilbert proposes but Anne rejects him. This part always breaks my heart, that Anne can't see this perfect love right in front of her. But for the first time since I've been reading these books, a different face flashes in my mind. It's not Hayes.

It's Whit.

I can picture the tilt of his chin, the hope in his warm eyes, the way his dark hair would swoop over his forehead when he looks down, trying to hide his shattering disappointment. He probably should have known Anne's answer after she sent him that awful text. I close the book and sigh against the cover.

"Marnie!" It's Mom, her voice filtering back to me from what sounds like the living room. "Can you get the door?"

"Can't you get it?" I yell back at her.

"I'm painting my toenails!"

Is there a memo I missed? With a grumble, I roll off my bed and pass Kat at the dining room table and Mom on the couch with her toes perched on the coffee table. All of their legs are tragically broken, apparently.

I pull the door open and blink.

"Adhira?"

A wide, laughing grin lights up her face and fills me with warmth. "Surprise!"

I stand back and open the door wider. There's so much I want to talk to her about. So much I want her advice on. So much that—

Are those garment bags?

"Is she here?" Mom darts around me—she can walk again! A miracle!—and squeals. "Yay! Adhira, I'm so happy you're here!"

"Wait."

Confusion is a dense Karl-esque fog around my head.

"Are those the dresses?" Mom asks.

The fog thickens.

Adhira flicks her eyes toward me, and her smile grows guilty. "They are, Mrs. Barnes."

Mom jostles past me for the garment bags. "Oh, I can't wait!"

"For what?" I'm still standing in my doorway, staring at my friend. Who certainly should still be in Toronto, right? School doesn't start for another three days.

"Come in, come in!" Mom hauls Adhira inside and leaves me standing there like a statue.

Dully, I realize Adhira has grabbed my wrist and is dragging me with them. I lean against the back of the couch and sort of stare. Adhira is here . . . with dresses . . . and Mom knew about it?

Adhira searches through her black leather tote and pulls out a square card. There's an emerald-green tassel hanging from one side, and the calligraphy on the face of the card swoops and swirls. She presses the card into my hands. "Your Christmas present from me."

I have to put the card practically against my nose to decipher the calligraphy.

The honor of your presence is requested at the annual Bay Area Regency Society's Austen Ball. Refreshments and dancing will commence promptly at six o'clock in the evening, on the twelfth of January.

"Wait. What?"

I have lost all capacity for understanding.

"I got us an invite to the Austen Ball!"

The what now?

Mom straight up shrieks with glee. "Adhira brought it up to me at Thanksgiving, and I've been *dying* to tell you, Marnie! Oh, a ball! I love a ball!"

Maybe she can go instead, then?

The confusion is dripping away, leaving behind a strange sediment of fear mixed with . . . *excitement.* A ball. I've pictured a dozen different balls in my mind through the years, Regency resplendence and Victorian pomp and Edwardian confections.

A ball. Oh, I suddenly very much hope this is real.

That realization uncovers another truth: Mary Bennet hated

balls. She would moan about the needlessly ornate dresses and lecture about the importance of studious conversation over dancing. Right now, I want none of those things. I *want* to get dressed up and dance.

This must be it. I've once and for all kicked Mary to the curb. A charge of energy zigzags from my scalp to my toes.

"Is this for real?" I search Adhira's face for confirmation.

She holds up one of the garment bags and unzips it. "It is very much for real, Mar."

Inside the garment bag hangs the cream dress, a come-to-life version of the sketch I'd so loved, made from my great-grandmother's cloth. Adhira didn't just surprise me with the invite, she *made* this gown. My mouth opens and closes wordlessly, breathlessly. My heart threatens to up and take its leave.

"Do you like it?" she asks, her voice quiet.

Hesitantly, I step forward and touch the dress's neckline. "It's . . . it's . . ."

It's *perfect*. Excitement thrills through my bones, bubbles in my blood. I'll wear this dress wholly as Marnie, and that thought is a wonderful thing.

"I love it, Adhira," I almost whisper.

Yesterday after Adhira gave me a series of small heart attacks with her sudden appearance and invitation, we queued up dances on YouTube and practiced things like the quadrille and the Scotch reel. And when I say "we," I mean me, Adhira, and Mom. Kat and Lola even joined for some of it. Don't tell Mom, but it was actually kind of fun. She ordered us Chinese takeout, and we watched Adhira's favorite costume drama in the media room and all got up to dance along during the big ball scene.

It wasn't until later that I thought of Whit. He was going to a dance too. Surely it wasn't the *same* ball, right? Despite telling myself that, Whit invaded my dreams, sweeping me around a ballroom and whispering against my neck that I was his Anne Girl.

Now, standing in front of Mom's dressing room mirror in a bathrobe, full face of makeup, and hair coiled into a chignon, nerves rattle. What if I can't remember any dances? What if I spill punch down the front of someone's cravat? What if, what if, what if.

Adhira catches my eyes in the mirror. "I've wanted to attend one of these *forever*! I'm so happy you're going with me."

I squeak in reply. There are industrial-strength lightbulbs encasing the mirror, so powerful I can hear them humming. That can't be healthy.

Mom flits into the dressing room and sinks onto a tufted stool with a dreamy sigh. "A ball. I've been longing to dance. Not that any eligible man would dance with an old lady like me. . . ." She pauses and looks to us to contradict her.

After a second, Adhira jumps in. "I'm sure there'd be plenty of people who'd love to dance with you, Mrs. Barnes."

Mom titters. "Oh, you're only being nice. They'd pass right by me when you're an option, you lovely girl." Mom pats at her hair and gives us a little smile. Her gaze lingers on Adhira, who's finishing her eye makeup, before sliding to me. "You're beautiful too, my dear."

"Yes, it only takes three pounds of makeup, false eyelashes, and Adhira magic."

"There's no need to be sarcastic. I got that enough with your older sister." Mom crosses to me and tucks a stray lock of hair behind my ear. "You're always beautiful, Marnie."

Hearing my mom say this—actually say it aloud and seem to mean it—flutters in my chest. I touch Mom's shoulder, and she looks back at me. When I was little, I used to curl up on a wing-back chair upholstered in peach she kept in her dressing room and read books while she got ready. I can still smell the powdery scent of her makeup, the lemony perfume she used to spritz in her updos. It wasn't about learning all that girly stuff my little sisters seemed to love, but being physically close to my mom. Before I started struggling with this notion she didn't want me around.

"You're beautiful too, Mom." She smiles and kisses my cheek. Then she holds up a finger and hustles into the enormous closet attached to her dressing room. She's back a minute later with two things: one beautiful and one horrific.

"Nope." I point at the corset in her right hand. "Under no

circumstances. I'm not wearing your lingerie, Mom."

"Don't be silly, Marnie. It's *shapewear*, not lingerie."

Yeah, *her* shapewear. But Adhira, the traitor, fiddles with her fingers, then says, "I actually think you should wear it. You can't wear a normal bra with this neckline, so you'll feel more pulled together."

My eyes promise murder, but I'm clearly outnumbered, so there's nothing to do but grimace and get cinched into the thing.

I focus instead on the other thing my Mom brought out— delicate pearl earrings—which are admittedly lovely.

Then the dress slides over my head, and Adhira buttons it up the back, since, as she explained, zippers didn't yet exist in the Regency era. I inform her neither did cars, so we probably should have arranged a horse and carriage to take us north to San Francisco, but she ignores this.

"Oh, girls." Mom hugs my bathrobe to her chest. She looks like she's getting misty, and as I stand back and take in Adhira and myself in the big mirror, I'm kind of right there with her.

"Adhira, thank you." I grab her hand and hold tight. "I can't believe you made this for me. I just . . . thank you."

It's almost too much, the way this gown makes me feel— beautiful and excited and *loved*. I feel like Mary is nothing but a bad memory. The soft cream fabric somehow makes my pale skin glow with a slight pink tinge (my god, is that a *healthy blush?*) and gracefully curves around my body and whispers to the ground in heavy folds. The sleeves are capped and have a tiny, pearl button detail, and Adhira helps me pull on opera-length cream gloves that make me feel downright elegant.

Mom is sighing so much, I'm not sure how she's still standing. Surely she's hyperventilated by now.

I take one last look in the mirror, then grin at Adhira. "Call up the horse and buggy. We've got a ball to get to."

Mom sits down heavily on the cushioned stool. "Sigh."

TWENTY-FOUR

AN OLD LADY STARES AT US. So does the hipster couple next to her. The fluorescent train lights wince and the cheap blue seats squeak. We really should have taken a horse and carriage. At least we'd fit in.

"Adhira, I love you, but we look ridiculous."

We're both perched at the edge of our seats, straight-backed and wearing legit *gowns* on a BART train.

She shrugs. "Then maybe stop grabbing your boobs, eh?"

"I'm not grabbing." I hiss, lift my palms where they've been cupping my chest, then clamp them back down. "I'm making sure a nipple doesn't pop out."

Adhira rolls her eyes. "You're such a prude."

"It's not prudish to want to keep one's bosom under wraps!"

The old lady across from us titters. Good for her. Hopefully she never exposes a breast in public.

"You're completely covered, Mar. That's what the lace is for! I swear, you are *so* Victorian, not Regency."

I feel like this should offend me. It doesn't. The corset has shoved my minuscule endowment practically up to my collarbones, my boobs plump over the creamy muslin and straining against the lace like two Christmas game hens.

Adhira uses the thick invitation to bat my hand away. "Come on, this is our stop. We're going to dance with eligible men. One may even have ten thousand pounds a year!"

"Ten thousand," I deadpan. "Be still, my beating heart."

But off the train and onto the twilight streets, a smile curls. Out here, surrounded by the stone buildings, it's easier to pretend. I even notice a few others in gowns drifting toward the opulent ballroom. A thrill jitters through me, at the anticipation, the *fantasy* of it all.

Before us, the imposing building is all marble and columns, but through the open glass doors, sound trips and trills around me. Violins and talking and clinking crystal. A shiver rolls over my lace-bound décolletage, and it has nothing to do with the January air. Through these doors, the modern world melts away to something I've only ever experienced in books. It's like I'm stepping into a story come to life. My trembling fingers go tight against Adhira's arm, and the grin she sneaks at me speaks of a magic we're sharing.

"Ladies." A stern voice makes us stop short, right inside the door. "Ah, no men with you, I see? Pity." The woman is dressed in so much tulle and feathers she looks like an unpleasant dove. She holds her hands out for our invitations and inspects them with a pair of pince-nez clipped to the tip of her rather large beak.

"Welcome, Miss Fitz and Miss Barnes. I'm your hostess, Mrs. Fiddle. I'm sorry to say we have quite a few more women in attendance tonight than men, but there are still plenty of enviable dance partners within the atrium hall." She rattles off all this with a practiced air, her eyes trained somewhere above our foreheads. "Please avail yourselves of the punch and hors d'oeuvres and revel in tonight's festivities." Her affected accent drops suddenly. "And don't forget to tip the band."

And then we're in. With, perhaps, slightly tarnished magic.

Candles—electric, if you look closely—are set in splendid candelabras along the perimeter of the narrow hall. Overhead, the arched glass ceiling lets in the diffuse San Francisco evening. The floor underfoot is marble, as are the walls, and the space echoes with the musicians romping through a lively tune and the foot-stomping dancers frolicking up and down in lines at the far end of the long hall. Women and a handful of men— most are occupied on the dance floor—float along the edges of the room, sipping punch from delicate crystal cups and making small talk.

In a corner, two women take a selfie together. The modern

butts up against this facade of manners and pomp, somehow smearing both things together into something not *quite* right. Disappointment worms its way into my logical mind.

I pat my chignon and smooth out my gown again. What does one actually *do* at a ball dominated by women? I guess we could start fomenting unrest at the plight of nineteenth-century women, though I have a feeling Mrs. Fiddle wouldn't take too kindly to that.

Adhira, too, has drooped. "It's all lovely," she tries, valiantly. She takes a turn fussing with her hair.

"Maybe we should get some punch?"

Adhira jumps at the idea, and soon we're back at the perimeter, though now with Hawaiian punch masquerading as posh Regency drinks.

"So . . . ," she starts.

I take a swig of punch and search the room. Most of the attendees are middle-aged, but they're laughing with their partners and circulating the room. A few snippets of attempted British accents float over me. I turn to Adhira and lift my nose in the air.

"My dear friend," I say in my most unctuous tone, "did you hear the gossip about Miss . . . er, Bayside?"

Her eyes flick up to me, a frown between her brows. "Who?"

"You know, Miss Bayside! The heiress who made all the papers in London when she cut off her engagement."

Adhira blinks quickly, but then dimples carve into her cheeks. "Oh, my darling Miss Barnes! How could I forget! Her stodgy old fiancé was caught"—she leans in—"*in flagrante delicto.*"

"That's the one!" Oh, this game is a bit of fun! I hook my arm through Adhira's to take a turn about the room. They're always taking turns about the room and strolls in the garden in my books. We deposit our empty cups, and I curtsy to her. "Shall we dance, Miss Fitz?"

She tilts her head to listen. "Oh, the quadrille! We practiced this one!"

"Of course we did, Miss Fitz. We are ladies of breeding, after all."

Adhira accepts my hand, and we join the foursomes converging on the dance floor. The dance is lively, and even though I'm truly awful at it, I'm laughing by the end. We clap for the orchestra and waltz over for more drinks. Now I understand the need for Ye Olde Kool-Aid—the oodles of sugar give us energy to dance.

We've just settled at a little table when Adhira startles at something behind me. Her eyes go big at the same moment as someone clears his throat and taps me on the shoulder.

It's Whit.

I jump out of my seat so fast I nearly topple the table. Vivid pink sloshes onto the white tablecloth, but I'm too busy staring.

Oh. My. God. Whit. In an impeccable black tailcoat and dark gray waistcoat. A white cravat is tied simply around his neck, and I can barely allow myself to venture a gaze southward to his slim-fitting gray trousers. Heat prickles up my neck and creeps into my cheeks. The candlelight sparkles against Whit's dark eyes and glints off his thick hair. My thumping heart nearly cracks my ribs apart at the look on his face, his lips quirked in something between surprise and joy.

"I didn't know you'd be here!" I blurt out with the grace of a fishmonger.

"How many formal dances are there? What are *you* doing here?" His voice is tinged with laughter, and his eyes dance over my ball gown. My heaving breath is hemmed in by the abominable corset, pressing my breasts against their sheer prison until I'm positive I'll split the lace.

"I . . . ," I croak. As in, like a frog, not as in keel over and die. Though that also is a distinct possibility. "I mean, Adhira and I . . ."

Adhira, who has abandoned me.

A woman with glossy black hair twisted up high and an inquisitive smile like Whit's approaches, two cups of punch in hand. It must be his sister. Her gaze shifts between me and Whit. She clears her throat, and Whit nearly startles. He steps back an inch. "Hana."

"Whit." She pairs his name with a healthy dose of suspicion.

He accepts one of the cups and takes a drink. His fingers against the crystal are clenched, knuckles blanching. "This is one of my partners with Bark Books."

Hana dips into a little curtsy. "Pleased to meet you."

"I mean, this is Marnie Barnes," Whit adds, emphasizing my name.

Hana's eyes go wide.

My face is on fire. Like, literal fire. Spontaneous human combustion and all that.

Hana grabs the cup of punch from Whit's hands. "Hey, I wasn't done with that."

Her grin is practically devious. "You can't dance with punch in your hands."

Then she melts away, leaving me alone with her brother.

My fingers twist, twist, twist. "I should have texted you to see if you'd be here. It was all a surprise."

Whit tilts his chin to one side. "A surprise I'm here?"

Those twisting fingers wrench apart. "Yes—I mean, no. I mean, Adhira got us tickets for Christmas, and showed up at my house to surprise me. But you're here with your sister. I don't want to bother you."

"Nothing about you is a bother, Marnie." He says it with such conviction, I jerk my face upward, my breath lodged in my throat. How can he be so sure about me? I don't understand how, when I feel unmoored in who I am.

Somewhere distant, like hearing notes waft over the ocean,

violins trill up the scale. Around us, couples gather on the dance floor in anticipation.

Whit sketches a small bow. "Join me in the waltz, Miss Barnes?"

The world tilts under my feet, but Whit's hand against my gloved arm steadies me, if only for a moment. Someone grab the smelling salts because I daresay I'm about to swoon. I try to laugh, but it comes out more like a choke. "Oh, I can't waltz. You should have seen me dancing with Adhira."

"I did see you."

The entirety of the ballroom is surely tipping into the sea. I'm dizzy with the sensation of it.

Whit, though, doesn't stagger. He holds up his arm and lets his palm hover inches from my waist. "Dance with me, Marnie?" His voice is deep and low and tinged with hope. "Please?"

I purse my lips and nod. Whit's hand brushes against my waist and settles there. Ripples of shock spread from the warmth of his palm against my body, until I'm nearly consumed with that single point of contact between us. His other hand grips mine and lifts it high, and I snake my palm up to his shoulder. He steps, and I step with him, curl my fingers against his shoulder and revel at the feel of muscles flexing and stretching under the fabric of his coat.

He knows the steps, and I let him lead. We turn and dip and glide around the room, a swirl of color and movement around us.

The dance is slow and smooth, but I'm struggling to breathe by the end of it. Whit, too, has a brightness in his eyes I've never noticed before and red staining his high cheeks. He licks his lips, his tongue running along the seam.

"Marnie . . ."

The song has ended, but his hands are still on me. I suck in a breath. "Whit. I . . . that was . . ."

Far away, the music starts anew.

"Ah, ah, ah," someone tsks, invading our world. We both wrench at the sound.

It's Mrs. Fiddle, and her feathers are bristled. Whit drops his hand from my waist. "Mr. Whitlock, need I remind you of all the eligible young ladies awaiting a dance partner."

Whit frowns and shares a look with me.

"It'd be highly unseemly to dance two in a row with a single partner, now don't you agree?"

"Of course, Mrs. Fiddle," Whit concedes. "I forgot my manners."

"Yes, indeed," she sniffs.

"Miss Barnes." Whit squares his shoulders toward me and inclines his head in a subtle bow. Then he lifts his eyes to mine, dark and intense, and my body quakes.

"Mr. Whitlock." It's a whisper as he goes, and a hope that he'll return.

Mrs. Fiddle drags Whit away to one of the many "eligible young ladies," this one a silver-haired crone wearing gold brocade and enough diamonds to fund a small nation-state.

I spin in a daze, searching for Adhira or even Hana. Someone to tether me back down to earth. My fingertips fizz and
my skin is electric. A space opens before me, and I lean against
the cool marble wall, thankful for the support. Out on the
dance floor, Whit is leading the stooped old woman in a stately
dance, but his eyes pick mine out from the crowd. They land
on me again and again, until I nearly sway with the sensation
that I'm still dancing with him.

As soon as the music fades, Whit bows to the woman and
weaves through the crowd to me, purposely sidestepping
Mrs. Fiddle, who's on the hunt for more male partners for her
female attendees.

Whit's chest rises sharply as he comes to stand before me.
The lines of his face are taut, his fingers flexing and curving
over and over. I push off from the wall and look up at him.
"Would you care to d—"

"I have to know. What is Hayes to you?"

The question buffets me right back against the wall, and
my throat closes up tight. Whit is so close, and my heart is a
jackrabbit. I want to dance with him again, feel his hands on
me again. My skin heats and my tongue is fat when I stammer,
"Hayes? He's always been a big part of my life. He saved—"

Whit wilts before me, his mouth going slack and his hands
falling. "Ah. I understand." He turns away, and fear tears
through me.

"Wait. Please, Whit."

He stops, twists his head to look at me. His eyebrows draw

upward, awaiting my explanation. But nothing comes out. The thought is burning up my mind—*I think I'm falling for you*—but I don't know how to say it. I've never uttered it aloud to anyone.

He waits for me, gives me a chance. And I fail. All this time, I'd thought I was changing, digging Mary up and throwing her out. But she's here, inside me. She's all I am.

Whit draws his shoulders back, draws shutters over the emotion in his face. "Hana is looking for me. Goodbye, Marnie."

I'm tossed at sea and reaching for any lifeline when I find Adhira. "I need to go home. To PCA."

TWENTY-FIVE

"MARNIE, I *CANNOT* ACCEPT YOU would choose Hayes over Whit."

The big wooden door into Hawthorne Hall bumps against my shoulder, jostling me inside.

"I already told you, I wasn't *choosing* Hayes. I just—"

I just didn't have the right answer. Or any answer. Or maybe *I'm* not the right answer. My eyes are bleary and my dress heavy and suffocating. How is it only an hour ago I was waltzing around a grand ballroom with a beautiful boy in a Regency-era suit and now . . .

"So text him." Adhira scoops up the mail from our box, gathers her hem into her hand, and starts climbing the stairs. The dorm is dim and almost eerie with most students still on break.

The vision of Whit walking away from me suffuses my thoughts. It was punctuation at the end of our sentence. It was a period, not a comma. Final. And the thought of not talking to him again, of losing our friendship because of Hayes . . .

I press the fingertips of my gloved hands against my forehead, trying to massage out the image of him walking away, but it remains. It burrows deep and promises to become a headache.

"I don't think a text would do anything."

Adhira's jaw is set, her eyebrows winging low when she cuts a look over her shoulder. "You won't know if you don't try."

"Drop it, okay?" I snap. We've reached our hall, and I'm suddenly weary.

And she does, but only because she's stopped outside our door, where a piece of paper with the Pacific Crest Academy insignia is taped. I squint to read the notice, but Adhira snatches it off the door.

"What the hell is this, Marnie?" Her fingers clench the paper.

A bead of concern drips down my throat, but it isn't enough to douse my annoyance. "What the hell is what? Can I go to bed and wallow in peace?"

She shakes the paper under my nose, then reads aloud: *Adhira Fitz and Marnie Barnes, please see Ms. Johnson for your room reassignments.*

Oh no. My request for a single room has finally been

granted. I didn't know, didn't realize. I'd *forgotten* about it all.

Down at the end of the hall, Ms. Johnson, our dorm RA, sticks her head around the door to the common area and kitchen. "Oh, good! You're both back early!"

She's a young British teacher—poetry, I think—and she's in a furry gray bathrobe and Coke-bottle glasses. And right now, I want her to turn that fuzzy butt around and toddle back to her room.

Instead, she smiles and starts walking our way. "It'll be easier moving rooms without all the other students out and about, don't you agree? Let me grab my out-process forms, and I'll be with you both in a tick."

I slice a look to Adhira, but she's gone statue-still. The notice is crumpled in her hands.

"It's a mistake, right?" Her voice is tight as she watches Ms. Johnson disappear into another room.

"No, not a mistake," I say to the floor.

Maybe if we just sit down, talk about it. I dig at my side, where the corset is probably piercing one of my lungs. Also, change into pajamas. Maybe we can do that first.

Adhira, though, throws the notice onto the hallway floor and rifles through our mail. She yanks out one clearly addressed to me from the PCA Housing Board and rips it open.

"That's actually a federal—" She glares me into silence. ". . . never mind."

Her lips thin out as she reads the letter, and when she looks at me, there are tears in her eyes. "You wrote them on October twenty-third? *After* I took you out for your birthday? *After* I thought we'd become friends?"

"My dad had paid for a single—"

Adhira swipes her hand through the air. "I don't give a flying fuck what your millionaire daddy paid for."

She pushes the door open so hard it slams against the closet and stalks into the room, ripping off her gown as she does. She's down to a corset and bloomers, and pretty soon I am too, the two of us undressing in silence. It'd be pretty comical—fighting in this ridiculous underwear—if I wasn't also terrified. Inside, I'm reaching for the strings, trying to keep them from unraveling, but I'm not sure how. I tug on cloth shorts and a T-shirt Grammy sent me last year with a grinning cartoon wolf sporting an Arizona-emblazoned cowboy hat. Yes, that's much more dignified.

Adhira's shoulders deflate and she stumbles back against the edge of her desk. "After how much work I put into trusting someone else again, and then it's all a damn lie." She glares at me, her face tight with anger. "You let me believe we were matched up as roommates for a reason; that's why I put so much stupid effort into being your friend, because I *believed* our applications found a connection between us." She slaps a hand against her chest, like she's proving how I've wounded her. "But you betrayed me, Marnie. You stabbed me in the back."

That makes my chin jerk up. It's not Adhira I see in front

of me. It's Lola, my mom, all the times they took one tiny thing and blew it out of proportion. All the times they made everything about them, with no regard for the rest of their family. "Betrayed?" I shake my head and twist up my mouth in a grimace. "Don't be silly. Just because I'm in my own room doesn't mean we won't be friends. I prefer my solitude. You know that about me. It's just a room."

"Yeah, like you and Whit are *just friends*. Oh, except you ruined that with your impossible obsession with a greasy, sniveling con artist."

It puts my back up, the way she's never even *tried* to understand what I see—saw—in Hayes. "He saved my life, Adhira. As in, literally."

"And I *literally* don't believe it. That guy—*that guy*—ran into the ocean to save you when your sisters wouldn't? What a load of crap."

My breath is tight, my emotions tearing through me. They burst out of me: "What the hell happened to you in Toronto to make you so bitter! You never even gave him a chance!"

"Because he doesn't deserve a chance!" she screams. "Don't you see how he's using you? How he's going to hurt you if you give him even an inch? He'll take everything from you, your old life, your friends . . . You'll be left . . ." The air whistles out of her, leaving her chest caved in.

It sucks the anger out of me, to see her shriveled and small like this.

"Adhira?" I take a step closer. This isn't about me or Hayes or even this room anymore. It's about whatever made her move across the continent. She's my best friend, and I've hurt her. I hurt her, then made it worse. The realization steals my breath, my anger, my stupid self-righteousness. "Adhira, please. What happened—"

"All right!" Ms. Johnson bustles in with a clipboard, but her broad face quickly loses its smile. "Oh dear."

Adhira ignores Ms. Johnson. Her dark eyes find mine, and they're flint. "You want your own room? Fine. Get out of *my* room, then."

"Now, Adhira," Ms. Johnson says, still hovering near the doorway. "Let's talk this through. There are plenty of room-mate situations that don't work out."

Adhira shoves past me toward the bathroom and slams the door.

Ms. Johnson *hmms* and shuffles from foot to foot. "Perhaps we should all sit down and talk about this."

"I don't want to talk," Adhira yells through the door.

And because I'm ultimately a coward, I don't push it. I don't try. Even as I hate myself for it, I don't knock on that bathroom door even though I can hear Adhira crying. I can't be a friend to her. Quietly, Ms. Johnson helps me pack my meager belongings to move to my new room down the hall.

The room is narrow and chilly; the walls are bare. This is what I wanted, right? I came to PCA to be an academic, after all.

I slump onto the naked mattress with my chignon falling down and my hands curled in my lap, but Ms. Johnson interrupts my sulking. "A couple more things, then you're all settled." She tries for a smile, but gives up halfway there. She pats my shoulder twice, then steps back. "Maybe you could try to smooth things over with Ms. Fitz. I'd hate for that to be how you end things."

I choke on a laugh and shrug.

In stocking feet, I pad back down the hall and into my room—my *former* room. Adhira is still in the bathroom, so I stand close and knock.

"Can I explain?" I say against the wood.

"Go. Away." Her response is muffled and sticky with tears.

Her words sink like needles into my skin. My friend—my best friend, my *only* friend—wants me out of her life. And it's my fault. I bite down hard against the realization, but it's still there. This is entirely my fault. I've been so selfish, so consumed with my own issues that I've ruined one of the most important relationships of my life. I press my forehead to the door and squeeze my eyes shut so hard stars pop through the dark.

Through the wood, I can still hear Adhira crying. A good friend would open the door and give her comfort. But I am not a good friend. I don't even know how to be a passable one. So instead, I do the best thing I can: I leave her alone.

As silently as possible, I stack the last of my books on my desk, then untack a few photos from my corkboard. The contract I wrote is still there, mocking me.

I, Marnie Elizabeth Barnes, hereby do swear to root out and destroy Mary Bennet.

Root out. More like I dug in. I failed at everything I tried to accomplish. And I failed at being a real friend to Adhira, who supported me every step of the way. All to end up here—alone. Why did I even try? Mary Bennet is here to stay. I wriggle my fingers under the top of the paper and rip it down.

I shove the paper into one of the books, clamp them under one arm, and drape the last of my clothes over the other. The hallway is mercifully empty. You know what, Ms. Johnson was right about one thing: I'm glad I'm doing this walk of shame without any witnesses.

Scratch that. Down the hall, the kitchen microwave dings. And Lia—*effing Lia*—comes around the corner. I tuck my chin and try to hurry past her, but my muscles seize up and the books pop out from under my arm and tumble to the floor. Without looking, Lia balances her microwave dinner on an oven mitt, kneels down, and picks up one of the books to hand to me.

It's only then she looks up and freezes. "Oh, it's you."

"Unfortunately."

Lia peers down the hall toward my—*Adhira's* room. "Lovers' quarrel?"

My stomach sours. "Something like that."

Lia stands, still balancing that Lean Cuisine, and shoves the book at me. She smirks. "Adhira always seemed too cool to be friends with you."

I blink slowly and look from Lia's frozen dinner up to her face. "I don't exactly see you surrounded by friends, Ms. Meal for One."

Red blotches spread up Lia's neck, and she scowls and scurries away. My triumph lasts for approximately two seconds, then it oozes away and leaves me just as tired and disappointed as before.

Back in the room I sit on the edge of the bed and stare out the window. There's nothing but blackness and my own sallow face reflected back.

I pull out my phone and flick through my contacts. Adhira: Obviously not. Whit: Also no. Hayes: Ha. Lindy . . .

You around?

I need to hear some kind words.

My phone pings. *About to board jet for Sara's bach weekend. What's up?*

I hesitate over the keypad. There's so much I want to say, and I have no earthly idea how to say it. A niggling at the back of my neck makes me stop, delete my attempts, pause again. I don't want to be a bother.

Nothing major. Have a great time!

I set my phone down and stretch out on the bare mattress. My hand falls to the book on top of a stack next to my bed:

Wide Sargasso Sea. I read the inscription again: *To us tower-bound women. Break free.*

But how does one escape a tower of one's own making? I did this to myself, and there's no way to tear it down. There's no escape. I'm surrounded by my books. And I've never felt more alone in my entire life.

For a few wonderful months, I tasted what it was to have friends. People who *chose* to be around me because they liked me, not because of the obligations of birth.

But in the end, they all saw the real me. The unrelenting, unlikable me. Whit, now Adhira.

I'm Mary, and Mary's no heroine.

We're nobody.

TWENTY-SIX

THE FIRST WEEK AFTER THE Austen Ball, Whit called in sick to Bark Books and left me making small talk with the actual volunteer coordinator. January marched along horrifically bright, the weather entirely unsympathetic to my misery.

The second week after the Austen Ball, Whit returned to Bark Books but, if he wasn't shunning me, it was shunning-adjacent. Even Sir Pat gave me the cold paw. Five Hunt Prize judges made an unannounced visit, and I had to make Edgar the spaniel my example for "reading to dogs" success.

The third week after the Austen Ball, Adhira walked right by me in the cafeteria and sat with Shelby Anderson, who looked so pleased with the new seating arrangements I wanted to throw nachos in her face. It rained that afternoon, but only because I'd forgotten my raincoat in my dorm room. I trudged all the way from the still-unnamed science building back to my single room and took a ridiculously long, hot shower and told myself I'd never be able to do that if I had a roommate.

Three weeks.

Three weeks of having my failures on display at school and at Bark Books.

Each passing day, the fluttering hope and fragile endearment I felt for Whit dissolves a little bit more. We had a sort-of thing, a thing-in-training, but now that's gone. With Adhira, the gnawing ache in the pit of my stomach fades every time I pass her on campus or sit across the room from her in class. The wounds are scabbed over and sore . . . but healing. That's the worst thing of all: I *had* a best friend, but apparently my solitary, lonely life can return so easily. Was I really so hopelessly unchanged by the past months of trying to escape my Mary-ness?

I'm too nervous I'll run into Adhira at Bardo, so I thread my way over a cushion of moss through the garden, where the rhododendrons are starting to wake up for the spring. Just beyond the headmaster's residence hides a rounded gate that only opens from the inside. I discovered it the first lonely weekend here at PCA. And now here I am again, pushing the resistant hinges, stepping out onto the Greenwich Garden Path. I follow the staircase carved into the hillside and start walking.

I've never explored this snug neighborhood sandwiched

between Russian Hill and North Beach, but I amble my way around the park and duck into a narrow coffee shop. There are so many unknowns—is there Wi-Fi, where should I sit, do they call my name when my drink is ready—but I refuse to let myself turn around and scurry back to PCA. Maybe a little unknown is a lot okay.

There's a small table by the window, so I arrange my notepad, books, and highlighters. I said I was cool with a *little* bit of the unknown, I'm not becoming—*shudder*—laid-back.

The big Hunt Prize presentation is in less than two months, so I hunch over my notebook and start prepping. I'm getting an early start, but what else do I have going on? Also, I'm about as good at public speaking as I am at lasting friendship; I need all the prep time I can get. One hour drags into two. My butt aches, and my eyes are grimy. I pull off my glasses and lean back in my chair, stretching.

Outside the window, Lia walks by. It's such a jarring intrusion that I jam my glasses back on. Her golden-blond hair trails down her back, and her face is tilted toward me, open and laughing. And the man at her elbow is . . .

Hayes.

Spiders skitter down my spine. My muscles twitch, spurring me on to act, do something.

I dash out of the coffee shop and skid to a stop on the sidewalk.

"Hayes!" Except I'm no longer excited to see him. I haven't

been in a long time. The realization is sunshine seeping into a darkened room.

He mutters something to Lia I can't hear, and she shrugs and flounces off. What are they doing together on a Thursday afternoon? The Hunt Prize fair is over, so it's not like Bright Star Capital is still assisting Lia with anything, right?

He walks closer, settling his features as he does. His tight mouth loosens, and he bares his teeth in a smile. It's all a calculation—that's so obvious now. It's like opening an old toy to see the clockwork.

"Marnie. What a surprise." He saunters closer, but the cologne I once tracked down and spritzed on my pillow now makes my throat slick with scent. He's wearing too much of it. Has it always been that way?

I want nothing more than to back away, mumble a goodbye, and bolt. But I force my spine straight. "What were you doing with Lia?"

His smile falters for half a heartbeat. "What do you mean?"

"I mean, just now. Shouldn't you be at your office?"

He blinks, blinks again. "Oh, that! It's for her Hunt Prize." He chuckles and nudges my shoulder. "Marnie, are you jealous? You know I love my Barnes girls."

The way he says *love* releases writhing worms in my stomach. But I play along. *What* was he doing with Lia? "Is there something to be jealous of?"

He chuckles again and runs a hand through his hair. It's tiny, barely there, but this is a man I've studied for years: the tension in his shoulders unwinds by the barest margin. He thinks he's charmed me. He really is quite stupid, isn't he?

"With Lia? Don't be ridiculous." Hayes presses his lips together, leans closer—

And pulls his phone from his pocket. "Now that we finally have a minute, can I show you my app? You said you'd talk to your dad about it, Mar. Remember? We can figure this out together, right?"

He doesn't wait for my answer. He steps closer, so close I have to fight the urge to step away. He holds out his phone and lightly rests his hand on the small of my back.

"I'm so glad you're finally seeing it, Mar. You know you're one of the most important people to me, right? Not even Sara has seen this." He speaks in a low voice I'm assuming is meant to make me weak-kneed. But the beta version of his app is doing enough of that, and for all the wrong reasons. It's called Hack the Help. The tagline is "Because who wants the pro-letariat parking your Porsche?" I think I'm going to be sick.

I swallow back the nausea and point at a slider bar. "And what's that for?"

Hayes settles into his routine, his smile oozing. The hand at my back slides to my hip, and I shiver in disgust. "Oh, I'm really proud of that. You can select for all sorts of metrics and choose how diverse you want the hired help to be. So, say you want all minorities so you look woke, or you don't want any old men or fat chicks."

And I don't know why, I don't know what makes *this*

repulsive moment worse than all the others, but that's it. I push his hand off my hip and step away. I've wasted five years obsessed, not in love. And even then, I was in love with the *idea* of him, not Hayes himself. I've projected all my desires for the romantic hero in my life onto Hayes, who is wholly undeserving.

I've been such an idiot. Adhira has tried making me see the truth. Even Lola, months ago at The Shack. She said I was remembering the day Hayes saved me all wrong. The reality has been staring me in the face for years: There's no possible way this man put himself in harm's way for another human being.

He was my world for years. *Years.* I'd spend our moments together breathless, and the weeks afterward replaying every word, every look between us. And for what—for some social climber who probably *lied* about being my savior? A shudder rolls down my spine. How many times have I made excuses for his behavior? How many times have I been willfully obtuse so as not to shatter the illusion of him as the hero befitting my unrequited obsession? My cheeks burn with it all.

"Mar, what's wrong? I need your help on this." He tries to come closer, but I hold a palm up between us.

Shame twists and churns throughout my body. I'm molten at the edges, burning with incandescent rage. It all bubbles up and up and up until I can't hold it in any longer.

"Dammit, Hayes. I fantasized about this moment, about

you, for how long? But the reality is . . . ." I rake hands through my hair. "You're not a fantasy. You're not the hero. I am."

He stumbles over himself, trying to recover. There's a perfect smile on his lips, but terror in his eyes. I've got the power right now. And that terrifies him. *Good*. He should be afraid. He should be afraid of all of us.

"You're right, you are. Totally. But, Marnie, you make me want to be a better man." His smile is rabid, and tendons stick out in his neck from the strain of it.

"It's not my job to make you a better person."

All these years I thought he was a better person because of a single moment. My finger again goes to the scar at my hairline, long the reminder of who I'd falsely built Hayes up to be—my savior, my hero. Hayes's eyes track my movement, and his face juts closer, triumph in his eyes.

"I saved your life. Or did you forget that?"

"Did you? Did you really?"

His eyes darken with anger. "Why are you being such a bitch?"

Bitch. The word settles between us, but it doesn't hurt. I earned this one, and *my god*, does it feel good. I smile, and it makes Hayes's lips thin to a slit. I should tell him to smile more. He's quite unattractive when he's angry.

"Have you ever thought I went in when no one else would?" He spits the words at me. "Maybe I wanted to spare you the knowledge that your own sisters would have let you drown."

The thought turns over in my head, but it doesn't settle right. I may have had my differences with my sisters, but we're family. They love me. The memory of that day flares bright, the story I've twisted and replayed a million times. But now I'm seeing it through a different lens. The shock on his face when he hit me with his board. The way he swore, not in fear . . . but in surprise.

"You're lying." Finally uncovering the truth is a sharp pain that jabs my gut, so hard it nearly steals my breath. But it subsides in ripples and knits my muscles and bones and brain back together stronger, confident. I'm finally clear of the lie. "You had no idea I was there. It was all dumb luck."

The truth of it is plain in his face, in the way he sucks breath. His cheeks prickle pink, and he licks his lips. "I *did* save you, Marnie." His voice is a whine, a plea. It hits me that Hayes believes his own lie. I almost feel bad for him.

I push my shoulders back and stare Hayes right in the eyes. "Good for you. Now go explain to your *fiancée* that you're a piece of shit and leave me the hell alone."

TWENTY-SEVEN

SO, IN A TWIST NO ONE saw coming, Hayes apparently *did* go grovel to Sara. I know, because I finally worked up the courage to call her the very next morning. In what was surely one of the most awkward conversations in human history—up there with Oedipus chatting with his new wife about family history—I told Sara that Hayes had made some questionable comments to me and seemed to be spending a lot of time with Lia Lawson.

Sara had sighed, then said she appreciated my concern, but she and Hayes had talked. He knew he'd screwed up, but he'd promised her nothing had ever crossed the line and they were devoted to building a stronger relationship. When I started to tell her about the app—Sara would surely be just as grossed out about that diversity slider!—she interrupted and pointedly asked me to give them time to heal together.

So yeah, guess I've still got a wedding to attend in two weeks.

Sara's not the only one who doesn't want me around. Whit was a no-show again at Bark Books, and Adhira has been MIA all weekend. At least Lindy's back from Sara's bachelorette weekend, but there's so much to tell her I don't even know where to start.

Which all leaves me here: sitting alone in the PCA caf telling myself to cut the pity party.

The caf is all big windows and blond wood and white walls, like a high-end Ikea. In the brochures enticing parents to send their daughters off to PCA, a big deal is made about the head chef and the kitchen garden. But today, I'm definitely eating cheese pizza and French fries with a chocolate milk. I'm fairly sure none of what's on my plate started life in the kitchen garden.

You know what else didn't start life in a cute organic garden? Lia. Everyone knows hell spawn are reared on factory farms.

Beelzebub's favorite daughter drops her tray at the next table over and perches at a seat, her gaggle of friends around her. Lia picks at her salad one leaf at a time and loudly brags about a recent weekend in Milan. I know a Lean Cuisine that begs to differ.

She catches me staring and nudges her friend. "We'd ask you to join us, Marnie, since you're already listening, but there's no room." There are three empty chairs at her table. So it's going to be *that* sort of day, then. "Though," she continues, "not being wanted didn't stop you from chasing after Hayes the other day."

She's baiting me. I roll my eyes and stick a fry in my mouth.

She pulls a plummy little smirk that would incite murder in the hearts of nuns. "Did you see the press release?"

I chew slowly. "For what?"

I shouldn't have taken the bait, I realize as soon as I close my mouth. Lia lights up with evil. "Oh, Daddy is officially getting the science building named after him. Too bad for your dad, huh? I guess the Barnes don't win *everything* in the end."

"I have no idea why I should care."

But I do, and she knows I do. Dad has never admitted it, but he wanted his name on that building. He's given years of his time, talents, and money to the tech incubator here at PCA, and he *deserved* the recognition. At a table near Lia, Adhira glances up at me, then away. My table suddenly seems big and empty with just me and my tray and my invisible friends. I tuck back into my food and do my best to ignore everyone.

This, apparently, is unacceptable. Through eyes cast downward, I see Lia stomp away with her tray, then circle back to stop at my shoulder. I swallow a bite of pizza before I look up at her. Her dress today is bubble-gum pink, and the afternoon light flashes off the enormous diamond studs in her ears.

She makes fun of me because I'm an easy target, that's what I told Adhira all those months ago. When Adhira promised we'd be difficult women, it'd shocked my cells into action. Into *becoming* someone new. Yet Lia still finds me a soft body she can kick when she's down.

Her eyes sharpen, and her smile bares her teeth. "Is it true your sister dropped out of all those film festivals because she's in rehab? That's what caused her accident, right? She was high?"

"Hey!" Adhira jolts upright, her chair scraping the tile. "That's enough."

Lia goes still, tension crackling around us. But confidence surges through me, and I share a look with Adhira. My bones are sure and steady as I stand up and face Lia. "Don't you have small animals to torture or something?"

Lia turns on a heel and stalks out, and Adhira rushes over. "Are you—"

"I'm sorry!" I blurt at her. "I was wrong about the whole thing, and stupid, and I miss you. I miss sharing a room with you. And being friends, obviously. I miss that most of all."

A smile slowly crawls across her face. "I missed you too, Mar." It's like weeks of loneliness melting away.

To us tower-bound women. Break free.

The inscription comes to me in a flash of realization. My tower was built of bricks with many names—my jealousy of Lindy; my obsession with Hayes; my fear of accepting myself—but *I* built it.

And I can tear it down.

I grab Adhira in a hug and squeeze tight, then pull back. Beyond us, Lia is shoving her way through the cafeteria doors, pulling a raincoat over her shoulders. "I want to catch up with you. But right now, I need to go murder Lia."

Adhira grins. "Can I be your accomplice?"

"Obviously."

"Lia!" My clogs slip on the slick flagstone as I push out the rain-splattered doors, but I run toward her. "Lia, you want to know what Hayes said about you?"

That makes her freeze. Maybe we both know how to get under the other's skin. Adhira is at my side as we skid to a stop in front of Lia, and she grabs hold of my rain jacket to keep from slipping on the grass.

Lia's back is still turned, but her shoulders have gone stiff under her raincoat.

"Nothing," I say, raising my voice over the rain. "He didn't mention you at all."

She twists to sneer at me over her shoulder. "Why would I care?"

"I suspect for the same reason I did. You know he's getting married in, like, two weeks, right?"

Pain ripples down her face, but she schools it. "And like I said," she intones, obviously working to make herself appear bored as she steps closer. "Why would I care? I'm not an obsessed little weirdo like you, chasing after a guy who is, like, way too old and doesn't give a shit about you."

Her words glance off me like the rain. Sliding down to the ground, forgotten. I could walk away right now. But I've wasted so many damn years walking away from Lia. I can't do it anymore.

"What the hell is your problem with me? You've been awful to me for years, and I don't know why."

Lia's eyes narrow to slits. "Oh, don't act like you have no clue."

I throw up my hands. "I really effing don't!"

I know our dads don't like each other, that . . . *something* happened more than a decade ago between them. But that's it. Every search I've done has come up empty. And, honestly, it's hard to imagine how Dad—gentle, absent-minded Dad—could do something to a peacock like Casper Lawson that would cause his daughter to hold such a grudge.

Around us, the sky hunkers down low and the rain pelts down, misting the concrete under our feet. Most of our classmates are eating lunch or in class, but the few who are out are slowing, staring. Lia stalks closer, close enough I can see her neck red with blotches where her makeup fades.

"Your family ruined my life." The careful boredom is gone. It's been burned away by a hatred so strong I nearly stumble. It takes every last ounce of courage not to back away, but I can feel Adhira beside me. I've got my best friend by my side; I'm not afraid of Lia Lawson.

I arch one eyebrow and throw boredom back in her face. "I

hardly think I ruined your life, Lia."

She's the one who made my life hell. She's the one who showed back up at Crenshaw in fifth grade with me in her crosshairs. Lia, giggling and whispering with her friends whenever I'd walk by. Lia, looking at me like I was worse than scum.

Lia, who, right now, has gone rigid with rage.

"You ruined everything," she absolutely bellows.

The storm of her anger buffets me, knocking me unsteady. Adhira grabs hold of my elbow, an anchor. Lia's crying now, sobs rolling out of her and big, fat tears streaming out of her puffy eyes. This isn't a show.

"You're the reason my mom left." Her voice is filled with anguish, and my heart twists. "You're the reason we lost everything. I even had to sell my pony, Marnie. My fucking pony!"

Lia drags in a ragged breath I feel deep in the pit of my stomach. How long has she been holding that in? I understand all too well the horrible ache of staying quiet, of papering over the cracks inside yourself with bravado.

I take a small step closer, hold out my hand. I truly have no idea how or why my family decimated hers so completely, but I want to understand. I want to make this right, if I can.

Lia lifts her chin and glares. "Yeah," she says, her voice quiet and raw. "So don't act like you have some perfect little family. Don't you dare."

TWENTY-EIGHT

⟡

MY FINGERS TWIST TOGETHER, SQUEEZING WORRY into my skin. How did Dad cause so much damage to the Lawsons? If it were so awful, wouldn't there be some paper trail? Articles, blog posts, *something*.

"Do you truly not know what happened?" Adhira asks after Lia flees.

I cast my memories back, but it's like swimming through pea soup. Finally, I shake my head. But there must be *some* record of it.

The library. I had to have missed something. My shoes squeak against the floor as we stomp inside, and the librarian, Ms. Parnell, shushes me. I grind to a halt. How have I never thought to ask? All the hours I've spent in this library, and I've never even considered *asking* the librarian to help. If I weren't scoured so raw from the worry, I'd give myself a scolding about my misuse of library resources.

We stop in front of the main desk, and I clear my throat. Ms. Parnell has a squishy, lined face and a stern attitude toward book-lending that I appreciate.

"Ms. Parnell, I need your help."

She takes a moment before looking up at me over the top of her glasses. "Do you, Ms. Barnes." It isn't a question, it's a toleration.

"I need to know what happened between my dad and Casper Lawson. Something more than ten years ago. I can't find anything online, but I know something happened."

One corner of her flat mouth twitches. "Oh, there's a reason for that." Ms. Parnell groans as she pushes herself out of her chair, but she marches toward a back corner of the library with the air of someone much younger. Or maybe she's just that aggrieved.

Through a door marked "Archives—Special Access Only," Ms. Parnell reveals a squat room surrounded on three sides by cabinets and a small table with two wooden chairs in the middle. The lights are dim, hidden in recesses along the edges of the wall, and there's a single green-shaded lamp on the table.

"Position and money can do a lot to scrub your history online, but the printed word is harder to erase," explains Ms. Parnell as she runs a hand along the labeled filing cabinets.

Finally, she stops and yanks a drawer open, then selects a folder and drops it on the table between me and Adhira. "When Mr. Lawson joined the board, he tried to get us to remove these, but I refused. He didn't like that much." She shrugs, and continues. "Then I threw his daughter's phone out the window, and he didn't like that much either. But I've seen plenty of Casper Lawsons in my time, and I'm sure I'll see plenty more."

Adhira is already opening the long, greenish-gray hanging folder when Ms. Parnell stops at the door. "Look for a full-page ad in each of those, and make sure you follow the filing system when you put them back."

Then she's gone, and I'm rubbing the confusion away from my forehead. An ad?

Adhira frowns at me, but we dig in. I choose an August 2007 issue of *Wired* magazine, and she chooses *Businessweek* from around the same time. The room is filled with silence and the whisper of turning pages, then—

"Found it."

I scramble around to Adhira's side of the table and read over her shoulder.

Beware Casper Lawson, founder of Lawson Logistics

My heart thumps hard, and I lean close to read the words under the glaring headline. It's essentially an article, but it's written by my father. I fly through the whole thing once, then slowly one more time.

According to this piece, Casper founded a company that promised cut-rate prices on high-end goods and a delivery service. He approached Dad for funding and to lend credibility, but Dad said no. He said the tech didn't hold up. Yet Casper went to other possible investors and lied, saying Dad was attached to the fledgling company. He used the power of Dad's name to bilk investors out of millions. Some of them had been Dad's friends and former colleagues. When Dad found out, he apparently tried to meet with Casper, but the man refused. So Dad took out ads in *Wired, Businessweek*, and the *New York Times*.

"Whoa," Adhira breathes out. "That was intense."

I jab a finger at one word in particular. "He called him not technical. That's a Silicon Valley slap in the face."

Adhira grabs the *Times* and locates the ad in that one too. "But how does this track with Lia losing a pony?"

Moving quickly, I refile the evidence Casper Lawson worked so hard to erase. "I'm going to find out."

Adhira follows me to the library door, then stops. "You should talk to your dad alone. Meet me back at the room?"

"Your room?"

Adhira shakes her head. "Our room."

Our room. Happiness surges through me, and with the confidence of a reinstated best friend, I march across campus toward Dad's office.

"I know what happened with Casper." I'm barely in the door when I announce this.

Dad's entire body seems to slump. "Can we talk about this another time, Marnie?"

"Lia just screamed at me outside the caf about losing a pony, so no."

"Not my finest hour," Dad says, scrubbing his jaw. He braces his hands on his knees and looks at me. "Have you heard the term 'proportionate response'?"

"It means calibrating your response based on what your adversary does."

Dad nods. "And me taking out three full-page ads was a disproportionate response. It ruined his family. His wife walked out on him and their two young girls. They had to sell everything and move in with his parents. Look, what Casper did was wrong. People I respect lost a lot of money because he used my name. But I wish I would have handled it all a bit more . . . delicately."

I frown. "But he came back."

"He came back," Dad echoes me. "He disappeared for about five years, then burst back on the scene. And as much as I don't like the man, he seems to be all aboveboard now."

It all slots into place—the way Lia has treated me, the way Casper has appeared to want me to fail. Somehow, knowing there's a reason for it lessens the hurt. I mean, I'm not about to start inviting Lia over for slumber parties, but at least her hatred for me makes sense. And goodness knows I like sensible things.

Adhira is sketching when I get back to Hawthorne Hall. I fill her in while she makes us both tea with her electric kettle. She takes a sip, fiddles with the teabag, then says, "I feel like I owe you an explanation. About the room thing and how much it hurt me."

We're both sitting on her bed, and it feels nice to see the other bed—*my* bed—empty and waiting for me to return. "I screwed up. That's on me."

"Well, you did kind of screw up spectacularly."

"Thank you, thank you." I twirl my wrist in a mock bow.

"But it's more than that," Adhira starts. She chews on a nail and stares out the window, and I give her room to find the words. "It *is* about Toronto. I used to attend this amazing performing arts school. It was great, and I had all these friends, and it was . . . it was everything it was supposed to be, right? And then . . ." Her breath is shaky, and her fingers tremble when she moves to tuck hair behind her ear. "There was this teacher, head of the theater department and a big name in Toronto. Everyone loved him. *I* loved him. But then he started saying things to me, like totally innocent at first, and I felt flattered he was singling me out. I feel like such an idiot now."

"You're not an idiot, Adhira."

She smiles, but it's thin. "It got worse . . . the things he was saying. He made me lead designer on the big fall play and kept finding ways to get me alone."

Sourness rises in my throat, searing on my tongue. I reach across and clench Adhira's hand.

"I was supposed to go to this costuming workshop in Montreal, and he was going to drive me. Everyone thought it was this amazing opportunity. But I got sick right before we were supposed to leave, like puking everywhere. I think it was my body trying to protect me, to prevent me from going. Even though I was scared of what was going to happen, I still thought he saw something in me." Adhira trails off, her chest rising and falling featherlight.

"Did he . . . hurt you?" My stomach is in knots at the thought that my effervescent, optimistic, beautiful friend was hurt by someone.

Her mouth is tight, but she shakes her head no, and relief pours through me.

"I showed my mom all his texts and she started crying. My mom never cries. We went straight to the administration, but they questioned whether I was leading him on, and then it got out, and . . . everyone saw *me* as the reason this beloved teacher was fired. My parents pulled me out and I was homeschooled for a semester before I applied here."

"I'm so sorry. I'm sorry it took me so long to ask about your past."

Adhira squeezes my fingers. "I probably should have just told you. It's not like I can pretend it didn't happen. But I . . . I still missed so much about my old life. And then I felt guilty about missing those things. So when I found out you didn't *actually* want to be my roommate, it was like being abandoned all over again."

Her hand goes limp in mine.

The old me would have let her pull away. But if I'm going to change, I need to take hold of my story, my future. I need to show Adhira what she means to me.

"Adhira, there may not have been some board or algorithm or whatever that matched us together, but you are my best friend because you're *you*. I am infinitely better because you're in my life." The words spill out of me, my love for her. It's a bit awkward and it's hard to say aloud, but it's important. No more hiding. "I'm sorry that I've made it harder than it should be for you to move all the way here."

Her face lifts to mine, and there are tears there, but a smile too. "Marnie Barnes, I do believe you've kicked Mary Bennet to the curb."

I shrug, and snatches of an idea that've been flitting around the back of my mind finally form into a coherent thought. "You know what? I think it's more that Mary and I are cool with each other now."

"Good. I always thought Mary deserved more credit." A lopsided smile carves a dimple into her cheek. "Well, now you know why I judged Hayes harshly."

A loud *pfffft* makes my lips vibrate. "Oh, you didn't judge him harshly enough, I think."

I fill her in while we move my belongings back to our room, and Adhira claps in all the appropriate places.

The last thing I do is unearth the contract that I shoved into the pages of a book. I'm about to tack it back up, rips and all, then stop. I wrote this when I thought Mary was a bad thing, but we've changed, me and Mary. So it's about time this contract did too. I grab a pen off Adhira's desk to amend the contract, then tape up the imperfections and stick it to the middle of my corkboard.

I, Marnie Elizabeth Barnes, hereby do swear to live with and accept ~~root out and destroy~~ Mary Bennet. I will not allow myself to be ~~pedantic, conceited, or insensible. I will~~ so concerned with the opinions of others, unless they've earned it. not allow myself to die alone with fifteen cats, having never been kissed. I will NOT change who I am, ~~no matter~~ (Okay, yeah, that one can stay.) ~~the cost, to cast off Mary Bennet.~~ but will choose to become whoever I want to be.

ReSigned,

Marnie Barnes / ~~October 28~~ February 6

And that, ladies and gentlemen, is how Mary Bennet found her voice.

TWENTY-NINE

MARY BENNET FOUND HER VOICE. Then promptly got laryngitis.

Because eight days later—yes, on Valentine's Day—I'm standing outside a chapel in Sausalito bursting with pink peonies and dripping with twinkly lights, and there's a string quartet playing for Hayes and Sara's wedding guests.

I've woven in and out of plans so much over the past week I've become a beautiful tapestry of nerves. Sara said she and Hayes talked, but why should I trust that Hayes *actually* told Sara the truth? And what even *is* the truth? It's not like he tried to kiss me or anything, it just felt . . . wrong. Ugh. See? Tapestry.

I called Lindy twice and then talked about the weather. I

even called Mom, but she was in the middle of a bespoke millinery disaster (her words).

Overhead, the twilight sky broods. It's been spitting rain off and on all day, so my hair is truly one for the frizziness record books. The invitations asked all attendees to wear either black or pink, and without Adhira's help when I ordered this dress a few weeks ago, the baby pink, bateau-neck dress fits like a sack. There's room to smuggle in a half-dozen sliders and eat my way through this mess.

Adhira tried to help me cinch the waist with a narrow patent-leather belt before she left for *Hamlet*, the play she's costuming, but the dress sags over my chest and lands right below my knees, so I look about three inches tall. We're not even going to discuss the shoes I picked out, but let's just say Mom gasped when she saw them and started muttering things about spinsters.

The rain picks up, so I duck inside. Hayes's mom is there, greeting guests. She spots me and calls out, but I am prepared to talk with zero Wellesleys at present. I spin on a sensible heel and lurch through a side door, only to trip headlong into a foamy sea of tulle.

It's the dressing room, a flurry of gowns, bubbling laughter, and scent of rose perfume. Sara's mom, aunts, and a cousin are there, along with Joss and Lindy. Sara's mom yells for me to shut the door so the men don't see, and I wordlessly obey. Humiliation shivers from my scalp down to my toes.

My attention snaps to Sara, with her perfect dewy skin and glossy hair swept over one graceful shoulder and gown that makes her look like a fancy mermaid. I should talk to her again. I *need* to talk to her again. But how do you tell a woman *on her wedding day* that she really, really needs to rethink her choice of groom?

I'm uncomfortable in this dress, in my skin. My insides are shriveled up and my voice is gone. Sara glances at me, beams in happiness, then returns to her toilette.

Frustration builds in my chest. Why couldn't Hayes have gone Full Asshole and just said *I will sleep with you if you get me your dad's money*. That'd make this so much easier, instead of this awful, murky sensation of something being wrong without any concrete reason.

Lindy's watching me closely. My words stink with desperation when I focus on my sister and say, "I need to talk to you."

"Of course, Mar." She grabs her cane and leads me toward a small chamber at the back of the dressing room. One whole wall is stained glass, and there are three boxes of tissues on three separate delicate tables.

The door shuts behind us with a quiet click. Lindy tilts her chin. "Is everything okay with Bark Books?"

"What? Oh yeah, that's fine. I—"

"Because Dad said Whit hasn't been there, so I wanted to make sure everything's fine."

A groan works its way up my throat. "That's sort of related."

There's a knock at the door, and it startles me back to my mission. "Just a minute!"

Okay, Marnie. Say it. Just say it.

Except when I did just say it, Sara promised me this wasn't a big deal, that I was fussed about nothing. My gut twists. No, this isn't *nothing*.

Lindy's attention slides to the door. Beyond, someone calls her name. "Can we talk about this later?"

"No!"

"Okay . . ."

Say it. Say it. "It's about—"

The door cracks open, and Sara's mom sticks her head in. "Pictures!" she trills like a songbird, sending panic through my blood. "The photographer is waiting. We need our matron of honor!"

"Lindy." My voice is a whisper.

She puts weight back on her cane. "I hate being called matron," she mutters to me. Sara's mom loops a hand around her wrist, but Lindy turns back to me. "After the wedding, I'm all yours. Will saved you a seat."

Then she's gone, and when I peek out of the antechamber, the room is deserted, except for two bottles of champagne chilling in an ice bucket.

My fingers slip along the neck of one bottle, condensation prickling cold. My grip tightens and I'm out the door with my new plus-one, a bottle of Veuve Clicquot. Walking blindly, I rush down a hall, my ugly heels thumping, and push out an arched wooden door. There's a portico overhead to protect from the driving rain, and I plop ever so gracefully on the flagstone steps and take my first ever sip of champagne.

Bubbles tickle my throat and warmth rises from my belly. I've only ever had a bit of red wine with holiday meals and a few sips of the awful craft beer Will and Lindy stock at The Shack. Oh, I may like champagne very much! Even better, another two swigs of the champagne, and the guilt inside me seems to pop and float away. Swig—*pop!* Swig—*pop!* I may be completely healed by the bottom of this bottle!

I've done my due diligence, right? What else can I do, run down the aisle and physically stop this wedding?

The bottle is to my lips again when someone collapses onto the steps next to me. I swivel my head and have to blink a few times before I recognize Lia. Her rosy pink dress is so tight I'm not entirely certain she can breathe. The last time I saw her, she screamed at me. Now, her nose is a bit red and her limbs loose. She sniffles, then yanks the bottle out of my hands and tips it back to her lips.

After a long draw from the bottle, she hands it back over. "They sprang for the good stuff."

I nod once, but the world doesn't stop bobbing for quite a long time. I do believe I may be tipsy.

Lia fiddles with the straps of her heeled sandals. "I'm sorry," she says quietly.

I'm what now?

Lia tilts her face to look at me. "I'm sorry for what I said about Lindy. I had no idea. My mom had a miscarriage a few years ago after she remarried. It was . . . it was awful. I'm sorry your family had to go through that too."

"Oh." I shove hands into my dress pockets and blink away the memories. "And I'm sorry about your pony. I truly didn't know."

Lia shrugs. "I know you didn't. How could you? It's . . . easier to blame you than my dad."

We fall silent, sharing the bottle between us. The rain beats a staccato against the roof, and the world smells of freshly turned earth.

"I can't believe this shit is happening," Lia finally says, eyes trained on the rain outside our little porch. "I snuck two shots of tequila from Dad's liquor cabinet before we came here to cope. I'm already half-drunk."

She holds the bottle out to me, but I wave it away. My stomach is already sloshing with bubbles and some stubborn guilt. I slump my cheek into my hand and grimace. "He doesn't deserve her."

"He doesn't deserve any of us, but we're the dumbasses who all fell for him." She presses her lips together for a moment. "I never told him, just so you know."

I eye the bottle, then grab it from Lia and gulp back another long drink. I swipe the back of my hand across my lips. "I was in love with him for an embarrassingly long time."

The words feel slow and sticky in my mouth, but Lia seems to understand all the same. I have the distinct feeling I should be worried by how easily I'm confirming all this to Lia—who knows what she's capable of when she's drunk, or what she'll do with this information when she sobers up—but she slings an arm around my neck, camaraderie personified.

"At least you didn't . . ." She trails off, shudders, and sticks her tongue out in disgust. "Ugh, I don't even want to think about it."

It takes a second for the implication to sink in. Oh. *Oh.* They slept together. A shudder rolls through me and Lia nods in affirmation. He's a damn adult and he slept with a girl still in high school. It might technically be legal since Lia's eighteen, but it's also technically super skeezy. So this is that concrete proof I wanted. Wish it would have had the decency to show up before I was three-quarters of the way through a bottle of champagne. I hand the bottle back over. She accepts it gratefully.

"We shouldn't have even come," I groan.

"And let him think he can steamroll us? No, I'm here and I'm going to look fucking fantastic while I'm at it. God, that's such bullshit, right?" Lia slides her gaze over me, lingering on my shoes. I tuck them under me as far as I can without falling face-first off the steps. "Are you going more for the martyr look, then?"

Ah, there it is. The Lia I know. She takes one last drink and stumbles to her feet, leaving the dregs of the bottle with me. "I better get back to Daddy and get this over with."

Lia tilts through the door, and I'm restored to the enjoyment of all my former dislike. A shiver rolls over my bare arms. The world has gone blurry at the edges, and the door handle isn't where I last put it when I stand and try to duck back into the church. The floor buckles under my feet, and I have to hold myself steady against the wall on the search for my family.

The music is swelling—quite too loud, actually—and the guests are standing when I plop into the end of the pew next to Will.

Everything is a bit . . . sloshy. Slooshy. Mushy. My bones, my eyelids, the minister saying whatever it is he's saying at the front of the chapel.

Why isn't this over yet? They're not even Catholic. We should be in and out and halfway to bed by now. I need a burger. I smash my hands against my pockets, but they are horrifically burger-free. Useless pockets. Next to me, Will clears his throat and I sort of . . . grunt? No, I surely didn't grunt in the middle of these never-ending nuptials. It was definitely more a delicate mew.

The sound rolls up my throat again. It's the tiniest of kitten burps.

Will's eyes have gone big, but my focus goes sideways as the minister's words float toward me: "speak now" and "forever" and "peace."

And then everything is quite suddenly *not* sloshy. Oh god, it's so not sloshy. I grab the back of the pew in front of me and try to swallow, but my stomach is currently a one-way trip. In the wrong direction.

It's volcanic, tectonic. Coming up *now*. Right now.

"Oh, god. No! Don't!" I lurch to my feet, but the chapel spins madly and my hand slips when I try to grab Will and the world is edged with black.

So much black. And my stomach has relocated to my throat and the ground is so near.

Blurry, blurry, blurry pink. A flap of air and a screech and a shoot of pain at the back of my head.

Mom swims into view before me. Bends over me, the tasseled ends of her pink wrap shivering over my eyes. What happened? My head feels like murder and my throat is on fire and there's a warm wetness on my neck and shoulder. The last thing I remember is Sara standing at the altar with Resident Dickhead Hayes. And now I'm . . .

I'm not entirely sure where I am.

"Did she call it off?" I croak to Mom.

"What?" Her voice is tinny, like I'm hearing it through the wall.

"The wedding. Did Sara call it off? I hope so. I tried to tell her, but Hayes is a creep. He hit on me and I think he *slept* with Lia Lawson." My confession pours out of me like so much champagne-flavored vomit. It's cathartic, honestly. I almost feel like myself again. Myself with a head split in two.

I push my glasses back into position. The shapes and colors

around me harden into focus beyond Mom. Arched beams overhead. Wooden pews along either side.

And a woman with glossy dark hair and a mermaid silhouette. A groan starts deep, deep in my emptied stomach and rolls up my throat.

Oh, *shit*.

From tiles to rafters, the silence hollers. It's so loud I'm afraid it'll pull the whole place down around us. Someone do something! Doesn't the minister have a line for this? I squeeze my eyes shut and push up to my elbows just as the silence finally breaks.

Sara sobs, then she throws her bouquet to the ground and sprints past me.

Behind me, a door slams. My skin prickles with the accusation of a hundred pairs of eyes.

"What's wrong with you, Marnie?" Hayes growls.

Pounding feet against altar steps, then Will jumps in front of me so Hayes is nothing but legs and anger.

"Not another damn word," he spits at Hayes. "Do you hear me, you little shit?"

"Er, gentlemen," the minister adds. *Yeah, too late, dude.*

Through the staring crowd, Lindy's mouth hangs open with horror. Above me, Mom glares down in fury. Somewhere off to my left, Dad's voice breaks with disappointment. "Oh, Marnie."

And I can't do this. I can't.

I grab the shawl from around Mom's neck to clean the puke

off me and shove myself to my feet. I can't face them. So I don't.

I run. Out into the rain and into the dark. Down the slippery gravel hill toward the glowing streetlights on Sausalito's main drag. Guess who's thankful for sturdy orthopedic heels now, *Mom*.

I dash through lamplight and dive under a striped awning. It's a bookstore, the windows dark and the door locked tight. A car crawls by, but it doesn't stop. I huddle under the awning and scrub at my frigid arms. My glasses are speckled with rain, but I've nothing to dry them with. I've got my phone on me, but no money for the last ferry across the bay back to San Francisco. I guess I could walk back across the Golden Gate Bridge, but that seems too tragic, even for me.

"Marnie!" I whirl toward the voice and groan. Lola skids under the awning.

"Not now, Lola."

A frown crumples my little sister's face for a second, then she holds out a bottle of water and a tin of mints. "Thought you could use this. I've puked in public before and it's . . . not fun."

My shoulders sag, and I gratefully accept the water and take a cleansing swig. "Yeah," I finally say, "but did you also object to a wedding at the same time? God, I made such a mess of everything."

"It was pretty spectacular," Lola admits, then she grins. "I'm gonna have to up my game so I don't lose my title as family screw-up." But her smile drops as she steps closer and toes the ground. "Why don't you come back to the chapel? Trust me, everyone knows you're not the bad guy here."

I *definitely* don't believe that. "I can't, Lola. I just *can't*."

"Do you have someone to come pick you up? I can wait with you."

"Adhira's coming," I lie. "You should head back."

Lola rolls her lips together and glances back toward the darkness where the chapel hides. "Are you sure?"

She turns away when I nod, but before she makes it a step, I reach out and squeeze her hand. "Thanks for this." I shake the water bottle and mints in my other hand, but I hope she knows I also mean her coming to check on me.

Lola shrugs. "That's what sisters do."

And then she leaves and I'm struck with the realization that Lindy isn't the only Barnes sister I need to get to know better. I'm also struck with the realization that I'm cold, alone, and definitely lied about Adhira picking me up.

Okay, think, Marnie.

My fingers tremble, but I flick my phone on. My teeth gnaw at my lips. There's no way I'm bugging Adhira on a play night. I'd consider Dev, but I don't know his number. That leaves . . . I select his number before I can think too hard about it. Whit picks up on the first ring.

"I need help," I say, and then I burst into tears. They're hot and salty and probably mascara-tinged.

"Where are you?"

I turn in a circle and tell him the name of the bookstore emblazoned in gold letters on the window.

"I'm leaving now. Don't move."

The sparkling water Lola brought me is encircled with a personalized label in looping cursive: *Hayes + Sara // A day to remember.* Heh. I've corrected enough misuse of the word ironic to know it's coincidental, but that declaration still feels prophetic. I dig my nail under the paper and rip it away, then I crumple it up in the tiniest ball possible and smash it under my heel.

The rain on my skin has dried, but it's left a deep, bitter cold in its wake by the time Whit makes it across the bridge to me. When I open the door, his dark eyes search me. "Are you hurt?" There's urgency in his voice, and he rakes both hands through his hair before setting them back on the steering wheel. His jaw is so tight, I can pick out the jump of his pulse in his neck.

Wordlessly, I shake my head, then crawl into the passenger seat of his little blue hatchback and wrap myself up in my arms. Whit twists in his seat, and I think—hope—for a second he's going to hug me, but instead he reaches into the back seat and grabs a Paws & Claws sweater and tosses it into my lap, along with some tissue and another bottle of water.

"Thanks," I mumble. Gratefully, I tug the sweatshirt over my dress and huddle down into the seat. It smells like him, fresh sea air and green tea. The scent calms the jumbled emotions. We haven't been alone like this since he asked me what Hayes meant to me and I royally screwed it up.

Whit starts driving and glances at me. "Really, Marnie. Are you okay?"

I burrow my hands into the sleeves so just my fingertips stick out to worry at the hem. "Oh, you know. I embarrassed myself so thoroughly I'll never be able to show my face in polite society, but other than that."

A half smile ghosts across Whit's lips. "Other than that."

The lights of the bridge blur across the windows in the rain, but there's something beautiful about crossing the bay back toward home. San Francisco sits snug against the water, the dark of the Presidio giving way to the milky yellow glow of the city at night.

"You want to talk about what happened?" he asks as he winds the car through the streets, pointing us toward the PCA campus.

A groan pushes against the back of my teeth. "It's, uh . . . I actually . . ." I chug the rest of the water and scrub at the makeup surely streaking my face. His mouth screws to one side.

"I stood up at Hayes's wedding and objected."

A long, slow sigh issues out of Whit, and his knuckles where he grips the steering wheel bulge white. He glances at me, red taillights glinting against his eyes, but they're shuttered. Unreadable. His voice is tentative when he asks, "And did it work?"

A rueful laugh escapes me. "It wasn't intentional. Although, it should have been to stop Sara from marrying someone awful like him."

Whit's chin jerks, but he doesn't say anything.

I clear my throat and rub at the end of my nose. "Ah, a bit of advice. Don't drink an entire bottle of champagne. Not that this happened to me, but you might puke in the middle of a wedding and shame your entire family."

Whit sucks in a breath. "Really?"

"Really."

He slows the car. Past the rain lashing the windows, the iron gates of PCA glow with passing traffic. I go to tug the sweater over my head, but Whit stops me with a fleeting hand on my arm.

"Keep it."

I pick at the hem. "Thank you. For everything, I mean."

A hush gathers between us. Whit's hand resting on the gearshift catches my attention. My heart, soggy until now, crackles with a rush of warmth, until there is fire in my belly and embers on my tongue. I already embarrassed myself once today; why not really go for it? I reach for his hand and hold it between my own. And Whit holds on tight.

A muscle jumps in his jaw, and he stares straight ahead for a ragged breath before he turns to me. His fingers are warm and sure and work confidence into my bones. The fire inside me flares, spreads, until I'm nearly consumed.

"Why is it I can talk to you so easily, Whit? Why is it I miss you the second you're gone? Why is it I can't stop thinking about you? No one else but you?"

"Marnie, don't." But he doesn't pull away from me when I lean closer, when I run my fingers through his thick hair like I've wanted to for far longer than I even knew.

And I can't stop. I need him to know how I feel. I need to *show* him. My fingers that are caught up in his hair whisper down to his neck, and I grab hold and draw him closer. Close enough to kiss.

Whit dips his chin and takes my hand and presses his lips to my palm in a way that surely should be described in all the best classic romance novels. The heat of his mouth against my skin sends prickles of shock all the way down to my toes. But then he tilts his head back, away from me. He tugs his hand free from mine and a sigh rustles through him.

"I can't, Marnie. You must know how much I . . . but I can't be your backup plan."

His words shudder over me. "I know how to answer you now, about Hayes, I mean. I don't love him, Whit. I don't think I ever did."

And it's true. Because back there at the wedding, I didn't even think about Hayes. I only feared I'd hurt Sara.

But Whit is shaking his head. "I've spent months being jealous of that pompous asshole. I believe you, but I . . ." He heaves in another breath and scrubs one hand down his face. "You just worked through something really big. It's best for both of us if I give you some room to breathe, figure out what's next. But, Marnie. You're pretty amazing exactly how you are. I wish you'd realize that."

Then he turns the ignition over to start his car and puts both hands on his steering wheel. It's over. It's truly over.

Except when I get back to my room in Hawthorne Hall, I can still smell him around me, still feel the texture of his hair against my fingertips. And I can still hear him, his words to me. I've been so awash with guilt and regret and this awful certainty I'll never be good enough for anyone.

But I will. I am. It's simply up to me to choose.

Right now, I choose myself. I choose my friends. I choose my family.

I pull out my phone and call Lindy.

THIRTY

IN THE FORTY-EIGHT HOURS SINCE the Wedding That Wasn't, I've learned three things.

One: tech blogs are calling it Puke and Punishment. Turns out, plenty of people in Palo Alto didn't much care for Hayworth Wellesley. The fact that he took advantage of a girl more than five years younger has rendered him a stain most are trying to scrub out. I've been painted as something of a Robin Hood figure, swooping in (though that should be staggering in, let's be honest) to cut down the high and mighty. It hasn't stopped my mother from telling everyone I had a bad reaction to shellfish, but you can't win them all.

Two: Whit has put in his notice at Paws & Claws of Outer Richmond. The morning after the wedding, nursing one hell of a hangover, I schlepped out to Bark Books only to find

Whit absent once again. Though this time, it was because he was moving into a new apartment with his college friends. I tried hard to be happy for him, then teared up when I overheard a kid reading *The Poky Little Puppy* to Sir Pat.

And three: my family doesn't hate me. I mean, Mom isn't about to hire a skywriter to declare her undying love for her suddenly notorious middle daughter, but no one has disowned me. In fact—

"Mar?" Lindy leans hard on her cane as she sidesteps along the row of theater seats. She eases into the seat next to mine, the pocket of her dress crinkling with plastic. She fishes out a bag of Sour Patch Kids. "Want to share? You like the yellow ones, right?"

I rip open the bag and shove a lemony Sour Patch Kid into my mouth. "Yesh," I say around the gummy.

On either side of us, theater patrons chat and stretch through the intermission. It's closing night for *Hamlet*. According to theater blogs, two of the city's publications, and me, it's been a rousing success.

Ophelia is devastating as the girl who gives up everything for a guy who deserves nothing. Yeah, the comparison hasn't escaped me. She could be Lia or me or even Sara. The yellow gummy is a big lump, sticky in my throat, when I turn to Lindy. "How is she?" I ask with a wince, like I'm ripping off a Band-Aid.

Lindy's dark eyebrows scrunch. "Sara? Will and I were actually with her right before I came here. We all signed up for sailing lessons because I guess big traumatic events mean we should go live on the water. According to Will."

She glances at me and grins, but I hold my breath. "And?"

"And," Lindy says, then sighs. "She wishes *how* she found out about the bastard was a tad less dramatic, but I think she's relieved she found out before it was too late. The stuff about sleeping with Casper Lawson's daughter . . . anyway, she's going on her honeymoon—solo—and she hired movers to get all of Hayes's stuff out of their apartment."

There's urgency in my voice when I say, "I'm sorry for it all. Not for stopping the wedding, but for . . . everything."

Lindy rustles the bag of candy for a second, then plucks two yellows for me. "How are you handling it?"

I take a second to chew, considering my answer. "Um . . . I'm embarrassed, obviously, but more about how long I spent obsessed. It's . . ." Words bubble up—*regret, shame, disappointment*—but I scrub them away. "I'm not going to waste any more time thinking about him."

Lindy wrinkles her nose. "Good. It was obvious after your accident that you were smitten, but, I don't know, you were young and it seemed to fade fast."

"I just got good at hiding it. I got good at hiding all of my emotions."

"Well, next time you're into someone, tell me, so I can vet them." She nudges my shoulder and grins.

I grin back. "Yeah, next time." I wonder what she'd think of Whit.

Then the lights dim, the murmuring crowd hushes, and I'm pulled back into Adhira's play. After the final applause quiets an hour later, Adhira finds me in the theater's lobby. Her cheeks are pink and her eyes bright. When she asks me and Lindy to come celebrate with her, Dev, and Tilda, I don't hesitate for even a second before I say yes.

The morning of the very last Bark Books dawns like a jewel box—golden citrine sun, dazzling sapphire sky, diamond-floss clouds. I yawn and stretch out, pressing the heels of my hands into my headboard.

A hard knot of bittersweet takes root in my chest. But Adhira, who's already up and dressed, makes that knot shift to accommodate joy. She's wearing my wiener-dog button-down tucked into a knee-length black leather skirt.

"Can I borrow this?" She catches my eye in the reflection of her makeup mirror and picks at the cuff of my shirt.

"No." My voice creaks, and I clear it with a laugh. "I wish you could be there today."

Adhira sits at the edge of my bed and kicks her legs out, one ankle hooked over the other. "I'll be cheering you on from across the bay."

I scramble up to my elbows. "Oh! That's right!" She was accepted into UC Berkeley and is in the running for a costume design scholarship. "I will literally die of happiness if you stay in California."

Adhira pokes at my calf under the covers but grins.

"That's not what literally means."

I beam at her. "It does in this instance." I got into Stanford like Lindy before me, but I've realized it's not the right fit, so I've accepted a spot at USF to study English in the fall. Adhira and I get ready side by side, then head over to Bardo for Earl Grey and an Americano before peeling off in separate directions.

An hour later, Booker lumbers up Balboa toward Paws & Claws, moving a bit slower today with all the bodies in it. Daniel's at the wheel, with Beth next to him; Dad sits atop a closed book cabinet, and Lindy is in the fold-down seat across from me.

"Are you excited?" Lindy peers over the top of her George Eliot novel.

"Yes, and also sad. I'll miss coming here, working with everyone."

Whit, my mind whispers.

"The end of a chapter," she says, closing her book. "But I'm pretty sure there's a lot more to go before the end of your book, Marnie."

Outside, the cheery awning goes up and the book display slowly takes shape. For the final day, I chose all the favorites the kids have been drawn to over the months. There are silly books about a moose on the loose and sweet books about orphan dogs; there are beautiful books about forests and hilarious books about elephants. In honor of it all, I'm in my cat cardigan, but Adhira helped me make it slightly edgier with a narrow black minidress paired with tights and ankle boots.

The first kids are already waiting before we officially open, the parents mingling and chatting and the kids being little-kid picky when it comes to choosing books. I try to soak it all in, these final hours with Bark Books. My smile hasn't budged from my face since the second we pulled up, but it doesn't hurt my cheeks anymore, doesn't feel unnatural. My smile is part of me. Part of the me that has slowly surfaced over the past months. I'm happy to have finally found it. To have found *her*.

The day goes quickly, and the children are starting to thin out, the parents packing up to head home. A lot of them stop to say goodbye to me, to even thank me. It fills me with a warmth that is hard to describe, like a dozen fresh-from-the-oven cupcakes from Edie's bakery, iridescent sprinkles on top.

I'm stowing away the books when a shadow falls over me.

"Got anything on orca whales?"

His voice blooms within me, pushing tendrils all through my body. I pull a face and squint up at Whit.

"Maybe try Fins and Flippers of Outer *Outer* Richmond."

Whit nods thoughtfully and taps the table twice with the edge of his hand. "Right. Goodbye, then."

He pauses for half a heartbeat, then grins.

"I didn't know you'd be here today," I say. "I heard you got an apartment with your friends. I'm happy for you."

His smile softens and he hooks a hand behind his neck.

"I wanted to come say goodbye." His voice is low, meant only for me.

I step out from behind the book table and wrap Whit in a hug that lasts less time than I want, but is more than I expected today. In the car, he said something that has replayed in my mind during quiet moments: that I need space to figure out what comes next. He's right. I need time on my own, just being comfortable in this life of mine.

I hope someday I'm ready to make room for Whit, or someone like him. But as much as I want to grab his chin and tug his mouth down to mine, I don't. I uncurl my fingers from his soft T-shirt and step back.

"Good luck, Eugene Whitlock, Jr."

Whit sighs. "You too, Anne Girl."

Then we both busy our hands with all the things we should be doing instead of holding each other. Whit fiddles with the keys in his hand, and I sort out books I'm meant to be putting away.

"Okay," Whit says, almost to himself. "Okay." He turns away, takes a step, then another.

Then he's gone. And I feel like crying, but I won't.

Daniel steps out from Booker and nudges my shoulder. He holds up his phone. "I want to show you something."

It's the pictures taken from that first Bark Books months ago, and he finds one in particular: me and Whit sitting in front of Sir Pat's kennel. My hand is through the bars, fingers buried in the fur behind the mutt's floppy ear. Sir Pat's only got eyes for Whit, but Whit . . . his attention is on me. His mouth is open, the corner curled up in the beginning of a smile, and his hand rests on the cushion, like he's reaching out to touch me. Like he *wants* to. I didn't see it for too long, and I wish it could have gone a different way, but it didn't, and there's no going back now. Only forward. Regret doesn't have mastery over time, after all. Simply mastery over our memories.

I stare for a long time at that photo before I look up at Daniel. I'll miss him. He's been a fantastic advisor during my time at the library. But that is coming to a close, too, like so many other things.

For the last time, I head inside to Paws & Claws, and I go straight to a kennel at the far end of the room. It's quiet, the children gone and the dogs resting.

"Hi, Sir Pat," I say, folding my legs under me in front of the curious, strange-looking dog. I wonder if he knows this all ends today. So many of his brethren were adopted, but the right person for him is still out there somewhere.

He nudges his pink nose against the bars of the kennel, and I push my hand through to stroke at the wiry fur atop his head. He whines and leans into my palm, his eyes on me.

"I know," I say to him. "We'll both miss him." And I think he agrees.

THIRTY-ONE

HEADMASTER FINCH'S RESIDENCE IS DECKED out like a wedding cake. Floral garlands swoop around the turret and pastel streamers flutter from the gables. The rhododendrons are blooming in the early spring warmth, and the air is sweet and cloying. I pause on the gravel walkway for a second, just taking it all in.

This is it. The end of everything I've worked toward for months. My nerves spark, but the joyful atmosphere douses the anxiety. Before me, my fellow finalists and their families chat with faculty and judges, the sunshine smiling down on a hundred people eating petit fours and cradling fine bone china.

The Hunt Prize Tea is a tradition dating back to Theodora Hunt's days. Back then, girls wore their loveliest gowns so the "judges" could gossip through town about who would become the most sought-after bride. Today, we're in our uniforms. Though not official, we're supposed to avoid talking about our projects during the tea, simply enjoy each other's company. Then we'll process down the walk to the Ed for our final presentations.

Dad and Lindy pause next to me. Lindy's no longer using her cane, but she holds tight to Dad's arm. The rest of my family is meeting us at the Ed in an hour. Kat texted me earlier to warn that Lola is in costume, but it just made me smile.

Through the crowd, Adhira and her mom are flapping their hands at each other, but they're both grinning. Mrs. Fitz's teal sari nearly glows in the sun, and Adhira's gold bracelets glitter where they peek out of her blazer. She catches my eye and waves.

"Ready?" Dad squeezes my arm.

Am I ready? I face him and nod decisively. Because you know what? I've created and carried out a fantastic project. I've helped twelve animals (eight dogs, two cats, one bunny, and Ralph the iguana) find their forever homes. I've grown closer to my dad and sister. I've forged a best-friendship. I've met an amazing guy who, yeah, I also want to kiss, but hopefully I'll settle for friendship.

I've got a lot to be proud of, so let's go celebrate Bark Books.

The Ancient One and Lady Orange bustle over first, though I'm pretty sure they just want to talk to Lindy. My sister, to her eternal credit, steers the conversation back toward Sir Pat and the animals at the shelter. I thank the judges for supporting me throughout my project and step away across the carpet of grass.

When I started this, all I could see was winning. A lemon rind twist in my stomach says that's still sort of true. I can't deny the recognition for my hard work would feel amazing. But there's something else there now, something softer. I want to live in this moment and be proud. I want to *enjoy* myself.

So I sidestep a judge I recognize who stopped by Bark Books, pile a delicate china plate with minty green petit fours, and go to find Adhira. I spot her beyond a white canvas tent bustling with families and servers. She's with her parents by the house steps and surrounded by a gaggle of smiling judges. I scoot around the hubbub, threading through a clutch of flowering rhododendrons at the edge of the party.

But a voice stops me. "This attitude is unacceptable, young lady. Get out there and sell your project."

It's Casper Lawson, and when I peek through the bushes, I see his profile standing over Lia, his spray-tanned face nearly purple with anger. They're hidden from the rest of the celebration, standing in the shadows of the mansion.

Lia huffs an enormous sigh and crosses her arms. "Dad, stop having a hissy fit. I'm trying my best."

That makes her father's shoulders go rigid. "Well, your best is clearly not good enough. Why would anyone want anything to do with a failure? You need to win this to make up for that wedding stunt."

My fingers go tight against the china. How dare he act like she was in any way responsible for the wedding disaster—that blame lies with Hayes.

I take a step toward them to tell Casper as much, but Lia throws her shoulders back. "Don't project your problems on me, Dad. You want me to win so bad, go out there and beg people yourself. I'm done."

Lia stomps toward me, and I stumble back into the bush, but she catches me and goes still. There's a branch poking me in my butt, a flower jammed against my jaw. Lia's eyebrows shoot high, and her lips jerk, almost like she's going to smile. Then she rolls her eyes and stalks off.

Whatever; good for her standing up to her bridge troll of a father. After this is all over, I hope she treats herself to her fanciest frozen dinner.

But standing in a bush, clutching a plate of desserts, an idea pops into my head. An idea that bursts through me, makes me jittery at the possibility.

I spent so long obsessed with the idea of winning, but that seems small-minded now. What would winning the prize mean at this point, anyway? An accolade? A few words to add to my resumé? If *this* is a highlight in my future, then I haven't lived enough. And I fully intend on making my moments count.

My mind is a hive, buzzing with each new idea. Could it work? Does it matter either way?

Us finalists troop up the walkway toward the Ed, a crowd of cheering students, teachers, and families lining the way. The shouts and claps blend into white noise, and I focus on what's coming.

But one cheer winnows through the rest. Catches at my focus and pulls me back to this moment. At the end of the procession, standing on the steps of the Ed, my family chants for me: Marnie! Marnie! Marnie!

Goose bumps prickle down my arms, and I jump out of line to join them. We spill into the lobby, families and finalists jostling and hugging. Other families chant their daughters' names, still others hold up homemade signs or bouquets of flowers.

My family is going more for general, cheerful chaos. Lola's in a fuzzy brown dog onesie, complete with a floppy-eared hood, Kat next to her in dog ears. Edie's got Elle thrown over her shoulder so her dress has flopped over her back and exposed her white-tighted bottom; Theo and Jonah are clamped onto Joss's legs, roaring at passing adults like tiny dragons. Will has his arm around Lindy's waist, and Dad just stands at the edge beaming at us all.

Then there's Mom, who I haven't seen since Puke and Punishment and who, instead of saying hello, asks where Adhira is. But she's also wearing a giant gold button with my name on it. And yeah, it kind of makes her look like those kindergartners whose parents pin their names on their shirts the first day of school, but the effort stirs flutters of love in my chest. My family is here for me, and pride seals itself up along my spine, making me stand straighter.

Less lovely is Casper Lawson when he pushes past us. He shoves at Lola's puppy shoulder and she grimaces and snaps, "Uh, excuse you."

Casper slices a glare at us and stomps away, but it makes me smile. He is so predictable, the poor man.

"Ew," Lola whines. "Why is he so orange?"

Mom purses her surgically enhanced lips. "It's the toxins, dear," she says sagely.

The lights along the wall dim once, twice, and the talking intensifies for one moment—the last hugs and good lucks rippling through us.

"Okay, this is it," Lindy says, swinging her attention to me. "You have your speech memorized?"

I rub at the tip of my nose. I have my old speech memorized. "Ah, yup."

"I saw on the program you're going second-to-last, right before Lia, so try to relax," Lindy adds. Why do I feel she's about two seconds from handing me a towel and a water bottle?

Mom squeezes my shoulder. "She'll do her best. It's the only way Marnie knows."

In months past, I probably would have taken this as a dig at my character, but Mom is smiling and nodding, and I know all the way down to my toes she means it. I *am* going to do what I think is best. I hope it's not a disappointment to them.

I'm crushed in a big group hug, then Dad and I split off toward marked seats for the finalists and mentors in the front rows. The thick program someone handed me worries under my fingers and my nerves fizz. PCA bunting hangs from the stage, the rafters, even the balcony behind us, which is already filling with supporters. The spotlights onstage are turned up to intensity level "smite," and in place of the orchestra pit, there are two long tables laden with score sheets, water bottles, and the twenty-person Hunt Prize judging committee.

We find our seats, and the lights go down. My heart hammers in my chest, and I focus on my plan.

Headmaster Finch takes the stage and welcomes us all, and I absently clap when those around me do. There's a reading of the official rules—three minutes each to talk about our projects, no props, no crowd support until we're done—and an introduction of the judges that seems to last longer than rush-hour traffic on Highway 101. Then it starts, and I'm entirely unprepared. But also brimming with determination.

A girl whose project was something called Interpretive Street Art is onstage, but my mind wanders. Dad, Lindy, and I walked through my speech last night over burgers and fries. I know it by heart, though Dad also has a printout of it sitting on his lap just in case. I won't need it.

I peer up and spot a clutch of silver balloons bobbing around against the ceiling.

Two nights ago was the premiere of the school's spring play, and Adhira was lead designer on all the costumes. It was too late to be included in her Hunt Prize effort, but she sketched all the designs for *Pygmalion* and oversaw the costume class's implementation of her designs. I attended opening night with Adhira's parents and Dev, and I didn't even cringe when her mom gave me a hug that lasted well past the acceptable three-second mark. Dev declared the actress playing Eliza Doolittle was too pitchy, but I thought she did fine. And the costumes were absolutely spot-on, both Dev and I agreed on that.

Afterward, I presented Adhira with a bouquet of periwinkle, edelweiss, and bluebells, then spent so much time explaining their meaning according to the Victorian language of flowers—fond memories, thanking a friend for their courage, and good luck, respectively—she eventually told me to shut up already so we could all walk over to Bardo for some late-night coffee and dessert. They're sitting proud on the windowsill of our room right now. The flowers, I mean, not the dessert. There wasn't a crumb left of any of that.

Speaking of, Adhira is next onstage, and I cheer as she ascends the steps. I'm nearly as loud as Dev, Tilda, and her parents wolf-whistling. All these months we've worked side by side on the Hunt Prize. We both deserve a win, but I think one of us deserves it more.

"Marnie Barnes," the voice calls out.

My turn. My three minutes to impress the judges.

Dad squeezes my hand. "Good luck up there. You want the notes?"

I glance at the printed speech, and behind me to where I know the rest of my family is watching for me, *hoping* for me. Did they come all this way for nothing? I wanted them to gush about me like they do Lindy or Joss. I wanted them to *notice* me more than my sisters. But it's not a competition. We're family, and we Barnes sisters rise together.

At the back of the theater, the door opens, and springtime light floods in for a second. And I see him: Whit. Slipping in the door, standing along the back wall. My heart bursts, like a puffball of a dandelion dancing away on the breeze. He came. I texted him the other day to invite him, but he never responded. But he's here, and it makes what I'm about to do seem tolerable. Not tolerable, *right*. I'm *certain* I'm making the right choice.

"Marnie Barnes," the voice calls out again, a bit sharper now. "Take the stage, please."

I turn to Dad, who's holding up my speech. "I don't need it. Thank you for everything. I'm so glad you were my mentor. And, uh, sorry if this isn't what you expected."

Yet, somehow, I know he'll be proud.

My seat groans under me as I stand and I feel an auditorium

full of eyes on my back. All my life, I've been desperate to impress, desperate to prove my worth. But I've proved it to myself, and that's what matters most, I think.

I step into the glow of the stage light and squint out at the judges. They're bathed in shadows, like I'm addressing the void. But at the back of the auditorium—past Dad calling my name, past Adhira and her family and Dev and Tilda clapping for me, past the rest of my family cheering—Whit stands in the light of the open door and grins.

I settle my shoulders, take a deep breath, and begin.

"I'm here to tell you why you should award the Hunt Prize to Adhira Fitz."

I am *proud* of my project, of myself. But objectively, Adhira deserves this win. Not just because I fully believe she's created the best project, but because she followed her passion. She didn't calculate what would play best with the judges. Like Lindy did when she won, Adhira will use her win as the cornerstone of her career. Even though I eventually fell in love with my project, I wanted to win because of the accolade.

This is the truth, and it's what I tell the judges and audience. I say it to the utter, shocked silence, and I say it to the judges swathed in darkness, and I say it to Whit, watching me at the edge of the open door.

"So, in conclusion." My speech has unfurled on my tongue, poured from me with a passion that's left me sweating in the spotlight with clenched hands. I've been emptied of my doubts and need to impress and filled back up with certainty, happiness, excitement.

And I have no earthly idea how to end this thing.

"Um, yeah." I wrinkle my nose to resettle my glasses and fidget onto the outer edge of my clogs. My heart pounds so hard I swear I can hear it reverberating back to me over the loud speakers. "Vote for Adhira Fitz. Um, thank you."

The silence hangs in the air for a moment, then shatters. Some people clap, a few even cheer, but a lot more are hissing with whispers. I make myself walk steadily out of the spotlight, then bolt toward the stairs. I clatter down them and nearly collide with Lia waiting at the bottom. The noise grows, and a judge asks for calm.

My stomach has been turned inside out and I sort of want to crawl into a hole and sleep for the next three to six months.

"Well, that's one way to leave an impression on the judges," Lia says.

"Fuck them," I force out, which surprises a laugh out of both of us. I take another step down, so we're at eye level. "Hey, good luck."

Her eyebrows twitch, like she's deciding which delightfully nasty bon mot she'll deploy. But then her mouth settles into something like a smile and she says, "Thank you."

I stride up the aisle and pause where Adhira is standing, her mouth agape, but I motion for her to sit down. My grand declaration to vote for her won't go over well if the contestant flees with me. Instead, I head for the exit as a desperate judge taps on a microphone and pleads for quiet. My family pays him no attention and troops out behind me, talking and laughing and congratulating me. I feel bright as a star, burning, burning, burning across the sky.

Whit catches my attention near the back door, and the smile on his lips makes my thumping heart twist and thrum with a feeling I'm not quite ready to name. But the tumult and jostle of my family carries me past him. Out through the lobby and into the spring sunshine. I spin, searching for him through the pats and hugs and "oh my *god*, Marnie"s.

Whit's eyes find mine as he steps out of the auditorium doors, and he holds up his hand in a wave, then he turns a corner and is gone.

Later. I'll find him later. I've got a few things I need to say to him. A few things I need to *do*.

Now, I focus on my family. Who love me. Who are proud of me. Their love washes over me, and I lift my chin and smile.

And a few minutes later, when Adhira bursts outside wearing a shiny gold medal around her neck, I scream and fling my arms around her.

THIRTY-TWO

I CAN BARELY KEEP UP with Sir Pat. He tugs and lunges on his leash, snapping at blades of spring-green grass and jumping after butterflies like a puppy. We're both a bit rumpled after the long walk through Golden Gate Park and toward this part of San Francisco, but we're both definitely showing our smiley canines. Every few seconds, Sir Pat bounds back to me and plants his paws on my thighs, as if he's making sure he's really here with me.

I kneel down in front of him and scratch behind his ears. "I promise, Sir Pat, this is real." He pushes his muzzle up to my face and gives me a sloppy lick from my jaw to my temple, but it makes me love him all the more.

I had to call in Dev to help me pull this off, but I've got a timetable and a map, and now, I wait.

Wait, and hope.

The building in front of me is quiet, a few people lounging under trees with books or spread out on blankets in the grass to soak up the sunshine. But my eyes are on the doors. I count my heartbeats with my breath, my nerves buzzing.

Then the door pushes open, and people start pouring out. A rumble of feet on concrete, of calls and texts being made, of bikes being unlocked. My eyes dart through the crowd for the right person. The *only* person.

There.

Whit stops on the top stair and gapes at us, his shoulders jostled by the other students. Even from here, I can see him blink quickly, see his mouth drop open. He shakes his head, like he's coming to, and clatters down the steps toward me.

Sir Pat explodes toward him so hard I lose hold of his leash. The mutt tears over the grass toward Whit and leaps on him, until they're such a frenzy of hands and paws and wagging tails and laughter that I can't tell where Sir Pat ends and Whit begins. Whit crouches in the grass and ruffles the fur around Sir Pat's neck, his fingers catching at the new collar and tags— the tag engraved with Sir Pat's full name and Whit's cell phone number.

And I wait, and hope.

Whit takes his time standing, picking up Sir Pat's leash and leading him back to me.

"You adopted him?" There is awe coloring his voice, the words coming out like honey.

I'm beaming as I say, "Your roommates approved."

Whit's eyebrows shoot high. "My roommates knew?"

"And Dev and his brother, who helped me with the schedule. And I guess Adhira, who knows all."

Whit stares at me, his face full of wonder. It was meant to be goodbye, that final day at Bark Books. A start to new chapters for both of us. But, well, I've turned the page, and I very much want Eugene Whitlock Jr. to continue on in my story. And I hope, and I hope, and I hope.

"I was an idiot," I say before I can lose my nerve. But, honestly, my nerves have been anything but lost lately. It's a nice feeling.

Whit reaches out for me, but I stop him.

"No, let me say this. I've practiced it a hundred times in the mirror." Okay, so I may have embraced new, confident Marnie, but it's not like I'm taking up improv. I mean, come on. Improv is terrifying.

He laughs and Sir Pat yelps and paws at his leg, but Whit only stares at me.

"I was absolutely blind to what we have, Whit. I was stupid and blind and . . ." I have to stop to take a deep breath before I say this next part. "Whit, you're one of my best friends. You're kind and funny and you make me feel like . . . like there's a universe contained within us. You make me feel like starlight, and wow, I can't believe I said that out loud but it's true. People write stories about what we have. They write songs about it. And definitely some really bad poetry."

He steps nearer, closes the distance between us until I can count his eyelashes. He hesitates for only a moment, then brushes a lock of hair away from my forehead.

"Is that the end of your speech?"

I tilt my chin and look up at him. My heart is so big, the air in my lungs struggles for space. "Yeah, I think it is. I just . . . I needed you to know . . ."

"Know what?" His voice is low and deep in his throat, and I swear I can feel the rumble of it all the way through me. His hand on my face traces down my shoulder, my arm, leaving a wake of heat. He catches up my fingers between his own and pulls my hand to his lips.

I breathe around my heart and say, "How much I love you, you stupid boy."

His mouth is on mine in an instant, his lips warm and searching, so hungry I can feel every bit of his love for me returned tenfold. I wrap my arms up his back and hold tight, lean into this kiss, into him. I kiss him until I can scarcely breathe, until my heart threatens to split in two from happiness.

Until the only thing keeping us from floating away is Sir Pat's tangled leash tethering our legs to the earth.

Whit tips his forehead against mine, our chests rising and falling in unison. His face cracks wide in a smile, matching my own. "Now what?"

"Now," I begin, pressing upward to steal another kiss. It's a marvel the way Whit's mouth fits seamlessly against mine.

I slide my hand down his arm and twine my fingers with his. Before us, the city beckons. There is so much I want to do, to explore. So much *life* in this wondrous place I want to share with this person.

"Now," I say, leading him and Sir Pat onward. "We turn the page. I can't wait to see what comes next."

Acknowledgments

Hi, friends! It's me, your quietly freaking out debut author who's got a lot of people to thank for making this book possible. So let's get to it.

First, to my agent, Amy Bishop, and my editor, Alice Jerman. Thank you for laughing at my jokes and championing Marnie. I'm so grateful to you both for your support, thoughtful edits, and general awesomeness. To the entire team at HarperCollins for turning a thing that lived on my laptop into a real book—Clare Vaughn (that tagline!), Jessica White (thank your copy editors, friends), Alexandra Rakaczki, Catherine Lee, Jenna Stempel-Lobell, Lisa Calcasola, Mitchell Thorpe, Natasha Razi, and Misa Sugiura. And a big thank-you to Jacqueline Li for cover art that made me screech with excitement the first time I saw it.

To my indomitable, badass Pitch Wars mentors Carrie Allen and Sabrina Lotfi, for helping me fall in love with Marnie's story all over again. You're both generous, smart, and talented women. Another big shout-out to the rest of the Pitch Wars 2019 class for being supportive and amazing.

Okay, strap in. There's more. To Victoria Hanley and the wonderful writers at Lighthouse Writers Workshop here in Denver. To the Lilys—Melisa Ford, Cory Chambers, Alex Swanson, and Kelly Crowe. To Kristen Dickson for the always great feedback and just *getting it* when I need to complain about writing + children. The MUGs for their encouragement—Taylor L.W. Ross, Ana Ellickson, Aleese Lin, and Genevieve Sinha. To Pablo's, for the endless supply of tea and scones while I wrote. The Denver chapter of FYA Book Club, for their hours of YA discussions and weird tangents. And to my nonwriter friends who've patiently listened to me *go on* and supported me forever—Megan, Traci, and the rest of my OKC people (you know who you are . . . not you, Andy); Liz, Haley, Katie, and Lauren.

Lastly, to the people who are stuck with me. To my parents for never telling me to get my nose out of a book. To my children, Nico and Gus, for gracefully and without complaint giving me all the uninterrupted writing time I needed . . . jokes! Hahaha*sob*. And most important, to Ian—my best friend and hands-down the only guy with whom I'd ever want to survive another pandemic. Here's to tolerating my love of puns, being my adventure partner, and absolutely crushing it as #1 stage husband.

Finally *finally* to Jane Austen, obviously. And to all us Marys out there, figuring out our place in our own stories. Let's be difficult women, shall we?